BARRON'S
BUSINESS
TRAVELERS

FRENCH
FOR THE
BUSINESS
TRAVELER

Annie Heminway
Faculty, Alliance Française

BARRON'S

All inquiries should be addressed to:
Barron's Educational Series, Inc.
250 Wireless Boulevard
Hauppauge, NY 11788

Library of Congress Catalog Card No. 93-6289

International Standard Book No. 0-8120-1768-4

Library of Congress Cataloging-in-Publication Data

Heminway, Annie.
    [Talking business in French]
    French for the business traveler / Annie Heminway.—2nd ed.
       p.   cm.—(Barron's bilingual business guides)
    ISBN 0-8120-1768-4
    1. Business—Dictionaries. 2. English language—Dictionaries—
French. 3. Business—Dictionaries—French. 4. French language—
Dictionaries—English. I. Title. II. Series.
HF1002.H37 1994
650'.03—dc20
                                      93-6289
                                      CIP

PRINTED IN THE UNITED STATES OF AMERICA

4567 9692 987654321

CONTENTS

PREFACE

It is the nature of business to seek out new markets for its products and to find efficient ways to bring goods and services to more people. In the global marketplace, this often means travel to foreign countries, where language and customs are different. Even when a business person knows the language of the host country, the specific and often idiosyncratic terminology of the business world can be an obstacle to successful negotiations in a foreign language.

This phrase book is an essential pocket reference for any seasoned business traveler. Whether your business is manufacturing or finance, communications or sales, this three-part guide will help you express yourself in your business dealings and in your correspondence. You will want to carry this book with you on every trip and take it to every meeting. But it is also the reference you will keep on your desk at the office. This is the ultimate business dictionary for conducting your business in French.

Acknowledgments

1990 Demographic Yearbook, United Nations
The Europa World Yearbook 1992
The Statesman's Yearbook 1992–3
French and International Acronyms and Initials
Multi-lingual Dictionary of Commerce and International Trade and Shipping, 1990
Business Babble
Algerian Consulate General, Belgian-American Chamber of Commerce, Inc., Belgian Consulate General, Canadian Consulate General, Délégation Général du Québec (Alden Prouty, Commercial Attaché), French-American Foundation, French Embassy, The French West Indies Tourist Board, Haitian Consulate, Embassy of Luxembourg, Moroccan Embassy, Swiss Consulate General, U.S. Public Health Service, International Vaccination Information, Social Republic of Vietnam Mission to the United Nations, Vietnam Travel Center.

I. PRONUNCIATION GUIDE

This book assumes you are already somewhat familiar with the basic pronunciation rules of French but for those whose knowledge is a little rusty, here are some tips. Below are tables which give the sounds represented by each French letter.

Stress

Since all French syllables have approximately the same amount of stress, pronounce each syllable with equal emphasis and put a slightly stronger emphasis on the last syllable of a word group.

Consonants

In French, final consonants are usually silent, except for final C, R, F, and L (as in CaReFuL), which are usually pronounced.

FRENCH LETTER	ENGLISH SOUND	EXAMPLE
b, d, f, k, l, m, n,	same as English	
p, s, t, v, z	same as English	
c (before e, i, y)	SS (S at beginning of word)	cigare *see-gahr*
ç (before a, o, u)	SS (S at beginning of word)	garçon *gahr-ssohn*
c (before a, o, u)	K	comme *kohm*

FRENCH LETTER	ENGLISH SOUND	EXAMPLE
g (before e, i, y)	S as in pleasure	rouge *roozh*
ge (before a, o)	S as in pleasure	mangeons *mahn-zhohn*
g (before a, o, u)	G	gant *gahn*
gn	nyuh as in onion	oignon *oh-nyohn*
h	always silent	hôtel *oh-tehl*
j	S as in pleasure	je *zhuh*
qu, final q	K	cinq *sank*

NOTE: When combined with a word beginning with a vowel or *h*, *x* has a *z* sound. Before a word beginning with a consonant, it is silent. The underscored n means there is a nasalized pronunciation of the "n" sound.

FRENCH LETTER	ENGLISH SOUND	EXAMPLE
r	Roll the R at the top back of the mouth as if you were gargling or spitting.	rue *rew*
ss	S	poisson *pwah-ssohn*
s	beginning of word	six *sees*
s	next to consonant	disque *deessk*
s	between vowels	poison *pwah-zohn*
th	T	thé *tay*
x	S in these words only	six *seess*, dix *deess*, soixante *swah-ssahnt*
x	X	excellent *ehkss-eh-lahn*

FRENCH LETTER	ENGLISH SOUND	EXAMPLE
a, à, â	A as in yacht or A in after	la *lah*
é, final er, final ez, et	A as in day	musée *mew-zay*
e + 2 consonants	E as in ever	sept *seht*
e + final pronounced consonant		
e, ê, è		
e	sometimes like E of early with no R sound	le *luh*
i (î), y	EE as in meet	île *eel*
i + vowel or ll	Y as in yes	famille *fah-mee*
o + final pronounced consonant	O as in for	homme *ohm*
o, o before se, o last sound in word, au, eau	O as in open	au *oh*
ou	OO as in tooth	où *oo*
oy, oi	WA as in watch	trois *trwah*
U	There is none. Round lips and say E and U at same time.	du *dew*
U + vowel	WEE as in wee	huit *weet*

Nasal Sounds

Nasal sounds are produced through the mouth and the nose at the same time. Nasal sounds occur when N or M follow a vowel in the same syllable. There is NO nasal sound for VOWEL + NN, VOWEL + MM, VOWEL + N + VOWEL, VOWEL + M + VOWEL. NOTE: n̲ means there is a nasalized pronunciation of the "N" sound. The tip of the tongue does not touch the roof of the mouth.

FRENCH LETTER	ENGLISH SOUND	EXAMPLE
AN, AM, EN, EM	similar to on	France *Frahn̲ss*
IN, IM, AIN, AIM	similar to an	pain *pan̲*
IEN	Similar to y̲a̲n̲ of Yankee	bein *byan̲*
ON, OM	similar to o̲n̲ of lo̲n̲g	bon *bohn̲*
UN, UM	similar to u̲n̲ of u̲n̲der	un *uhn̲*

Liaison and Elision

Liaison and elision are two linguistic devices that add to the beauty and fluidity of the French language.

Liaison means linking. In French, the final consonant of a word is usually not pronounced. Sometimes, however, when the final consonant of one word is followed by a beginning vowel or "h" of the next word, liaison occurs.

Nous arrivons. *noo zah-ree-vohn̲*

With the following words in French, the final vowel is dropped if the next word starts with a vowel or "H." The dropped vowel is replaced by an apostrophe. This is called elision.

la auto = l'auto *(loh-toh)*
le homme = l'homme *(lohm)*

DOING BUSINESS IN FRENCH-SPEAKING COUNTRIES

Doing business in French-speaking countries is often greeted with a degree of trepidation by non-native speakers. Language differences and cultural dictates are often disorienting for those unfamiliar with the customs of the country.

Learning about the accepted cultural practices will help you to feel more confident conducting business in French-speaking countries. This book contains information on prevalent customs that will increase both your comfort level and success quotient for managing business in these countries.

Usual Hours of Operation

France	Monday to Friday 9:00 AM to 12:00 PM and 2:00 PM to 6:00 PM
Belgium	Monday to Friday 9:00 AM to 12:00 PM and 1:00 PM to 5:00 PM
Canada (Québec)	Monday to Friday 9:00 AM to 12:30 PM and 1:30 PM to 5:00 PM
French Caribbean	Monday to Friday 8:00 AM to 3:00 PM
Luxembourg	Monday to Friday 8:30 AM to 12:00 PM and 2:00 PM to 5:30 PM
North Africa	Monday 8:30 PM to 11:30 PM and 3 PM to 6 PM With variations according to countries.
Southeast Asia	Monday to Friday 8:30 AM to 12:00 PM and 1:00 PM to 5:00 PM
Switzerland	Monday to Friday 8:30 AM to 12:00 PM and 2:00 PM to 5:00 PM

Business Customs

France: French business is still conducted in a rather formal and conservative manner. Although a more relaxed attitude seems to be the trend among younger executives, business partners do not address each other on a first name basis. Do not forget to shake hands when meeting someone or taking leave.

During negotiations in all French-speaking countries, the pace is usually slower and it would be advisable not to use the hard-sell method. As elsewhere, an appointment is preferred and a phone call is recommended if detained. Courtesy goes a long way in smoothing the relationship.

Belgium: The above recommendations for France can be applied to Belgium.

Canada (Québec):   Customs are similar to the United States. As the Québecois are proud of their French heritage, it is preferable that business be conducted in French.

French Caribbean: Customs tend to be rather formal but once a business relationship has been established, a more casual rapport can be expected.

Luxembourg: Same remarks as for Québec.

North Africa: Never forget that personal relationships are of the utmost importance. Most business may take a great deal of time; however, punctuality is always expected. Once you have established a relationship, the interaction will tend to be warm and more casual. A letter of introduction from a mutual acquaintance will help open doors.

Switzerland: Discretion and formality are highly valued in all circumstances. Punctuality is important for any occasion, business or social.

Vietnam: A certain formality is still the norm. While French is widely used socially, business is usually conducted in English.

General Government Policy and Economic Situation

(Statistics given in this section are generally accurate through 1992.)

France: Apart from the Republic of France, four overseas departments (D.O.M.) fall under French jurisdiction, and a number of overseas territories (T.O.M.) have limited French involvement. The French economy combines free enterprise and nationalized companies such as the railroads, the electric and gas utilities, and the telephone system. The television industry is an example of privatization and has created an explosion of successful cable networks.
Main imports: Machinery, transport equipment, basic manufactured products, and miscellaneous manufactured products.
Main exports: Machinery, transport equipment, miscellaneous manufactured products, road vehicles, armaments, and chemicals.
Inflation rate: 3%.
Future development in trade policies: An effort to develop a trade surplus. The transfer of state owned enterprises to the private sector. In line with the European Economic Community (EC), trade policies are experiencing change. France has already implemented approximately 86% of the EC measures, surpassed only by Denmark.
Principal trading partners: Italy, Belgium, Luxembourg, the Netherlands, and the United States.
Population: 56,556,000.
Language: French.
Religion: 80% are Roman Catholic, plus other Christian denominations. Muslim and Jewish communities.
GDP: $1,000,866 million.
GDP per inhabitant: $17,830.
Unemployment rate: 11%.

Belgium: Still a kingdom with a monarch, industries are privately owned and export driven. Belgium has been the mediator in Europe since World War II. It is the home of the Council of Europe, NATO, and the Benelux Economic Union.

Main imports: Machinery, transportation equipment, basic manufactures, chemicals, and related products.

Main exports: Basic manufactures including gem diamonds, iron and steel, machinery, transportation equipment, chemicals, and foodstuffs.

Inflation rate: 3.7%.

Future development in trade policies: Economic prosperity in Flanders has offset a decline in Wallonia. Dependent on external trade, Belgium has been vulnerable to price fluctuations internationally.

Principal trading partners: Germany, France, and the Netherlands.

Population: 9,986,475.

Language: Flemish is spoken in the northern region of Flanders, accounting for approximately 57% of the population, while French is spoken in the south, Wallonia, making up 43% of the population.

Religion: The majority is Roman Catholic.

GDP: $162,026 million.

GDP per inhabitant: $16,390.

Unemployment rate: 9.8%.

Luxembourg: The Grand Duchy of Luxembourg, a small, but highly industrialized country relying heavily upon foreign markets. With favorable banking laws, Luxembourg is home to many banks and holding companies, including "Aciéries Réunies de Burbach-Esch-Dudelange," the steel and iron foundry. Luxembourg is the European leader in steel production.

Main imports: Minerals, base metals and manufactured metals, chemicals, and transportation equipment.

Main exports: Iron and steel, mineral and chemical production, base metals and manufactures, rubber, plastics, machinery, and apparatus.

Inflation rate: 4.4%.

Future development in trade policies: Continued diversification away from dependence on finance; steel and iron industries maintain a trade balance.

Principal trading partners: Germany, Belgium, and France.

Population: 384,400.

Language: The national language, Letzeburgish, is spoken by nearly everyone. French is generally used for administrative purposes while German is the written language for trade and the press.

Religion: 95% Roman Catholic.

GDP: $10,875 million.

GDP per inhabitant: $28,770.

Unemployment rate: 1.3%.

Switzerland: The Swiss Confederation is composed of 20 cantons and 6 half cantons. Banking plays a major role in the Swiss free market economy which has six stock exchanges.

Main imports: Mineral fuels for power, motor vehicles, chemical elements, metal products, and machinery.

Main exports: Precision engineering, watches and clocks, heavy engineering, machine building, textiles, chocolates, chemicals, and pharmaceuticals.
Inflation rate: 5.9%.
Future development in trade policies: With the development of a single European market, Switzerland is pursuing a more liberalized and deregulated economy. In 1990, a 10 year moratorium was passed on the construction of nuclear power stations, thereby forcing the government to rethink its energy needs. The adoption in 1991 of the Energy 2000 program concentrates on the conservation of energy and the stabilization of imported energy.
Principal trading partners: the United States, Germany, France, and all the other EC member countries.
Population: 6,750,693.
Language: Switzerland is divided into three major language regions: German 73.5%, French 20.1 %, Italian 4.5%, plus an additional group of 1% that speaks Romansch.
Religion: 50.4% Protestant, 43.6% Roman Catholic.
GDP: $219,337 million.
GDP per inhabitant: $32,790.
Unemployment rate: 1.8%. 25% of the Swiss work force are foreigners, the highest percentage in Europe.

Canada: Among the provinces of Canada is Québec, with more than 6.5 million French-speaking inhabitants. Québec is recognized as a distinct society in terms of its language, culture, and legal system in the same way each of the other English-speaking provinces has control of their own cultural affairs. The government encourages the development of small and medium-sized businesses.
Main imports: Foodstuffs, crude petroleum, chemicals, machinery motor vehicles, and computers.
Main exports: Lumber forest products, motor vehicles and aircraft parts, fish and seafood, furs, wheat, and mineral fuels.
Inflation rate: 5.8%.
Future development in trade policies: An open trade agreement between the United States and Canada has been in effect since late 1993. NAFTA, the North American Free Trade Agreement, allows companies that set up shop in Québec unlimited access to North American markets. Foreign investment is heavily relied upon for industry while major amounts of investment capital go to the United States.
Principal trading partners: The United States accounts for the majority of imports and exports with the EC while Japan makes up the balance.
Population: 26,991,000.
Language: Although 98% of the population speak English, 62.7% consider themselves English-speaking and 25.4% consider themselves French-speaking.
Religion: 45% Roman Catholic, with numerous other religious denominations.
GDP: $500,337 million.
GDP per inhabitant: $19,070.
Unemployment rate: 8.1%.

French Caribbean: Guadeloupe, Martinique, Haiti, St. Vincent and Grenadines make up a group of islands in the Caribbean settled by the French in the late 17th Century. Some are still under French rule and have retained a relaxed French culture that seems to be most often defined by the beach and sun.

Main imports: Food, live animals, mineral fuels, machinery, transportation equipment, and basic manufactured products.

Main exports: Sugar, coffee, rum, exotic fruits, and tropical oils for cosmetics and pharmaceuticals.

Inflation rate: Ranges from 3.3% to 7%.

Future development in trade policies: While the economies of these countries are generally dependent on tourism, their governments have attempted to boost light manufacturing, especially in the area of assembled goods. Other than Haiti, these islands depend heavily on aid and support from France. Since 1992, Haiti, the poorest economy in the Western Hemisphere, has had embargos placed upon it, causing many industries to shut down or relocate.

Principal trading partners: United States, Japan, Canada, Italy, France, and other Caribbean countries.

Population: Guadeloupe 344,000; Martinique 341,000; Haiti 5,963,000; St. Vincent et Grenadines 116,000.

Language: French is the official language, but each island has creole and patois dialects that are widely spoken.

Religion: Roman Catholic majority, other Christian denominations, and Voodoo, a form of folk religion.

GDP: $2,114 million to $2,556 million.

GDP per inhabitant: $400 to $6,320.

Unemployment rate: Ranges from 12.7% to 24%.

North Africa: Algeria, Morocco, Tunisia. Although independent of French rule since the second half of this century, French culture and language are still part of everyday life and business.

Main imports: Transportation equipment, basic manufactured products, and food.

Main exports: Natural gas and petroleum, iron ore, phosphates, and lead.

Inflation rate: 9.3%–11.8%.

Future development in trade policies: Even though rich in exportable hydrocarbons, these nations are trying to decrease their reliance on agricultural imports and increase the production of other basic manufactures for export.

Principal trading partners: France, Italy, Germany, the United States, and the Netherlands.

Population: Algeria 24,961,000; Morocco 25,061,000; Tunisia 8,300,000.

Language: Although Arabic is the national language, French is widely used.

Religion: Islam.

GDP: $53,116 million.

GDP per inhabitant: $2,170.

Unemployment rate: 25%.

Vietnam: In 1986 a policy of renovation was adopted. In 1987 the Law on Foreign Investment was introduced. Since then, positive developments in almost all aspects of Vietnam's economy have been achieved. The United States embargo was lifted in 1994 and trade relations have been restored.

Main imports: Fuel, capital equipment, vehicles, fertilizers, and consumer goods.

Main exports: Rice, crude oil, textiles, and garments.
Inflation rate: 15%.
Principal trading partners: Taiwan, Japan and other East and Southeast
   Asian countries.
Population: 68.1 million.
Language: Vietnamese.
Religion: Buddhism.

BEFORE YOU GO...

Passports

All permanent U.S. residents must carry a valid passport when traveling
abroad, excluding trips to Canada where a birth certificate or a voter's registra-
tion card is sufficient. Application should be made by mail or in person at least
eight weeks in advance to either:

1. a U.S. Passport Agency office located in twelve major cities and
   Washington, D.C.
2. designated U.S. post offices throughout the country.
3. state and federal courthouses.

You may also consult your travel agent or international airline office to
find out what documents you need and the proper procedures to follow.
Requirements for citizens and non-citizens differ. No international travel tickets will be issued by an airline or travel agent to persons without valid passports. Currently, passports are issued for ten years for a fee of $55.00.

Visas

Visas are not required by France, Belgium, Luxembourg, or Switzerland
for travelers with U.S. passports whose stay does not exceed three months.
Requirements for a long term visa (stays over three months) may require up to
a three-month processing period and must be obtained in the country of
residence.

Travel requirements to Africa and the Middle East vary; however, visas
are often required and are issued by each embassy for a small fee. It may be
necessary to have a corporate letter stating the purpose of the trip and the company contact at your destination as well as a financial statement for travel
expenses. Visas to Arab countries vary; therefore, check with the consulate
when making travel plans.

The French Caribbean Islands have the same visa requirements as France.
Travel in Southeast Asia is similar to the Middle East.

Additional information for each country can be obtained at the consulate
general or the embassy of that country prior to departure from the U.S.

Immunizations

There are no immunization requirements for entry into the European
countries or upon return to the United States. If you plan to include travel to
Asia, Africa, or the Middle East, consult your doctor or the nearest U.S. Public
Health Service office.

Customs and Currency Regulations

In general, travelers with U.S. passports are allowed to bring in $400 of duty-free items for their own personal use. These items include tobacco, alcohol, and perfumes, and are allowed in the following quantities (there are, however, local variations):

400 cigarettes or 100 cigars or 500 grams of tobacco (about 1 pound)
2 liters of wine
1 liter of liquor
2 ounces of perfume

If you are not in excess of these amounts, a simple statement of "nothing to declare" will be respected by most customs officials.

For gifts whose final destination is the country you are entering, the rules are a bit stricter and vary greatly among the different countries. It would be wise to check on the duty-free limits beforehand and to declare whatever is in excess. Gifts worth $50 or less may be sent home subject to certain restrictions. For further up-to-date details, ask your travel agent or airline to provide a copy of U.S. Customs regulations.

For personal valuables such as jewelry, furs, watches, cameras, computers, CD players, and tape recorders (acquired before your trip), you should have proof of prior possession or register same with United States Customs before departure. This will ensure that they are not subject to duty either by the United States upon return, or by any country you visit.

Restrictions on the amount of foreign currency (or checks) that foreign nationals may bring into these countries may vary. European countries have no restrictions. If in doubt, consult your travel agent.

The Franc Zone

The Franc Zone is a group of countries that had political ties with France as far back as the seventeenth century and have chosen to maintain an economic link with today's French Franc. These countries have currencies that are linked to the French Franc at a fixed rate of exchange.

While each of these nations has its own issuing bank, they hold reserves mainly in the form of French Francs. These francs are freely convertible with the exchange rate determined by the Paris stock market.

The participating countries are Benin, Burkina Faso, Cameroon, Central African Republic, Chad, Congo, Côte d'Ivoire, Equatorial Guinea, Mayotte, St. Pierre et Miquelon and the overseas French departments and territories, Gabon, Mali, Niger, Sénégal, and Togo.

For more information, contact Service de la Zone Franc, Banque de France, 39 rue Croix-des-Petits-Champs, BP 140-01 Paris, Tel. (1) 42.92.31.26 Fax. (1) 42.96.47.

Traveler's Checks, Credit Cards, Foreign Exchange

All major international traveler's checks and credit cards are accepted by most of the hotels, restaurants, and shops. The most recognized are American

Express, Barclays, Citibank, and Bank of America. The cards most accepted are American Express, MasterCard, Visa, and Diner's Club.

However, be advised that the exchange rate on dollar traveler's checks is almost always disadvantageous. You can buy foreign currency checks or actual currency in the United States before leaving at rates equivalent to or better than the bank rate you will get abroad. Currency or checks may be purchased from retail foreign currency dealers. For further information, contact Thomas Cook at 630 Fifth Avenue, New York, NY 10111. Tel: (212) 757 6915.

To credit card users: When charging, make sure that the following information appears on the original and all copies of your bill: the correct date; the type of currency being charged (francs, Canadian dollars, etc.); the official exchange rate for that currency on that date (if possible); and, the total amount of the bill. Without this information, you may end up paying at an exchange rate less favorable to you and more favorable to your overseas host, and for a larger bill than you thought!

Driver's Licenses

A valid American license is usually respected. However, if you plan to stay for any length of time, and want to avoid language problems on the road, it is a good idea to get an international driver's document through the Automobile Association of America (AAA), or a local automobile club.

Electrical Appliances

If you plan to bring along any small electrical appliances for use without batteries, be aware that Europe's system of electric current and voltage differs from ours. If your appliance has no special internal adapters or converters made specifically for use in Europe, you will have to supply your own. For most appliances, you will need plug adapters that provide correctly shaped prongs for European outlets. Different American-made appliances (irons, hair dryers, razors, radios, battery rechargers, etc.) need either adapters or converters to change European voltage and frequency levels. In France, Switzerland, and Belgium, 220-230 volts AC is almost standard, although 110-115 can still be found in some places.

III. BASIC WORDS AND PHRASES

Fundamental Expressions

Yes.	Oui. (wee)
No.	Non. (noh<u>n</u>)
Maybe.	Peut-être. (puh-teh-truh)
Please.	S'il vous plaît. (seel voo pleh)
Thank you very much.	Merci beaucoup. (mehr-ssee-boh-koo)
Excuse me.	Excusez-moi. (ehkss-kew-zay mwah)
I am sorry.	Je suis désolé(e). (zhuh swee day-zoh-lay)
Just a second.	Un instant, s'il vous plaît. (Uh<u>n</u> ans-tahnt, seel voo pleh)
That's all right.	Ça va. (sah-vah)
O.K.	D'accord. (dah-kohr), Bien entendu. (bya<u>n</u> nah<u>n</u>-tah<u>n</u>-dew)
It doesn't matter.	Ça ne fait rien. (sah nuh feh rya<u>n</u>)
Sir.	Monsieur. (muh-ssyuh)
Madame (Mrs.)	Madame. (muh-dahm)
Miss	Mademoiselle. (mahd-mwah-zehl)
Good morning.	Bonjour. (boh<u>n</u>-zhoor)
Good afternoon.	Bonjour. (boh<u>n</u>-zhoor)
Good evening.	Bonsoir. (boh<u>n</u>-swahr)
Good night.	Bonne nuit. (boh<u>n</u>-nwee)
Good-bye.	Au revoir. (oh-ruh-vwahr)
Glad to meet you.	Enchanté de faire votre connaissance. (ah<u>n</u>-shah<u>n</u>-tay duh fehr voh-truh koh-neh-ssah<u>n</u>ss)
How are you?	Comment allez-vous? (koh-mah<u>n</u> tah-lay-voo)
Very well, thank you.	Très bien, merci. (treh bya<u>n</u> mehr-ssee)
And you?	Et vous? (ay voo)
Fine.	Bien. (bya<u>n</u>)
Allow me to introduce myself.	Permettez-moi de me présenter. (pehr-meh-tay mwah duh muh pray-zah<u>n</u>-tay)
My name is…	Je m'appelle… (zhuh mah-pehl)
How do you do? (Glad to meet you.)	Enchanté de faire votre connaissance. (ah<u>n</u>-shah<u>n</u>-tay duh fehr voh-truh koh-neh-ssah<u>n</u>ss)
Glad to meet you, too.	Moi de même. (meh-wah duh mameh)
Where are you from?	D'où venez-vous? (doh ven-ehz-voo)
Where do you live?	Où habitez-vous? (oo ah-bee-tay voo)
How long will you be staying in Paris?	Combien de temps resterez-vous à Paris? (koh<u>n</u>-bya<u>n</u> duh tah<u>n</u> rehss-tray voo ah pa-ree)
Where are you staying in town?	Où êtes-vous descendu? (oo eht voo dehss-sah<u>n</u>-dew)

Where can I reach you?	Où puis-je vous joindre? (oo pwee-zhuh voo zhwah<u>n</u>-druh)
Here's my address and my telephone number.	Voici mon adresse et mon numéro de téléphone. (vwah-ssee moh<u>n</u> nah-drehss ay moh<u>n</u> new-may-roh duh tay-lay-fohn)
Could you pick me up at my hotel this evening?	Pouvez-vous passer me prendre à mon hôtel ce soir? (poo-vay voo pass-say muh prah<u>n</u>-druh ah moh<u>n</u> noh-tehl ssuh swahr)
See you tomorrow.	À demain. (ah duh-ma<u>n</u>)
See you later.	À tout à l'heure. (ah toot ah luhr)

Communications

Do you speak English?	Parlez-vous anglais? (pahr-lay voo ah<u>n</u>-gleh)
I don't speak French.	Je ne parle pas français. (zhuh nuh pahrl pah frah<u>n</u>-sseh)
I speak a little French.	Je parle un peu français. (zuh pahrl uh<u>n</u> puh frah<u>n</u>-sseh)
Is there anyone here who speaks English?	Y a-t-il quelqu'un qui parle anglais ici? (ee ah teel kehl-kuh<u>n</u> kee pahrl ah<u>n</u>-gleh ee-ssee)
Please write it down.	Notez-le s'il vous plaît. (noh-tay-luh seel voo pleh)
Please speak more slowly.	Parlez plus lentement, s'il vous plaît. (pahr-lay plew lah<u>n</u>t-mah<u>n</u> seel voo pleh)
Please repeat.	Répétez, s'il vous plaît. (ray-pay-tay seel voo pleh)
How do you say that in French?	Comment dit-on ça en français? (koh-mah<u>n</u> dee toh<u>n</u> sah ah<u>n</u> frah<u>n</u>-sseh)
What does this mean?	Qu'est-ce que ça veut dire? (kehss kuh sah vuh deer)
What is your name?	Comment vous appelez-vous? (koh-mah<u>n</u> voo zah-play voo)
Do you understand?	Comprenez-vous? (koh<u>n</u>-pruh-nay-voo)
I don't understand.	Je ne comprends pas. (zhuh nuh koh<u>n</u>-prah<u>n</u> pah)
What did you say?	Qu'est-ce-que vous avez dit? (kehss kuh voo zah-vay dee)

Common Questions and Phrases

Where is the _____?	Où est le/la _____? (oo eh luh/lah _____)
When?	Quand? (kah<u>n</u>)
How?	Comment? (koh-mah<u>n</u>)
How much?	Combien? (koh<u>n</u>-bya<u>n</u>)
Who?	Qui? (kee)
Why?	Pourquoi? (poor-kwah)
Which?	Quel/quelle? (kehl/kehl-luh)
Here is _____ .	Voici _____ . (vwah-ssee)
There is _____ .	Voilà _____ . (vwah-lah)
It/that is _____ .	C'est _____ . (seh)

Useful Nouns

address	l'adresse (lah drehss)
amount	le montant (luh moh<u>n</u>-tah<u>n</u>)
appointment	le rendez-vous (luh rah<u>n</u>-day voo)
bill	la facture (lah fahk-tuhr), l'addition (lah dee-syo<u>n</u>)
business	les affaires (lay zah-fehr)
car	la voiture (lah vwah-tewr)
cashier	la caisse (lah kehss)
check	le chèque (luh shehk), la vérification (lah veh-ree-fee-kah-ssyoh<u>n</u>)
city	la ville (lah veel)
customs	la douane (lah dwahn)
date	la date (lah daht)
document	le document (luh doh-kew-mah<u>n</u>)
elevator	l'ascenseur (lah-sah<u>n</u>-suhr)
fax	la télécopie (lah tay-lay-koh-pee), le fax (luh fahx)
flight	le vol (luh vohl)
friend	l'ami, l'amie (lah-mee)
hanger	le cintre (luh sa<u>n</u>-truh)
key	la clé, la clef (lah klay)
list	la liste (lah leesst)
magazine	la revue (la ruh-vew)
maid	la femme de chambre (lah fahm duh shah<u>n</u>-bruh)
manager	le directeur (luh dee-rehk-tuhr)
map	la carte (lah kahrt), le plan (luh plahn)
mistake	l'erreur (leh-ruhr)
money	l'argent (lahr-zhah<u>n</u>)
name	le nom (luh noh<u>n</u>)
newspaper	le journal (luh zhoor-nahl)
office	le bureau (luh bew-roh)
package	le colis (luh koh-lee), le paquet (luh pah-keht)
paper	le papier (luh pah-pyay)
passport	le passeport (luh pahss-pohr)
pen	le stylo (luh stee-loh)
pencil	le crayon (luh kreh-yoh<u>n</u>)
porter	le porteur (luh pohr-tuhr)
post office	la poste (lah pohsst)
postage	l'affranchissement (lah frah<u>n</u>-sheess-mah<u>n</u>)
price	le prix (luh pree), le tarif (luh tah-reef)
raincoat	l'imperméable (la<u>n</u>-pehr-may-ah-bluh)
reservation	la réservation (la ray-zehr-va-sioh<u>n</u>)
rest room	les toilettes (lay twah-leht)
restaurant	le restaurant (luh rehss-toh-rah<u>n</u>)
road	la route (lah root)
room	la chambre (lah shah<u>n</u>-bruh)

shirt	la chemise (lah shuh-meez)
shoes	les chaussures (lay shoh-ssewrs)
shower	la douche (lah doosh)
store	le magasin (luh mah-gah-za<u>n</u>)
street	la rue (lah rew)
suit	le costume (luh kohs-tewm)
suitcase	la valise (lah vahl-eehz)
taxi	le taxi (luh tahk-ssee)
telegram	le télégramme (luh tay-lay-grahm)
telephone	le téléphone (luh tay-lay-foh<u>n</u>)
terminal (railroad)	la gare (lah gahr)
ticket	le billet (luh bee-yey)
time	le temps (luh ta<u>n</u>), l'heure (luhr)
tip	le pourboire (luh poor-bwahr)
train	le train (luh tra<u>n</u>)
trip	le voyage (luh vwah-yahzh)
umbrella	le parapluie (luh pah-rah-plwee)
waiter	le serveur (luh sehr-vuhr)
waitress	la serveuse (lah sehr-vuhz)
watch	la montre (lah moh<u>n</u>-truh)
water	l'eau (loh)

Useful Verbs (infinitive forms)

accept	accepter (ak-ssehp-tay)
answer	répondre (ray-poh<u>n</u>-druh)
arrive	arriver (ah-ree-vay)
ask	demander (duh-mah<u>n</u>-day)
assist	aider (ay-day)
be	être (eh-truh)
begin	commencer (koh-mah<u>n</u>-ssay)
bring	apporter (ah-pohr-tay), amener (ah-muh-nay)
buy	acheter (ahsh-tay)
call	appeler (ah-peh-lay)
carry	porter (pohr-tay)
change	changer (shah<u>n</u>-zhay)
close	fermer (fehr-may)
come	venir (vuh-neer)
confirm	confirmer (koh<u>n</u>-feer-may)
continue	continuer (koh<u>n</u>-tee-new-ay)
cost	coûter (koo-tay)
deliver	livrer (lee-vray)
do	faire (fehr)
eat	manger (ma<u>n</u>-zhay)
end	terminer (tehr-mee-nay)
enquire	s'adresser (s'ah-dreh-ssay)
enter	entrer (ah<u>n</u>-tray)
examine	examiner (ehkss-ah-mee-nay)
exchange	échanger (ay-sha<u>n</u>-zhay)

feel	sentir (ssah<u>n</u>-teer)
finish	finir (fee-neer)
fix	réparer (ray-pah-ray), fixer (feekss-say)
follow	suivre (swee-vruh)
forget	oublier (oo-blee-yay)
get	obtenir (ohb-tuh-neer)
give	donner (doh-nay)
go	aller (ah-lay)
hear	entendre (ah<u>n</u>-tah<u>n</u>-druh)
help	aider (eh-day), assister (ah-sees-tay)
intend	avoir l'intention (ah-vwahr la<u>n</u>-tah<u>n</u>-ssyoh<u>n</u>)
keep	garder (gahr-day)
know	savoir (sah-vwahr), connaître (koh-neh-truh)
learn	apprendre (ah-prah<u>n</u>-druh)
leave	quitter (kee-tay)
like	aimer (eh-may)
listen	écouter (ay-koo-tay)
look	regarder (ruh-gahr-day)
lose	perdre (pehr-druh)
make	faire (fehr), construire (koh<u>n</u>-strew-eer)
mean	vouloir dire (voo-lwahr deer)
meet	rencontrer (rah<u>n</u>-koh<u>n</u>-tray), rejoindre (reh-zhwah<u>n</u>-dreh)
miss	manquer (mah<u>n</u>-kay)
need	avoir besoin de (ah-vwahr buhz-wa<u>n</u> duh)
open	ouvrir (oo-vreer)
order	commander (koh-mah<u>n</u>-day)
park	garer (gah-ray), stationner (stah-ssyoh<u>n</u>-nay)
pay	payer (peh-yay)
prefer	préférer (pray-fehr-ray)
prepare	préparer (pray-pah-ray)
present	présenter (pray-zah<u>n</u>-tay)
prove	prouver (proo-vay)
pull	tirer (tee-ray)
purchase	acheter (ahsh-tay)
put	mettre (meh-truh)
read	lire (leer)
receive	recevoir (ruh-suh-vwahr)
recommend	recommander (ruh-koh-mah<u>n</u>-day)
register	enregistrer (ah<u>n</u>-reh-zhee-sstray)
remain	rester (rehss-tay)
repair	réparer (ray-pah-ray)
repeat	répéter (ray-pay-tay)
rest	se reposer (suh ruh-poh-zay)
return	retourner (ruh-toor-nay)
run	courir (koo-reer)
say	dire (deer)
see	voir (vwahr)
send	envoyer (ah<u>n</u>-vwah-yay)
show	montrer (moh<u>n</u>-tray)

sit	s'asseoir (sah-sswahr)
speak	parler (pahr-lay)
stand	se lever (suh-luh-vay)
start	commencer (koh-mah<u>n</u>-ssay)
stop	arrêter (ah-reh-tay)
take	prendre (prah<u>n</u>-druh)
talk	parler (pahr-lay)
tell	dire (deer), raconter (rah-koh<u>n</u>-tay)
think	penser (pah<u>n</u>-ssay)
try	essayer (eh-sseh-yay)
turn	tourner (toor-nay)
use	employer (ah<u>n</u>-plwah-yay)
visit	visiter (vee-zee-tay)
wait	attendre (ah-tah<u>n</u>-druh)
walk	marcher (mahr-shay)
want	vouloir (voo-lwahr)
wear	porter (pohr-tay)
work	travailler (trah-vah-yay)
write	écrire (ay-kreer)

Useful Adjectives and Adverbs

above/below	au-dessus/au-dessous (oh duh-ssew/oh duh-sseow)
ahead/back	en avant/en arrière (ah<u>n</u> ah-vah<u>n</u>/ah<u>n</u> nah-ryehr)
best/worst	meilleur(eure)/pire (meh-yuhr/peer)
big/small	grand(e)/petit(e) (grah<u>n</u>[d]/puh-tee[t])
early/late	tôt/tard (toh/tahr)
easy/difficult	facile/difficile (fah-seel/dee-fee-seel)
few/many	peu/beaucoup (puh/boh-koo)
first/last	premier/dernier (pruh-myay/dehr-nyay)
front/back	devant/derrière (duh-vah<u>n</u>/dehr-ryehr)
full/empty	plein/vide (pla<u>n</u>/veed)
good/bad	bon(ne)/mauvais(e) (boh<u>n</u> [nuh]/moh-veh[z])
hot/cold	chaud(e)/froid(e) (shoh[d]/frwah[d])
high/low	haut(e)/bas(se) (oh[t]/bah[ss])
inside/outside	dedans/dehors (duh-dah<u>n</u>/duh-ohr)
large/small	gros(se)/petit(e) (groh[ss]/puh-tee[t])
more/less	plus/moins (plew/mwa<u>n</u>)
near/far	près/loin (preh/lwa<u>n</u>)
old/new	vieux (vieille)/nouveau (nouvelle) (vyuh/vyay)/(noo-voh/noo-vehl)
open/shut	ouvert(e)/fermé(e) (oo-vehr/fehr-may)
slow/fast	lent(e)/rapide (lah<u>n</u>[t]/rah-peed)
thin/thick	mince/épais(se) (ma<u>n</u>ss/ay-peh[ss])

Other Useful Words

a, an	un (uh<u>n</u>), une (ewn)
about	environ (ah<u>n</u>-vee-roh<u>n</u>)

across	en face de (ah<u>n</u> fahss duh), de l'autre côté (duh doh-truh koh-tay)
after	après (ah-preh)
again	de nouveau (duh noo-voh)
all	tout(e) (too[t])
almost	presque (prehss-kuh)
also	aussi (oh-ssee)
always	toujours (too-zhoor)
among	parmi (pahr-mee)
and	et (ay)
another	un(e) autre (uh<u>n</u> [ewn] oh-truh)
around	autour (oh-toor), vers (vehr)
at	à (ah)
away	loin (lwa<u>n</u>)
back (of)	derrière (dehr-ryehr)
because	parce que (pahrss kuh)
before	avant (ah-vah<u>n</u>), devant (duh-vah<u>n</u>)
behind	derrière (deh-ryehr)
between	entre (ah<u>n</u>-truh)
both	tous (les) deux (too [leh] duh), l'un(e) et l'autre (luh<u>n</u> [lewn] ay loh-truh)
but	mais (meh)
down	en bas (ah<u>n</u>-bah)
each	chaque (shahk)
enough	assez (ah-ssay)
even	même (mehm)
every	chaque (shahk), tout (too)
except	sauf (sohf)
few	peu de (puh duh)
for	pour (poor)
from	de (duh)
however	cependant (ssuh-pah<u>n</u>-dah<u>n</u>)
if	si (see)
in	dans (dah<u>n</u>)
instead (of)	au lieu de (oh lyuh duh)
into	dans (dah<u>n</u>)
maybe	peut-être (puh teh-truh)
more	plus (de…) (plew [duh…]), encore (de…) (ah<u>n</u>-kor [duh…])
much	beaucoup (boh-koo)
next (to)	à côté de (ah koh-tay duh)
not	pas (pah)
now	maintenant (ma<u>n</u>t-nah<u>n</u>)
of	de (duh)
often	souvent (soo-vah<u>n</u>)
only	seulement (suhl-mah<u>n</u>)
or	ou (oo)
other	autre (oh-truh)
perhaps	peut-être (puh teh-truh)
same	même (mehm)

since	depuis (duh-pwee)
some	quelque (kehl-kuh)
soon	bientôt (bya<u>n</u>-toh)
still (yet)	encore (ah<u>n</u>-kohr), toujours (too-zhoor)
that/this	ce/cet/cette (ssuh/sseht/sseht)
these	ces (sseh)
to	à (ah)
until	jusqu'à (zhewss-kah)
very	très (treh)
with	avec (ah-vehk)

Directions

north	le nord (luh nohr)
south	le sud (luh sewd)
east	l'est (lehsst)
west	l'ouest (lwehsst)
around the corner	au coin (oh kwa<u>n</u>)
straight ahead	tout droit (too drwah)
left	à gauche (ah gohsh)
in the middle	au milieu (oh mee-lyuh), au centre (oh sah<u>n</u>-truh)
right	à droite (ah drwaht)

Days of the Week

Sunday	dimanche (dee-mah<u>n</u>sh)
Monday	lundi (luh<u>n</u>-dee)
Tuesday	mardi (mahr-dee)
Wednesday	mercredi (mehr-kruh-dee)
Thursday	jeudi (zhuh-dee)
Friday	vendredi (vah<u>n</u>-druh-dee)
Saturday	samedi (sahm-dee)

today	aujourd'hui (oh-zhoor-dwee)
yesterday	hier (yehr)
tomorrow	demain (duh-ma<u>n</u>)
before, previously	antérieurement (ah<u>n</u>-teh-ryehr-mah<u>n</u>)
next week	la semaine prochaine (lah suh-meh<u>n</u> proh-shehn)
next month	le mois prochain (luh mwah proh-sha<u>n</u>)
the day after tomorrow	après-demain (ah-preh duh-ma<u>n</u>)
the weekend	le week-end (luh week-eh<u>n</u>d)
What day is today?	Quel jour est-ce aujourd'hui? (kehl zhoor ess oh-zhoor-dwee)
	Quel jour sommes-nous aujourd'hui? (kehl zhoor sohm noo oh-zhoor-dwee)
Today is _____.	C'est aujourd'hui _____. (seh toh-zhoor-dwee)
	Nous sommes _____. (noo sohm)
2 days ago	il y a deux jours (eel-yah duh zhoor)

in 2 days	dans deux jours (dah<u>n</u> duh zhoor)
every day	tous les jours (too lay zhoor)
day off	(le) jour de congé ([luh] zhoor duh koh<u>n</u>-zhay)
holiday	(le) jour de fête ([luh] zhoor duh feht)
birthday	l'anniversaire (lah-nee-vehr-ssehr)
per day	par jour (pahr zhoor)
during the day	pendant la journée (pah<u>n</u>-dah<u>n</u> lah zhoor-nay)
from this day on	dès aujourd'hui (deh zoh-zhoor-dwee)
the week	la semaine (lah suh-meh<u>n</u>)
a week day	un jour de semaine (uh<u>n</u> zhoor duh suh-meh<u>n</u>)
the week end	le week-end (luh week-ehnd)
last week	la semaine passée (lah suh-meh<u>n</u> pah-ssay)
this week	cette semaine (seht suh-meh<u>n</u>)
next week	la semaine prochaine (lah suh-meh<u>n</u> proh-sheh<u>n</u>)
a week from today	aujourd'hui en huit (oh-zhoor-dwee ah<u>n</u> weet)
2 weeks from tomorrow	demain en quinze (duh-ma<u>n</u> ah<u>n</u> ka<u>n</u>z)
during the week	pendant la semaine (pah<u>n</u>-dah<u>n</u> lah suh-meh<u>n</u>)

Months of the Year

January	janvier (zha<u>n</u>-vee-yay)
February	février (fay-vree-yay)
March	mars (mahrss)
April	avril (ah-vreel)
May	mai (meh)
June	juin (zhwa<u>n</u>)
July	juillet (zhwee-yeh)
August	août (oo *or* oot)
September	septembre (sehp-tah<u>n</u>-bruh)
October	octobre (ohk-toh-bruh)
November	novembre (noh-vah<u>n</u>-bruh)
December	décembre (day-sah<u>n</u>-bruh)
the month	le mois (luh mwah)
2 months ago	il y a deux mois (eel yah duh mwah)
last month	le mois dernier (luh mwah dehr-nyay)
this month	ce mois (suh mwah)
next month	le mois prochain (luh mwah proh-sha<u>n</u>)
during the month of	pendant le mois de (pah<u>n</u>-dah<u>n</u> luh mwah duh)
since the month of	depuis le mois de (duh-pwee luh mwah duh)
for the month of	pour le mois de (poor luh mwah duh)
every month	tous les mois (too lay mwah)
per month	par mois (pahr mwah)

What is today's date?	Quelle est la date aujourd'hui? (kehl ay lah daht zhoor-dwee?)
Today is _____ .	C'est aujourd'hui _____ . (seht oh-zhoor-dwee)
• Monday, May 1	• lundi, le premier mai (luhn-dee luh pruh-myay may)
• Tuesday, June 2	• mardi, le deux juin (mahr-dee luh duh zhwan)

(NOTE: Use the ordinal number only for the first of the month.)

the year	l'an/l'année (lahn/lah-nay)
per year	par an (pahr ahn)
all year	toute l'année (toot lah-nay)
every year	chaque année (shahk ah-nay)
during the year	pendant l'année (pahn-dahn lah-nay)

The Four Seasons

spring	le printemps (luh pran-tan)
summer	l'été (lay-tay)
autumn	l'automne (loh-tohn)
winter	l'hiver (lee-vehr)

Time

What time is it?	Quelle heure est-il? (kehl uhr eh teel)
It is _____ .	Il est _____ . (eel eh)
• noon	• midi (mee-dee)
• 1:05	• une heure cinq (ewn-uhr sank)
• 2:10	• deux heures dix (duh-zuhr deess)
• 3:15	• trois heures et quart (trwah zuhr ay kahr)
• 4:20	• quatre heures vingt (kah-truh-uhr van)
• 5:25	• cinq heures vingt-cinq (sank-uhr van sank)
• 6:30	• six heures et demie (seez-uhr ay duh-mee)
• 7:35	• sept heures trente-cinq (seht-uhr trahnt-sank)
• 8:40	• neuf heures moins vingt (nuhv-uhr mwan van)
• 9:45	• dix heures moins le quart (deez-uhr mwan luh kahr)
• 10:50	• onze heures moins dix (ohnz uhr mwan deess)
• 11:55	• minuit moins cinq (mee-nwee mwan sank)
• 8:00	• huit heures (weet-uhr)
• 2:30	• deux heures et demie (duhz-uhr ay duh-mee)

- 7:15
- sept heures et quart (seht-uhr ay kahr)

per hour
par heure (pahr uhr)

three hours ago
il y a trois heures (eel yah trwah-zuhr)

early
tôt (toh), de bonne heure (duh bohn-uhr)

late
tard (tahr)

late (in arriving)
en retard (ahn ruh-tahr)

on time
à l'heure (ah luhr)

noon
midi (mee-dee)

midnight
minuit (mee-nwee)

in the morning
le matin (luh mah-tan)

in the afternoon
l'après-midi (lah-preh mee-dee)

in the evening
le soir (luh swahr)

at night
la nuit (lah nwee)

second
une seconde (ewn suh-gohnd)

minute
une minute (ewn mee-newt)

hour
une heure (ewn uhr)

a quarter of an hour
un quart d'heure (uhn kahr duhr)

a half hour
une demi-heure (ewn duh-mee uhr)

Arrival/Hotel

My name is _____.
Je m'appelle _____. (zhuh mah-pehl)

I am American.
Je suis américain. (zhuh swee zah-may-ree-kan)

I'm staying at _____.
Je suis à _____. (zhuh swee zah)

Here is my passport.
Voici mon passeport. (vwah-ssee mohn pahss-pohr)

- business card.
- ma carte de visite (mah kahrt duh vee-zeet)

I'm on a business trip.
Je suis en voyage d'affaires. (zhuh swee zahn vwah-yahzh dah fehr)

I'm just passing through.
Je suis de passage. (zhuh swee duh pah-ssazh)

I'll be staying here a few days.
Je reste ici quelques jours. (zhuh rehss-tay ee-ssee kehl-kuh zhoor)

- a week.
- une semaine. (ewn suh-mehn)

- a few weeks.
- quelques semaines. (kehl kuh suh-mehn)

- a month.
- un mois. (uhn mwah)

I have nothing to declare.
Je n'ai rien à déclarer. (zhuh nay ryan ah day-klah-ray)

I'd like to go to the _____ hotel.
Je voudrais aller à l'hôtel _____. (zhu voo-dreh zah-lay ah loh-tehl)

Where can I get a taxi?
Où puis-je trouver un taxi? (oo pweezh troo-vay uhn tahk-ssee)

I have a reservation.
J'ai retenu une chambre. (zhay ruh-tuh-new ewn shan-bruh)

I need a room for one night.
Je voudrais une chambre pour une nuit. (zhuh voo-dreh zewn shan-bruh poor ewn nwee)

I want a double room with a bath.

Je voudrais une chambre à deux lits avec salle de bains. (zhuh voo-dreh zewn shan-bruh ah duh lee ah-vehk sahl duh ban)

What is the rate for the room without meals?

Quel est le tarif pour la chambre sans repas? (kehl eh luh tah-reef poor lah shan-bruh sahn ruh-pah)

What is the rate with breakfast?

Quel est le tarif petit déjeuner compris? (kehl eh luh tah-reef puh-tee day-zhuh-nay kohn-pree)

Where is the elevator?

Où est l'ascenseur? (oo eh lah-sahn-suhr)

Please send up some mineral water.

Veuillez m'apporter de l'eau minérale. (vuh-yay mah-pohr-tay duh loh mee-nay-rahl)

Please wake me tomorrow at _____ .

Réveillez-moi demain matin à ____ , s'il vous plaît. (ray-veh-yay mwah duh-man mah-tan ah seel voo pleh)

Did anyone call for me?

Est-ce que quelqu'un m'a téléphone? (ehss-kuh kehl-kuhn mah tay-lay-foh-nay)

I'd like to put this in the hotel safe.

Je voudrais mettre ceci dans le coffre-fort de l'hôtel. (zhuh voo-dreh meh-truh ssuh-ssee dahn luh koh-fruh fohr duh loh-tehl)

Can you please make this call for me?

Pouvez-vous faire un appel téléphonique pour moi, s'il vous plaît? (poo-vay voo fehr uhn-nah-pehl tay-lay-foh-neek poor mwah seel vous pleh)

Please send someone up for the bags.

Envoyez quelqu'un pour descendre mes bagages, s'il vous plaît. (ahn-vwah-yay kehl-kuhn poor day-ssahn-druh may bah-gahzh seel vous pleh)

Is my bill ready?

Est-ce que ma note est prête? (ehss kuh mah noht eh preht)

Transportation

bus

l'autobus or le bus (loh-toh-bewss) (luh bewss)

train

le train (luh tran)

subway

le métro (luh may-troh)

ticket

le billet (luh bee-yeh)

I would like to rent a small car.

Je voudrais louer une petite voiture. (zhuh voo-dreh loo-ay ewn puh-teet vwah-tewr)

...with automatic transmission

...avec transmission automatique (ah-vehk trahnz-mee-ssyohn oh-toh-mah-teek)

How much does it cost per day?

Quel est le tarif par jour? (kehl eh luh tah-reef pahr zhoor)

• per week?

• par semaine? (pahr suh-mehn)

• per kilometer?

• par kilomètre? (pahr kee-loh-meh-truh)

How much is the insurance?

Combien coûte l'assurance? (kohn-byan koo-teh lah-ssew-rahnss)

Do you accept credit cards?

Acceptez-vous les cartes de crédit? (ahk-ssehp-tay voo lay kahrt duh kray-dee)

Do I have to leave a deposit?	Dois-je verser des arrhres? (dwahzh vehr-ssay day zahr)
I want to rent the car here and leave it some place else.	Je voudrais louer la voiture ici et la laisser ailleurs. (zhuh voo-dreh loo-ay lah vwah-tewr ee-ssee ay lah leh-ssay ah-yuhr)
I am looking for a gas station.	Je cherche une station-service. (shuh shehrsh ewn stah-ssyohn sehr-veess)
Fill'er up with premium.	Faites le plein s'il vous plaît, avec du super. (feht-luh plan seel voo-pleh ah-vehk dew sew-pehr)
Please check the battery.	Veuillez vérifier la batterie. (vuh-yay vay-ree-fyay lah bah-tree)

- the brakes.
- the carburetor.
- the oil.
- the spark plugs.
- the tires.
- the water.

- les freins. (lay fran)
- le carburateur. (luh kahr-bew-rah-tuhr)
- le niveau d'huile. (luh nee-voh dweel)
- les bougies. (lay boo-zhee)
- les pneus. (lay pnuh)
- le niveau d'eau. (luh nee-voh doh)

Could you show me the way on this road map?	Pouvez-vous me montrer le chemin sur cette carte routière? (poo-vay voo muh mohn-tray luh chuh-man sewr seht kahrt roo-tyehr)
Where is my hotel on this map?	Où se trouve mon hôtel sur ce plan? (oo suh troov mohn oh-tehl sewr sseh plahn)

Familiarize yourself with these traffic signs:

No U-turn

No passing

Border crossing

Traffic signal ahead

Speed limit

Traffic circle (roundabout) ahead

Minimum speed limit

All traffic turns left

End of no passing zone

One-way street   Detour

Danger ahead   Entrance to expressway   Expressway ends

Gasoline (petrol) ahead   Right of way   Dangerous intersection ahead

Parking   No vehicles allowed   Dangerous curve

Pedestrian crossing   Oncoming traffic has right of way   No bicycles allowed

| No parking allowed | No entry | No left turn |

| Guarded railroad crossing | Yield | Stop |

Where is the subway station?

How much is a ticket?

• a book

Where can I buy a ticket?

Does this train go to _____ ?

Please tell me when we get there.

Do I have to change trains?

Is this seat taken?

Taxi! Are you available?

Take me to this address.

How much is it?
Wait for me. I'll be right back.

At what time is there a flight to _____ ?
I would like a round-trip ticket in coach.

• in first class.

I would like a seat in the

Où se trouve la station de métro? (oo suh troov lah stah-ssyohn duh may-troh)
Combien coûte un ticket (kohn-byan koo-tay uhn tee-keht)

• un carnet (uhn kahr-neh)

Où puis-je acheter un billet? (oo pweezh ahsh-tay uhn bee-yeh)

Est-ce que ce train va à _____ ? (ehss kuh suh tran vah ah)

S'il vous plaît, dites-moi quand nous y arriverons. (seel voo pleh, deet mwah kahn noo zee ah-ree-vrohn)

Dois-je changer de train? (dwahzh shahn-zhay duh tran)

Est-ce que cette place est occupée? (ehss kuh seht plahss eh toh-kew-pay)

Taxi! Etes-vous libre? (tahk-ssee! eht voo lee-bruh)

Conduisez-moi à cette adresse. (kohn-dwee-zay mwah ah seht-ah-drehss)

C'est combien? (seh kohn-byan)
Attendez-moi s'il vous plaît. Je reviens tout de suite. (ah-tahn-day mwah seel voo pleh. Zhuh ruh-vyan toot sweet)

À quelle heure y a-t-il un vol pour _____ ? (ah kehl uhr ee ah-teel uhn vohl poor)
Je voudrais un aller et retour en classe touriste. (zhuh oo-dreh zuhn ah-lay ay ruh-toor ahn toor-istee klahss)

• en première classe. (ahn pruh-myehr klahss)

Je voudrais une place dans la section

non-smoking section.	non-fumeurs. (zhuh voo-dreh zewn plahss dah<u>n</u> lah sehk-ssoh<u>n</u> noh<u>n</u>-few-muhr)
• near the window.	• près d'une fenêtre. (pray dewn fuh-neh-truh)
• on the aisle.	• côté couloir. (koh-tay koo-lwahr)
At what time does the plane leave?	À quelle heure part l'avion? (ah kehl uhr pahr lah vyoh<u>n</u>)
What is my flight number?	Quel est le numéro de mon vol? (kehl eh luh new-may-roh duh moh<u>n</u> vohl)
What gate do we leave from?	De quelle porte partons-nous? (duh kehl pohrt pahr-toh<u>n</u> noo)

Leisure Time

Is there a discotheque here?	Y a-t-il une discothèque? (ee ah teel ewn deess-koh-tehk)
Is there one at the hotel?	Y en-a-t-il une dans l'hôtel? (ee-ah<u>n</u>-ah teel ewn dah<u>n</u> loh-tehl)
I would like to reserve a table.	Je voudrais réserver une table. (zhuh voo-dreh ray-sehr-veh ewn tah-bluh)
Where is the checkroom?	Où est le vestiaire? (oo eh luh vehss-tyehr)
Where can I buy English-language newspapers?	Où puis-je me procurer des journaux en anglais? (oo pweezh muh proh-kew-ray day zhoor-noh ah<u>n</u> ah<u>n</u>-gleh)
I would like to see a soccer match.	Je voudrais voir un match de football. (zhuh voo-dreh vwahr uh<u>n</u> mahtch duh foot-bohl)
Where can I buy tickets?	Où puis-je acheter des billets? (oo pwee-zhuh ahsh-tay day bee-yeh)
Where is the stadium?	Où est le stade? (oo eh luh stahd)
What teams are going to play?	Quelles équipes vont jouer? (kehl zay-keep voh<u>n</u> zhoo-ay)
Is there a pool near the hotel?	Y a-t-il une piscine près de l'hôtel? (ee-ah-teel ewn pee-seen pray duh loh-tehl)
Is it far?	Est-ce que c'est loin? (ehss kuh seh lwa<u>n</u>)

Restaurants

Breakfast	le petit déjeuner (luh puh-tee day-zhuh-nay)
Lunch	le déjeuner (luh day-zhuh-nay)
Dinner	le dîner (luh dee-nay)
Do you know a good restaurant?	Connaissez-vous un bon restaurant? (koh-neh-ssay voo uh<u>n</u> boh<u>n</u> rehss-toh-rah<u>n</u>)
Is it very expensive?	Est-ce très cher? (ehss treh shehr)
Waiter!	Monsieur! (muh ssyuh)
We would like to have lunch.	Nous voudrions déjeuner (noo voo-dree-yoh<u>n</u> day-zhuh-nay)
The menu, please.	La carte (le menu) s'il vous plaît. (lah kahrt [luh muh-new] seel voo pleh)

What's today's special?

What do you recommend?

To begin, bring us a cocktail...

...and also a bottle of mineral water...

...and a beer.

I would like to order.

Do you have a house wine?

- a knife
- a fork
- a spoon
- a teaspoon

- a glass
- a cup
- a plate
- a napkin

I would like an espresso without sugar, please.

Do you mind if I smoke?

Do you have American cigarettes?

What brands?

Please give me a pack of matches also.

The check, please.

Is the tip included?

Do you accept credit cards?

Which ones?

I don't think this is right.

We are in a hurry.

Where are the rest rooms?

Quel est le plat du jour? (kehl eh luh plah dew zhoor)

Que me recommandez-vous? (kuh muh ruh-koh-mahn-day voo)

Pour commencer, apportez-nous un apéritif...(poor koh-mahn-ssay, ah-pohr-tay noo uhn nah-pay-ree-teef)

...et aussi une bouteille d'eau minérale... (ay oh-see ewn boo-tehy doh mee-nay-rahl)

...et une bière. (ay ewn byehr)

Je voudrais commander. (zhuh voo-dreh koh-mahn-day)

Avez-vous du vin ordinaire? (ah-vay voo dew van ohr-dee-nehr)

- un couteau (uhn-koo-toh)
- une fourchette (ewn foor-sheht)
- une cuiller (ewn kwee-yehr)
- une cuiller à café (ewn kwee-yehr ah kah-fay)

- un verre (uhn vehr)
- une tasse (ewn tahss)
- une assiette (ewn ah-ssyeht)
- une serviette (ewn sehr-vyeht)

Je voudrais un café espress sans sucre s'il vous plaît. (zhuh voo-dreh zuhn kah-fay ehss-prehss sahn sew-kruh seel voo pleh)

Ça vous dérange si je fume? (sah voo day-rahnzh see zhuh fewm)

Avez-vous des cigarettes américaines? (ah-vay voo day see-gah-reht ah-may-ree-kehn)

Quelles marques? (kehl mahrk)

Donnez-moi aussi une boîte d'allumettes, s'il vous plaît. (doh-nay mwah oh-see ewn bwaht dah-lew-meht, seel voo pleh)

L'addition, s'il vous plaît. (lah-dee-ssyohn seel voo pleh)

Le pourboire est-il compris? (luh poohr-bwahr kohn-pree)

Acceptez-vous les cartes de crédit? (ahk-ssehp-tay voo lay kahrt duh kray-dee)

Lesquelles? (lay-kehl)

Je crois qu'il y a une erreur. (zhuh krwah keel yah ewn ehr-ruhr)

Nous sommes pressés. (Noo sohm preh-ssay)

Où sont les toilettes? (oo sohn lay twah-leht)

Shopping

How much is it?	C'est combien? (seh kohn-byan)
Where could I find _____?	Où pourrais-je trouver _____? (oo poo-rehzh troo-vay)
Can you help me?	Pouvez-vous m'aider? (poo-vay meh-day)
I need _____.	J'ai besoin de _____. (zhay buh-zwan duh)
Do you have any others?	En avez-vous d'autres? (ahn nah-vay voo doh-truh)
Can I pay with a traveler's check?	Puis-je payer avec un chèque de voyage? (pweezh peh-yay ah-vehk uhn shehk duh vwah-yahzh)
Do you have anything smaller?	Avez-vous quelque chose de plus petit? (ah-vay voo kehl kuh shohz duh plew puh-teet)
• larger	• de plus grand (duh plew grahn)

Medical Care

Where is the nearest pharmacy?	Où se trouve la pharmacie la plus proche? (oo suh troov lah fahr-mah-ssee lah plew prohsh)
I need something for a cold.	Il me faut quelque chose pour un rhume. (eel muh foh kehl-kuh shohz poor uhn rewm)
• constipation.	• la constipation. (lah kohn-stee-pah-ssyohn)
• a cough.	• la toux. (lah too)
• diarrhea.	• la diarrhée. (lah dee-ah-ray)
• a headache.	• un mal de tête. (uhn mahl duh teht)
• insomnia.	• l'insomnie. (lan-sohm-nee)
• a toothache.	• un mal de dents. (uhn mahl duh dahn)
• an upset stomach.	• une indigestion. (uhn-zan-dee-shehss-tyohn)
I don't feel well. I need a doctor who speaks English.	Je ne me sens pas bien. Je voudrais voir un médecin qui parle anglais. (zhuh nuh muh sahn pah byan. Zhuh voo-drey vwahr unn mayd-ssan kee pahrl ahn-gleh)
I am dizzy.	J'ai des vertiges. (zhai day vehr-teezh)
I feel weak.	Je me sens faible. (zhuh muh sahn feh-bluh)
I have a pain in my chest, around my heart.	J'ai une douleur à la poitrine, près du coeur. (zhai ewn doo-luhr ah lah pwah-treen preh dew kuhr)
I had a heart attack a few years ago.	J'ai eu une crise cardiaque il y a quelques années. (zhai ew ewn kreez kahr-dyahk eel yah kehl kuh zahn-nay)
I am taking this medicine.	Je prends ce médicament. (zhuh prahn suh may-dee kah-mahn)
Do I have to go to the hospital?	Dois-je aller à l'hôpital? (dwahzh al-lay al loh-pee-tahl)

I have a toothache. Could you recommend a dentist?	J'ai un mal de dents. Pouvez-vous me recommander un dentiste? (zhai uhn mahl duh dahn. Poo-vay voo muh ruh-koh-mahn-day uhn dahn-teesst)
I just broke my glasses. Can you repair them while I wait?	Je viens de casser mes lunettes. Pouvez-vous les réparer pendant que j'attends? (zhuh vee-ahn duh kah-ssay may lew-neht. Poo-vay voo lay ray-pah-ray pahn-dahn kuh zha-tahn)

Telephone

Is there a phone booth?	Y a-t-il une cabine téléphonique? (ee ah-teel ewn kah-been tay-lay-foh-neek)
Do you have a telephone directory?	Avez-vous un annuaire téléphonique? (ah-veh voo-zuhn ah-new-ehr tay-lay-foh-neek)
I want to make a person to person call.	Je voudrais téléphoner en préavis. (zhuh voo-dreh tay-lay-foh-nay ahn pray-ah-vee)
How do you call the United States?	Que faites-vous pour téléphoner aux États-Unis? (kuh feht voo poor tay-lay-foh-nay oh zeh-tah zew-nee)
I would like to talk to the operator.	Je voudrais parler à l'opératrice. (zhuh voo-dreh pahr-leh ah loh-peh-rah-treess)
May I speak to...	Pourrais-je parler à... (poor-rayzh pahr-lay ah)
Who is calling?	Qui est à l'appareil? (kee eh tah-lah-pah-rehy)
Speak louder.	Parlez plus fort. (pahr-lay plew fohr)
Hold on.	Ne quittez pas. (nuh kee-tay pah)
You gave me a wrong number.	Vous m'avez donné le mauvais numéro. (voo mah-vay doh-nay luh moh-veh new-may-roh)
I was disconnected.	J'ai été coupé. (zhai ay-tay koo-pay)
I would like to leave a message.	Je voudrais laisser un message. (zhuh voo-dreh leh-ssay uhn meh-ssahzh)

Postal Service

Post Office	Le bureau de poste (luh bew-roh duh pohsst)
A postcard	une carte postale (un kahrt pohss-tahl)
a letter	une lettre (ewn leh-truh)
a telegram	un télégramme (uhn tay-lay-grahm)
air-mail letter	une lettre par avion (ewn leh-truh pahr ah-vyohn)
a registered letter	une lettre recommandée (ewn leh-truh ruh-koh-mahn-day)
a special delivery letter	une lettre exprès (ewn leh-truh ehkss-prehss)
a package	un colis (uhn koh-lee)

I would like to buy some stamps.	Je voudrais acheter des timbres. (zhuh voo-dreh zahsh-tay day tah<u>n</u>-bruh)
What is the postage to the United States?	Quel est l'affranchissement pour les États-Unis? (kehl ey lah-frah<u>n</u>-sheess-mah<u>n</u> poor lay zay-tah-zew-nee)
Where is the letter box?	Où se trouve la boîte aux lettres? (oo suh troov lah bwaht oh leh-truh)
I would like to send a telex.	Je voudrais envoyer un télex. (zhuh voo-dreh zah<u>n</u>-vwah-yay uh<u>n</u> teh-lehks)
How late are you open?	Jusqu'à quelle heure êtes-vous ouvert? (zhewss-kah kehl uhr eht voo zoo-vehr)
How much is it per minute? Or per word?	Quel est le tarif par minute? Ou par mot? (kehl eh luh tah-reef pahr mee-newt? Oo pahr moh?)

Signs

For Rent	À louer (ah loo-ay)
For Sale	À vendre (ah vah<u>n</u>-druh)
Elevator	Ascenseur (ah-sah<u>n</u>-ssuhr)
Careful	Attention (ah-tah<u>n</u>-ssyoh<u>n</u>)
Ladies	Dames (dahm)
Danger	Danger (dah<u>n</u>-zhay)
Do Not Enter	Défense d'entrer (day-fah<u>n</u>ss dah<u>n</u>-tray)
No Smoking	Défense de fumer (day-fah<u>n</u>ss-duh few-may)
Keep Off the Grass	Défense de marcher sur la pelouse (day-fah<u>n</u>ss duh mahr-shay sewr lah pehl-oos)
Don't Drink the Water	Eau non potable (oh noh<u>n</u> poh-tah-bluh)
Entrance	Entrée (ah<u>n</u>-tray)
Closed	Fermé (fehr-may)
Men	Hommes (ohm)
Information	Renseignements (rah<u>n</u>-seh-nyuh-mah<u>n</u>), Information (a<u>n</u>-fohr-mah-ssyoh<u>n</u>)
Free *or* Unoccupied	Libre (lee-bruh)
Occupied	Occupé (oh-kew-pay)
Open	Ouvert (oo-vehr)
Push	Poussez (poo-ssay)
Private	Privé (pree-vay)
Waiting Room	Salle d'attente (sahl dah-tah<u>n</u>t)
Exit	Sortie (sohr-tee)
No Parking	Stationnement interdit (stah-ssyoh<u>n</u>-mah<u>n</u> a<u>n</u>-tehr-dee)
Pull	Tirez (tee-ray)

Numbers

Cardinal Numbers: Numerals of more than three figures have a period in French, instead of a comma. Thus, 1,000 will appear as 1.000.

0	zéro (zay-roh)
1	un (uh<u>n</u>)

2	deux (duh)
3	trois (trwah)
4	quatre (kah-truh)
5	cinq (sank)
6	six (seess)
7	sept (seht)
8	huit (weet)
9	neuf (nuhf) ·
10	dix (deess)
11	onze (ohnz)
12	douze (dooz)
13	treize (trehz)
14	quatorze (kah-tohrz)
15	quinze (kanz)
16	seize (sehz)
17	dix-sept (dee-seht)
18	dix-huit (dee-zweet)
19	dix-neuf (deez-nuhf)
20	vingt (van)
21	vingt et un (van-tay-uhn)
22	vingt-deux (van-duh)
23	vingt-trois (van-trwah)
24	vingt-quatre (van-kah-truh)
25	vingt-cinq (van-sank)
26	vingt-six (van-seess)
27	vingt-sept (van-seht)
28	vingt-huit (van-tweet)
29	vingt-neuf (van-nuhf)
30	trente (trahnt)
31	trente et un (trahn-tay-uhn)
32	trente-deux (trahn-duh)
40	quarante (kah-rahnt)
41	quarante et un (kah-rahn-tay-uhn)
42	quarante-deux (kah-rahnt-duh)
50	cinquante (san-kahnt)
51	cinquante et un (san-kahn-tay-uhn)
52	cinquante-deux (san-kahnt-duh)
60	soixante (swah-ssahnt)
61	soixante et un (swah-ssahn-tay-uhn)
62	soixante-deux (swah-ssahnt-duh)
70	soixante-dix (swah-ssahnt-deess)
71	soixante et onze (swah-ssahn-tay-ohnz)
72	soixante-douze (swah-ssahnt-dooz)
73	soixante-treize (swah-ssahnt-trehz)
74	soixante-quatorze (swah-ssahnt-kah-tohrz)
75	soixante-quinze (swah-ssahnt-kanz)
76	soixante-seize (swah-ssahnt-sehz)
77	soixante-dix-sept (swah-ssahnt-dee-seht)
78	soixante-dix-huit (swah-ssahnt-dee-zweet)
79	soixante-dix-neuf (swah-ssahnt-deez-nuhf)

80	quatre-vingts (kah-truh-van)
81	quatre-vingt-un (kah-truh-van-uhn)
82	quatre-vingt-deux (kah-truh-van-duh)
90	quatre-vingt-dix (kah-truh-van-deess)
91	quatre-vingt-onze (kah-truh-van-ohnz)
92	quatre-vingt-douze (kah-truh-van-dooz)
100	cent (sahn)
101	cent un (sahnt uhn)
102	cent deux (sahn duh)
110	cent dix (sahn deess)
120	cent vingt (sahn-van)
200	deux cents (duh-sahn)
300	trois cents (trwah-sahn)
400	quatre cents (kah-truh-sahn)
500	cinq cents (sank-sahn)
600	six cents (see-sahn)
700	sept cents (seht-sahn)
800	huit cents (weet-sahn)
900	neuf cents (nuhf-sahn)
1,000	mille (meel)
2,000	deux mille (duh-meel)
3,000	trois mille (trwah-meel)
4,000	quatre mille (kah-truh-meel)
5,000	cinq mille (sank-meel)
6,000	six mille (sees-meel)
7,000	sept mille (seht-meel)
8,000	huit mille (wee-meel)
9,000	neuf mille (nuhf-meel)
10,000	dix mille (dee-meel)
20,000	vingt mille (van-meel)
30,000	trente mille (trahnt-meel)
40,000	quarante mille (kah-rahnt-meel)
50,000	cinquante mille (san-kahnt-meel)
60,000	soixante mille (swah-sahnt-meel)
70,000	soixante dix mille (swah-sahnt-dee-meel)
80,000	quatre-vingt mille(kah-truh-van-meel)
90,000	quatre-vingt dix mille (kah-truh-van-deess-meel)
100,000	cent mille (sahn-meel)
200,000	deux cent mille (duh-sahn-meel)
300,000	trois cent mille (trwah-sahn-meel)
400,000	quatre cent mille (kah-truh-sahn-meel)
500,000	cinq cent mille (sank-sahn-meel)
600,000	six cent mille (see-sahn-meel)
700,000	sept cent mille (seht-sahn-meel)
800,000	huit cent mille (wee-sahn-meel)
900,000	neuf cent mille (nuhf-sahn-meel)
1,000,000	un million (uhn-mee-lyohn)
2,000,000	deux millions (duh-mee-lyohn)
10,000,000	dix millions (dee-mee-lyohn)

100,000,000	cent millions (sah<u>n</u>-mee-lyoh<u>n</u>)
1,000,000,000	un milliard (uh<u>n</u> mee-lyarh)

Examples:

540	cinq cent quarante (sa<u>n</u>k-sah<u>n</u>-kah-rah<u>n</u>t)
1540	mille cinq cent quarante (meel-sa<u>n</u>k-sah<u>n</u>-kah-rah<u>n</u>t)
11,540	onze mille cinq cent quarante (oh<u>n</u>z-meel-sa<u>n</u>k-sah<u>n</u>-kah-rah<u>n</u>t)
611,540	six cent onze mille cinq cent quarante (see-sah<u>n</u>-oh<u>n</u>z-meel-sa<u>n</u>k-sah<u>n</u>-kah-rah<u>n</u>t)
1,611,540	un million six cent onze mille cinq cent quarante (uh<u>n</u> meellyoh<u>n</u> see-sah<u>n</u>-oh<u>n</u>z-sa<u>n</u>k-sah<u>n</u>-kah-rah<u>n</u>t)

Years:

1900	mille neuf cent (meel-<u>n</u>uhf-sah<u>n</u>)
1987	mille neuf cent quatre-vingt sept (meel-<u>n</u>uhf-sah<u>n</u>-kah-truh-va<u>n</u>-seht)
1988	mille neuf cent quatre vingt huit (meel-<u>n</u>uhf-sah<u>n</u>-kah-truh-va<u>n</u>-weet)
1989	mille neuf cent quatre-vingt neuf (meel-<u>n</u>uhf-sah<u>n</u>-kah-truh-va<u>n</u>-nuhf)
1990	mille neuf cent quatre-vingt dix (meel-nuhf-sah<u>n</u>-kah-truh-va<u>n</u>-deess)
1999	mille neuf cent quatre-vingt dix neuf (meel-nuhf-sah<u>n</u>-kah-truh-va<u>n</u>-deess-nuhf)

Ordinal Numbers:

first	premier/première (1er) (pruh-myay/pruh-myehr)
second	deuxième (2e) (duh-zyehm)
third	troisième (trwah-zyehm)
fourth	quatrième (kah-tree-yehm)
fifth	cinquième (sa<u>n</u>-kyehm)
sixth	sixième (see-zyehm)
seventh	septième (seh-tyehm)
eighth	huitième (wee-tyehm)
ninth	neuvième (nuh-vyehm)
tenth	dixième (dee-zyehm)

Quantities:

a half	une moitié (ewn mwah-tyay)
half a	un/une demi/e (uh<u>n</u>/ewn duh-mee)
half of	la moitié de (lah mwah-tyay duh)
a quarter	un quart (uh<u>n</u> kahr)
three quarters	trois quarts (trwah kahr)
a third	un tiers (uh<u>n</u> tyehr)
two thirds	deux tiers (duh tyehr)
a cup of	une tasse de (ewn tahss duh)

a dozen of	une douzaine de (ewn doo-zehn duh)
a kilo of	un kilo de (uhn kee-loh duh)
a liter of	un litre de (uhn lee-truh duh)
a little bit of	un peu de (uhn puh duh)
a lot of	beaucoup de (boh-koo duh)
a pair of	une paire de (ewn pehr duh)
enough of	assez de (ah-ssay duh)
too much of	trop de (troh duh)

Useful Abbreviations

B.M.	Banque Mondiale	World Bank
c.-à-d.	c'est-à-dire	that is to say *or* i.e.
CE	Communauté Européenne	E.C.
Cie.	Compagnie	Company
EU	États-Unis	United States
F.M.I.	Fonds Monétaire International	International Monetary Fund
h.	heure(s)	hour or o'clock
M.	Monsieur	Mr.
Mlle	Mademoiselle	Miss
MM.	Messieurs	Gentlemen
Mme	Madame	Mrs.
O.C.D.E.	Organisation de Coopération Économique	Organization for Economic Cooperation and Development
ONU	Organisation des Nations Unies	United Nations
p. ex.	par exemple	for example
P et T	Postes et Télécom-munications	Post Office and Telecom-munications
RATP	Régie Autonome des Transports Parisiens	Paris Transport Authority
RD	Route Départementale	local road
RN	Route Nationale	national road
SA	Société anonyme	Ltd., Inc.
SI	Syndicat d'Initiative	Tourist Information Office
SNCF	Société Nationale des Chemins de Fer Français	French National Railways
s.v.p.	s'il vous plaît	please
T.T.C.	toutes taxes comprises	taxes included

Business Schools

H.E.C.	(École des) Hautes Études Commerciales (exchange program with N.Y.U.)
ENA	École Nationale ut'Administration
ESSEC	École Supérieure de Sciences Économiques et Commerciales
SUPdeCo	École Supérieure de Commerce

IV. BUSINESS DICTIONARY

The 3,000-entry list of basic business terms is presented first in English to French, with the pronunciation in the last column, and later in French to English, with the pronunciation in the middle column. The pronunciation for each word is clearly indicated in italics. If the pronunciation is the same as the English pronunciation, however, the pronunciation column will be blank.

A

abandon (v)	abandonner	*(ah-bãhn-dœ-nEh)*
abandonment	l'abandon (prime, option), le délaissement (assurance maritime)	*(ah-bãhn-dÕhn), (prEEhm, ohp-syÕh), (deh-lehs-mÃh), (ah-sooh-rÃhns mah-reeh-tEEhm)*
abatement	l'abattement	*(ah-baht-mÃh)*
abide by a provision (v)	respecter une disposition	*(rœhs-pehk-tEh oohn deehs-poh-zeeh-syÕhn)*
ability-to-pay concept	la capacité contributive	*(kah-pah-seeh-tEh kõhn-treeh-booh-tEEhv)*
abortion	l'avortement, (m) l'IVG	*(ah-vohrt-mÃhn)*
above par	au-dessus du pair	*(oh dœ-sOOh dooh pEhr)*
above the line	au-dessus de la ligne	*(oh dœ-sOOh dœ lah lEEh-nyœ)*
abovementioned	susmentionné	*(sooh-mÃh-syoh-nEh)*
absentee ownership	l'absentéisme du propriétaire, le propriétaire absent	*(ahb-sãhn-teh-EEhz-mœ dooh proh-pryeh-tEhr), (proh-pryeh-tEhr ahb-sÃhn)*
absenteeism	l'absentéisme	*(ahb-sãhn-teh-EEhz-mœ)*
absorb (v)	absorber	*(ahb-zohr-bEh)*
absorb the loss (v)	apurer la perte	*(ah-pooh-rEh lah pEhrt)*
absorption costing	le prix de revient complet	*(prEEh dœ rœ-vyÁhn kohm-plEh)*
abstract of title	l'extrait du titre de proprieté	*(eks-trEh dooh tEEh-trœ dœ proh-preeh-eh-tEh)*
accelerated depreciation	l'amortissement accéléré	*(lah-mohr-eehs-mÃh ak-seh-leh-rEh)*
acceleration clause	la clause de remboursement anticipé	*(klOhz dœ rãhm-boohrs-mÃh ãhn-teeh-seeh-pEh)*
acceleration premiun	la prime de remboursement anticipé	*(prEEhm dœ rãhm-boohrs-mÃh ãhn-teeh-seeh-pEh)*
accept (v)	accepter	*(ahk-sehp-tEh)*
acceptable quality level	le niveau de qualité acceptable	*(neeh-vŒ dœ dœ kah-leeh-tEh ahk-sehp-tÁhblœ)*
acceptance	l'acceptation	*(ahk-sehp-tah-syÕh)*
acceptance agreement	l'accord d'acceptation	*(ah-kOhr dahk-sehp-tah-syÕh)*
acceptance bill	la traite documents contre acceptation	*(trEht doh-kooh-mÃh kõhn-trœ ahk-sehp-tah-syÕh)*
acceptance credit	le crédit par acceptation	*(kreh-dEEh pahr ahk-sehp-tah-syÕh)*
acceptance house	la banque d'escompte d'effets étrangers	*(bÃhnk del s-kÕhnt deh-fEht eh-trãhn-zhEh)*
acceptance sampling	l'échantillonnage pour acceptation	*(eh-shãhn-teeh-yoh-nAzh poohr lahk-sehp-tah-syÕh)*

acceptance test	le test en vue d'acceptation	*(læ tehst āhn vOOh dahk-sehp-tah-syŌh)*
acceptor	l'accepteur	*(ahk-sehp-tŒr)*
accession rate	le taux d'accession	*(tOh dahk-seh-syŌh)*
accidental damage	les dommages fortuits	*(doh-mAhzh fohr-twEEh)*
accommodation bill	la traite de complaisance	*(trEht dæ kõhn-pleh-zÃhns)*
accommodation credit	le crédit de complaisance	*(kreh-dEEh dæ kõhn-pleh-zÃhns)*
accommodation endorsement	l'endossement de complaisance	*(āhn-dohs-mÃh dæ kõhn-pleh-zÃhns)*
accommodation paper	le billet de complaisance	*(beeh-yEh dæ kõhn-pleh-zÃhns)*
accommodation parity	la parité de complaisance	*(pah-reeh-tEh dæ kõhn-pleh-zÃhns)*
accommodation platform	le programme de complaisance	*(proh-grAhm dæ kõhn-pleh-zÃhns)*
accompanied goods	les marchandises accompagnées	*(mahr-shāhn-dEEhz ah-kõhm-pah-nyEh)*
accord and satisfaction	l'accord général	*(ah-kOhr zheh-neh-rAhl)*
account	le compte	*(kŌhnt)*
account balance	le solde d'un compte	*(sOhld dæhn kŌhnt)*
account day	le jour de liquidation	*(zhOOhr dæ leeh-keeh-dah-syŌh)*
account executive	le chef de publicité, le gestionnaire de compte, la personne en charge de comptes déterminés (responsable du budget)	*(shef dæ pooh-bleeh-seeh-tEh), (zhehs tyohn-nEhr dæ kŌhnt), (pehr-sŌhn āhn shAhrzh dæ kŌhnt deh-tehr-meeh-nEh)*
account for (v)	tenir compte de	*(tæ-nEEhr kŌhnt dæ)*
account number	le numéro de compte	*(nooh-meh-rOh dæ kŌhnt)*
account, current	le compte courant	*(kŌhnt kooh-rÃhn)*
accountability	la responsabilité	*(ræs-pohn-sah-beeh-leeh-tEh)*
accountant	la, le comptable	*(kõhn-tAh-blæ)*
accountant, chief	le chef comptable	*(shEhf kõhn-tAh-blæ)*
accounting department	le service de comptabilité	*(sær-vEEhs dæ kõhn-tah-beeh-leeh-tEh)*
accounting method	la méthode comptable	*(meh-tOhd kõhn-tAh-blæ)*
accounting period	l'exercice comptable	*(ehk-sær-sEEhs kõhn-tAh-blæ)*
accounting ratio	le ratio comptable	*(rAh-syoh kõhn-tAh-blæ)*
accounting, cost	la comptabilité de prix de revient	*(kõhn-tah-beeh-leeh-tEh dæ prEEh dæ ræ-vyÃhn)*
accounting, management	la comptabilité de gestion	*(kõhn-tah-beeh-leeh-tEh dæ zhæhs-tyŌh)*
accounts payable	les dettes passives, les dettes à court terme	*(DEht pah-sEEhv), (dEht ah koohr tEhrm)*

A

accounts receivable	les dettes actives, les valeurs réalisables à court terme	*(DEht ahk-tEEhv), (vah-lŒhr reh-ah-leeh-zAh-blœ ah koohr tEhrm)*
accounts, group	les comptes groupés	*(kÕhnt grooh-pEh)*
accounts, secured	les comptes garantis	*(kÕhnt gah-rähn-tEEh)*
accretion	l'accroissement	*(ah-krwahs-mÃh)*
accrual	l'accumulation des intérêts	*(ah-kooh-mooh-lah-syÕh dehz æhn-teh-rEh)*
accrual method	la méthode du report variable	*(meh-tOhd dooh ræh-pŒhr vah-ryAh-blœ)*
accrue (v)	courir	*(kooh-rEEhr)*
accrued assets	les éléments d'actif courus et non échus	*(eh-leh-mÃh dahk-tEEf kooh-rOOh eh nõhn eh-shOOh)*
accrued depreciation	l'amortissement couru	*(ah-mohr-eehs-mÃh kooh-rOOh)*
accrued expenses	les charges courues	*(shAhrzh kooh-rOOh)*
accrued interest	les intérêts courus et non échus	*(æhn-teh-rEh kooh-rOOh eh nõhn eh-shOOh)*
accrued revenue	le revenu couru	*(ræhv-nOOh kooh-rOOh)*
accrued taxes	les impôts courus, la provision pour impôts	*(æhm-pOh kooh-rOOh), (proh-veeh-zyÕhn poohr æhm-pOh)*
accumulated depreciation	l'amortissement accumulé	*(ah-mohr-eehs-mÃh ah-kooh-mooh-lEh)*
acetic acid	l'acide acétique	*(ah-sEEhd ah-seh-tEEhk)*
acetone	l'acétone	*(ah-seh-tOhn)*
acid	l'acide	*(ah-sEEhd)*
acid content	le degré d'acidité	*(deh-grEh dah-seeh-deeh-tEh)*
acid rain	la pluie acide	*(plwEEh ah-sEEhd)*
acid-test ratio	le ratio de liquidité immédiate	*(rAh-syoh dœ leeh-keeh-deeh-tEh eeh-meh-dyAht)*
acknowledge (v)	reconnaître, admettre	*(ræ-koh-nEh-trœ), (ahd-mEh-trœ)*
acknowledge receipt of (v)	accuser réception de	*(ah-kooh-zEh reh-sehp-syÕh dœ)*
acknowledgment	le remerciement	*(ræh-mehr-seeh-mÃh)*
acoustic coupler	le coupleur acoustique	*(kooh-plŒr ah-koohs-tEEhk)*
acquire (v)	acquérir	*(ah-keh-rEEhr)*
acquired rights	les droits acquis	*(drwAh ah-kEEh)*
acquisition	l'acquisition	*(ah-keeh-zehh-syÕh)*
acquisition profile	le profil des acquisitions	*(proh-fEEhl dehz ah-keeh-zehh-syÕh)*
acquisition, data	l'acquisition des informations, la saisie des données	*(ah-keeh-zehh-syÕh dehz æhn-fohr-mah-syÕh), (seh-zEEh deh doh-nEh)*

acreage allotment	la superficie maximale de terrains dont la production donne droit à subvention	*(sooh-pehr-feeh-sEEh mahk-seeh-mAhl dœ tœr-Æhn dŌhn lah proh-doohk-syŌh dOhn drwAh ah soohb-vāhn-syŌh)*
acronym	le sigle	*(sEEh-glœ)*
across-the-board settlement	l'accord unanime	*(ah-kOhr ooh-nah-nEEhm)*
across-the-board tariff negotiations	les négociations tarifaires générales	*(neh-goh-syah-syŌh tah-reeh-fEhr zheh-neh-rAhl)*
act of God	le cas de force majeure	*(kAh dœ fOhrs mah-zhŒhr)*
action plan	le programme d'action	*(proh-grAhm dahk-syŌh)*
action research	l'investigation	*(æn-vehs-teeh-gah-syŌh)*
active account	le compte actif	*(kŌhnt ahk-tEEf)*
active assets	les éléments d'actif productifs	*(eh-leh-mÃh dahk-tEEf proh-doohk-tEEhf)*
active debt	la dette active	*(DEht ahk-tEEhv)*
active trust	la fiducie active	*(feeh-dooh-sEEh ahk-tEEhv)*
activity chart	le graphique des activités	*(graf-fEEhk dehz ahk-teeh-veeh-tEh)*
actual cash value	la valeur réelle au comptant	*(vah-lŒhr reh-Ehl oh kōhn-tÃhn)*
actual cost	le coût réel	*(kOOht reh-Ehl)*
actual income	le revenu réel	*(rœhv-nOOh reh-Ehl)*
actual liability	la dette réelle	*(DEht reh-Ehl)*
actual market volume	le volume réel du marché	*(voh-lOOhm reh-Ehl dooh mahr-shEh)*
actual total loss	la perte totale réelle	*(pEhrt toh-tAhl reh-Ehl)*
actuals	les chiffres réels	*(shEEh-frœ reh-Ehl)*
actuary	l'actuaire	*(ahk-twEhr)*
ad	la pub	*(poohb)*
add-on sales	les ventes complémentaires	*(vÃhnt kōhn-pleh-mÃh-tEhr)*
addendum	l'additif	*(ah-deeh-tEEf)*
additional payment	le paiement supplémentaire	*(peh-mÃh sooh-pleh-mÃh-tEhr)*
additive	l'additif	*(ah-deeh-tEEhf)*
address commission	la commission d'adresse	*(koh-meeh-syŌh dah-drEhs)*
adjudge (v)	prononcer un jugement	*(proh-nōhn-sEh œhn zhoohzh-mÃh)*
adjudication	le jugement	*(zhoohzh-mÃh)*
adjust (v)	ajuster	*(ah-zhOOhs-tEh)*
adjustable peg	la parité fixe, mais ajustable	*(pah-reeh-tEh fEEhks meh ah-zhOOhs-tAh-blœ)*
adjusted CIF price	le prix CAF ajusté	*(prEEh ah-zhOOhs-tEh)*
adjusted earned income	le revenu salarial ajusté	*(rœhv-nOOh sah-lah-ryAl ah-zhOOhs-tEh)*

A

adjusted rate	le taux ajusté	*(tOh ah-zhOOhs-tEh)*
adjusting entry	l'inscription comptable d'ajustement	*(æhn-skreehp-syŌ kõhn-tAh-blœ dah-zhOOhstœ-mÃh)*
adjustment process	le processus d'ajustement	*(proh-seh-sOOh dah-zhOOhstœ-mÃh)*
adjustment trigger	le déclenchement d'un processus d'ajustement	*(deh-cklãhnsh-mÃh dæhn proh-seh-sOOh dah-zhOOhstœ-mÃh)*
administration	l'administration, la gestion	*(ad-meeh-neehs-trah-syŌh), (zhœhs-tyŌh)*
administrative	administratif	*(ad-meeh-neehs-trah-tEEhf)*
administrative expenses	les frais d'administration	*(frEh dad-meeh-neehs-trah-syŌh)*
administrator	l'administrateur, le gestionnaire	*(ad-meeh-neehs-trah-tŒhr), (zhehs-tyohn-nEhr)*
administratrix	l'administratrice, la gestionnaire	*(ad-meeh-neehs-trah-trEEhs), (zhehs-tyohn-nEhr)*
advance (v)	avancer	*(ah-vãhn-sEh)*
advance notice	le préavis	*(preh-ah-vEEh)*
advance payments	les paiements anticipés	*(peh-mÃh ãhn-teeh-seeh-pEh)*
advance refunding	le remboursement anticipé	*(rãhm-boohrs-mÃh ãhn-teeh-seeh-pEh)*
advantage, competitive	l'avantage concurrentiel	*(ah-vãhn-tAhzh kõhn-kooh-rãhn-syEhl)*
adverse balance	la balance déficitaire	*(bah-lÃhns deh-feeh-seeh-tEhr)*
advertising	la publicité, la réclame	*(pooh-bleeh-seeh-tEh), (reh-klAhm)*
advertising agency	l'agence de publicité	*(ah-zhÃhns dœ pooh-bleeh-seeh-tEh)*
advertising budget	le budget publicitaire	*(booh-zhEh pooh-bleeh-see-tEhr)*
advertising campaign	la campagne de publicité	*(kãh-pÃh-nyœ dœ pooh-bleeh-seeh-tEh)*
advertising drive	la campagne publicitaire	*(kãh-pÃh-nyœ pooh-bleeh-seeh-tEhr)*
advertising expenses	les frais de publicité	*(frEh dœ pooh-bleeh-seeh-tEh)*
advertising manager	le chef de publicité	*(shEhf dœ pooh-bleeh-seeh-tEh)*
advertising media	les médias publicitaires	*(meh-dyAh pooh-bleeh-seeh-tEhr)*
advertising rates	les tarifs publicitaires	*(tah-rEEhf pooh-bleeh-see-tEhr)*
advertising research	la recherche publicitaire	*(rœ-shEhrsh pooh-bleeh-seeh-tEhr)*

advertising strategy	la stratégie publicitaire	*(strah-teh-zhEEh pooh-bleeh-seeh-tEhr)*
advice note	la lettre d'avis	*(lEh-trœ dah-vEEh)*
advise (v)	informer, conseiller	*(æhn-fohr-mEh), (kõh-seh-yEh)*
advisory council	le comité consultatif	*(koh-meeh-tEh kõh-soohl-tah-tEEhf)*
advisory funds	les fonds consultatifs	*(fÕhn kõh-soohl-tah-tEEhf)*
advisory service	le service de documentation	*(sœr-vEEhs dœ doh-kooh-mÃh-tah-syÕh)*
aerosol spray	l'aérosol	*(ah-eh-roh-sOhl)*
affidavit	l'affidavit, l'attestation par écrit	*(ah-feeh-dah-vEEh), (ah-tehs-tah-syÕh pahr eh-krEEh)*
affiliate	l'affilié, la filiale	*(ah-feeh-lyEh), (feeh-lyAhl)*
affirmative action	l'action positive	*(ahk-syÕh poh-zeeh-tEEhv)*
affreightment	l'affrètement	*(ah-freht-mÃh)*
afloat	à flot	*(ah flOh)*
after-hours trading	le commerce après-bourse	*(koh-mEhrs ah-prEh-bOOhrs)*
after-sales service	le service après-vente	*(sœr-vEEhs ah-prEh-vÃhnt)*
after-tax real rate of return	le taux de rentabilité net	*(tOh dœ rãhn-tah-beeh-leeh-tEh nEht)*
aftersight	à . . . jours de vue	*(ah zhOOhr dœ vOOh)*
aftertaste	l'arrière-goût	*(ah-ryEhr gOOht)*
against all risks	contre tous les risques	*(kõhn-trœ tooh leh rEEhs-kœ)*
agency	l'agence	*(ah-zhÃhns)*
agency fee	la commission d'agence	*(koh-meeh-syÕh dah-zhÃhns)*
agenda	l'ordre du jour	*(Ohr-drœ dooh zhOOhr)*
agent	l'agent, le mandataire	*(ah-zhÃh), (mÃhn-dah-tEhr)*
aggregate demand	la demande globale, l'offre globale	*(dæh-mÃhnd gloh-bAhl), (Oh-frœ gloh-bAhl)*
aggregate risk	le risque consolidé	*(rEEhs-kœ kõh-soh-leeh-dEh)*
aggregate supply	la production globale, l'offre globale	*(proh-doohk-syÕh gloh-bAhl), (Oh-frœ gloh-bAhl)*
aging	le vieillissement	*(vyeh-yeehs-mÃh)*
agreement	l'accord	*(ah-kOhr)*
agricultural paper	le journal agricole	*(zhOOhr-nAhl ah-greeh-kOhl)*
agriculture	l'agriculture	*(ah-greeh-koohl-tOOhr)*
AIDS	le sida	*(see-dAh)*

air date	la date de diffusion	(daht dœ deer-fooh-ZyÕhn)
air express	par express aérien	(pahr ek-sprEhs ah-eh-ryÊhn)
air filter	le filtre à air	(fEEhl-trœ ah Ehr)
air freight	le fret aérien	(frEht ah-eh-ryÊhn
air pollution	la pollution de l'air	(poh-looh-syÕhn dœ lEhr)
air shipments	le transport aérien	(trãhns-pOhr ah-eh-ryÊhn)
aircraft	l'avion, l'appareil	(ah-vyÕhn, ah-pah-rEhy)
airlock	le sas	(sAh)
air-to-air missile	le missile air-air	(meeh-sEEhl ehr-Ehr)
air-to-surface missile	le missile air-sol	(meeh-sEEhl ehr-sOhl)
alcohol	l'alcool	(ahl-kOhl)
alcohol-free	sans alcool	(sãhnz ahl-kOhl)
alcoholic content	la teneur en alcool	(tœ-nŒr ahn ahl-kOOl)
algorithm	l'algorithme	(ahl-goh-rEEht-mœ)
algorithmic language	le langage algorithmique	(lãhn-gAhzh ahl-goh-reeht-mEEhk)
alien corporation	la société étrangère	(soh-syeh-tEh eh-trãhn-zhEhr)
all in cost	tous frais compris	(tooh frEh kõh-prEEh)
all or none	tout ou rien	(tooht ooh ryÊh)
allergic reaction	la réaction allergique	(reh-ahk-syÕhn ah-lehr-zhEEhk)
allocation of costs	la répartition des coûts	(reh-pahr-teeh-syÕh deh kOOht)
allocation of responsibilities	la répartition des responsabilités	(reh-pahr-teeh-syÕh deh rœs-pohn-sah-beeh-leeh-tEh)
allocation, resource	la répartition des ressources	(reh-pahr-teeh-syÕh deh rœh-sOOhrs)
allot (v)	attribuer, répartir	(ah-treeh-booh-Eh), (reh-pahr-tEEhr)
allotment	l'attribution, l'affectation, la répartition, la part, la position	(ah-treeh-booh-syÕh), (ah-fehk-tah-syÕh), (reh-pahr-teeh-syÕh), (pAhr), (poh-zeeh-syÕh)
allotment letter	l'avis d'attribution	(ah-vEEh dah-treeh-booh-syÕh)
allow (v)	permettre, allouer, accorder	(pehr-mEh-trœ), (ah-looh-Eh), (ah-kohr-dEh)
allowance	l'allocation, la remise, la franchise, la tolérance	(ah-loh-kah-syÕh), (rœh-mEEhz), (frãh-shEEhz), (toh-leh-rÃhns)
allowance (tax)	l'abattement	(ah-baht-mÃhn)
allowance, depreciation	l'indemnité de dépréciation	(ãhn-dehm-neeh-tEh dœ deh-preh-syah-syÕh)

alloy steel	l'acier allié	*(ah-syEh ah-lyEh)*
ally	l'allié	*(ah-yEh)*
aloe vera	l'aloès	*(ah-loh-Eh)*
alongside	le long du bord	*(lŌh dooh bOhr)*
alteration	le changement, la modification	*(shāhnzh-mĀh), (mohdeeh-feeh-kah-syŌh)*
alternating current	le courant alternatif	*(kooh-rĀhnt ahl-tehr-nahtEEhf)*
alternative order	la commande alternative	*(koh-mĀhnd ahl-tehr-nahtEEhv)*
alternator	l'alternateur	*(ahl-tehr-nah-tŒhr)*
amalgamation	la fusion	*(fooh-zyŌh)*
amend (v)	amender, rectifier	*(ah-māhn-dEh), (rehkteeh-feeh-Eh)*
amendment	l'amendement	*(ah-māhnd-mĀh)*
amine	l'amine	*(ah-mEEhn)*
amino acid	l'acide aminé	*(ah-seehd ah-mEEhn)*
ammonia	l'ammoniac	*(ah-moh-nyAhk)*
ammunition	la munition	*(mooh-neeh-sŌhn)*
amortization	l'amortissement	*(ah-mohr-eehs-mĀh)*
amount	le montant, la somme	*(mōhn-tĀh), (sOhm)*
amount due	la somme due, le montant dû	*(sOhm dooh), (mōhn-tĀh dooh)*
amplifier	l'amplificateur	*(ahm-pleeh-feeh-kah-tŒhr)*
amplitude modulation (AM)	la modulation d'amplication	*(moh-dooh-lah-syŌh dahm-pleeh-kah-syŌh)*
analgesic	l'analgésique	*(āh-nahl-zheh-zEEhk)*
analog computer	l'ordinateur analogique	*(ohr-deeh-nah-tŒhr ahnah-loh-zhEEhk)*
analysis	l'analyse	*(āh-nah-lEEhz)*
analysis, break-even	l'analyse du point d'équilibre, le point de sensibilité	*(āh-nah-lEEhz dooh pwÆh deh-keeh-lEEhbrœ), (pwÆh dœ sāhseeh-beeh-leeh-tEh)*
analysis, competitor	l'analyse de la concurrence	*(āh-nah-lEEhz dœ lah kōhn-kooh-rĀhns)*
analysis, cost	l'évaluation des coûts	*(eh-vah-lwah-syŌh deh kOOht)*
analysis, cost-benefit	l'analyse coût/profit	*(āh-nah-lEEhz kOOht /proh-fÆEh)*
analysis, critical path	l'analyse du chemin critique	*(āh-nah-lEEhz dooh shœmÆh kreeh-tEEhk)*
analysis, depth	l'analyse en profondeur	*(āh-nah-lEEhz āhn prohfōhn-dŒhr)*
analysis, financial	l'analyse financière	*(āh-nah-lEEhz feeh-nāhnsyEhr)*
analysis, functional	l'analyse fonctionnelle	*(āh-nah-lEEhz fōhnk-syohnEhl)*

A

analysis, input-output	l'analyse des entrées et sorties	*(āh-nah-lEEhz dehz ãhn-trEh eh sohr-tEEh)*
analysis, investment	l'étude de la rentabilité des investissements	*(eh-tOOhd dœ lah rãhn-tah-beeh-leeh-tEh dehz æhn-vehs-teehs-mÃh)*
analysis, job	l'analyse de l'emploi	*(āh-nah-lEEhz dœ lãhm-plwAh)*
analysis, needs	l'analyse des besoins	*(āh-nah-lEEhz deh bœh-zwÆhn)*
analysis, product	l'analyse des produits	*(āh-nah-lEEhz deh proh-dwEEh)*
analysis, profitability	l'étude de rentabilité	*(eh-tOOhd dœ rãhn-tah-beeh-leeh-tEh)*
analysis, risk	l'étude du risque	*(eh-tOOhd dooh rEEhs-kœ)*
analysis, sales	l'étude des ventes	*(eh-tOOhd deh vÃhnt)*
analysis, systems	l'étude des méthodes	*(eh-tOOhd deh meh-tOhd)*
analyst	l'analyste	*(āh-nah-lEEhst)*
analytic chemistry	la chimie analytique	*(sheeh-mEEh āh-nah-leeh-tEEhk)*
anchorage (dues)	les droits de mouillage	*(drwAh dœ mweeh-yAhzh)*
ancillary operation	l'opération annexe	*(oh-peh-rah-syÕh ah-nEhks)*
anesthesia	l'anesthésie	*(ah-nehs-teh-zEEh)*
anesthetic	l'anesthétique	*(āh-nehs-teh-tEEhk)*
angle of incidence	l'angle d'incidence	*(ãhn-glœ dãhn-seeh-dÃhns)*
angora	l'angora	*(ãhn-goh-rAh)*
ankle boots	les bottines	*(boh-tEEhn)*
annealing	recuit	*(reh-kwEEh)*
annual	annuel	*(ah-nwEhl)*
annual accounts	les comptes annuels	*(kÕhnt ah-nwEhl)*
annual audit	la vérification annuelle	*(veh-reeh-feeh-kah-syÕh ah-nwEhl)*
annual report	le rapport annuel	*(rah-pOhr ah-nwEhl)*
annuitant	le rentier, la rentière	*(rãh-tyEh), (rãh-tyEhr)*
annuity	l'annuité, la rente à terme	*(ah-nweeh-tEh), (rãhnt ah tEhrm)*
antacid	l'antiacide	*(ahn-teeh-ah-sEEhd)*
antenna	l'antenne	*(ãhn-tEhn)*
anti-dumping duty	le droit antidumping	*(drwAh antidumping)*
anti-inflammatory	l'anti-inflammatoire	*(ahn-teeh-æhn-flah-mah-twAhr)*
antibiotic	l'antibiotique	*(ahn-teeh-beeh-oh-tEEhk)*
anticholinergic	l'anticholinergique	*(ahn-teeh-koh-leeh-nehr-zhEEhk)*
anticoagulant	l'anticoagulant	*(ahn-teeh-koh-ah-gooh-lÃh)*
antidepressant	l'anti-dépresseur	*(ahn-teeh-deh-preh-sŒhr)*
antique authenticity certificate	le certificat d'authenticité	*(sehr-teeh-feeh-kAh doh-tãhn-teeh-see-tEh)*

antiseptic	l'antiseptique	*(ahn-teeh-sehp-tEEhk)*
antitrust laws	les lois anti-trust	*(lwAh anti-trust)*
A.O.C.	Appellation d'Origine Contrôlée	*(ah-peh-lay-syÕhn doh-reeh-zheehn kõhn troh-lEh)*
apparel	les vêtements	*(vEht-mÃh)*
application form	le bulletin de souscription, le formulaire	*(booh-læ-t˜Æhn dæ sooh-skreehp-syÕh), (fohr-mooh-lEhr)*
applied proceeds swap	le solde d'application d'une opération d'échange	*(sOhld dah-pleeh-kah-syÕh doohn oh-peh-rah-syÕh deh-shÃhnzh)*
apply (v)	appliquer	*(ah-pleeh-kEh)*
appointment	la nomination, le rendez-vous	*(noh-meeh-nah-syÕh), (rãhn-deh-vOOh)*
appraisal	l'évaluation, l'estimation	*(eh-vah-lwah-syÕh), (ehs-teeh-mah-syÕh)*
appraisal, capital expenditure	l'estimation des immobilisations	*(ehs-teeh-mah-syÕh dehz eeh-moh-beeh-leeh-zah-syÕh)*
appraisal, financial	l'évaluation financière	*(eh-vah-lwah-syÕh feeh-nãhn-syEhr)*
appraisal, investment	l'évaluation des investissements	*(eh-vah-lwah-syÕh dehz æhn-vehs-teehs-mÃh)*
appraisal, market	l'évaluation du marché	*(eh-vah-lwah-syÕh dooh mahr-shEh)*
appraisal, self-	l'auto-appréciation	*(oh-toh-ah-preh-syah-syÕh)*
appreciation	la plus-value, l'evaluation	*(plooh-vah-lOOh), (eh-vah-lwah-syÕh)*
apprentice	l'apprenti	*(ah-prãhn-tEEh)*
appropriation	le prélèvement, l'affectation	*(preh-lehv-mÃh), (ah-fehk-tah-syÕh)*
approval	l'approbation, l'agrément	*(ah-proh-bah-syÕh), (ah-greh-mÃh)*
approve (v)	approuver, agréer	*(ah-prooh-vEh), (ah-greh-Eh)*
approved delivery facility	le service de livraison approuvé	*(sær-vEEhs dæ leeh-vreh-zÕh ah-prooh-vEh)*
approved securities	les garanties approuvées	*(gah-rãhn-tEEh ah-prooh-vEh)*
arbitrage	l'arbitrage	*(ahr-beeh-trAhzh)*
arbitration	l'arbitrage de litiges	*(ahr-beeh-trAhzh dæ leeh-tEEhzh)*
arbitration agreement	l'accord d'arbitrage	*(ah-kOhr dahr-beeh-trAhzh)*
arbitrator	l'arbitre	*(ahr-bEEh-træ)*
area manager	le chef de secteur	*(shEhf dæ sehk-tŒhr)*
arithmetic mean	la moyenne arithmétique	*(mwah-yEhn areeht-meh-tEEhk)*

A

armaments	les armements	(ahr-mœh-mÃhn)
arms length	à des conditions normales	(ah deh kõhn-deeh-syÕh nohr-mAhl)
aroma	l'arôme	(ah-rOhm)
around (exchange term)	environ	(ãhn-veeh-rÕh)
arrears	l'arriéré, l'arrérage	(ah-ryeh-rEh), (ah-reh-rAhzh)
art department	le service de création	(sœr-vEEhs dœ kreh-sh-syÕhn)
art director	le directeur artistique	(deeh-rehk-tŒhr ahr-teehs-tEEhk)
arthritis	l'arthrite	(ahr-trEEht)
as soon as possible	aussitôt que possible	(oh-seeh-tOh kœ poh-sEEh-blœ)
as, if and when	sous les réserves d'usage	(sooh leh reh-zEhrv dooh-zAhz)
as-is goods	les marchandises telles quelles	(mahr-shãhn-dEEhz tehl kEhl)
ashtray	le cendrier	(sãhn-dryEh)
asking price	le prix demandé	(prEEh dœh-mãhn-dEh)
aspirant member	le candidat à l'adhésion	(kãhn-deeh-dah ah lah-deh-zyÕhn)
aspirin	l'aspirine	(ahs-peeh-rEEhn)
assay	l'essai	(eh-sEh)
assemble (v)	assembler	(ah-sãhm-blEh)
assembly	l'assemblée, l'assemblage	(ah-sãhm-blEh), (ah-sãhm-blAhzh)
assembly line	la chaîne de montage	(shEhn dœ mõhn-tAhzh)
assess (v)	estimer	(ehs-teeh-mEh)
assessed valuation	la valeur estimée	(vah-lŒhr ehs-teeh-mEh)
assessment	l'évaluation, l'imposition d'office	(eh-vah-lwah-syÕh), (æhm-poh-zeeh-syÕh doh-fEEhs)
asset	l'actif, la valeur, le capital	(ahk-tEEf), (vah-lŒhr), (kah-peeh-tAhl)
asset turnover	la rotation des capitaux	(roh-tah-syÕh deh kah-peeh-tOh)
asset value	la valeur en capital	(vah-lŒhr ãhn kah-peeh-tAhl)
assets, accrued	les éléments d'actif courus	(eh-leh-mÃh dahk-tEEf kooh-rOOh)
assets, current	l'actif disponible	(ahk-tEEf deehs-poh-nEEh-blœ)
assets, deferred	les capitaux différés	(kah-peeh-tOh deeh-feh-rEh)
assets, fixed	les immobilisations	(eeh-moh-beeh-leeh-zah-syÕh)
assets, intangible	les valeurs intangibles	(vah-lŒhr æhn-tãhn-zhEEh-blœ)

assets, liquid	les disponibilités	*(deehs-poh-neeh-beeh-leeh-tEh)*
assets, net	l'actif net	*(ahk-tEEf nEht)*
assets, tangible	les valeurs matérielles, tangibles	*(vah-lŒhr mah-teh-ryEhl), (tāhn-zhEEh-blœ)*
assign (v)	céder, transmettre, assigner	*(seh-dEh), (trāhnz-mEh-trœ), (ah-seeh-nyEh)*
assignee	la, le cessionnaire	*(seh-syoh-nEhr)*
assignment	l'affectation	*(ah-fehk-tah-syÕh)*
assignment (personnel)	l'affectation à un poste	*(ah-fehk-tah-syÕh ah œhn pOhst)*
assignor	le cedant	*(seh-dÃh)*
assistant	l'adjoint	*(ad-zhwÆhn)*
assistant general manager	l'adjoint au directeur général	*(ad-zhwÆhn oh deeh-rehk-tŒhr zheh-neh-rAhl)*
assistant manager	le sous-directeur	*(sooh-deeh-rehk-tŒhr)*
associate company	la société affiliée	*(soh-syeh-tEh ah-feeh-lyEh)*
assumed liability	le passif pris en charge	*(pah-sEEhf preehz āhn shAhrzh)*
astrakan	l'astrakan	*(ahs-trah-kāhn)*
astronaut	l'astronaute	*(ahs-troh-nOht)*
at and from	à et de	*(ah eh dœ)*
at best	au mieux	*(oh myŒh)*
at call	sur demande à vue	*(soohr dœh-mÃhnd ah vOOh)*
at or better	au moins	*(oh mwÆh)*
at par	au pair	*(oh pEhr)*
at sight	à vue	*(ah vOOh)*
at the close	à la fermeture	*(ah lah fehrm-tOOhr)*
at the market	au cours du marché	*(oh kOOhr dooh mahr-shEh)*
at the opening	à l'ouverture	*(ah looh-vehr-tOOhr)*
atmosphere	l'atmosphere	*(aht-mohs-fEhr)*
atom	l'atome	*(ah-tOhm)*
atomic	atomique	*(ah-toh-mEEhk)*
attach (v)	annexer, joindre	*(ah-nehk-sEh), (zhwÆn-drœ)*
attaché case	l'attaché-case	*(ah-tah-shEh kAhs)*
attain unity (v)	réaliser l'unité	*(reh-ah-leeh-zEh looh-neeh-tEh)*
attended time	le temps de présence	*(tÃh dœ preh-zÃhns)*
attestation	l'attestation; la légalisation (signature)	*(ah-tehs-tah-syÕh), (leh-gal-leeh-zah-syÕh)*
attorney	l'avocat	*(ah-voh-kAh)*
attorney in fact	le fondé de pouvoir	*(fõhn-dEh dœ pooh-vwAhr)*
attorney, power of	la procuration	*(proh-kooh-rah-syÕh)*
attrition	l'usure, l'érosion	*(ooh-zOOhr), (eh-roh-zyÕh)*

A

audience rating	l'indice d'écoute	(Æhn-deehs deh-kOOht)
audience research	l'étude d'opinion	(eh-tOOhd doh-peeh-nyÕhn)
audio mixing	le mixage	(meehks-Ahzh)
audit (v)	vérifier	(veh-reeh-feeh-Eh)
audit trail	la direction d'investigation	(deeh-rehk-syÕh dæn-vehs-teeh-gah-syÕh)
audit, internal	le contrôle interne	(kõhn-trOhl æhn-tEhrn)
auditing balance sheet	le bilan de contrôle	(beeh-lÃh dœ kõhn-trOhl)
auditor	le commissaire aux comptes	(koh-meeh-sEhr oh kÕhnt)
authenticity (gold)	l'authentification	(oh-tãhn-teeh-feeh-kah-syÕh)
authority, to have (v)	avoir qualité de	(ah-vwAhr kah-leeh-tEh dœ)
authorize (v)	autoriser	(oh-toh-reeh-zEh)
authorized dealer	le concessionnaire agréé	(kõhn-seh-syoh-nEhr ah-greh-Eh)
authorized shares	les parts nominales	(pAhr noh-meeh-nAhl)
authorized signature	la signature autorisée	(seehg-nah-tOOhr oh-toh-reeh-zEh)
auto-pilot	le pilote automatique	(peeh-lOhl oh-toh-mah-tEEhk)
automatic	automatique	(oh-toh-mah-tEEhk)
automatic gearshift	l'embrayage automatique	(ãhm-brah-yAhzh oh-toh-mah-tEEhk)
automatic weapons	les armes automatiques	(Ahrm oh-toh-mah-tEEhk)
automation	l'automatisation	(oh-toh-mah-teeh-zah-syÕh)
automobile	l'automobile	(oh-toh-moh-bEEhl)
automotive worker	l'ouvrier mécanicien	(ooh-vryEh meh-kah-neeh-syÆhn)
autonomous	autonome	(oh-toh-nOhm)
availability, subject to	sous réserve de disponibilité	(sooh reh-zEhrv dœ deehs-poh-neeh-beeh-leeh-tEh)
average	la moyenne, l'avarie (transport maritime)	(mwah-yEhn), (ah-vah-rEEh [trãhnz-pOhr mah-reeh-tEEhm])
average cost	le coût moyen	(kOOht mwah-yEhn)
average life	la durée de vie moyenne	(dooh-rEh dœ vEEh mwah-yEhn)
average price	les cours moyens	(kOOhr mwah-yEhn)
average unit cost	le prix unitaire moyen	(prEEh ooh-neeh-tEhr mwah-yEhn)
averaging	l'établissement d'une moyenne	(eh-tah-bleehs-mÃh mwah-yEhn)
avoidable costs	les frais évitables	(frEh eh-veeh-tAh-blœ)

B

back a venture (v)	soutenir une entreprise	(sooh-tœh-nEEhr oohn ãhn-trœh-prEEhz)
back haul	le fret de retour	(frEht dœ rœh-tOOhr)
back order	la commande en souffrance	(koh-mÃhnd ãhn sooh-frÃhns)
back selling	la revente	(rœ-vÃhnt)
back taxes	le rappel d'impôts	(rah-pEhl dœ̃hm-pOh)
backdate (n)	la date antérieure	(dAht ãhn-teh-ryŒhr)
backdate (v)	antidater	(ãhn-teeh-dah-tEh)
backed note	l'effet avalisé	(eh-fEht ah-vah-leeh-zEh)
background	l'arrière-plan	(ah-ryEhr plÃhn)
background music	le fond sonore	(fÕhn soh-nOhr)
backing and filling	l'aval et l'enregistrement	(ah-vAhl eh lãhn-rœh-zheehs-trœ-mÃh)
backing support	le soutien	(sooh-tyÆh)
backlog	les commandes en carnet	(koh-mÃhnd ãhn kahr-nEh)
backup	la copie de sauvegarde	(koh-pEEh dœ sohv-gAhrd)
backup bonds	les cautions de soutien	(koh-syÕh dœ sooh-tyÆh)
backwardation	le déport	(deh-pOhr)
backwash effect	le contrecoup	(kõhn-trœ-kOOh)
bacterial infection	l'infection bactérienne	(æ̃hn-fehk-syÕhn bahk-teh-ryEhn)
bad debt	la mauvaise créance	(moh-vEhz kreh-Ãhns)
balance	le solde	(sOhld)
balance of payments	la balance des paiements	(bah-lÃhns deh peh-mÃh)
balance of trade	la balance commerciale	(bah-lÃhns koh-mehr-syAhl)
balance ratios	le ratio de bilan	(rAh-syoh dœ beeh-lÃh)
balance sheet	le bilan	(beeh-lÃh)
balance, bank	le solde en banque	(sOhld ãhn bÃhnk)
balance, credit	le solde créditeur	(sOhld kreh-deeh-tŒr)
bale capacity	la capacité balles	(kah-pah-seeh-tEh bAhl)
bale cargo	le chargement en balles	(shahrz-mÃh ãhn bAhl)
ballast bonus	l'indemnité de lest	(æ̃hn-dehm-neeh-tEh dœ lEhst)
balloon (payment)	le prêt à échéance de remboursement différée	(prEht ah eh-sheh-Ãhns dœ rãhm-boohrs-mÃh deeh-feh-rEh)
balloon note	le paiement en bloc	(peh-mÃh ãhn blOhk)
balm	le baume	(bOhm)
bank	la banque	(bÃhnk)
bank acceptance	l'acceptation bancaire	(ahk-sehp-tah-syÕh bãhn-kEhr)
bank account	le compte en banque	(kÕhnt ãhn bÃhnk)
bank balance	le solde en banque	(sOhld ãhn bÃhnk)
bank charges	les frais bancaires, les frais de banque	(frEh bãhn-kEhr), (frEh dœ bÃhnk)

bank check	le chèque bancaire	*(shEhk bãhn-kEhr)*
bank deposit	le dépôt bancaire	*(deh-pOh bãhn-kEhr)*
bank draft	la traite bancaire	*(trEht bãhn-kEhr)*
bank examiner	l'inspecteur de banque	*(ãehns-pehk-tŒhr dœ bÃhnk)*
bank exchange	l'échange bancaire	*(eh-shÃhnzh bãhn-kEhr)*
bank holiday	le jour férié	*(zhOOhr feh-ryEh)*
bank letter of credit	la lettre de crédit bancaire	*(lEh-trœ dœ kreh-dEEh bãhn-kEhr)*
bank loan	le prêt bancaire	*(prEht bãhn-kEhr)*
bank money order	le mandat bancaire	*(mãhn-dAh bãhn-kEhr)*
bank note	le billet de banque	*(beeh-yEh dœ bÃhnk)*
bank rate	le taux de base bancaire	*(tOh dœ bAhz bãhn-kEhr)*
bank release	l'acquittement bancaire	*(ah-keeht-mÃh bãhn-kEhr)*
bank statement	le relevé bancaire	*(rœh-lœh-vEh bãhn-kEhr)*
bankruptcy	la faillite, la banqueroute	*(feh-yEEht), (bãhnk-rOOht)*
bar chart	le graphique en tuyaux d'orgue	*(graf-fEEhk ãhn tooh-yOh d'Ohr-gœ)*
barbiturate	le barbiturique	*(bahr-beeh-tooh-rEEhk)*
bareboat charter	l'affrètement coque nue	*(ah-freht-mÃh kOhk nOOh)*
bargain	la bonne affaire	*(bOhn ah-fEhr)*
bargaining power	le pouvoir de négociation	*(pooh-vwAhr dœ neh-goh-syah-syÕh)*
bargaining, collective	la convention collective	*(kÕhn-vÃhn-syÕh koh-lehk-tEEhv)*
barge transportation	le chalandage	*(shah-lahn-dAhzh)*
barratry	la baraterie	*(bah-rah-tœh-rEEh)*
barrel	le tonneau	*(toh-nOh)*
bars	les barres	*(bAhr)*
barter (n)	le troc	*(trOhk)*
barter (v)	troquer	*(troh-kEh)*
base	le fond de teint	*(fÕhn dœ tÃEhnt)*
base currency	la devise de référence	*(dœh-vEEhz dœ reh-feh-rÃhns)*
base price	le prix de base	*(prEEh dœ bAhz)*
base rate	le taux de base	*(tOh dœ bAhz)*
base year	l'année de référence	*(ah-nEh dœ reh-feh-rÃhns)*
basis point (1/100%)	le point de référence	*(pw ÃEh dœ reh-feh-rÃhns)*
batch	la cuvée	*(kooh-vEh)*
batch processing	le traitement par lots	*(treht-mÃh pahr lOh)*
batch production	la production en lot	*(proh-doohk-syÕh ãhn lOh)*
batiste	la batiste	*(bah-tEEhst)*
batten fitted	fixé avec des lattes	*(feehk-sEh ah-vEhk deh lAht)*
battery	la batterie	*(bah-teh-rEEh)*
beam	le rayon	*(rah-yÕh)*
bear	le baissier	*(beh-syEh)*

bear market	le marché à la baisse	*(mahr-shEh ah lah ah lah bEhs)*
bearer	le porteur	*(pohr-tŒhr)*
bearer bond	le bon au porteur	*(bŌh oh pohr-tŒhr)*
bearer security	l'action au porteur	*(ahk-syŌh oh pohr-tŒhr)*
beaver	le castor	*(kahs-tOhr)*
bed	le lit	*(lEEh)*
bell-shaped curve	la courbe en forme de cloche	*(kOOhrb āhn fOhrm dœ klOsh)*
below par	au-dessous du pair	*(oh dœ-sOOh dooh pEhr)*
below the line	au-dessous de la ligne	*(oh dœ-sOOh dœ lah lEEh-nyœ)*
belt	la ceinture, la courroie	*(sǽhn-tOOhr), (kooh-rwAh)*
bends	les courbes, la maladie des caissons	*(kOOhrb), (mah-kah-dEEh deh keh-sŌh)*
beneficiary	la, le bénéficiaire	*(beh-neh-feeh-syEhr)*
benzene	le benzène	*(bāhn-zĔhn)*
bequest	le legs	*(lEhg)*
berth terms	le fret à la cueillette	*(frEht ah lah kœh-yEht)*
bid (takeover)	l'offre publique d'achat	*(Oh-frœ pooh-blEEhk dah-shAh)*
bid and asked	à l'achat et à la vente	*(ah lah-shAh eh ah la vÃhnt)*
bill	l'effet, la facture, la note	*(eh-fEht), (fahk-tOOhr), (nOht)*
bill broker	le courtier d'escompte	*(koohr-tyEh dehs-kŌhnt)*
bill of exchange	la lettre de change, la traite	*(lĔh-trœ dœ shÃnzh), (trEht)*
bill of lading	le connaissement	*(koh-nEhs-mÃh)*
bill of sale	l'acte de vente	*(Ahk-tœ dœ vÃhnt)*
bill of sight	la déclaration provisoire	*(deh-klah-rah-syŌh proh-veeh-zwAhr)*
billboard	le panneau d'affichage	*(pah-nOh dah-feeh-shAhzh)*
billets	les billettes	*(beeh-yEht)*
billfold	le porte-billets	*(pohrt-beeh-yEh)*
binary code	le code binaire	*(kOhd beeh-nEhr)*
binary notation	la notation binaire	*(noh-tah-syŌh beeh-nEhr)*
binder	la lettre de couverture	*(lĔh-trœ dœ kooh-vehr-tOOhr)*
biochemistry	la biochimie	*(beeh-oh-sheeh-mEEh)*
biodegradable	biodégradable	*(beeh-oh-grah-dÁh-blœh)*
biopsy	la biopsie	*(beeh-ohp-sEEh)*
biological diacidizing	la fermentation malolactique	*(fehr-mãhn-tah-syŌh mah-loh-lahk-tEEhk)*
biologist	le biologiste	*(beeh-oh-loh-zhEEhst)*
biology	la biologie	*(beeh-oh-loh-zhEEh)*
biosphere	la biosphère	*(beeh-oh-sfEhr)*

birth control	le contrôle des naissances	(kõhn-trOhl deh neh-sÃhns)
birth defect	la malformation congénitale	(mahl-fohr-mah-syÕhn kõhn-zheh-neh-tAhl)
bit	le bit, unité binaire	(ooh-neeh-teh beeh-nEhr)
bitter	amer	(ah-mEhr)
black and white	le noir et blanc	(nwAhr eh blÃhn)
black hole	le trou noir	(trooh nwAhr)
black market	le marché noir	(mahr-shEh nwAhr)
blade	la lame	(lAhm)
blanket bond	le cautionnement global	(koh-syohn-mÃh gloh-bAhl)
blanket order	la déclaration d'intention d'achat	(deh-klah-rah-syÕh dãhn-tãhn-syÕh dah-shAh)
blast furnace	le haut-fourneau	(oht-foohr-nOh)
blazer	la veste	(vehst)
bleed (v)	saigner	(seh-nyEh)
blemish	l'imperfection, le défaut	(æhm-pehr-fehk-syÕhn, deh-fOh)
blend (v)	mélanger	(meh-lãhn-zhEh)
blender	le mixeur	(meek-sŒhr)
block (to)	faire obstacle	(fehr ohb-stAh-klœh)
blockade	le blocus	(bloh-kOOh)
blockage of funds	le blocage de fonds	(bloh-kAhzh dœ fÕhn)
blocked currency	la devise bloquée	(dæh-vEEhz bloh-kEh)
blood	le sang	(sÃhn)
blood pressure	la tension artérielle	(tãhn-syÕhn ahr-teh-ryEhl)
blood test	l'analyse de sang	(ah-nah-lEEhz deh sAhn)
blotchy	couvert de taches, taché	(kooh-vEhr dœ tAhsh), (tah-shEh)
blotter	le sous-main	(sooh-mÆhn)
blouse	le chemisier	(shœh-meeh-zyEh)
blowup	l'agrandissement	(ah-grãhn-deehs-mÃh)
blue chip stock	les valeurs de premier ordre	(vah-lŒhr dœ prœh-myEh Ohr-drœ)
blue-collar worker	le travailleur manuel	(trah-vah-yŒhr mah-nwEhl)
blueprint	le projet	(proh-zhEh)
board meeting	la réunion du conseil	(reh-ooh-nyÕh dooh kõhn-sEh-yœ)
board of directors	le conseil d'administration	(kõhn-sEh-yœ dad-meeh-neehs-trah-syÕh)
board of supervisors	le conseil de surveillance	(kõhn-sEh-yœ dœ soohr-veh-yÃhns)
board, executive	le conseil de direction	(kõhn-sEh-yœ dœ deeh-rehk-syÕh)
boardroom	la salle du conseil	(sAhl dooh kõhn-sEh-yœ)
body	la carrosserie, le corps	(kah-roh-seh-rEEh), (kOhr)
boilerplate	la tôle à chaudière	(tOhl ah shoh-dyEhr)

boldface	en gras	*(ãhn grAh)*
		pOh)
bomb (v)	bombarder	*(bohm-bahr-dEh)*
bomber	le bombardier	*(bohm-bahr-dyEh)*
bond	l'obligation, la caution	*(oh-bleeh-gah-syŌh),*
		(koh-syŌh)
bond areas	les zones d'entrepôt	*(zOhn dãhn-træ-*
bond issue	l'émission d'obligations	*(eh-meeh-syŌh doh-bleeh-*
		gah-syŌh)
bond market	le marché des obligations	*(mahr-shEh dehz oh-bleeh-*
		gah-syŌhn)
bond power	le pouvoir d'émettre des	*(pooh-vwAhr deh-mEh-træ*
	obligations	*dehz oh-bleeh-gah-syŌh)*
bond rating	le classement des	*(klahs-mÃh dehz oh-bleeh-*
	obligations	*gah-syŌh)*
bonded carrier	le transporteur couvert par	*(trãhnz-pohr-tŒhr kooh-*
	une caution	*vEhrt pahr oohn koh-*
		syŌh)
bonded goods	les marchandises sous	*(mahr-shãhn-dEEhz*
	douane	*sooh dooh-Ahn)*
bonded warehouse	l'entrepôt sous contrôle	*(ãhn-træ-pOh sooh kõhn-*
	douanier	*trOhl dooh-ah-nyEh)*
bonds (and stocks)	les valeurs mobilières	*(vah-lŒhr moh-beeh-*
		lyEhr)
bone china	la porcelaine	*(pohr-seh-lEhn)*
bone scan	la scintigraphie osseuse	*(sãehn-teeh-grah-fEEh ohs-*
		Œhz)
bonus (premium)	la prime	*(prEEhm)*
book	le livre	*(lEEh-vræ)*
book inventory	l'inventaire comptable	*(ãhn-vãhn-tEhr kõhn-tAh-*
		blæ)
book value	la valeur comptable	*(vah-lŒhr kõhn-tAh-blæ)*
book value per	la valeur comptable par	*(vah-lŒhr kõhn-tAh-blæ*
share	action	*pahr ahk-syŌh)*
bookkeeping	la comptabilité	*(kõhn-tah-beeh-leeh-tEh)*
boom	l'essor économique	*(eh-sOhr eh-koh-moh-*
		mEEhk)
boost (v)	impulser, lancer	*(ãehm-poohl-sEh, lãhn-*
		sEh)
booster rocket	la fusée de lancement	*(fooh-zEh dæ lãhns-mÃhn)*
boot shop	la botterie	*(boh-teh-rEEh)*
bootmaker	le bottier	*(boh-tyEh)*
boots	les bottes	*(bOht)*
border	la limite, la frontière	*(leeh-mEEht), (frõhn-*
		tyEh)
border tax	l'ajustement fiscal aux	*(ah-zhOOhstœ-mÃh feehs-*
adjustment	frontières	*kAhl oh frõhn-tyEhr)*
borrow (v)	emprunter	*(ãehm-prãehn-tEh)*
botanic	la botanique	*(boh-tah-nEEhk)*
bottle	la bouteille	*(booh-tEh-yœ)*

bouquet	le bouquet	*(booh-kEh)*
bow tie	le nœud papillon	*(nŒh pah-peeh-yŌh)*
bowl	le bol	*(bOhl)*
boycott	le boycottage	*(bohy-koh-tAhzh)*
brain tumor	la tumeur au cerveau	*(tooh-mŒhr oh sehr-vOh)*
brainstorming	le brainstorming	
brake	le frein	*(frÃÉhn)*
brake pedal	la pédale de frein	*(peh-dAhl dœ frÃÉhn)*
branch office	la succursale	*(sooh-koohr-sAhl)*
brand	la marque	*(mAhr-kœ)*
brand acceptance	l'acceptation de la marque	*(ahk-sehp-tah-syŌh dœ lah mAhr-kœ)*
brand image	l'image de marque	*(eeh-mAhzh dœ mAhr-kœ)*
brand loyalty	la fidélité à la marque	*(feeh-deh-leeh-tEh ah lah mAhr-kœ)*
brand manager	le chef de produit	*(shEhf dœ proh-dwEEh)*
brand recognition	l'identification de la marque	*(eeh-dãhn-teeh-feeh-kah-syŌh dœ lah mAhr-kœ)*
breadbasket	la corbeille à pain	*(kohr-bEh-yœ ah pÃÉhn)*
breakthrough	la percée	*(pehr-sEh)*
break-even (v)	atteindre le seuil de rentabilité	*(ah-tÃÉhn-drœ lœ sŒhyœ dœ rãhn-tah-beeh-leeh-tEh)*
break-even analysis	l'analyse du point d'équilibre	*(ãh-nah-lEEhz dooh pwÃÉh deh-keeh-lEEh-brœ)*
break-even point	le point d'équilibre, le seuil de rentabilité	*(pwÃÉh deh-keeh-lEEh-brœ), (sŒhyœ dœ rãhn-tah-beeh-leeh-tEh)*
breast cancer	le cancer du sein	*(kãhn-sEhr dooh sÃÉhn)*
breathe (v)	respirer	*(rœhs-peeh-rEh)*
broadcast (v)	diffuser	*(deeh-fooh-zEh)*
broken lot	la fin de série	*(fÃÉhn dœ seh-rEEh)*
broken stowage	le désarrimage	*(deh-zah-reeh-mAhzh)*
broker	le courtier, le cambiste	*(koohr-tyEh), (kahm-bEEhst)*
broker, software	le revendeur de logiciel	*(rœh-vãhn-dŒhr dœ loh-zheeh-syEhl)*
budget appropriation	l'affectation au budget	*(ah-fehk-tah-syŌh oh booh-zhEh)*
budget forecast	la prévision budgétaire	*(preh-veeh-zyŌh booh-zheh-tEhr)*
budget investment	l'investissement budgétaire	*(ÃÉhn-vehs-teehs-mÃÃh booh-zheh-tEhr)*
budget, advertising	le budget de publicité	*(booh-zhEh dœ pooh-bleeh-seeh-tEh)*
budget, capital	le budget d'investissement	*(booh-zhEh dãhn-vehs-teehs-mÃÃh)*

budget, cash	le budget de trésorerie	*(booh-zhEh dœ treh-zoh-reh-rEEh)*
budget, marketing	le budget de marketing	*(booh-zhEh dœ marketing)*
budget, sales	le budget commercial	*(booh-zhEh koh-mehr-syAhl)*
bull	le haussier	*(oh-syEh)*
bull market	le marché haussier	*(mahr-shEh oh-syEh)*
bullet	la balle	*(bAhl)*
bumper	le pare-choc	*(pahr-shOhk)*
burden rate	le coefficient d'imputation des frais généraux	*(koh-eh-feeh-sÃhnt dæhm-pooh-tah-syÕh deh frEh zheh-neh-rOh)*
burn	la brûlure	*(brooh-lOOhr)*
burning	la brûlure	*(brooh-lOOhr)*
bureaucrat	le bureaucrate	*(booh-roh-krAht)*
buret	la burette	*(booh-rEht)*
business activity	l'activité commerciale	*(ahk-teeh-veeh-tEh koh-mehr-syAhl)*
business card	la carte de visite	*(kAhrt dœ veeh-zEEht)*
business cycle	le cycle économique	*(sEEh-klœ eh-koh-noh-mEEhk)*
business management	la gestion d'entreprise	*(zhœhs-tyÕh dãhn-trœh-prEEhz)*
business plan	le projet commercial	*(proh-zhEh koh-mehr-syAhl)*
business policy	la politique de l'entreprise	*(poh-leeh-tEEhk dãhn-trœh-prEEhz)*
business strategy	la stratégie de l'entreprise	*(strah-teh-zhEEh dœ lãhn-trœh-prEEhz)*
butter dish	le beurrier	*(bœh-ryEh)*
button	le bouton	*(booh-tÕh)*
buttonhole	la boutonnière	*(booh-toh-nyEhr)*
buy at best (v)	acheter au meilleur prix	*(ahsh-tEh oh meh-yŒhr prEEh)*
buy back (v)	racheter	*(rahsh-tEh)*
buy on close (v)	acheter en clôture	*(ahsh-tEh ãhn kloh-tOOhr)*
buy on opening (v)	acheter en ouverture	*(ahsh-tEh ãhn ooh-vehr-tOOhr)*
buy out (v)	racheter	*(rah-shtEhr)*
buyer	l'acheteur	*(ahsh-tŒhr)*
buyer, chief	l'acheteur principal	*(ahsh-tŒhr prãhn-seeh-pAhl)*
buyer, credit	l'acheteur de créance	*(ahsh-tŒhr dœ kreh-Ãhns)*
buyer, potential	l'acheteur potentiel	*(ahsh-tŒhr poh-tãhn-syEhl)*
buyer's market	le marché acheteur	*(mahr-shEh ahsh-tŒhr)*
buyer's option	l'option d'achat	*(ohp-syÕh dah-shAh)*
buyer's premium	la prime pour l'acheteur	*(prEEhm poohr lahsh-tŒhr)*

B

B

buyer's responsibility	la responsabilité de l'acheteur	(ræs-pohn-sah-beeh-leeh-tEh dœ lahsh-tŒhr)
buyout	le désintéressement	(dehz-æhn-teh-rehs-mÃh)
bypass	le pontage	(põhn-tahzh)
by-laws	les statuts (d'une société)	(stah-tOOh doohn soh-syeh-tEh)
by-product	le sous-produit	(sooh proh-dwEEh)
byte	le multiplet, le mot, l'octet	(moohl-teeh-plEh), (mOh), (ohk-tEht)

C

cable	le câble	(kAh-blœ)
cable television	la télévision à câble	(teh-leh-veeh-zyÕh ah kAh-blœ)
cable transfer	le virement par câble	(veehr-mÃh pahr kAh-blœ)
calcium	le calcium	(kahl-syOOhm)
calculator	la calculatrice	(kahl-kooh-lah-trEEhs)
calfskin	la peau de veau	(pOh dœ vOh)
call (v)	convoquer	(kõhn-voh-kEh)
call feature	la clause de remboursement anticipé	(klOhz dœ rãhm-boohrs-mÃh ãhn-teeh-seeh-pEh)
call loan	le prêt remboursable sur demande	(prEht rãhm-boohr-sAh-blœ soohr dœh-mÃhnd)
call money	l'argent au jour le jour	(ahr-zhÃhn oh zhOOhr lœ zhOOhr)
call option	la prime à la hausse	(prEEhm ah lah Ohs)
call price	le prix de rachat	(prEEh dœ rah-shAh)
call protection	la protection contre le risque de remboursement anticipé	(proh-tehk-syÕh kõhn-trœ lœ rEEhs-kœ dœ rãhm-boohrs-mÃh ãhn-teeh-seeh-pEh)
call rate	le taux de l'argent au jour le jour	(tOh dœ lahr-jÃhn oh zhOOhr lœ zhOOhr)
call rule	la règle du remboursement	(rEh-glœ dooh rãhm-boohrs-mÃh)
callback	le rappel	(rah-pEhl)
camel's hair	le poil de chameau	(pwAhl dœ shAh-mOh)
campaign, advertising	la campagne publicitaire	(kãh-pÃh-nyœ pooh-bleeh-seeh-tEhr)
campaign, productivity	la campagne de productivité	(kãh-pÃh-nyœ dœ proh-doohk-teeh-veeh-tEh)
camshaft	l'arbre à came	(Ahr-brœ ah kAhm)
can opener	l'ouvre-boîtes	(Œhv-ræh bwAht)
cancel (v)	annuler	(ah-nooh-lEh)
cancelled check	le chèque annulé	(shEhk ah-nooh-lEh)
candlestick	le chandelier	(shãhn-dœh-lyEh)

capacity	la capacité, la capacité de mémoire, le pouvoir	*(kah-pah-seeh-tEh), (kah-pah-seeh-tEh dœ meh-mwAhr), (pooh-vwAhr)*
capacity, manufacturing	la capacité de fabrication	*(kah-pah-seeh-tEh dœ fah-breeh-kah-syÕh)*
capacity, plant	la capacité de production	*(kah-pah-seeh-tEh dœ proh-doohk-syÕh)*
capacity, utilization	la capacité d'exploitation	*(kah-pah-seeh-tEh dehks-plwah-tah-syÕh)*
capital account	le compte de capital	*(kÕhnt dœ kah-peeh-tAhl)*
capital allowance	l'allocation en capital	*(ah-loh-kah-syÕh ãhn kah-peeh-tAhl)*
capital asset	le capital fixe	*(kah-peeh-tAhl fEEhks)*
capital budget	le budget d'investissement	*(booh-zhEh dãhn-vehs-teehs-mÃh)*
capital expenditure appraisal	l'estimation des immobilisations	*(ehs-teeh-mah-syÕh dehz eeh-moh-beeh-leeh-zah-syÕh)*
capital expenditure	les immobilisations	*(eeh-moh-beeh-leeh-zah-syÕh)*
capital exports	les exportations de capitaux	*(ehks-pohr-tah-syÕh dœ kah-peeh-tOh)*
capital gain (loss)	la plus-value	*(plooh-vah-lOOh)*
capital goods	les biens d'équipement	*(byÃh deh-keehp-mÃh)*
capital increase	l'augmentation du capital	*(ohg-mãhn-tah-syÕh dœ kah-peeh-tAhl)*
capital letter	la majuscule	*(mah-yoohs-kOOhl)*
capital market	le marché des capitaux	*(mahr-shEh deh kah-peeh-tOh)*
capital stock	le capital actions	*(kah-peeh-tAhl ahk-syÕh)*
capital structure	la structure du capital	*(stroohk-tOOhr dooh kah-peeh-tAhl)*
capital surplus	le surplus en capital	*(soohr-plOOh ãhn kah-peeh-tAhl)*
capital, raising	la mobilisation de capitaux	*(moh-beeh-leeh-zah-syÕh dœ kah-peeh-tOh)*
capital, return on	le rendement du capital	*(rãhnd-mÃh dooh kah-peeh-tAhl)*
capital, risk	le capital à risque	*(kah-peeh-tAhl ah rEEhs-kœ)*
capital, spending	le capital d'achat	*(kah-peeh-tAhl ah-shAh)*
capital, working	le capital de roulement	*(kah-peeh-tAhl dœ roohl-mÃh)*
capital-intensive	à capitaux élevés	*(ah kah-peeh-tOh eh-leh-vEh)*
capital-output ratio	le taux de rendement du capital	*(tOh dœ rãhnd-mÃh dooh kah-peeh-tAhl)*

capitalism	le capitalisme	*(kah-peeh-tahl-EEhz-mœ)*
capitalization	la capitalisation	*(kah-peeh-tah-leeh-zah-syÕh)*
capsule	la capsule	*(kahp-sOOhl)*
caption	la légende	*(leh-zhÃhnd)*
car	la voiture	*(vwah-tOOhr)*
carbon	le carbone	*(kahr-bOhn)*
carbon steel	l'acier au carbone	*(ahs-yEh oh kahr-bOhn)*
carburetor	le carburateur	*(kahr-booh-rah-tŒhr)*
card case	le porte-cartes	*(pohrt-kAhrt)*
cargo	la cargaison	*(kahr-geh-zÕh)*
carload	le chargement	*(shahrzh-mÃh)*
carrier	le transporteur	*(trãhnz-pohr-tŒhr)*
carrier's risk	le risque du transporteur	*(rEEhs-kœ dooh trãhnz-pohr-tŒhr)*
carryback	le report sur exercice précédent	*(rœh-pŒhr soohr ehk-sœr-sEEhs preh-seh-dÃh)*
carryforward	le report à nouveau	*(rœh-pŒhr ah nooh-vOh)*
carrying charge	la charge	*(shAhrzh)*
carrying value	la valeur du chargement	*(vah-lŒhr dooh shahrzh-mÃh)*
carryover	le report	*(rœh-pŒhr)*
cartel	le cartel	*(kahr-tEhl)*
cartridge	la cartouche	*(kahr-tOOsh)*
carving knife	le couteau à découper	*(kooh-tOh ah dœh-kooh-pEh)*
case	la caisse	*(kEhs)*
cash	les espèces, la caisse	*(ehs-pEhs), (kEhs)*
cash and carry	le paiement comptant des marchandises emportées	*(peh-mÃh kõhn-tÃhn mahr-shãhn-dEEhz æhm-pohr-tEh)*
cash balance	le solde de caisse	*(sOhld dœ kEhs)*
cash basis	la position de caisse	*(poh-zeeh-syÕh dœ kEhs)*
cash before delivery	le paiement avant livraison	*(peh-mÃh ah-vÃh leeh-vreh-zÕh)*
cash budget	le budget de trésorerie	*(booh-zhEh dœ treh-zoh-reh-rEEh)*
cash discount	l'escompte au comptant	*(ehs-kÕhnt kõhn-tÃhn)*
cash dividend	le dividende en espèces	*(deeh-veeh-dÃhnd ãhn ehs-pEhs)*
cash entry	l'encaissement	*(ãhn-kehs-mÃh)*
cash flow	la marge brute d'autofinancement (M.B.A.)	*(mAhrzh brOOht doh-toh-feeh-nãhns-mÃh)*
cash flow statement	le relevé de la marge brute	*(rœh-lœh-vEh dœ lah mAhrzh brOOht)*
cash in advance	le paiement d'avance	*(peh-mÃh dah-vÃhns)*
cash management	la gestion de trésorerie	*(zhœhs-tyÕh dœ treh-zoh-reh-rEEh)*

cash on delivery (C.O.D.)	le paiement à la livraison	*(peh-mÃh ah lah leeh-vreh-zÕh)*
cash payment	le paiement en espèces	*(peh-mÃh ãhn ehs-pEhs)*
cash reserves	les liquidités	*(leeh-keeh-deeh-tEh)*
cash surrender value	la valeur de rachat	*(vah-lŒhr dœ rah-shAh)*
cashbook	le livre de caisse	*(lEEh-vrœ dœ kEhs)*
cashier's check	le chèque de caisse	*(shEhk dœ kEhs)*
cashmere	le cachémire	*(kahsh-eh-mEEhr)*
cask (225 litres)	la barrique	*(bah-rEEhk)*
cassette	la cassette	*(kah-sEht)*
cast iron	la fonte coulée	*(fÕhnt kooh-lEh)*
casualty insurance	l'assurance contre les accidents corporels	*(ah-sooh-rÃhns kõhn-trœ lehz ahk-seeh-dÃhn kohr-poh-rEhl)*
catalog	le catalogue	*(kah-tah-lOhg)*
catalyst	le catalyseur	*(kah-tah-leeh-zŒhr)*
catch (v)	attraper	*(ah-trah-pEh)*
cathode	la cathode	*(kah-tOhd)*
ceiling	le plafond	*(plah-fÕhn)*
cell	la cellule	*(seh-lOOhl)*
center spread	la double page centrale	*(dooh-blœ pah-zh sãhn-trAhl)*
centiliter	le centilitre	*(sãhn-teeh-lEEh-trœ)*
central bank	la banque d'émission	*(bÃhnk deh-meeh-syÕh)*
central processing unit	l'unité de traitement centrale	*(looh-neeh-tEh dœ treht-mÃh sãhn-trAhl)*
central rate	le taux central	*(tOh sãhn-trAhl)*
centralization	la centralisation	*(sãhn-trah-leeh-zah-syÕh)*
certificate	le certificat	*(sehr-teeh-feeh-kAh)*
certificate of deposit	le certificat de dépôt	*(sehr-teeh-feeh-kAh dœ deh-pOh)*
certificate of incorporation	le certificat d'incorporation	*(sehr-teeh-feeh-kAh dæhn-kohr-poh-rah-syÕh)*
certificate of origin	le certificat d'origine	*(sehr-teeh-feeh-kAh doh-reeh-zhEEhn)*
certified check	le chèque visé	*(shEhk veeh-zEh)*
certified public accountant	l'expert-comptable	*(ex-pEhr-kõhn-tAh-blœ)*
cervical cancer	le cancer du col	*(kãhn-sEhr dooh kOhl)*
chafing dish	le chauffe-plat	*(shOht plAh)*
chain of command	la voie hiérarchique	*(vwAh yeh-rahr-kEEhk)*
chain store	le magasin à succursales multiples	*(mah-gah-zÆhn ah sooh-koohr-sAhl moohl-tEEh-plœ)*
Chairman of the Board	le président du conseil d'administration, Président-directeur général	*(preh-zeeh-dÃh dooh kõhn-sEh-yœ dad-meeh-neehs-trah-syÕh), (preh-zeeh-dÃh deeh-rehk-tŒhr zheh-neh-rAhl)*

C

chalky	crayeux	*(kreh-yŒh)*
chamber of commerce	la chambre de commerce	*(shÃhm-brœ dœ koh-mEhrs)*
champagne glass	la flûte à champagne	*(flOOht ah sham-pÃh-nyœ)*
champagne method	la méthode champenoise	*(meh-tOhd shãhm-peh-nwAhz)*
channel	le canal	*(kah-nAhl)*
channel of distribution	le réseau de distribution	*(reh-zOh dœ deehs-treeh-booh-syÕh)*
Channel tunnel	le tunnel sous la Manche	*(tooh-nEhl sooh lah mÃhnsh)*
chapter	le chapitre	*(shah-pEEh-trœ)*
character	le caractère	*(kah-rahk-tEhr)*
character font	la police des caractères	*(poh-lEEhs deh kah-rahk-tEhr)*
charge account (in a store)	le compte d'un client	*(kÕhnt dœhn kleeh-Ãhn)*
charge chrome	le ferrochrome de charge	*(feh-roh-krOhm dœ shAhrzh)*
charge-off	les charges exclues	*(shAhrzh ehks-klOOh)*
charges	les frais	*(frEh)*
chart, activity	le graphique d'activité	*(graf-fEEhk dahk-teeh-veeh-tEh)*
chart, bar	le graphique en tuyaux d'orgue	*(graf-fEEhk ãhn tooh-yOh dOhr-gœ)*
chart, flow	le graphique de flux	*(graf-fEEhk dœ flOOhks)*
chart, management	le tableau de gestion	*(tah-blOh dœ zhœhs-tyÕh)*
charter	la charte, l'affrètement	*(shAhrt), (ah-freht-mÃh)*
charter party agent	l'agent de charte-partie	*(ah-zhÃh dœ shAhrt-pahr-tEEh)*
chartered accountant (Brit.)	l'expert-comptable	*(ex-pEhr kõhn-tAh-blœ)*
chassis	le châssis	*(shah-sEEh)*
chattel	les biens mobiliers	*(byÆhn moh-beeh-lyEh)*
chattel mortgage	l'hypothèque sur des biens mobiliers	*(eeh-poh-tEhk soohr deh byÆhn moh-beeh-lyEh)*
cheap	bon marché	*(bÕhn mahr-shEh)*
check	le chèque, la vérification	*(shEhk), (veh-reeh-feeh-kah-syÕh)*
check (v)	vérifier, contrôler	*(veh-reeh-fyEh), (kõhn-troh-lEh)*
checking account	le compte chèques	*(kÕhnt shEhk)*
checklist	la liste de contrôle	*(leehst dœ kõhn-trOhl)*
cheese tray	le plateau à fromage	*(plah-tOh ah froh-mAhzh)*
chemical	le produit chimique	*(proh-dwEEh keeh-mEEhk)*
chemistry	la chimie	*(sheeh-mEEh)*
chief accountant	le chef comptable	*(shEhf kõhn-tAh-blœ)*

chief buyer	l'acheteur principal	*(ahsh-tŒhr præ̃hn-seeh-pAhl)*
chief executive	le directeur général	*(deeh-rehk-tŒhr zheh-neh-rAhl)*
chief executive officer (C.E.O.)	le directeur exécutif	*(deeh-rehk-tŒhr ehk-seh-kooh-tEEhf)*
chief financial officer (C.F.O.)	le directeur financier	*(deeh-rehk-tŒhr feeh-nãhn-syEh)*
chief operating officer (C.O.O.)	le directeur opérationnel	*(deeh-rehk-tŒhr oh-peh-rah-syoh-nEhl)*
china	la porcelaine	*(pohr-seh-lEhn)*
chinaware	la faïence	*(fah-eeh-Ãhns)*
chip	la puce, la plaquette la puce (informatique)	*(pOOhs), (plah-kEht lah pOOhs/æ̃hn-fohr-mah-tEEhk)*
chloride	le chlorure	*(kloh-rOOhr)*
chloroform	le chloroforme	*(kloh-roh-fOhrm)*
chromium	le chrome	*(krOhm)*
cigarette case	l'étui à cigarettes	*(eh-twEEh ah seeh-gah-rEht)*
circuit	le circuit	*(seehr-kwEEh)*
circulation	le tirage	*(teeh-rAhzh)*
cirrhosis of the liver	la cirrhose du foie	*(seehr-Ohz dooh fwAh)*
civil action	l'action civile	*(ahk-syÕh seeh-vEEhl)*
civil engineering	le génie civil	*(zheh-nEEh seeh-vEEhl)*
claim	la réclamation	*(reh-klah-ma-syÕh)*
classified ad	la petite annonce	*(pœh-tEEht ah-nÕhns)*
classified sparkling wine	le champagne	*(shahm-pAh-nyœ)*
clause	la clause	*(klOhz)*
clean (v)	nettoyer	*(nœh-twah-yEh)*
clean document	le document net, le document sans reserve	*(doh-kooh-mÃh nEht), (doh-kooh-mÃh sÃh rœh-zEhrv)*
clean technology	les techniques non-pollutantes	*(tehk-nEEhk nõhn poh-looh-tÃhnt)*
clean-up	le nettoyage	*(neh-twah-yAzh)*
cleanser	le démaquillant	*(deh-mah-keeh-yÃhn)*
clear off a debt	s'acquitter d'une dette	*(sah-keeh-tEh doohn dEht)*
clearing	le collage	*(koh-lAhzh)*
clearinghouse	la chambre de compensation	*(shÃhm-brœ dœ kõhm-pãhn-sah-syÕh)*
climate	le climat	*(kleeh-mAh)*
closed account	le compte inactif, le compte clos	*(kÕhnt eehn-ahk-tEEf), (kÕhnt klOh)*
closely held corporation	la société contrôlée par un petit nombre d'actionnaires	*(soh-syeh-tEh kõhn-trOh-lEh pahr œhn pœh-tEEh nÕhm-brœ dahk-syoh-nEhr)*

C

close-up	le gros plan	*(groh plãhn)*
closing entry	l'écriture de clôture	*(eh-kreeh-tOOhr dœ kloh-tOOhr)*
closing price	le cours de clôture	*(kOOhr dœ kloh-tOOhr)*
cloudy	nuageux, trouble	*(nwah-zhŒh), (trOOh-blœh)*
cluster bomb	la bombe à fragmentation	*(bOhmb ah frahg-mãhn-tah-syÕhn)*
clutch	l'embrayage	*(ãhm-brah-yAhzh)*
clutch pedal	la pédale d'embrayage	*(peh-dAhl dãhm-brah-yAhzh)*
co-ownership	la co-propriété	*(koh-proh-pryeh-tEh)*
coal	le charbon	*(shahr-bÕh)*
coaster	les dessous de verre	*(dœ-sOOh dœ vEhr)*
coat	le manteau	*(mãhn-tOh)*
coated paper	le papier glacé	*(pah-pyEh glah-sEh)*
coaxial cable	le câble coaxial	*(kAh-blœ koh-ahk-syAhl)*
codicil	le codicille	*(koh-deeh-sEEhyœ)*
coffee break	la pause-café	*(pOhz-kah-fEh)*
coffeepot	la cafetière	*(kah-feh-tyEhr)*
cohesion funds	le fonds de cohésion	*(fÕhn dœ koh-eh-zyÕhn)*
coil	la bobine	*(boh-bEEhn)*
coinsurance	la coassurance	*(koh-ah-sooh-rÃhns)*
cold call	la visite impromptue d'un vendeur	*(veeh-zEEht ãhm-prohm-tOOh dœhn vÃhn-dŒhr)*
cold rolling	le laminé à froid	*(lah-meeh-nEh ah frwAh)*
collagen	le collagène	*(koh-lah-jEhn)*
collar	le col	*(kOhl)*
collateral	la garantie	*(gah-rãhn-tEEh)*
colleague	la, le collègue	*(koh-lEhg)*
collect on delivery	payable à la livraison, contre remboursement	*(pah-yAh-blœ ah lah leeh-vreh-zÕh), (kõhn-trœ rãhm-boohrs-mÃh)*
collection	la collection	*(koh-lehk-syÕh)*
collection agent	l'agent de recouvrement	*(ah-zhÃh dœ rœh-kooh-vrœ-mÃh)*
collection period	le délai d'encaissement	*(deh-lEh dãhn-kehs-mÃh)*
collective agreement	la convention collective	*(kÕhn-vÃhn-syÕh koh-lehk-tEEhv)*
collective bargaining	la négociation paritaire de convention collective	*(neh-goh-syah-syÕh pah-reeh-tEhr dœ kÕhn-vÃhn-syÕh koh-lehk-tEEhv)*
collector of customs	le receveur des douanes	*(rœh-seh-vŒhr deh dooh-Ahn)*
colloquium	le colloque	*(koh-lOhk)*
color	la couleur	*(kooh-lŒhr)*
color separation	la séparation couleur	*(seh-pah-rah-syÕh kooh-lŒhr)*
color transparency	la diapositive couleurs	*(deeh-ah-poh-zeeh-tEEhv kooh-lŒhr)*

combat power	la puissance de combat	*(pweeh-sÃhns dœ kohm-bAh)*
combination	la combinaison, l'association	*(kõhm-beeh-neh-zÕh), (ah-soh-syah-syÕh)*
combination duty	les droits combinés	*(drwAh kõhm-beeh-nEh)*
come into force (v)	entrer en vigueur	*(ãhn-trEh ãhn veeh-gŒhr)*
command	la commande	*(koh-mÃhnd)*
command station	le poste de commandement	*(pOhst dœ koh-mãhnd-mÃhn)*
commerce	le commerce	*(koh-mEhrs)*
commercial	le spot publicitaire	*(sphot pooh-bleeh-seeh-tEhr)*
commercial ad	le spot publicitaire	*(spot pooh-bleeh-seeh-tEhr)*
commercial bank	la banque commerciale	*(bÃhnk koh-mehr-syAhl)*
commercial grade	la qualité commerciale	*(kah-leeh-tEh koh-mehr-syAhl)*
commercial invoice	la facture commerciale	*(fahk-tOOhr koh-mehr-syAhl)*
commission (agency)	la commission	*(koh-meeh-syÕh)*
commission (fee)	la commission, la guelte	*(koh-meeh-syÕh), (gEhlt)*
commitment	l'engagement	*(ãhn-gahzh-mÃh)*
commodity	le produit de base, la denrée	*(proh-dwEEh dœ bAhz), (dãhn-rEh)*
commodity exchange	la bourse des denrées	*(bOOhrs deh dãhn-rEh)*
common agricultural policy (CAP)	la politique agricole commune (PAC)	*(poh-leeh-tEEhk ah-greeh-kOhl koh-mOOhn)*
common carrier	le transporteur public	*(trãhnz-pohr-tŒhr pooh-blEEhk)*
common drug policy	la politique communautaire sur la drogue	*(poh-leeh-tEEhk koh-mooh-noh-tEhr soohr lah drOhg)*
common gun law	la loi communautaire sur les armes à feu	*(lwah koh-mooh-noh-tEhr soohr lehz Ahrm ah fŒh)*
common market	le marché commun	*(mahr-shEh koh-mOOhn)*
common stock	l'action ordinaire	*(ahk-syÕh ohr-deeh-nEhr)*
company	la société	*(soh-syeh-tEh)*
company goal	le but	*(bOOh)*
company policy	la politique de la société	*(poh-leeh-tEEhk dœ lah soh-syeh-tEh)*
company, holding	la société de portefeuille	*(soh-syeh-tEh dœ pohrt-fŒhyœ)*
company, parent	la maison mère	*(meh-zÕh mEhr)*
compatible	compatible	*(kõhn-pah-tEEh-blœh)*

compensating balance	la balance compensatoire	*(bah-lĀhns kohm-pāhn-sah-twAhr)*
compensation	la compensation, la rémunération, l'indemnité	*(kõhm-pāhn-sah-syŌh), (reh-mooh-neh-rah-syŌh), (æhn-dehm-neeh-tEh)*
compensation trade	le commerce de compensation	*(koh-mEhrs dæ kõhm-pāhn-sah-syŌh)*
competition	la concurrence	*(kõhn-kooh-rĀhns)*
competitive advantage	l'avantage concurrentiel	*(ah-vāhn-tAhzh kõhn-kooh-rāhn-syEhl)*
competitive edge	léger avantage concurrentiel	*(leh-zhEh ah-vāhn-tAhzh kõhn-kooh-rāhn-syEhl)*
competitive price	le prix compétitif, le prix concurrentiel	*(prEEh kohm-peh-teeh-tEEhf), (prEEh kõhn-kooh-rāhn-syEhl)*
competitive strategy	la stratégie concurrentielle	*(strah-teh-zhEEh kõhn-kooh-rāhn-syEhl)*
competitor	le concurrent	*(kõhn-kooh-rĀh)*
competitor analysis	l'analyse des concurrents	*(āh-nah-lEEhz kõhn-kooh-rĀh)*
complexion	le teint	*(tĒhnt)*
complimentary copy	le spécimen	*(speh-seeh-mEhn)*
comply with EC legislation (v)	se plier à la législation européenne	*(sæ pleeh-Eh ah lah leh-zheehs-lay-syŌhn eh-roh-peh-Ehn)*
component	le composant	*(kohm-poh-zĀh)*
composite index	l'indice composite	*(æhn-dEEhs kohm-poh-zEEht)*
composite package	la vente jumelée	*(vĀhnt zhooh-mæh-lEh)*
composition	la composition	*(kõhm-poh-zeeh-syŌh)*
compound interest	l'intérêt composé	*(æhn-teh-rEh kohm-poh-zEh)*
compound	le composé	*(kõhm-poh-zEh)*
compounds	les composés	*(kõhm-poh-zEh)*
comptroller	le commissaire aux comptes	*(koh-meeh-sEhr oh kŌhnt)*
computer	l'ordinateur	*(ohr-deeh-nah-tŒhr)*
computer bank	la banque informatique	*(bĀhnk æhn-fohr-mah-tEEhk)*
computer center	le centre informatique	*(sĀhn-træ æhn-fohr-mah-tEEhk)*
computer input	l'entrée (d'ordinateur)	*(āhn-trEh dohr-deeh-nah-tŒhr)*
computer language	le langage informatique	*(lāhn-gAhzh æhn-fohr-mah-tEEhk)*
computer memory	la mémoire	*(meh-mwAhr)*
computer output	la sortie	*(sohr-tEEh)*
computer program	le programme	*(proh-grAhm)*

computer science	l'informatique	*(æhn-fohr-mah-tEEhk)*
computer storage	la mémoire	*(meh-mwAhr)*
computer terminal	le terminal d'ordinateur	*(tehr-meeh-nAhl dohr-deeh-nah-tŒhr)*
computer, analog	l'ordinateur analogique	*(ohr-deeh-nah-tŒhr ah-nah-loh-zhEEhk)*
computer, digital	l'ordinateur numérique	*(ohr-deeh-nah-tŒhr nooh-meh-rEEhk)*
computer-assisted	assisté par ordinateur	*(ah-seeh-tEh pahr ohr-deeh-nah-tŒhr)*
concentration	le titre (d'une solution)	*(tEEh-trœ doohn soh-looh-syÕh)*
conditional acceptance	l'acceptation conditionnelle	*(ahk-sehp-tah-syÕh kõhn-deeh-syoh-nEhl)*
conditional sales contract	le contrat de vente sous conditions	*(kõhn-trAh dœ vÃhnt sooh kõhn-deeh-syÕh)*
condom	le préservatif	*(preh-zehr-vah-tEEhf)*
conductor	le conducteur	*(kõhn doohk-tŒhr)*
conference room	la salle de conférence	*(sAhl dœ kõhn-feh-rÃhns)*
confidential	confidentiel	*(kõhn-feeh-dãhn-syEhl)*
confirmation of order	la confirmation de commande	*(kohn-feehr-mah-syÕh dœ koh-mÃhnd)*
conflict of interest	le conflit d'intérêts	*(kõhn-flEEh dæhn-teh-rEh)*
conglomerate	le conglomérat	*(kõhn-gloh-meh-rAh)*
connect (v)	raccorder	*(rah-kohr-dEh)*
connecting rod	la bieille	*(byEh-yœ)*
conservation	la défense de l'environnement	*(deh-fÃhns dœ lõhn-veeh-rõhn-mÅhn)*
consideration (business law)	la contrepartie	*(kõhn-trœ-pahr-tEEh)*
consignee	la, le destinataire	*(dehs-teeh-nah-tEhr)*
consignment	l'expédition	*(ehks-peh-deeh-syÕh)*
consolidated financial statement	le bilan consolidé	*(beeh-lÃh kõh-soh-leeh-dEh)*
consolidation	la consolidation	*(kõh-soh-leeh-dah-synOh)*
consortium	le consortium	*((kõh-sohr-tyOOhm)*
consultant	le consultant	*(kõhn-soohl-tÃh)*
consultant, management	l'organisateur conseil, le conseiller en gestion	*(ohr-gah-neeh-zah-tŒhr kõhn-sEh-yœ), (kõh-seh-yEh ãhn zhœhs-tyÕh)*
consumer	le consommateur	*(kõhn-soh-mah-tŒhr)*
consumer acceptance	la faveur du public	*(fah-vŒhr dooh pooh-blEEhk)*
consumer credit	le crédit à la consommation	*(kreh-dEEh ah lah kõhn-soh-mah-syÕh)*
consumer goods	les biens de consommation	*(by˜Æn dœ kõhn-soh-mah-syÕh)*
consumer price index	l'indice des prix à la consommation	*(æhn-dEEhs deh prEEh ah lah kõhn-soh-mah-syÕh)*

C

C

consumer research	l'étude des besoins des consommateurs	*(eh-tOOhd deh bœh-zwÆhn deh kõhn-soh-mah-tŒhr)*
consumer satisfaction	la satisfaction des consommateurs	*(sah-teehs-fahk-syÕh deh kõhn-soh-mah-tŒhr)*
contact sheet	la planche de contact	*(plÃhnsh dœ kõhn-tAhkt)*
container	le conteneur	*(kõhn-tœh-nŒhr)*
contagious	contagieux	*(kõhn-tah-zhŒh)*
contaminate (v)	contaminer	*(kõhn-tah-meeh-nEh)*
content	la teneur	*(tœh-nŒhr)*
contingencies	les faux frais divers	*(fOh frEh deeh-vEhr)*
contingent fund	le fonds de prévoyance	*(fÕhn dœ preh-vwah-yÃhns)*
contingent liability	le passif éventuel	*(pah-sEEhf eh-vãhn-twEhl)*
continuous caster	la coulée continue	*(kooh-lEh kõhn-teeh-nOOh)*
contraceptive	le contraceptif	*(kõhn-trah sehp-tEEhf)*
contract	le contrat	*(kõhn-trAh)*
contract carrier	le transporteur sous contrat	*(trãhnz-pohr-tŒhr sooh kõhn-trAh)*
contract month	le mois de contrat	*(mwAh dœ kõhn-trAh)*
contraindication	la contre-indication	*(kõhn-trœh-æhn-deeh-kah-syÕhn)*
control key	la touche de commande	*(tOOhsh dœ koh-mÃhnd)*
control lever	le levier de commande	*(lœh-vyEh dœ koh-mÃhnd)*
control tower	la tour de contrôle	*(toohr dœ kõhn-trOhl)*
control, cost	le contrôle des prix de revient	*(kõhn-trOhl deh prEEh dœ rœ-vyÃhn)*
control, financial	le contrôle financier	*(kõhn-trOhl feeh-nãhn-syEh)*
control, inventory	le contrôle des stocks	*(kõhn-trOhl deh stocks)*
control, manufacturing	le contrôle de fabrication	*(kõhn-trOhl dœ fah-breeh-kah-syÕh)*
control, production	la planification de la production	*(plah-neeh-feeh-kah-syÕh dœ lah proh-doohk-syÕh)*
control, quality	le contrôle de qualité	*(kõhn-trOhl dœ kah-leeh-tEh)*
control, stock	la gestion des stocks, la vérification des stocks	*(zhæhs-tyÕh deh stocks), (veh-reeh-feeh-kah-syÕh deh stocks)*
controllable costs	les dépenses contrôlables	*(deh-pãhns kõhn-troh-lAh-blœ)*
controller	le directeur des services comptables	*(deeh-rehk-tŒhr deh sœr-vEEhs kõhn-tAhb-lœ)*
controlling interest	la participation majoritaire	*(pahr-teeh-seeh-pah-syÕh mah-zhoh-reeh-tEhr)*
conventional product	le produit classique	*(proh-dwEEh klah-sEEhk)*

conventional warfare	la guerre conventionnelle	*(gEhr kõhn-vãhn-syoh-nEhl)*
convertible	la décapotable	*(deh-kah-poh-tAh-blœ)*
convertible debentures	les obligations convertibles	*(oh-bleeh-gah-syÕh kõhn-vehr-tEEh-blœ)*
convertible preferred stock	les actions privilégiées convertibles	*(ahk-syÕh preeh-veeh-leh-zhyEh kõhn-vehr-tEEh-blœ)*
conveyor	le transporteur	*(trãhnz-pohr-tah-tŒhr)*
conveyor belt	la chaîne de montage	*(shEhn dœ mõhn-tAhzh)*
cooper	le tonnelier	*(toh-neh-lyEh)*
cooperation agreement	l'accord de coopération	*(ah-kOhr dœ koh-oh-peh-rah-syÕh)*
cooperative	la coopératif	*(koh-oh-peh-rah-tEEhf)*
cooperative advertising	la publicité conjointe	*(pooh-bleeh-seeh-tEh kõhn-jwÆhnt)*
copper	le cuivre	*(kwEEh-vrœ)*
copy (text)	l'exemplaire	*(ehk-sãhm-plEhr)*
copy (v)	copier	*(koh-pyEhr)*
copy testing	l'évaluation de l'impact d'une publicité	*(eh-vah-lwah-syÕh dœ lǣhm-pAh doohn pooh-bleeh-seeh-tEh)*
copyright	le droit d'auteur	*(drwAh doh-tŒhr)*
copywriter	le rédacteur (-trice) publicitaire	*(reh-dahk-tŒhr pooh-bleeh-seeh-tEhr)*
cork	le bouchon	*(booh-shÕh)*
corkscrew	le tire-bouchon	*(teehr-booh-shÕh)*
corn	le maïs	*(mah-EEh)*
corporate growth	la croissance d'une entreprise	*(krwah-sÅhns doohn ãhn-trœh-prEEhz)*
corporate image	l'image de marque d'une société	*(eeh-mAhzh dœ mAhr-kœ doohn soh-syeh-tEh)*
corporate planning	la planification d'entreprise	*(plah-neeh-feeh-kah-syÕh dãhn-trœh-prEEhz)*
corporate structure	la structure de l'entreprise	*(stroohk-tOOhr dãhn-trœh-prEEhz)*
corporation	la société anonyme	*(soh-syeh-tEh ah-noh-nEEhm)*
corporation tax	l'impôt sur les entreprises	*(ǣhm-pOh soohr lehz ãhn-trœh-prEEhz)*
corpus	le corpus	*(kohr-pOOhs)*
correspondence	la correspondance	*(koh-rehs-põhn-dÃhns)*
correspondent bank	la banque correspondante à l'étranger	*(bÃhnk koh-rehs-põhn-dÃhnt ah leh-trãhn-zhEh)*
cortisone	la cortisone	*(kohs-teeh-zOhn)*
cost (n)	le coût, les frais	*(kOOht), (frEh)*
cost (v)	coûter	*(kooh-tEh)*
cost accounting	la comptabilité prix de revient	*(kõhn-tah-beeh-leeh-tEh prEEh dœ rœ-vyÃhn)*

cost analysis	la comptabilité analytique	*(kõhn-tah-beeh-leeh-tEh ah-nah-leeh-tEEhk)*
cost and freight	le coût et le fret	*(kOOht eh læ frEht)*
cost control	le contrôle coûts	*(kõhn-trOhl deh kOOht)*
cost effective	rentable	*(rãhn-tAh-blœ)*
cost factor	le facteur coût	*(fahk-tŒhr kOOht)*
cost of capital	le coût du capital	*(kOOht dooh kah-peeh-tAhl)*
cost of goods sold	le coût des marchandises vendues	*(kOOht deh mahr-shãhn-dEEhz vãhn-dOOh)*
cost of living	le coût de la vie	*(kOOht dœ lah vEEh)*
cost reduction	la compression des coûts	*(kõhm-preh-syÕh deh kOOht)*
cost, average	le coût moyen	*(kOOht mwah-yEhn)*
cost, direct	les frais directs	*(frEh deeh-rEhkt)*
cost, indirect	les frais indirects	*(frEh ˜æhn-deeh-rEhkt)*
cost, replacement	les frais de remplacement, la valeur à neuf	*(frEh dœ rãhm-plahs-mÃh), (vah-lŒhr ah nŒhf)*
cost, variable	les frais variables	*(frEh vah-ryAh-blœ)*
cost-benefit analysis	l'étude du rapport coûts/profits	*(eh-tOOhd dooh rah-pOhr kOOht /proh-fEEh)*
cost-plus contract	le contrat à prix coûtant majoré	*(kõhn-trAh ah prEEh kooh-tÃhn mah-zhoh-rEh)*
cost-price squeeze	la compression des prix de revient	*(kõhm-preh-syÕh deh prEEh dœ ræ-vyÃhn)*
costs, allocation of	la répartition des coûts	*(reh-pahr-teeh-syÕh deh kOOht)*
costs, fixed	les coûts fixes	*(kOOht fEEhks)*
costs, managed	les frais contrôlés	*(frEh kõhn-troh-lEh)*
costs, production	le coût de production	*(kOOht dœ proh-doohk-syÕh)*
costs, set-up	les frais d'installation	*(frEh dæhn-stah-lah-syÕh)*
costs, standard	les frais normaux	*(frEh nohr-mOh)*
cotton	le coton	*(koh-tÕhn)*
couch	le canapé	*(kah-nah-pEh)*
cough (v)	tousser	*(tooh-sEh)*
cough drop	la pastille pour la toux	*(pahs-tEEh-yœ poohr lah tOOh)*
cough syrup	le sirop pour la toux	*(seeh-rOhp poohr lah tOOh)*
Council of Europe	le Conseil de l'Europe	*(kõhn-sEh dœ leh-ooh-rOhp)*
countdown	le compte à rebours	*(kohmt ah ræh-bOOhr)*
counter check	le chèque omnibus	*(shEhk ohrn-neeh-bOOhs)*
counterfeit	la contrefaçon	*(kõhn-træ-fah-sÕh)*
countervailing duty	le droit compensateur	*(drwAh kõhm-pãhn-sah-tŒhr)*

country	la région	*(reh-zhŌh)*
country of origin	le pays d'origine	*(pah-EEh doh-reeh-zhEEhn)*
country of risk	le pays de risque	*(pah-EEh dœ rEEhs-kœ)*
coupon (bond interest)	le coupon	*(kooh-pŌh)*
courier service	le service du courrier	*(sœr-vEEhs dœ kooh-ryEh)*
covenant (promises)	la convention	*(kŌhn-vÃhn-syŌh)*
cover	la couverture	*(kooh-vehr-tOOhr)*
cover charge	les frais de couverture	*(frEh dœ kooh-vehr-tOOhr)*
cover letter	la lettre de couverture	*(lEh-trœ dœ kooh-vehr-tOOhr)*
cover ratio	le coefficient de couverture	*(koh-eh-feeh-sÃhnt dœ kooh-vehr-tOOhr)*
coverage	la couverture	*(kooh-vehr-tOOhr)*
cowhide	la vachette	*(vah-shEht)*
coyote	le coyote	*(koh-yOht)*
cracking	le cracking	
crankshaft	le vilebrequin	*(vEEhl-brœh-kEEhn)*
crawling peg	la parité à crémaillère	*(pah-reeh-tEh ah kreh-mah-yEhr)*
cream jar	le pot de crème	*(poh dœ krEhm)*
creamy	onctueux	*(õhnk-tŒh)*
credit (n)	le crédit	*(kreh-dEEh)*
credit (v)	créditer	*(kreh-deeh-tEh)*
credit balance	le solde créditeur	*(sOhld kreh-deeh-tŒr)*
credit bank	la banque de crédit	*(bÃhnk dœ kreh-dEEh)*
credit bureau	l'institution de crédit	*(æhn-steeh-tooh-syŌh dœ kreh-dEEh)*
credit card	la carte de crédit	*(kAhrt dœ kreh-dEEh)*
credit control	le contrôle des crédits	*(kõhn-trOhl deh kreh-dEEh)*
credit insurance	l'assurance de crédit, l'assurance contre les mauvaises créances	*(ah-sooh-rÃhns dœ kreh-dEEh), (ah-sooh-rÃhns kõhn-trœ leh moh-vEhz kreh-Ãhns)*
credit line	la ligne de crédit	*(lEEh-nyœ dœ kreh-dEEh)*
credit management	la gestion des crédits	*(zhœhs-tyŌh deh kreh-dEEh)*
credit note	la note de crédit	*(nOht dœ kreh-dEEh)*
credit rating	l'évaluation de la solvabilité	*(eh-vah-lwah-syŌh dœ lah sohl-vah-beeh-leeh-tEh)*
credit reference	la référence de crédit	*(reh-feh-rÃhns dœ kreh-dEEh)*
credit terms	les conditions de crédit	*(kõhn-deeh-syŌh dœ kreh-dEEh)*
credit union	le syndicat de crédit	*(seehn-deeh-kAh dœ kreh-dEEh)*
creditor	le créancier	*(kreh-ãhn-syEh)*

critical path analysis	l'analyse de la trajectoire	*(āh-nah-lEEhz dœ lah trah-zhehk-twAhr)*
crop	la coupe	*(kOOhp)*
cross-licensing	l'échange de brevets	*(eh-shĀhnzh dœ brœh-vEht)*
crucible	le creuset	*(krœh-zEht)*
crude	non raffiné	*(nõh rah-feeh-nEh)*
crystal	le cristal	*(kreehs-tAhl)*
crystal glass manufacturing	la cristallerie	*(kreehs-tah-lœh-rEEh)*
crystallization	la cristallisation	*(kreehs-tah-leeh-zah-syÕh)*
cuff link	le bouton de manchette	*(booh-tÕhn dœ māhn-shEht)*
cultural export permit	l'autorisation d'exportation d'œuvres d'art	*(oh-toh-reeh-zah-syÕh dehks-pohr-tah-syÕh dŒhvrœ dAhr)*
cultural property	la propriété culturelle	*(proh-pryeh-tEh koohl-tooh-rEhl)*
cum dividend	le dividende attaché	*(deeh-veeh-dĀhnd ah-tah-shEh)*
cumulative	cumulatif	*(kooh-mooh-lah-tEEhf)*
cumulative preferred stock	les valeurs de priorité cumulatives	*(vah-lŒhr dœ preeh-oh-reeh-tEh kooh-mooh-lah-tEEhv)*
cup	la tasse	*(tAhs)*
cupola	le cubilot	*(kooh-beeh-lOh)*
cure (v)	guérir	*(geh-rEEhr)*
currency	le cours, la devise	*(kOOhr), (dœh-vEEhz)*
currency band	la marge de fluctuation entre monnaies	*(mAhrzh dœ floohk-twah-sÕh Āhn-trœ moh-nEh)*
currency clause	la clause de change	*(klOhz dœ shĀhnzh)*
currency conversion	la conversion de devises	*(kõhn-vehr-zyÕh dœ dœh-vEEhz)*
currency exchange	le cours des devises	*(kOOhr deh dœh-vEEhz)*
currency unit	l'unité monétaire	*(ooh-neeh-tEh moh-neh-tEhr)*
current	le courant	*(kooh-rĀhn)*
current assets	l'actif réalisable	*(ahk-tEEf reh-ah-leeh-zAh-blœ)*
current liabilities	la dette à court terme	*(DEht ah koohr tEhrm)*
current ratio	le taux du jour	*(tOh dooh zhOOhr)*
current yield	le rendement courant	*(rāhnd-mĀh kooh-rĀhn)*
cursor	le curseur	*(koohr-sŒhr)*
curved	incurvé	*(ãhn-koohr-vEh)*
customer	le client	*(kleeh-Āhn)*
customer profile	le profil de la clientèle	*(proh-fEEhl dœ lah kleeh-ãhn-tEhl)*
customer service	le service clients	*(sœr-vEEhs kleeh-Āhn)*
customs	la douane	*(dooh-Ahn)*

customs broker	le courtier en douane	*(koohr-tyEh ãhn dooh-Ahn)*
customs duty	les droits de douane	*(drwAh dœ dooh-Ahn)*
customs entry	la déclaration en douane	*(deh-klah-rah-syÕh ãhn dooh-Ahn)*
customs union	l'union douanière	*(ooh-nyÕh dooh-ah-nyEhr)*
cut (v)	tailler	*(tah-yEh)*
cutback	la réduction	*(reh-doohk-syÕh)*
cutlery	la coutellerie	*(kooh-teh-lœh-rEEh)*
cycle billing	la facturation périodique	*(fahk-tooh-rah-syÕh peh-ryoh-dEEhk)*
cycle, business	le cycle économique	*(sEEh-klœ eh-koh-moh-mEEhk)*
cycle, life (of a product)	le cycle de vie	*(sEEh-klœ dœ vEEh)*
cycle, work	le cycle de production	*(sEEh-klœ dœ proh-doohk-syÕh)*
cylinder	le cylindre	*(seeh-lãhn-drœ)*
cyst	le kyste	*(kEEhst)*

D

daily	quotidien	*(koh-teeh-dyEhn)*
dairy products	les produits laitiers	*(proh-dwEEh leh-tyEhr)*
damage	les dommages	*(doh-mAhzh)*
data	les données	*(doh-nEh)*
data acquisition	la saisie des données	*(seh-zEEh deh doh-nEh)*
data bank	la banque de données	*(bÃhnk dœ doh-nEh)*
data base	la base de données	*(bAhz dœ doh-nEh)*
data processing	le traitement des données	*(treht-mÃh deh doh-nEh)*
date of delivery	la date de livraison	*(dAht dœ leeh-vreh-zÕh)*
day cream	la crème de jour	*(krEhm dœ zhOOhr)*
day loan	le prêt au jour le jour	*(prEht oh zhOOhr lœ zhOOhr)*
day order	l'ordre journalier	*(Ohr-drœ zhoohr-nah-lyEh)*
dead freight	le faux fret	*(fOh frEht)*
dead rent	la créance irrécouvrable	*(kreh-Ãhns eeh-reh-kooh-vrAh-blœ)*
deadline	la date limite	*(dAht leeh-mEEht)*
deadlock	l'impasse	*(ãhm-pAhs)*
deal	la transaction	*(trãhn-zahk-syÕh)*
deal, package	le contrat global, le forfait	*(kõhn-trAh gloh-bAhl), (fohr-fEh)*
dealer	le courtier de change, le marchand	*(koohr-tyEh dœ shÃhnzh), (mahr-shÃhnd)*

dealership	l'exclusivité des opérations de change	*(ehks-klooh-seeh-veeh-tEh dehz oh-peh-rah-syÕh dœ shÃhnzh)*
debentures	les obligations non garanties	*(oh-bleeh-gah-syÕh nõh gah-rãhn-tEEh)*
debit	le débit	*(deh-bEEh)*
debit entry	l'entrée passive	*(ãhn-trEh pah-sEEhv)*
debit note	la note de débit	*(nOht dœ deh-bEEh)*
debt	la dette	*(DEht)*
debtlessness	la situation de non-endettement	*(seeh-twah-syÕh dœ nõhn-ãhn-deht-mÃh)*
debug (v)	mettre au point, dépanner	*(mEh-trœ oh pw~Æh), (deh-pah-nEh)*
decanter	la carafe	*(kah-rAhf)*
decontamination	la décontamination	*(deh-kõhn-tah-meeh-nah-syÕhn)*
deductible	déductible	*(deh-doohk-tEEh-blœ)*
deduction	la déduction, la réduction	*(deh-doohk-syÕh), (reh-doohk-syÕh)*
deed	l'acte, le contrat	*(Ahk-tœ), (kõhn-trAh)*
deed of sale	l'acte de vente	*(Ahk-tœ dœ vÃhnt)*
deed of transfer	l'acte de cession	*(Ahk-tœ dœ seh-syÕh)*
deed of trust	l'acte de confiance, le contrat fiduciaire	*(Ahk-tœ dœ kõhn-feeh-Ãhns), (kõhn-trAh feeh-dooh-syEhr)*
deep dish	le plat creux	*(plah krŒh)*
default (n)	le défaut	*(deh-fOh)*
default (v)	manquer à ses engagements	*(mãhn-kEh ah sehz ãhn-gahzh-mÃh)*
defective	défectueux	*(deh-fehk-tŒh)*
deferred	différé	*(deeh-feh-rEh)*
deferred annuities	les annuités différées	*(ah-nweeh-tEh deeh-feh-rEh)*
deferred assets	les capitaux différés	*(kah-peeh-tOh deeh-feh-rEh)*
deferred charges	les dépenses différées	*(deh-pÃhns deeh-feh-rEh)*
deferred deliveries	les livraisons différées	*(leeh-vreh-zÕh deeh-feh-rEh)*
deferred income	le revenu différé	*(rœhv-nOOh deeh-feh-rEh)*
deferred liabilities	les dettes différées	*(DEht deeh-feh-rEh)*
deferred tax	l'impôt différé	*(ãhm-pOh deeh-feh-rEh)*
deficit	le déficit	*(deh-feeh-sEEht)*
deficit financing	le financement par le déficit	*(feeh-nãhns-mÃh pahr lœ deh-feeh-sEEht)*
deficit spending	les dépenses supérieures aux recettes	*(deh-pÃhns sooh-peh-ryŒhr oh rœh-sEht)*
deflation	la déflation	*(deh-flah-syÕh)*
deforestation	la déforestation	*(deh-foh-rehs-tah-syÕhn)*
defroster	le dégivreur	*(deh-geeh-vrŒhr)*
degree	le degré	*(dœh-grEh)*

D

delay	le retard, le délai	*(ræh-tAhr)*, *(deh-lEh)*
delay (v)	retarder	*(ræh-tahr-dEh)*
delete (v)	effacer	*(eh-fah-sEh)*
delinquent account	le compte douteux	*(kŌhnt dooh-tŒh)*
delivered price	le prix rendu	*(prEEh rāhn-dOOh)*
delivery	la livraison, l'accouchement	*(leeh-vreh-zŌh)*, *(ah-koohsh-mĀhn)*
delivery date	la date de livraison	*(dAht dæ leeh-vreh-zŌh)*
delivery notice	l'avis de livraison	*(ah-vEEh dæ leeh-vreh-zŌh)*
delivery points	les points de livraison	*(pw¯Æh dæ leeh-vreh-zŌh)*
delivery price	le prix à la livraison	*(prEEh ah lah leeh-vreh-zŌh)*
demand	la demande	*(dæh-mĀhnd)*
demand (v)	exiger	*(ehk-seeh-zhEh)*
demand assessment	l'évaluation de la demande	*(eh-vah-lwah-syŌhn dæ lah dæh-mĀhd)*
demand deposit	le dépôt à vue	*(deh-pOh ah vOOh)*
demand line of credit	la ligne de crédit à vue	*(lEEh-nyæ dæ kreh-dEEh ah vOOh)*
demilitarize	démilitariser	*(deh-meeh-leeh-tah-leeh-zEh)*
demographic	démographique	*(deh-moh-graf-fEEhk)*
demotion	la rétrogradation	*(reh-troh-grah-dah-syŌh)*
demurrage	la surestarie	*(sooh-rehs-tah-rEEh)*
density	la densité	*(dāhn-seeh-tEh)*
department	le service	*(sær-vEEhs)*
department store	le grand magasin	*(grĀhn mah-gah-z¯Æhn)*
deplete (v)	épuiser	*(eh-pweeh-zEh)*
depletion accounting	la comptabilité d'épuisement	*(kōhn-tah-beeh-leeh-deh deh-pweehz-mĀh)*
depletion control	le contrôle d'épuisement	*(kōhn-trOhl deh deh-pwee hz-mĀh)*
deposit	le depôt	*(deh-pOh)*
deposit, account	le compte de dépôt à vue	*(kŌhnt dæ deh-pOh ah vOOh)*
deposit, bank	le dépôt bancaire	*(deh-pOh bāhn-kEhr)*
depository	le dépôt, l'entrepôt	*(deh-pOh)*, *(āhn-træ-pOh))*
depreciation	la dépréciation, l'amortissement	*(deh-preh-syah-syŌh)*, *(ah-mohr-eehs-mĀh)*
depreciation allowance	l'indemnité de dépréciation	*(æhn-dehm-neeh-tEh dæ deh-preh-syah-syŌh)*
depreciation of currency	la dépréciation de la monnaie	*(deh-preh-syah-syŌh dæ lah moh-nEh)*
depreciation, accelerated	l'amortissement accéléré	*(ah-mohr-eehs-mĀh ak-seh-leh-rEh)*
depreciation, accrued	l'amortissement couru	*(ah-mohr-eehs-mĀh kooh-rOOh)*

depression	la crise	*(krEEhz)*
depth analysis	l'analyse en profondeur	*(āh-nah-lEEhz ãhn proh-fōhn-dŒhr)*
deputy chairman	le vice-président	*(veehs-preh-zeeh-dÃh)*
deputy manager	le directeur adjoint	*(deeh-rehk-tŒhr ad-zhwÆhn)*
deregulated	suspendu (le règlement, la règlementation)	*(soohs-pāhn-dOOh), (reh-glœh-mÃh), (reh-glœh-mãhn-tah-syÕh)*
deregulation	la déréglementation	*(deh-reh-glœh-mahn-tah-syÕhn)*
dermatologically tested	testé par les dermatologues	*(tehs-tEh pahr leh dœhr-mah-toh-logh)*
desertification	la désertification	*(deh-sehr-teeh-feeh-kah-syÕhn)*
design (v)	dessiner	*(dœh-seeh-nEh)*
design engineering	l'étude de conception	*(eh-tOOhd dœ kõhn-sehp-syÕh)*
designer	le couturier, le dessinateur	*(kooh-tooh-ryEh), (deh-seeh-nah-tŒhr)*
dessert plate	l'assiette à dessert	*(ah-syEht ah dœh-sEhr)*
detector	le détecteur	*(deh-tehk-tŒhr)*
detonator	le détonateur	*(deh-toh-nah-tŒhr)*
devaluation	la dévaluation	*(deh-vah-lwah-syÕh)*
devalue (v)	dévaluer	*(deh-vah-lwEh)*
developing country	pays en développement	*(pah-EEh ãhn deh-veh-lohp-mÃh)*
device	le dispositif	*(deehs-poh-zeeh-tEEhf)*
diabetes	le diabète	*(deeh-ah-bEht)*
diesel	le diésel	*(deeh-zEhl)*
differential, price	l'écart de prix	*(eh-kAhr dœ prEEh)*
differential, tariff	l'écart de tarif	*(eh-kAhr dœ tah-rEEhf)*
differential, wage	la grille des salaires	*(grEEhyœ deh sah-lEhr)*
digital	le digital, numérique	*(deeh-zheeh-tAhl), (nooh-meh-rEEhk)*
digital computer	l'ordinateur numérique	*(ohr-deeh-nah-tŒhr nooh-meh-rEEhk)*
digitalis	la digitaline	*(deeh-zheeh-tah-lEEhn)*
dilution of equity	la dilution du capital	*(deeh-looh-syÕh dooh kah-peeh-tAhl)*
dilution of labor	la dévalorisation du travail	*(deh-vah-loh-reeh-zah-syÕh dooh trah-vAhyœ)*
dinner plate	l'assiette plate	*(ah-syEht plAht)*
dinnerware set	le service	*(sœhr-vEEhs)*
diode	la diode	*(deeh-Ohd)*
direct access storage	la mémoire à accès direct	*(meh-mwAhr ah ahk-sEh deeh-rEhkt)*
direct cost	le coût direct	*(kOOht deeh-rEhkt)*
direct expenses	les frais proportionnels	*(frEh proh-pohr-syoh-nEhl)*

direct investment	l'investissement direct	(*ãhn-vehs-teehs-mÃh deeh-rEhkt*)
direct labor (accounting)	le coût du travail	(*kOOht dooh trah-vAhyœ*)
direct mail	le courrier direct, la vente par correspondance	(*kooh-ryEh deeh-rEhkt), (vÃhnt pahr koh-rehs-põhn-dÃhns*)
direct mail advertising	la publicité directe par correspondance	(*pooh-bleeh-seeh-tEh deeh-rEhkt pahr koh-rehs-põhn-dÃhns*)
direct paper	le papier direct	(*pah-pyEh deeh-rEhkt*)
direct quotation	la cotation directe	(*koh-tah-syÕh deeh-rEhkt*)
direct selling	la vente directe	(*vÃhnt deeh-rEhkt*)
director	l'administrateur	(*ad-meeh-neehs-trah-tŒhr*)
disability	l'invalidité	(*ãhn-vah-leeh-deeh-tEh*)
disarmament	le désarmement	(*dehz-ahr-mœh-mÃhn*)
disbursement	le débours	(*deh-bOOhr*)
disc	le disque	(*dEEhsk*)
discharge (v)	décharger	(*deh-shahr-zEh*)
discount (n)	l'escompte	(*ehs-kÕhnt*)
discount cash flow	la marge brute actualisée	(*mAhrzh brOOht ahk-twah-leeh-zEh*)
discount rate	le taux d'escompte	(*tOh dehs-kÕhnt*)
discount securities	l'action au-dessous du pair	(*ahk-syÕh oh dœ-sOOh dooh pEhr*)
discounting	la pratique de l'escompte	(*prah-tEEhk dehs-kÕhnt*)
discretionary account	le compte géré en vertu a d'un contrat de gestion	(*kÕhnt zheh-rEh ãhn vœhr-tOOh doohn kõhn-trAh dœ zhœhs-tyÕh*)
discretionary order	l'ordre à appréciation	(*Ohr-drœ ah ah-preh-syah-syÕh*)
disease	la maladie	(*mah-lah-dEEh*)
dishes	la vaisselle	(*veh-sEhl*)
dishonor (as a check)	le refus d'acceptation	(*rœh-fOOh dahk-sehp-tah-syÕh*)
dish towel	le torchon	(*tohr-shÕhn*)
dishwasher safe	garanti lave-vaisselle	(*gah-rãhn-tEEh lahv-veh-sEhl*)
disk	le disque	(*dEEhsk*)
disk drive	le lecteur de disques	(*lehk-tŒhr dœ dEEhsk*)
dispatch	l'expédition	(*ehks-peh-deeh-syÕh*)
displacement	la cylindrée	(*seeh-l~ehn-drEh*)
disposable	jetable	(*zhœh-tAh-blœh*)
disposable income	le revenu disponible	(*rœhv-nOOh deehs-poh-nEEh-blœ*)
dispute (n)	la contestation	(*kõhn-tehs-tah-syÕh*)
dispute (v)	débattre	(*deh-bAh-trœ*)
dispute, labor	le conflit du travail	(*kõhn-flEEh dooh trah-vAhyœ*)

D

distil (v)	distiller	*(deehs-teeh-lEh)*
distillation	la distillation	*(deehs-teeh-lah-syÕh)*
distribution	la distribution	*(deehs-treeh-booh-syÕh)*
distribution costs	les frais de distribution	*(frEh dœ deehs-treeh-booh-syÕh)*
distribution network	le réseau de distribution	*(reh-zOh dœ deehs-treeh-booh-syÕh)*
distribution policy	la politique de distribution	*(poh-leeh-tEEhk dœ deehs-treeh-booh-syÕh)*
distribution, channels of	les canaux de distribution	*(kah-nOh dœ deehs-treeh-booh-syÕh)*
distributor	le distributeur	*(deehs-treeh-booh-tŒhr)*
diuretic	la diurétique	*(deeh-ooh-reh-tEEhk)*
diversification	la diversification	*(deeh-vehr-seeh-feeh-kah-syÕh)*
divestment	la dépossession	*(deh-poh-seh-syÕh)*
dividend	le dividende	*(deeh-veeh-dÃhnd)*
dividend yield	le rendement d'un dividende	*(rãhnd-mÃh doohn deeh-veeh-dÃhnd)*
division of labor	la division du travail	*(deeh-veeh-zyÕh dooh trah-vAhyœ)*
dock (ship's receipt)	le dock	
dock handling charges	les droits de dock	*(drwAh dœ dock)*
document	le document	*(doh-kooh-mÃh)*
documentary	le documentaire	*(doh-kooh-mãhn-tEhr)*
dollar cost averaging	le calcul du prix moyen en dollars	*(kahl-kOOhl dooh prEEh mwah-yEhn ãhn doh-lAhr)*
domestic bill	la traite intérieure	*(trEht ãhn-teh-reyŒhr)*
domestic corporation	la société nationale	*(soh-syeh-tEh nah-syoh-nAhl)*
donor	le donneur	*(doh-nŒhr)*
door-to-door (sales)	le porte-à-porte	*(pOhrt ah pOhrt)*
dosage	le dosage	*(doh-zAhzh)*
dose	la dose	*(dOhz)*
double dealing	le double jeu	*(dOOh-blœ zhŒh)*
double pricing	le double étiquetage	*(dOOh-blœ eh-teeh-keh-tAhzh)*
double taxation	la double imposition	*(dOOh-blœ ãhm-poh-zeeh-syÕh)*
double time	la double paie	*(dOOh-blœ pEh)*
double-entry bookkeeping	la comptabilité en partie double	*(kõhn-tah-beeh-leeh-tEh ãhn pahr-EEh dOOh-blœ)*
down payment	l'acompte, les arrhes	*(ah-kÕhnt), (Ahr)*

down the line	subalterne (en descendant la voie hiérarchique)	*(soohb-ahl-tEhrn ãhn deh-sãhn-dÃhn lah vwAh yeh-rahr-kEEhk)*
downswing	en phase descendante	*(fÃhz deh-sãhn-dÃhnt)*
downtime	le temps mort, la période de fermeture pour travaux	*(tÃh mOhr), (peh-ryOhd dœ fehr-mœh-tOOhr poohr trah-vOh)*
downturn	la récession, la baisse	*(reh-seh-syÕh), (bEhs)*
draft	l'effet de commerce, la traite	*(eh-fEht dœ koh-mEhrs), (trEht)*
drape (v)	draper	*(drah-pEh)*
draw off	soutirer, tirer une cuve	*(sooh-teeh-rEh), (teeh-reh oohn kOOhv)*
drawback	le remboursement lors de l'exportation des droits de douane payés à l'importation	*(rãhm-boohrs-mÃh lOhr dœ lehks-pohr-tah-syÕh deh drwAh dœ dooh-Ahn pah-yEh ah lãhm-pohr-tãh-syÕh)*
drawdown	la moins-value	*(mwãh-vah-lOOh)*
drawdown date	la date de tirage	*(dAht dœ teeh-rAhzh)*
drawee	le tiré d'une traite	*(teeh-rEh doohn trEht)*
drawer	le tireur d'une traite, le tireur d'un chèque	*(teeh-rŒhr doohn trEht), (teeh-rŒhr dœhn shEhk)*
drayage	le camionnage	*(kah-myoh-nAhzh)*
dregs	le moût	*(mOOht)*
dress	la robe	*(rOhb)*
dressing	le pansement	*(pãhns-mÃh)*
dried up well	le puits asséché	*(pwEEhz ah-seh-shEh)*
drink (v)	boire	*(bwAhr)*
driver	le conducteur	*(kõhn-doohk-tŒhr)*
drop	la goutte, la pastille	*(gOOht), (pahs-tEEh-yœ)*
drop out (v)	retirer	*(rœh-teeh-rEh)*
drop shipment	l'expédition directe	*(ehks-peh-deeh-syÕh deeh-rEhkt)*
drought	la sécheresse	*(seh-sheh-rEhs)*
drowsiness	la somnolence	*(sohm-noh-lÃns)*
drug	la drogue, le stupéfiant	*(drOhg), (stooh-peh-feeh-Ãh)*
drug addiction	la toximanie	*(tohk-seeh-mah-nEEh)*
drugstore	la pharmacie	*(fahr-mah-sEEh)*
dry	sec	*(sEhk)*
dry cargo	la cargaison ordinaire	*(kahr-geh-zÕh ohr-deeh-nEhr)*
dry goods	les marchandises sèches (les tissus, les étoffes)	*(mahr-shãhn-dEEhz sEhsh), (teeh-sOOh, eh-tOhf)*
dry skin	la peau sèche	*(poh sEhsh)*
dry wine	le vin sec	*(vÆhn sEhk)*
dryness	le dessèchement	*(doeh-sehsh-mÃhn)*
dubbing	le doublage	*(dooh-blAzh)*

D

dummy	la maquette	*(mah-kEht)*
dump	la décharge	*(deh-shAhrzh)*
dump (v)	déverser	*(deh-vehr-sEh)*
dumping	le déversement	*(deh-vehrs-mÃhn)*
dumping (goods in foreign market)	le dumping	
dunnage	le fardage	*(fahr-dAhzh)*
duopoly	le duopole	*(dooh-oh-pOhl)*
durable goods	les biens durables	*(byÆh dooh-rAh-blœ)*
duress	la contrainte	*(kõhn-trÆhnt)*
duty	la taxe, les droits	*(tAhks), (drwAh)*
duty ad valorem	le droit ad valorem	*(drwAh ad valorem)*
duty free	en franchise	*(ãhn frãh-shEEhz)*
duty, anti-dumping	les droits anti-dumping	*(drwAh anti-dumping)*
duty, combination	les droits combinés	*(drwAh kõhm-beeh-nEh)*
duty, countervailing duty	le droit compensateur	*(drwAh kõhm-pãhn-sah-tŒhr)*
duty, export	la taxe à l'exportation	*(tAhks ah lehks-pohr-tah-syÕh)*
duty, remission	la remise de droits	*(rœh-mEEhz dœ drwAh)*
duty, specific	le droit spécifique	*(drwAh speh-seeh-fEEhk)*
dye (v)	teindre	*(tÆhn-drœ)*
dynamics, group	la dynamique de groupe	*(deeh-nah-mEEhk dœ grOOhp)*
dynamics, market	la dynamique du marché	*(deeh-nah-mEEhk dooh mahr-shEh)*
dynamics, product	la dynamique des produits	*(deeh-nah-mEEhk deh proh-dwEEh)*

E

earmark (v)	affecter	*(ah-fehk-tEh)*
earnings	le revenu	*(rœhv-nOOh)*
earnings on assets	le rendement de fonds propres	*(rãhnd-mÃh dœ fÕhn prOh-prœ)*
earnings per share	les bénéfices par action	*(beh-neh-fEEhs pahr ahk-syÕh)*
earnings performance	la rentabilité	*(rãhn-tah-beeh-leeh-tEh)*
earnings report	le compte-rendu des bénéfices	*(kÕhnt-rãhn-dOOh deh beh-neh-fEEhs)*
earnings yield	le rendement	*(rãhnd-mÃh)*
earnings, retained	les bénéfices non distribués	*(beh-neh-fEEhs nõh deehs-treeh-bwEh)*
earnings/price ratio	le coefficient de capitalisation des résultats	*(koh-eh-feeh-sÃhnt dœ kah-peeh-tah-leeh-zah-syÕh deh reh-soohl-tAh)*
earthenware	la faïence	*(fah-eeh-Ãhns)*

earthy	terreux	*(teh-rOe)*
EC national	le ressortissant de la CE	*(rœh-sohr-teeh-sÃhn dœ lah seh-Eh)*
EC passport holder	le titulaire d'un passeport de la CE	*(teeh-tooh-lEhr dœhn pahs-pOhr dœ lah seh-Eh)*
ecological	écologique	*(eh-koh-loh-zhEEhk)*
ecology	l'écologie	*(eh-koh-loh-zhEEh)*
econometrics	l'économétrie	*(eh-koh-noh-meh-trEEh)*
economic	économique	*(eh-koh-moh-mEEhk)*
economic indicators	les indicateurs économiques	*(æhndeeh-kah-tŒhrz eh-koh-moh-mEEhk)*
economic life	la vie économique	*(vEEh eh-koh-moh-mEEhk)*
economic order quantity	la quantité économique d'approvisionnement	*(kãhn-teeh-tEh eh-koh-moh-mEEhk dah-proh-veeh-zyohn-mÃh)*
economy	l'économie	*(eh-koh-noh-mEEh)*
economy of scale	l'économie d'échelle	*(eh-koh-noh-mEEh deh-shEhl)*
edit (v)	éditer	*(eh-deeh-tEh)*
edition	l'édition	*(eh-deeh-syÕh)*
editor	le rédacteur	*(reh-dahk-tŒhr)*
effective yield	le rendement réel	*(rãhnd-mÃh reh-Ehl)*
efficiency	l'efficacité	*(eh-feeh-kah-seeh-tEh)*
ejection seat	le siège éjectable	*(syEhzh eh-zhehk-tAh-blœh)*
elasticity (of supply or demand)	l'élasticité	*(eh-lahs-teeh-seeh-tEh)*
electric arc furnace	le four électrique	*(fOOhr eh-lehk-trEEhk)*
electrical engineering	la technique électrique	*(tehk-nEEhk eh-lehk-trEEhk)*
electricity	l'électricité	*(eh-lehk-treeh-seeh-tEh)*
electrode	l'eléctrode	*(eh-lehk-trOhd)*
electrolysis	l'électrolyse	*(eh-lehk-troh-lEEhz)*
electrolytic process	le procéde électrolytique	*(proh-seh-dEh eh-leh-troh-leeh-tEEhk)*
electron	l'électron	*(eh-lehk-trÕh)*
electronic	l'électronique	*(eh-lehk-troh-nEEhk)*
electronic whiteboard	le tableau électronique	*(tah-blOh eh-lehk-troh-nEEhk)*
electrostatic	l'électrostatique	*(eh-lehk-troh-stah-tEEhk)*
elegance	l'élégance	*(eh-leh-gÃhns)*
element	l'élément	*(eh-leh-mÃh)*
embargo	l'embargo	*(æhm-bahr-goh)*
embezzlement	le détournement de fonds	*(deh-toohr-nœ-mÃh dœ fÕhn)*
emergency	l'urgence	*(oohr-zhÃhns)*
emission	l'émission	*(eh-meeh-syÕhn)*

employee	l'employé(e)	(ãhm-plwah-yEh)
employee counseling	l'orientation professionnelle	(oh-ryãhn-tah-syÕh proh-feh-syoh-nEhl)
employee relations	les relations professionnelles	(ræh-lah-syÕh proh-feh-syoh-nEhl)
employment agency	le bureau de placement	(booh-rOh dæ plahs-mÃh)
empowered to	abilité à	(ah-beeh-leeh-tEh ah)
emulsion	l'émulsion	(eh-mohl-syÕhn)
encumbrance (liens, liabilities, commitments)	l'engagement	(ãhn-gahzh-mÃh)
end of period	la fin de l'exercice	(fÆhn dæ ehk-sær-seEhs)
end product	le produit fini	(proh-dwEEh feeh-nEEh)
end use certificate	le certificat d'utilisation finale	(sehr-teeh-feeh-kAh dooh-teeh-zah-syÕh feeh-nAhl)
endorse (v)	endosser	(ãhn-doh-sEh)
endorsee	l'endossataire	(ãhn-doh-sah-tEhr)
endorsement	l'endossement	(ãhn-dohs-mÃh)
endowment	la dotation	(doh-tah-syÕh)
energy conservation	les économies d'énergie	(eh-koh-noh-mEEh deh-nehr-zhEEh)
enforce (v)	appliquer, mettre en vigueur	(ah-pleeh-kEh, mEh-træh ãhn veeh-gŒhr)
engine	le moteur	(moh-tŒhr)
engineer	l'ingénieur	(ãhn-zheh-nyŒhr)
engineering	l'ingénierie	(ãhn-zheh-nyeh-rEEh)
engineering and design department	le bureau d'études	(booh-rOh deh-tOOhd)
engineering, design	l'étude de conception	(eh-tOOhd dæ kõhn-sehp-syÕh)
engineering, industrial	l'organisation industrielle	(ohr-gah-neeh-zah-syÕh ãhn-doohs-tryEhl)
engineering, systems	l'organisation des systèmes	(ohr-gah-neeh-zah-syÕh deh seehs-tEhm)
engineering, value	l'étude de la valeur	(eh-tOOhd dæ lah vah-lŒhr)
engrave (v)	graver	(grah-vEh)
enlarge (v)	agrandir	(ah-grãhn-dEEhr)
enterprise	l'entreprise	(ãhn-træh-prEEhz)
entrepreneur	l'entrepreneur	(ãhn-træh-præh-nŒhr)
entry permit	la déclaration d'importation	(deh-klah-rah-syÕh dæhm-pohr-tah-syÕh)
entry, cash	l'encaissement	(ãhn-kehs-mÃh)
entry, debit	l'écriture au passif	(eh-kree-tOOhr oh pah-sEEhf)
entry, ledger	l'écriture au grand livre	(eh-kree-tOOhr oh grÃn lEEh-vræ)
environment	l'environnement	(ãhn-veeh-rohn-mÃhn)

environmental advantage	l'atout écologique	*(ah-tOOht eh-koh-loh-zhEEhk)*
environmental assessment	l'évaluation de l'environnement	*(eh-vah-lwah-syÕn dœ lœhn-veeh-rohn-mÃhn)*
environmental damage	les atteintes à l'environnement	*(ah-tœhnt ah lœhn-veeh-rohn-mÃhn)*
environmental impact	l'impact sur l'environnement	*(œhm-pAhkt soohr lœhn-veeh-rohn-mÃhn)*
environmental management	la gestion de l'environnement	*(zhehs-tyÕhn dœ lœhn-veeh-rohn-mÃhn)*
environmentalist	l'écologiste	*(eh-koh-loh-zhEEhst)*
environmentally friendly	écologique	*(eh-koh-loh-zhEEhk)*
enzyme	l'enzyme	*(œhn-zhEEhm)*
equal pay for equal work	l'égalité des salaires	*(eh-gah-leeh-tEh deh sah-lEhr)*
equipment	l'équipement	*(eh-keehp-mÃh)*
equipment leasing	l'affermage, le crédit-bail	*(ah-fehr-mAhzh), (kreh-dEEh-bEhl)*
equity	l'action à revenu variable	*(ahk-syÕh ah rœhv-nOOh vah-ryAh-blœ)*
equity investments	les investissements en capital	*(œhn-vehs-teehs-mÃh ãhn kah-peeh-tAhl)*
equity, dilution of	la dilution du capital	*(deeh-looh-syÕh dooh kah-peeh-tAhl)*
equity, return on	le rendement du capital	*(rãhnd-mÃh dooh kah-peeh-tAhl)*
equity, share	l'action en capital	*(ahk-syÕh ãhn kah-peeh-tAhl)*
erase (v)	effacer	*(eh-fah-sEh)*
ergonomics	l'ergonomie	*(ehr-goh-noh-mEEh)*
erode top soil (v)	ronger la couche arable	*(rõhn-zhEh lah kOOhsh ah-rAh-blœh)*
error	l'erreur	*(eh-rŒhr)*
escalator clause	la clause d'échelle mobile, la clause d'escalation	*(klOhz deh-shEhl moh-bEEhl), (klOhz deh-skah-lah-syÕh)*
escheat	la déshérence	*(dehz-eh-rÃhns)*
escrow	le gage de garantie confié à un tiers	*(gAhzh dœ gah-rãhn-tEEh kõhn-fyEh ah œhn tyEhrs)*
escrow account	le compte de garantie (confié à un tiers), le compte bloqué	*(kÕhnt dœ gah-rãhn-tEEh kõhn-fyEh ah œhn tyEhrs), (kÕhnt bloh-kEh)*
estate	la proprieté foncière, le bien immobilier	*(proh-preeh-eh-tEh fõhn-syEhr), (byÃh eeh-moh-beeh-lyEh)*
estate (or chateau)	le château	*(shah-tOh)*
estate agent	l'agent immobilier	*(ah-zhÃh eeh-moh-beeh-lyEh)*

estate bottled	mis en bouteille au château	*(mEEhz ãhn booh-tEh-yœ oh shah-tOh)*
estate tax	les droits de succession	*(drwAh dœ sooh-seh-syÕh)*
estimate (n)	l'estimation, le devis	*(ehs-teeh-mah-syÕh),*
estimate (v)	estimer	*(ehs-teeh-mEh)*
estimate, sales	la prévision de vente	*(preh-veeh-zyÕh dœ vÃhnt)*
estimated price	l'estimation de prix	*(ehs-teeh-mah-syÕh dœ prEEh)*
estimated time of arrival	l'heure prévue d'arrivée	*(Œhr preh-vOOh dah-reeh-vEh)*
estimated time of departure	l'heure prévue de départ	*(Œhr preh-vOOh dœ deh-pAhr)*
ethane	l'éthane	*(eh-tAhn)*
ether	l'éther	*(eh-tEh)*
Eurobond	l'Euro-obligation	*(eh-roh-oh-bleeh-gah-syÕh)*
Eurocheque	l'eurochèque	*(eh-ooh-roh-shEhk)*
Eurocrat	l'eurocrate	*(eh-ooh-roh-krAht)*
Eurocurrency	les Eurodevises	*(eh-roh-dœh-vEEhz)*
Eurodollar	l'Eurodollar	*(eh-roh-doh-lAhr)*
Euromarket	l'euromarché	*(eh-ooh-roh-mahr-shEh)*
European citizenship	la citoyenneté européenne	*(seeh-twah-yehn-tEh eh-ooh-roh-peh-Ehn)*
European Community (EC)	la Communauté européenne (CE)	*(koh-mooh-noh-tEh eh-ooh-roh-peh-Ehn)*
European Currency Unit	l'ÉCU	*(eh-kOOh)*
European Monetary System	le système monétaire européen	*(seehs-tEhm moh-neh-tEhr eh-ooh-roh-peh-Ehn)*
European Parliament	le Parlement européen	*(pahr-lœh-mÃhn eh-ooh-roh-peh-Ehn)*
euthanasia	l'euthanasie	*(eh-ooh-tah-nah-zEEh)*
evaluation	l'évaluation	*(eh-vah-lwah-syÕh)*
evaluation, job	l'évaluation de poste	*(eh-vah-lwah-syÕh dœ pOhst)*
evaporation	l'evaporation	*(eh-vah-poh-rah-syÕh)*
ex dividend	ex-dividende	*(ex-deeh-veeh-dÃhnd)*
ex dock	la marchandise rendue au port d'importation	*(mahr-shãhn-dEEhz rãhn-dOOh oh pOhr dæhm-pohr-tah-syÕh)*
ex factory	départ usine	*(deh-pAhr ooh-zEEhn)*
ex mill	départ fabrique	*(deh-pAhr fah-brEEhk)*
ex mine	départ mine	*(deh-pAhr meehn)*
ex rights	ex-droits	*(ex-drwAh)*
ex warehouse	départ entrepôt	*(deh-pAhr ãhn-træ-pOh)*
ex works	départ usine	*(deh-pAhr ooh-zEEhn)*

exchange (n) (stock, commodity)	la bourse	*(bOOhrs)*
exchange (v)	échanger	*(eh-shãhn-zhEh)*
exchange control	le contrôle des changes	*(kõhn-trOhl deh shÃhnzh)*
exchange discount	la perte de conversion	*(pEhrt dœ kõhn-vehr-zyÕhn)*
exchange loss	la perte sur le change	*(pEhrt soohr lœ shÃhnzh)*
exchange rate	le taux de change	*(tOh dœ shÃhnzh)*
exchange risk	le risque de change	*(rEEhs-kœ dœ shÃhnzh)*
exchange value	la valeur d'échange	*(vah-lŒhr deh-shÃhnzh)*
excise duty	le droit de régie	*(drwAh dœ reh-zhEEh)*
excise license	le droit de l'accise	*(drwAh dœ lahk-sEEhz)*
excise tax	la taxe à la consommation	*(tAhks ah lah kõhn-soh-mah-syÕh)*
exclusive	en exclusivité	*(ãhn ehks-klooh-seeh-veeh-tEh)*
exclusive representative	le représentant exclusif	*(rœh-preh-zãhn-tÃhnt ehks-klooh-sEEhf)*
executive	le dirigeant	*(deeh-reeh-zhÃh)*
executive board	le conseil de direction	*(kõhn-sEh-yœ dœ deeh-rehk-syÕh)*
executive committee	le comité de direction	*(koh-meeh-tEh dœ deeh-rehk-syÕh)*
executive compensation	l'indemnité de direction	*(ãhn-dehm-neeh-tEh dœ deeh-rehk-syÕh)*
executive director	l'administrateur	*(ad-meeh-neehs-trah-tŒhr)*
executive line	la ligne de direction	*(lEEh-nyœ dœ deeh-rehk-syÕh)*
executive search	la recherche de cadres	*(rœ-shEhrsh dœ kAh-drœ)*
executive secretary	la, le secrétaire de direction	*(seh-kreh-tEhr dœ deeh-rehk-syÕh)*
executive, chief	le directeur d'une entreprise	*(deeh-rehk-tŒhr doohn ãhn-trœh-prEEhz)*
executor	l'exécuteur testamentaire	*(ehk-seh-kooh-tŒhr tehs-tah-mãhn-tEhr)*
exemption	l'exemption	*(ehk-zãhm-syÕh)*
exhaust	l'échappement	*(eh-shAhp-mÃh)*
expectations, up to our	à la hauteur de nos prévisions, conformément à notre attente	*(ah lah oh-tŒhr dœ noh preh-veeh-zyÕh), (kõhn-fohr-meh-mÃh ah nOh-trœ ah-tÃhnt)*
expected results	les résultats attendus	*(reh-soohl-tAh ah-tãhn-dOOh)*
expenditure	la dépense	*(deh-pãhns)*
expense account	l'indemnité pour frais professionnels, les frais de représentation	*(ãhn-dehm-neeh-tEh poohr frEh proh-feh-syoh-nEhl), (frEh dœ rœh-preh-zãhn-tah-syÕh)*

E

E

expenses	les frais généraux	(frEh zheh-neh-rOh)
expenses, direct	les dépenses directes	(deh-pÃhns deeh-rEhkt)
expenses, indirect	les dépenses indirectes	(deh-pÃhns æhn-deeh-rEhkt)
expenses, running	les dépenses courantes	(deh-pãhns kooh-rÃhnt)
expenses, shipping	les frais d'expédition	(frEh dehks-peh-deeh-syÕh)
experiment	l'expérience	(ehks-peh-ryÃhns)
experimental	expérimental	(ehks-peh-reeh-mãhn-tAhl)
expiry date	la date d'échéance	(dAht deh-sheh-Ãhns)
export (v)	exporter	(ehks-pohr-tEh)
export agent	le commissionnaire-exportateur	(kohm-meeh-syoh-nEhr ehks-pohr-tah-tŒhr)
export credit	le crédit à l'exportation	(kreh-dEEh ah lehks-pohr-tah-syÕh)
export duty	les droits d'exportation	(drwAh dehks-pohr-tah-syÕh)
export entry	la déclaration d'exportation	(deh-klah-rah-syÕh dehks-pohr-tah-syÕh)
export house	l'entreprise d'exportation	(ãhn-trœh-prEEhz dehks-pohr-tah-syÕh)
export manager	le directeur de l'exportation	(deeh-rehk-tŒhr dœ lehks-pohr-tah-syÕh)
export middleman	l'intermédiaire d'exportation	(æhn-tehr-meh-dyEhr dehks-pohr-tah-syÕh)
export permit	la licence d'exportation	(leeh-sÃhns dehks-pohr-tah-syÕh)
export quota	les contingents à l'exportation	(kõhn-teehn-zhÃhnt ah lehks-pohr-tah-syÕh)
export regulations	les réglementations à l'exportation	(reh-glœh-mãhn-tah-syÕh ah lehks-pohr-tah-syÕh)
export sales contract	le contrat de vente à l'exportation	(kõhn-trAh dœ vÃhnt ah lehks-pohr-tah-syÕh)
export taxes	les taxes à l'exportation	(tAhks ah lehks-pohr-tah-syÕh)
export, for	destiné à l'exportation	(dehs-teeh-nEh ah lehks-pohr-tah-syÕh)
export-import bank	la banque d'import-export	(bÃhnk dæhm-pOhr-ehks-pOhr)
expresso cup	la demi-tasse	(dœh-mEEh tAhs)
expropriation	l'expropriation	(ehks-proh-pryah-syÕh)
extra dividend	super-dividende	(super-deeh-veeh-dÃhnd)
extract	l'extrait	(ehks-trEht)
eye contour	le pourtour des yeux	(poohr-tOOhr dehz yŒh)
eye cream	la crème pour les yeux	(krEhm poohr lehz yŒh)
eye shadow	l'ombre à paupières	(Ohm-brœh ah poh-pyEhr)
eyebrow	le sourcil	(soohr-sEEhl)
eyedrop	le collyre	(koh-lEEhr)
eyelash	le cil	(sEEhl)
eyeglass case	l'étui à lunettes	(eh-twEEh ah looh-nEht)
eye-catching	accrocheur	(ah-kroh-shŒhr)

F

fabric	le tissu	*(teeh-sOOh)*
face cream	la crème pour le visage	*(krEhm poohr lœ veeh-zAhzh)*
face powder	la poudre de riz	*(pOOh-drœh dœ rEEhs)*
face value	la valeur nommale	*(vah-lŒhr noh-mAhl)*
facilities	l'équipement, les moyens, les locaux	*(eh-keehp-mÃh), (mwah-yEhn), (loh-kOh)*
fact sheet	la feuille de renseignements	*(fŒh-yœ dœ rãhn-seh-nyœ-mÃh)*
factor (n)	le facteur, le coefficient, le mandataire, l'intermédiaire (souvent ducroire)	*(fahk-tŒhr), (koh-eh-feeh-sÃhnt), (mÃhn-dah-tEhr), (ãhn-tehr-meh-dyEhr sooh-vÃh dooh-krwAhr)*
factor analysis	l'analyse factorielle	*(ãh-nah-lEEhz fahk-toh-ryEhl)*
factor rating	l'évaluation des facteurs	*(eh-vah-lwah-syÕh deh fahk-tŒhr)*
factor, cost	le facteur coût	*(fahk-tŒhr kOOht)*
factor, load	le coefficient de remplissage	*(koh-eh-feeh-sÃhnt dœ rãhm-pleeh-sAhzh)*
factor, profit	le facteur profit	*(fahk-tŒhr proh-fEEh)*
factoring	l'affacturage	*(ah-fahk-tooh-rAhzh)*
factory	l'usine	*(ooh-zEEhn)*
factory overhead	les frais généraux d'usinc	*(frEh zheh-neh-rOh dooh-zEEhn)*
fail (v)	échouer, manquer	*(eh-shooh-Eh), (mãhn-kEh)*
failure	l'insuccès, le défaut	*(ãhn-soohk-sEh), (deh-fOh)*
fair market value	la valeur marchande moyenne	*(vah-lŒhr mahr-shÃhnd mwah-yEhn)*
fair return	le rendement moyen	*(rãhnd-mÃh mwah-yEhn)*
fair trade	le libre échange réciproque	*(lEEh-brœ eh-shÃhnzh reh-seeh-prOhk)*
fall off (v)	se détacher	*(sœh deh-tah-shEh)*
farm out (v)	donner en sous-traitance	*(doh-nEh ãhn sooh-treh-tÃhns)*
fashion	la mode	*(mOhd)*
fashionable	à la mode	*(ah lah mOhd)*
feed ratio	le taux d'approvisionnement	*(tOh dah-proh-veeh-zyohn-mÃh)*
feedback	l'auto-contrôle, la réaction	*(oh-toh-kõhn-trOhl), (reh-ahk-syÕh)*
fender	l'aile	*(Ehl)*
ferment	le ferment	*(fehr-mÃh)*
ferritic	ferritique	*(feh-reeh-tEEhk)*
ferroalloys	les ferro-alliages	*(feh-roh-ah-lyAhzh)*
ferromanganese	le ferromanganese	*(feh-roh-mahn-gah-nEhz)*

fever	la fièvre	*(fyEh-vrœh)*
fiber optic	la fibre optique	*(fEEh-brœ ohp-tEEhk)*
fidelity bond	l'assurance protégeant un employeur contre un détournement de fonds commis par un employé	*(ah-sooh-rÃhns proh-teh-zhÃh œhn æhm-plwah-yŒhr kõhn-trœ œhn deh-toohrn-mÃh dœ fÕhn koh-mEEh pahr œhn æhm-plwah-yEh)*
fiduciary	le fiduciaire	*(feeh-dooh-syEhr)*
fiduciary issue	l'émission fiduciaire	*(eh-meeh-syÕh feeh-dooh-syEhr)*
fiduciary loan	le prêt fiduciaire	*(prEht feeh-dooh-syEhr)*
field warehousing	l'entreposage surveillé	*(ãhn-trœ-poh-sAhzh soohr-veh-yEh)*
fight (v)	lutter	*(looh-tEh)*
filament	le filament	*(feeh-lah-mÃh)*
file	le dossier, le fichier	*(doh-syEh), (fee-shyEh)*
filter	le filtre	*(fEEhl-trœ)*
finance (v)	financer	*(feeh-nãhn-sEh)*
finance company	la société de financement	*(soh-syeh-tEh dœ feeh-nãhns-mÃh)*
financial analysis	l'analyse financière	*(ãh-nah-lEEhz feeh-nãhn-syEhr)*
financial appraisal	l'évaluation financière	*(eh-vah-lwah-syÕh feeh-nãhn-syEr)*
financial backing	le soutien financier	*(sooh-tyẼhn feeh-nãhn-syEh)*
financial control	le contrôle financier	*(kõhn-trOhl feeh-nãhn-syEh)*
financial director	le directeur financier	*(deeh-rehk-tŒhr feeh-nãhn-syEh)*
financial highlight	la principale donnée financière	*(prãhn-seeh-pAhl doh-nEh feeh-nãhn-syEhr)*
financial incentive	le stimulant financier	*(steeh-mooh-lÃh feeh-nãhn-syEh)*
financial management	la gestion financière	*(zhœhs-tyÕh feeh-nãhn-syEh)*
financial period	l'exercice financier	*(ehk-sœr-sEEhs feeh-nãhn-syEh)*
financial planning	la planification budgétaire	*(plah-neeh-feeh-kah-syÕh booh-zheh-tEhr)*
financial services	les services financiers	*(sœr-vEEhs feeh-nãhn-syEh)*
financial standing	la solvabilité	*(sohl-vah-beeh-leeh-tEh)*
financial statement	l'état financier, le rapport financier	*(eh-tAh feeh-nãhn-syEh), (rah-pOhr feeh-nãhn-syEh)*
financial year	l'exercice financier	*(ehk-sœr-sEEhs feeh-nãhn-syEh)*
fine (penalty)	l'amende	*(ah-mÃhnd)*

fine line	la ridule	*(reeh-dOOhl)*
finish	la finition	*(feeh-neeh-syÕhn)*
finished goods inventory	le stock des produits finis	*(stock deh proh-dwEEh feeh-nEEh)*
finished products	les produits finis	*(proh-dwEEh feeh-nEEh)*
finishing mill	les laminoirs de finition	*(lah-meeh-nwAhr deh-feeh-neeh-syÕh)*
fire (v)	tirer	*(teeh-rEh)*
firm	la firme	*(fEEhrm)*
firm (v)	raffermir	*(rah-fœhr-mEEhr)*
first in, first out	premier entré, premier sorti	*(prœh-myEh ãhn-trEh),* *(prœh-myEh sohr-tEEh)*
first preferred stock	le titre privilégié de premier ordre	*(tEEh-trœ preeh-veeh-leh-zhyEh dœ prœh-myEh Ohr-drœ)*
fiscal agent	l'agent fiscal	*(ah-zhÃh feehs-kAhl)*
fiscal drag	la ponction fiscale	*(põhnk-syÕh feehs-kAhl)*
fiscal year	l'année fiscale	*(ah-nÉh feehs-kAhl)*
fishy-back service (container)	le service mer-route	*(sœr-vEEhs mehr-rOOht)*
fitch	le putois	*(pooh-twAh)*
fixed assets	les capitaux fixes, les immobilisations	*(kah-peeh-tOh fEEhks),* *(eeh-moh-beeh-leeh-zah-syÕh)*
fixed capital	le capital fixe	*(kah-peeh-tAhl fEEhks)*
fixed charges	les charges fixes	*(shAhrzh fEEhks)*
fixed costs	les frais fixes	*(frEh fEEhks)*
fixed expenses	les dépenses fixes	*(deh-pãhns fEEhks)*
fixed income security	la valeur à revenu fixe	*(vah-lŒhr ah rœhv-nOOh fEEhks)*
fixed investment	le placement à rendement fixe	*(plahs-mÃh ah rãhnd-mÃh fEEhks)*
fixed rate of exchange	le taux de change fixe	*(tOh dœ shÃhnzh fEEhks)*
fixed term	le délai fixe	*(deh-lEh fEEhks)*
fixture (on balance sheet)	le poste	*(pOhst)*
flannel	la flanelle	*(flah-nEhl)*
flat bond	l'obligation à rendement fixe	*(oh-bleeh-gah-syÕh ah rãhnd-mÃh fEEhks)*
flat rate	le taux uniforme	*(tOh ooh-neeh-fOhrm)*
flat yield	le rendement forfaitaire	*(rãhnd-mÃh fohr-feh-tEhr)*
flatcar	le véhicule-plateau	*(veh-eeh-kOOhl plah-tOh)*
flats products	les produits plats	*(proh-dwEEh plAh)*
flatware	les couverts	*(kooh-vEhr)*
flaw	le défaut	*(deh-fOht)*
flawless	sans défaut, sans imperfection	*(sãhn deh-fOh), (sãhns œhm-pœhr-fehk-syÕhn)*
fleet policy	la police flotte	*(poh-lEEhs flOht)*
flexible tariff	le tarif variable	*(tah-rEEhf vah-ryAh-blœ)*

F

F

flight deck	la cabine de pilotage	*(kah-bEEhn dœ peeh-loh-tAhzh)*
float (n) (outstanding checks, stock)	les chèques non encaissés	*(shEhk nõhn-ãehn-kah-sEh)*
float (v) (issue stock)	émettre	*(eh-mEh-trœ)*
floater	la police flottante	*(poh-lEEhs floh-tÃhnt)*
floating asset	le capital variable	*(kah-peeh-tAhl vah-ryAh-blœ)*
floating change rate	le taux de change flottant	*(tOh dœ shÃhnzh loh-tÃhn)*
floating charge	les frais variables	*(frEh vah-ryAh-blœ)*
floating debt	la dette flottante	*(DEht loh-tÃhnt)*
floating rate	le taux mobile	*(tOh moh-bEEhl)*
floor (of exchange)	le plancher (à la Bourse)	*(plãhn-shEh bOOhrs)*
floppy disk	la disquette	*(deehs-kEht)*
flow chart	le graphique	*(graf-fEEhk)*
flute	la flûte à champagne	*(flOOht ah sham-pÃh-nyœ)*
fly (v)	voler	*(voh-lEh)*
FOB plant	le départ usine	*(deh-pAhr ooh-zEEhn)*
follow up (v)	relancer, poursuivre	*(rœh-lãhn-sEh), (poohr-swEEhv-rœ)*
follow-up order	la commande complémentaire	*(koh-mÃhnd kõhm-pleh-mÃh-tEhr)*
font	la fonte	*(fÕhnt)*
foodstuffs	les denrées alimentaires	*(dãhn-rEh ah-leeh-mãhn-tEhr)*
footage	le métrage	*(meh-trAhzh)*
footing (accounting)	l'addition	*(ah-deeh-syÕh)*
for export	destiné à l'exportation	*(dehs-teeh-nEh ah lehks-pohr-tah-syÕh)*
forecast (n)	la prévision	*(preh-veeh-zyÕh)*
forecast (v)	prévoir	*(preh-vwAhr)*
forecast, budget	la prévision budgétaire	*(preh-veeh-zyÕh booh-zheh-tEhr)*
forecast, market	la prévision du marché	*(preh-veeh-zyÕh dooh mahr-shEh)*
forecast, sales	la prévision de vente	*(preh-veeh-zyÕh dœ vÃhnt)*
forehead	le front	*(frÕhn)*
foreign affairs	les affaires étrangères	*(ah-fEhr eh-trãhn-zhEhr)*
foreign bill of exchange	la lettre de change sur l'étranger	*(lEh-trœ dœ shÃhnzh soohr leh-trãhn-zhEh)*
foreign change	le change	*(shÃhnzh)*
foreign corporation	la société étrangère, la société à capitaux étrangers	*(soh-syeh-tEh eh-trãhn-zhEhr), (soh-syeh-tEh ah kah-peeh-tOh eh-trãhn-zhEh)*

foreign currency	la devise étrangère	*(dœh-vEEhz eh-trãhn-zhEhr)*
foreign debt	la dette extérieure	*(DEht ehks-teh-ryŒhr)*
foreign securities	les valeurs étrangères	*(vah-lŒhr eh-trãhn-zhEhr)*
foreign tax credit	le crédit pour impôt acquitté à l'étranger	*(kreh-dEEh poohr ãhm-pOh ah-keeht-tEh ah leh-trãhn-zhEh)*
foreign trade	le commerce extérieur	*(koh-mEhrs ehks-teh-ryŒhr)*
foreman	le contremaître	*(kõhn-trœ-mEh-trœ)*
forgery	la contrefaçon	*(kõhn-trœ-fah-sÕh)*
fork	la fourchette	*(foohr-shEht)*
form	l'imprimé	*(ãehm-preeh-mEh)*
form letter	l'imprimé	*(ãehm-preeh-mEh)*
format	le format	*(fohr-mAh)*
format (v)	formater	*(fohr-mah-tŒhr)*
formula	la formule	*(fohr-mOOhl)*
forward contract	le contrat à terme	*(kõhn-trAh ah tEhrm)*
forward cover	la couverture à terme	*(kooh-vehr-tOOhr ah tEhrm)*
forward forward	l'opération simultanée à terme	*(oh-peh-rah-syÕh ah tEhrm)*
forward margin	la marge à terme	*(mAhrzh ah tEhrm)*
forward market	le marché à terme	*(mahr-shEh ah tEhrm)*
forward purchase	l'achat à terme	*(ah-shAh ah tEhrm)*
forward shipment	la livraison à terme	*(leeh-vreh-zÕh ah tEhrm)*
forwarding agent	le commissionnaire de transport, le groupeur, le transitaire	*(koh-meeh-syoh-nEhr dœ trãhns-pOhr), (grooh-pŒhr), (trãhn-zeeh-tEhr)*
fossil fuel	le combustible fossile	*(kohm-boohs-tEEh-blœh foh-sEEhl)*
foul bill of lading	le connaissement avec réserves	*(koh-nEhs-mÃh ah-vEhk reh-zEhrv)*
foundry	la fonderie	*(fõhn-dœh-rEEh)*
four colors	la quadrichromie	*(kah-dreeh-kroh-mEEh)*
four-cylinder engine	le moteur à 4 cylindres	*(moh-tŒhr ah kÆh-trœ seeh-lˉÆhn-drœ)*
fox	le renard	*(rœh-nAhr)*
fragrance-free	inodore	*(æhn-oh-dOhr)*
franchise	la franchise	*(frãh-shEEhz)*
fraud	la fraude	*(frOhd)*
free alongside ship	franco long du bord (F.L.B.), franco quai	*(frÃhn-koh lÕh dooh bOhr), (frÃhn-koh kEh)*
free and clear	quitte et libre	*(kEEht eh lEEh-brœ)*
free enterprise	la libre entreprise	*(lEEh-brœ ãhn-trœh-prEEhz)*
free list (commodities without duty)	la liste d'exemptions	*(lEEhst dehk-zãhm-syÕh)*

F

free market	le marché libre	*(mahr-shEh lEEh-brœ)*
free market industry	l'industrie à prix libres	*(æhn-doohs-trEEh ah prEEh lEEh-brœ)*
free movement	la libre circulation	*(lEEh-brœh seehr-koohlah-syÕhn)*
free of particular average	franc d'avaries particulières	*(frÃnk dah-vah-rEEh pahrteeh-kooh-lyEhr)*
free on board	franco à bord	*(frAhn-koh ah bOhr)*
free on rail	franco wagon	*(frAhn-koh vah-gÕh)*
free port	le port franc	*(pOhr frÃhnk)*
free time	le temps libre	*(tÃh lEEh-brœ)*
free trade	le libre-échange	*(leeh-brœh-eh-shÃhnzh)*
free trade zone	la zone franche	*(zOhn frÃhnsh)*
freeboard	franc-bord	*(frAhnk-bOhr)*
freelance	indépendant	*(æhn-deh-pãhn-dÃhnt)*
freight	le fret	*(frEht)*
freight all kinds	le fret en tous genres	*(frEht ãhn tooh zhÃhn-rœ)*
freight allowance	allocation pour frais de transport accordée au client	*(ah-loh-kah-syÕh poohr frEh dœ trãhns-pOhr ahkohr-dEh oh kleeh-Ãhn)*
freight collect	port dû	*(pohrt dOOh)*
freight forwarder	le transitaire	*(trãhn-zeeh-tEhr)*
freight included	le fret inclus	*(frEht æhn-klOOh)*
freight prepaid	port payé d'avance	*(pohrt pah-yEh ah-vÃhns)*
French cuff	le poignet mousquetaire	*(pwah-nyEh moohs-kehtEhr)*
frequency	la fréquence	*(freh-kÃhns)*
frequency curve	la courbe de la cloche	*(kOOhrb dœ lah klOsh)*
frequency modulation (FM)	la modulation de fréquence	*(moh-dooh-lah-syÕh dœ freh-kÃhns)*
freshness	la fraîcheur	*(freh-shŒEhr)*
fringe benefits	les avantages hors salaire	*(ah-vãhn-tAhzh ohr sahlEhr)*
fringe market	le débouché marginal	*(deh-booh-shEh mahrzheeh-nAhl)*
front-end fee	la commission de montage	*(koh-meeh-syÕh dœ mõhntAhzh)*
front-end financing	le financement de départ	*(feeh-nãhns-mÃh dœ dehpAhr)*
front-end loading	le prélèvement des frais d'achat sur les premiers versements	*(preh-lehv-mÃh deh frEh dah-shAh soohr leh prœh-myEh vehrs-mÃh)*
front-wheel drive	la traction avant	*(trahk-syÕh ah-vÃh)*
frozen assets	les fonds bloqués	*(fÕhn bloh-kEh)*
frozen credit	le crédit bloqué	*(kreh-deeh bloh-kEh)*
fruity	fruité	*(frweeh-tEh)*
full settlement	pour solde de tout compte	*(poohr sOhld tooh kÕhnt)*
functional analysis	l'analyse fonctionnelle	*(ãh-nah-lEEhz fõhnk-syohnEhl)*

fulfill the obligations (v)	remplir les obligations	*(rāhm-plEEhr lehz oh-bleeh-gah-syÕhn)*
full-bodied	corsé	*(kohr-sEh)*
function key	la touche de fonction	*(tOOhsh dœ fõhnk-syÕhn)*
fund	le fonds	*(fÕhn)*
fund, contingent	le fonds de prévoyance	*(fÕhn dœ preh-vwah-yÃhns)*
fund, sinking	la caisse d'amortissement	*(kEhs dah-mohr-eehs-mÃh)*
fund, trust	le fonds mutuel	*(fÕhn mooh-twEhl)*
funded debt	la dette consolidée	*(DEht kõh-soh-leeh-dEh)*
funds, public	les fonds publics	*(fÕhn pooh-blEEhk)*
funds, working	les fonds de roulement	*(fÕhn dœ roohl-mÃh)*
fungible goods	les marchandises fongibles	*(mahr-shãhn-dEEhz fõhn-zhEEh-blœ)*
furnace	le four	*(fOOhr)*
fuselage	le fuselage	*(fooh-sœh-lAhzh)*
futures	les marchandises vendues à terme	*(mahr-shãhn-dEEhz vãhn-dOOh uh tEhrm)*
futures option	l'option à terme	*(ohp-syÕh ah tEhrm)*

G

G.N.P. (Gross National Product)	P.N.B. (Produit National Brut)	*(proh-dwEEh nah-syoh-nAhl brOOh)*
galley	l'épreuve	*(eh-prŒhv)*
galvanizing	la galvanisation	*(gahl-vah-neeh-zah-syÕh)*
garment bag	la housse de voyage	*(OOhs dœ vwah-yAhzh)*
garnishment	la saisie-arrêt	*(seh-zEEh-ah-rEht)*
gas consumption	la consommation	*(kõhn-soh-mah-syÕh)*
gas pedal	l' accélérateur	*(ahk-seh-leh-rah-tŒhr)*
gasoline	l'essence	*(eh-sÃhns)*
gasoline tank	le réservoir	*(reh-zehr-vwAhr)*
gearing	le levier	*(lœh-vyEh)*
gearshift	le changement de vitesse	*(shãhnzh-mÃh dœ veeh-tEhs)*
gel	le gel	*(zlEhl)*
general acceptance	l'acceptation sans réserves	*(ahk-sehp-tah-syÕh sÃh reh-zEhrv)*
general average loss	la perte d'avarie commune	*(pEhrt dah-vah-rEEh kohm-mOOhn)*
general manager	le directeur général	*(deeh-rehk-tŒhr zheh-neh-rAhl)*
general meeting	l'assemblée générale	*(ah-sãhm-blEh zheh-neh-rAhl)*
general partnership	la société commerciale en nom collectif	*(soh-syeh-tEh koh-mehr-syAhl ãhn nOhm koh-lehk-tEEhf)*
general strike	la grève générale	*(grEhv zheh-neh-rAhl)*

generator	le générateur	*(zheh-neh-rah-tŒhr)*
gentleman's agreement	l'accord à l'amiable	*(ah-kOhr ah lah-myAh-blœ)*
gilded	doré	*(doh-rEh)*
gilt (Brit. govt. security)	la valeur de premier ordre	*(vah-lŒhr dœ Ohr-drœ*
glass	le verre	*(vEhr)*
global warming	le réchauffement de la planète	*(reh-shohf-mÃhn dœ lah plah-nEht)*
glossy	brillant	*(breeh-yÃh)*
gloves	les gants	*(gÃhn)*
glow	l'éclat	*(eh-klAh)*
glowing	éclatant	*(eh-klah-tÃhn)*
glut	la pléthore	*(pleh-tOhr)*
go around (v)	faire appel à des capitaux flottants	*(fEhr ah-pEhl ah deh kah-peeh-tOh floh-tÃh)*
go public (v)	faire appel à des capitaux publics	*(fEhr ah-pEhl ah deh kah-peeh-tOh pooh-blEEhk)*
go-down	l'effondrement	*(eh-fõn-drœ-mÃh)*
go-go fund	les fonds hautement spéculatifs	*(fÕhnz oht-mÃhn speh-kooh-lah-tEEhf)*
going concern value	la valeur saine	*(vah-lŒhr sEhn)*
going rate (or price)	le taux (ou prix) en vigueur	*(tOh [ooh prEEh] ãhn veeh-nyŒhr)*
gold clause	la clause or	*(klOhz Ohr)*
gold price	le cours de l'or	*(kOOhr dœ lOhr)*
gold reserves	les réserves d'or	*(reh-zEhrv dOhr)*
good delivery (securities)	de bonne livraison	*(dœ bOhn leeh-vreh-zÕh)*
goods	les marchandises	*(mahr-shãhn-dEEhz)*
goods, capital	les biens d'équipement	*(byÆhn deh-keehp-mÃh)*
goods, consumer	les biens de consommation	*(byÆhn dœ kõhn-soh-mah-syÕh)*
goods, durable	les marchandises durables	*(mahr-shãhn-dEEhz dooh-rAh-blœ)*
goods, industrial	les produits industriels	*(proh-dwEEh ãhn-doohs-tryEhl)*
goodwill	la réputation, la clientèle	*(reh-pooh-tah-syÕh), (kleeh-ãhn-tEhl)*
government	le gouvernement	*(gooh-vehrn-mÃh)*
government agency	l'agence gouvernementale	*(ah-zhÃhns gooh-vehrn-mãhn-tAhl)*
government bank	la banque d'état	*(bÃhnk deh-tAh)*
government bonds	les obligations d'état	*(oh-bleeh-gah-syÕh deh-tAh)*
grace period	le délai de grâce	*(deh-lEh dœ grAhs)*
grade, commercial	la qualité commerciale	*(kah-leeh-tEh koh-mehr-syAhl)*

graft	la corruption	*(koh-roohp-syÕh)*
grain	le grain, les céréales	*(grÆhn), (seh-reh-Ahl)*
gram	le gramme	*(grAhm)*
grant (v)	accorder	*(ah-kohr-dEh)*
grant an overdraft (v)	consentir un découvert	*(kõhn-sãhn-tEEhr œhn deh-kooh-vEhrt)*
grape	le raisin	*(reh-zÆhn)*
grape bunch	la grappe	*(grAhp)*
grape harvest	les vendanges	*(vãhn-dAhzh)*
graph	le graphique	*(graf-fEEhk)*
gratuity	la gratification	*(grah-teeh-feeh-kah-syÕh)*
gravy boat	la saucière	*(soh-syEhr)*
gray market	le marché parallèle	*(mahr-shEh pah-rah-lEhl)*
greenhouse effect	l'effet de serre	*(eh-fEh dœ sEhr)*
greenhouse gas	le gaz entraînant l'effet de serre	*(gAhz æhn-treh-nÃhn leh-fEh sEhr)*
grid	la grille	*(grEEh-yœ)*
grievance procedure	la procédure d'arbitrage	*(proh-seh-dOOhr dahr-beeh-trAhzh)*
grille	la calandre	*(kah-lÃhn-drœ)*
grinding	le meulage	*(mœh-lAhzh)*
gross domestic product	le produit intérieur brut	*(proh-dwEEh æhn-teh-rèyŒhr brOOh)*
gross income	le revenu brut	*(rœhv-nOOh brOOh)*
gross investment	l'investissement brut	*(æhn-vehs-teehs-mÃh brooh)*
gross loss	la perte brute	*(pEhrt brOOht)*
gross margin	la marge brute	*(mAhrzh bOOht)*
gross national product	le produit national brut	*(proh-dwEEh nuh-syoh-nAhl brOOh)*
gross price	le prix brut	*(prEEh brOOh)*
gross profit	le bénéfice brut	*(beh-neh-fEEhs brOOh)*
gross sales	le chiffre d'affaires brut	*(shEEh-frœ dah-fEhr brOOh)*
gross spread	l'écart des cours brut	*(eh-kAhr deh kOOhr brOOh)*
gross weight	le poids brut	*(pwAh brOOh)*
gross yield	le rendement brut	*(rãhnd-mÃh brOOh)*
ground	moulu	*(mooh-lOOh)*
groundwater reserves	les nappes phréatiques	*(nAhp freh-ah-tEEhk)*
group accounts	les comptes groupés	*(kÕhnt grooh-pEh)*
group dynamics	la dynamique de groupe	*(deeh-nah-mEEhk dœ grOOhp)*
group insurance	l'assurance de groupe, l'assurance collective	*(ah-sooh-rÃhns dœ grOOhp), (ah-sooh-rÃhns koh-lehk-tEEhv)*
group training	la formation de groupe	*(fohr-mah-syÕh dœ grOOhp)*
group, product	le groupe de produits	*(grOOhp dœ proh-dwEEh)*

G

growth	la croissance	*(krwah-sÃhns)*
growth index	l'indice de croissance	*(ãhn-dEEhs dœ krwah-sÃhns)*
growth industry	l'industrie de croissance	*(ãhn-doohs-trEEh dœ krwah-sÃhns)*
growth potential	le potentiel de croissance	*(poh-tãhn-syEhl dœ krwah-sÃhns)*
growth rate	le taux de croissance	*(tOh dœ krwah-sÃhns)*
growth stock	les valeurs d'avenir	*(vah-lŒhr dah-vœh-nEEhr)*
growth, corporate	l'expansion de l'entreprise	*(ehks-pãhn-syÕh dœ lãhn-trœh-prEEhz)*
guarantee	la garantie	*(gah-rãhn-tEEh)*
guaranteed classified vintage	l'appellation contrôlée	*(ah-peh-lah-syÕh kõhn-troh-lEh)*
guaranty bond	le bon de cautionnement	*(bÕh dœ koh-syohn-mÃh)*
guaranty company	la société de cautionnement	*(soh-syeh-tEh dœ koh-syohn-mÃh)*
guesstimation	l'estimation au jugé	*(ehs-teeh-mah-syÕh oh zhooh-zhEh)*
guidance system	le système de guidage	*(seehs-tEhm dœ geeh-dAhzh)*
guidelines	les directives	*(deeh-rehk-tEEhv)*
gun fire	le feu d'artillerie	*(fœh dahr-teeh-yeh-rEEh)*

H

half-life (bonds)	la demi-vie	*(dœh-meeh-vEEh)*
hand cream	la crème pour les mains	*(krEhm poohr leh mÆhn)*
hand-blown glass	le verre soufflé	*(vEhr sooh-flEh)*
hand-glued handles	les anses collées à la main	*(Ahns koh-lEh ah lah mÆhn)*
hand-painted	peint(e) à la main	*(pãhnt ah lah mÆhn)*
handbag	le sac à main	*(sAhl ah mÆhn)*
handicap	le handicap	
handkerchief	le mouchoir	*(mooh-shwAhr)*
handler	le manutentionnaire	*(mah-nooh-tãhn-syoh-nEhr)*
harbor dues	les droits portuaires	*(drwAh pohr-twEhr)*
hard copy	le document en clair	*(doh-kooh-mÃh ãhn klEhr)*
hard currency	la devise forte	*(dœh-vEEhz fOhrt)*
hard disk	le disque dur	*(deehsk dOOhr)*
hard sell	la vente de choc	*(vÃhnt dœ shOhk)*
hardcover	cartonné	*(kahr-toh-nEh)*
hardness	le diamètre	*(deeh-ah-meh-trEEh)*
hardware	le matériel, le hardware	*(mah-teh-ryEhl), (hard-wahr)*
harmful	nuisible	*(nweeh-zEEh-blœh)*
head office	la maison-mère, le siège social	*(meh-zÕh mEhr), (syEhzh soh-syAhl)*
headache	le mal à la tête	*(mahl ah lah tEht)*

headhunter	le chasseur de têtes	*(shah-sŒhr dœ tEht)*
headline	à la une	*(ah lah OOhn)*
headload	la commission de courtier	*(koh-meeh-syÕh dœ koohr-tyEh)*
headquarters	le siège social, la maison-mère	*(syEhzh soh-syAhl), (meh-zÕh mEhr)*
heady	capiteux	*(kah-peeh-tOh)*
health hazard	le risque pour la santé	*(rEEhsk poohr lah sãhn-tEh)*
healthy	sain, en bonne santé	*(sÆhn), (ãhn bohn sãhn-tEh)*
heart attack	la crise cardiaque	*(krEEhz kahr-deeh-Ahk)*
heat	la charge	*(shAhrzh)*
heavy industry	l'industrie lourde	*(ãhn-doohs-trEEh lOOhrd)*
heavy lift charges	le chargement lourd	*(shahrzh-mÃh lOOhr)*
hectare	l'hectare	*(ehk-tAhr)*
hedge (v)	se couvrir	*(sœ kooh-vrEEhr)*
helicopter	l'hélicoptère	*(eh-leeh-kohp-tEhr)*
helmet	le casque	*(kAhsk)*
hem	l'ourlet	*(oohr-lEht)*
hexachlorophene	l'hexachlorophène	*(ehk-sah-kloh-roh-fEhn)*
hidden assets	les actifs occultés	*(ahk-tEEf oh-koohl-tEh)*
high fashion designer	le grand couturier	*(grãhn kooh-tooh-ryEh)*
high fidelity	la haute fidélité	*(Oht feeh-deh-leeh-tEh)*
high technology firm	l'entreprise de pointe	*(ãhn-trœh-prEEhz dœ pwÆht)*
highest bidder	le plus offrant	*(ploohz oh-frÃhn)*
hire (v)	embaucher	*(ãhm-boh-shEh)*
HIV	VIH	*(vay-ash-eeh)*
hoard (v)	thésauriser	*(teh-zoh-reeh-zEh)*
holder (negotiable instruments)	le détenteur	*(deh-tãhn-tŒhr)*
holder in due course	le tiers porteur	*(tyEhrs pohr-tŒhr)*
holding company	le holding	*(hol-deeng)*
holding period	la période de détention	*(peh-ryOhd dœ deh-tãhn-syÕh)*
hole in ozone layer	le trou dans la couche d'ozone	*(trooh dãhn lah kOOhsh doh-zOhn)*
holster	l'étui à revolver	*(eh-twEEh ah rœh-vohl-vEh)*
home market	le marché intérieur	*(mahr-shEh ãhn-teh-reyŒhr)*
homeopathy	l'homéopathie	*(oh-meh-oh-pah-tEEh)*
homogeneity	l'homogénéité	*(oh-moh-zheh-neh-eeh-tEh)*
hood	la capuche	*(kah-pOOhsh)*
hormone	l'hormone	*(ohr-mOhn)*
horsepower	les chevaux	*(shœ-vOh)*

hospitalization	l'hospitalisation	*(ohs-peeh-tah-leh-zah-syÕhn)*
hot money	les capitaux fébriles	*(kah-peeh-tOh feh-brEEhl)*
hot rolling	le laminé à chaud	*(lah-meeh-nEh ah shOhd)*
hourly earnings	le gain horaire	*(gĒEhn oh-rEhr)*
housing authority	le service du logement	*(sœr-vEEhs dooh lohzh-mÃh)*
human resources	les ressources humaines	*(rœh-sOOhrs ooh-mEhn)*
human rights	les droits de l'homme	*(drwAh dœ lOhm)*
hybrid computer	l'ordinateur hybride	*(ohr-deeh-nah-tŒhr eeh-brEEhd)*
hydrocarbon	l'hydrocarbure	*(eeh-droh-kahr-bOOhr)*
hydrochloric acid	l'acide chloridrique	*(ah-sEEhd kloh-rEEhk)*
hydrolysis	l'hydrolyse	*(eeh-droh-lEEhz)*
hydrosulfate	le sulfhydrate	*(soohlf-eeh-drAht)*
hyphenate (v)	césurer	*(seh-sooh-rEh)*
hypothecation	la prise d'hypothèque mobilière	*(prEEhz deeh-poh-tEhk moh-beeh-lyEhr)*

I

ice bucket	le seau à glace	*(sOh ah glAhs)*
idle capacity	le potentiel inutilisé	*(poh-tãhn-syEhl æhn-ooh-teeh-leeh-zEh)*
ignition	le contact	*(kõhn-tAhkt)*
ill	malade	*(mah-lAhd)*
illegal	illégal	*(eeh-leh-gAhl)*
illegal shipments	les expéditions illégales	*(ehks-peh-deeh-syÕh eeh-leh-gAhl)*
illustration	l'illustration	*(eeh-loohs-trah-syÕh)*
imitation	l'imitation	*(eeh-meeh-tah-syÕh)*
immune system	le système immunitaire	*(seehs-tEhm eeh-moh-neeh-tEhr)*
impact on (v)	influencer	*(æhn-flooh-ãhn-sEh)*
impact, profit	l'incidence sur le profit	*(æhn-seeh-dÃhns soohr lœ proh-fEEh)*
impending changes	les changements imminents	*(shãhnzh-mÃh eeh-meeh-nÃh)*
implement (to)	metter en œuvre	*(mEh-trœh ãhn Œh-vrœh)*
implementation	la mise en œuvre	*(mEEhz ãhn Œh-vrœh)*
implication	l'implication	*(æhm-pleeh-kah-syÕh)*
implied agreement	l'accord tacite	*(ah-kOhr tah-sEEht)*
import (n)	l'importation	*(æhm-pohr-tah-syÕh)*
import (v)	importer	*(æhm-pohr-tEh)*
import declaration	la déclaration d'importation	*(deh-klah-rah-syÕh dæhm-pohr-tah-syÕh)*
import deposits	les dépôts à l'importation	*(deh-pOh ah læhm-pohr-tah-syÕh)*

import duty	les droits d'importation, les arrhes	(drwAh dǣhm-pohr-tah-syŌh), (Ahr)
import entry	la déclaration d'importation	(deh-klah-rah-syŌh ǣhm-pohr-tah-syŌh)
import license	la licence d'importation	(leeh-sÃhns dǣhm-pohr-tah-syŌh)
import quota	les contingents à l'importation	(kõhn-teehn-zhÃhnt ah lǣhm-pohr-tah-syŌh)
import regulations	les réglementations à l'importation	(reh-glǣh-mãhn-tah-syŌh ah lǣhm-pohr-tah-syŌh)
import tariff	les droits de douane à l'importation	(drwAh dœ dooh-Ahn ah lǣhm-pohr-tah-syŌh)
importer of record	l'importateur inscrit	(ǣhm-pohr-tah-tŒhr ǣhn-skrEEh)
impound (v)	saisir, confisquer	(seh-zEEhr), (kõhn-feehs-kEh)
improve upon (v)	enchérir sur	(ãhn-sheh-rEEhr soohr)
improvements	les améliorations	(ah-meh-lyoh-rah-syŌh)
impulse buying	l'achat spontané	(ah-shAh spõhn-tah-nEh)
impurity	l'impureté	(ǣhm-pooh-reh-tEh)
imputed	imputé	(ǣhm-pooh-tEh)
in the red	dans le rouge	(dãhn lœ rOOhzh)
in transit	en transit	(ãhn trÃhn-zEEht)
inadequate	inadéquat	(ǣhn-ah-dœh-kAht)
incentive	le stimulant	(steeh-mooh-lÃh)
inch	le pouce	(pOOhs)
inchoate interest	l'intérêt incomplet	(ǣhn-teh-rEh ǣhn-kohm-plEh)
incidental expenses	les faux fais	(foh fEh)
incineration	l'incinération	(ǣhn-seeh-neh-rah-syŌhn)
income	le revenu	(rœhv-nOOh)
income account	le compte de revenu	(kÕhnt dœ rœhv-nOOh)
income bonds	les obligations à intérêt conditionnel	(oh-bleeh-gah-syŌh ah ǣhn-teh-rEh kõhn-deeh-syoh-nEhl)
income bracket	la tranche de revenus	(trÃhnsh dœ rœhv-nOOh)
income statement	le compte d'exploitation	(kÕhnt dehks-plwah-tah-syŌh)
income tax	l'impôt sur le revenu	(ǣhm-pOh soohr lœ rœhv-nOOh)
income yield	le rendement du revenu	(rãhnd-mÃh dooh rœhv-nOOh)
income, gross	le revenu brut	(rœhv-nOOh brOOh)
income, net	le revenu net	(rœhv-nOOh nEht)
incorporate (v)	incorporer, constituer (une société)	(ǣhn-kohr-poh-rEh), (kõhn-steeh-tooh-Eh [oohn soh-syeh-tEh])
increase (n)	la majoration, la hausse	(mah-zhoh-rah-syŌh), (Ohs)

I

increase (v)	augmenter	*(ohg-māhn-tEh)*
increase tension (v)	accroître la tension	*(ah-krwAh-trœh lah tāhn-syÕhn)*
increased costs	la hausse des prix	*(Ohs deh prEEh)*
incremental cash flow	l'autofinancement marginal	*(oh-toh-feeh-nāhns-mÃh mahr-zheeh-nAhl)*
incremental cost	le prix de revient marginal	*(prEEh dœ rœ-vyÃhn mahr-zheeh-nAhl)*
indebtedness	l'endettement	*(āhn-deht-mÃh)*
indemnity	l'indemnité	*(æ̃hn-dehm-neeh-tEh)*
indenture	le contrat d'apprentissage	*(kõhn-trAh dah-prãhn-teeh-sAzh)*
index (indicator)	l'indice	*(æ̃hn-dEEhs)*
index (v)	répertorier	*(reh-pehr-toh-ryEh)*
index option	l'option indice	*(ohp-syÕh æ̃hn-dEEhs)*
index, growth	l'indice de croissance	*(æ̃hn-dEEhs dœ krwah-sÃhns)*
index-linked guaranteed minimum wage	le S.M.I.C.	
indexing	l'indexation	*(æ̃hn-dehks-ah-syÕh)*
indirect claim	la réclamation indirecte	*(reh-klah-mah-syÕh æ̃hn-deeh-rEhkt)*
indirect cost	les frais indirects	*(frEh æhn-deeh-rEhkt)*
indirect expenses	les dépenses indirectes	*(deh-pÃhns æ̃hn-deeh-rEht)*
indirect labor	le travail indirect	*(trah-vAhyœ æ̃hn-deeh-rEht)*
indirect tax	l'impôt indirect	*(æ̃hm-pOh æ̃hn-deeh-rEht)*
induction	l'induction	*(æ̃hn-doohk-syÕh)*
induction furnace	le four à induction	*(fOOhr ah æ̃hn-doohk-synOh)*
industrial accident	l'accident du travail	*(ahk-seeh-dÃh dooh trah-vAhyœ)*
industrial arbitration	l'arbitrage industriel	*(ahr-beeh-trAhzh æ̃hn-doohs-tryEhl)*
industrial engineering	l'ingéniérie industrielle	*(æ̃hn-zheh-nyeh-rEEh æ̃hn-doohs-tryEhl)*
industrial goods	les biens manufacturés	*(byÆhn mah-nooh-fahk-tooh-rEh)*
industrial insurance	l'assurance du travail	*(ah-sooh-rÃhns dooh trah-vAhyœ)*
industrial planning	la planification industrielle	*(plah-neeh-feeh-kah-syÕh æ̃hn-doohs-tryEhl)*
industrial relations	les relations industrielles	*(rœh-lah-syÕh æ̃hn-doohs-tryEhl)*
industrial union	le syndicat industriel	*(seehn-deeh-kAh æ̃hn-doohs-tryEhl)*
industry	l'industrie	*(æ̃hn-doohs-trEEh)*

industrywide	dans l'ensemble de l'industrie	*(dāh lãhn-sÃhm-blœ dœ lǽhn-doohs-trEEh)*
inefficient	inefficace	*(eehn-eh-feeh-kAhs)*
inelastic demand or supply	l'inélasticité de l'offre et de l'emploi	*(ǽhn-eh-lahs-teeh-seeh-tEh dœ lOh-frœ eh dœ lãhm-plwAh)*
infant industry	l'industrie naissante	*(ǽhn-doohs-trEEh neh-sÃhnt)*
inflation	l'inflation	*(ǽhn-flah-syÕh)*
inflationary	inflationniste	*(ǽhn-flah-syoh-nEEhst)*
infrastructure	l'infrastructure	*(eehn-frah-stroohk-tOOhr)*
ingot	le lingot	*(lǽhn-gOh)*
ingot mold	la lingotière	*(lǽhn-goh-tyEhr)*
inheritance tax	le droit de succession	*(drwAh dœ sooh-seh-syÕh)*
injection	la piqûre	*(peeh-kOOhr)*
injector	l'injecteur	*(ǽhn-zhehk-tŒhr)*
injunction	l'injonction	*(ǽhn-zhõhnk-syÕh)*
ink	l'encre	*(Ãhn-krœ)*
inland bill of lading	le connaissement intérieur, la lettre de voiture	*(koh-nEhs-mÃh ǽhn-teh-ryŒhr), (lEh-trœ dœ vwah-tOOhr)*
innovation	l'innovation	*(ǽh-noh-vah-syÕh)*
inorganic chemistry	la chimie minerale	*(sheeh-mEEh meeh-neh-rAhl)*
input	l'entrée	*(ãhn-trEh)*
input-output analysis	l'analyse des entrées et sorties	*(ãh-nah-lEEhz dehz ãhn-trEh eh sohr-tEEh)*
insert	l'insertion	*(ǽhn-sehr-synOh)*
insert (v)	insérer	*(ǽhn-seh-rEh)*
insolvent	insolvable	*(ǽhn-sohl-vAh-blœ)*
inspection	l'inspection	*(ǽhns-pehk-syÕh)*
inspector	l'inspecteur	*(ǽhns-pehk-tŒhr)*
instability	l'instabilité	*(ǽhns-stah-beeh-leeh-tEh)*
install (v)	installer	*(ǽhns-tah-lEh)*
installment	le versement	*(vehrs-mÃhn)*
installment credit	la vente à tempérament	*(vÃhnt ah tehm-peh-rah-mÃh)*
installment plan	le calendrier des échéances	*(kah-lãhn-dryEh dehz eh-sheh-Ãhns)*
institutional advertising	la publicité de prestige	*(pooh-bleeh-seeh-tEh dœ prehs-tEEhzh)*
institutional investor	l'investisseur institutionnel	*(ǽhn-vehs-teeh-sŒhr ǽhn-steeh-tooh-syÕh-nEhl)*
instruct (v)	donner des instructions	*(doh-nEh dehz ǽhn-stroohk-syÕh)*
instrument	l'instrument	*(ǽhn-strooh-mÃhn)*
instrument panel	le tableau de bord	*(tah-blOh dœ bOhr)*
instrumental capital	le capital productif	*(kah-peeh-tAhl proh-doohk-tEEhf)*

I

insulator	l'insulateur	*(æhn-sooh-lah-tŒhr)*
insulin	l'insuline	*(æhn-sooh-lÆhn)*
insurance	l'assurance	*(ah-sooh-rÃhns)*
insurance broker	le courtier d'assurance	*(koohr-tyEh dah-sooh-rÃhns)*
insurance company	la compagnie d'assurance	*(kõhm-pah-nyEEh dah-sooh-rÃhns)*
insurance fund	le fonds d'assurance	*(fÕhn dah-sooh-rÃhns)*
insurance policy	la police d'assurance	*(poh-lEEhs dah-sooh-rÃhns)*
insurance premium	la prime d'assurance	*(prEEhm dah-sooh-rÃhns)*
insurance underwriter	le souscripteur (d'assurance)	*(sooh-skreehp-tŒhr dah-sooh-rÃhns)*
insured	l'assuré	*(ah-sooh-rEh)*
intangible assets	les valeurs incorporelles	*(vah-lŒhr æhn-kohr-poh-rEhl)*
integrated circuit	le circuit intégré	*(seehr-kwEEht æhn-teh-grEh)*
integrated management system	le système de direction intégré	*(seehs-tEhm dœ deeh-rehk-syÕh æhn-teh-grEh)*
interact (v)	réagir réciproquement	*(reh-ah-zhEEhr reh-seeh-prohk-mÃh)*
interbank	de banque à banque	*(dœ bÃhnk ah bÃhnk)*
interest	l'intérêt	*(æhn-teh-rEh))*
interest arbitrage	l'arbitrage des taux d'intérêt	*(ahr-beeh-trAhzh deh tOh dæhn-teh-rEh)*
interest expenses	les dépenses d'intérêt	*(deh-pãhns dæhn-teh-rEh)*
interest income	la rente	*(rãhnt)*
interest parity	la parité des taux d'intérêt	*(pah-reeh-tEh deh tOh dæhn-teh-rEh)*
interest period	la période d'intérêt	*(peh-ryOhd dæhn-teh-rEh)*
interest rate	le taux d'intérêt	*(tOh dæhn-teh-rEh)*
interest, compound	l'intérêt composé	*(æhn-teh-rEh kohm-poh-zEh)*
interest-free loan	le crédit gratuit	*(kreh-dEEh grah-twEEh)*
interface (v)	communiquer	*(koh-mooh-neeh-kEh)*
interim	l'intérim	*(æhn-teh-rEEhm)*
interim budget	le budget provisoire	*(booh-zhEh proh-veeh-zwAhr)*
interim statement	le relevé provisoire	*(rœh-lœh-vEh proh-veeh-zwAhr)*
interlocking directorate	les directions imbriquées	*(deeh-rehk-syÕh æhm-breeh-kEh)*
intermediary	l'intermédiaire	*(æhn-tehr-ɹeh-dyEhr)*
intermediary goods	les biens intermédiaires	*(byÆhnz æɪn-tehr-meh-dyEhr)*
internal	interne	*(æhn-tEhrn)*
internal audit	le contrôle interne	*(kõhn-trOhl æhn-tEhrn)*

I

internal funding	la consolidation interne	*(kōh-soh-leeh-dah-synOh ǣhn-tEhrn)*
internal rate of return	le taux interne de rentabilité	*(tOh ǣhn-tEhrn dœ rãhn-tah-beeh-leeh-tEh)*
internal revenue tax	la recette fiscale	*(rœh-sEht feehs-kAhl)*
International Date Line	la ligne internationale de changement de date	*(lEEh-nyœ ǣhn-tehr-nah-syoh-nAhl dœ shãhnzh-mÃh dœ dAht)*
interstate commerce	le commerce entre les états des États-Unis	*(koh-mEhrs ãhn-trœ lehz eh-tahz-ooh-nEEh)*
intervene (v)	intervenir	*(ǣhn-tehr-vœh-nEEhr)*
interview	l'entrevue	*(ãhn-trœ-vOOh)*
intravenous feeding	l'alimentation intraveineuse	*(ah-leeh-mãhn-tah-syÕhn œhn-trah-veh-nŒhz)*
intestate	intestat	*(ǣhn-tehs-tAh)*
intrinsic value	la valeur intrinsèque	*(vah-lŒhr)*
invalidate (v)	invalider	*(ǣhn-vah-leeh-dEh)*
inventory	l'inventaire, les stocks	*(ǣhn-vãhn-tEhr)*
inventory control	la gestion des stocks	*(zhœhs-tyÕh deh stocks)*
inventory turnover	la rotation des stocks	*(roh-tah-syÕh deh stocks)*
inventory, perpetual	l'inventaire tournant	*(ǣhn-vãhn-tEhr toohr-nÃh)*
inventory, physical	l'inventaire physique	*(ǣhn-vãhn-tEhr feeh-zEEhk)*
inverted market	le marché inversé	*(mahr-shEh ǣhn-vœhr-sEh)*
invest (v)	investir	*(ǣhn-vœhs-tEEhr)*
invested capital	le capital investi	*(kah-peeh-tAhl ǣhn-vœhs-tEEhr)*
investigator	l'enquêteur	*(ãhn-keh-tŒhr)*
investment	l'investissement	*(ǣhn-vehs-teehs-mÃh)*
investment adviser	le conseiller en investissement	*(kōh-seh-yEh ãhn ǣhn-vehs-teehs-mÃh)*
investment analysis	l'analyse des investissements	*(ãh-nah-lEEhz dehz ǣhn-vehs-teehs-mÃh)*
investment appraisal	l'évaluation des investissements	*(eh-vah-lwah-syÕh dehz ǣhn-vehs-teehs-mÃh)*
investment bank	la banque de placement	*(bÃhnk dœ plahs-mÃhn)*
investment budget	le budget d'investissement	*(booh-zhEh dǣhn-vehs-teehs-mÃh)*
investment company	la société d'investissement	*(soh-syeh-tEh dǣhn-vehs-teehs-mÃh)*
investment credit	le crédit d'investissement	*(kreh-dEEh dǣhn-vehs-teehs-mÃh)*
investment criteria	les critères d'investissement	*(kreeh-tEhr dǣhn-vehs-teehs-mÃh)*
investment grade	le niveau d'investissement	*(neeh-vŒ dǣhn-vehs-teehs-mÃh)*

I

investment letter	la déclaration d'investissement	*(deh-klah-rah-syÕh dǽhn-vehs-teehs-mÃh)*
investment policy	la politique d'investissement	*(poh-leeh-tEEhk dǽhn-vehs-teehs-mÃh)*
investment program	le programme d'investissement	*(proh-grAhm dǽhn-vehs-teehs-mÃh)*
investment strategy	la stratégie de l'investissement	*(strah-teh-zhEEh dœ lǽhn-vehs-teehs-mÃh)*
investment trust	la coopérative de placement	*(koh-oh-peh-rah-tEEhv dœ plahs-mÃh)*
investment, return on	le rendement d'un investissement	*(rãhnd-mÃh doohn ǽhn-vehs-teehs-mÃh)*
investors relations	les relations avec les investisseurs	*(ræh-lah-syÕh ah-vehk leh ǽhn-vehs-teeh-sŒhr)*
invigorate (v)	revitaliser	*(ræh-veeh-tah-leeh-zEh)*
invisibles	les importations, les exportations invisibles	*(ǽhm-pohr-tah-syÕh), (ehks-pohr-tah-syÕh ǽhn-veeh-zEEh-blœ)*
invitation to bid	l'appel d'offre	*(ah-pEhl dOh-frœ)*
invoice	la facture	*(fahk-tOOhr)*
invoice cost	le coût de facturation	*(kOOht DŒ fahk-tooh-rah-syÕh)*
invoice pro forma	la facture pro forma	*(fahk-tOOhr proh-fOhr-mah)*
invoice, commercial	la facture commerciale	*(fahk-tOOhr koh-mehr-syAhl)*
iodine	l'iode	*(yOhd)*
iron	le fer, le fer à repasser	*(fEhr), (fEhr ah ræh-pah-sEh)*
iron ore	le minerai de fer	*(meeh-neh-rEh dœ fEhr)*
irritant agent	l'agent irritant	*(ah-zhÃhn eeh-reeh-tÃhn)*
irritation	l'irritation	*(eeh-reeh-tah-syÕhn)*
isotope	l'isotope	*(eeh-zoh-tOhp)*
issue (n) (stock)	l'émission	*(eh-meeh-syÕh)*
issue (v)	émettre	*(eh-mEh-trœ)*
issue price	le prix d'émission	*(prEEh deh-meeh-syÕh)*
issued shares	les actions émises	*(ahk-syÕh eh-mEEhz)*
italic	l'italique	*(eeh-tah-lEEhk)*
item	l'article	*(ahr-tEEhk-lœ)*
itemize (v)	détailler	*(deh-tah-yEh)*
itemized account	le compte spécifié	*(kÕhnt speh-seeh-fyEh)*
itching	la démangeaison	*(deh-mãhn-zheh-sÕhn)*

J

jacket	la jaquette	*(zhah-kEht)*
Jason clause	clause Jason	*(klOhz Jason)*
jawbone (v)	intervenir personnellement	*(ǽhn-tehr-væh-nEEhr pehr-soh-nehl-mÃh)*

jet lag	la fatigue due au décalage horaire	*(fah-tEEhg dOOh oh deh-kah-lAzh oh-rEhr)*
jewel	le bijou	*(beeh-zhOOh)*
jig (production)	le calibre	*(kah-lEEh-brœ)*
job	l'emploi	*(āhm-plwAh)*
job analysis	l'analyse d'un emploi	*(āh-nah-lEEhz dœhn āhm-plwAh)*
job description	la définition d'un poste	*(deh-feeh-neeh-syŌh dœhn pOhst)*
job evaluation	l'évaluation d'un emploi	*(eh-vah-lwah-syŌh dœhn āhm-plwAh)*
job hopper	le travailleur à grande mobilité	*(trah-vah-yŒhr ah grāhnd moh-beeh-leeh-tEh)*
job lot	les soldes	*(sOhld)*
job performance	la compétence	*(kōhm-peh-tĀhns)*
job security	la sécurité de l'emploi	*(seh-kooh-reeh-tEh dāhm-plwAh)*
job shop	le fournisscur à la commande	*(ſuuhr-neeh-zŒhr ah lah koh-mĀhnd)*
jobber	l'intermédiaire, le marchand de titres	*(æhn-tehr-meh-dyEhr), (mahr-shĀhnd dœ tEEh-trœ)*
jobber's turn	le bénéfice du marchand de titres	*(beh-neh-fEEhs dooh mahr-shĀhnd dœ tEEh-trœ)*
joint account	le compte commun, le compte collectif	*(kŌhnt koh-mOOhn), (kŌhnt koh-lehk-tEEhf)*
joint cost	les frais communs	*(frEh koh-mOOhn)*
joint estate	la coproprićtć	*(koh-proh-pryeh-tEh)*
joint liablity	l'obligation conjointe	*(oh-bleeh-gah-syŌh kōhn-zhwÆhnt)*
joint owner	le copropriétaire	*(koh-proh-pryeh-tEhr)*
joint stock company	la société anonyme par actions	*(soh-syeh-tEh ah-noh-nEEhm pahr ahk-syŌh)*
joint venture	l'entreprise commune, l'association	*(āhn-trœh-prEEhz koh-mOOhn), (ah-soh-syah-syŌh)*
journal	le journal	*(zhOOhr-nAhl)*
journeyman	l'homme de peine	*(Ohm dœ pEhn)*
joystick	le levier de commande	*(lœh-vyEh dœ koh-mĀhnd)*
junior partner	l'associé en second	*(ah-soh-syEh āhn sœh-kŌhnd)*
junior security	le titre de second ordre	*(tEEh-trœ dœ sœh-kŌhnd Ohr-drœ)*
jurisdiction	la juridiction	*(zhooh-reeh-deehk-syŌh)*
justify (v)	justifier	*(zhoohs-teeh-fyEh)*

K

keep posted (v)	tenir au courant	*(tœ-nEEhr oh kooh-rĀhn)*

kettle	la bouilloire	*(booh-lwAhr)*
key	la touche	*(tOOhsh)*
key case	le porte-clés	*(pOhrt klEh)*
key exports	l'exportation-clé	*(ehks-pohr-tah-syÕh klEh)*
key-man insurance	l'assurance de l'homme-clé	*(ah-sooh-rÃhns dœ lOhm klEh)*
keyboard	le clavier	*(klah-vyEh)*
Keynesian economics	la théorie keynésienne	*(teh-oh-rEEh keh-neh-zyEhn)*
keypunch	la perforatrice à clavier	*(pehr-foh-rah-trEEhs ah klah-vyEh)*
kickback	le pot-de-vin	*(poh-dœ-vÃ̃Ehn)*
kidskin	le chevreau	*(shœh-vrOh)*
kilowatt	le kilowatt	
kiting (banking)	le tirage à découvert	*(teeh-rAzh ah deh-kooh-vEhrt)*
knife	le couteau	*(kooh-tOh)*
knife handle	le manche de couteau	*(mÃhnsh dooh kooh-tOh)*
knife rest	le porte-couteau	*(pOhrt-kooh-tOh)*
knot (nautical)	le nœud	*(nŒh)*
know-how	le savoir-faire	*(sah-vwAhr fEhr)*

L

label	l'étiquette	*(eh-teeh-kEht)*
labor	le travail, la main-d'œuvre	*(trah-vAhyœ), (mÃ̃Ehn dŒh-vrœ)*
labor code	le Code du travail	*(kOhd dooh trah-vAhyœ)*
labor dispute	le conflit ouvrier	*(kõhn-flEEh ooh-vryEh)*
labor force	la population active	*(poh-pooh-lah-syÕh ahk-tEEhv)*
labor law	le législation du travail	*(leh-zheehs-lah-syÕh dooh trah-vAhyœ)*
labor leader	le chef syndicaliste	*(shEhf seehn-deeh-kah-lEEhst)*
labor market	le marché de l'emploi	*(mahr-shEh dœ lãhm-plwAh)*
labor relations	les relations professionnelles	*(rœh-lah-syÕh proh-feh-syoh-nEhl)*
labor turnover	les fluctuations de personnel	*(floohk-twah-syÕh dœ pehr-soh-nEhl)*
labor union	le syndicat ouvrier	*(seehn-deeh-kÃh ooh-vryEh)*
labor-intensive	le consommateur de main-d'œuvre	*(kõhn-soh-mah-tŒhr dœ mÃ̃Ehn dŒh-vrœ)*
labor-saving	l'économie de main-d'œuvre	*(eh-koh-noh-mEEh dœ mÃ̃Ehn dŒh-vrœ)*
laboratory	le laboratoire	*(lah-boh-rah-twAhr)*
laboratory technician	le laborantin(e)	*(lah-boh-rahn-tEEhn)*

laborer	le travailleur	*(trah-vah-yŒhr)*
lace	la dentelle	*(dāhn-tEhl)*
lagging indicator	le clignotant économique	*(kleeh-nyoh-tÃhnt eh-koh-moh-mEEhk)*
laissez-faire	laisser faire	*(leh-seh-fEhr)*
lambskin	l'agneau	*(ah-nyOh)*
land	la terre	*(tEhr)*
land grant	la concession (de terrain)	*(kõhn-seh-syÕh dœ tœ-rÆhn)*
land reform	la réforme agraire	*(reh-fOhrm ah-grEhr)*
land tax	l'impôt foncier	*(æhm-pOh fõhn-syEhr)*
landed cost	les frais fonciers	*(frEh fõhn-syEhr)*
landfill site	la décharge	*(deh-shAhrzh)*
landing	l'atterrissage	*(ah-teh-reeh-sAhzh)*
landing certificate	le certificat de débarquement	*(sehr-teeh-feeh-kAh dœ deh-bahrk-mÃh)*
landing charges	les frais de débarquement	*(frEh dœ deh-bahrk-mÃh)*
landing costs	les dépenses de débarquement	*(deh-pāhns dœ deh-bahrk-mÃh)*
landowner	le propriétaire foncier	*(proh-pryeh-tEhr fõhn-syEhr)*
laptop	le portatif	*(pohr-tah-tEEhf)*
large-scale	à grande échelle	*(grāhnd eh-shEhl)*
laser	le laser	*(lah-zEh)*
laser guidance	guidage par laser	*(geeh-dAhzh pahr lah-zEhr)*
laser printer	l'imprimante à laser	*(æhn-preeh-mÃhnt ah lah-zEh)*
lash	le navire porte-allège	*(nah-vEEhr pohrt-ah-lEhzh)*
last in, first out	dernier entré, premier sorti	*(dehr-nyEh āhn-trEh), (præh-myEh sohr-tEEh)*
lather (v)	étaler en faisant mousser	*(eh-tah-lEh āhn feh-zÃhn mooh-sEh)*
launch (v)	lancer	*(lāhn-sEh)*
law	la loi, la jurisprudence	*(lwAh), (zhooh-reehs-prooh-dÃhns)*
law of diminishing returns	la loi des rendements décroissants	*(lwAh deh rāhnd-mÃh deh-krwah-sÃhn)*
lawsuit	le procès	*(proh-sEh)*
lawyer	l'avocat	*(ah-voh-kAh)*
lay time	le délai de planche	*(deh-lEh dœ plÃhnsh)*
lay up (v)	désarmer (un navire)	*(deh-zahr-mEh [œhn nah-vEEhr])*
laydays	les jours de planche, les surestaries	*(zhOOhr dœ plÃhnsh), (sooh-rehs-tah-rEEh)*
layer	la couche	*(kOOhsh)*
layoff	le licenciement	*(leeh-sāhn-seeh-mÃh)*
layout	le modèle, les débours	*(moh-dEhl), (deh-bOOhr)*

lead content	la teneur en plomb	*(teh-nŒhr ãhn plÕhm)*
lead time	le délai d'approvisionnement	*(deh-lEh dah-proh-veeh-zyohn-mÃh)*
leader	le meneur	*(mœh-nŒhr)*
leader bank	la banque chef de file	*(bÃhnk shEhf dœ feEhl)*
leadfree	sans plomb	*(sãhn plÕhm)*
leading firm	l'entreprise de pointe	*(ãhn-trœh-prEEhz dœ pwÆht)*
leading indicator	l'indicateur de marché	*(æhn-deeh-kah-tŒhr dœ mahr-shEh)*
leads and lags	le termaillage	*(tehr-mah-yAhzh)*
leakage	la fuite	*(fwEEht)*
learning curve	la courbe d'accoutumance	*(kOOhrb dah-kooh-tooh-mãhns)*
lease (n)	le bail	*(bAh-yœ)*
lease (v)	louer	*(looh-Eh)*
leased department	le rayon d'un grand magasin affermé en concession	*(rah-yÕh dœhn grãhn mah-gah-zÆhn ah-fehr-mEh ãhn kõhn-seh-syÕh)*
leather	le cuir	*(kwEEhr)*
leather goods	la maroquinerie	*(mah-roh-keeh-neh-rEEh)*
leather jacket	le blouson de cuir	*(blooh-zÕh dœ kwEEhr)*
leather strap	la lanière	*(lah-nyEhr)*
leave of absence	le congé	*(kõhn-zhEh)*
ledger	le grand livre	*(grãhn lEEh-vrœ)*
ledger account	le compte du grand livre	*(kÕhnt dooh grãhn lEEh-vrœ)*
ledger entry	l'entrée du grand livre	*(ãhn-trEh dooh grãhn lEEh-vrœ)*
legacy	le legs	*(lEhg)*
legal capital	le capital légal	*(kah-peeh-tAhl leh-gAhl)*
legal entity	la personne morale	*(pehr-sÕhn moh-rAhl)*
legal holiday	la fête légale	*(fEht leh-gAhl)*
legal list (fiduciary investments)	la liste légale	*(lEEhst leh-gAhl)*
legal monopoly	le monopole légale	*(moh-noh-pOhl leh-gAhl)*
legal tender	la monnaie légale	*(moh-nEh leh-gAhl)*
lend (v)	prêter	*(preh-teh)*
lending margin	la marge de prêt	*(mAhrzh dœ prEht)*
length	la longueur	*(lõhn-gŒhr)*
lesion	la lésion	*(leh-zyÕhn)*
less-than-carload	le chargement incomplet	*(shahrzh-mÃh æhn-kohm-plEh)*
less-than-truckload	le chargement incomplet	*(shahrzh-mÃh æhn-kohm-plEh)*
lessee	le locataire à bail	*(loh-kah-tEhr ah bAh-yœ)*
lessor	le bailleur	*(bah-yŒhr)*

letter	la lettre, le caractère	*(lEh-trœ), (kah-rahk-tEhr)*
letter of credit	la lettre de crédit	*(lEh-trœ dœ kreh-dEEh)*
letter of guaranty	la lettre de garantie	*(lEh-trœ dœ gah-rãhn-tEEh)*
letter of indemnity	le cautionnement	*(koh-syohn-mÃh)*
letter of introduction	la lettre d'introduction	*(lEh-trœ dæhn-troh-doohk-syÕh)*
letterpress	la typographie	*(teeh-poh-grah-fEEh)*
leukemia	la leucémie	*(leh-ooh-seh-mEEh)*
level out (v)	égaliser	*(eh-gah-leeh-zEh)*
lever	le levier	*(lœh-vyEh)*
leverage	l'effet de levier	*(eh-fEht dœ lœh-vyEh)*
leveraged lease	le financement spéculatif	*(feeh-nãhns-mÃh speh-kooh-lah-tEEhf)*
levy taxes (v)	lever des taxes	*(lœh-vyEh dœ tAhks)*
liability	la responsabilité, le passif	*(rœs-pohn-sah-beeh-leeh-tEh), (pah-sEEhf)*
liability insurance	l'assurance en responsabilité civile	*(ah-sooh-rÃhns ãhn rœs-pohn-sah-beeh-leeh-tEh seeh-vEEhl)*
liability, actual	la dette réelle	*(DEht reh-Ehl)*
liability, assumed	le passif pris en charge	*(pah-sEEhf preehz ãhn shAhrzh)*
liability, contingent	le passif éventuel	*(pah-sEEhf eh-vãhn-twEhl)*
liability, current	la dette à court terme	*(DEht ah koohr tEhrm)*
liability, fixed	la dette fixe	*(DEht fEEhks)*
liability, secured	la dette garantie	*(DEht gah-rãhn-tEEh)*
liability, unsecured	la dette sans garantie	*(DEht sãh gah-rãhn-tEEh)*
liable for tax	assujetti à l'impôt	*(ah-sooh-zheh-tEEh ah lãhm-pOh)*
liable to	passible de	*(pah-sEEh-blœ dœ)*
libel	la diffamation	*(deeh-fah-mah-syÕh)*
license	le permis	*(pehr-mEEh)*
license fee	la redevance	*(rœh-dœh-vÃhns)*
licensed warehouse	l'entrepôt autorisé	*(ãhn-trœ-pOh oh-toh-reeh-zEh)*
lid	le couvercle	*(kooh-vEhr-klœh)*
lien	le privilège	*(preeh-veeh-lEhzh)*
life cycle (of product)	la durée de vie	*(dooh-rEh dœ vEEh)*
life insurance policy	la police d'assurance-vie	*(poh-lEEhs dah-sooh-rÃhns vEEh)*
life member	le membre à vie	*(mÃhm-brœ ah vEEh)*
life of a patent	la durée d'un brevet, d'une patente	*(dooh-rEh dæhn brœh-vEh), (doohn pah-tÃhnt)*
light	léger	*(leh-zhEh)*
limestone	la pierre à chaux	*(pyEhr ah shOh)*

L

limited liability	la responsabilité limitée	(ræhs-pohn-sah-beeh-leeh-tEh leeh-meeh-tEh)
limited order (stock market)	l'ordre avec limites	(Ohr-dræ ah-vEhk leeh-mEEht)
limited partnership	la société en commandite	(soh-syeh-tEh ãhn koh-mãhn-dEEht)
line	la ligne	(lEEh-nyæ)
line drawing	l'esquisse	(ehs-kEEhs)
line executive	le chef de secteur	(shEhf dæ sehk-tŒhr)
line of business	la spécialité (d'une affaire)	(speh-syah-leeh-tEh doohn ah-fEhr)
line, assembly	la chaîne de montage	(shEhn dæ mõhn-tAhzh)
line, product	la gamme de produits	(gAhm dæ proh-dwEEh)
lineal estimation	l'estimation linéaire	(ehs-teeh-mah-syÕh leeh-neh-Ehr)
linear	linéaire	(leeh-neh-Ehr)
linear programming	la programmation linéaire	(proh-grah-mah-syÕh leeh-neh-Ehr)
linear terms	les termes linéaires	(tEhrm leeh-neh-Ehr)
linen	la toile de lin	(twAhl dæ lEEhn)
lining	la doublure	(dooh-blOOhr)
lipstick	le rouge à lèvres	(rOOhzh ah lEh-vræh)
liquid assets	les disponibilités	(deehs-poh-neeh-beeh-leeh-tEh)
liquidate (v)	liquider	(leeh-keeh-dEh)
liquidation	la liquidation	(leeh-keeh-dah-syÕh)
liquidation value	la valeur de liquidation	(vah-lŒhr dæ leeh-keeh-dah-syÕh)
liquidity	la liquidité, les espèces	(leeh-keeh-deeh-tEh), (ehs-pEhs)
liquidity preference	la préférence pour la liquidité	(preh-feh-rÃhns poohr la leeh-keeh-deeh-tEh)
liquidity ratio	le coefficient de liquidité	(koh-eh-feeh-sÃhnt dæ leeh-keeh-deeh-tEh)
list price	le prix courant	(prEEh kooh-rÃhn)
listed securities	les valeurs inscrites	(vah-lŒhr æ̃hn-skrEEht)
listing	l'établissement d'une liste, la cotation, la liste	(eh-tah-bleehs-mÃh doohn lEEhst), (koh-tah-syÕh), (lEEhst)
liter	le litre	(lEEh-træ)
litigation	le litige	(leeh-tEEhzh)
live program	l'émission en direct	(eh-meeh-syÕhn ãhn deeh-rEhkt)
living trust	la société de gestion active	(soh-syeh-tEh dæ zhæhs-tyÕh ahk-tEEhv)
lizard (skin)	la peau de lézard	(pOh dæ leh-zAhr)
load (sales charge)	la commission	(koh-meeh-syÕh)
load factor	le coefficient de charge	(koh-eh-feeh-sÃhnt dæ shAhrzh)
load, work	la charge de travail	(shAhrzh dæ trah-vAhyæ)

L

loan	le prêt, l'emprunt	*(prEht), (æ̃hm-pr̃(Ẽhn)*
loan stock (govt.	les valeurs d'emprunt	*(vah-lŒhr dæ̃hm-*
bonds)		*pr̃(Ẽhn)*
lobbying	l'action d'un groupe de	*(ahk-syÕh dœhn grOOhp*
	pression	*dœ preh-syÕh)*
local customs	les usages locaux	*(ooh-zAhz loh-kOh)*
local taxes	les impôts locaux	*(æ̃hm-pOh loh-kOh)*
local wine	le vin du cru, du terroir	*(vÃEhn dooh krOOh),*
		(dooh teh-rwAhr)
lock in (rate of	le blocage	*(bloh-kAhzh)*
interest)		
lockout	la grève	*(grEhv)*
logistics	la logistique	*(loh-zheehs-tEEhk)*
logo	le logo	*(loh-gOh)*
long hedge	le contrat à long terme	*(kõhn-trAh ah lÕh tEhrm)*
long product	le produit long	*(proh-dwEEh lÕh)*
long sleeves	les manches longues	*(mÃhnsh lÕhng)*
long ton	la tonne métrique	*(tUhn meh-trEEhk)*
long-range	à longue portée	*(ah lÕhng pohr-tEh)*
long-range	la planification à long terme	*(plah-neeh-feeh-kah-syÕh*
planning		*ah lÕh tEhrm)*
long-term capital	le compte de capital à long	*(kÕhnt dœ kah-peeh-tAhl*
account	terme	*ah lÕh tEhrm)*
long-term debt	la dette à long terme	*(DEht ah ah lÕh tEhrm)*
long-term	le traitement de longue	*(treht-mÃhn dœ lÕhng*
treatment	durée	*dooh-rEh)*
loss	la perte	*(pEhrt)*
loss leader	l'article-appât	*(ahr-tEEhk-lœ ah-pAh)*
loss, gross	la perte brute	*(pEhrt brOOht)*
loss, net	la perte nette	*(pEhrt nEht)*
loss-loss ratio	le ratio sinistres-primes	*(rAh-syoh seeh-nEEhst-rœ*
		prEEhm)
lot	le lot	*(lOht)*
lotion	la lotion	*(loh-syÕhn)*
low-income	à faible rendement	*(ah fEh-blœ rãhnd-mÃh)*
low-interest loans	les prêts à faible intérêt	*(prEht ah fEh-blœ æ̃hn-*
		teh-rEh)
low-yield bond	l'obligation à faible	*(oh-bleeh-gah-syÕh ah*
	rendement	*fEh-blœ rãhnd-mÃh)*
lower case	la minuscule	*(meeh-neehs-kOOhl)*
lubrication	le graissage	*(greh-sAhzh)*
lump sum	le montant forfaitaire	*(mõhn-tÃh fohr-feh-tEhr)*
lung cancer	le cancer du poumon	*(kãhn-sEhr dooh pooh-*
		mÕhn)
luscious	savoureux, succulent	*(sah-vooh-rŒh)*
luster	la patine	*(pah-tEEhn)*
luxury goods	les marchandises de luxe	*(mahr-shãhn-dEEhz dœ*
		lOOhks)
luxury tax	la taxe de luxe	*(tAhks dœ lOOhks)*
lynx	le lynx	*(lÆ̃hnks)*

M

Maastricht Treaty	le Traité de Maastricht	*(treh-tEh dœh mehs-trEEht)*
machine gun	la mitrailleuse	*(meeh-trah-yŒhz)*
machinery	le mécanisme, les machines	*(meh-kah-nEEhz-mœ), (mah-shEEhn)*
machining	l'usinage	*(ooh-zeeh-nAhzh)*
macroeconomics	la macroéconomie	*(mah-kroh-eh-koh-noh-mEEh)*
magazine	le magazine	*(mah-gah-zEEhn)*
magnetic memory	la mémoire magnétique	*(meh-mwAhr mah-nyeh-tEEhk)*
magnetic tape	la bande magnétique	*(bÃhnd mah-nyeh-tEEhk)*
magnum (2 bottles in one)	le magnum	*(mahg-nOOhm)*
mail order	la vente par correspondance	*(vÃhnt pahr koh-rehs-põhn-dÃhns)*
mailing list	la liste d'adresses	*(lEEhst dah-drEhs)*
main memory	la mémoire principale	*(meh-myAhr prãhn-seeh-pAhl)*
mainframe computer	unité centrale de traitement	*(ooh-neeh-tEh sãhn-trAhl dœ treht-mÃh)*
maintenance	l'entretien	*(ãhn-trœh-tyEhn)*
maintenance contract	le contrat de maintenance	*(kõhn-trAh dœ mãhn-tœh-nÃhns)*
maintenance margin	la marge d'entretien	*(mAhrzh dãhn-trœh-tyÆhn)*
maize	le maïs	*(mah-EEh)*
majority interest	la participation majoritaire	*(pahr-teeh-seeh-pah-syÕh mah-zhoh-reeh-tEhr)*
majority voting	le vote majoritaire	*(vOht mah-zhoh-reeh-tEhr)*
make available (v)	mettre à disposition	*(mEh-trœ ah deehs-poh-zeeh-syÕh)*
make oneself up	maquiller (se)	*(mah-keeh-leh)*
make-or-buy decision	la décision d'achat ou de fabrication	*(lah deh-seeh-zyÕh dah-shAh ooh dœ fah-breeh-kah-syÕh)*
make-ready	la mise en forme	*(mEEhz ãhn fOhrm)*
maker (of check, draft, etc.)	le tireur	*(teeh-rŒhr)*
makeshift	le moyen de fortune	*(mwah-yEhn dœ fohr-tOOhn)*
makeup	le maquillage	*(mah-keeh-lAhzh)*
makeup case	la trousse à maquillage	*(trOOhs ah mah-keeh-yAhzh)*
malleability	la malléabilité	*(mah-leh-ah-beeh-leeh-tEh)*

malolactic fermentation	la fermentation malolactique	*(fehr-māhn-tah-syŌh mah-loh-lahk-tEEhk)*
man (gal) Friday	le, la factotum	*(fahk-tOh-toohm)*
man-hours	les heures de main-d'œuvre	*(Œhr dœ mǼhn dŒhvrœ)*
manage (v)	gérer	*(zheh-rEh)*
managed costs	les frais contrôlés	*(frEh kõhn-troh-lEh)·*
managed economy	l'économie dirigée	*(eh-koh-noh-mEEh deeh-reeh-zhEh)*
managed float	le flottement dirigé	*(floht-mÃh deeh-reeh-zhEh)*
management	la gestion	*(zhœhs-tyŌh)*
management accounting	la comptabilité de gestion	*(kõhn-tah-beeh-leeh-tEh dœ zhœhs-tyŌh)*
management by objectives	la direction par objectifs	*(deeh-rehk-syŌh pahr ohb-zhehk-tEEhf)*
management chart	le tableau de bord	*(tah-blOh dœ bOhr)*
management consultant	l'expert en gestion, le conseiller en gestion	*(ehks-pEhr ãhn zhœhs-tyŌh), (kõh-seh-yEh ãhn zhœhs-tyŌh)*
management fee	la commission de gestion	*(koh-meeh-syŌh dœ zhœhs-tyŌh)*
management group	le groupe de gestion	*(grOOhp dœ zhœhs-tyŌh)*
management team	l'équipe de gestion	*(eh-kEEhp dœ zhœhs-tyŌh)*
management, business	la gestion d'entreprise	*(zhœhs-tyŌh dãhn-trœh-prEEhz)*
management, credit	la gestion de crédits	*(zhœhs-tyŌh dœ kreh-dEEh)*
management, financial	la gestion financière	*(zhœhs-tyŌh feeh-nãhn-syEh)*
management, line	la gestion de lignes	*(zhœhs-tyŌh dœ lEEh-nyœ)*
management, market	la gestion commerciale	*(zhœhs-tyŌh koh-mehr-syAhl)*
management, middle	les cadres moyens	*(kAh-drœ mwah-yEhn)*
management, office	la direction administrative	*(deeh-rehk-syŌh ad-meeh-neehs-trah-tEEhv)*
management, personnel	la direction du personnel	*(deeh-rehk-syŌh dooh pehr-soh-nEhl)*
management, product	la gestion de produit	*(zhœhs-tyŌh dœ proh-dwEEh)*
management, sales	la direction des ventes	*(deeh-rehk-syŌh deh vÃhnt)*
management, systems	la gestion des systèmes	*(zhœhs-tyŌh deh seehs-tEhm)*
management, top	les cadres supérieurs	*(kAh-drœ sooh-peh-ryŒhr)*
manager	le directeur	*(deeh-rehk-tŒhr)*
mandate	le mandat	*(māhn-dAh)*

mandatory redemption	le remboursement obligatoire	*(rãhm-boohrs-mÃh oh-bleeh-gah-twAhr)*
manganese ore	le minerai de manganèse	*(meeh-neh-rEh dœ mãhn-gah-nEhz)*
manicuring kit	la trousse à manucure	*(trOOhs ah mah-nooh-kOOhr)*
manifest	le manifeste	*(mah-neeh-fEhst)*
manmade fibers	les fibres synthétiques	*(fEEh-brœ seehn-teh-tEEhk)*
manpower	la main-d'œuvre	*(mÆhn dŒh-vrœ)*
manual workers	les travailleurs manuels	*(trah-vah-yŒhr mah-nwEhl)*
manufacturer	le fabricant, l'industriel	*(fah-breeh-kÃh), (æhn-doohs-tryEhl)*
manufacturer's agent	l'agent	*(ah-zhÃh)*
manufacturer's representative	le représentant	*(rœh-preh-zãhn-tÃh)*
manufacturing capacity	la capacité de fabrication	*(kah-pah-seeh-tEh dœ fah-breeh-kah-syÕh)*
manufacturing control	le contrôle de fabrication	*(kõhn-trOhl dœ fah-breeh-kah-syÕh)*
margin call	l'appel de marge	*(ah-pEhl dœ mAhrzh)*
margin of safety	la marge de sécurité	*(mAhrzh dœ seh-kooh-reeh-tEh)*
margin requirements	les marges requises	*(mAhrzh reh-kEEhz)*
margin, gross	la marge brute	*(mAhrzh brOOht)*
margin, net	la marge nette	*(mAhrzh nEht)*
margin, profit	la marge bénéficiaire	*(mAhrzh beh-neh-feeh-syEhr)*
marginal account	le compte marginal	*(kÕhnt mahr-zheeh-nAhl)*
marginal cost	le coût marginal	*(kOOht mahr-zheeh-nAhl)*
marginal pricing	la fixation du prix marginal	*(feehk-sah-syÕh dooh prEEh mahr-zheeh-nAhl)*
marginal productivity	la productivité marginale	*(proh-doohk-teeh-veeh-tEh mahr-zheeh-nAhl)*
marginal revenue	le rendement marginal	*(rãhnd-mÃh mahr-zheeh-nAhl)*
marine cargo insurance	l'assurance maritime	*(ah-sooh-rÃhns mah-reeh-tEEhm)*
marine underwriter	l'assureur maritime	*(ah-sooh-rŒhr mah-reeh-tEEhm)*
markdown	le démarquage	*(deh-mahr-kAhzh)*
market	le marché	*(mahr-shEh)*
market (v)	commercialiser	*(koh-mehr-syahl-eeh-zEh)*
market access	le débouché	*(deh-booh-shEh)*
market appraisal	l'évaluation du marché	*(eh-vah-lwah-syÕh dooh mahr-shEh)*
market concentration	la concentration du marché	*(kõhn-sãhn-trah-syÕh dooh mahr-shEh)*

market dynamics	la dynamique du marché	*(deeh-nah-mEEhk dooh mahr-shEh)*
market forces	les tendances du marché	*(tãhn-dÃhns dooh mahr-shEh)*
market forecast	la prévision de marché	*(preh-veeh-zyÕh dœ mahr-shEh)*
market index	l'indice du marché	*(æhn-dEEhs dooh mahr-shEh)*
market management	la gestion commerciale	*(zhœhs-tyÕh koh-mehr-syAhl)*
market penetration	la pénétration du marché	*(peh-neh-trah-syÕh dooh mahr-shEh)*
market position	la position sur le marché	*(poh-zeeh-syÕh soohr lœ mahr-shEh)*
market potential	le potentiel du marché	*(poh-tãhn-syEhl dooh mahr-shEh)*
market price	le prix du marché	*(prEEh doof mahr-shEh)*
market rating	la classification des marchés	*(klah-seeh-feeh-kah-syÕh deh mahr-shEh)*
market report	l'analyse de marché	*(ãh-nah-lEEhz dœ mahr-shEh)*
market research	l'étude de marché	*(eh-tOOhd dœ mahr-shEh)*
market saturation	la saturation du marché	*(sah-tooh-rah-syÕh dooh mahr-shEh)*
market share	la part du marché	*(pAhr dooh mahr-shEh)*
market survey	l'étude des débouchés	*(eh-tOOhd deh deh-booh-shEh)*
market trends	les tendances du marché	*(tãhn-dÃhns dooh mahr-shEh)*
market value	la valeur marchande	*(vah-lŒhr mahr-shÃnd)*
market, buyer's	le marché acheteur	*(mahr-shEh ahsh-tŒhr)*
market, fringe	le marché marginal	*(mahr-shEh mahr-zheeh-nÃhl)*
market-maker (securities)	les valeurs de référence	*(vah-lŒhr dœ reh-feh-rÃhns)*
marketable securities	les titres réalisables	*(tEEh-trœ reh-ah-leeh-zÃh-blœ)*
marketing	la commercialisation	*(koh-mehr-syah-leeh-zah-syÕh)*
marketing budget	le budget commercial	*(booh-zhEh koh-mehr-syAhl)*
marketing concept	la démarche commerciale	*(deh-mÃhrsh koh-mehr-syAhl)*
marketing plan	le plan commercial, le programme de commercialisation, le projet commercial	*(plÃh koh-mehr-syAhl), (proh-grÃhm dœ koh-mehr-syah-leeh-zah-syÕh), (proh-zhEh koh-mehr-syAhl)*
marketplace	le marché, le monde des affaires	*(mahr-shEh), (mÕhnd dehz ah-fEhr)*

markup	le taux de marge	*(tOh dœ mAhrzh)*
marmot	la marmotte	*(mahr-mOht)*
mascara	le mascara	*(mahs-kah-rah)*
mask	le masque	*(mAhsk)*
mass communications	les communications de masse	*(koh-mooh-neeh-kah-syÕh dœ mAhs)*
mass marketing	la distribution de masse	*(deehs-treeh-booh-syÕh dœ mAhs)*
mass media	le média, la presse en général	*(meh-dyAh), (prEhs ãhn zheh-neh-rAhl)*
mass production	la fabrication en série	*(fah-breeh-kah-syÕh ãhn seh-rEEh)*
mat	mat	
matched samples	les échantillons provenant d'un même univers	*(eh-shãhn-teeh-yÕh prohvœh-nÃh dœhn mEhm ooh-neeh-vEhrs)*
materials	les matériaux	*(mah-teh-ryOh)*
maternity leave	le congé de maternité	*(kõhn-zhEh dœ mah-tehr-meeh-tEh)*
mathematical model	la représentation mathématique	*(rœh-preh-zãhn-tah-syÕh mah-teh-mah-tEEhk)*
matrix	la matrice	*(mah-trEEhs)*
matrix management	la méthode des matrices	*(meh-tOhd deh mah-trEEhs)*
maturity	l'échéance	*(eh-sheh-Ãhns)*
maturity date	la date de remboursement	*(dAht dœ rãhm-boohrs-mÃh)*
maximize (v)	amplifier	*(ãhm-pleeh-fyEh)*
mean (average)	la moyenne	*(mwah-yEhn)*
measure (v)	mesurer	*(mœh-zooh-rEh)*
mechanic	le mécanicien	*(meh-kah-neeh-syÆhn)*
mechanic's lien	le privilège du constructeur, le droit de nantissement	*(preeh-veeh-lEhzh dooh kõhn-stroohk-tŒhr), (drwAh dœ nãhn-teehs-mÃh)*
mechanical engineer	l'ingénieur mécanicien	*(ãhn-zheh-nyŒhr meh-kah-neeh-syÆhn)*
mechanical engineering	l'industrie mécanique	*(ãhn-doohs-trEEh meh-kah-nEEhk)*
mechanical	la maquette	*(mah-kEht)*
media coverage	le reportage des médias, la couverture	*(rœh-pohr-tAhzh deh meh-dyAh), (kooh-vehr-tOOhr)*
median	la médiane	*(meh-dyAhn)*
mediation	la médiation	*(meh-dyah-syÕh)*
medication	le médicament	*(meh-deeh-kah-mÃh)*
medicine	le médicament	*(meh-deeh-kah-mÃh)*
medium of exchange	le moyen d'échange	*(mwah-yEhn eh-shÃhnzh)*
medium term	le moyen terme	*(mwah-yEhn tEhrm)*

meet the price (v)	être compétitif	*(Eh-træ kohm-peh-teeh-tEEhf)*
meeting	la réunion, l'assemblée, le colloque	*(reh-ooh-nyÕh), (ah-sãhm-blEh), (koh-lOhk)*
meeting, board	la réunion du conseil d'administration	*(reh-ooh-nyÕh dooh kõhn-sEh-yæ dad-meeh-neehs-trah-syÕh)*
member firm	la filiale	*(feeh-lyAhl)*
member of firm	la, le sociétaire	*(soh-syeh-tEhr)*
member state	l'État membre	*(eh-tAh mãhm-bræh)*
memorandum	le mémorandum	*(meh-moh-rãhndOOhm)*
MEP	le député européen	*(deh-pooh-tEh eh-ooh-roh-peh-Ehn)*
mercantile	mercantile	*(mehr-kãhn-tEEhl)*
mercantile agency	l'agence de renseignements commerciaux	*(ah-zhÃhns dæ rãhn-seh-nyæh-mÃh koh-mehr-syOh)*
mercantile law	le droit commercial	*(drwAh koh-mehr-syAhl)*
merchandise	la marchandise, le produit	*(mahr-shãhn-dEEhz), (proh-dwEEh)*
merchandising	le négoce	*(neh-gOhs)*
merchant	le marchand	*(mahr-shÃhn)*
merchant bank	la banque d'affaires	*(bÃhnk dah-fEhr)*
merchant guild	la corporation marchande	*(kohr-poh-rah-syÕh mahr-shÃnd)*
merger	la fusion	*(fooh-zyÕhn)*
metals	les métaux	*(meh-tOh)*
methane	le méthane	*(meh-tAhn)*
method	la méthode	*(meh-tOhd)*
metrication	l'adoption du système métrique	*(ah-dohp-syÕh dooh seehs-tEhm meh-trEEhk)*
microchip	la microplaquette	*(meeh-kroh-plah-kEht)*
microcomputer	le micro-ordinateur	*(meeh-kroh-ohr-deeh-nah-tŒhr)*
microfiche	la microfiche	*(meeh-kroh-fEEhs)*
microfilm	le microfilm	*(meeh-kroh-fEEhlm)*
microprocessor	le micro-processeur	*(meeh-kroh-proh-seh-sŒhr)*
microwave	le micro-onde	*(meeh-kroh-Ohnd)*
microwave safe	garanti four à micro-ondes	*(gah-rãhn-tEEh foohr ah meeh-kroh-Õhnd)*
middle management	les cadres moyens	*(kAh-dræ mwah-yEhn)*
middleman	l'intermédiaire	*(æhn-tehr-meh-dyEhr)*
mileage	le kilométrage	*(keeh-loh-meh-trAhzh)*
military	l'armée	*(ahr-mEh)*
minicomputer	le mini-ordinateur	*(meeh-neeh-ohr-deeh-nah-tŒhr)*
minimum reserves	la réserve de sécurité	*(reh-zEhrv dæ seh-kooh-reeh-tEh)*

minimum wage	le salaire minimum	*(sah-lEhr meeh-neeh-mOOhm)*
mink	le vison	*(veeh-zÕh)*
minority interest	la participation minoritaire	*(pahr-teeh-seeh-pah-syÕh meeh-noh-reeh-tEhr)*
mint	la monnaie	*(moh-nEh)*
miscalculation	l'erreur de calcul	*(eh-rŒhr dœ kahl-kOOhl)*
miscellaneous	divers	*(deeh-vEhr)*
misleading	trompeur, mensonger	*(trõhm-pŒhr), (mãhn-sõhn-zhEh)*
misunderstanding	le malentendu, le désaccord	*(mah-lãhn-tãhn-dOOh), (deh-zah-kOhr)*
mixed cost	les frais mixtes	*(frEh mEEhks-tœ)*
mixed sampling	l'échantillonnage divers	*(leh-shãhn-teeh-yoh-nAzh deeh-vEhr)*
mixer	le mélangeur	*(meh-lãhn-zhŒhr)*
mobility of labor	la mobilité de l'emploi	*(moh-beeh-leeh-tEh dœ lãhm-plwAh)*
mock-up	la maquette	*(mah-kEht)*
mode	le mode	*(mOhd)*
model	le mannequin, le modèle	*(mah-nœh-kÆhn), (moh-dEhl)*
modem	le modem	*(moh-dEhm)*
modular production	la production modulaire	*(proh-doohk-syÕh moh-dooh-lEhr)*
moire	la moire	*(mwAhr)*
moisten (v)	humecter	*(ooh-mehk-tEh)*
moisturize (v)	hydrater	*(eeh-drah-tEh)*
moisturizing	hydratant	*(eeh-drah-tÃhn)*
molar	molaire	*(moh-lEhr)*
mold	le moule	*(mOOhl)*
moldy taste	le goût de moisi	*(gOOh dœ mwah-zEEh)*
mole	la mole	*(mOhl)*
molecule	la molécule	*(moh-leh-kOOhl)*
molybdenum	le molybdène	*(moh-leehb-dEhn)*
monetary base	la base monétaire	*(bAhz moh-neh-tEhr)*
monetary credits	les crédits monétaires	*(kreh-dEEh moh-neh-tEhr)*
monetary policy	la politique monétaire	*(poh-leeh-tEEhk moh-neh-tEhr)*
money	l'argent	*(ahr-zhÃh)*
money manager	le gérant de fonds à court terme	*(zheh-rÃhn dœ fÕhn ah koohr tEhrm)*
money market	le marché monétaire	*(mohr-shEh mah-neh-tEhr)*
money order	le mandat-poste	*(mãhn-dAh pOhst)*
money shop	le centre financier	*(sÃhn-trœ feeh-nãhn-syEh)*
money supply	la masse monétaire	*(mAhs moh-neh-tEhr)*
monitor	l'appareil de contrôle	*(ah-pah-rEh-yœ dœ kõhn-trOhl)*

monitor (v)	surveiller, observer	*(soohr-veh-yEh), (ohbsehr-vEh)*
monogram	le monogramme	*(moh-roh-grAhm)*
monopoly	le monopole	*(moh-noh-pOhl)*
monopsony	le marché monopsone	*(mahr-shEh moh-nohpsOhn)*
Monte Carlo technique	la méthode de Monte Carlo	*(meh-tOhd dœ Monte Carlo)*
moonlighting	le travail au noir, le cumul d'emplois	*(trah-vAhyœ oh nwAhr), (kooh-mOOhl dãhmplwAh)*
morale	le moral	*(moh-rAhl)*
moratorium	le moratoire	*(moh-rah-twAhr)*
morphine	la morphine	*(mohr-fEEhn)*
Morroco leather	le maroquin	*(mah-roh-kEEhn)*
mortgage	l'hypothèque	*(eeh-poh-tEhk)*
mortgage bank	la banque hypothécaire	*(bÃhnk eeh-poh-teh-kEhr)*
mortgage bond	l'obligation hypothécaire	*(oh-bleeh-gah-syÕh eehpoh-teh-kEhr)*
mortgage certificate	le certificat hypothécaire	*(sehr-teeh-feeh-kAh eehpoh-teh-kEhr)*
mortgage debenture	l'obligation hypothécaire	*(oh-bleeh-gah-syÕh eehpoh-teh-kEhr)*
mortgage loan	le prêt hypothécaire	*(prEht eeh-poh-teh-kEhr)*
most favored nation clause	la clause de la nation la plus favorsée	*(klOhz dœ lah nah-syÕh lah plooh fah-voh-reehzEh)*
motion	la motion	*(moh-syÕh)*
motivation study	l'étude de motivations	*(eh-tOOhd dœ moh-teehvah-synOh)*
motor	le moteur	*(moh-tŒhr)*
mouse	la souris	*(sooh-rEEh)*
mousse	la mousse	*(mOOhs)*
movement of goods	la rotation des stocks	*(roh-tah-syÕh deh stocks)*
moving average	la moyenne mobile	*(mwah-yEhn moh-bEEhl)*
moving expenses	les dépenses variables, les frais de déménagement	*(deh-pãhns vah-ryAh-blœ), (frEh dœ deh-meh-nahz-mÃh)*
moving parity	la parité mobile	*(pah-reeh-tEh moh-bEEhl)*
MRI	la résonance magnétique nucléaire (RMN)	*(reh-soh-nÃhns mah-nyeh-tEEhk nooh-kleh-Ehr)*
multicurrency	multidevises	*(moohl-teeh-dœh-vEEhz)*
multilateral agreement	l'accord multilatéral	*(ah-kOhr moohl-teeh-lah-teh-rAhl)*
multilateral trade	le commerce multilatéral	*(koh-mEhrs moohl-teeh-lah-teh-rAhl)*
multinational corporation	la société multinationale	*(soh-syeh-tEh moohl-teeh-nah-syoh-nAhl)*

multiple exchange rate	le taux de change multiple	*(tOh dœ shÃhnzh moohl-tEEh-plœ)*
multiple taxation	l'imposition multiple	*(æhm-poh-zeeh-syÕh moohl-tEEh-plœ)*
multiples	les multiples	*(moohl-tEEh-plœ)*
multiplier	le multiplicateur	*(moohl-teeh-pleeh-kah-tŒhr)*
multiprogramming	la programmation multiple	*(proh-grah-mah-syÕh moohl-tEEh-plœ)*
municipal bond	l'obligation municipale	*(oh-bleeh-gah-syÕh mooh-neeh-seeh-pAhl)*
muscle relaxant	le relaxant musculaire	*(reh-lahk-sÃhn moohs-kooh-lEhr)*
muslin	la mousseline	*(moohs-lEEhn)*
mustard pot	le moutardier	*(mooh-tahr-dyEh)*
mutual fund	la société d'investissement à capital variable (SICAV)	*(soh-syeh-tEh dæn-vehs-teehs-mÃh ah kah-peeh-tAhl vah-ryAh-blœ)*
mutual savings bank	la mutuelle d'épargne	*(mooh-twEhl deh-pAhr-nyœ)*
mutually exclusive classes	les catégories d'exclusion réciproque	*(kah-teh-goh-rEEh dehks-klooh-zyÕh reh-seeh-prOhk)*

N

NAFTA	l'ALÉNA	*(ah-leh-nAh)*
named inland point in country of importation	le point de débarquement convenu	*(pwÆh dœ deh-bahrk-mÃh kõhn-vœh-nOOh)*
named point of destination	le lieu de destination convenu	*(lyŒh dœ dehs-teeh-nah-syÕh kõhn-vœh-nOOh)*
named point of exportation	le lieu d'exportation convenu	*(lyŒh dehks-pohr-tah-syÕh kõhn-vœh-nOOh)*
named point of origin	le lieu d'origine désigné	*(lyŒh doh-reeh-zhEEhn deh-zeeh-nyEh)*
named port of importation	le port d'importation convenu	*(pOhr dæhm-pohr-tah-syÕh kõhn-vœh-nOOh)*
named port of shipment	le port d'expédition convenu	*(pOhr dehks-peh-deeh-syÕh kõhn-vœh-nOOh)*
napkin	la serviette	*(sœhr-vyEht)*
napkin ring	le rond de serviette	*(rõhnd dœ sœhr-vyEht)*
narcotic	le narcotique	*(nahr-koh-tEEhk)*
national bank	la banque nationale	*(bÃhnk nah-syoh-nAhl)*
national debt	la dette publique	*(DEht pooh-blEEhk)*
nationalism	le nationalisme	*(nah-syoh-nah-lEEhz-mœ)*
nationalization	la nationalisation	*(nah-syoh-nah-leeh-zah-syÕh)*

native produce	les produits du pays	*(proh-dwEEh dooh pah-EEh)*
NATO	l'OTAN	*(oh-tAhn)*
natural gas	le gaz naturel	*(gAhz nah-tooh-rEhl)*
natural resources	les ressources naturelles	*(rœh-sOOhrs nah-tooh-rEhl)*
near money	la quasi-monnaie	*(kAh-zeeh moh-nEh)*
neck (of bottle)	le goulot	*(gooh-lOh)*
needle	l'aiguille	*(eh-gEEh-yœ)*
needs analysis	l'évaluation des besoins	*(eh-vah-lwah-syŌh deh bœh-zwÆhn)*
negative	le négatif	*(neh-gah-tEEhf)*
negative cash flow	la marge brute négative	*(mAhrzh brOOht neh-gah-tEEhv)*
negative pledge	l'engagement négatif	*(āhn-gahzh-mÃh neh-gah-tEEhf)*
negligent	négligent, fautif	*(neh-gleeh-zhÃn), (foh-tEEhf)*
negotiable	commercialisable, négociable	*(koh-mehr-syah-leeh-zAh-blœ), (neh-goh-syAh-blœ)*
negotiable securities	les titres négociables	*(tEEh-trœ neh-goh-syAh-blœ)*
negotiate (v)	négocier	*(neh-goh-syEh)*
negotiated sale	la vente négociée	*(vÃhnt neh-goh-syEh)*
negotiation	la négociation	*(neh-goh-syah-syŌh)*
negotiator	le négociateur	*(neh-goh-syah-tŒhr)*
nerve gas	le gaz asphyxiant	*(gAhz ahs-feehks-yÃhn)*
net asset value	la valeur nominale nette	*(vah-lŒhr noh-meeh-nAhl nEht)*
net asset worth	la valeur réelle nette	*(vah-lŒhr reh-Ehl nEht)*
net assets	les actifs nets	*(ahk-tEEhf nEht)*
net borrowed reserves	les emprunts nets	*(æhm-prŒhn nEht)*
net cash flow	la marge brute nette	*(mAhrzh brooht nEht)*
net change	l'écart net du cours	*(eh-kAhr nEht dooh kOOhr)*
net equity assets	la valeur nette des placements en actions	*(vah-lŒhr nEht deh plahs-mÃh āhn ahk-syŌh)*
net income	le revenu net	*(rœhv-nOOh nEht)*
net investment	l'investissement net	*(æhn-vehs-teehs-mÃh nEht)*
net loss	la perte nette	*(pEhrt nEht)*
net margin	la marge nette	*(mAhrzh nEht)*
net position (of a trade)	la position nette	*(poh-zeeh-syŌh nEht)*
net present value	la valeur actuelle nette	*(vah-lŒhr ahk-twEhl nEht)*
net profit	le bénéfice net	*(beh-neh-fEEhs nEht)*
net sales	le chiffre d'affaires net	*(shEEh-frœ dah-fEhr nEht)*

net working capital	les fonds de roulement nets	(fÕhn dœ roohl-mÃh nEht)
net worth	la valeur nette	(vah-lŒhr nEht)
network	le réseau	(reh-zOh)
network (v)	étendre à l'ensemble du réseau	(eh-tÃhn-drœ ah lãhn-sÃhm-blœ dooh reh-zOh)
neutral	neutre	(nŒh-trœ)
neutralization	la neutralisation	(nœh-trah-leeh-zah-syÕh)
neutron	le neutron	(nœh-trÕh)
new issue	la nouvelle émission	(nooh-vEhl eh-meeh-syÕh)
new money	les capitaux frais	(kah-peeh-tOh frEh)
new product development	le lancement de nouveaux produits	(lãhns-mÃh dœ nooh-vOh proh-dwEEh)
newsprint	le papier journal	(pah-pyEh zhoohr-nAhl)
night cream	la crème de nuit	(krEhm dœ nwEEh)
night depository	le coffre de nuit	(kOh-frœ dœ nwEEh)
nitrate	le nitrate	(neeh-trAht)
nitric acid	l'acide nitrique	(ah-sEEhd neeh-trEEhk)
nitrite	le nitrite	(neeh-trEEht)
nitrogen	l'azote	(ah-zOht)
no fly zone	la zone d'exclusion aérienne	(zohn dehks-klooh-zyÕhn ah-eh-ryEhn)
no par value	sans valeur nominale	(sÃh vah-lŒhr noh-meeh-nAhl)
no problem	sans problème	(sÃh proh-blEhm)
no-load fund	le titre sans frais de commission	(tEEh-trœ sãh frEh dœ koh-meeh-syÕh)
noise pollution	la pollution par le bruit	(poh-looh-syÕhn pahr lœ brwEEh)
nominal price	le prix nominal	(prEEh noh-meeh-nAhl)
nominal yield	le rendement nominal	(rãhnd-mÃh noh-meeh-nAhl)
noncumulative preferred stock	le titre de priorité non cumulatif	(tEEh-trœ dœ preeh-oh-reeh-tEh nõh kooh-mooh-lah-tEEhf)
noncurrent assets	les valeurs non exigibles	(vah-lŒhr nõhn ehk-seeh-zhEEh-blœ)
nondurable goods	les biens périssables	(byÆhn peh-reeh-sAh-blœ)
nonfeasance	délit d'abstention	(deh-lEEh dahb-stãhn-syÕh)
nonmember	non membre	(nõh mÃhm-brœ)
nonpolluting energy	l'énergie non polluante	(eh-nehr-zhEEh nohn poh-looh-Ãhnt)
nonprofit	à but non lucratif	(ah bOOh nõh looh-krah-tEEhf)
nonresident	non-résident	(nõhn-reh-zeeh-dÃh)
nontoxic	non toxique	(nõhn tohk-sEEhk)
nonvoting stock	les titres sans droit de vote	(tEEh-trœ sãh drwAh dœ vOht)

norm	la norme	(nOhrm)
normal skin	la peau normale	(pOh nohr-mAhl)
not otherwise indicated by name	non mentionné par ailleurs	(nõh mãhn-syoh-nEh pahr ah-yŒhr)
notary	le notaire	(noh-tEhr)
note, credit	l'avoir	(ah-vwAhr)
note, debit	le bordereau de débit	(bohr-dœ-rOh dœ deh-bEEh)
note, promissory	le billet à ordre	(beeh-yEh ah Ohr-drœ)
note, receivable	l'effet à recevoir	(eh-fEht ah rœ-seh-vwAhr)
novation	la novation	(noh-vah-syÕh)
noxiousness	la nocivité	(noh-seeh-veeh-tEh)
nuclear build-up	l'escalade des armes nucléaires	(ehs-kah-lAhd dehz Ahrm nooh-kleh-Ehr)
nuclear war	la guerre nucléaire	(gEhr nooh-kleh-Ehr)
nuclear waste	les déchets nucléaires	(deh-shEh rooh-kleh-Ehr)
null and void	nul et non avenu	(nOOhl eh nõhn ah-vœh-nOOh)
nullify (v)	annuler	(ah-nooh-lEh)
numerical control	le contrôle numérique	(kõhn-trOhl nooh-meh-rEEhk)
nutria	le ragondin	(rah-gõhn dÃEhn)

O

oak barrel	le fût de chêne	(fOOh dœ shEhn)
obligation	l'obligation	(oh-bleeh-gah-syÕh)
obsolescence	le vieillissement, la désuétude	(vyeh-yeehs-mÃh), (deh-sweh-tOOhd)
occupation	le métier	(meh-tyEh)
occupational accident	l'accident du travail	(ahk-seeh-dÃh dooh trah-vAhyœ)
occupational hazard	le risque du métier	(rEEhs-kœ dooh meh-tyEh)
odd lot	le lot irrégulier	(lOht eeh-reh-gooh-lyEh)
odd lot broker	l'agent en lots irréguliers	(ah-zhÃh ãhn lOht eeh-reh-gooh-lyEh)
odometer	le compte-tours	(kÕnt-tOOhr)
off board	(stock market) hors-bourse	(ohr-bOOhrs)
off-line	autonome	(oh-toh-nOhm)
off-the-books	non-comptabilisé	(nõhn-kõhm-tah-beeh-leeh-zEh)
offer (v)	offrir	(oh-frEEhr)
offer for sale	la proposition de vente	(proh-poh-zeeh-syÕh dœ vÃhnt)
offered price	le prix offert	(prEEh oh-fEhr)
offered rate	le taux consenti	(tOh kõhn-sãhn-tEEh)
office	le bureau	(booh-rOh)

office management	la direction administrative	*(deeh-rehk-syŌh ad-meeh-neehs-trah-tEEhv)*
office, branch	la succursale	*(sooh-koohr-sAhl)*
office, head	le siège social	*(syEhzh soh-syAhl)*
official channels	la voie hiérarchique	*(vwAh yeh-rahr-kEEhk)*
off-peak rate	le tarif de faible écoute	*(tah-rEEhf dœ ƒEh-blœ eh-kOOht)*
offset printing	l'impression offset	*(æhm-prœh-syŌh offset)*
offshore company	la compagnie de forage en mer	*(kõhm-pah-nyEEh dœ foh-rAhzh ãhn mEhr)*
ohm	l'ohm	
oil filter	le filtre à huile	*(ƒEEhl-trœ ah wEEhl)*
oil pump	la pompe à huile	*(pOhmp ah wEEhl)*
oilcloth	la toile cirée	*(twAhl seeh-rEh)*
oily	gras	*(grAh)*
oily skin	la peau grasse	*(pOh grAhs)*
ointment	l'onguent	*(õhn-gÃh)*
oligopoly	l'oligopole	*(oh-leeh-goh-pOhl)*
oligopsony	l'oligopsonie	*(oh-leeh-gohp-soh-nEEh)*
omit (v)	omettre, supprimer	*(œh-mEhtrœ), (sooh-preeh-mEh)*
on account	en compte	*(ãhn kÕhnt)*
on board	à bord	*(ah bOhr)*
on consignment	en dépôt, en consignation	*(ãhn deh-pOh), (ãhn kõhn-seeh-nyah-syŌh)*
on demand	sur demande, à vue	*(soohr dæh-mÃhnd), (ah vOOh)*
on location	en extérieur	*(ãhn ehks-teh-ryŒhr)*
on the agenda	à l'ordre du jour	*(ah lOhr-drœh dooh zhOOhr)*
on the back	au verso	*(oh vehr-sOh)*
on-line	en ligne	*(ãhn lEEhn-yœh)*
on-the-job training	la formation dans l'entreprise, sur le tas	*(fohr-mah-syŌh dãhn lãhn-trœh-prEEhz), (soohr lœ tAh)*
open account	le compte ouvert	*(kÕhnt ooh-vEhr)*
open cover	FACOB (traité facultatif obligatoire)	*(treh-tEh fah-koohl-tah-tEEhf oh-bleeh-gah-twAhr)*
open door policy	la politique de la porte ouverte	*(poh-leeh-tEEhk dœ lah pOhrt ooh-vEhrt)*
open market	le marché libre	*(mahr-shEh lEEh-brœ)*
open market operations	les opérations sur le marché libre	*(oh-peh-rah-syŌh soohr lœ mahr-shEh lEEh-brœ)*
open order	l'ordre révocable	*(Ohr-drœ reh-voh-kAh-blœ)*
open shop	l'entreprise non syndicalisée	*(ãhn-trœh-prEEhz nõh seehn-deeh-kah-leeh-zEh)*
opening balance	le bilan d'entrée, le solde à l'entrée	*(beeh-lÃh dãhn-trEh), (sOhld ah lãhn-trEh)*

opening price	le cours d'ouverture	*(kOOhr dooh-vehr-tOOhr)*
operating budget	le budget d'exploitation	*(booh-zhEh dehks-plwah-tah-syÕh)*
operating expenses	les frais d'exploitation	*(frEh dehks-plwah-tah-syÕh)*
operating income	le revenu d'exploitation	*(ræhv-nOOh dehks-plwah-tah-syÕh)*
operating profit	le bénéfice net avant impôts	*(beh-neh-fEEhs nEht ah-vÃhnt ëhm-pOh)*
operating statement	le relevé d'exploitation	*(ræh-læh-vEh dehks-plwah-tah-syÕh)*
operations audit	les contrôles de gestion	*(kõhn-trOhl dæ zhæhs-tyÕh)*
operations headquarters	le siège opérationnel	*(syEzh oh-peh-rah-syoh-nEhl)*
operations management	le contrôle d'exploitation	*(kõhn-trOhl dehks-plwah-tah-syÕh)*
operator	l'exploitant	*(ehks-plwah-tÃhnt)*
opium	l'opium	
opossum	l'opossum	
opportunity costs	le coût d'opportunité	*(kOOht doh-pohr-tooh-neeh-tEh)*
optic	l'optique	*(ohp-tEEhk)*
option	l'option	*(ohp-syÕh)*
option, stock	l'option de souscription	*(ohp-syÕh dæ sooh-skreehp-syÕh)*
optional	facultatif	*(fah-koohl-tah-tEEhf)*
oral bid (stock exchange)	à la criée (à la bourse)	*(ah lah kreeh-Eh), (ah lah bOOhrs)*
order (n)	la commande	*(koh-mÃhnd)*
order (v)	commander	*(koh-mãhn-dEh)*
order form	le bon de commande	*(bÕh dæ koh-mÃhnd)*
order number	le numéro de commande	*(nooh-meh-rOh dæ koh-mÃhnd)*
order of the day	l'ordre du jour	*(Ohr-dræ dooh zhOOhr)*
order, place an (v)	passer une commande	*(pah-sEh oohn koh-mÃhnd)*
ordinary capital	le capital ordinaire	*(kah-peeh-tAhl ohr-deeh-nEhr)*
ore	le minerai	*(meeh-neh-rEh)*
organic chemistry	la chimie organique	*(sheeh-mEEh ohr-gah-nEEhk)*
organization	l'organisation	*(ohr-gah-neeh-zah-syÕh)*
organization chart	l'organigramme	*(ohr-gah-neeh-grAhm)*
original cost	le coût initial	*(kOOht eeh-neeh-syAhl)*
original entry	l'enregistrement initial	*(ãhn-ræh-zheehs-træ-mÃh eeh-neeh-syAhl)*
original maturity	l'échéance originelle	*(eh-sheh-Ãhns oh-reeh-zheeh-nEhl)*
oscillator	l'oscillateur	*(oh-seeh-lah-tŒhr)*

ostrich (skin)	l'autruche	(oh-trOOhsh)
other assets (and liabilities)	autre actif (et passif)	(Oh-træ ahk-tEEf eh pah-sEEhf)
otter	la loutre	(lOOh-træ)
out of style	démodé	(deh-moh-dEh)
out-of-pocket expenses	les débours	(deh-bOOhr)
outbid (v)	surenchérir	(sooh-rãhn-sheh-rEEhr)
outlay	la mise de fonds	(mEEhz dœ fÕhn)
outlet	le débouché, le point de vente	(deh-booh-shEh), (pwÆh dœ vÃhnt)
outlook	la perspective	(pehrs-pehk-tEEhv)
output	le rendement, la production	(rãhnd-mÃh), (proh-doohk-syÕh)
outsized articles	les articles de taille exceptionnelle	(ahr-tEEhk-læ dœ tAh-yœ ehk-sehp-syoh-nEhl)
outstanding contract	le contrat à remplir	(kõhn-trAh ah rahm-plEEhr)
outstanding debt	la créance à recouvrir	(kreh-Ãhns ah ræh-kooh-vrEEhr)
outstanding stock	les titres en circulation	(tEEh-træ ãhn seehr-kooh-lah-syÕh)
outturn	le déchet	(deh-shEht)
over-the-counter quotation	la cotation officieuse (hors marché)	(koh-tah-syÕh oh-feeh-syŒhz [ohr mahr-shEh])
overage	l'excédent	(ehk-seh-dÃhn)
overbought	survendu	(soohr-vãhn-dOOh)
overcapitalized	surcapitalisé	(soohr-kah-peeh-tah-leeh-zEh)
overcharge	la surcharge	(soohr-shAhrzh)
overdraft	le découvert	(deh-kooh-vEhr)
overdue	en retard	(ãhn ræh-tAhr)
overhang	le surplomb, le porte-à-faux	(soohr-plOhm), (pOhrt ah fOh)
overhaul regulations (v)	refondre les réglementations	(ræh-fÕhn-dræh leh reh-glæh mãhn-tah-syÕhn)
overhead	général	(zheh-neh-rAhl)
overhead charges	les frais généraux	(frEh zheh-neh-rOh)
overlap (v)	chevaucher	(shœh-voh-shEh)
overnight	du jour au lendemain	(dooh zhOOhr oh lãhnd-mÆhn)
overpaid	surpayé	(soohr-pah-yEh)
oversold	survendu	(soohr-vãhn-dOOh)
overstock	le surplus de stock	(soohr-plOOh dœ stock)
oversubscribed	sur-souscrit	(soohr sooh-skrEEh)
oversupply	la fourniture excédentaire	(foohr-neeh-tOOhr ehk-seh-dãhn-tEhr)
overtime	les heures supplémentaires	(Œhr sooh-pleh-mÃh-tEhr)
overvalued	surévalué	(sooh-reh-vah-lwEh)
owner	le propriétaire	(proh-pryeh-tEhr)

owner's equity	les capitaux propres	*(kah-peeh-tOh prOh-prœ)*
ownership	la propriété	*(proh-pryeh-tEh)*
ownership, absentee	l'absentéisme (du propriétaire), le propriétaire absent	*(ahb-sãhn-teh-EEhz-mœ dooh proh-pryeh-tEhr), (proh-pryeh-tEhr ahb-sÃhn)*

P

p/e ratio	le coefficient de capitalisation des résultats	*(koh-eh-feeh-sÃhnt dœ kah-peeh-tah-leeh-zah-syÕh deh reh-soohl-tAh)*
package deal	le contrat global	*(kõhn-trAh gloh-bAhl)*
packaging	l'emballage	*(æhm-bah-lAhzh)*
packing case	la caisse d'emballage	*(kEhs dæhm-bah-lAhzh)*
packing list	le colisage	*(koh-leeh-zAhzh)*
page makeup	la mise en page	*(mEEhz ãhn pAhzh)*
pagination	la pagination	*(pah-zheeh-nah-syÕhn)*
paging	la pagination	*(pah-zheeh-nah-syÕhn)*
paid holiday	les congés payés	*(kõhn-zhEh pah-yEh)*
paid in full	entièrement payé	*(ãhn-tyehr-mÃh pah-yEh)*
paid up capital	le capital versé	*(kah-peeh-tAhl vehr-sEh)*
paid up shares	les actions libérées	*(ahk-syÕh leeh-beh-rEh)*
paid-in surplus	le surplus versé	*(soohr-plOOh vehr-sEh)*
paint	la peinture	*(pæhn-tOOhr)*
pallet	la palette	*(pah-lEht)*
palletized freight	le fret transporté sur palettes	*(frEht trãhnz-pohr-tEh soohr pah-lEht)*
pamphlet	la brochure	*(broh-shOOhr)*
panel	le panneau	*(pah-nOh)*
pants	le pantalon	*(pãhn-tah-lÕh)*
paper	le papier	*(pah-pyEh)*
paper holder	le serre-papier	*(sEhr pah-pyEh)*
paper profit	le profit fictif	*(proh-fEEh feehk-tEEhf)*
paper tape	le papier gommé	*(pah-pyEh goh-mEh)*
paperback	broché	*(broh-shEh)*
par	le pair	*(pEhr)*
par value	la valeur au pair	*(vah-lŒhr oh pEhr)*
par, above	au-dessus du pair	*(oh deh-sOOh dooh pEhr)*
par, below	au-dessous du pair	*(oh dæh-sOOh dooh pEhr)*
parallel circuit	le circuit parallèle	*(seehr-kwEEh pah-rah-lEhl)*
parcel post	le paquet-poste	*(pah-keh-pOhst)*
parent company	la maison mère	*(meh-zÕh mEhr)*
parity	la parité	*(pah-reeh-tEh)*
parity income ratio	le rapport parité/revenu	*(rah-pOhr pah-reeh-tEh /ræhv-nOOh)*
parity price	le prix de parité	*(prEEh dœ pah-reeh-tEh)*
part cargo	le chargement partiel	*(shahrzh-mÃh pahr-syEhl)*

partial payment	le paiement partiel	*(peh-mÃh pahr-syEhl)*
participating preferred stock	les titres privilégiés de participation	*(tEEh-trœ preeh-veeh-leh-zhyEh dœ pahr-teeh-seeh-pah-syÕh)*
participation fee	les honoraires de participation	*(oh-noh-rEhr dœ pahr-teeh-seeh-pah-syÕh)*
participation loan	le prêt en participation	*(prEht ãhn pahr-teeh-seeh-pah-syÕh)*
particular average loss	la perte d'avarie particulière	*(pEhrt dah-vahrEEh pahr-teeh-kooh-lyEhr)*
partner	l'associé(e)	*(ah-soh-syEh)*
partnership	l'association (de personnes)	*(ah-soh-syah-syÕh [dœ pehr-sÕhn])*
parts	les parts, les pièces	*(pAhr), (pyEhs)*
passbook	le carnet de compte, le livret de banque	*(kahr-nEh dœ kÕhnt), (lEEh-vrœ dœ bÃhnk)*
passed dividend	le dividende passé	*(deeh-veeh-dÃhnd pah-sEh)*
passport case	le porte-passeport	*(pohrt-pahs-pOhrt)*
past due	en souffrance	*(ãhn sooh-frÃhns)*
pasteurized	pasteurisé	*(pahs-tœh-reeh-zEh)*
pastry server	la pelle à tarte	*(pEhl ah tAhr-tœ)*
patent	le brevet	*(brœh-vEh)*
patent application	le dépôt de brevet	*(deh-pOh dœ brœh-vEh)*
patent law	la loi sur les brevets	*(lwAh soohr leh brœh-vEh)*
patent pending	brevet en attente d'homologation	*(brœh-vEh ãhn ah-tÃhnt doh-moh-loh-gah-syÕh)*
patent registering	le dépôt des brevets	*(deh-pOh deh brœh-vEht)*
patent royalty	la redevance sur un brevet	*(rœh-deh-vÃhns soohr œhn brœh-vEh)*
patented process	la méthode brevetée	*(meh-tOhd brœh-veh-tEh)*
pattern	le modèle, le patron	*(moh-dEhl), (pah-trÕh)*
pay (v)	payer	*(pah-yEh)*
pay as you go	(système) de retenue à la source, méthode de forfait avec rectifications périodiques	*(seehs-tEhm dœ rœh-tœh-nOOh ah lah sOOhrs), (meh-tOhd dœ fohr-fEh ah-vEhk rehk-teeh-feeh-kah-syÕh peh-ryoh-dEEhk)*
pay back a loan (v)	rembourser un prêt	*(rœhn-boohr-sEh œhn prEht)*
pay off (v)	régler, payer sous la table	*(reh-glEh), (pah-yEh sooh lah tAh-blœ)*
pay up (v)	acquitter, libérer	*(ah-keeh-tEh), (leeh-beh-rEh)*
payable on demand	payable sur demande	*(pah-yAh-blœ soohr dœh-mÃhnd)*
payable to bearer	payable au porteur	*(pah-yAh-blœ oh pohr-tŒhr)*

payable to order	payable à la commande	*(pah-yAh-blœ ah lah koh-mÃhnd)*
payback period	le délai d'amortissement	*(deh-lEh dah-mohr-eehs-mÃh)*
payee	la, le bénéficiaire	*(beh-neh-feeh-syEhr)*
payer	le payeur	*(pah-yŒhr)*
payload	les charges salariales	*(shAhrzh sah-lah-ryAl)*
paymaster	le trésorier-payeur	*(treh-zoh-ryEh pah-yŒhr)*
payment	le paiement	*(peh-mÃh)*
payment in full	le règlement intégral	*(reh-glœh-mÃh æhn-teh-grAhl)*
payment refused	le paiement refusé	*(peh-mÃh ræh-fooh-zEh)*
payout period	le délai de paiement	*(deh-lEh dœ peh-mÃh)*
payroll	l'ensemble des salaires	*(ãhn-sÃhm-blœ deh sah-lEhr)*
payroll tax	l'impôt sur les salaires	*(æhm-pOh soohr leh sah-lEhr)*
peace-keeping force	la force de maintien de la paix	*(fohrs dœ mæhn-tyEhn dœ lah pEh)*
peak load	la charge maximum	*(shAhrzh mahk-seeh-mOOhm)*
pegged price	le prix contrôlé	*(prEEh kõhn-troh-lEh)*
pegging	le blocage, l'indexation	*(bloh-kAhzh), (æhn-dehk-sah-syÕh)*
pellet	le grain	*(grÆhn)*
penalty clause	la clause pénale	*(klOhz peh-nAhl)*
penalty-fraud action	le procès intenté en cas de fraude	*(proh-sEh æhn-tãhn-tEh ãhn kAh dœ frOhd)*
penicillin	la pénicilline	*(peh-neeh-seeh-lEEhn)*
penny stock	les actions cotées en cents	*(ahk-syÕh koh-tEh ãhn sÃhnt)*
pension fund	la caisse de retraite	*(kehs dœ ræh-trEht)*
pepper mill	le moulin à poivre	*(mooh-lÆhn ah pwAh-vrœ)*
pepper shaker	la poivrière	*(pwah-vryEhr)*
per capita	par habitant	*(pahr ah-beeh-tÃh)*
per diem	par jour	*(pahr zhOOhr)*
per share	par action	*(pahr ahk-syÕh)*
percentage earnings	les gains au pourcentage	*(gÆhn oh poohr-sãhn-tAhzh)*
percentage of profit	le tantième	*(tãhn-tyEhm)*
perfect binding	la reliure	*(ræh-lyOOhr)*
performance bond	la garantie de bonne exécution	*(gah-rãhn-tEEh dœ bOhn ehk-zeh-kooh-syÕh)*
perfume bottle	le flacon de parfum	*(flah-kÕhn dœ pahr-fOOhm)*
periodic inventory	l'inventaire périodique	*(æhn-vãhn-tEhr peh-ryoh-dEEhk)*
peripherals	les périphériques	*(peh-reeh-feh-rEEhk)*

perks	les petits profits	*(pæh-tEEh proh-fEEh)*
permit	le permis	*(pehr-mEEh)*
perpetual inventory	l'inventaire perpétuel	*(æhn-vãhn-tEhr pæhr-peh-twEhl)*
personal deduction	le nombre d'exemption par individu	*(nÕhm-bræ dehk-zãhm-syÕh pahr æhn-deeh-veeh-dOOh)*
personal exemption	l'exemption personnelle	*(ehk-zãhm-syÕh pehr-soh-nEhl)*
personal income tax	l'impôt sur le revenu des personnes physiques (IRPP)	*(æhm-pOh soohr ræhv-nOOh deh pehr-sÕhn feeh-zEEhk)*
personal liability	la responsabilité individuelle	*(ræhs-pohn-sah-beeh-leeh-tEh æhn-deeh-veeh-dwEhl)*
personal property	les biens meubles	*(byÆhn mŒh-blœ)*
personality test	le test psychologique	*(tesh seeh-koh-loh-zhEEhk)*
personnel administration	l'administration du personnel	*(ad-meeh-neehs-trah-syÕh dooh pehr-soh-nEhl)*
personnel department	le service du personnel	*(sær-vEEhs dooh pehr-soh-nEhl)*
personnel management	la direction du personnel	*(deeh-rehk-syÕh dooh pehr-soh-nEhl)*
pesticide	le pesticide	*(pehs-teeh-sEEhd)*
petrochemical	pétrochimique	*(peh-troh-keeh-mEEhk)*
petrodollars	les pétrodollars	*(peh-troh-doh-lAhr)*
petroleum	le pétrole	*(peh-trOhl)*
pharmaceutical	pharmaceutique	*(fahr-mah-seh-ooh-tEEhk)*
pharmacist	le pharmacien(ne)	*(fahr-mah-syÆhn)*
phase in (v)	introduire graduellement	*(æhn-troh-dwEEhr grah-dwehl-mÃh)*
phase out (v)	supprimer peu à peu	*(sooh-preeh-mEh pŒh ah pŒh)*
phenol	le phénol	*(feh-nOhl)*
phosphate	le phosphate	*(fohs-fAht)*
photographer	le photographe	*(foh-toh-grAhf)*
physical inventory	l'inventaire des marchandises	*(æhn-vãhn-tEhr deh mahr-shãhn-dEEhz)*
physician	le médecin, le physicien	*(mehd-sÆhn), (feeh-zeeh-syÆhn)*
phytosanitary regulations	les réglementations phytosanitaires	*(reh-glœ-mãhn-tah-syÕh feeh-toh-sah-neeh-tEhr)*
pica	le cicéro	*(seeh-seh-rOh)*
pick-up and delivery	le ramassage et la livraison	*(rah-mah-sAhzh eh lah leeh-vreh-zÕh)*
picket line	le piquet	*(peeh-kEh)*
pickling	le décapage	*(deh-kah-pAhzh)*
pie chart	le graphique circulaire "camembert"	*(graf-fEEhk seehr-kooh-lEhr)*

piecework	le travail à la pièce	*(trah-vAhyœ ah lah pyEhs)*
pig iron	la fonte	*(fŌhnt)*
piggyback service	le service de ferroutage	*(sœr-vEEhs dœ feh-rooh-tAhzh)*
pigment	le pigment	*(peehg-mÃh)*
pigskin	la porc	*(pOhr)*
pilferage	le larcin	*(lahr-sǼhn)*
pill	la pilule	*(peeh-lOOhl)*
pillowcase	la taie d'oreiller	*(tEh doh-reh-yEh)*
pilotage	les droits de pilotage	*(drwAh dœ peeh-loh-tAhzh)*
pinion	le pignon	*(peeh-nyŌh)*
pipage	la canalisation	*(kah-nah-leeh-zah-syŌh)*
pipes and tubes	les tubes et tuyauteries	*(tOOhb eh tooh-yah-tœh-rEEh)*
piston	le piston	*(peehs-tŌh)*
pitcher	le pichet	*(peeh-shEh)*
place an order (v)	passer commande	*(pah-sEh koh-mÃhnd)*
place of business	le lieu d'affaires, l'adresse d'une entreprise	*(lyŒh dah-fEhr), (ah-drEhs doohn ãhn-trœh-prEEhz)*
place setting	le couvert	*(kooh-vEhr)*
plan	le projet	*(proh-zhEh)*
plan, action	le plan d'action	*(plÃhn dahk-syŌh)*
plan, market	le projet commercial	*(proh-zhEh koh-mehr-syAhl)*
planned obsolescence	le vieillissement calculé	*(vyeh-yeehs-mÃh kahl-kooh-lEh)*
plant (n)	l'usine	*(ooh-zEEhn)*
plant capacity	la capacité de production	*(kah-pah-seeh-tEh dœ proh-doohk-syŌh)*
plant location	l'implantation d'une usine	*(ãhm-plãhn-tah-syŌh dooh ooh-zEEhn)*
plant manager	le directeur d'une usine	*(deeh-rehk-tŒhr doohn ooh-zEEhn)*
plants	les plantes	*(plÃhnt)*
plate	l'assiette, le cliché, la plaque	*(ah-syEht), (kleeh-shEh), (plAhk)*
play host (v)	accueillir	*(ah-kweh-yEEhr)*
pleat	la pli	*(pleeh)*
pleated	plissé(e)	*(pleeh-sEh)*
pledge	l'engagement, le gage	*(ãhn-gahzh-mÃh), (gAhzh)*
plenary meeting	la réunion plénière	*(reh-ooh-nyŌh pleh-nyEhr)*
plenary session	la session plénière	*(seh-syŌhn pleh-nyEhr)*
plowback (earnings)	le réinvestissement	*(reh-ǽhn-vehs-teehs-mÃh)*
plus accrued interest	intérêt couru supplémentaire	*(ǽhn-teh-rEh kooh-rOOh sooh-pleh-mÃh-tEhr)*
pocketbook	le porte-feuille	*(pohrt-fŒh-yœ)*

point (percentage, mortgage term)	le point	*(pwÆh)*
point	le corps, le point	*(kOhr), (pwÆhn)*
point of order	le point de procédure	*(pwÆh dœ proh-seh-dOOhr)*
point-of-sale	le point de vente	*(pwÆhn dœ vÃhnt)*
policy	la politique	*(poh-leeh-tEEhk)*
policyholder	l'assuré	*(ah-sooh-rEh)*
political framework	le cadre politique	*(kAh-drœh poh-leeh-tEEhk)*
pollutant	polluant	*(poh-lwÃhn)*
pollute (v)	polluer	*(poh-lwEh)*
pollution	la pollution	*(poh-looh-syÕhn)*
pollution-free	non polluant	*(nõhr poh-lwÃhn)*
polyester	le polyester	*(poh-leeh-ehs-tEhr)*
polymer	le polymère	*(poh-leeh-mEhr)*
pool (of funds)	la mise en commun	*(meehz ãhn koh-mOOhn)*
pool (v)	mettre en commun	*(mEh-trœ ãhn koh-mOOhn)*
pool one's resources (v)	mettre en commun ses ressources	*(meh-trœh ãhn koh-mOOhn seh-rœh-soohrs)*
pop a cork (v)	faire sauter le bouchon	*(fehr soh-tEh loe booh-shÕhn)*
pooling of interest	la mise en commun d'intérêts	*(meehz ãhn koh-mOOhn dæhn-teh-rEh)*
poplin	la popeline	*(pohp-lEEhn)*
portfolio	le porte-documents, le portefeuille	*(pohrt-doh-kooh-mÃh), (pohrt-fŒh-yœ)*
portfolio management	la gestion des portefeuilles	*(zhœhs-tyÕh deh pohrt-fŒh-yœ)*
portfolio theory	la théorie de portefeuille	*(teh-oh-rEEh dœ pohrt-fŒh-yœ)*
portfolio, stock	le portefeuille de titres	*(pohrt-fŒh-yœ dœ tEEh-trœ)*
portion	la tranche	*(trÃhnsh)*
position limit	la position-limite	*(poh-zeeh-syÕh leeh-mEEht)*
positive	positif	*(poh-zeeh-tEEhf)*
positive cash flow	la trésorie positive	*(treh-soh-rœh-rEEh poh-zeeh-tEEhf)*
post (book-keeping) (v)	porter en compte, inscrire	*(pohr-tEh ãhn kÕhnt), (æhn-skrEEhr)*
postdate (v)	postdater	*(pohst-dah-tEh)*
postdated	postdaté	*(pohst-dah-tEh)*
poster	l'affiche	*(ah-fEEhsh)*
postpone (v)	ajourner	*(ah-zhoohr-nEh)*
potential buyer	l'acheteur potentiel	*(ahsh-tŒhr poh-tãhn-syEhl)*
potential sales	les ventes potentielles	*(vÃhnt poh-tãhn-syEhl)*
pottery	la poterie	*(poh-teh-rEEh)*

powder	la poudre	*(pOOh-drœ)*
power	la puissance, l'énergie	*(pweeh-sÃhns, eh-nehr-jEEh)*
power of attorney	la procuration	*(proh-kooh-rah-syÕh)*
power steering	la direction assistée	*(deeh-rehk-syÕh ah-seehs-tEh)*
practical	pratique	*(prah-tEEhk)*
preemptive right	le droit de préemption	*(drwAh dœ preh-ehmp-syÕh)*
prefabrication	la préfabrication	*(preh-fah-breeh-kah-syÕh)*
preface	la préface	*(preh-fAhs)*
preferential debts	les dettes privilégiées	*(DEht preeh-veeh-leh-zhyEh)*
preferred stock	les valeurs privilégiées	*(vah-lŒhr preeh-veeh-leh-zhyEh)*
preferred tariff	le tarif préférentiel	*(tah-rEEhf preh-feh-rãhn-syEhl)*
pregnancy	la grossesse	*(grohs-Ehs)*
preliminary prospectus	l'avant-projet de prospectus	*(ah-vÃhn-proh-zhEh dœ prohs-pehk-tOOh)*
premises	les locaux	*(loh-kOh)*
premium offer	l'offre supplémentaire	*(Oh-frœ sooh-pleh-mÃh-tEhr)*
premium pricing	l'établissement de la prime	*(eh-tah-bleehs-mÃh dœ lah prEEhm)*
premium, acceleration	la prime de remboursement anticipé	*(prEEhm dœ rãhm-boohrs-mÃh ãhn-teeh-seeh-pEh)*
premium, insurance	la prime d'assurance	*(prEEhm dah-sooh-rÃhns)*
prenatal care	les soins prénataux	*(swÆhn preh-nah-tOh)*
prepaid expenses (balance sheet)	les frais payés d'avance (bilan)	*(frEh pah-yEh dah-vÃhns [beeh-lÃh])*
prepay (v)	payer d'avance	*(pah-yEh dah-vÃhns)*
prescription	l'ordonnance	*(ohr-doh-nÃhns)*
preservation	la préservation	*(preh-sœhr-vah-syÕhn)*
president	le directeur général	*(deeh-rehk-tŒhr zheh-neh-rAhl)*
press book	l'exemplaire de presse	*(ehk-zãhm-plEhr dœ prEhs)*
press campaign	la campagne de presse	*(kahm-pÃhnyœ dœ prEhs)*
press clipping	la coupure de presse	*(kooh-pOOhr dœ prEhs)*
press release	le communiqué de presse	*(koh-mooh-neeh-kEh dœ prEhs)*
pressure	la pression	*(prœh-syÕh)*
prevent (v) aging	prévenir le vieillissement	*(preh-vœh-nEEhr lœ vyeh-yeehs-mÃhn)*
preventive maintenance	l'entretien préventif	*(ãhn-trœh-tyÆhn preh-vãhn-tEEhf)*

P

P

preventive medicine	la médecine préventive	*(meh-deeh-sEEhn preh-vãhn-tEEhv)*
price (n)	le prix, le cours	*(prEEh), (kOOhr)*
price (v)	établir un prix	*(eh-tah-blEEhr œhn prEEh)*
price cutting	le rabais	*(rah-bEh)*
price differential	le différentiel des prix	*(deeh-feh-rãhn-syEhl deh prEEh)*
price elasticity	l'élasticité des prix	*(eh-lahs-teeh-seeh-tEh deh prEEh)*
price fixing	la fixation du prix	*(feehk-sah-syÕh dooh prEEh)*
price index	l'indice de prix	*(ãhn-dEEhs dœ prEEh)*
price limit	le prix limite	*(prEEh leeh-mEEht)*
price list	le barème, le tarif	*(bah-rEhm), (tah-rEEhf)*
price range	la gamme des prix, la fourchette des prix	*(gAhm deh prEEh), (foohr-shEht deh prEEh)*
price support	le soutien des prix	*(sooh-tyÆh deh prEEh)*
price tick	le pointage des prix	*(pwãhn-tAhzh deh prEEh)*
price war	la guerre des prix	*(gEhr deh prEEh)*
price, competitive	le prix compétitif	*(prEEh kohm-peh-teeh-tEEhf)*
price, market	le prix du marché	*(prEEh dooh mahr-shEh)*
price-earnings ratio	le coefficient de capitalisation des résultats	*(koh-eh-feeh-sÃnt dœ kah-peeh-tah-leeh-zah-syÕh deh reh-soohl-tAh)*
primary market	le marché préliminaire	*(mahr-shEh preh-leeh-meeh-nEhr)*
primary reserves	les réserves de base	*(reh-zEhrv dœ bAhz)*
prime costs	le prix de revient	*(prEEh dœ rœ-vyÃhn)*
prime rate	le taux préférentiel de l'escompte	*(tOh preh-feh-rãhn-syEhl deh lehs-kÕhnt)*
prime time	l'heure de grande écoute	*(Œhr dœ grÃhnd eh-kOOht)*
principal	le capital	*(kah-peeh-tAhl)*
print	l'imprimé	*(ãhm-preeh-mEh)*
print run	la tirage	*(teeh-rAhzh)*
printer	l'imprimante	*(ãhn-preeh-mÃhnt)*
printed circuit	le circuit imprimé	*(seehr-kwEEht ãhm-preeh-mEh)*
printed matter	les imprimés	*(ãhm-preeh-mEh)*
printing	l'impression	*(ãhm-preh-syÕh)*
printout	la liste imprimée	*(lEEhst ãhm-preeh-mEh)*
priority	la priorité	*(preeh-oh-reeh-tEh)*
private fleet	la flotte privée	*(flOht preeʰ-vEh)*
private label (or brand)	la marque du distributeur	*(mAhr-kœ dooh deehs-treeh-booh-tŒhr)*
private placement (finance)	l'investissement privé	*(ãhn-vehs-teehs-mÃh preeh-vEh)*

pro forma invoice	la facture pro forma	*(fahk-tOOhr proh-fOhr-mah)*
pro forma statement	le relevé pro forma	*(ræh-læh-vEh proh-fOhr-mah)*
probate	la validation	*(vah-leeh-dah-syÕh)*
problem	le problème	*(proh-blEhm)*
problem solving	la résolution des problèmes	*(reh-zoh-looh-syÕh deh proh-blEhm)*
proceeds	le produit de la vente	*(proh-dwEEh dæ lah vÃhnt)*
process (v)	traiter	*(treh-tEh)*
process	le procédé	*(proh-seh-dEh)*
process, production	la production	*(proh-doohk-syÕh)*
processing error	l'erreur de traitement	*(eh-rŒhr dæ treht-mÃh)*
processor	le processeur	*(proh-seh-SŒhr)*
procurement	l'acquisition	*(ah-keeh-zeeh-syÕh)*
product	le produit	*(proh-dwEEh)*
product analysis	l'étude du produit	*(eh-tOOhd dooh proh-dwEEh)*
product design	la conception du produit	*(kõhn-sehp-syÕh dooh proh-dwEEh)*
product development	la mise au point du produit	*(mEEhz oh pwÆh dooh proh-dwEEh)*
product dynamics	la dynamique des produits	*(deeh-nah-mEEhk deh proh-dwEEh)*
product group	le groupe de produits	*(grOOhp dæ proh-dwEEh)*
product life	la durée de vie d'un produit	*(dooh-rEh dæ vEEh dæhn proh-dwEEh)*
product line	la ligne de produits	*(lEEh-nyæ dæ proh-dwEEh)*
product management	la gestion des produits	*(zhæhs-tyÕh deh proh-dwEEh)*
product profitability	la rentabilité d'un produit	*(rãhn-tah-beeh-leeh-tEh dæhn proh-dwEEh)*
production	la production	*(proh-doohk-synOh)*
production control	le contrôle de la production	*(kõhn-trOhl dæ lah proh-doohk-syÕh)*
production costs	le coût de la production	*(kOOht dæ proh-doohk-syÕh)*
production line	la ligne de production	*(lEEh-nyæ dæ proh-doohk-syÕh)*
production process	le processus de production	*(proh-seh-sOOh dæ proh-doohk-syÕh)*
production schedule	le programme de production	*(proh-grAhm dæ proh-doohk-syÕh)*
productivity	la productivité	*(proh-doohk-teeh-veeh-tEh)*
productivity campaign	la campagne de productivité	*(kãh-pÃh-nyæ dæ proh-doohk-teeh-veeh-tEh)*

profession	la profession	*(proh-feh-syÕh)*
profit	le bénéfice	*(beh-neh-fEEhs)*
profit factor	le facteur rentabilité	*(fahk-tŒhr rãhn-tah-beeh-leeh-tEh)*
profit impact	l'incidence sur les bénéfices	*(æhn-seeh-dÃhns soohr leh beh-neh-fEEhs)*
profit margin	la marge bénéficiaire	*(mAhrzh beh-neh-feeh-syEhr)*
profit projection	la prévision des bénéfices	*(preh-veeh-zyÕh deh beh-neh-fEEhs)*
profit sharing	la participation aux bénéfices	*(pahr-teeh-seeh-pah-syÕh oh beh-neh-fEEhs)*
profit, gross	le bénéfice brut	*(beh-neh-fEEhs brOOh)*
profit, net	le bénéfice net	*(beh-neh-fEEhs nEht)*
profit-and-loss account	le compte des pertes et profits	*(kÕhnt deh pEhrt eh proh-fEEh)*
profit-and-loss statement	l'état des pertes et profits	*(eh-tAh deh pEhrt eh proh-fEEh)*
profit-taking	la prise de bénéfices	*(prEEhz dœ beh-neh-fEEhs)*
profitability	la rentabilité	*(rãhn-tah-beeh-leeh-tEh)*
profitability analysis	l'étude de rentabilité	*(eh-tOOhd dœ rãhn-tah-beeh-leeh-tEh)*
profitable	rentable	*(rãhn-tAh-blœh)*
program (n)	le programme	*(proh-grAhm)*
program (v)	programmer	*(proh-grah-mEh)*
prohibited goods	les marchandises prohibées	*(mahr-shãhn-dEEhz proh-eeh-bEh)*
project (n)	le projet	*(proh-zhEh)*
project (v)	projeter	*(proh-zheh-tEh)*
project planning	la planification	*(plah-neeh-feeh-kah-syÕh)*
promissory note	le billet à ordre	*(beeh-yEh ah Ohr-drœ)*
promotion	la promotion, l'avancement	*(proh-moh-syÕh), (ah-vãhns-mÃh)*
promotion, sales	les ventes promotionnelles	*(vÃhnt proh-moh-syoh-nEhl)*
promotional activity	l'activité de promotion	*(ahk-teeh-veeh-tEh dœ proh-moh-syÕh)*
prompt	rapide	*(rah-pEEhd)*
proof	l'épreuve	*(eh-prŒhv)*
proof of loss	la pièce justificative de perte	*(pyEhs zhoohs-teeh-feeh-kah tEEv dœ pEhrt)*
proofreading	la relecture	*(rœh-lehk-tOOhr)*
property	la propriété	*(proh-pryeh-tEh)*
proprietary	détenu par le propriétaire, propriété exclusive	*(deh-tœ-nOOh pahr lœ proh-pryeh-tEhr), (proh-pryeh-tEh ehks-klooh-sEEhv)*
proprietor	la, le propriétaire	*(proh-pryeh-tEhr)*
propulsion	la propulsion	*(proh-poohl-syÕh)*

prospective consumer	le consommateur potentiel	*(kõhn-soh-mah-tŒhr poh-tãhn-syEhl)*
prospectus	le prospectus	*(prohs-pehk-tOOh)*
protect (v)	protéger	*(proh-teh-zhEh)*
protectionism	le protectionnisme	*(proh-tehk-syoh-nEEhz-mœ)*
protest (banking, law)	la protestation, le protêt	*(proh-tehs-tah-syÕh), (proh-tEht)*
proton	le proton	*(proh-tÕh)*
prototype	le prototype	*(proh-toh-tEEhp)*
provide that (v)	stipuler que	*(steeh-pooh-lEh kœh)*
proxy	le fondé de pouvoir, la procuration	*(fõhn-dEh dœ pooh-vwAhr), (proh-kooh-rah-syÕh)*
proxy statement	la circulaire d'information	*(seehr-kooh-lEhr œhn-fohr-mah-syÕh)*
prudent man rule	la règle sage	*(rEh-glœ sAhzh)*
public auction	la vente aux enchères	*(vÃhnt oh ãhn-shEhr)*
public company	la société anonyme par actions	*(soh-syeh-tEh ah-noh-mEEhm pahr ahk-syÕh)*
public domain	le domaine public	*(doh-mEhn pooh-blEEhk)*
public funds	les fonds publics	*(fÕhn pooh-blEEhk)*
public offering	l'offre publique	*(Oh-frœ pooh-blEEhk)*
public opinion poll	le sondage	*(sõhn-dAhzh)*
public property	la propriété publique	*(proh-pryeh-tEh pooh-blEEhk)*
public relations	les relations publiques	*(rœh-lah-syÕhn pooh-blEEhk)*
public sale	la vente publique	*(vÃhnt pooh-blEEhk)*
public sector	le secteur public	*(sehk-tŒhr pooh-blEEhk)*
public utility	le service public	*(sœr-vEEhs pooh-blEEhk)*
public works	les travaux publics	*(trah-vOh pooh-blEEhk)*
publicity	la publicité	*(pooh-bleeh-seeh-tEh)*
publisher	l'éditeur	*(eh-deeh-tŒhr)*
pump priming	les mesures de relance de l'économie	*(mœh-zOOhr dœ rœh-lÃhns dœ leh-koh-noh-mEEh)*
punch card	la carte perforée	*(kAhrt pehr-foh-rEh)*
purchase (v)	acheter	*(ahsh-tEh)*
purchase money mortgage	l'hypothèque consentie au vendeur d'un immeuble par l'acheteur en garantie du montant du prêt non liquidé	*(eeh-poh-tEhk kõhn-sãhn-tEEh oh vÃhn-dŒhr dœhn eeh-mŒh-blœ pahr ahsh-tŒhr ãhn gah-rãhn-tEEh dooh mõhn-tÃh dooh prEht nõh leeh-keeh-dEh)*
purchase order	le bon de commande, l'ordre d'achat	*(bÕh dœ koh-mÃhnd), (Ohr-drœ dah-shAh)*
purchase price	le prix d'achat	*(prEEh dah-shAh)*

purchasing manager	le directeur des achats	*(deeh-rehk-tŒhr dehz ah-shAh)*
purchasing power	le pouvoir d'achat	*(pooh-vwAhr dah-shAh)*
pure risk	le risque pur	*(rEEhs-kœ pOOhr)*
purgative	le purgatif	*(poohr-gah-tEEhf)*
purification	la purification	*(pooh-reeh-feeh-kah-synOh)*
purse	le porte-monnaie	*(pohrt-moh-nEh)*
put and call	la double option, le stellage	*(dOOh-blœ ohp-syŌh), (stœh-lAhzh)*
put in a bid (v)	faire une offre	*(fEhr oohn Oh-frœ)*
put into orbit	mettre en orbite	*(mEht-rœh ãhn ohr-bEEht)*
put option	l'option de vente	*(ohp-syŌh dœ vÃhnt)*
pyramid selling	la vente pyramidale	*(vÃhnt peeh-rah-meeh-dAhl)*
pyramiding	la technique pyramidale	*(tehk-nEEhk peeh-rah-meeh-dAhl)*

Q

qualifications	les compétences	*(kõhm-peh-tÃhns)*
qualified acceptance endorsement	l'acceptation sous réserve	*(ahk-sehp-tah-syŌh sooh reh-zEhrv)*
quality control	le contrôle de qualité	*(kõhn-trOhl dœ kah-leeh-tEh*
quality goods	les marchandises de qualité	*(mahr-shãhn-dEEhz dœ kah-leeh-tEh)*
quantity	la quantité	*(kãhn-teeh-tEh)*
quantity discount	la remise pour quantité importante	*(rœh-mEEhz poohr kãhn-teeh-tEh æhm-pohr-tÃhnt)*
quasi-public company	la société quasi-publique	*(soh-syeh-tEh kah-zeeh-pooh-blEEhk)*
quench (v)	tremper	*(trãhm-pEh)*
quick assets	l'actif disponible	*(ahk-tEEf deehs-poh-nEEh-blœ)*
quit claim deed	l'acte de transfert d'un droit	*(Ahk-tœ dœ trãhnz-fEhr dœhn drwAh)*
quorum	le quorum	
quota	les contingents	*(kõhn-teehn-zhÃhn)*
quota system	le système des contingents	*(seehs-tEhm dœ kõhn-teehn-zhÃh)*
quota, export	les contingents à l'exportation	*(kõhn-teehn-zhÃhnt ah lehks-pohr-tah-syŌh)*
quota, sales	les contingents de vente	*(kõhn-teehn-zhÃhn dœ vÃhnt)*
quotation	la cotation	*(koh-tah-syŌhn)*

R

rabbit	le lapin	*(lah-pÆhn)*
raccoon	le raton laveur	*(rah-tÕh lah-vŒhr)*
rack jobber	le grossiste-étalagiste	*(groh-sEEhst-eh-tah-lah-zhEEhst)*
radar	le radar	*(rah-dAhr)*
radial tire	le pneu radial	*(nŒh rah-dyAhl)*
radio	la radio	*(rah-dyOh)*
radioactivity	la radioactivité	*(rah-dyoh-ahk-teeh-veeh-tEh)*
rail shipment	l'expédition ferroviaire	*(ehks-peh-deeh-syÕh feh-roh-vyEhr)*
railway transportation	le transport ferroviaire	*(trãhns-pOhr feh-roh-vyEhr)*
rain check	la partie remise	*(pahr-tEEh rœh-mEEhz)*
rain forest	la forêt tropicale	*(foh-rÉh troh-peeh-kAhl)*
raincoat	l'imperméable	*(ãhm-pehr-meh-Ah-blœ)*
rainfall	les précipitations	*(preh-seeh-peeh-tah-syÕhn)*
raising capital	le capital en accroissement	*(kah-peeh-tAhl ãhn ah-krwahs-mÃh)*
rally	la reprise	*(rœh-prEEhz)*
random access	l'accès aléatoire	*(ahk-sEh ah-leh-ah-twAhr)*
random access memory	la mémoire vive	*(meh-mwAhr vEEhv)*
random sample	l'échantillon aléatoire	*(eh-shãhn-teeh-yÕhn ah-leh-ah-twAhr)*
range	la tranche	*(trÃhnsh)*
rash	la rougeur	*(rooh-zhŒr)*
rate	le taux	*(tOh)*
rate of growth	le taux de croissance	*(tOh dœ krwah-sÃhns)*
rate of increase	le taux de croissance	*(tOh dœ krwah-sÃhns)*
rate of interest	le taux d'intérêt	*(tOh dæhn-teh-rÉh)*
rate of return	le taux de rentabilité	*(tOh dœ rãhn-tah-beeh-leeh-tEh)*
rate, base	le taux de base	*(tOh dœ bAhz)*
rating, credit	l'évaluation de la solvabilité	*(eh-vah-lwah-syÕh dœ lah sohl-vah-beeh-leeh-tEh)*
rating, market	l'évaluation du marché	*(eh-vah-lwah-syÕh dooh mahr-shEh)*
ratio	le coefficient	*(koh-eh-feeh-sÃhnt)*
rationing	le rationnement	*(rah-syohn-mÃh)*
raw materials	les matières premières	*(mah-tyEhr prœh-myEhr)*
rayon	la rayonne	*(rah-yOhn)*
re-export	la réexportation	*(reh-ehks-pohr-tah-syÕh)*
reach a consensus (v)	parvenir à un consensus	*(pahr-vœh-nEEhr ah æhr kõhn-sãhn-sooh)*
reactant	le réactif	*(reh-ahk-tEEhf)*

R

ready cash	l'argent comptant	*(ahr-zhÃh kõhn-tÃhn)*
ready-to-wear	le prêt-à-porter	*(prEht ah pohr-tEh)*
real assets	les biens immobiliers	*(byÆhn eeh-moh-beeh-lyEh)*
real estate	la propriété immobilière	*(proh-pryeh-tEh eeh-moh-beeh-lyEhr)*
real income	le revenu réel	*(ræhv-nOOh reh-Ehl)*
real investment	l'investissement réel	*(æhn-vehs-teehs-mÃh reh-Ehl)*
real price	le prix réel	*(prEEh reh-Ehl)*
real time	le temps réel	*(tÃh reh-Ehl)*
real wages	le salaire réel	*(sah-lEhr reh-Ehl)*
ream	la rame	*(rAhm)*
rear axle	l'essieu arrière	*(leh-see-oo ah-ryEhr)*
reasonable care	la gestion raisonnable	*(zhæhs-tyÕh reh-soh-nAh-blæ)*
rebars	le fer à béton	*(fehr ah beh-tÕh)*
rebate	la remise	*(ræh-mEEhz)*
recapitalization	la recapitalisation	*(ræh-kah-peeh-tah-leeh-zah-syÕh)*
receipt	le reçu	*(ræh-sOOh)*
receiver	le récepteur	*(reh-sæhp-tŒhr)*
recession	le recul, la recession	*(ræh-kOOhl), (ræh-seh-syÕh)*
reciprocal trading	le commerce croisé	*(koh-mEhrs krwah-zEh)*
record	le disque	*(dEEhsk)*
record (v)	enregistrer	*(ãhn-ræh-zheehs-trEh)*
record date	la date d'inscription	*(dAht dãhn-skreehp-syÕ)*
record player	l'électrophone	*(eh-lehk-troh-fÕhn)*
recourse	le recours	*(ræh-kOOhr)*
recovery	le recouvrement	*(æh-kooh-vræ-mÃh)*
recovery of expenses	le remboursement des dépenses	*(rãhm-boohrs-mÃh deh deh-pãhns)*
recyclable	recyclable	*(ræh-seeh-klAh-blæh)*
recycle	recycler	*(ræh-seeh-klEh)*
recycling center	le centre de recyclage	*(sÃhn-træ dæ ræh-seeh-klAhzh)*
recycling plant	l'usine de traitement	*(ooh-zEEhn dæ treht-mÃhn)*
red tape	la paperasserie	*(pah-peh-rah-seh-rEEh)*
redeemable bond	l'obligation amortissable	*(oh-bleeh-gah-syÕh ah-mohr-teeh-sAh-blæ)*
redemption allowance	l'allocation de l'amortissement	*(ah-loh-kah-syÕh dah-mohr-eehs-mÃh)*
redemption fund	le fonds d'amortissement	*(fÕhn dah-mohr-eehs-mÃh)*
redemption premium	la prime de remboursement	*(prEEhm dæ rãhm-boohrs-mÃh)*
rediscount rate	le taux de réescompte	*(tOh dæ reh-ehs-kÕhnt)*
reduce (v)	réduire	*(reh-dwEEhr)*

reduction	la réduction	*(reh-doohk-syŌh)*
reference number	le numéro de référence	*(nooh-meh-rOh dœ reh-feh-rÃhns)*
reference, credit	la référence de crédit	*(reh-feh-rÃhns dœ kreh-dEEh)*
refinancing	le refinancement	*(rœh-feeh-nãhns-mÃh)*
refine (v)	raffiner	*(rah-feeh-nEh)*
refinery	la raffinerie	*(rah-feeh-neh-rEEh)*
reflation	la relance par l'augmentation de la masse monétaire	*(rœh-lÃhns pahr lohg-mãhn-tah-syŌh dœ lah mAhs moh-neh-tEhr)*
refractories	les produits réfractaires	*(proh-dwEEh reh-frahk-tEhr)*
refund	le remboursement	*(rãhm-boohrs-mÃh)*
refuse acceptance (v)	refuser l'acceptation	*(rœh-fooh-zEh lahk-sehp-tah-syŌh)*
refuse payment (v)	refuser le paiement	*(rœh-fooh-zEh lœ peh-mÃh)*
regard (with regard to)	rapport (par rapport à)	*(rah-pOhr [pahr rah-pOhr ah])*
register marks	les repères	*(rœh-pEhr)*
registered check	le chèque enregistré	*(shEhk ãhn-rœh-zheehs-trEh)*
registered mail	le courrier recommandé	*(kooh-ryEh rœh-koh-mãhn-dEh)*
registered representative	le représentant agréé	*(rœh-preh-zãhn-tÃh ah-grEh)*
registered security	le titre nominatif	*(tEEh-trœ noh-meeh-nah-tEEhf)*
registered trademark	la marque déposée	*(mAhr-kœ deh-poh-zEh)*
regression analysis	l'analyse de régression	*(ãh-nah-lEEhz dœ reh-greh-syŌh)*
regressive tax	l'impôt régressif	*(ǽhm-pŌh reh-greh-sEEhf)*
regular warehouse	l'entrepôt régulier	*(ãhn-trœ-pŌh reh-gooh-lyEh)*
regulation	la réglementation	*(reh-glœh-mãhn-tah-syŌh)*
reimburse (v)	rembourser	*(rãhm-boohr-sEh)*
reinsure	le réassurer	*(reh-ah-sooh-rEhr)*
rejuvenate (v)	rajeunir	*(rah-zhooh-nEEhr)*
relaxation of restraints	l'assouplissement des restrictions	*(ah-sooh-pleehs-mÃhn deh rœhs-treehk-syŌhn)*
reliable source	la source digne de confiance	*(sOOhrs dEEh-nyœ dœ kõhn-feeh-Ãhns)*
remainder	le reliquat	*(reh-leeh-kAh)*
remedies	les remèdes	*(rœh-mEhd)*
remedy (law)	le recours	*(rœh-kOOhr)*
remission of a tax	la détaxe	*(deh-tAhks)*

remission of duty	le droit de remise	*(drwAh dœ ræh-mEEhz)*
remote control	la télécommande	*(teh-leh-koh-mÃhnd)*
remove frontier controls (v)	supprimer les contrôles douaniers	*(sooh-preeh-mEh leh kõhn-trOhl dooh-ah-nyEh)*
remuneration	la rémunération	*(reh-mooh-neh-rah-syÕh)*
renegotiate (v)	renégocier	*(ræh-neh-goh-syEh)*
renew (v)	renouveler	*(ræh-noohv-lEh)*
renewable resources	les ressources renouvelables	*(ræh-soohrs ræh-nooh-vAh-blœh)*
rent	le loyer, la rente	*(loh-yEh), (rãhnt)*
rent (v)	louer, prendre en location	*(looh-Eh), (prÃhn-dræ ãhn loh-kah-syÕh)*
reorder (v)	passer commande	*(pah-sEh koh-mÃhnd)*
reorganization	la réorganisation	*(reh-ohr-gah-neeh-zah-syÕh)*
repair (v)	réparer	*(ræh-pah-rEh)*
repay (v)	rembourser	*(rãhm-boohr-sEh)*
repeat order	la commande de renouvellement	*(koh-mÃhnd dœ ræh-nooh-vehl-mÃh)*
replacement cost	le coût de remplacement	*(kOOht dœ rãhm-plahs-mÃh)*
replacement parts	les pièces de rechange	*(pyEhs dœ ræh-shÃhnzh)*
reply (v)	répondre	*(reh-pÕhn-dræ)*
reply, in . . . to	en réponse à	*(ãhn reh-pÕhns ah)*
report	le rapport	*(rah-pOhr)*
repossess (v)	reprendre possession	*(ræh-prÃhn-dræ poh-seh-syÕh)*
representative	le représentant	*(ræh-preh-zãhn-tÃh)*
reproduction costs	les frais de reproduction	*(frEh dœ ræ-proh-doohk-syÕh)*
request for bid	l'appel d'offre	*(ah-pEhl dOh-fræ)*
requirements	les besoins	*(bœh-zwÆhn)*
resale	la revente	*(ræ-vÃhnt)*
research and development	la recherche et le développement	*(ræ-shEhrsh eh lœ deh-veh-lohp-mÃh)*
research	la recherche	*(ræ-shEhrsh)*
reserve	la réserve	*(reh-sEhrv)*
resident buyer	l'acheteur résident	*(ahsh-tŒhr reh-zeeh-dÃh)*
residue	le résidu	*(reh-zeeh-dOOh)*
resilience	l'élasticité	*(eh-lahs-teeh-seeh-tEh)*
resistance	la résistance	*(reh-seehs-tÃhns)*
resolution (legal documents)	la résolution	*(reh-zoh-looh-syÕh)*
resonance	la résonance	*(reh-zoh-nÃhns)*
resource allocation	la répartition des ressources	*(reh-pahr-teeh-syÕh deh ræh-sOOhrs)*
response	la réaction	*(reh-ahk-syÕhn)*

restrictions on export	les restrictions à l'exportation	*(rœh-streehk-syÕh ah lehks-pohr-tah-syÕh)*
restrictive labor practices	la discrimination à l'embauche	*(deehs-kreeh-meeh-nah-syÕh ah lǽhm-bOhsh)*
restructure (v)	restructurer	*(rœh-stroohk-tooh-rEh)*
resume (v)	reprendre	*(rœh-prÃhn-drœ)*
résumé (n)	le curriculum vitae	
retail	la vente au détail	*(vÃhnt oh deh-tAhyœ)*
retail bank	la banque de détail	*(bÃhnk dœ deh-tAhyœ)*
retail merchandise	la marchandise de détail	*(mahr-shãhn-dEEhz dœ deh-tAhyœ)*
retail outlet	le magasin de détail, le point de vente	*(mah-gah-zǼhn dœ deh-tAhyœ), (pwǼh dœ vÃhnt)*
retail price	le prix de détail	*(prEEh dœ deh-tAhyœ)*
retail saìes tax	l'impôt sur les ventes au détail	*(ǽhm-pOh soohr leh vÃhnt oh deh-tAhyœ)*
retaiì trade	le commerce de détail	*(koh-mEhrs dœ deh-tAhyœ)*
retained earnings	les gains non distribués	*(gÉhn nõh deehs-treeh-bwEh)*
retained profits	les bénéfices non distribués	*(beh-neh-fEEhs nõh deehs-treeh-bwEh)*
retirement	la retraite	*(rœ-trEht)*
retrieve (v)	récupérer	*(reh-kooh-peh-rEh)*
retroactive	rétroactif	*(reh-troh-ahk-tEEf)*
return on assets managed	la rentabilité du capital investi	*(rãhn tah beeh leeh tEh dooh kah-peeh-tAhl ǽhn-vœhs-tEEh)*
return on capital	la rémunération du capital	*(reh-mooh-neh-rah-syÕh dooh kah-peeh-tAhl)*
return on equity	la rentabilité des capitaux propres	*(rãhn-tah-beeh-leeh-tEh deh kah-peeh-tOh prOh-prœ)*
return on investment	le rendement d'un investissement	*(rãhnd-mÃh dœhn œhn-vehs-teehz-mÃh)*
return on sales	le produit des ventes	*(proh-dwEEh deh vÃhnt)*
return, rate of	le taux de rendement	*(tOh dœ rãhnd-mÃh)*
reusable	réutilisable	*(reh-ooh-teeh-zAh-blœh)*
revaluation	la réévaluation	*(reh-eh-vah-lwah-syÕh)*
revenue	le revenu, les recettes	*(rœhv-nOOh), (rœh-sEht)*
revenue bond	l'obligation à intérêt conditionnel	*(oh-bleeh-gah-syÕh ah ǽhn-teh-rEh kõhn-deeh-syoh-nEhl)*
reverse stock split	la consolidation du capital	*(kõh-soh-leeh-dah-synOh dooh kah-peeh-tAhl)*
review (v)	examiner	*(eh-zah-meeh-nEh)*
revocable trust	la fiducie révocable	*(feeh-dooh-sEEh reh-voh-kAh-blœ)*

R

R

revolving credit	le crédit par acceptation renouvelable, le crédit tournant	*(kreh-dEEh pahr ahk-sehp-tah-syŌh ræh-nooh-veh-lAh-blœ), (kreh-dEEh toohr-nÃh)*
revolving fund	le fonds de roulement, le fonds tournant	*(fŌhn dœ roohl-mÃh), (fŌhn toohr-nÃh)*
reward	la rétribution	*(reh-treeh-booh-syŌh)*
rider (documents)	l'avenant, l'allonge	*(ah-væh-nÃh), (ah-lŌhnzh)*
right of recourse	le droit de recours	*(drwAh dœ ræh-kOOhr)*
right of way	le droit de passage	*(drwAh dœ pah-sAhzh)*
rights	les droits	*(drwAh)*
ring	le segment	*(seg-mnAhn)*
rinse (v)	rincer	*(ræhn-sEh)*
ripe	mûr	*(mOOhr)*
riot	l'émeute	*(eh-mŒht)*
risk	le risque	*(rEEhs-kœ)*
risk analysis	l'analyse du risque	*(ãh-nah-lEEhz dooh rEEhs-kœ)*
risk assessment	l'appréciation des risques	*(ah-preh-syah-syŌh deh rEEhs-kœ)*
risk capital	le capital de risque	*(kah-peeh-tAhl dœ rEEhs-kœ)*
risk-free	sans risque	*(sãhn rEEhsk)*
robot	le robot	*(roh-bOh)*
robust	charpenté, robuste	*(shahr-pãhn-tEh)*
rod	la baguette	*(bah-gEht)*
rollback	la baisse des prix imposés	*(bEhs deh prEEh æhm-poh-zEh)*
rolling mill	le laminoir	*(lah-meeh-nwAhr)*
rolling stock	le matériel roulant	*(mah-teh-ryEhl rooh-lÃh)*
rollover	le crédit à taux revisable	*(kreh-dEEh ah tOh ræh-veeh-zAh-blœ)*
roman (lettering)	romain	*(roh-mÃh)*
room temperature	chambré	*(shãhm-brEh)*
rosé wine	le rosé	*(roh-zEh)*
rough draft	l'esquisse	*(ehs-kEEhs)*
rough estimate	le devis approximatif	*(dœh-vEEh ah-prohk-seeh-mah-tEEhf)*
round lot	la quotité	*(koh-teeh-tEh)*
round platter	le plat rond	*(plAh rŌhn)*
routine	la routine	*(rooh-tEEhn)*
royalty (payment)	la redevance	*(ræh-dœh-vÃhns)*
royalties	les droits d'auteur	*(drwAh doh-tŒhr)*
rubbery	le goût de caoutchouc	*(gOOh dœ kah-oh-shOOh)*
rug	le tapis	*(tah-pEEh)*
run an ad (v)	faire passer une annonce	*(fehr pah-sEh oohn ah-nŌhns)*
running expenses	les dépenses courantes	*(deh-pãhns kooh-rÃhnt)*
runway	la piste	*(pEEhst)*
rush order	la commande urgente	*(koh-mÃhnd oohr-zhÃhnt)*

S

sable	la zibeline	*(zeeh-beh-lEEhn)*
saccharin	la saccharine	*(sah-kah-rEEhn)*
saddle	la selle de cheval	*(sEhl dœ shœh-vAhl)*
saddler	le sellier	*(seh-lyEh)*
safe deposit box	le compartiment d'un coffre-fort	*(kõhm-pahr-teeh-mÃh dœhn kOhf-rœ fOhr)*
safe investment	les valeurs de père de famille, les valeurs sûres	*(vah-lŒhr dœ pEhr dœ fah-mEEh-yœ), (vah-lŒhr sOOhr)*
safeguard	la sauvegarde	*(sohv-gAhrd)*
salad bowl	le saladier	*(sah-lah-dyEh)*
salad plate	l'assiette à salade	*(ah-syEht ah sah-lAhd)*
salary	le traitement, les émoluments, les gages, la rétribution	*(treht-mÃh), (eh-moh-looh-mÃh), (gAzh), (reh-treeh-booh-syÕh)*
sale and leaseback	la cession-bail	*(seh-syÕh beh)*
sale through mail order	la vente par correspondance	*(vÃhnt pahr koh-rehs-põhn-dÃhns)*
sales	les ventes	*(vÃhnt)*
sales analysis	l'analyse des ventes	*(ãh-nah-lEEhz deh vÃhnt)*
sales budget	le budget des ventes	*(booh-zhEh deh vÃhnt)*
sales estimate	l'estimation des ventes	*(ehs-teeh-mah-syÕh deh vÃhnt)*
sales force	l'équipe des vendeurs	*(eh-kEEhp deh vÃhn-dŒhr)*
sales forecast	la prévision de vente	*(preh-veeh-zyÕh dœ vÃhnt)*
sales management	le service des ventes	*(sœr-vEEhs deh vÃhnt)*
sales promotion	la promotion des ventes	*(proh-moh-syÕh deh vÃhnt)*
sales quota	les contingents de vente	*(kõhn-teehn-zhÃhn dœ vÃhnt)*
sales tax	l'impôt sur le chiffre d'affaires, la taxe á l'achat	*(ãhm-pOh soohr lœ shEEh-frœ dah-fEhr), (tAhks ah lah-shAh)*
sales territory	le secteur des ventes	*(sehk-tŒhr deh vÃhnt)*
sales volume	le volume des ventes, le chiffre d'affaires	*(voh-lOOhm deh vÃhnt), (shEEh-frœ dah-fEhr)*
salt	le sel	*(sEhl)*
salt shaker	la salière	*(sah-lyEhr)*
salts	les sels	*(sEhl)*
salvage (v)	récupérer	*(reh-kooh-peh-rEh)*
salvage charges	la prime de sauvetage, les frais de sauvetage	*(prEEhm dœ soh-veh-tAhzh), (frEh dœ soh-veh-tAhzh)*
salvage value	la valeur résiduelle, la valeur de liquidation	*(vah-lŒhr reh-zeeh-dwEhl), (vah-lŒhr dœ leeh-keeh-dah-syÕh)*

salve	la pommade	*(poh-mAhd)*
sample (v)	échantillonner	*(eh-shãhn-teeh-yoh-nEh)*
sample line	la ligne d'échantillons	*(lEEh-nyœ eh-shãhn-teeh-yÕh)*
sample size	le format échantillon	*(fohr-mAht eh-shãhn-teeh-yÕh)*
saponification	la saponification	*(sah-poh-neeh-feeh-kah-synOh)*
satellite	le satellite	*(sah-teh-lEEht)*
satellite TV	la télévision par satellite	*(teh-leh-veeh-zyÕhn pahr sah-teh-lEEht)*
saucer	la soucoupe	*(sooh-kOOhp)*
savings	l'épargne	*(eh-pAhr-nyœ)*
savings account	le compte épargne	*(kõhnt eh-pAhr-nyœh)*
savings bank	la banque d'épargne, la caisse d'épargne	*(bÃhnk deh-pAhr-nyœ), (kEhs deh-pAhr-nyœ)*
savings bond	le bon d'épargne	*(bÕh deh-pAhr-nyœ)*
scale	la balance	*(bsah-lÃhns)*
scanner	le scanneur	*(skah-nŒhr)*
scanning	le balayage	*(bah-lah-yAhzh)*
scarf	le foulard	*(fooh-lAhr)*
schedule	le programme	*(proh-grAhm)*
scissor case	l'étui à ciseaux	*(eh-twEEh ah seeh-zOh)*
scoring	la coordination	*(koh-ohr-deeh-nah-syÕh)*
scrap	les déchets ou la ferraille	*(deh-shEht ooh feh-rAh-yœ)*
screen	l'écran	*(eh-krÃhn)*
screening	le filtrage, le dépistage	*(feehl-trAhzh), (deh-peehs-tAhzh)*
script	le document original, le manuscrit	*(doh-kooh-mÃh oh-reeh-zheeh-nAhl), (mah-nooh-srEEh)*
sealed bid	le pli cacheté contenant une offre, la soumission	*(pleeh kash-tEh kõhn-tœh-nÃhnt oohn Oh-frœ), (sooh-meeh-syÕh)*
sealskin	la peau de phoque	*(pOh dœ fOhk)*
seasonal	saisonnier	*(seh-soh-nyEh)*
seat	le siège	*(syEhzh)*
second mortgage	la deuxième hypothèque	*(dœh-zyEhm eeh-poh-tEhk)*
second position	la deuxième position	*(dœh-zyEhm poh-zeeh-syÕh)*
secondary market (securities)	le marché secondaire	*(mahr-shEh sœ-kõhn-dEhr)*
secondary offering (securities)	l'offre secondaire	*(Oh-frœ sœ-kõhn-dEhr)*
secretary	la, le secrétaire	*(seh-kreh-tEhr)*
secured accounts	les comptes garantis	*(kÕhnt gah-rãhn-tEEh)*
securities	les titres, les valeurs	*(tEEh-trœ), (vah-lŒhr)*
security	la garantie, la sécurité	*(gah-rãhn-tEEh), (seh-kooh-reeh-tEh)*
sedan	la berline	*(behr-lEEhn)*

sedative	le sédatif	(seh-dah-tEEhf)
self-appraisal	l'auto-appréciation	(oh-toh-ah-preh-syah-syÕh)
self-employed	indépendant	(æhn-deh-pãhn-dÃhnt)
self-financing	l'autofinancement	(oh-toh-freeh-nahns-mÃhn)
self-management	l'autogestion	(oh-toh-zhœhs-tyÕh)
self-service	le libre-service	(lEEh-brœ sœr-vEEhs)
self-sufficiency	l'autarcie	(oh-tahr-sEEh)
sell (v)	vendre	(vÃhn-drœ)
sell direct (v)	vendre directement	(vÃhn-drœ deeh-rehkt-mÃh)
sell, hard	la vente par des méthodes agressives	(vÃhnt pahr deh meh-tOhd ah-greh-sEEhv)
sell, soft	la vente par des méthodes de suggestion	(vÃhnt pahr deh meh-tOhd dœ sooh-zhœhs-tyÕh)
semiconductor	le semi-conducteur	(sœh-meeh-kõhn-doohk-tŒhr)
semis	les semis	(sœh-mEEh)
semivariable costs	les dépenses semi-variables	(deh-pãhns sœ-meeh-vah-ryAh-blœ)
senior issue	l'émission de premier rang	(eh-meeh-syÕh dœ prœh-myeh rÃhng)
seniority	l'ancienneté	(ãhn-syeh-nœh-tEh)
sensitive skin	la peau sensible	(pOh sãhn-sEEh-blœh)
separation	la séparation	(seh-pah-rah-syÕh)
serial bonds	les obligations échéant en série	(oh-bleeh-gah-syÕh eh-sheh-Ãhnt ãhn seh-rEEh)
serial film	le feuilleton	(fœhy-tÕhn)
serial storage	la mémoire par série	(meh-mwAhr pahr seh-rEEh)
serum	le sérum	(seh-rOOhm)
service (v)	assurer l'entretien	(ah-sooh-rEh lãhn-trœh-tyÆhn)
service contract	le contrat d'entretien	(kõhn-trAh dãhn-trœh-tyÆhn)
service, advisory	le service de conseil	(sœr-vEEhs dœ kõhn-sEh-yœ)
service, customer	le service clients	(sœr-vEEhs kleeh-Ãhn)
set-up costs	les frais d'installation	(frEh dãhn-stah-lah-syÕh)
settlement	le règlement	(reh-glœh-mÃh)
settlement, full	la liquidation totale, la liquidation solde de tout compte	(leeh-keeh-dah-syÕh toh-tAhl), (leeh-keeh-dah-syÕh sOhld dœ tooh kÕhnt)
severance pay	l'indemnité de licenciement	(æhn-dehm-neeh-tEh dœ leeh-sãhn-seeh-mÃh)
sew (v)	coudre	(kOOh-drœ)

S

sewing kit	la trousse à couture	(trOOhs ah kooh-tOOhr)
sewing machine	la machine à coudre	(mah-shEEhn ah kOOh-drœ)
sewn	broché	(broh-shEh)
shade	l'abat-jour	(ah-bah-zhOOhr)
shareholder	l'actionnaire	(ahk-syoh-nEhr)
shareholder's equity	les capitaux propres de l'actionnaire	(kah-peeh-tOh prOh-prœ dœ lahk-syoh-nEhr)
shareholders' meeting	l'assemblée des actionnaires	(ah-sāhm-blEh dehz ahk-syoh-nEhr)
shares	les actions	(ahk-syŌh)
sheet	la feuille, le drap	(fŒh-yœ), (drAh)
sheets	la tôle	(tOhl)
shell	l'obus	(oh-bOOhs)
shift (labor)	l'équipe	(eh-kEEhp)
shipment	l'expédition	(ehks-peh-deeh-syŌh)
shipper	l'expéditeur	(ehks-peh-deeh-tŒhr)
shipping agent	l'agent maritime	(ah-zhÃh mah-reeh-tEEhm)
shipping charges	les frais d'expédition	(frEh dehks-peh-deeh-syŌh)
shipping expenses	les dépenses d'expédition	(deh-pāhns dehks-peh-deeh-syŌh)
shipping instructions	les instructions d'expédition	(āhn-stroohk-syŌh dehks-peh-deeh-syŌh)
shipping memo	le bordereau d'expédition	(bohr-dœ-rOh dehks-peh-deeh-syŌh)
shirt	la chemise	(shœh-mEEhz)
shock absorber	l'amortisseur	(ah-mohr-teeh-sŒhr)
shoe	la chaussure	(shoh-sOOhr)
shoot	le tournage	(toohr-nAhzh)
shoot (film) (v)	tourner	(toohr-nEh)
shopping center	le centre commercial	(sÃhn-trœ koh-mehr-syAhl)
short delivery	la livraison incomplète	(leeh-vreh-zŌh āhn-kohm-plEht)
short film	le court-métrage	(koohr-meh-trAzh)
short of, be (v)	être à court de	(Eh-trœ ah kOOhr dœ)
short position	la position à la baisse	(poh-zeeh-syŌh ah lah bEhs)
short sale	la vente à découvert	(vÃhnt ah deh-kooh-vEhrt)
short shipment	le chargement incomplet	(shahrzh-mÃh āhn-kohm-plEh)
short sleeves	les manches courtes	(mÃhnsh kOOhrt)
short supply	l'approvisionnement insuffisant	(ah-proh-veeh-zyohn-mÃh āhn-sooh-feeh-zÃh)
short wave	l'onde courte	(Ohnd-kOOhrt)
short-range	à courte portée	(ah koohrt pohr-tEh)
short-term capital account	le compte de capital à court terme	(kŌhnt dœ kah-peeh-tAhl ah koohr tEhrm)
short-term debt	la dette à court terme	(DEht ah koohr tEhrm)

short-term financing	le financement à court terme	*(feeh-nãhns-mÃh ah koohr tEhrm)*
shortage	la pénurie	*(peh-nooh-rEEh)*
shoulder pad	l'épaulette	*(eh-poh-lEht)*
shrink-wrapped	emballé sous film rétractable	*(ãhm-bah-lEh sooh fEEhlm reh-trahk-tAh-blœ)*
shuttle	la navette	*(nah-vEht)*
sick leave	le congé de maladie	*(kõhn-zhEh dœ mah-kah-dEEh)*
side effect	l'effet secondaire (m)	*(eh-fEh seh-kohn-dEhr)*
sight draft	la traite à vue	*(trEht ah vOOh)*
signature	la signature	*(seehg-nah-tOOhr)*
silent partner	le commanditaire	*(koh-mahn-deeh-tEhr)*
silicon	le silicone	*(seeh-leeh-kÕhn)*
silk	la soie	*(swAh)*
silk factory	la soirie	*(swah-rEEh)*
silk goods	les soiries	*(swah-rEEh)*
silk manufacturers (Lyon)	les soyeux	*(soh-yOh)*
silkworm	le ver à soie	*(vEhr ah swAh)*
silky	soyeux	*(swah-yŒh)*
silverware	l'argenterie	*(ahr-zhãhn-tœh-rEEh)*
simulate (v)	simuler	*(seeh-mooh-lEh)*
single market	le marché unique	*(mahr-shEh ooh-neeh-kEh)*
sinking fund	le fonds d'amortissement	*(fÕhn dah-mohr-eehs-mÃh)*
sinus	le sinus	*(seeh-nOOhs)*
six-cylinder engine	le moteur à six cylindres	*(moh-tŒhr ah sEEhs seeh-lÃhn-drœ)*
size	la dimension, la taille	*(deeh-mãhn-syÕh), (tAh-yœ)*
skilled labor	la main-d'œuvre qualifiée	*(mÃhn dŒh-vrœ kah-leeh-feeh-Eh)*
skin	l'épiderme, la peau	*(eh-peeh-dEhr-mœh), (pOh)*
skin tone	la tonicité	*(toh-neeh-seeh-tEh)*
skirt	la jupe	*(zhOOhp)*
slabs	les brames	*(brAhm)*
sleeping pill	le somnifère	*(sohm-nee-fEhr)*
slice	la tranche	*(trÃhnsh)*
sliding parity	la parité mobile	*(pah-reeh-tEh moh-bEEhl)*
sliding scale	l'échelle mobile	*(eh-shEhl moh-bEEhl)*
slippers	les chaussons	*(shoh-sÕh)*
slogan	le slogan	*(sloh-gÃhn)*
slump	l'effondrement, le marasme	*(eh-fõn-drœ-mÃh), (mah-rAhz-mœ)*
small business	la petite entreprise	*(pœh-tEEht ãhn-trœh-prEEhz)*
smell (v)	humer	*(ooh-mEh)*
smoky smell	l'odeur de fumée	*(oh-dŒhr dœ fooh-mEh)*
smooth	lisse	*(lEEhs)*

S

snakeskin	la peau de serpent	*(pOh dœ sœhr-pÃh)*
sneak preview	l'avant-première	*(ah-vÃhn-prœh-myEhr)*
sneeze (v)	éternuer	*(eh-tœhr-nwEh)*
socks	les chaussettes	*(shoh-sEht)*
soft	doux (ce)	*(dOOh)*
soft cover	la couverture souple	*(kooh-vehr-tOOhr sOOh-plœ)*
soft currency	la devise faible	*(dœh-vEEhz fEh-blœ)*
soft goods	les tissus	*(teeh-sOOh)*
soft loan	le crédit à taux privilégié	*(kreh-dEEh ah tOh preeh-veeh-leh-zhyEh)*
soft sell	la vente par des méthodes de suggestion	*(vÃhnt pahr deh meh-tOhd dœ sooh-zhœhs-tyÕh)*
software	le logiciel, le software	*(loh-zheeh-syEhl)*
software broker	le courtier en logiciel	*(koohr-tyEh ãhn loh-zheeh-syEhl)*
soil erosion	l'érosion des sols	*(eh-roh-zyÕhn deh sOhl)*
solar energy	l'énergie solaire	*(eh-nehr-zhEEh soh-lEhr)*
soldier	le soldat	*(sohl-dAh)*
sole agent	l'agent exclusif	*(ah-zhÃh ehks-klooh-sEEhf)*
sole proprietorship	l'entreprise individuelle	*(ãhn-trœh-prEEhz æhn-deeh-veeh-dwEhl)*
sole rights	les droits exclusifs	*(drwAh ehks-klooh-sEEhf)*
solubility	la solubilité	*(soh-looh-beeh-leeh-tEh)*
solute	le soluté	*(soh-looh-tE)*
solution	la solution	*(soh-looh-synOh)*
solvency	la solvabilité	*(sohl-vah-beeh-leeh-tEh)*
solvent	le solvant	*(sohl-vÃh)*
sort (v)	trier	*(treeh-Eh)*
sound	le son	*(sÕh)*
sound effects	les trucages sonores	*(trooh-kAhzh soh-nOhr)*
sound track	la bande son	*(bÃhnd sÕhn)*
soup dish	l'assiette creuse	*(ah-syEht krŒhz)*
soup ladle	la louche	*(lOOhsh)*
soup tureen	la soupière	*(sooh-pyEhr)*
sour	âcre	*(Ah-krœ)*
sovereignty	la souveraineté	*(sooh-vræhn-oeh-tEh)*
space buying	l'achat d'espace	*(ah-shAh dehs-pAhs)*
space station	la station spatiale	*(stah-syÕhn spah-syAhl)*
spacecraft	le vaisseau spatial	*(veh-sOh spah-syAhl)*
spacelab	le laboratoire spatial	*(lah-boh-rah-twAhr spah-syAhl)*
spacesuit	le scaphandre	*(skah-fAhn-drœh)*
spacewalk	la marche dans l'espace	*(mAhrsh dãhn leh-spAhs)*
spare tire	la roue de secours	*(rOOh dœ sœh-kOOhr)*
spark plug	la bougie	*(booh-zhEEh)*
sparkle	l'éclat	*(eh-klAh)*
sparkling wine	le vin mousseux	*(vÆhn mooh-sOh)*
speaker	le haut-parleur	*(Oht pahr-lŒhr)*

S

specialist (stock exchange)	le spécialiste en certaines valeurs	*(speh-syah-lEEhst āhn sœhr-tEhn vah-lŒhr)*
specialty goods	les produits spéciaux	*(proh-dwEEh speh-syOh)*
specialty steels	les aciers spéciaux	*(ahs-yEh speh-syOh)*
specific duty	le droit spécifique	*(drwAh speh-seeh-fEEhk)*
spectrum	le spectre	*(spEhk-trœ)*
speculator	le spéculateur, l'accompagnateur	*(speh-kooh-lah-tŒhr), (ah-kõhm-ah-nyah-tŒhr)*
speech bubble	la bulle	*(bOOhl)*
speed up (v)	accélérer	*(ahk-seh-leh-rEh)*
speedometer	le compteur de vitesse	*(kõhmp-tŒhr dœ veeh-tEhs)*
spellcheck	le contrôle orthographique	*(kõhn-trOhl ohr-toh-grah-fEEhk)*
spin-off	la retombée	*(rœh-tõhm-bEh)*
spine	le dos	*(dOhs)*
split, stock	le fractionnement des actions	*(frahk-syohn-mĀh dehz ahk syÕh)*
spoilage	les déchets	*(deh-shEht)*
spoiled	altéré, souillé	*(ahl-teh-rEh), (swee-yEh)*
sponsor (v)	commanditer, parrainer	*(koh-māhn-deeh-tEhr), (pah-reh-nEh)*
sponsor (of fund, partnership)	le répondant	*(reh-pōhn-dĀhn)*
spoon	la cuiller, cuillère	*(kooh-yEhr)*
sportswear	les vêtements de sport	*(veht-mĀh dœ spOhr)*
spot delivery	la livraison immédiate, l'opération au comptant	*(leeh-vreh-zÕh eeh-meh-dyAht), (oh peh-rah-syÕh oh kõhn-tĀhn)*
spot market	le marché du disponible, le marché au comptant	*(mahr-shEh dooh deehs-poh-nEEh-blœ), (mahr-shEh oh kõhn-tĀhn)*
spout	le bec verseur	*(bEhk vehr-sŒhr)*
spray	le vaporisateur, l'atomiseur	*(vah-poh-reeh-zah-tŒhr), (ah-toh-meeh-zŒhr)*
spread	l'écart des cours	*(eh-kAhr deh kOOhr)*
spreadsheet	le tableau financier	*(tah-blOh feeh-nāhn-syEh)*
spring	le ressort	*(rœh-sOhr)*
staff	le personnel, l'état-major	*(pehr-soh-nEhl), (eh-tAh mah-zhOhr)*
staff and line	organisation mixte (état-major et responsables sur le terrain)	*(ohr-gah-neeh-zah-syÕh meehk-stœ), (eh-tAh mah-zhOhr rehs-põhn-sAh-blœ soohr lœ tœ-rÆhn)*
staff assistant	le cadre adjoint	*(kAh-drœ ad-zhwÆhn)*
staff organization	la direction du personnel	*(deeh-rehk-syÕh dooh pehr-soh-nEhl)*
stagflation	la stagflation	*(stahg-flah-syÕh)*

S

stainless steel	l'acier inoxydable	*(ahs-yEh ãehn-ohk-seeh-dAh-blœ)*
stale check	le chèque périmé	*(shEhk peh-reeh-mEh)*
stalking	l'égrappage	*(eh-grah-pAhzh)*
stand in line (v)	faire la queue	*(fEhr la kOOh)*
stand-alone text processor	la machine à traitement de texte autonome	*(mah-shEEhn ah treht-mÃh dœ tEhk-stœ oh-toh-nOhm)*
stand-alone workstation	le poste de travail autonome	*(pOhst dœ trah-vAhyœ oh-toh-nOhm)*
standard	la norme	*(nOhrm)*
standard costs	les coûts standard	*(kOOht stahn-dAhr)*
standard deviation	l'écart type	*(eh-kAhr tEEhp)*
standard of living	le niveau de vie	*(neeh-vŒ dœ vEEh)*
standard practice	le procédé type	*(proh-seh-dEh tEEhp)*
standard time	le temps normal, l'heure normale	*(tÃh nohr-mAhl), (Œhr nohr-mAhl)*
standardization	la normalisation	*(nohr-mah-leeh-zah-syÕh)*
standardize (v)	homogénéiser	*(oh-moh-zheh-neh-eeh-zEh)*
standing charges	les frais permanents	*(frEh pehr-mah-nÃh)*
standing costs	les frais fixes	*(frEh fEEhks)*
standing order	l'ordre permanent	*(Ohr-drœ pehr-mah-nÃh)*
starch	l'amidon	*(ah-meeh-dÕh)*
start-up cost	les frais d'établissement	*(frEh deh-tah-bleehs-mÃh)*
starter	le démarreur	*(deh-mah-rŒhr)*
statement	l'état	*(eh-tAh)*
statement of account	le relevé de compte	*(rœh-lœh-vEh dœ kÕhnt)*
statement, financial	l'état financier	*(eh-tAh feeh-nãhn-syEh)*
statement, pro forma	l'état pro forma	*(eh-tAh proh-fOhr-mah)*
statement, profit-and-loss	l'état des pertes et profits	*(eh-tAh deh pEhrt eh proh-fEEh)*
statistics	les statistiques	*(stah-teehs-tEEhk)*
statute	le statut	*(stah-tOOh)*
statute of limitations	la prescription légale	*(prehs-kreehp-syÕh leh-gAhl)*
stay separate (v)	faire cavalier seul	*(fehr kah-vah-lyEh sŒhl)*
steel mill	l'acierie	*(ahs-yeh-rEEh)*
steering	la direction	*(deeh-rehk-syÕh)*
steering wheel	le volant	*(voh-lÃh)*
stereophonic	stéréophonique	*(steh-reh-oh-foh-nEEhk)*
stimulant	le stimulant	*(steeh-mooh-lÃh)*
stitch	le point	*(pwÆhn)*
stock	les valeurs, les titres, le stock, l'action	*(vah-lŒhr), (tEEh-trœ), (ahk-syÕhn)*
stock certificate	le titre de bourse	*(tEEh-trœ dœ bOOhrs)*
stock control	la gestion des stocks	*(zhœhs-tyÕh deh stocks)*

Stock Exchange	la Bourse	*(bOOhrs)*
stock index	l'indice des actions	*(ãhn-dEEhs dehz ahk-syŌh)*
stock market	le marché des actions, la bourse	*(mahr-shEh dehz ahk-syŌh), (bOOhrs)*
stock option	l'option en bourse	*(ohp-syŌh ãhn bOOhrs)*
stock power	le pouvoir pour le transfert et la vente d'actions	*(pooh-vwAhr poohr lœ_ trãhnz-fEhr eh lah vÃhnt dahk-syŌh)*
stock profit	la plus-value des titres	*(plooh-vah-lOOh deh tEEh-trœ)*
stock purchase	l'achat de titres	*(ah-shAh dœ tEEh-trœ)*
stock split	le fractionnement des actions	*(frahk-syohn-mÃh dehz ahk-syŌh)*
stock takeover	le rachat	*(rah-shAh)*
stock turnover	la rotation des stocks	*(roh-tah-syŌh des stocks)*
stock-in-trade	stocks et fournitures en magasin ct fabrication en cours	*(stocks eh foohr-neeh-tOOhr ãhn mah-gah-zÆhn eh fah-breeh-kah-syŌh ãhn kOOhr)*
stockbroker	l'agent de bourse	*(ah-zhÃhn dœ bOOhrs)*
stockholder	l'actionnaire	*(ahk-syoh-nEhr)*
stockholder's equity	le capital propre	*(kah-peeh-tAhl prOh-prœ)*
stockings	les bas	*(bAh)*
stocks (and bonds)	les valeurs mobilières	*(vah-lŒhr moh-beeh-lyEhr)*
stoneware	la poterie en grès	*(poh-teh-rEEh ãhn grEh)*
stop-payment	le paiement bloqué	*(peh-mÃh bloh-kEh)*
storage	l'entreposage, la mise en mémoire	*(ãhn-trœ-poh-sAhzh), (meehz ãhn meh-mwAhr)*
store	le magasin, la réserve	*(mah-gah-zÆhn), (reh-zEhrv)*
stowage	l'arrimage	*(ah-reeh-mAhzh)*
stowage charges	les frais d'arrimage	*(frEh dah-reeh-mAhzh)*
straddle	l'opération mixte (option d'achat plus option à la vente)	*(oh-peh-rah-syŌh mEEhks-tœ), (ohp-syŌh dah-shAh ploohz ohp-syŌh ah lah vÃhnt)*
strapping	l'opération mixte (une vente, deux achats)	*(oh-peh-rah-syŌh mEEhks-tœ), (oohn vÃhnt dŒhz ah-shAh)*
strategic articles	les articles stratégiques	*(ahr-tEEh-klœ strah-teh-zhEEhk)*
streamline (v)	rationaliser	*(rah-syoh-nah-leeh-zEh)*
stress management	la tension des dirigeants	*(tãhn-syŌh deh deeh-reeh-zhÃhn)*
strike (v)	faire la grève	*(fEhr lah grEhv)*
strike day	le jour de grève	*(zhOOhr dœ grEhv)*

S

strike, wildcat	la grève sauvage	*(grEhv soh-vAhzh)*
strikebreaker	le briseur de grève	*(breeh-zŒhr dœ grEhv)*
stripping	le montage	*(mõhn-tAhzh)*
structural shapes	l'acier de construction	*(ahs-yEh dœ kõhn-stroohk-syÕh)*
stuffing	le bourrage	*(booh-rAhzh)*
style	le style	*(stEEhl)*
stylist	le styliste	*(steeh-lEEhst)*
subcontract	le contrat de sous-traitance	*(kõhn-trAh dœ sooh-treh-tÃhns)*
subcontractor	le sous-traitant	*(sooh-treh-tÃh)*
sublet (v)	sous-louer	*(sooh-looh-Eh)*
subscriber	l'abonné (e)	*(ah-boh-nEh)*
subscription price	le prix de souscription, le prix de l'abonnement	*(prEEh dœ sooh-skreehp-syÕh), (prEEh dœ lah-bohn-mnAh)*
subsidiary	la filiale	*(feeh-lyAhl)*
subsidize (v)	subventionner	*(soohb-vãhn-syoh-nEh)*
subsidy	la subvention	*(soohb-vãhn-syÕhn)*
subtle	subtile	*(soohb-tEEhl)*
substandard	au-dessous de la norme	*(oh dœ-sOOh dœ lah nOhrm)*
suede	le suède	*(swEhd)*
suede jacket	le blouson de daim	*(blooh-zÕh dœ dEhm)*
sugar bowl	le sucrier	*(sooh-kryEh)*
sugar content	le pourcentage de sucre	*(poohr-sãhn-tAhzh dœ sOOh-krœ)*
sugar tongs	la pince à sucre	*(pÆhns ah sOOh-krœh)*
suit	le complet	*(kõhm-plEh)*
suitcase	la valise	*(vah-lEEhz)*
sulfite (n)	sulfiter	*(soohl-feeh-tEh)*
sulfuric acid	l'acide sulfurique	*(ah-sEEhd soohl-fooh-rEEhk)*
sulphamide	le sulfamide	*(soohl-fah-mEEhd)*
sum-of-the-year digits	l'amortissement proportionnel à l'ordre numérique inversé des années	*(ah-mohr-eehs-mÃh proh-pohr-syoh-nEhl ah lOhr-drœ nooh-meh-rEEhk æhn-vœhr-sEh dehz ah-nEh)*
summit meeting	la réunion au sommet	*(reh-ooh-nyÕhn oh soh-mEh)*
sun block	l'écran solaire	*(eh-krÃhn soh-lEhr)*
sun lotion	la lotion solaire	*(loh-syÕhn soh-lEhr)*
super alloys	les super alliages	*(sooh-pehr ah-lyAhzh)*
supersede (v)	remplacer	*(rãhm-plah-sEh)*
supervisor	le chef d'atelier	*(shEhf dah-teh-lyEh)*
supple	souple	*(sOOh-plœh)*
supplier	le fournisseur	*(foohr-neeh-sŒhr)*
supply and demand	l'offre et la demande	*(Oh-frœ eh lah dœh-mÃhnd)*

S

supply services	les services d'intendance	*(sœr-vEEhs dǽhn-tāhn-dĀhns)*
support activities	les activités de soutien	*(ahk-teeh-veeh-tEh dœ sooh-tyǼh)*
surcharge	la surcharge	*(soohr-shAhrzh)*
surety company	la société de cautionnement	*(soh-syeh-tEh dœ koh-syohn-mĀh)*
surgery	la chirurgie	*(sheeh-roohr-zhEEh)*
surplus capital	le capital de réserve	*(kah-peeh-tAhl dœ reh-zEhrv)*
surplus goods	les excédents	*(ehk-seh-dĀhn)*
surrogate mother	la mère porteuse	*(mEhr pohr-tŒhz)*
surtax	la surtaxe	*(soohr-tAhks)*
suspended payment	le paiement en souffrance	*(peh-mĀh ãhn sooh-frĀhns)*
suspension	la suspension	*(soohs-pãhn-syÕh)*
sustainable resources	les ressources soutenables	*(rœh-soohrs seeh-teh-nAh-blœh)*
sweater	le pull-over	
sweet and sour	aigre-doux	*(Eh-greoh dOOh)*
switch	le commutateur, l'interrupteur	*(koh-mooh-tah-tŒhr), (ǽhn-teh-roohp-tŒhr)*
switching charges	les frais reportés	*(frEh rœh-pœhr-tEh)*
sworn	assermenté	*(ah-sœhr-mãhn-tEh)*
symptom	le symptome	*(sœhn-tOhm)*
syndicate	le syndicat, le consortium	*(seehn-deeh-kAh), (kõhn-sohr-tyOOhn)*
synthesis	la synthèse	*(seehn-tEhz)*
synthetic	synthétique	*(sǽhn-teeh-tEEhk)*
syringe	la seringue	*(sœh-rǼhng)*
systems analysis	l'analyse des systèmes	*(ãh-nah-lEEhz deh seehs-tEhm)*
systems design	la conception de systèmes	*(kõhn-sehp-syÕh dœ seehs-tEhm)*
systems engineering	l'organisation des systèmes	*(ohr-gah-neeh-zah-syÕh deh seehs-tEhm)*
systems management	la gestion des systèmes	*(zhœhs-tyÕh deh seehs-tEhm)*

T

table of contents	la table des matières	*(tAh-blœ deh mah-tyEhr)*
tablecloth	la nappe	*(nAhp)*
tablespoon	la cuiller à soupe	*(kooh-yEhr ah sOOhp)*
tablet	la tablette	*(tah-blEht)*
taffeta	le taffetas	*(tah-feh-tAh)*
tailor	le tailleur	*(tah-yŒhr)*
take	la prise de vue	*(prEEhz dœ vOOh)*
take down (v)	prendre note	*(prĀhn-drœ nOht)*

take off (v)	décoller, faire un rabais	*(deh-koh-lEh), (fEhr œhn rah-bEh)*
take out (v)	contracter	*(kõhn-trAhk-tEh)*
take-home pay	le salaire net	*(sah-lEhr nEht)*
takeover	le rachat	*(rah-shAh)*
takeover bid	l'offre publique d'achat (OPA)	*(Oh-frœ pooh-blEEhk dah-shAh)*
talks	les pourparlers	*(poohr-pahr-lEh)*
tamperproof package	l'emballage inviolable	*(æhm-bah-lAhzh æhn-vyoh-lAh-blœh)*
tan (v)	tanner	*(tah-nEh)*
tangible assets	les valeurs matérielles	*(vah-lŒhr mah-teh-ryEhl)*
tank	le char	*(shAhr)*
tanker	le wagon-citerne, le bateau-citerne, le camion-citerne	*(vah-gÕh seeh-tEhrn), (bah-tOh seeh-tEhrn), (kah-myÕh seeh-tEhrn)*
tanner	le tanneur	*(tah-nŒhr)*
tannery	la tannerie	*(tah-neh-rEEh)*
tannin (tanin)	le tannin (le tanin)	*(tah-nÆhn)*
tap the forest's wealth	exploiter les ressources forestières	*(ehks-plwah-tEh leh ræh-soohrs foh-rehs-tyEhr)*
tape recorder	l'enregistreur	*(āhn-ræh-zheehs-trŒhr)*
target audience	le public-cible	*(pooh-blEEhk sEEh-blœh)*
target market	le marché-cible	*(mahr-shEh sEEh-blœh)*
target price	le prix cible	*(prEEh sEEh-blœ)*
tariff	le tarif	*(tah-rEEhf)*
tariff barriers	les barrières tarifaires	*(bah-ryEhr tah-reeh-fEhr)*
tariff charge	les charges tarifaires	*(shAhrzh tah-reeh-fEhr)*
tariff classification	la classification tarifaire	*(klah-seeh-feeh-kah-syÕh tah-reeh-fEhr)*
tariff commodities	les produits figurant au tarif douanier	*(proh-dwEEh feeh-gooh-rÃhnt oh tah-rEEhf dooh-ah-nyEh)*
tariff differential	l'écart tarifaire	*(eh-kAhr tah-reeh-fEhr)*
tariff war	la guerre tarifaire	*(gEhr tah-reeh-fEhr)*
tart	acide, âpre	*(ah-sEEhd), (Ah-prœh)*
task force	le groupe de travail	*(grOOhp dœ trah-vAhyœ)*
taste (v)	déguster	*(deh-goohs-tEh)*
tasteless	fade	*(fAhd)*
tasting	la dégustation	*(deh-goohs-tah-syÕh)*
tax	l'impôt, la taxe	*(æhm-pOh), (tAhks)*
tax allowance	l'exonération fiscale, l'abattement fiscal	*(ehks-oh-neh-rah-syÕh feehs-kAhl), (ah-baht-mÃh feehs-kAhl)*
tax base	l'assiette de l'impôt	*(ah-syEht dœ læhm-pOh)*
tax break	l'avantage fiscal	*(ah-vāhn-tAhzh feehs-kAhl)*
tax burden	la pression fiscale	*(prœh-syÕh feehs-kAhl)*
tax collector	le percepteur	*(pehr-sehp-tŒhr)*

tax deduction	la déduction fiscale	*(deh-doohk-syÕh feehs-kAhl)*
tax evasion	la fraude fiscale	*(frOhd feehs-kAhl)*
tax haven	le paradis fiscal	*(pah-rah-dEEh feehs-kAhl)*
tax relief	le dégrèvement	*(deh-grehv-mÃh)*
tax shelter	le paradis fiscal	*(pah-rah-dEEh feehs-kAhl)*
tax, excise	le droit d'accise	*(drwAh dahk-sEEhz)*
tax, export	la taxe à l'exportation	*(tAhks ah lehks-pohr-tah-syÕh)*
tax, import	la taxe à l'importation	*(tAhks ah lǽhm-pohr-tah-syÕh)*
tax, sales	la taxe sur le chiffre d'affaires	*(tAhks soohr lœ shEEh-frœ dah-fEhr)*
tax-free	exempt d'impôts	*(ek-zÃhn dǽhn-pOh)*
tax-free income	le revenu libre d'impôt	*(rœhv-nOOh lEEh-brœ dǽhm-pOh)*
taxable	imposable	*(ǽhn-poh-zAh-blœh)*
taxation	l'imposition, la taxation	*(ǽhm-poh-zeeh-syÕh), (tahks-ah-syÕh)*
teacup	la tasse à thé	*(tAhs ah tEh)*
team management	l'équipe de gestion	*(eh-kEEhp dœ zhœhs-tyÕh)*
teapot	la théière	*(teh-yEhr)*
teaspoon	la cuiller à cafe	*(kooh-yEhr ah kah-fEh)*
telecommunications	les télécommunications	*(teh-leh-koh-mooh-neeh-kah-syÕh)*
telemarketing	le télémarketing	*(teh-leh marketing)*
teleprocessing	le télétraitement	*(teh-leh-treht-mÃh)*
television	la télévision	*(teh-leh-veeh-zyÕhn)*
teller	le guichetier	*(geehsh-tyEh)*
temperature	la température	*(tãhm-peh-rah-tOOhr)*
tender	la soumission, l'offre	*(sooh-meeh-syÕh), (Oh-frœ)*
tender offer	l'adjudication	*(ad-zhooh-deeh-kah-syÕh)*
tender, legal	la monnaie légale	*(moh-nEh leh-gAhl)*
term bond	l'obligation à terme	*(oh-bleeh-gah-syÕh ah tEhrm)*
term insurance	l'assurance à terme	*(ah-sooh-rÃhns ah tEhrm)*
term loan	le prêt à terme fixe	*(prEht ah tEhrm fEEhks)*
terminal	le terminal	*(tehr-meeh-nAhl)*
terminate (v)	terminer, résilier	*(tehr-meeh-nEh), (reh-zeeh-lEh)*
terms of sale	les clauses de vente	*(klOhz dœ vÃhnt)*
territorial waters	les eaux territoriales	*(Œh teh-reeh-toh-ryAhl)*
territory	le territoire	*(teh-reeh-twAhr)*
test	l'essai	*(eh-sEh)*
test tube	l'éprouvette	*(eh-prooh-vEht)*
thick	épais	*(eh-pEh)*
thin	mince	*(mǼhns)*
thin market	le marché réduit	*(mahr-shEh reh-dwEEh)*

third window	le troisième guichet	*(trwah-zyEhm geeh-shEht)*
third-party exporter	l'exportateur tiers, l'intermédiaire	*(ehks-pohr-tah-tŒhr tyEhrs), (æhn-tehr-meh-dyEhr)*
thread	le fil	*(fEEhl)*
threaten	menacer	*(meh-nah-sEh)*
three-pronged fork	la fourchette à trois dents	*(foohr-shEht ah trwah dÃhn)*
through bill of lading	le connaissement direct	*(koh-nEhs-mÃh deeh-rEhkt)*
throughput	la capacité de traitement, le rendement	*(kah-pah-seeh-tEh dœ treht-mÃh), (rãhnd-mÃh)*
tick, price	le pointage des prix	*(pwæhn-tAhzh deh prEEh)*
ticker tape	la bande de téléscripteur	*(bÃhnd dœ teh-leh-skreehp-tŒhr)*
tie	la cravate	*(krah-vAht)*
tied aid	l'aide conditionnelle	*(Ehd kõhn-deeh-syoh-nEhl)*
tied loan	le prêt conditionnel	*(prEht kõhn-deeh-syoh-nEhl)*
tight market	le marché difficile	*(mahr-shEh deeh-feeh-sEEhl)*
time and motion	l'organisation scientifique du travail	*(ohr-gah-neeh-zah-syÕh syÃhn-teeh-fEEhk dooh trah-vAhyœ)*
time bill (of exchange)	l'effet à terme	*(eh-fEht ah tEhrm)*
time deposit	le dépôt à terme	*(deh-pOh ah tEhrm)*
time order	l'ordre à terme	*(Ohr-drœ ah tEhrm)*
time segment	la tranche horaire	*(trÃhnsh oh-rEhr)*
time sharing	le temps partagé	*(tÃh pahr-tah-zhEh)*
time zone	le fuseau horaire	*(fooh-zOh oh-rEhr)*
time, down	le temps mort	*(tÃh mOhr)*
time, lead	le délai de livraison	*(deh-lEh dœ leeh-vreh-zÕh)*
timetable	l'emploi du temps, l'horaire	*(ãhm-plwAh dooh tÃh), (oh-rEhr)*
tint	la teinte, la couleur	*(tÆhnt), (kooh-lŒhr)*
tip (inside information)	le tuyau	*(tooh-yOh)*
tip	le pourboire	*(poohr-bwAhr)*
tire	le pneu	*(nŒh)*
titanium	le titane	*(teeh-tAhn)*
title	le titre	*(tEEh-trœ)*
title insurance	l'assurance de titres de propriété	*(ah-sooh-rÃhns dœtEEh-trœ dœ proh-pryeh-tEh)*
titration	le titrage	*(teeh-trAzh)*
to the bearer	au porteur	*(oh pohr-tŒhr)*
toaster	le grille-pain	*(grEEh-yœh-pÆhn)*

toilet kit	la trousse de toilette	*(trOOhs dœ twah-lEht)*
tombstone	l'annonce de placement	*(ah-nÕhns dœ plahs-mÃh)*
tone	la tonalité	*(toh-nah-leeh-tEh)*
tonnage	le tonnage	*(toh-nAhzh)*
tools	les outils, les instruments	*(ooh-tEEhl), (ãhn-strooh-mÃhn)*
top management	les cadres supérieurs	*(kAh-drœ sooh-peh-ryŒhr)*
top of the line	haut de gamme	*(Oht dœ gAhm)*
top price	le prix fort	*(prEEh fOhr)*
top quality	la qualité supérieure	*(kah-leeh-tEh sooh-peh-ryŒhr)*
topping up	le complément	*(kõhm-pleh-mÃh)*
torpedo (v)	torpiller	*(tohr-peeh-yEh)*
torque	le couple	*(kOOh-plœ)*
tort	le dommage	*(doh-mAhzh)*
tote bag	le sac de voyage	*(sahk dœ vwah-yAhzh)*
toughness	la dureté	*(dooh-rœh-tEh)*
toxicity level	le niveau de toxicité	*(neeh-vOh dœ tohk-seeh-tEh)*
toxicology	la toxicologie	*(tohk-seeh-koh-loh-zhEEh)*
toxin	la toxine	*(tohk-sEEhn)*
tracking station	la station de observation	*(stah-syÕhn dœ ohb-sehr-vah-syÕhn)*
trade (n)	le commerce	*(koh-mEhrs)*
trade (v)	commercer	*(koh-mehr-sEh)*
trade acceptance	l'acceptation commerciale	*(ahk-sehp-tah-syÕh koh-mehr-syAhl)*
trade agreement	l'accord commercial	*(ah-kOhr koh-mehr-syAhl)*
trade association	l'association commerciale	*(ah-soh-syah-syÕh koh-mehr-syAhl)*
trade barrier	la barrière douanière	*(bah-ryEhr dooh-ah-nyEhr)*
trade commission	la commission commerciale	*(koh-meeh-syÕh koh-mehr-syAhl)*
trade credit	le crédit commercial	*(kreh-dEEh koh-mehr-syAhl)*
trade date	la date de transaction	*(dAht dœ trãhn-zahk-syÕh)*
trade discount	l'escompte d'usage	*(ehs-kÕhnt dooh-zAhz)*
trade house	la maison de commerce	*(meh-zÕh dœ koh-mEhrs)*
trade union	le syndicat ouvrier	*(seehn-deeh-kAh ooh-vryEh)*
trade, fair	le libre-échange réciproque	*(lEEh-brœ eh-shÃhnzh reh-seeh-prOhk)*
trade-off	l'échange	*(eh-shÃhnzh)*
trademark	la marque de fabrique	*(mAhr-kœ dœ fah-brEEhk)*
trader	le négociant, l'opérateur en bourse, le cambiste	*(neh-goh-syÃh), (oh-peh-rah-tŒhr ãhn bOOhrs), (kãhn-bEEhst)*

trading company	la société de commerce	*(soh-syeh-tEh dœ koh-mEhrs)*
trading floor	la corbeille (à la bourse)	*(kohr-bEhyœ), (ah lah bOOhrs)*
trading limit	la limite de négociation	*(leeh-mEEht dœ neh-goh-syah-syÕh)*
trainee	la, le stagiaire	*(stah-zhEhr)*
tranquilizer	le calmant	*(kahl-mÃh)*
transaction	l'opération	*(oh-peh-rah-syÕhn)*
transfer	le transfert	*(trãhnz-fEhr)*
transfer agent	l'agent de transfert	*(ah-zhÃh dœ trãhnz-fEhr)*
transfer of powers	le transfert des pouvoirs	*(trãhns-fEhr deh pooh-vwAhr)*
transferred	muté	*(mooh-tEh)*
transformer	le transformateur	*(trãhnz-fohr-mah-tŒhr)*
transit, in	en transit	*(ãhn trÃhn-zEEht)*
transit advertising	l'affichage transport	*(ah-feeh-shAhzh trãhns-pOhr)*
translator	le traducteur, la traductrice	*(trah-doohk-tŒhr), (trah-doohk-trEEhs)*
transmission frame	la trame de transmission	*(trAhm dœ trãhnz-meeh-syÕhn)*
transmitter	le transmetteur	*(trãhnz-meht-tŒhr)*
transplant	la greffe	*(grEhf)*
traveler's check	le chèque de voyage	*(shEhk dœ vwah-yAhzh)*
tray	le plateau	*(plah-tŒh)*
treasurer	le trésorier	*(treh-zoh-ryEh)*
treasury bill	le bon du trésor	*(bõhn dooh treh-zOhr)*
treasury bonds	les bons du trésor (échéance à plus de dix ans)	*(bõh dooh treh-zOhr) , (eh-sheh-Ãhns ah plooh dœ deehs Ãhn)*
treasury notes	les bons du Trésor (échéance entre un et dix) ans	*(bõh dooh treh-zOhr), (eh-sheh-Ãhns ãhn-trœ œhn eh deehs Ãhn)*
treasury stock	les actions de trésorerie	*(ahk-syÕh dœ treh-zoh-reh-rEEh)*
treaty	le traité, l'accord, le contrat	*(treh-tEh), (ah-kOhr), (kõhn-trÃh)*
trend	la tendance	*(tãhn-dÃhns)*
trial balance	la balance de vérification	*(bah-lÃhns dœ veh-reeh-feeh-kah-syÕh)*
trigger (v)	déclencher	*(deh-klãhn-shEh)*
troubleshoot (v)	concilier	*(kõhn-seeh-lyEh)*
troubleshooter	le médiateur, le dépanneur, l'enquêteur	*(meh-dyah-tŒhr), (deh-pah-nŒhr), (ãhn-keh-tŒhr)*
truckload	le chargement complet	*(shahrzh-mÃh kohm-plEh)*
trunk	la malle	*(mAhl)*
trust	le trust, le fidéicommis	*(feeh-deh-eeh-koh-mEEh)*

trust company	la compagnie fiduciaire	*(kõhm-pah-nyEEh feeh-dooh-syEhr)*
trust fund	le fonds de dépôt	*(fÕhn dœ deh-pOh)*
trust receipt	la recette fiduciaire	*(ræh-sEht feeh-dooh-syEhr)*
trustee	le curateur, le mandataire, l'administrateur	*(kooh-rah-tŒhr), (mÃhn-dah-tEhr), (ad-meeh-neehs-trah-tŒhr)*
tungsten	le tungstène	*(toohng-stEhn)*
turbine	la turbine	*(toohr-bEEhn)*
tureen	la terrine	*(teh-rEEhn)*
turnkey	clefs en main	*(klEhf ãhn mÆhn)*
turnover	la rotation des stocks	*(roh-tah-syÕh deh stocks)*
turnover asset	la rotation de l'actif	*(roh-tah-syÕh dœ lahk-tEEf)*
turnover stock	le stock de roulement	*(stock dœ roohl-mÃh)*
turnover, sales	les ventes d'écoulement	*(vÃhnt deh-koohl-mÃh)*
tuxedo	le smoking	
two-name paper	le papier à deux noms	*(pah-pyEh ah dŒh nÕhm)*
two-tiered market inventory	le marché à deux niveaux	*(mahr-shEh ah dŒh neeh-vŒ)*
type of vine	le cépage	*(seh-pAhzh)*

U

ultra vires acts	les excès de pouvoir	*(ehk-sEh dœ pooh-vwAhr)*
unaccompanied goods	les marchandises non accompagnées	*(mahr-shãhn-dEEhz nõhn ah-kõhm-pah-nyEh)*
unbleached linen	la toile écrue	*(twAhl eh-krOOh)*
unbreakable	incassable	*(æhn-kah-sAh-blœh)*
uncollectible accounts	les comptes non recouvrables	*(kÕhnt nõh ræh-kooh-vrAh-blœ)*
uncork	déboucher	*(deh-booh-shEh)*
underate (v)	sous-estimer	*(soohs-ehs-teeh-mEh)*
undercapitalized	sous-capitalisé	*(sooh-kah-peeh-tah-leeh-zEh)*
undercut (v)	vendre moins cher	*(vÃhn-drœ mwÆ shEhr)*
underpaid	sous-payé	*(sooh-pah-yEh)*
undersigned	soussigné	*(sooh-seeh-nyEh)*
understanding (agreement)	l'entente, l'accord verbal	*(ãhn-tÃhnt), (ah-kOhr vehr-bAhl)*
undertake (v)	entreprendre	*(ãhn-trœ-prÃhn-drœ)*
undervalue (v)	sous-évaluer	*(soohs-eh-vah-looh-Eh)*
underwriter	l'assureur, le membre d'un syndicat de garantie	*(ah-sooh-rŒhr), (mÃhm-brœ dœhn seehn-deeh-kAh dœ gah-rãhn-tEEh)*
undeveloped	inexploité	*(æhn-ehks-plwah-tEh)*
unearned increment	la plus-value	*(plooh-vah-lOOh)*

unearned revenue	la rente	(rāhnt)
unemployment	le chômage	(shoh-mAhzh)
unemployment compensation	l'indemnité de chômage	(ǣhn-dehm-neeh-tEh dœ shoh-mAhzh)
unfair	injuste, déloyal	(ǣhn-zhOOhst), (deh-lwah-yAhl)
unfavorable	défavorable	(deh-fah-voh-rAh-blœ)
unfeasible	irréalisable	(eeh-reh-ah-leeh-zAh-blœ)
unfermented grape juice	le jus de raisin	(zhOOhs dœ reh-zǢhn)
union contract	le contrat syndical	(kōhn-trAh seehn-deeh-kAhl)
union label	l'appartenance syndicale	(ah-pahr-tœh-nÃhns seehn-deeh-kAhl)
union, labor	le syndicat ouvrier	(seehn-deeh-kAh ooh-vryEh)
unit cost	le prix de revient unitaire	(prEEh dœ rœ-vyÃhn ooh-neeh-tEhr)
unit load discount	la remise à l'unité	(rœh-mEEhz ah looh-neeh-tEh)
unit of data transmission speed	le baud	(bOh)
unit price	le prix à l'unité	(prEEh ah looh-neeh-tEh)
unlisted	non coté, hors coté	(nōh koh-tEh), (ohr koh-tEh)
unload (v)	décharger	(deh-shahr-zhEh)
unsecured loan	le prêt non garanti	(prEht nōhn gah-rāhn-tEEh)
unskilled labor	la main-d'œuvre non qualifiée	(mǢhn dŒh-vrœ nōh kah-leeh-feeh-Eh)
up to our expectations	à la hauteur de nos prévisions, à la hauteur de notre attente	(ah la oh-tŒhr dœ noh preh-vee-zyŌhn), (ah lah oh-tŒhr dœ nOh-trœ ah-tÃhnt)
update (v)	mettre à jour	(mEh-trœh ah zhOOhr)
upgrade (v)	augmenter la puissance	(ohg-māhn-tEh lah pweeh-sÃhns)
upmarket	le haut de gamme	(oh dœ gAhm)
upturn	la reprise (économique), le redressement	(rœh-prEEhz eh-koh-moh-mEEhk), (rœh-drehs-mÃh)
upward trend	la tendance à la hausse	(tāhn-dÃhns ah lah Ohs)
urban renewal	la rénovation des zones urbaines	(reh-noh-vah-syŌh deh zOhn oohr-bEhn)
urban sprawl	l'urbanisation effrénée	(oohr-bah-neeh-zah-syŌh eh-freh-nEh)
use tax	la taxe à la consommation	(tAhks ah lah kōhn-soh-mah-syŌh)

useful life	la durée utile	(dooh-rEh ooh-tEEhl)
user-friendly	favorable à l'utilisateur, d'une utilisation agréable	(fah-voh-rAh-blœ ah looh-teeh-leeh-zah-tŒhr), (doohn ooh-teeh-leeh-zah-syŌh ah-greh-Ah-blœ)
usury	l'usure	(ooh-zOOhr)
utility	l'utilité; le service public	(ooh-teeh-leeh-tEh), (sœr-vEEhs pooh-blEEhk)

V

VCR	le magnétoscope	(mah-nyeh-toh-skOhp)
V8 engine	le moteur V.8	(moh-tŒhr veh wEEht)
vaccine	le vaccin	(vahk-sEEhn)
vacuum	le vide	(vEEhd)
vacuum cleaner	l'aspirateur	(ahs-peeh-rah-tŒhr)
vacuum melting furnace	le four sous vide	(fOOhr sooh vEEhd)
valid	valide, valable	(vah-lEEhd), (vah-lAh-blœ)
validate (v)	valider	(vah-leeh-dEh)
valuation	l'évaluation; l'estimation	(eh-vah-lwah-syŌh), (ehs-teeh-mah-syŌh)
value	la valeur	(vah-lŒhr)
value engineering	l'analyse de la valeur	(āh-nah-lEEhz dœ lah vah-lŒhr)
value for duty	la valeur douanière	(vah-lŒhr dooh-ah-nyEhr)
value, asset	la valeur en capital	(vah-lŒhr āhn kah-peeh-tAhl)
value, book	la valeur comptable	(vah-lŒhr kōhn-tAh-blœ)
value, face	la valeur nominale	(vah-lŒhr noh-meeh-nAhl)
value, market	la valeur marchande, le cours	(vah-lŒhr mahr-shÃnd), (kOOhr)
value-added tax	la taxe à la valeur ajoutée	(tAhks ah la vah-lŒhr ah-zhooh-tEh)
valve	la soupape	(sooh-pAhp)
vanadium	le vanadium	(vah-nah-dyOOhm)
variable annuity	l'annuité variable	(ah-nweeh-tEh vah-ryAh-blœ)
variable costs	les frais variables	(frEh vah-ryAh-blœ)
variable import levy	l'impôt variable à l'importation	(ǣhm-pOh vah-ryAh-blœ ah lǣhm-pohr-tah-syŌh)
variable margin	la marge variable	(mÅhrzh vah-ryAh-blœ)
variable rate	le taux variable	(tOh vah-ryAh-blœ)
variable rate mortgage	l'hypothèque à taux variable	(eeh-poh-tЀhk ah tOh vah-ryAh-blœ)

V

variable yield investment	le placement à revenu variable	*(plahs-mÃhn ah rœh-vœh-nOOh vah-ryAh-blœh)*
variance	l'écart	*(eh-kAhr)*
vat	la cuve	*(kOOhv)*
vector	le vecteur	*(vehk-tŒhr)*
veil	la voilette	*(vwah-lEht)*
velocity of money	la vitesse de circulation	*(veeh-tEhs dœ seehr-kooh-lah-syÕh)*
velvety	velouté	*(vœh-looh-tEh)*
vendor	le fournisseur, le vendeur	*(foohr-neeh-sŒhr), (vÃhn-dŒhr)*
vendor's lien	le privilège du fournisseur	*(preeh-veeh-lEhzh dooh foohr-neeh-sŒhr)*
venture capital	le capital-risque	*(kah-peeh-tAhl rEEhsk)*
vertical integration	l'intégration verticale	*(ãhn-teh-grah-syÕh vehr-teeh-kAhl)*
vest	le gilet	*(zheeh-lEh)*
vested interests	les intérêts acquis	*(ãhn-teh-rEh ah-kEEh)*
vested rights	les droits acquis	*(drwAh ah-kEEh)*
veto	le veto	*(veh-tOh)*
veto (v)	mettre son veto	*(mEh-trœh sÕhn veh-tOh)*
vice-president	le vice-président	*(veehs-preh-zeeh-dÃh)*
videocassette player	le magnetophone	*(mah-nyeh-toh-fÕhn)*
vine	le cep	*(sEhp)*
vinegar taste	le goût de vinaigre	*(gOOh dœ vãhn-Eh-greoh)*
vineyard	le vignoble	*(veeh-nyOh-blœ)*
vintage	le cru	*(krOOh)*
vintage year	le millésime	*(meeh-lEh-zEEhm)*
vintner	le négociant en vins	*(neh-goh-syÃh ãhn vÆhn)*
vintry	le chais	*(shEh)*
virus	le virus	*(veeh-rOOhs)*
visible balance of trade	la balance commerciale visible	*(bah-lÃhns koh-mehr-syAhl veeh-zEEh-blœ)*
vitamin	la vitamine	*(veeh-tah-mEEhn)*
viticulture	la viticulture	*(veeh-teeh-koohl-tOOhr)*
voice-activated	à commande vocale	*(ah koh-mÃhnd voh-kAhl)*
void	vide, nul	*(vEEhd), (nOOhl)*
voided check	le chèque annulé	*(shEhk ah-nooh-lEh)*
volatile market	le marché instable	*(mahr-shEh ãhn-stAh-blœ)*
voltage	la voltage	*(vohl-tAhzh)*
volume discount	la remise pour quantité importante	*(rœh-mEEhz poohr kãhn-teeh-tEh ãhm-pohr-tÃhnt)*
volume	le volume	*(voh-lOOhm)*
volume, sales	le volume des ventes	*(voh-lOOhm deh vÃhnt)*
voting right	le droit de vote	*(drwAh dœ vOht)*
voucher	la pièce justificative, le reçu	*(pyEhs zhoohs-teeh-kah-tEEhv), (rœh-sOOh)*

V

W

wage	le salaire	*(sah-lEhr)*
wage differential	l'écart de salaire	*(eh-kAhr sah-lEhr)*
wage dispute	le conflit salarial	*(kõhn-flEEh sah-lah-ryAl)*
wage drift	la dérive des salaires	*(deh-rEEhv deh sah-lEhr)*
wage earner	le salarié	*(sah-lah-ryEh)*
wage freeze	le blocage des salaires	*(bloh-kAhzh deh sah-lEhr)*
wage level	le niveau des salaires	*(neeh-vŒ deh sah-lEhr)*
wage scale	l'échelle des salaires	*(eh-shEhl deh sah-lEhr)*
wage structure	la structure des salaires	*(stroohk-tOOhr deh sah-lEhr)*
wage-price spiral	la spirale des prix et des salaires	*(speeh-rAhl deh prEEh eh deh sah-lEhr*
wages	les salaires	*(sah-lEhr)*
waiver clause	la clause d'abandon	*(klOhz dah-bãhn-dÕhn)*
walkman	le baladeur	*(bah-lah-dŒhr)*
walkout	le débrayage	*(deh-brah-yAhzh)*
want ad	la demande ou l'offre d'emploi (petites annonces)	*(dæh-mÃhnd ooh lOh-frœ dãhm-plwAh [pœh-tEEht ah-nÕhns])*
warehouse	l'entrepôt	*(ãhn-trœ-pOh)*
warehouseman	le manutentionnaire	*(mah-nooh-tãhn-syoh-nEhr)*
warhead	l'ogive	*(oh-zhEEhv)*
warning indicator	l'indicateur d'alcrtc	*(æhn-deeh-kah-tŒhr dah-lEhrt)*
warrant	la garantie, le certificat	*(gah-rãhn-tEEh), (sehr-teeh-feeh-kAh)*
warranty	la garantie	*(gah-rãhn-tEEh)*
warship	le navire de guerre	*(nah-vEEhr dœ gEhr)*
washing machine	la machine à laver	*(mah-shEEhn ah lah-vEh)*
waste disposal	l'élimination de déchets	*(eh-leeh-meeh-nah-syÕhn deh deh-shEt)*
waste disposal unit	le broyeur des déchets	*(brwah-yŒhr deh deh-shEt)*
waste management	la gestion des déchets	*(zhehs-tyÕhn deh deh-shEt)*
wasting asset	l'actif défectible	*(ahk-tEEf deh-fehk-tEEh-blœ)*
watch strap	le bracelet de montre	*(brah-sœh-lEht dœ mÕhn-trœ)*
water pollution	la pollution des eaux	*(poh-looh-syÕhn dez Œh)*
water pump	la pompe à eau	*(pOhmp-ah Oh)*
water treatment	le traitement des eaux	*(treat-mÃh dez Œh)*
waterbased	à base d'eau	*(ah bAhz dOh)*
waterproof	imperméable	*(æhm-pœhr-meh-Ah-blæh)*
watt	le watt	

wave	l'onde	*(Ohnd)*
wave of the future	la tendance future	*(tãhn-dÃhns fooh-tOOhr)*
waybill	le bordereau d'expédition, la lettre de voiture	*(bohr-dœ-rOh dehks-peh-deeh-syÕh), (lEh-trœ dœ vwah-tOOhr)*
wealth	la richesse	*(reeh-shEhs)*
weapon	l'arme	*(Ahrm)*
wear and tear	l'usure	*(ooh-zOOhr)*
weaver	le tisserand	*(teeh-sœh-rÃh)*
web offset	la rotative offset	*(roh-tah-tEEhv offset)*
weekly return	le bilan hebdomadaire	*(beeh-lÃh ehb-doh-mah-dEhr)*
weight	le poids	*(pwAh)*
weighted average	la moyenne pondérée	*(mwah-yEhn põhn-deh-rEh)*
weightlessness	l'apesanteur	*(ah-peh-sãh-tŒhr)*
well-rounded	moelleux, onctueux	*(mœh-yŒh), (õhnk-tŒh)*
wharfage charge	les frais de quayage, les droits de bassin	*(frEh dœ keh-yAhzh), (drwAh dœ bah-sÆhn)*
wheel	la roue	*(rOOh)*
when issued	au moment de l'émission	*(oh moh-mÃh dœ leh-meeh-syÕh)*
whip	le fouet	*(fooh-Eh)*
white collar workers	les employés de bureau	*(æhm-plwah-yEh dœ booh-rOh)*
white porcelain	la porcelaine blanche	*(pohr-sœh-lEhn blÃhnsh)*
wholesale market	le marché de gros	*(mahr-shEh dœ grOh)*
wholesale price	le prix de gros	*(prEEh dœ grOh)*
wholesale trade	le commerce de gros	*(koh-mEhrs dœ grOh)*
wholesaler	le grossiste	*(groh-sEEhst)*
widen the gap (v)	élargir le fossé	*(eh-lahr-zhEEhr lœh foh-sEh)*
wildcat strike	la grève sauvage	*(grEhv soh-vAhzh)*
will	la volonté, le testament	*(voh-lõhn-tEh), (tehs-tah-mÃh)*
windfall profits	l'aubaine	*(oh-bÊhn)*
window dresser	l'étalagiste	*(eh-tah-lah-zhEEhst)*
window dressing	l'art de l'étalage, la présentation d'une vitrine	*(Ahr dœ leh-tah-lAhzh), (preh-zãhn-tah-syÕh doohn veeh-trEEhn)*
windowing	le fenêtrage	*(fœh-neh-trAhzh)*
windshield	le pare-brise	*(pahr brEEhz)*
wine	le vin	*(vÆhn)*
wine cellar	la cave à vin	*(kahv ah vÆhn)*
wine cooperative	la coopérative vinicole	*(koh-oh-peh-rah-tEEhv veeh-nee'h-kOhl)*
wine glass	le verre à vin	*(vEhr ah vÆhn)*
wine steward	le sommelier	*(soh-meh-lyEh)*
winegrower	le vigneron, le viticulteur	*(veeh-nyeh-rÕh), (veeh-teeh-koohl-tŒhr)*

W

winemaker	le maître de chais, le viticulteur, le vigneron	*(mEh-trœ dœ shEh), (veeh-tee-koohl-tŒhr), (veeh-nyeh-rÕh)*
winepress	le pressoir	*(preh-swAhr)*
winery	la maison de production de vin	*(meh-zÕhn dœ proh-doohk-syÕhn dœ vÆhn)*
wire	le fil	*(fEEhl)*
wire transfer	le transfert télégraphique	*(trãhnz-fEhr teh-leh-graf-fEEhk)*
with average	avec avarie particulière	*(ah-vEhk ah-vah-rEEh pahr-teeh-kooh-lyEhr)*
withdraw (v)	retirer	*(rœh-teeh-rEh)*
withdrawal	le retrait	*(rœh-trEh)*
withholding tax	la retenue à la source (impôts)	*(rœh-tœh-nOOh ah lah sOOhrs [æhm-pOh])*
witness	le témoin	*(teh-mwÆhn)*
wool	la laine	*(lEhn)*
word processing	le traitement de texte	*(treht-mÃhn dœ tEhkst)*
word processor	l'équipement de traitement de texte	*(eh-keehp-mÃh dœ treht-mÃh dœ tEhk-stœ)*
work (v)	travailler	*(trah-vah-yEh)*
work by contract	le travail sous contrat	*(trah-vAhyœ sooh kõhn-trAh)*
work commitee	le comité d'entreprise	*(koh-meeh-tEh dãhn-trœh-prEEhz)*
work council	le comité d'entreprise	*(koh-meeh-tEh dãhn-trœh-prEEhz)*
work cycle	le cycle du travail	*(sEEh-klœ dooh trah-vAhyœ)*
work day	le jour ouvrable	*(zhOOhr ooh-vrAh-blœ)*
work in progress	les travaux en cours	*(trah-vOh ãhn kOOhr)*
work load	la charge de travail	*(shAhrzh dœ trah-vAhyœ)*
work order	l'ordre de fabrication	*(Ohr-drœ dœ fah-breeh-kah-syÕh)*
work schedule	l'emploi du temps, l'horaire	*(ãhm-plwAh dooh tÃh), (oh-rEhr)*
work station	le poste de travail	*(pOhst dœ trah-vAhyœ)*
work stoppage	le temps chômé	*(tÃh shoh-mEh)*
workforce	la main-d'œuvre	*(mÆhn dŒh-vrœ)*
working assets	l'actif de roulement	*(ahk-tEEf dœ roohl-mÃh)*
working balance	le solde de roulement	*(sOhld dœ roohl-mÃh)*
working capital	le fonds de roulement	*(fÕhn dœ roohl-mÃh)*
working class	la classe ouvrière	*(klAhs ooh-vryEhr)*
working contract	le contrat de travail	*(kõhn-trAh dœ trah-vAhyœ)*
working funds	les fonds d'exploitation	*(fÕhn dehks-plwah-tah-syÕh)*
working hours	l'horaire de travail	*(oh-rEhr dœ trah-vAhyœ)*
working papers	le permis de travail	*(pehr-mEEh dœ trah-vAhyœ)*

W

working tools	les outils de travail	*(ooh-tEEhl dœ trah-vAhyœ)*
workplace	le lieu de travail	*(lyŒh dœ trah-vAhyœ)*
workshop	l'atelier	*(ah-teh-lyEh)*
World Bank	la Banque Mondiale	*(bĀhnk mõhn-dyAhl)*
worth, net	la valeur nette	*(vah-lŒhr nEht)*
worthless	sans valeur	*(sāh vah-lŒhr)*
wrinkle	la ride	*(rEEhd)*
writ	l'acte judiciaire	*(Ahk-tœ zhooh-deeh-syEhr)*
write-off	la déduction	*(deh-doohk-syÕh)*
writedown	la réduction	*(reh-doohk-syÕh)*
written agreement	l'accord écrit	*(ah-kOhr eh-krEEh)*
written bid (stock exhange)	par casier (à la bourse)	*(pahr kah-zyEh ah lah bOOhrs)*

X

| **x-ray** | la radiographie | *(rah-dyoh-grah-fEEh)* |

Y

yardstick	l'étalon	*(eh-tah-lÕh)*
yarn	le fil	*(fEEhl)*
year	l'année	*(ah-nEh)*
year, fiscal	l'année budgétaire, l'exercice financier	*(ah-nEh booh-zheh-tEhr), (ehk-sœr-sEEhs feeh-nāhn-syEh)*
year-end	la fin d'année	*(fĀĒhn dah-nEh)*
yeast	la levure	*(lœh-vOOhr)*
yield	la récolte, le rendement, le rapport	*(reh-kOhlt), (rāhnd-mĀh), (rah-pOhr)*
yield to maturity	le rendement à l'échéance	*(rāhnd-mĀh ah leh-sheh-Āhns)*

Z

zero coupon	le coupon zéro	*(kooh-pÕh zeh-rOh)*
zinc	le zinc	*(zĀĒhnk)*
zip code	le code postal	*(kOhd pohs-tAhl)*
zipper	la fermeture éclair	*(fehr-mœh-tOOhr eh-klEhr)*
zone	la zone	*(zOhn)*
zoning law	la réglementation d'urbanisation	*(reh-glœh-māhn-tah-syÕh doohr-bah-neeh-zah-syÕh)*

A

à … jours de vue	*(ah zhOOhr dœ vOOh)*	aftersight
à base d'eau	*(ah bAhz dŒh)*	waterbased
à bord	*(ah bOhr)*	on board
à but non lucratif	*(ah bOOh nõh looh-krah-tEEhf)*	nonprofit
à commande vocale	*(ah koh-mÃhnd voh-kAhl)*	voice-activated
à courte portée	*(ah koohrt pohr-tEh)*	short-range
à des conditions normales	*(ah deh kõhn-deeh-syÕh nohr-mAhl)*	arms length
à et de	*(ah eh dœ)*	at and from
à flot	*(ah flOh)*	afloat
à grande échelle	*(ah grãhnd eh-shEhl)*	large scale
à l'achat et à la vente	*(ah lah-shAh eh a lah vÃhnt)*	bid and asked
à l'ordre du jour	*(ah lOhr-drœh dooh zhOOhr)*	on the agenda
à l'ouverture (f)	*(ah looh-vehr-tOOhr)*	at the opening
à la chaîne (f)	*(ah lah shEhn)*	assembly line
à la criée (à la bourse)	*(ah lah kreeh-Eh [ah lah bOOhrs])*	oral bid (stock exchange)
à la fermeture	*(ah lah fehrm-tOOhr)*	at the close
à la hauteur de nos prévisions	*(ah lah oh-tŒhr dœ noh preh-vee-zyÕhn)*	up to our expectations
à la mode	*(ah lah mOhd)*	fashionable
à la une	*(ah lah OOhn)*	headline
à longue portée	*(ah lõhng pohr-tEh)*	long-range
à vue	*(ah vOOh)*	at call, at sight, on demand
abandon (m)	*(ah-bãhn-dõhn-mÃh), (prEEhm, ohp-syÕh)*	abandonment (prime, option)
abandonner	*(ah-bãhn-dõhn-Eh)*	abandon (v)
abat-jour (m)	*(ah-bah zhOOhr)*	shade
abattement (m)	*(ah-baht-mÃhn)*	abatement, allowance (tax)
abattement (m) fiscal	*(ah-baht-mÃh feehs-kAhl)*	tax allowance
abilité à	*(ah-beeh-leeh-tEh ah)*	empowered to
abonné (e)(m)	*(ah-boh-nEh)*	subscriber
absentéisme du propriétaire (m)	*(ahb-sãhn-teh-EEhz-mœ proh-pryeh-tEhr)*	absenteeism, absentee ownership
absorber	*(ahb-zohr-bEh)*	absorb (v)
accélérateur (m)	*(ahk-seh-leh-rah-tŒhr)*	gas pedal
accélérer	*(ahk-seh-leh-rEh)*	speed up (v)
acceptation (f)	*(ahk-sehp-tah-syÕh)*	acceptance
acceptation bancaire	*(ahk-sehp-tah-syÕh bãhn-kEhr)*	bank acceptance

A

acceptation commerciale	*(ahk-sehp-tah-syŌh koh-mehr-syAhl)*	trade acceptance
acceptation conditionnelle	*(ahk-sehp-tah-syŌh kõhn-deeh-syoh-nEhl)*	conditional acceptance
acceptation sans réserves	*(ahk-sehp-tah-syŌh sãh reh-zEhrv)*	general acceptance
acceptation sous réserve	*(ahk-sehp-tah-syŌh sooh reh-zEhrv)*	qualified acceptance endorsement
accepter	*(ahk-sehp-tEh)*	accept (v)
accepteur (m)	*(ahk-sehp-tŒhr)*	acceptor
accès (m) aléatoire	*(ahk-sEhs ah-leh-ah-twAhr)*	random access
accident (m) du travail	*(ahk-seddh-dÃh dooh trah-vAhyœ)*	work injury
accompagnateur (m)	*(ah-kõhm-ah-nyah-tŒhr)*	speculator
accord (m)	*(ah-kOhr)*	agreement, treaty
accord à l'amiable	*(ah-kOhr ah lah-myAh-blœ)*	gentleman's agreement
accord commercial	*(ah-kOhr koh-mehr-syAhl)*	trade agreement
accord d'acceptation	*(ah-kOhr dahk-sehp-tah-syŌh)*	acceptance agreement
accord d'arbitrage	*(ah-kOhr dœ ahr-beeh-trAhzh)*	arbitration agreement
accord de coopération	*(ah-kOhr dœ koh-oh-peh-rah-syŌh)*	cooperation agreement
accord écrit	*(ah-kOhr eh-krEEh)*	written agreement
accord général	*(ah-kOhr zheh-neh-rAhl)*	accord and satisfaction
accord multilatéral	*(ah-kOhr moohl-teeh-lah-teh-rAhl)*	multilateral agreement
accord tacite	*(ah-kOhr tah-sEEht)*	implied agreement
accord unanime	*(ah-kOhr ooh-nah-nEEhm)*	across-the-board settlement
accord verbal	*(ah-kOhr vehr-bAhl)*	understanding (agreement)
accorder	*(ah-kohr-dEh)*	allow (v), grant (v)
accouchement (m)	*(ah-koohsh-mÃhn)*	delivery
accrocheur	*(ah-kroh-shŒhr)*	eye-catching
accroissement (m)	*(ah-krwahs-mÃh)*	accretion
accroître la tension	*(ah-krwAh-trœh lah tãhn-syŌhn)*	increase tension (v)
accueillir	*(ah-kweh-yEEhr)*	welcome, host (v)
accumulation (f) des intérêts	*(ah-kooh-mooh-lah-syŌh dehz æhn-teh-rEh)*	accrual
accuser réception de	*(ah-kooh-zEh reh-sehp-syŌh dœ)*	acknowledge receipt of (v)
acétone (m)	*(ah-seh-tOhn)*	acetone
achat (m) à terme	*(ah-shAh ah tEhrm)*	forward purchase
achat (m) d'espace	*(ah-shAh dehs-pAhs)*	space buying

achat de titres	*(ah-shAh dœ tEEh-trœ)*	stock purchase
achat par correspondance	*(ah-shAh pahr koh-rehs-põhn-dÃhns)*	mail order purchase
achat spontané	*(ah-shAh spõhn-tah-nEh)*	impulse buying
acheter	*(ahsh-tEh)*	purchase (v)
acheter au meilleur prix	*(ahsh-tEh oh meh-yŒhr prEEh)*	buy at best (v)
acheter en clôture	*(ahsh-tEh ãhn kloh-tOOhr)*	buy on close (v)
acheter en ouverture	*(ahsh-tEh ãhn ooh-vehr-tOOhr)*	buy on opening (v)
acheteur (m)	*(ahsh-tŒhr)*	buyer
acheteur de créance	*(ahsh-tŒhr dœ kreh-Ãhns)*	credit buyer
acheteur potentiel	*(ahsh-tŒhr poh-tãhn-syEhl)*	potential buyer
acheteur principal	*(ahsh-tŒhr prãhn-seeh-pAhl)*	chief buyer
acheteur résident	*(ahsh-tŒhr reh-zeeh-dÃh)*	resident buyer
acide (m)	*(ah-sEEhd)*	acid, tart
acide acétique	*(ah-sEEhd ah-seh-tEEhk)*	acetic acid
acide (m) aminé	*(ah-sEEhd ah-meeh-nEh)*	amino acid
acide chloridrique	*(ah-sEEhd kloh-rEEhk)*	hydrochloric acid
acide nitrique	*(ah-sEEhd neeh-trEEhk)*	nitric acid
acide sulfurique	*(ah-sEEhd soohl-fooh-rEEhk)*	sulfuric acid
acier (m) allié	*(ah-syEh ah-lyEh)*	alloy steel
acier (m) au carbone	*(ahs-yEh oh kahr-bOhn)*	carbon steel
acier (m) de construction	*(ahs-yEh dœ kÕhn-stroohk-syÕh)*	structural shapes
acier (m) inoxydable	*(ahs-yEh æhn-ohk-seeh-dΛh blœ)*	stainless steel
acierie (f)	*(ahs-yeh-rEEh)*	steel mill
aciers (mpl) spéciaux	*(ahs-yEh speh-syOh)*	specialty steels
acompte (m)	*(ah-kÕhnt)*	down payment
acquérir	*(ah-keh-rEEhr)*	acquire (v)
acquisition (f)	*(ah-keeh-zeeh-syÕh)*	acquisition, procurement
acquisition des informations	*(ah-keeh-zeeh-syÕh dehz æhn-fohr-mah-syÕh)*	data acquisition
acquittement (m) bancaire	*(ah-keeht-mÃh bãhn-kEhr)*	bank release
acquitter	*(ah-keeh-tEh)*	pay up (v)
acquitter (s') d'une dette	*(ah-keeh-tEh doohn dEht)*	clear off a debt (v)
âcre	*(Ah-krœ)*	sour
acte (m)	*(Ahk-tœ)*	deed
acte de cession	*(Ahk-tœ dœ seh-syÕh)*	deed of transfer
acte de confiance	*(Ahk-tœ dœ kõhn-feeh-Ãhns)*	deed of trust
acte de transfert d'un droit	*(Ahk-tœ dœ trãhnz-fEhr dæhn drwAh)*	quit claim deed
acte de vente	*(Ahk-tœ dœ vÃhnt)*	deed of sale, bill of sale

A

acte judiciaire	(Ahk-tœ zhooh-deeh-syEhr)	writ
actif (m)	(ahk-tEEf)	asset, assets
actif circulant	(ahk-tEEf seehr-kooh-lÃh)	turnover asset
actif de roulement	(ahk-tEEf dœ roohl-mÃh)	working assets
actif défectible	(ahk-tEEf deh-fehk-tEEh-blœ)	wasting asset
actif disponible	(ahk-tEEf deehs-poh-nEEh-blœ)	current assets, quick assets
actif net (m)	(ahk-tEEhf nEht)	net asset
actif réalisable	(ahk-tEEf reh-ah-leeh-zAh-blœ)	current assets
actifs occultés	(ahk-tEEf oh-koohl-tEh)	hidden assets
action (f)	(ahk-syÕhn)	stock
action (f) à revenu variable	(ahk-syÕh ah rœhv-nOOh vah-ryAh-blœ)	equity
action au porteur	(ahk-syÕh oh pohr-tŒhr)	bearer security
action civile	(ahk-syÕh seeh-vEEhl)	civil action
action d'un groupe de pression	(ahk-syÕh dœhn grOOhp dœ prœh-syÕh)	lobbying
action en capital	(ahk-syÕh ãhn kah-peeh-tAhl)	share equity
action ordinaire	(ahk-syÕh ohr-deeh-nEhr)	common stock
action positive	(ahk-syÕh poh-zeeh-tEEhv)	affirmative action
actionnaire (m)	(ahk-syoh-nEhr)	shareholder
actions (fpl)	(ahk-syÕh)	shares
actions cotées au-dessous du pair	(ahk-syÕh koh-tEh oh dœh-sOOh dooh pEhr)	discount securities
actions cotées en cents	(ahk-syÕh koh-tEh ãhn sÃhnt)	penny stock
actions émises	(ahk-syÕh eh-mEEhz)	issued shares
actions libérées	(ahk-syÕh leeh-beh-rEh)	paid up shares
actions privilégiées convertibles	(ahk-syÕh preeh-veeh-leh-zhyEh kõhn-vehr-tEEh-blœ)	convertible preferred stock
activité (f) commerciale	(ahk-teeh-veeh-tEh koh-mehr-syAhl)	business activity
activité de promotion	(ahk-teeh-veeh-tEh dœ proh-moh-syÕh)	promotional activity
activités (fpl) de soutien	(ahk-teeh-veeh-tEh dœ sooh-tyÆh)	support activities
actuaire (m)	(ahk-twEhr)	actuary
additif (m)	(ah-deeh-tEEf)	addendum, additive
addition (f)	(ah-deeh-syÕh)	footing (accounting), bill (restaurant)
adjoint (m)	(ad-zhwÆhn)	assistant
adjoint au directeur général	(ad-zhwÆhn oh deeh-rehk-tŒhr zheh-neh-rAhl)	assistant general manager

adjudication (f)	*(ad-zhooh-deeh-kah-syÕh)*	tender offer
admettre	*(ahd-mEh-trœ)*	acknowledge (v)
administrateur (m)	*(ad-meeh-neehs-trah-tŒhr)*	trustee, administrator, executive director
administratif	*(ad-meeh-neehs-trah-tEEhf)*	administrative
administration (f)	*(ad-meeh-neehs-trah-syÕh)*	administration
administration du personnel	*(ad-meeh-neehs-trah-syÕh dooh pehr-soh-nEhl)*	personnel administration
administratrice (f)	*(ad-meeh-neehs-trah-trEEhs)*	administratrix
adoption (f) du système métrique	*(ah-dohp-syÕh dooh seehs-tEhm meh-trEEhk)*	metrication
adresse (f) d'une entreprise	*(ah-drEhs doohn ãhn-trœh-prEEhz)*	place of business
aérosol (m)	*(ah-eh-roh-sOhl)*	aerosol spray
affacturage (m)	*(ah fahk tooh-rΛhzh)*	factoring
affaires (fpl) étrangères	*(ah-fEhr eh-trãhn-zhEh)*	foreign affairs
affectation (f)	*(ah-fehk-tah-syÕh)*	appropriation, assignment, allotment
affectation à un poste	*(ah-fehk-tah-syÕh ah œhn pOhst)*	assignment (personnel)
affectation au budget	*(ah-fehk-tah-syÕh oh booh-zhEh)*	budget appropriation
affecter	*(ah-fehk-tEh)*	earmark (v)
affermage (m)	*(ah fehr mΛhzh)*	equipment leasing
affichage (m) transport	*(ah fœh shΛhzh trãhns pOhr)*	transit advertising
affiche (f)	*(ah-feehsh)*	poster
affidavit (m)	*(ah-feeh-dah-vEEh)*	affidavit
affilié (m)	*(ah-feeh-lyEh)*	affiliate
affrètement (m)	*(ah-freht-mÃh)*	affreightment, charter
affrètement coque nue	*(ah-freht-mÃh kOhk nOOh)*	bareboat charter
agence (f)	*(ah-zhÃhns)*	agency, dealership
agence (f) de publicité	*(ah-zhÃhns dœ pooh-bleeh-seeh-tEh)*	advertising agency
agence de renseignements commerciaux	*(ah-zhÃhns dœ rãhn-seh-nyœh-mÃh koh-mehr-sOh)*	mercantile agency
agence gouvernementale	*(ah-zhÃhns gooh-vehrn-mãhn-tAhl)*	government agency
agent (m)	*(ah-zhÃh)*	agent
agent (m) de bourse	*(ah-zhÃhn dœ bOOhrs)*	stockbroker
agent de change	*(ah-zhÃh dœ shÃhnz)*	stockbroker
agent de charte-partie	*(ah-zhÃh dœ shAhrt-pahr-tEEh)*	charter-party agent

agent de recouvrement	*(ah-zhÃh dœ rœh-koohvrœ-mÃh)*	collection agent
agent de transfert	*(ah-zhÃh dœ trãhnz-fEhr)*	transfer agent
agent en lots irréguliers	*(ah-zhÃh ãhn lOht eeh-rehgooh-lyEh)*	odd lot broker
agent exclusif	*(ah-zhÃh ehks-kloohsEEhf)*	sole agent, manufacturer's agent
agent fiscal	*(ah-zhÃh feehs-kAhl)*	fiscal agent
agent immobilier	*(ah-zhÃh eeh-moh-beehlyEh)*	real estate agent
agent (m) irritant	*(ah-zhÃhn eeh-reeh-tAhn)*	irritant agent
agent maritime	*(ah-zhÃh mah-reehtEEhm)*	shipping agent
agneau (m)	*(ah-nyOh)*	lambskin
agrandir	*(ah-grãhn-dEEhr)*	enlarge (v)
agrandissement (m)	*(ah-grãhn-deehz-mÃh)*	blowup
agrément (m)	*(ah-greh-mÃh)*	approval
agriculture (f)	*(ah-greeh-koohl-tOOhr)*	agriculture
aide (f) conditionnelle	*(Ehd kõhn-deeh-syoh-nEhl)*	tied aid
aigre-doux	*(Eh-grœh dOOh)*	sweet and sour
aiguille (f)	*(eh-gEEh-yœ)*	needle
aile (f)	*(Ehl)*	fender
ajourner	*(ah-zhoohr-nEh)*	postpone (v)
ajustement fiscal (m) aux frontières	*(ah-zhOOhstœ-mÃh feehskAhl oh frõhn-tyEhr)*	border tax adjustment
ajuster	*(ah-zhOOhs-tEh)*	adjust (v)
alcool (m)	*(ahl-kOhl)*	alcohol
ALÉNA (m)	*(al-leh-nAh)*	NAFTA
algorithme (m)	*(ahl-goh-rEEht-mœ)*	algorithm
alimentation (f) intraveineuse	*(ah-leeh-mãhn-tah-syÕhn œhn-trah-veh-nŒhz)*	intravenous feeding
allié (m)	*(ah-lyEh)*	ally
allocation (f)	*(ah-loh-kah-syÕh)*	allowance
allocation de l'amortissement	*(ah-loh-kah-syÕh dœ lahmohr-eehs-mÃh)*	redemption allowance
allocation en capital	*(ah-loh-kah-syÕh ãhn kahpeeh-tAhl)*	capital allowance
allocation pour frais de transport accordée au client	*(ah-loh-kah-syÕh poohr frEh dœ dœ trãhnspOhr ah-kohr-dEh oh kleeh-Ãhn)*	freight allowance
allonge (f)	*(ah-lÕhnz)*	rider (documents)
allouer	*(ah-looh-Eh)*	allow (v)
aloès (m)	*(ah-loh-Ehs)*	aloe vera
altéré	*(ahl-teh-rEh)*	spoiled
alternateur (m)	*(ahl-tehr-nah-tŒhr)*	alternator
amélioration (f)	*(ah-meh-lyoh-rah-syÕh)*	improvement
amende (f)	*(ah-mÃhnd)*	fine (penalty)
amender	*(ah-mãhn-dEh)*	amend (v)
amendment (m)	*(ah-mãhnd-mÃh)*	amendment

amer	*(ah-mEhr)*	bitter
amidon (m)	*(ah-meeh-dÕh)*	starch
amine (f)	*(ah-mEEhn)*	amine
ammoniac (m)	*(ah-moh-nyAhk)*	ammonia
amortissement (m)	*(ah-mohr-tees-mÃhr)*	amortization
amortissement (matériel)	*(ah-mohr-eehs-mÃh), (mah-teh-ryEhl)*	depreciation
amortissement accéléré	*(ah-mohr-eehs-mÃh ak-seh-leh-rEh)*	accelerated depreciation
amortissement accumulé	*(ah-mohr-eehs-mÃh ah-kooh-mooh-lEh)*	accumulated depreciation
amortissement couru	*(ah-mohr-eehs-mÃh kooh-rOOh)*	accrued depreciation
amortissement proportionnel à l'ordre numérique inversé des années	*(ah-mohr-eehs-mÃh proh-pohr-syoh-nEhl ah lOhr-drœ nooh-meh-rEEhk æhn-vœhr-sEh dehz ah-nEh)*	sum-of-the-years digits
amortisseur (m)	*(ah-mohr-teeh-sŒhr)*	shock absorber
amplificateur (m)	*(ahm-pleeh-feeh-kah-tŒhr)*	amplifier
amplifier	*(ãhm-pleeh-fyEh)*	maximize
analgésique (m)	*(ãh-nahl-zheh-zEEhk)*	analgesic
analyse (f)	*(ãh-nah-lEEhz)*	analysis
analyse coût/profit	*(ãh-nah-lEEhz kOOht/ proh-fEEh)*	cost-benefit analysis
analyse d'un emploi	*(ãh-nah-lEEhz dœhn ãhm-plwAh)*	job analysis
analyse de la concurrence	*(ãh-nah-lEEhz dœ lah kÕhn-kooh-rÃhns)*	competitor analysis
analyse de la trajectoire	*(ãh-nah-lEEhz dœ lah trah-zhehk-twAhr)*	critical path analysis
analyse de la valeur	*(ãh-nah-lEEhz dœ lah vah-lŒhr)*	value engineering
analyse de marché	*(ãh-nah-lEEhz dœ mahr-shEh)*	market report
analyse de régression	*(ãh-nah-lEEhz dœ reh-greh-syÕh)*	regression analysis
analyse (f) de sang	*(ah-nah-lEEhz dœ sÃhn)*	blood test
analyse de ventes	*(ãh-nah-lEEhz dœ vÃhnt)*	sales analysis
analyse des besoins	*(ãh-nah-lEEhz DEH bœh-zwÆhn)*	needs analysis
analyse des entrées et sorties	*(ãh-nah-lEEhz ãhn-trEh eh sohr-tEEh)*	input-output analysis
analyse des investissements	*(ãh-nah-lEEhz dehz ãhn-vehs-teehs-mÃh)*	investment analysis
analyse des produits	*(ãh-nah-lEEhz deh proh-dwEEh)*	product analysis
analyse des systèmes	*(ãh-nah-lEEhz deh seehs-tEhm)*	systems analysis

A

analyse du point d'équilibre	*(ãh-nah-lEEhz dooh pwǼh deh-keeh-lEEh-brœ)*	break-even analysis
analyse du risque	*(ãh-nah-lEEhz dooh reEhs-kœ)*	risk analysis
analyse en profondeur	*(ãh-nah-lEEhz ãhn proh-fõhn-dŒhr)*	depth analysis
analyse factorielle	*(ãh-nah-lEEhz fahk-toh-ryEhl)*	factor analysis
analyse financière	*(ãh-nah-lEEhz feeh-nãhn-syEh)*	financial analysis
analyse fonctionnelle	*(ãh-nah-lEEhz fõhnk-syoh-nEhl)*	functional analysis
analyste (m/f)	*(ãh-nah-lEEhst)*	analyst
ancienneté (f)	*(ãhn-syeh-nœh-tEh)*	seniority
anesthésie (f)	*(ah-nehs-teh-zEEh)*	anesthesia
anesthétique (m)	*(ãh-nehs-teh-tEEhk)*	anesthetic
angle (m) d'incidence	*(ãhn-glœ dãhn-seeh-dÃhns)*	angle of incidence
angora	*(ãhn-goh-rAh)*	angora
année (f)	*(ah-nEh)*	year
année budgétaire	*(ah-nEh booh-zheh-tEhr)*	fiscal year
annexer (joindre)	*(ah-nehk-sEh), (zhwǼn-drœ)*	attach (v)
annonce (f)	*(ah-nÕhns)*	ad
annuel	*(ah-nwEhl)*	annual
annuité (f)	*(ah-nweeh-tEh)*	annuity
annuité variable	*(ah-nweeh-tEh vah-ryAh-blœ)*	variable annuity
annuités différées	*(ah-nweeh-tEh deeh-feh-rEh)*	deferred annuities
annuler (chèque)	*(ah-nooh-lEh), (shEhk)*	cancel, void (v)
annuler (contrat)	*(ah-nooh-lEh), (kõhn-trAh)*	nullify (v)
anses (fpl) collées à la main	*(Ãhns koh-lEh ah lah mǼhn)*	hand-glued handles
antenne (f)	*(ãhn-tEhn)*	antenna
anticoagulant (m)	*(ahn-teeh-koh-ah-gooh-lÃh)*	anticoagulant
antidépresseur (m)	*(ahn-teeh-deh-preh-sŒhr)*	antidepressant
anti-inflammatoire	*(ahn-teeh-ǽhn-flah-mah-twAhr)*	anti-inflammatory
antibiotique (m)	*(ahn-teeh-beeh-oh-tEEhk)*	antibiotic
anticholinergique	*(ahn-teeh-koh-leeh-nehr-zhEEhk)*	anticholinergic
antidater	*(ãhn-teeh-dah-tEh)*	backdate (v)
antiseptique (m)	*(ahn-teeh-sehp-tEEhk)*	antiseptic
apesanteur (f)	*(ah-peh-zãhn-tŒhr)*	weightlessness
appareil (m)	*(ah-pah-rEh-yŒ)*	aircraft
appareil (m) de contrôle	*(ah-pahr-Eh-yœ kõhn-trOhl)*	monitor

appartenance (m) syndicale	*(ah-pahr-tœh-nÃhns seehn-deeh-kAhl)*	union label
appel (m) de marge	*(ah-pEhl dœ mAhrzh)*	margin call
appel d'offre	*(ah-pEhl dOh-frœ)*	request for bid, invitation to bid
appellation (f) contrôlée	*(ah-peh-lah-syÕh kõhn-troh-lEh)*	guaranteed classified vintage
Appellation d'Origine Contrôlée	*(ah-peh-lay-syÕhn doh-reeh-zhEEhn kõhn troh-lEh)*	A.O.C.
appliquer	*(ah-pleeh-kEh)*	apply (v), enforce (v)
appréciation (f) des risques	*(ah-preh-syah-syÕh deh rEEhs-kœ)*	risk assessment
apprenti (m)	*(ah-prãhn-tEEh)*	apprentice
approbation (f)	*(ah-proh-bah-syÕh)*	approval
approuver	*(ah-prooh-vEh)*	approve (v)
approvisionnement (m) insuffisant	*(ah-proh-veeh-zyohn mÃh ãehn-sooh-feeh-zÃh)*	short supply
âpre	*(Ah-prœh)*	tart
apurer la perte	*(ah-pooh-rEh lah pEhrt)*	absorb (v) the loss
arbitrage (m)	*(ahr-beeh-trAhzh)*	arbitration
arbitrage des taux d'intérêt	*(ahr-beeh-trAhzh deh tOh dãehn-teh-rEh)*	interest arbitrage
arbitrage industriel	*(ahr-beeh-trAhzh ãehn-doohs-tryEhl)*	industrial arbitration
arbitre (m)	*(ahr-bEEh-trœ)*	arbitrator
arbre (m) à came	*(Ahr-brœ ah kAhm)*	camshaft
argent (m)	*(ahr-zhÃh)*	money
argent au jour le jour	*(ahr-zhÃh oh zhOOhr lœ zhOOhr)*	call money
argent comptant	*(ahr-zhÃh kõhn-tÃhn)*	ready cash
argenterie (f)	*(ahr-zhãhn-teh-rEEh)*	silverware
arme (f)	*(Ahrm)*	weapon
armée (f)	*(ahr-mEh)*	military
armements (mpl)	*(ahr-mœh-mÃhn)*	armaments
armes (fpl) automatiques	*(Ahrm oh-toh-mah-tEEhk)*	automatic weapons
arôme (m)	*(ah-rOhm)*	aroma
arrhes (fpl)	*(Ahr)*	deposit, down payment, import duty
arriéré (m)	*(ah-ryeh-rEh)*	arrears
arrière-goût (m)	*(ah-ryEhr gOOht)*	aftertaste
arrière-plan (m)	*(ah-ryEhr plÃhn)*	background
arrimage (m)	*(ah-reeh-mAhzh)*	stowage
art de l'étalage	*(Ahr dœ leh-tah-lAhzh)*	window dressing
arthrite (f)	*(ahr-trEEht)*	arthritis
article (m)	*(ahr-tEEhk-lœ)*	item
article-appât	*(ahr-tEEhk-lœ ah-pAh)*	loss leader

A

articles (mpl) de taille exceptionnelle	*(ahr-tEEhk-lœ dœ tAh-yœ ehk-sehp-syoh-nEhl)*	outsized articles
articles stratégiques	*(ahr-tEEhk-lœ strah-teh-zhEEhk)*	strategic articles
aspirateur (m)	*(ahs-peeh-rah-tŒhr)*	vacuum cleaner
aspirine (f)	*(ahs-peeh-rEEhn)*	aspirin
assemblée (f)	*(ah-sãhm-blEh)*	meeting, assembly
assemblée d'actionnaires	*(ah-sãhm-blEh dahk-syoh-nEhr)*	shareholders' meeting
assemblée générale	*(ah-sãhm-blEh zheh-neh-rAhl)*	general meeting
assembler	*(ah-sãhm-blEh)*	assemble (v)
assermenté	*(ah-sœhr-mãhn-tEh)*	sworn
assiette (f)	*(ah-syEht)*	plate
assiette à dessert	*(ah-syEht ah dœh-sEhr)*	dessert plate
assiette à salade	*(ah-syEht ah sah-lAhd)*	salad plate
assiette creuse	*(ah-syEht krŒhz)*	soup dish
assiette (f) de l'impôt	*(ah-syEht dœ lœ̃hm-pOh)*	tax base
assiette plate	*(ah-syEht plAht)*	dinner plate
assigner	*(ah-seeh-nyEh)*	assign
assisté par ordinateur	*(ah-seehs-tEh pahr ohr-deeh-nah-tŒhr)*	computer assisted
association (de personnes)	*(ah-soh-syah-syÕh dœ pehr-sÕhn)*	partnership
association (f) commerciale	*(ah-soh-syah-syÕh koh-mehr-syAhl)*	trade association
associé (m)	*(ah-soh-syEh)*	partner
associé en second	*(ah-soh-syEh ãhn sœh-kÕhnd)*	junior partner
assouplissement (m) des restrictions	*(ah-sooh-pleehs-mÃhn deh rœhs-treehk-syÕyn)*	relaxation of restraints
assujetti à l'impôt	*(ah-sooh-zheh-tEEh ah lœ̃hm-pOh)*	liable for tax
assurance (f)	*(ah-sooh-rÃhns)*	insurance
assurance à terme	*(ah-sooh-rÃhns ah tEhrm)*	term insurance
assurance collective	*(ah-sooh-rÃhns koh-lehk-tEEhv)*	group insurance
assurance contre le détournement de fonds	*(ah-sooh-rÃhns kõhn-trœ lœ deh-toohrn-mÃh dœ fÕhn)*	fidelity bond
assurance contre les accidents corporels	*(ah-sooh-rÃhns kõhn-trœ lehz ahk-seeh-dÃh kohr-poh-rEhl)*	casualty insurance
assurance contre les mauvaises créances	*(ah-sooh-rÃhns kõhn-trœ leh moh-vEhz kreh-Ãhns)*	credit insurance
assurance de crédit	*(ah-sooh-rÃhns dœ kreh-dEEh)*	credit insurance
assurance de groupe	*(ah-sooh-rÃhns dœ grOOhp)*	group insurance

assurance de l'homme-clé	*(ah-sooh-rÃhns dœ lOhm klEh)*	key-man insurance
assurance de titres de propriété	*(ah-sooh-rÃhns dœ tEEh-trœ dœ proh-pryeh-tEh)*	title insurance
assurance du travail	*(ah-sooh-rÃhns dooh trah-vAhyœ)*	industrial insurance
assurance en responsabilité civile	*(ah-sooh-rÃhns ãhn rœs-pohn-sah-beeh-leeh-tEh seeh-vEEhl)*	liability insurance
assurance maritime	*(ah-sooh-rÃhns mah-reeh-tEEhm)*	marine cargo insurance
assuré (m)	*(ah-sooh-rEh)*	policyholder, insured
assurer l'entretien	*(ah-sooh-rEh lãhn-trœh-tyEhn)*	service (v)
assureur (m)	*(ah-sooh-rŒhr)*	underwriter
assureur maritime	*(ah-sooh-rŒhr mah-reeh-tEEhm)*	marine underwriter
astrakan (m)	*(ahs-trah-kAhn)*	astrakan
astronaute (m)	*(ahs-troh-nOht)*	astronaut
atelier (m)	*(ah-teh-lyEh)*	workshop
atmosphère (f)	*(aht-moh-sfEhr)*	atmosphere
atome (m)	*(ah-tOhm)*	atom
atomiseur (m)	*(ah-toh-meeh-zŒhr)*	spray
atomique	*(ah-toh-mEEhk)*	atomic
atout (m) écologique	*(ah-tOOh eh-koh-loh-zhEEhk)*	environmental advantage
attaché-case (m)	*(ah-tah-shEh kAhs)*	attache case
atteindre le seuil de rentabilité	*(ah-tÃhn-drœ lœ sŒhyœ dœ rãhn-tah-beeh-leeh-tEh)*	break even
atteintes (fpl) à l'environnement	*(ah-tÆhnt ah lãhn-veeh-rohn-mÃhn)*	environmental damage
atterrissage (m)	*(ah-teh-reeh-sAhzh)*	landing
attestation (f)	*(ah-tehs-tah-syÕh)*	attestation
attestation par écrit	*(ah-tehs-tah-syÕh pahr eh-krEEh)*	affidavit
attraper	*(ah-trah-pEh)*	catch (v)
attribuer (répartir)	*(ah-treeh-booh-Eh), (reh-pahr-tEEhr)*	allot (v)
attribution (f)	*(ah-treeh-booh-syÕh)*	allotment
au cours du marché	*(oh kOOhr dooh mahr-shEh)*	at the market
au jour le jour	*(oh zhOOhr lœ zhOOhr)*	day to day
au mieux	*(oh myŒh)*	at best
au moins	*(oh mwÆh)*	at or better
au moment de l'émission	*(oh moh-mÃh dœ leh-meeh-syÕh)*	when issued
au pair	*(oh pEhr)*	at par
au porteur	*(oh pohr-tŒhr)*	to the bearer

A

au verso	*(oh vehr-sOh)*	on the back
au-dessous de la ligne	*(oh deh-sOOh dœ lah lEEh-nyœ)*	below the line
au-dessous de la norme	*(oh dœ-sOOh dœ lah nOhrm)*	substandard
au-dessous du pair	*(oh dœ-sOOh dooh pEhr)*	below par
au-dessus de la ligne	*(oh dœ-sOOh dœ lah lEEh-nyœ)*	above the line
au-dessus du pair	*(oh dœ-sOOh dooh pEhr)*	above par
aubaine (f)	*(oh-bEhn)*	windfall profits
augmentation (f) de capital	*(ohg-mãhn-tah-syÕh dœ kah-peeh-tAhl)*	capital increase
augmenter	*(ohg-mãhn-tEh)*	increase (v)
augmenter la puissance	*(ohg-mãhn-tEh lah pweeh-sÃhns)*	upgrade (v)
aussitôt que possible	*(oh-seeh-tOh kœ poh-sEEh-blœ)*	as soon as possible
autarcie (f)	*(oh-tahr-sEEh)*	self-sufficiency
authenticité (f)	*(oh-tãhn-teeh-see-tEh)*	authentification
auto-appréciation (f)	*(oh-toh-ah-preh-syah-syÕh)*	self-appraisal
auto-contrôle (m)	*(oh-toh-kõhn-trOhl)*	feedback
auto-gestion (f)	*(oh-toh-zhœhs-tyÕh)*	self-management
autofinancement (m)	*(ah-toh-feeh-nãhns-mÃhn)*	self-financing
autofinancement (m) marginal	*(oh-toh-feeh-nãhns-mÃh mahr-zheeh-nAhl)*	incremental cash flow
automatique	*(oh-toh-mah-tEEhk)*	automatic
automatisation (f)	*(oh-toh-mah-teeh-zah-syÕh)*	automation
automobile (f)	*(oh-toh-moh-bEEhl)*	automobile
autonome (non connecté)	*(oh-toh-nOhm [nõh koh-nehk-tEh])*	off-line
autorisation (f) d'exportation d'œuvres d'art	*(oh-toh-reeh-zah-syÕh dehks-pohr-tah-syÕh dŒhvrœ dAhr)*	cultural export permit
autoriser	*(oh-toh-reeh-zEh)*	authorize (v)
autre actif (et passif) (m)	*(Oh-trœ ahk-tEEf eh pah-sEEhf)*	other assets (and liabilities)
aval (m) et enregistrement	*(ah-vAhl eh lãhn-rœh-zheehs-trœ-mÃh)*	backing and filling
avancement (m)	*(ah-vãhns-mÃh)*	promotion
avancer	*(ah-vãhn-sEh)*	advance (v)
avant-première (f)	*(ah-vÃhn-prœh-myEhr)*	sneak preview
avant-projet (m) de prospectus	*(ah-vÃhn-proh-zhEh dœ prohs-pehk-tOOh)*	preliminary prospectus
avantage (m) concurrentiel	*(ah-vãhn-tAhzh kõhn-kooh-rãhn-syEhl)*	competitive advantage
avantage (m) fiscal	*(ah-vãhn-tAhzh feehs-kAhl)*	tax break

avantages (mpl) hors salaire	*(ah-vãhn-tAhzh ohr sah-lEhr)*	fringe benefits
avarie (f)	*(ah-vah-rEEh)*	average
avec avarie particulière	*(ah-vEhk ah-vah-rEEh pahr-teeh-kooh-lyEhr)*	with average
avenant (m)	*(ah-vœh-nÃh)*	rider (contracts)
avion (m)	*(ah-vyÕhn)*	aircraft
avis (m) d'attribution (de répartition)	*(ah-vEEh dah-treeh-booh-syÕh), (dœ reh-pahr-teeh-syÕh)*	allotment letter
avis de livraison	*(ah-vEEh dœ leeh-vreh-zÕh)*	delivery notice
avocat (m)	*(ah-voh-kAh)*	lawyer
avoir (m)	*(ah-vwAhr)*	credit, credit note
avortement (m)	*(ah-vohrt-mÃhn)*	abortion
azote	*(ah-zOht)*	nitrogen

B

baguette (f)	*(bah-gEht)*	rod
bail (m)	*(bAh-yœ)*	lease
bailleur (m)	*(bah-yŒhr)*	lessor
bailleur de fonds	*(bah-yŒhr dœ fÕhn)*	silent partner
baisse (f)	*(bEhs)*	downturn
baisse des prix imposée	*(bEhs deh prEEh æhm-poh-zÈh)*	rollback
baissier (m)	*(beh-syEh)*	bear
baladeur (m)	*(bah-lah-dŒhr)*	walkman
balance (f)	*(bah-lÃhns)*	scale
balance (f) commerciale	*(bah-lÃhns koh-mehr-syAhl)*	balance of trade
balance commerciale visible	*(bah-lÃhns koh-mehr-syAhl veeh-zEEh-blœ)*	visible balance of trade
balance compensatoire	*(bah-lÃhns kohm-pãhn-sah-twAhr)*	compensating balance
balance de vérification	*(bah-lÃhns dœ veh-reeh-feeh-kah-syÕh)*	trial balance
balance déficitaire	*(bah-lÃhns deh-feeh-seeh-tEhr)*	adverse balance
balance des paiements	*(bah-lÃhns deh peh-mÃh)*	balance of payments
balayage (m)	*(bah-lah-yAhzh)*	scanning
balle (f)	*(bAhl)*	bullet
bande (f) de téléscripteur	*(bÃhnd dœ teh-leh-skreehp-tŒhr)*	ticker tape
bande magnétique	*(bÃhnd mah-nyeh-tEEhk)*	magnetic tape
bande (f) son (m)	*(bÃhnd-sÕhn)*	sound track
banque (f)	*(bÃhnk)*	bank
banque à banque, de	*(bÃhnk ah bÃhnk)*	interbank

banque chef de file	*(bÃhnk shEhf dœ ʃEEhl)*	leader bank
banque commerciale	*(bÃhnk koh-mehr-syAhl)*	commercial bank
banque correspondante	*(bÃhnk koh-rehs-põhn-*	correspondent bank
à l'étranger	*dÃhnt ah leh-trãhn-*	
	zhEh)	
banque d'émission	*(bÃhnk deh-meeh-syÕh)*	central bank
banque d'escompte	*(bÃhnk dehs-kÕhnt [deh-*	acceptance house
(d'effets étrangers)	*ʃEht eh-trãhn-zhEh])*	
banque d'état	*(bÃhnk deh-tAh)*	government bank
banque d'import-export	*(bÃhnk dãhm-pOhr-ehks-*	export-import bank
	pOhr)	
banque d'investissements	*(bÃhnk d~œhn-vehs-teehs-*	merchant bank,
	mÃh)	investment bank
banque de crédit	*(bÃhnk dœ kreh-dEEh)*	credit bank
banque de détail	*(bÃhnk dœ deh-tAhyœ)*	retail bank
banque (f) de données	*(bÃhnk dœ doh-nEh)*	data bank
banque (f) de placement	*(bãhnk dœ plahs-mÃhn)*	investment bank
banque hypothécaire	*(bÃhnk eeh-poh-teh-kEhr)*	mortgage bank
banque informatique	*(bÃhnk ãhn-fohr-mah-*	computer bank
	tEEhk)	
Banque Mondiale	*(bÃhnk mõhn-dyAhl)*	World Bank
banque nationale	*(bÃhnk nah-syoh-nAhl)*	national bank
banqueroute (f)	*(bãhnk-rOOht)*	bankruptcy
baraterie (f)	*(bah-rah-tœh-rEEh)*	barratry
barbiturique (m)	*(bahr-beeh-tooh-rEEhk)*	barbiturate
barème, tarif (m)	*(bah-rEhm), (tah-rEEhf)*	price list
barres (fpl)	*(bAhr)*	bars
barrière (f) commerciale	*(bah-ryEhr koh-mehr-*	trade barrier
	syAhl)	
barrière (f) douanière	*(bah-reEhr dooh-ah-*	trade barrier
	nyEhr)	
barrières (fpl) tarifaires	*(bah-ryEhr tah-reeh-ʃEhr)*	tariff barriers
barrique (f)	*(bah-rEEhk)*	cask (225 litres)
bas (m)	*(bAh)*	stockings
base (f) de données	*(bAhz dœ doh-nEh)*	data base
base monétaire	*(bAhz moh-neh-tEhr)*	monetary base
bateau-citerne (m)	*(bah-tOh seeh-tEhrn)*	tanker
batiste (f)	*(bah-tEEhst)*	batiste
batterie (f)	*(bah-teh-rEEh)*	battery
baud (m)	*(bOh)*	unit of data trans-
		mission speed
baume (m)	*(bOhm)*	balm
bec (m) verseur	*(bEhk vehr-sŒhr)*	spout
bénéfice (m)	*(beh-neh-ʃEEhs)*	profit
bénéfice (m) brut	*(beh-neh-ʃEEhs)*	gross profit
bénéfice du marchand de	*(beh-neh-ʃEEhs dooh mahr-*	jobber's turn
titres	*shÃhnd dœ tEEh-trœ)*	
bénéfice net	*(beh-neh-ʃEEhs nEht)*	net profit
bénéfice net avant impôts	*(beh-neh-ʃEEhs nEht*	operating profit
	ah-vÃhnt ãhm-pOh)	

bénéfice par action	*(beh-neh-fEEhs pahr ahk-syÕh)*	earnings per share
bénéfices (mpl)	*(beh-neh-fEEhs)*	earnings
bénéfices non distribués	*(beh-neh-fEEhs nõh deehs-treeh-bwEh)*	retained profits, retained earnings
bénéficiaire (m/f)	*(beh-neh-feeh-syEhr)*	beneficiary, payee
benzène (m)	*(bãhn-zEhn)*	benzene
berline (f)	*(behr-lEEhn)*	sedan
besoins (mpl)	*(bœh-zwÆhn)*	requirements
beurrier (m)	*(bœh-ryEh)*	butter dish
bielle (f)	*(byEh-yœ)*	connecting rod
biens immobiliers (m)	*(byÆhn eeh-moh-beeh-lyEh)*	estate
biens (mpl) d'équipement	*(byÆhn deh-keehp-mÃh)*	capital goods
biens de consommation	*(byÆhn dœ kõhn-soh-mah-syÕh)*	consumer goods
biens de production	*(byÆhn dœ proh-doohk-syÕh)*	capital goods
biens durables (mpl)	*(byÆhn dooh-rAh-blœh)*	durable goods
biens immobiliers	*(byÆhn eeh-moh-beeh-lyEh)*	real assets
biens intermédiaires	*(byÆhnz æhn-tehr-meh-dyEhr)*	intermediary goods
biens manufacturés	*(byÆhn mah-nooh-fahk-tooh-rEh)*	industrial goods
biens meubles	*(byÆhn mŒh-blœ)*	personal property
biens mobiliers	*(byÆh moh-beeh-lyEh)*	chattel
biens périssables	*(byÆhn peh-reeh-sAh-blœ)*	nondurable goods
bijou (m)	*(beeh-zhOOh)*	jewel
bilan (m)	*(beeh-lÃh)*	balance sheet
bilan consolidé	*(beeh-lÃh kõh-soh-leeh-dEh)*	consolidated financial statement
bilan d'entrée	*(beeh-lÃh dãhn-trEh)*	opening balance
bilan de contrôle	*(beeh-lÃh dœ kõhn-trOhl)*	auditing balance sheet
bilan hebdomadaire	*(beeh-lÃh ehb-doh-mah-dEhr)*	weekly return
billet (m) à ordre	*(beeh-yEh ah Ohr-drœ)*	promissory note
billet de banque	*(beeh-yEh dœ bÃhnk)*	bank note
billet de complaisance	*(beeh-yEh dœ kõhn-pleh-zÃhns)*	accommodation paper
billettes (fpl)	*(beeh-yEht)*	billets
biochimie (f)	*(beeh-oh-sheeh-mEEh)*	biochemistry
biodégradable	*(beeh-oh-grah-dAh-blœh)*	biodegradable
biologie (f)	*(beeh-oh-loh-zhEEh)*	biology
biologiste (m)	*(beeh-oh-loh-zhEEhst)*	biologist
biopsie (f)	*(beeh-ohp-sEEh)*	biopsy
biosphère (f)	*(beeh-oh-sfEhr)*	biosphere
bit (m)		bit

blocage (m)	*(bloh-kAhzh)*	lock in (rate of interest)
blocage de fonds	*(bloh-kAhzh dœ fŌhn)*	blockage of funds
blocage de prix	*(bloh-kAhzh dœ prEEh)*	pegging
blocage des salaires	*(bloh-kAhzh deh sah-lEhr)*	wage freeze
blocus (m)	*(bloh-kOOh)*	blockade
blouson (m) de cuir	*(blooh-zŌh dœ kwEEhr)*	leather jacket
blouson de daim	*(blooh-zŌh dœ dEhm)*	suede jacket
bobine (f)	*(boh-bEEhn)*	coil
boire	*(bwAhr)*	drink (v)
bol (m)	*(bOhl)*	bowl
bombarder	*(bohm-bahr-dEh)*	bomb (v)
bombardier (m)	*(bohm-bahr-dyEh)*	bomber
bombe (f) à fragmentation	*(bOhmb ah frahg-māhn-tah-syŌhn)*	cluster bomb
bon (m) au porteur	*(bŌh oh pohr-tŒhr)*	bearer bond
bon d'épargne	*(bŌh deh-pAhr-nyœ)*	savings bond
bon de cautionnement	*(bŌh dœ koh-syohn-mĀh)*	guaranty bond
bon de commande	*(bŌh dœ koh-mĀhnd)*	order form, purchase order
bon marché	*(bŌhn mahr-shEh)*	cheap
bonne affaire (f)	*(bOhn ah-fEhr)*	bargain
bons du trésor (échéance à plus de dix ans)	*(bŌh dooh treh-zOhr [eh-sheh-Āhns ah plooh dœ deehs Āhn])*	treasury bonds, treasury bills
bon du trésor (échéance entre un et dix ans)	*(bŌh dooh treh-zOhr [eh-sheh-Āhns āhn-trœ œhn eh deehs Āhn])*	treasury note, treasury bill
bordereau (m) de débit	*(bohr-dœ-rOh dœ deh-bEEh)*	debit note
bordereau d'expédition	*(bohr-dœ-rOh dehks-peeh-deeh-syŌh)*	waybill, shipping memo
botanique (f)	*(boh-tah-nEEhk)*	botanic
botterie (f)	*(boh-teh-rEEh)*	boot shop
bottes (fpl)	*(bOht)*	boots
bottier (m)	*(boh-tyEh)*	bootmaker
bottines	*(bOh-tEEhn)*	ankle boots
bouchon (m)	*(booh-shŌh)*	cork
bougie (f)	*(booh-zhEEh)*	spark plug
bouilloire (f)	*(booh-lwAhr)*	kettle
bouquet (m)	*(booh-kEh)*	bouquet
bourrage (m)	*(booh-rAhzh)*	stuffing
Bourse (f)	*(bOOhrs)*	Stock Exchange
bourse des denrées	*(bOOhrs deh dāhn-rEh)*	commodity exchange
bourse des valeurs	*(bOOhrs deh vah-lŒhr)*	etock exchange
bouteille (f)	*(booh-tEh-yœ)*	bottle
bouton (m)	*(booh-tŌh)*	button
bouton (m) de manchette	*(booh-tŌhn dœ māhn-shEht)*	cuff link

boutonnière (f)	*(booh-toh-nyEhr)*	buttonhole
boycott (m)	*(bohy-kOht)*	boycott
bracelet (m) de montre	*(brahs-lEh dœ mÕhn-trœ)*	watch band
brainstorming (m)		brainstorming
brames (fpl)	*(brAhm)*	slabs
branche (f) d'affaires	*(brÃhnsh dah-fEhr)*	line of business
brevet (m)	*(brœh-vEh)*	patent
brevet en attente d'homologation	*(brœh-vEht ãhn ah-tÃhnt dœ oh-moh-loh-gah-syÕh)*	patent pending
brillant	*(breeh-yÃh)*	glossy
briseur (m) de grève	*(breeh-zŒhr dœ grEhv)*	strikebreaker
broché	*(broh-shEh)*	paperback, sewn
brochure (f)	*(broh-shOOhr)*	pamphlet
broyeur (m) de déchets	*(brwah-yŒhr deh deh-shEht)*	waste disposal unit
brûlure (f)	*(brooh-lOOhr)*	burn, burning
budget (m)	*(booh-zhEh)*	budget
budget commercial	*(booh-zhEh koh-mehr-syAhl)*	marketing budget
budget d'exploitation	*(booh-zhEh dehks-plwah-tah-syÕh)*	waybill, shipping memo
budget d'investissement	*(booh-zhEh dãehn-vehs-teehs-mÃh)*	investment budget, capital budget
budget de trésorerie	*(booh-zhEh dœ treh-zoh-reh-rEEh)*	cash budget
budget des ventes	*(booh-zhEh deh vÃhnt)*	sales budget
budget provisoire	*(booh-zhEh proh-veeh-zwAhr)*	interim budget
budget (m) publicitaire	*(booh-zhEh pooh-bleeh-seeh-tEhr)*	advertising budget
bulle (f)	*(bOOhl)*	speech bubble
bulletin (m) de souscription	*(booh-lœ-tÃÉhn dœ sooh-skreehp-syÕh)*	application form
bureau (m)	*(booh-rOh)*	office
bureau d'études	*(booh-rOh deh-tOOhd)*	engineering and design department
bureau de placement	*(booh-rOh dœ plahs-mÃh)*	employment agency
bureaucrate (m)	*(booh-roh-krAht)*	bureaucrat
burette (f)	*(booh-rEht)*	buret

C

cabine (f) de pilotage	*(kah-bEEhn dœ neeh-loh-tAhzh)*	flight deck
câble (m)	*(kAh-blœ)*	cable
câble (m) coaxial	*(kAh-blœ)*	coaxial cable

cachemire (m)	*(kahsh-eh-mEEhr)*	cashmere
cadre (m) adjoint	*(kAh-drœ ad-zhwÆhn)*	staff assistant
cadre (m) politique	*(kAh-drœ poh-leeh-tEEhk)*	political framework
cadres (mpl) moyens	*(kAh-drœ mwah-yEhn)*	middle management
cadres supérieurs	*(kAh-drœ sooh-peh-ryŒhr)*	top management
cafetière (f)	*(kah-feh-tyEhr)*	coffeepot
caisse (f)	*(kEhs)*	case
caisse (f) d'amortissements	*(kEhs dah-mohr-eehs-mÃh)*	sinking fund
caisse d'emballage	*(kEhs dæhm-bah-lAhzh)*	packing case
caisse d'épargne	*(kEhs deh-pAhr-nyœ)*	savings bank
caisse (f) de retraite	*(kEhs dœ rœh-trEh)*	pension fund
caisse, position de	*(kEhs, poh-zeeh-syÕh dœ)*	cash basis
calandre (f)	*(kah-lÃhn-drœ)*	grille
calcium (m)	*(kahl-syOOhm)*	calcium
calcul (m) du prix moyen en dollars	*(kahl-kOOhl dooh prEEh mwah-yEhn ãhn doh-lAhr)*	dollar cost averaging
calculatrice (f)	*(kahl-kooh-lah-trEEhs)*	calculator
calendrier (m) des échéances	*(kah-lãhn-dryEh dehz eh-sheh-Ãhns)*	installment plan
calibre (m)	*(kah-lEEh-brœ)*	jig
calmant (m)	*(kahl-mÃh)*	tranquilizer
cambiste (m)	*(kahm-bEEhst)*	trader, broker
camion-citerne (m)	*(kah-myÕh seeh-tEhrn)*	tanker
camionnage (m)	*(kah-myoh-nAhzh)*	drayage
campagne (f) de presse	*(kahm-pÃh-nyœh dœ prEhs)*	press campaign
campagne (f) de productivité	*(kãh-pÃh-nyœ dœ proh-doohk-teeh-veeh-tEh)*	productivity campaign
campagne de publicité	*(kãh-pÃh-nyœ dœ pooh-bleeh-seeh-tEh)*	advertising campaign, advertising drive
canal (m)	*(kah-nAhl)*	channel
canalisation (f)	*(kah-nah-leeh-zah-syÕh)*	pipage
canapé (m)	*(kah-nah-pEh)*	couch
canaux (mpl) de distribution	*(kah-nOh dœ deehs-treeh-booh-syÕh)*	channels of distribution
cancer (m) du col	*(kãhn-sEh dooh kOhl)*	cervical cancer
cancer du poumon	*(kãhn-sEh dooh pooh-mÕhn)*	lung cancer
cancer du sein	*(kãhn-sEh dooh sÆhn)*	breast cancer
candidat (m) à l'adhésion	*(kãhn-deeh-dAh ah lah-deh-zyÕhn)*	aspirant member
capacité (f)	*(kah-pah-seeh-tEh)*	capacity
capacité balles	*(kah-pah-seeh-tEh bAHl)*	bale capacity
capacité contributive	*(kah-pah-seeh-tEh kõhn-treeh-booh-tEEhv)*	ability to pay concept
capacité d'exploitation	*(kah-pah-seeh-tEh dehks-plwah-tah-syÕh)*	utilization capacity

capacité de fabrication	*(kah-pah-seeh-tEh dœ fah-breeh-kah-syÕh)*	manufacturing capacity
capacité (f) de mémoire	*(kah-pah-seeh-tEh dœ meh-mwAhr)*	capacity
capacité de production	*(kah-pah-seeh-tEh dœ proh-doohk-syÕh)*	plant capacity
capacité de traitement	*(kah-pah-seeh-tEh dœ treht-mÃh)*	throughput
capital (m)	*(kah-peeh-tAhl)*	capital, principal, assets
capital à risque	*(kah-peeh-tAhl ah rEEhs-kœ)*	risk capital
capital actions	*(kah-peeh-tAhl ahk-syÕh)*	capital stock
capital d'achat	*(kah-peeh-tAhl dah-shAh)*	spending capital
capital de réserve	*(kah-peeh-tAhl dœ reh-zEhrv)*	surplus capital
capital de roulement	*(kah-peeh-tAhl dœ roohl-mÃh)*	working capital
capital en accroissement	*(kah-peeh-tAhl ãhn ah-krwahs-mÃh)*	raising capital
capital fixe	*(kah-peeh-tAhl fEEhks)*	fixed capital, fixed assets
capital investi	*(kah-peeh-tAhl æhn-vœhs-tEEh)*	invested capital
capital légal	*(kah-peeh-tAhl leh-gAhl)*	legal capital
capital ordinaire	*(kah-peeh-tAhl ohr-deeh-nEhr)*	ordinary capital
capital productif	*(kah-peeh-tAhl proh-doohk-tEEhf)*	instrumental capital
capital propre	*(kah-peeh-tAhl prOh-prœ)*	stockholder's capital
capital spéculatif	*(kah-peeh-tAhl speh-koohlah-tEEhf)*	venture capital
capital variable	*(kah-peeh-tAhl vah-ryAh-blœ)*	floating assets
capital versé	*(kah-peeh-tAhl vehr-sEh)*	paid-up capital
capital-risque (m)	*(kah-peeh-tahl rEEhsk)*	venture capital
capitalisation (f)	*(kah-peeh-tah-leeh-zah-syÕh)*	capitalization
capitalisme (m)	*(kah-peeh-tah-lEEhz-mœ)*	capitalism
capitaux (mpl) différés	*(kah-peeh-tOh deeh-feh-rEh)*	deferred assets
capitaux élevés, à	*(kah-peeh-tOh eh-leh-vEh)*	capital intensive
capitaux fébriles	*(kah-peeh-tOh feh-brEEhl)*	hot money
capitaux fixes	*(kah-peeh-tOh fEEhks)*	fixed assets
capitaux flottants, faire appel à	*(kah-peeh-tOh floh-tÃhn, fEhr ah-pEhl ah)*	go around (v)
capitaux frais	*(kah-peeh-tOh frEh)*	new money
capitaux propres	*(kah-peeh-tOh prOh-prœ)*	shareholder's equity

capitaux publics, faire appel à des	(kah-peeh-tOh pooh-blEEhk), (fEhr ah-pEhl ah deh)	go public (v)
capiteux	(kah-peeh-tOh)	heady
capsule (f)	(kahp-sOOhl)	capsule
capuche (f)	(kah-pOOhsh)	hood
caractère (m)	(kah-rahk-tEhr)	character, letter
carafe (f)	(kah-rAhf)	decanter
carbone (m)	(kahr-bOhn) ·	carbon
carburateur (m)	(kahr-booh-rah-tŒhr)	carburetor
cargaison (f)	(kahr-geh-zÕh)	cargo
cargaison ordinaire	(kahr-geh-zÕh ohr-deeh-nEhr)	dry cargo
carnet (m) de compte	(kahr-nEh dœ kÕhnt)	passbook
carrosserie (f)	(kah-roh-seh-rEEh)	body
carte (f)	(kAhrt)	business card
carte de crédit	(kAhrt dœ kreh-dEEh)	credit card
carte perforée	(kAhrt pehr-foh-rEh)	punch card
cartel (m)	(kahr-tEhl)	cartel
cartonné	(kahr-toh-nEh)	hardcover
cartouche (f)	(kahr-tOOhsh)	cartridge
cas (m) de force majeure	(kAh dœ fOhrs mah-zhŒhr)	act of God
casque (m)	(kAhsk)	helmet
cassette (f)	(kah-sEht)	tape, cassette
castor (m)	(kahs-tOhr)	beaver
catalogue (m)	(kah-tah-lOhg)	catalog
catalyseur (m)	(kah-tah-leeh-zŒhr) ·	catalyst
catégories (fpl) d'exclusion réciproque	(kah-teh-goh-rEEh dehks-klooh-zyÕh reh-seeh-prOhk)	mutually exclusive classes
cathode (f)	(kah-tOhd)	cathode
cautionnement (m)	(koh-syohn-mÃh)	letter of indemnity
cautionnement global	(koh-syohn-mÃh gloh-bAhl)	blanket bond
cautions (fpl) de soutien	(koh-syÕh dœ sooh-tyÆh)	backup bonds
cave (f) à vin	(kahv ah vÆhn)	wine cellar
cédant (m)	(seh-dÃhn)	assignor
céder	(seh-dEh)	assign (v)
ceinture (f)	(sæhn-tOOhr)	belt
cellule (f)	(seh-lOOhl)	cell
cendrier (m)	(sãhn-dryEh)	ashtray
centilitre (m)	(sãhn-teeh-lEEh-trœ)	centiliter
centralisation (f)	(sãhn-trah-leeh-zah-syÕh)	centralization
centre (m) commercial	(sÃhn-trœ koh-mehr-syAhl)	shopping center
centre (m) de recyclage	(sÃhn-trœh dœ rœh-seeh-klAhzh)	recycling center
centre financier	(sÃhn-trœ feeh-nãhn-syEh)	money shop
centre informatique	(sÃhn-trœ æhn-fohr-mah-tEEhk)	computer center
cep (m)	(sEhp)	vine

C

cépage (m)	(seh-pAhzh)	type of vine
céréales (fpl)	(seh-reh-Ahl)	grain
certificat (m)	(sehr-teeh-feeh-kAh)	certificate
certificat d'authenticité d'une antiquité	(sehr-teeh-feeh-kAh doh-tãhn-teeh-see-tEh doohnãhn-teeh-kee-tEh)	antique authenticity certificate
certificat d'entrepôt	(sehr-teeh-feeh-kAh dãhn-træ-pOh)	warranty
certificat d'incorporation	(sehr-teeh-feeh-kAh dæhn-kohr-poh-rah-syÕh)	certificate of incorporation
certificat d'utilisation finale	(sehr-teeh-feeh-kAh dooh-teeh-zah-syÕh feeh-nAhl)	end use certificate
certificat de débarquement	(sehr-teeh-feeh-kAh dæ deh-bahrk-mÃh)	landing certificate
certificat de dépôt	(sehr-teeh-feeh-kAh dæ deh-pOh)	certificate of deposit
certificat hypothécaire	(sehr-teeh-feeh-kAh eeh-poh-teh-kEhr)	mortgage certificate
cessionnaire (m)	(seh-syoh-nEhr)	assignee
césurer	(seh-sooh-rEh)	hyphenate (v)
chai (m)	(shEh)	vintry
chaîne (f) de montage	(shEhn dæ mõhn-tAhzh)	assembly line, conveyor belt
chalandage (m)	(shah-lahn-dAhzh)	barge transportation
chambré	(shãhm-brEh)	room temperature
chambre (f) de commerce	(shÃhm-bræ dæ koh-mEhrs)	chamber of commerce
chambre de compensation	(shÃhm-bræ dæ kõhm-pãhn-sah-syÕh)	clearinghouse
champagne (m)	(sham-pAh-nyæ)	champagne
chandelier (m)	(shãhn-dæh-lyEh)	candlestick
change (m)	(shÃhnzh)	foreign exchange
changement (m)	(shãhnzh-mÃh)	alteration
changement (m) de vitesse	(shãhnzh-mÃh dæ veeh-tEhs)	gearshift
changements (mpl) imminents	(shãhnzh-mÃh eeh-meeh-nÃh)	impending changes
chapitre (m)	(shah-pEEh-træ)	chapter
char (m)	(shAhr)	tank
charbon (m)	(shahr-bÕh)	coal
charge (f)	(shAhrzh)	carrying charge, heat
charge de travail	(shAhrzh dæ trah-vAhyæ)	work load
charge maximum	(shAhrzh mahk-seeh-mOOhm)	peak load
chargement (m)	(shahrzh-mÃh)	carload
chargement complet	(shahrzh-mÃh kohm-plEh)	truckload

chargement en balles	*(shahrzh-mÃh ãhn bAhl)*	bale cargo
chargement incomplet	*(shahrzh-mÃh æhn-kohm-plEh)*	less-than-carload, less-than-truck-load, short shipment
chargement lourd	*(shahrzh-mÃh lOOhr)*	heavy lift charges
chargement partiel	*(shahrzh-mÃh pahr-syEhl)*	part cargo
charges (fpl) courues	*(shAhrzh kooh-rOOh)*	accrued expenses
charges exclues	*(shAhrzh ehks-klOOh)*	charge-off
charges fixes	*(shAhrzh fEEhks)*	fixed charges
charges salariales	*(shAhrzh sah-lah-ryAhl)*	payload
charges tarifaires	*(shAhrzh tah-reeh-fÉhr)*	tariff charge
chargeur (m)	*(shahr-zhŒhr)*	cartridge
charpenté	*(shahr-pãhn-tEh)*	robust
charte (f)	*(shAhrt)*	charter
charte-partie (f), agent de	*(shAhrt-pahr-tEEh, ah-zhÃh dœ)*	charter party agent
chasseur (m) de têtes	*(shah-sŒhr dœ tEht)*	head hunter
châssis (m)	*(shah-sEEh)*	chassis
château (m)	*(shah-tOh)*	estate (or chateau)
chauffe-plat (m)	*(shohf-plAh)*	chafing dish
chaussettes (m)	*(shoh-sEht)*	socks
chaussons (mpl)	*(shoh-sÕh)*	slippers
chaussure (f)	*(shoh-sOOhr)*	shoe
chef (m) comptable	*(shEhf kõhn-tAh-blœ)*	chief accountant
chef d'atelier	*(shEhf dah-teh-lyEh)*	supervisor
chef de produit	*(shEhf dœ proh-dwEEh)*	brand manager
chef (m) de publicité	*(shEhf dœ pooh-bleeh-seeh-tEh)*	account executive
chef de secteur	*(shEhf dœ sehk-tŒhr)*	line executive, area manager
chef syndicaliste	*(shEhf seehn-deeh-kah-lEEhste)*	labor leader
chemin (m) critique, analyse du	*(shœ-mÃh kreeh-tEEhk ãh-nah-lEEhz dooh)*	critical path analysis
chemise (f)	*(shœh-mEEhz)*	shirt
chemisier (m)	*(shœh-meeh-zyEh)*	blouse
chèque (m)	*(shEhk)*	check
chèque annulé	*(shEhk ah-nooh-lEh)*	cancelled check, voided check
chèque bancaire	*(shEhk bãhn-kEhr)*	bank check
chèque de caisse	*(shEhk dœ kEhs)*	cashier's check
chèque de voyage	*(shEhk dœ vwah-yAhzh)*	traveler's check
chèque enregistré	*(shEhk ãhn-rœh-zheehs-trEh)*	registered check
chèque omnibus	*(shEhk ohm-neeh-bOOhs)*	counter check
chèque périmé	*(shEhk peh-reeh-mEh)*	stale check
chèque visé	*(shEhk veeh-zEh)*	certified check
chèques (mpl) non encaissés	*(shEhk nõhn ãhn-keh-sEh)*	float

chevaucher (v)	*(shœh-voh-shEh)*	overlap
chevaux (mpl)	*(shœh-vOh)*	horsepower
chiffre (m) d'affaires	*(shEEh-frœ dah-fEhr)*	sales volume
chiffre d'affaires brut	*(shEEh-frœ dah-fEhr brOOh)*	gross sales
chiffre d'affaires net	*(shEEh-frœ dah-fEhr nEht)*	net sales
chiffres réels	*(shEEh-frœ reh-Ehl)*	actuals
chimie (f)	*(sheeh-mEEh)*	chemistry
chimie analytique	*(sheeh-mEEh āh-nah-leeh-tEEhk)*	analytic chemistry
chimie minérale	*(sheeh-mEEh meeh-neh-rAhl)*	inorganic chemistry
chimie organique	*(sheeh-mEEh ohr-gah-nEEhk)*	organic chemistry
chimique	*(sheeh-mEEhk)*	chemical
chirurgie (f)	*(sheeh-roohr-zhEEh)*	surgery
chloroforme (m)	*(kloh-roh-fOhrm)*	chloroform
chlorure (m)	*(kloh-rOOhr)*	chloride
chômage (m)	*(shoh-mAhzh)*	unemployment
chrome (m)	*(krOhm)*	chromium
cicéro (m)	*(seeh-seh-rOh)*	pica
cil (m)	*(sEEhl)*	eyelash
circuit (m)	*(seehr-kwEEh)*	circuit
circuit imprimé	*(seehr-kwEEht æhm-preeh-mEh)*	printed circuit
circuit intégré	*(seehr-kwEEht æhn-teh-grEh)*	integrated circuit
circuit parallèle	*(seehr-kwEEh pah-rah-lEhl)*	parallel circuit
circulaire (f) d'information	*(seehr-kooh-lEhr dæhn-fohr-mah-syÕh)*	proxy statement
cirrhose (f) du foie	*(seehr-Ohz dooh fwAh)*	cirrhosis of the liver
citoyenneté (f) européenne	*(seeh-twah-yehn-tEh eh-ooh-roh-peh-Ehn)*	European citizenship
classe (f) ouvrière	*(klahs ooh-vryEhr)*	working class
classement (m) des obligations	*(klahs-mÃh dehz oh-bleeh-gah-syÕh)*	bond rating
classification (f) des marchés	*(klah-seeh-feeh-kah-syÕh deh mahr-shEh)*	market rating
classification tarifaire	*(klah-seeh-feeh-kah-syÕh tah-reeh-fEhr)*	tariff classification
clause (f)	*(klOhz)*	clause
clause (f) d'abandon	*(klOhz dah-bãhn-dÕh)*	waiver clause
clause d'échelle mobile	*(klOhz deh-shEhl moh-bEEhl)*	escalator clause
clause d'escalation	*(klOhz deh-skah-lah-syÕh)*	escalator clause
clause de change	*(klOhz dœ shÃhnz)*	currency clause
clause de la nation la plus favorisée	*(klOhz dœ lah nah-syÕh lah plooh fah-voh-reeh-zEh)*	most-favored nation clause

C

clause de remboursement anticipé	*(klOhz dœ rãhm-boohrs-mÃh ãhn-teeh-seeh-pEh)*	call feature
clause dérogatoire	*(klOhz deh-roh-gah-twAhr)*	escape clause
clause Jason	*(klOhz Jason)*	Jason clause
clause or	*(klOhz Ohr)*	gold clause
clause pénale	*(klOhz peh-nAhl)*	penalty clause
clauses (fpl) de vente	*(klOhz dœ vÃhnt)*	terms of sale
clavier (m)	*(klah-vyEh)*	keyboard
clef (f) en main	*(klEhf ãhn mÆhn)*	turnkey
client (m)	*(kleeh-Ãhn)*	customer
clientèle (f)	*(kleeh-ãhn-tEhl)*	goodwill
clignotant (m) économique	*(kleeh-nyoh-tÃhnt eh-koh-moh-mEEhk)*	lagging indicator
climat (m)	*(kleeh-mAh)*	climate
coassurance (f)	*(koh-ah-sooh-rÃhns)*	coinsurance
Code (m) du travail	*(kOhd dooh trah-vAhyœ)*	labor code
code (m) binaire	*(kOhd beeh-nEhr)*	binary code
code postal	*(kOhd pohs-tAhl)*	zip code
codicille (m)	*(koh-deeh-sEEh-yœ)*	codicil
coefficient (m)	*(koh-eh-feeh-sÃhnt)*	ratio, factor
coefficient d'imputation des frais généraux	*(koh-eh-feeh-sÃhnt dæhm-pooh-tah-syÕh deh frEh zheh-neh-rOh)*	burden rate
coefficient de capitalisation des résultats	*(koh-eh-feeh-sÃhnt dœ kah-peeh-tah-leeh-zah-syÕh deh reh-soohl-tAh)*	price earnings ratio (p/e ratio)
coefficient de charge	*(koh-eh-feeh-sÃhnt dœ shAhrz)*	load factor
coefficient de couverture	*(koh-eh-feeh-sÃhnt dœ kooh-vehr-tOOhr)*	cover ratio
coefficient de liquidité	*(koh-eh-feeh-sÃhnt dœ leeh-keeh-deeh-tEh)*	liquidity ratio
coefficient de remplissage	*(koh-eh-feeh-sÃhnt dœ rãhm-pleeh-sAhzh)*	load factor
coffre (m) de nuit	*(kOh-frœ dœ nwEEh)*	night depository
col (m)	*(kOhl)*	collar
collage (m)	*(koh-lAhzh)*	clearing
collagène (m)	*(koh-lah-zhEhn)*	collagen
collection (f)	*(koh-lehk-syÕh)*	collection
collègue (m/f)	*(koh-lEhg)*	colleague
colloque (m)	*(koh-lOhk)*	meeting, colloquium
collyre (m)	*(koh-lEEhr)*	eyedrop
combinaison (f)	*(kõhm-beeh-neh-zÕh)*	combination
combustible (m) fossile	*(kõhm-boohs-tEEh-blœh foh-sEEhl)*	fossil fuel
comité (m) consultatif	*(koh-meeh-tEh kõh-soohl-tah-tEEhf)*	advisory council

comité d'entreprise	*(koh-meeh-tEh dãhn-trœh-prEEhz)*	work committee, work council
comité de direction	*(koh-meeh-tEh dœ deeh-rehk-syÕh)*	executive committee
commande (f)	*(koh-mÃhnd)*	order, command
commande alternative	*(koh-mÃhnd ahl-tehr-nah-tEEhv)*	alternative order
commande complémentaire	*(koh-mÃhnd kõhm-pleh-mãh-tEhr)*	follow-up order
commande de disque	*(koh-mÃhnd dœ dEEhsk)*	disk drive
commande de renouvellement	*(koh-mÃhnd dœ rœh-nooh-vehl-mÃh)*	repeat order
commande en souffrance	*(koh-mÃhnd ãhn sooh-frÃhns)*	back order
commande urgente	*(koh-mÃhnd oohr-jÃhnt)*	rush order
commande, passer une	*(koh-mÃhnd, pah-sEh oohn)*	place an order (v)
commandes (fpl) en attente	*(koh-mÃhnd ãhn ah-tÃhnt)*	backlog
commanditaire (m)	*(koh-mãhn-deeh-tEhr)*	silent partner
commerce (m)	*(koh-mEhrs)*	commerce, trade
commerce après-bourse	*(koh-mEhrs ah-preh-bOOhrs)*	after-hours trading
commerce croisé	*(koh-mEhrs krwah-zEh)*	reciprocal trading
commerce de compensation	*(koh-mEhrs dœ kõhm-pãhn-sah-syÕh)*	compensation trade
commerce de détail	*(koh-mEhrs dœ deh-tAhyœ)*	retail trade
commerce de gros	*(koh-mEhrs dœ grOh)*	wholesale trade
commerce entre les états d'un même	*(koh-mEhrs ãhn-trœ lehz eh-tAh dœhn mEhm)*	pays, commerce
commerce extérieur	*(koh-mEhrs ehks-teh-ryŒhr)*	foreign trade
commerce intérieur des États-Unis	*(koh-mEhrs ãehn-teh-ryŒhr dehz eh-tahz-ooh-nEEh)*	interstate commerce
commerce multilatéral	*(koh-mEhrs moohl-teeh-lah-teh-rAhl)*	multilateral trade
commercer	*(koh-mehr-sEh)*	trade (v)
commercialisable	*(koh-mehr-syah-leeh-zAh-blœ)*	negotiable
commercialisation	*(koh-mehr-syah-leeh-zah-syÕh)*	marketing
commercialiser	*(koh-mehr-syah-leeh-zEh)*	market (v)
commissaire aux comptes (m)	*(koh-meeh-sEhr oh kÕhnt)*	auditor, comptroller
commission (f)	*(koh-meeh-syÕh)*	commission
commission (pourcentage)	*(koh-meeh-syÕh [poohr-sãhn-tAhzh])*	load (sales charge)
commission commerciale	*(koh-meeh-syÕh koh-mehr-syAhl)*	trade commission

commission d'adresse	*(koh-meeh-syÕh dah-drEhs)*	address commission
commission d'agence	*(koh-meeh-syÕh dah-zhÃhns)*	agency fee
commission de courtier	*(koh-meeh-syÕh dœ koohr-tyEh)*	head load
commission de gestion	*(koh-meeh-syÕh dœ zhœhs-tyÕh)*	management fee
commission de montage	*(koh-meeh-syÕh dœ mõhn-tAhzh)*	front-end fee
commissionnaire (m) de transport	*(koh-meeh-syoh-nEhr dœ trãhns-pOhr)*	forwarding agent
commissionnaire-exportateur (m)	*(koh-meeh-syoh-nEhr ehks-pohr-tah-tŒhr)*	export agent
Communauté (f) Européenne (CE)	*(koh-mooh-noh-tEh eh-ooh-roh-peh-Ehn)*	European Community (EC)
communications (fpl) de masse	*(koh-mooh-neeh-kah-syÕh dœ mAhs)*	mass communications
communiqué (m) de presse	*(koh-mooh-neeh-kEh dœ prEhs)*	press release
communiquer	*(koh-mooh-neeh-kEh)*	interface (v)
commutateur (m), interrupteur (m)	*(koh-mooh-tah-tŒhr), (æhn-teh-roohp-tŒhr)*	switch
compagnie (f) d'assurance	*(kõhm-pah-nyEEh dah-sooh-rÃhns)*	insurance company
compagnie de forage en mer	*(kõhm-pah-nyEEh dœ foh-rAhzh ãhn mEhr)*	offshore company
compagnie fiduciaire	*(kõhm-pah-nyEEh feeh-dooh-syEhr)*	trust company
compartiment (m) de coffre-fort	*(kõhm-pahr-teeh-mÃh dæhn kOhf-rœ fOhr)*	safe deposit box
compatible	*(kõhn-pah-tEEh-blœh)*	compatible
compensation (f)	*(kõhm-pãhn-sah-syÕh)*	compensation
compétence (f)	*(kõhm-peh-tÃhns)*	job performance
compétences (fpl)	*(kõhm-peh-tÃhns)*	qualifications
complément (m)	*(kõhm-pleh-mÃh)*	topping up
complet (m)	*(kõhm-plEh)*	suit
composant (m)	*(kohm-poh-zÃh)*	component
composé (m)	*(kõhm-poh-zEh)*	compound
composés (mpl)	*(kõhm-poh-zEh)*	compounds
composition (f)	*(kõhm-poh-zeeh-syÕh)*	composition
compression (f) des coûts	*(kõhm-preh-syÕh deh kOOht)*	cost reduction
compression des prix de revient	*(kõhm-preh-syÕh deh prEEh dœ rœ-vyÃhn)*	cost-price squeeze
comptabilité (f)	*(kõhn-tah-beeh-leeh-tEh)*	bookkeeping
comptabilité analytique	*(kõhn-tah-beeh-leeh-tEh ah-nah-leeh-tEEhk)*	cost analysis

comptabilité d'épuisement	*(kõhn-tah-beeh-leeh-tEh deh deh-pweehz-mÃh)*	depletion accounting
comptabilité de gestion	*(kõhn-tah-beeh-leeh-tEh dœ zhœhs-tyÕh)*	management accounting
comptabilité du prix de revient	*(kõhn-tah-beeh-leeh-tEh dooh prEEh dœ rœh-vyÃhn)*	cost accounting
comptabilité en partie double	*(kõhn-tah-beeh-leeh-tEh ãhn pahr-tEEh dOOh-blœ)*	double-entry bookkeeping
comptable (m)	*(kõhn-tAh-blœ)*	accountant
compte (m)	*(kÕhnt)*	account
compte (m) à rebours	*(kOhmt ah rœh-bOOhr)*	countdown
compte actif	*(kÕhnt (ahk-tEEf)*	active account
compte bloqué	*(kÕhnt bloh-kEh)*	escrow account
compte (m) chèques	*(kÕhnt shEhk)*	checking account
compte clos	*(kÕhnt kloh)*	closed account
compte collectif	*(kÕhnt koh-lehk-tEEhf)*	joint account
compte courant	*(kÕhnt kooh-rÃhn)*	current account, checking account
compte (m) épargne	*(kÕhnt eh-pAhr-nyœh)*	savings account
compte d'exploitation	*(kÕhnt dehks-plwah-tah-syÕh)*	income statement
compte d'un client (dans un magasin)	*(kÕhnt dœhn kleeh-Ãhn [dÃhnz œhn mah-gah-zÆhn])*	charge account
compte de capital	*(kÕhnt dœ kah-peeh-tAhl)*	capital account
compte de capital à court terme	*(kÕhnt dœ kah-peeh-tAhl ah koohr tEhrm)*	short-term capital account
compte de capital à long terme	*(kÕhnt dœ kah-peeh-tAhl ah lÕh tEhrm)*	long-term capital account
compte de dépôt à vue	*(kÕhnt dœ deh-pOh ah vOOh)*	deposit account
compte de garantie confié à un tiers	*(kÕhnt dœ gah-rãhn-tEEh kõhn-fyEh ah œhn tyEhrs)*	escrow account
compte de revenus	*(kÕhnt dœ rœhv-nOOh)*	income account
compte des pertes et profits	*(kÕhnt deh pEhrt eh proh-fEEh)*	profit and loss account
compte douteux	*(kÕhnt dooh-tŒh)*	delinquent account
compte du grand livre	*(kÕhnt dooh grãhn lEEh-vrœ)*	ledger account
compte en banque	*(kÕhnt ãhn bÃhnk)*	bank account, checking account
compte géré en vertu d'un contrat de gestion	*(kÕhnt zheh-rEh ãhn vœhr-tOOh doohn kõhn-trÃh dœ zhœhs-tyÕh)*	discretionary account
compte inactif	*(kÕhnt ahk-tEEf)*	closed account
compte joint	*(kÕhnt zhwÆhnt)*	joint account
compte marginal	*(kÕhnt mahr-zheeh-nAhl)*	marginal account

compte ouvert	(kõhnt ooh-vEhr)	open account
compte spécifié	(kõhnt speh-seeh-fyEh)	itemized account
compte-rendu des bénéfices	(kõhnt-rãhn-dOOh deh beh-neh-fEEhs)	earnings report
compte-tours (m)	(kõnt-tOOhr)	odometer
comptes (mpl) annuels	(kõhnt ah-nwEhl)	annual accounts
comptes garantis	(kõhnt gah-rãhn-tEEh)	secured accounts
comptes groupés	(kõhnt grooh-pEh)	group accounts
comptes non recouvrables	(kõhnt ræh-kooh-vrAh-blœ)	uncollectible accounts
compteur (m) de vitesse	(kõhmp-tŒhr dœ veeh-tEhs)	speedometer
concentration (f) du marché	(kõhn-sãhn-trah-syÕh dooh mahr-shEh)	market concentration
conception (f) de systèmes	(kõhn-sehp-syÕh dœ seehs-tEhm)	systems design
conception du produit	(kõhn-sehp-syÕh dooh proh-dwEEh)	product design
concession (f) de terrain	(kõhn-seh-syÕh dœ tœ-rÆhn)	land grant, dealership
concessionnaire agréé (m)	(kõhn-seh-syoh-nEhr ah-greh-Eh)	authorized dealer
concurrence (f)	(kõhn-kooh-rÃhns)	competition
concurrent (m)	(kõhn-kooh-rÃh)	competitor
concurrentiel, avantage (m)	(kõhn-kooh-rãhn-syEhl, ah-vãhn-tAhzh)	competitive advantage
concurrentiel, léger avantage	(kõhn-kooh-rãhn-syEhl, leh-zhEh ah-vãhn-tAhzh)	competitive edge
concurrentielle, stratégie (f)	(kõhn-kooh-rãhn-syEhl, strah-teh-zhEEh)	competitive strategy
concurrents, analyse des	(kõhn-kooh-rÃh, ãh-nah-lEEhz deh)	competitor analysis
conditionnement (m)	(kõhn-deeh-syõhn-mÃh)	packaging
conditions de crédit (fpl)	(kõhn-deeh-syÕh dœ kreh-dEEh)	credit terms
conducteur (m)	(kõhn-doohk-tŒhr)	conductor, driver
confidentiel	(kõhn-feeh-dãhn-syEhl)	confidential
confirmation (f) de commande	(kõhn-feehr-mah-syÕh dœ koh-mÃhnd)	confirmation of order
confisquer (v)	(kõhn-feehs-kEh)	impound
conflit (m) d'intérêts	(kõhn-flEEh dãhn-teh-rEh)	conflict of interest
conflit ouvrier	(kõhn-flEEh ooh-vryEh)	labor dispute
conflit salarial	(kõhn-flEEh sah-lah-ryAhl)	wage dispute
conformément à notre attente	(kõhn-fohr-meh-mÃhn ah nOh-trœ ah-tÃhnt)	up to our expectations
congé (m)	(kõhn-zhEh)	leave of absence
congé de maternité	(kõhn-zhEh dœ mah-tehr-meeh-tEh)	maternity leave
congé de maladie	(kõhn-zhEh dœ mah-lah-dEEh)	sick leave
congés payés	(kõhn-zhEh pah-yEh)	paid holiday

congloméré (m)	(kõh-gloh-meh-rEh)	conglomerate
connaissement (m)	(koh-nEhs-mÃh)	bill of lading
connaissement avec réserves	(koh-nEhs-mÃh ah-vEhk reh-zEhrv)	foul bill of lading
connaissement direct	(koh-nEhs-mÃh deeh-rEhkt)	through bill of lading
connaissement intérieur	(koh-nEhs-mÃh æhn-teh-ryŒhr)	inland bill of lading
conseil (m) d'administration	(kõh-sEh-yœ dad-meeh-neehs-trah-syÕh)	board of directors
conseil de direction	(kõh-sEh-yœ dœ deeh-rehk-syÕh)	executive board
Conseil (m) de l'Europe	(kõh-sEh-yœh dœ leh-ooh-rOhp)	Council of Europe
conseil de surveillance	(kõh-sEh-yœ dœ soohr-veh-yÃhns)	board of supervisors
conseiller (informer)	(kõh-seh-yEh [æhn-fohr-mEh])	advise (v)
conseiller (m) en gestion	(kõh-seh-yEh ãhn zhœhs-tyÕh)	management consultant
conseiller en investissement	(kõh-seh-yEh ãhn æhn-vehs-teehs-mÃh)	investment adviser
consentir un découvert	(kõh-sãhn-tEEhr œhn deh-kooh-vEhrt)	grant an overdraft (v)
consolidation (f)	(kõh-soh-leeh-dah-synOh)	consolidation
consolidation du capital	(kõh-soh-leeh-dah-synOh dooh kah-peeh-tAhl)	reverse stock split
consolidation interne	(kõh-soh-leeh-dah-synOh æhn-tEhrn)	internal funding
consommateur (m)	(kõh-soh-mah-tŒhr)	consumer
consommateur de main-d'œuvre	(kõh-soh-mah-tŒhr dœ mÊhn dŒh-vrœ)	labor intensive
consommateur (m) potentiel	(kõh-soh-mah-tŒhr poh-tãhn-syEhl)	prospective consumer
consommation (f)	(kõh-soh-mah-syÕh)	gas consumption
consortium (m)	(kõh-sohr-tyOOhm)	consortium, syndicate
constituer une société	(kõh-steeh-tooh-Eh oohn soh-syeh-tEh)	incorporate (v)
consultant (m)	(kõh-soohl-tÃh)	consultant
contact (m)	(kÕhn-tAhkt)	ignition
contagieux	(kõh-tah-zhŒh)	contagious
contaminer	(kõh-tah-meeh-nEh)	contaminate (v)
conteneur (m)	(kõh-tæh-nŒhr)	container
contestation (f)	(kõh-tehs-tah-syÕh)	dispute
contingents (mpl)	(kõh-teehn-zhÃhn)	quota
contingents à l'exportation	(kõh-teehn-zhÃhn dehks-pohr-tah-syÕh)	export quota
contingents à l'importation	(kõh-teehn-zhÃhn ah læhm-pohr-tah-syÕh)	import quota

contingents de vente	*(kõhn-teehn-zhÃhn dœ vÃhnt)*	sales quota
contraceptif (m)	*(kõhn-trah-sehp-tEEhf)*	contraceptive
contracter	*(kõhn-trAhk-tEh)*	take out (v), contract
contre-indication (f)	*(kõhn-trœh-œhn-deeh-kah-syÕhn)*	contraindication
contrainte(f)	*(kõhn-trǼhnt)*	duress
contrat (m)	*(kõhn-trAh)*	contract, treaty
contrat à long terme	*(kohn-trAt ah lÕh tEhrm)*	long hedge
contrat à prix coûtant majoré	*(kõhn-trAh ah prEEh kooh-tÂhn mah-zhoh-rEh)*	cost-plus contract
contrat à remplir	*(kõhn-trAh ah rãhm-plEEhr)*	outstanding contract
contrat à terme	*(kõhn-trAh ah tEhrm)*	forward contract
contrat d'apprentissage	*(kõhn-trAh dah-prãhn-teeh-sAzh)*	indenture
contrat d'entretien	*(kõhn-trAh dãhn-trœh-tyǼhn)*	service contract
contrat de maintenance	*(kõhn-trAh dœ mãehn-tœh-nÃhns)*	maintenance contract
contrat de sous-traitance	*(kõhn-trAh dœ sooh-treh-tÃhns)*	subcontract
contrat de travail	*(kõhn-trAh dœ trah-vAhœ)*	working contract
contrat de vente à l'exportation	*(kõhn-trAh dœ vÃhnt ah lehks-pohr-tah-syÕh)*	export sales contract
contrat de vente sous condition	*(kõhn-trAh dœ vÂhnt sooh kõhn-deeh-syÕh)*	conditional sales contract
contrat fiduciaire	*(kõhn-trAh feeh-dooh-syEhr)*	deed of trust
contrat global	*(kõhn-trAh gloh-bAhl)*	package deal
contrat maritime	*(kõhn-trAh mah-reeh-tEEhm)*	maritime contract
contrat syndical	*(kõhn-trAh seehn-deeh-kAhl)*	union contract
contrat, mois de	*(kõhn-trAh mwAh dœ)*	contract month
contre tous risques	*(kõhn-trœ tooh rEEhs-kœ)*	against all risks
contre-partie (f)	*(kõhn-trœ-pahr-tEEh)*	consideration (business law)
contre-remboursement (m)	*(kõhn-trœ-rãhm-boohrs-mÃh)*	cash on delivery (C.O.D.)
contrecoup (m)	*(kõhn-trœ-kOOh)*	backwash effect
contrefaçon (f)	*(kõhn-trœ-fah-sÕh)*	forgery, counterfeit
contremaître (m)	*(kõhn-trœ-mEh-trœ)*	foreman
contrôle (m) d'épuisement	*(kõhn-trOhl deh deh-pweehz-mÃh)*	depletion control
contrôle d'exploitation	*(kõhn-trOhl ehks-plwah-tah-syÕh)*	operations management
contrôle de fabrication	*(kõhn-trOhl dœ fah-breeh-kah-syÕh)*	manufacturing control

contrôle de la production	*(kõhn-trOhl dœ lah proh-doohk-syÕh)*	production control
contrôle de qualité	*(kõhn-trOhl dœ kah-leeh-tEh)*	quality control
contrôle des changes	*(kõhn-trOhl deh shÃhnzh)*	exchange control
contrôle des crédits	*(kõhn-trOhl deh kreh-dEEh)*	credit control
contrôle (m) des naissances	*(kõhn-trOhl deh neh-sÃhns)*	birth control
contrôle des prix de revient	*(kõhn-trOhl dœ prEEh dœ rœ-vyÃhn)*	cost control
contrôle des stocks	*(kõhn-trOhl deh stocks)*	inventory control
contrôle financier	*(kõhn-trOhl feeh-nãhn-syEh)*	financial control
contrôle interne	*(kõhn-trOhl æhn-tEhrn)*	internal audit
contrôle numérique	*(kõhn-trOhl nooh-meh-rEEhk)*	numerical control
contrôle (m) orthographique	*(kohn-trOhl ohr-toh-grah-fEEhk)*	spellcheck
contrôler	*(kõhn-troh-lEh)*	check (v)
contrôles (mpl) de gestion	*(kõhn-trOhl dœ zhœhs-tyÕh)*	operations audit
convention (f)	*(kÕhn-vÃhn-syÕh)*	covenant (promises)
convention collective	*(kÕhn-vÃhn-syÕh koh-lehk-tEEhv)*	collective bargaining, agreement
conversion (f) de devises	*(kõhn-vehr-zyÕh dœ dæh-vEEhz)*	currency conversion
convoquer	*(kõhn-voh-kEh)*	call (v)
coopérative (f)	*(koh-oh-peh-rah-tEEhv)*	cooperative (n)
coopérative de placement	*(koh-oh-peh-rah-tEEhv dœ plahs-mÃh)*	investment trust
coopérative (f) vinicole	*(ko-oh-peh-rah-tEEhv veeh-neeh-kOhl)*	wine cooperative
coordination (f)	*(koh-ohr-deeh-nah-syÕh)*	scoring
copie (f) de sauvegarde	*(koh-pEEh dœ sohv-gAhrd)*	backup
copier	*(koh-pyEh)*	copy (v)
copropriétaire (m)	*(koh-proh-pryeh-tEhr)*	joint owner
copropriété (f)	*(koh-proh-pryeh-tEh)*	joint estate co-ownership
corbeille (f) (à la bourse)	*(kohr-bEhyœ), (ah lah bOOhrs)*	trading floor (stock exchange)
corbeille (f) à pain	*(kohr-bEh-yœ ah pÆhn)*	breadbasket
corporation (f) marchande	*(kohr-poh-rah-syÕh mahr-shÃhnd)*	merchant guide
corps (m)	*(kOhr)*	body, point
corpus (m)	*(kohr-pOOhs)*	corpus
correspondance (f)	*(koh-rehs-põhn-dÃhns)*	correspondence
corruption (f)	*(koh-roohp-syÕh)*	graft

corsé	*(kohr-sEh)*	full-bodied
cortisone (f)	*(kohr-teeh-zOhn)*	cortisone
cotation (bourse)	*(koh-tah-syÕh bOOhrs)*	listing
cotation (f)	*(koh-tah-syÕhn)*	quotation
cotation directe	*(koh-tah-syÕh deeh-rEhkt)*	direct quotation
cotation officieuse (hors marché)	*(koh-tah-syÕh oh-feeh-syŒhz [ohr mahr-shEh])*	over-the-counter quotation
coton (m)	*(koh-tÕhn)*	cotton
couche (f)	*(kOOhsh)*	layer
coudre	*(kOOh-drœ)*	sew (v)
coulée (f) continue	*(kooh-lEh kõhn-teeh-nOOh)*	continous caster
couleur (f)	*(kooh-lŒhr)*	color, tint
coupe (f)	*(kOOhp)*	crop
couple (m)	*(kOOh-plœ)*	torque
coupleur (m) acoustique	*(kooh-plŒr ah-koohs-tEEhk)*	acoustic coupler
coupure (f) de presse	*(kooh-pOOhr dœ prEhs)*	press clipping
coupon (m)	*(kooh-pÕh)*	coupon
coupon zéro	*(kooh-pÕh zeh-rOh)*	zero coupon
courant (m)	*(kooh-rÃh)*	current
courant alternatif	*(kooh-rÃhnt ahl-tehr-nah-tEEhf)*	alternating current
courbe (f) d'accoutumance	*(kOOhrb dah-kooh-tooh-mãhns)*	learning curve
courbe de la cloche	*(kOOhrb dœ lah klOsh)*	frequency curve
courbe en forme de cloche	*(kOOhrb ãhn fOhrm dœ klOsh)*	bell-shaped curve
courbes (fpl)	*(kOOhrb)*	bends
courir	*(kooh-rEEhr)*	accrue (v)
courrier (m) direct	*(kooh-ryEh deeh-rEhkt)*	direct mail
courrier recommandé	*(kooh-ryEh ræh-koh-mãhn-dEh)*	registered mail
courroie (f)	*(kooh-rwAh)*	belt
cours (m)	*(kOOhr)*	market value, price
cours d'ouverture	*(kOOhr dooh-vehr-tOOhr)*	opening price
cours de clôture	*(kOOhr dœ kloh-tOOhr)*	closing price
cours de l'or	*(kOOhr dœ lOhr)*	gold price
cours des devises	*(kOOhr dœ dœh-vEEhz)*	currency exchange rate
cours moyen	*(kOOhr mwah-yEhn)*	average price
court-métrage (m)	*(koohr-meh-trAhzh)*	short film
courtier (m)	*(koohr-tyEh)*	broker
courtier d'assurance	*(koohr-tyEh dah-sooh-rÃhns)*	insurance broker
courtier d'escompte	*(koohr-tyEh ehs-kÕhnt)*	bill broker
courtier de change	*(koohr-tyEh dœ shÃhnzh)*	dealer
courtier en bourse	*(koohr-tyEh ãhn bOOhrs)*	stock broker
courtier en douane	*(koohr-tyEh ãhn dooh-Ahn)*	customs broker

courtier en logiciel	*(koohr-tyEh āhn loh-zheeh-syEhl)*	software broker
coût (m)	*(kOOht)*	cost
coût d'opportunité	*(kOOht doh-pohr-tooh-neeh-tEh)*	opportunity costs
coût de facturation	*(kOOht dœ fahk-tooh-rah-syŌh)*	invoice cost
coût de la vie	*(kOOht dœ lah vEEh)*	cost of living
coût de production	*(kOOht dœ proh-doohk-syŌh)*	production costs
coût de remplacement	*(kOOht dœ rāhm-plahs-mĀh)*	replacement cost
coût des marchandises vendues	*(kOOht deh mahr-shāhn-dEEhz vāhn-dOOh)*	cost of goods sold
coût direct	*(kOOht deeh-rEhkt)*	direct cost
coût du capital	*(kOOht dooh kah-peeh-tAhl)*	cost of capital
coût du travail	*(kOOht dooh trah-vAhyœ)*	direct labor (accounting)
coût et fret	*(kOOht eh frEht)*	cost and freight
coût initial	*(kOOht eeh-neeh-syAhl)*	original cost
coût moyen	*(kOOht mwah-yEhn)*	average cost
coût réel	*(kOOht reh-Ehl)*	actual cost
couteau (m)	*(kooh-tOh)*	knife
couteau à découper	*(kooh-tOh ah deh-kooh-pEh)*	carving knife
coutellerie (f)	*(kooh-teh-yœh-rEEh)*	cutlery
coûter	*(kooht-tEh)*	cost (v)
coûts (mpl) fixes	*(kOOht fEEhks)*	fixed costs
coûts standard	*(kOOht stāhn-dAhr)*	standard costs
coûts, évaluation des	*(kOOht eh-vah-lwah-syŌh deh)*	cost analysis
coûts, répartition des	*(kOOht reh-pahr-teeh-syŌh deh)*	allocation of costs
couturier (m)	*(kooh-tooh-ryEh)*	designer
couvercle (m)	*(kooh-vEhr-klœh)*	lid
couvert (m)	*(kooh-vEhrt)*	place setting
couvert de taches	*(kooh-vEhr dœ tAhsh)*	blotchy
couverture (f)	*(kooh-vehr-tOOhr)*	cover, coverage (insurance)
couverture à terme	*(kooh-vehr-tOOhr ah tEhrm)*	forward cover
couverture (f) souple	*(kooh-vehr-tOOhr sOOh-plœ)*	soft cover
couvrir, se	*(kooh-vrEEhr)*	hedge (v)
coyote (m)	*(koh-yOht)*	coyote
cracking (m)		cracking
cravate (f)	*(krah-vAht)*	tie
crayeux	*(kreh-yŒh)*	chalky
créance (f) irrécouvrable	*(kreh-Āhns eeh-reh-kooh-vrAh-blœ)*	dead rent

C

créance à recouvrir	*(kreh-Ãhns ah ræh-kooh-vrEEhr)*	outstanding debt
créance mauvaise	*(kreh-Ãhns moh-vEhz)*	bad debt
créancier (m)	*(kreh-ãhn-syEh)*	creditor
crédit (m)	*(kreh-dEEh)*	credit
crédit à l'exportation	*(kreh-dEEh ah lehks-pohr-tah-syÕh)*	export credit
crédit à la consommation	*(kreh-dEEh ah lah kõhn-soh-mah-syÕh)*	consumer credit
crédit à taux privilégié	*(kreh-dEEh ah tOh preeh-veeh-leh-zhyEh)*	soft loan
crédit à taux révisable	*(kreh-dEEh ah tOh reh-veeh-zAh-blœ)*	rollover
crédit (m) bloqué	*(kreh-deeh bloh-kEh)*	frozen credit
crédit commercial	*(kreh-dEEh koh-mehr-syAhl)*	trade credit
crédit d'investissement	*(kreh-dEEh dãhn-vehs-teehs-mÃh)*	investment credit
crédit de complaisance	*(kreh-dEEh dœ kõhn-pleh-zÃhns)*	accommodation credit
crédit (m) gratuit	*(kreh-deeh grah-twEEh)*	interest-free loan
crédit par acceptation	*(kreh-dEEh pahr ahk-sehp-tah-syÕh)*	acceptance credit
crédit par acceptation renouvelable	*(kreh-dEEh pahr ahk-sehp-tah-syÕh ræh-nooh-veh-lAh-blœ)*	revolving credit
crédit pour impôt acquitté à l'étranger	*(kreh-dEEh poohr lãehm-pOh ah-keeh-tEh ah leh-trãhn-zhEh)*	foreign tax credit
crédit tournant	*(kreh-dEEh toohr-nÃh)*	revolving credit
crédit-bail	*(kreh-dEEh bAh-yœ)*	equipment leasing
créditer	*(kreh-deeh-tEh)*	credit (v)
crédits (mpl) monétaires	*(kreh-dEEh moh-neh-tEhr)*	monetary credits
crème (f) de jour	*(krEhm dœ zhOOhr)*	day cream
crème de nuit	*(krEhm dœ nweeh)*	night cream
crème pour le visage	*(krEhm poohr lœh veeh-zAhzh)*	face cream
crème pour les yeux	*(krEhm poohr lehz yŒh)*	eye cream
creuset (m)	*(krœh-zEht)*	crucible
crise (f)	*(krEEhz)*	depression
crise (f) cardiaque	*(krEEhz kahr-deeh-Ahk)*	heart attack
cristal (m)	*(kreehs-tAhl)*	crystal
cristallerie (f)	*(kreehs-tah-lœh-rEEh)*	crystal glass manufacturing
cristallisation (f)	*(kreehs-tah-leeh-zah-syÕh)*	crystallization
critères (mpl) d'investissement	*(kreeh-tEhr dãhn-vehs-teehs-mÃh)*	investment criteria
croissance (f)	*(krwa-sAhns)*	growth
croissance d'une entreprise	*(krwah-sÃhns doohn ãhn-træh-prEEhz)*	corporate growth

cru (m)	*(krOOh)*	vintage
cubilot (m)	*(kooh-beeh-lOh)*	cupola
cuiller (f) à cafe	*(kooh-yEhr ah kah-fEh)*	teaspoon
cuiller à soupe	*(kooh-yEhr ah sOOhp)*	tablespoon
cuiller, cuillère (f)	*(kooh-yEhr)*	spoon
cuir (m)	*(kwEEhr)*	leather
cuivre (m)	*(kwEEhv-rœ)*	copper
cumul (m) d'emplois	*(kooh-mOOhl dãhm-plwAh)*	moonlighting
cumulatif	*(kooh-mooh-lah-tEEhf)*	cumulative
curateur (m)	*(kooh-rah-tŒhr)*	trustee
curriculum vitae (m)		résumé
curseur (m)	*(koohr-sŒhr)*	cursor
cuve (f)	*(kOOhv)*	vat
cuvée (f)	*(kooh-vEh)*	batch
cycle (m) de production	*(sEEh-klœ dœ proh-doohk-syÕh)*	work cycle
cycle de vie	*(sEEh-klœ dœ vEEh)*	life cycle
cycle du travail	*(sEEh-klœ dooh trah-vAhyœ)*	work cycle
cycle économique	*(sEEh-klœ eh-koh-moh-mEEhk)*	business cycle
cylindre (m)	*(seeh-lÃEhn-drœ)*	cylinder
cylindrée (f)	*(seeh-lÃEhn-drEh)*	horsepower

D

dans l'ensemble de l'industrie	*(dãh lãhn-sÃhm-blœ dœ lãehn-doohs-trEEh)*	industrywide
dans le rouge	*(dãhn lœ rOOhzh)*	in the red
date (f) antérieure	*(dAht ãhn-teh-ryŒhr)*	back date
date d'échéance	*(dAht deh-sheh-Ãhns)*	expiry date
date d'inscription	*(dAht dãehn-skreehp-syÕh)*	record date
date (f) de diffusion	*(daht dœ deeh-fooh-zyÕhn)*	air date
date de livraison	*(dAht dœ leeh-vreh-zÕh)*	date of delivery
date de remboursement	*(dAht dœ rãhm-boohrs-mÃh)*	maturity date
date de tirage	*(dAht dœ teeh-rAhzh)*	drawdown date
date de transaction	*(dAht dœ trãhn-zahk-syÕh)*	trade date
date (f) limite	*(daht leeh-mEEht)*	deadline
débattre	*(deh-bAh-trœ)*	dispute (v)
débaucher	*(deh-boh-shEh)*	fire (v)
débit (m)	*(deh-bEEh)*	debit
débouché (m)	*(deh-booh-shEh)*	market access, outlet
débouché marginal	*(deh-booh-shEh mahr-zheeh-nAhl)*	fringe market
déboucher	*(deh-booh-shEh)*	uncork (v)

débours (m)	(deh-bOOhr)	disbursement, layout, out-of-pocket expenses
débrayage (m)	(deh-brah-yAhzh)	walkout
décapage (m)	(deh-kah-pAhzh)	pickling
décapotable (f)	(deh-kah-poh-tAh-blœ)	convertible
décharge (f)	(deh-shAhrzh)	dump
décharger	(deh-sharh-zhEh)	discharge (v), unload (v)
déchet (m)	(deh-shEht)	outturn
déchets (mpl)	(deh-shEht)	spoilage
déchets (mpl) nucléaires	(deh-shEht nooh-kleh-Ehr)	nuclear waste
déchets (m) ou ferraille (f)	(deh-shEht ooh feh-rAh-yœ)	scrap
décision (f) d'achat ou de fabrication	(deh-seeh-zyŌh dah-shAh ooh dœ fah-breeh-kah-syŌh)	make-or-buy decision
déclaration (f) d'exportation	(deh-klah-rah-syŌh dehks-pohr-tah-syŌh)	export entry
déclaration d'importation	(deh-klah-rah-syŌh dãehm-pohr-tah-syŌh)	import entry, import declaration, entry permit
déclaration d'intention d'achat	(deh-klah-rah-syŌh dãhn-tãhn-syŌh dah-shAh)	blanket order
déclaration d'investissement	(deh-klah-rah-syŌh dãehn-vehs-teehs-mÃh)	investment letter
déclaration en douane	(deh-klah-rah-syŌh ãhn dooh-Ahn)	customs entry
déclaration provisoire	(deh-klah-rah-syŌh proh-veeh-zwAhr)	bill of sight
déclenchement (m) d'un processus d'ajustement	(deh-klãhnsh-mÃh dœhn proh-seh-sOOh dah-zhoohs-tœ-mÃh)	adjustment trigger
déclencher	(deh-klãhn-shEh)	trigger (v)
décoller	(deh-koh-lEh)	take off (v)
décontamination (f)	(deh-kõhn-tah-meeh-nah-syŌhn)	decontamination
découvert (m)	(deh-kooh-vEhr)	overdraft
déductible	(deh-doohk-tEEh-blœ)	deductible
déduction (f)	(deh-doohk-syŌh)	write-off, deduction
déduction fiscale	(deh-doohk-syŌh feehs-kAhl)	tax deduction
défaut (m)	(deh-fOh)	failure, default, flaw, blemish
défavorable	(deh-fah-voh-rAh-blœ)	unfavorable
défectueux	(deh-fehk-tŒh)	defective
défense (f) de l'environnement	(deh-fÃhns dœ lãhn-veeh-rohn-mÃhn)	conservation
déficit (m)	(deh-feeh-sEEht)	deficit

définition (f) d'un poste	*(deh-feeh-neeh-syÕh dæhn pOhst)*	job description
déflation (f)	*(deh-flah-syÕh)*	deflation
déforestation (f)	*(deh-foh-rehs-tah-syÕhn)*	deforestation
dégivreur (m)	*(deh-geeh-vrŒhr)*	defroster
degré (m)	*(dæh-grEh)*	degree
degré (m) d'acidité	*(deh-grEh dah-seeh-deeh-tEh)*	acid content
dégrèvement (m)	*(deh-grehv-mÃh)*	tax relief
dégustation (f)	*(deh-goohs-tah-synOh)*	tasting
déguster	*(deh-goohs-tEh)*	taste (v)
délai (m)	*(deh-lEh)*	delay
délai (m) d'amortissement	*(deh-lEh dah-mohr-eehs-mÃh)*	payback period
délai d'approvisionnement	*(deh-lEh dah-proh-veeh-zyohn-mÃh)*	lead time
délai d'encaissement	*(deh-lEh dãhn-kehs-mÃh)*	collection period
délai de grâce	*(deh-lEh dœ grAhs)*	grace period
délai de livraison	*(deh-lEh dœ leeh-vreh-zÕh)*	lead time
délai de paiement	*(deh-lEh dœ peh-mÃh)*	payout period
délai de planche	*(deh-lEh dœ plÃhnsh)*	lay time
délai fixe	*(deh-lEh fEEhks)*	fixed term
délaissement (m)	*(deh-lehs-mÃh)*	abandonment (assurance maritime)
délit d'abstention	*(deh-lEEh dahb-stãhn-syÕh)*	nonfeasance
déloyal	*(deh-lwah-yAhl)*	unfair
demande (f)	*(dæh-mÃhnd)*	demand
demande globale	*(dæh-mÃhnd gloh-bAhl)*	aggregate demand
demande ou offre d'emploi (petites annonces)	*(dæh-mÃhnd ooh Oh-frœ dãhm-plwAh [pœh-tEEht ah-nÕhns])*	want ad
démangeaison (f)	*(deh-mãhn-zheh-sÕhn)*	itching
démaquillant (m)	*(deh-mah-keeh-yÃhn)*	cleanser
démarche (f) commerciale	*(deh-mAhrsh koh-mehr-syAhl)*	marketing concept
démarquage (m)	*(deh-mahr-kAhzh)*	markdown
démarreur (m)	*(deh-mah-rŒhr)*	starter
démilitariser	*(deh-meeh-leeh-tah-reel-zEh)*	demilitarize (v)
demi-tasse (f)	*(deh-mEEh tAhs)*	espresso cup
demi-vie (f)	*(dæh-meeh-vEEh)*	half life
démodé	*(deh-moh-dEh)*	out of style
démographique	*(deh-moh-graf-fEEhk)*	demographic
denrée (f)	*(dãhn-rEh)*	commodity
denrées (fpl) alimentaires	*(dãhn-rEh ah-leeh-mãhn-tEhr)*	foodstuffs
densité (f)	*(dãhn-seeh-tEh)*	density

D

dentelle (f)	*(dãhn-tEhl)*	lace
dépanner (v)	*(deh-pah-nEh)*	debug
dépanneur	*(deh-pah-nŒhr)*	troubleshooter
départ (m) entrepôt	*(deh-pAhr ãhn-træ-pOh)*	ex warehouse
départ fabrique	*(deh-pAhr fah-brEEhk)*	ex mill
départ mine	*(deh-pAhr mEEhn)*	ex mine
départ usine	*(deh-pAhr ooh-zEEhn)*	ex factory, FOB plant
dépense (f)	*(deh-pãhns)*	expenditure
dépenses (fpl) contrôlables	*(deh-pãhns kõhn-troh-lAh-blœ)*	controllable costs
dépenses courantes	*(deh-pãhns kooh-rÃhnt)*	running expenses
dépenses d'expédition	*(deh-pãhns dehks-peh-deeh-syÕh)*	shipping expenses
dépenses d'intérêt	*(deh-pãhns dæhn-teh-rEh)*	interest expenses
dépenses de déchargement	*(deh-pãhns dœ deh-sharhzh-mÃh)*	landing costs
dépenses différées	*(deh-pÃhns deeh-feh-rEh)*	deferred charges
dépenses directes	*(deh-pÃhns deeh-rEhkt)*	direct expenses
dépenses fixes	*(deh-pãhns fEEhks)*	fixed expenses
dépenses indirectes	*(deh-pÃhns æhn-deeh-rEhkt)*	indirect expenses
dépenses semi-variables	*(deh-pãhns vah-ryAh-blœ)*	semivariable costs
dépenses supérieures aux recettes	*(deh-pÃhns sooh-peh-ryŒhr oh ræh-sEht)*	deficit spending
dépenses variables	*(deh-pãhns vah-ryAh-blœ)*	moving expenses
dépistage (m)	*(deh-peehs-tAhzh)*	screening
déport (m)	*(deh-pOhr)*	backwardation
déposer une demande d'adhésion	*(deh-poh-zEh oon dœ-mÃhnd dah-deh-zyÕhn)*	apply (v)
dépossession (f)	*(deh-poh-seh-syÕh)*	divestment
dépôt (m)	*(dep-pOh)*	deposit
dépôt à terme	*(deh-pOh ah tEhrm)*	time deposit
dépôt à vue	*(deh-pOh ah vOOh)*	demand deposit
dépôt bancaire	*(deh-pOh bãhn-kEhr)*	bank deposit
dépôt de brevet	*(deh-pOh dœ bræh-vEh)*	patent application
dépôt de garantie	*(deh-pOh dœ gah-rãhn-tEEh)*	deposit
dépôts (mpl) à l'importation	*(deh-pOh ah læhm-pohr-tah-syÕh)*	import deposits
dépôt (m) des brevets	*(deh-pOh deh breh-vEht)*	patent registering
dépréciation (f)	*(deh-preh-syah-syÕh)*	depreciation
dépréciation de la monnaie	*(deh-preh-syah-syÕh dœ lah moh-nEh)*	depreciation of currency
député (m) européen	*(deh-pooh-tEh eh-ooh-roh-peh-Ehn)*	MEP
déréglementation (f)	*(deh-rehg-lœh-mãhn-tah-syÕhn)*	deregulation
dérive (f) des salaires	*(deh-rEEhv deh sah-lEhr)*	wage drift
dernier entré (m), premier sorti (m)	*(dehr-nyEh ãhn-trEh), (præh-myEh sohr-tEEh)*	last in, first out

désaccord (m)	*(deh-zah-kOhr)*	misunderstanding
désarmement (m)	*(dehz-ahr-mœh-mÃhn)*	disarmament
désarmer (un navire)	*(deh-zahr-mEh œhn nah-vEEhr)*	lay up (v)
désarrimage (m)	*(deh-zah-reeh-mAhzh)*	broken stowage
désertification	*(deh-sehr-teeh-feeh-kah-syÕhn)*	desertification
déshérance (f)	*(dehz-eh-rÃhns)*	escheat
désintéressement (m)	*(dehz-æhn-teh-rehs-mÃh)*	buyout
dessèchement (m)	*(deh-sehsh-mÃhn)*	dryness
dessinateur (m)	*(deh-seeh-nah-tŒhr)*	designer
dessiner	*(dœh-seeh-nEh)*	design (v)
dessous (m) de verre	*(dœh-sOOh dœ vEhr)*	coaster
destinataire (m)	*(dehs-teeh-nah-tEhr)*	consignee
destiné à l'exportation	*(dehs-teeh-nEh ah lehks-pohr-tah-syÕh)*	for export
désuétude (f)	*(deh-sweh-tOOhd)*	obsolescence
détacher (se)	*(deh-tah-shEh, sœh)*	fall off (v)
détailler	*(deh-tah-yEh)*	itemize (v)
détaxe (f)	*(deh-tAhks)*	remission of a tax
détecteur (m)	*(deh-tehk-tŒhr)*	detector
détenteur (m)	*(deh-tãhn-tŒhr)*	holder (negotiable instruments)
détenu par le propriétaire	*(deh-tœ-nOOh pahr lœ proh-pryeh-tEhr)*	proprietary
détonateur (m)	*(deh-toh-nah-tŒhr)*	detonator
détournement (m) de fonds	*(deh-toohr-nœ-mÃh dœ fÕhn)*	embezzlement
dette (f)	*(DEht)*	debt
dette à court terme	*(DEht ah koohr tEhrm)*	current liabilities, short-term debt
dette à long terme	*(DEht ah lÕh tEhrm)*	long-term debt
dette active	*(DEht ahk-tEEhv)*	active debt
dette consolidée	*(DEht kõh-soh-leeh-dEh)*	funded debt
dette extérieure	*(DEht ehks-teh-ryŒhr)*	foreign debt
dette fixe	*(DEht fEEhks)*	fixed liability
dette flottante	*(DEht floh-tÃhnt)*	floating debt
dette garantie	*(DEht gah-rãhn-tEEh)*	secured liability
dette publique	*(DEht pooh-blEEhk)*	national debt
dette réelle	*(DEht reh-Ehl)*	actual liability
dette sans garantie	*(DEht sãh gah-rãhn-tEEh)*	unsecured liability
dettes (fpl) actives	*(DEht ahk-tEEhv)*	accounts receivable
dettes différées	*(DEht deeh-feh-rEh)*	deferred liabilities
dettes passives	*(DEht pah-sEEhv)*	accounts payable
dettes privilégiées	*(DEht preeh-veeh-leh-zhyEh)*	preferential debts
deuxième position (f)	*(dœh-zyEhm poh-zeeh-syÕh)*	second position
dévalorisation (f) du travail	*(deh-vah-loh-reeh-zah-syÕh dooh trah-vAhyœ)*	dilution of labor

dévaluation	*(deh-vah-lwah-syÕhn)*	devalution
dévaluer	*(deh-vah-lwEh)*	devalue (v)
déversement (m)	*(deh-vehrs-mÃhn)*	dumping
déverser	*(deh-vehr-sEh)*	dump (v)
devis (m)	*(dœh-vEEh)*	estimate
devis approximatif	*(dœh-vEEh ah-prohk-seeh-mah-tEEhf)*	rough estimate
devise (f)	*(dœh-vEEhz)*	currency
devise bloquée	*(dœh-vEEhz bloh-kEh)*	blocked currency
devise de référence	*(dœh-vEEhz dœ reh-feh-rÃhns)*	base currency
devise étrangère	*(dœh-vEEhz eh-trãhn-zhEhr)*	foreign currency
devise faible	*(dœh-vEEhz fEh-blœ)*	soft currency
devise forte	*(dœh-vEEhz fOhrt)*	hard currency
diabète (m)	*(deeh-ah-bEht)*	diabetes
diamètre (m)	*(deeh-ah-mEh-trœ)*	hardness
diapositive (f) couleurs	*(deeh-ah-poh-zeeh-tEEhv kooh-lŒhr)*	color transparency
diésel (m)	*(dEEh-zehhl)*	diesel
diffamation (f)	*(deeh-fah-mah-syÕh)*	libel
différentiel (m) des prix	*(deeh-feh-rãhn-syEhl deh prEEh)*	price differential
différé	*(deeh-feh-rEh)*	deferred
diffuser	*(deeh-fooh-zEh)*	broadcast (v)
digital (m)	*(deeh-zheeh-tAhl)*	digital
digitaline (f)	*(deeh-zheeh-tah-lEEhn)*	digitalis
dilution (f) du capital	*(deeh-looh-syÕh dooh kah-peeh-tAhl)*	delution of equity
dimension (f)	*(deeh-mãhn-syÕh)*	size
diode (f)	*(deeh-Ohd)*	diode
directeur (m)	*(deeh-rehk-tŒhr)*	manager
directeur adjoint	*(deeh-rehk-tŒhr ad-zhwÆhn)*	deputy manager
directeur (m) artistique	*(deeh-rehk-tŒhr ahr-teehs-tEEhk)*	art director
directeur d'une entreprise	*(deeh-rehk-tŒhr doohn ãhn-trœh-prEEhz)*	chief executive
directeur d'une usine	*(deeh-rehk-tŒhr doohn ooh-zEEhn)*	plant manager
directeur de l'exportation	*(deeh-rehk-tŒhr dœ lehks-pohr-tah-syÕh)*	export manager
directeur des achats	*(deeh-rehk-tŒhr dehz ah-shAh)*	purchasing manager
directeur des services comptables	*(deeh-rehk-tŒhr deh sœr-vEEhs kõhn-tAh-blœ)*	controller
directeur exécutif	*(deeh-rehk-tŒhr ehk-seh-kooh-tEEhf)*	chief executive officer (C.E.O.)
directeur financier	*(deeh-rehk-tŒhr feeh-nãhn-syEh)*	chief financial officer (C.F.O.)

D

directeur général	*(deeh-rehk-tŒhr zheh-neh-rAhl)*	general manager, chief executive, president
directeur opérationnel	*(deeh-rehk-tŒhr oh-peh-rah-syoh-nEhl)*	chief operating officer (C.O.O.)
direction (f)	*(deeh-rehk-syÕh)*	steering
direction (f) administrative	*(deeh-rehk-syÕh ad-meeh-neehs-trah-tEEhv)*	office management
direction (f) assistée	*(deeh-rehk-syÕh ah-seehs-tEh)*	power steering
direction d'investigation	*(deeh-rehk-syÕh dæn-vehs-teeh-gah-syÕh)*	audit trail
direction des ventes	*(deeh-rehk-syÕh deh vÃhnt)*	sales management
direction du personnel	*(deeh-rehk-syÕh dooh pehr-soh-nEhl)*	personnel management, staff organization
direction par objectifs	*(deeh-rehk-syÕh pahr ohb-zhehk-tEEhf)*	management by objectives
directions (fpl) imbriquées	*(deeh-rehk-syÕh æhm-breeh-kEh)*	interlocking directorate
directives (fpl)	*(deeh-rehk-tEEhv)*	guidelines
dirigeant (m)	*(deeh-reeh-zhÃh)*	executive
discriminations (fpl) à l'embauche	*(deehs-kreeh-meeh-nah-syÕh ah læhm-bOhsh)*	restrictive labor practices
disponibilités (fpl)	*(deehs-poh-neeh-beeh-leeh-tEh)*	liquid assets
dispositif (m)	*(deehs-poh-zeeh-tEEhf)*	device
disque (m)	*(deehs-kœ)*	record
disque (m)	*(dEEhsk)*	disc, disk
disque (m) dur	*(deehsk dOOhr)*	hard disk
disquette (f)	*(deehs-kEht)*	floppy disk
disquette (f) souple	*(deehs-kEht sOOh-plœ)*	floppy disk
distiller	*(deehs-teeh-lEh)*	distill (v)
distillation (f)	*(deehs-teeh-lah-syÕh)*	distillation
distributeur (m)	*(deehs-treeh-booh-tŒhr)*	distributor
distribution (f)	*(deehs-treeh-booh-syÕh)*	distribution
distribution (f) de masse	*(deehs-treeh-booh-syÕh dœ mAhs)*	mass marketing
diurétique (f)	*(deeh-ooh-reh-tEEhk)*	diuretic
divers	*(deeh-vEhr)*	miscellaneous
diversification (f)	*(deeh-vehr-seeh-feeh-kah-syÕh)*	diversification
dividende (m)	*(deeh-veeh-dÃhnd)*	dividend
dividende attaché	*(deeh-veeh-dÃhnd ah-tah-shEh)*	cum dividend
dividende en espèces	*(deeh-veeh-dÃhnd ãhn ehs-pEhs)*	cash dividend
dividende passé	*(deeh-veeh-dÃhnd pah-sEh)*	passed dividend
division (f) du travail	*(deeh-veeh-zyÕh dooh trah-vAhyœ)*	dock (ship's receipt)

D

document (m) (acte)	*(doh-kooh-mÃh), (Ahk-tœ)*	document
document en clair	*(doh-kooh-mÃh ãhn klEhr)*	clear document
document net	*(doh-kooh-mÃh nEht)*	clean document
document original	*(doh-kooh-mÃh oh-reeh-zheeh-nAhl)*	script
document sans réserve	*(doh-kooh-mÃh sãh reh-zEhrv)*	clean document
documentaire (m)	*(doh-kooh-mãhn-tEhr)*	documentary
domaine (m) public	*(doh-mEhn pooh-blEEhk)*	public domain
dommage (m)	*(doh-mAhzh)*	tort
dommages (mpl)	*(doh-mAhzh)*	damage
dommages fortuits	*(doh-mAhzh fohr-twEEh)*	accidental damage
données (fpl)	*(doh-nEh)*	data
donner des instructions	*(doh-nEh dehz æhn-stroohk-syÕh)*	instruct
donneur (m)	*(doh-nŒhr)*	donor
doré	*(doh-rEh)*	gilded
dos (m)	*(dOhs)*	back
dosage (m)	*(deehs-teeh-lah-syÕh)*	dosage
dose (f)	*(dOhz)*	dose
dossier (m)	*(doh-syEh)*	file
dotation (f)	*(doh-tah-syÕh)*	endowment
douane (f)	*(dooh-Ahn)*	customs
doublage (m)	*(dooh-blAhzh)*	dubbing
double étiquetage (m)	*(dOOh-blœ eh-teeh-keh-tAhzh)*	double pricing
double imposition (f)	*(dOOh-blœ æhm-poh-zeeh-syÕh)*	double taxation
double jeu (m)	*(dOOh-blœ zhŒh)*	double dealing
double option (f)	*(dOOh-blœ ohp-syÕh)*	put and call
double page (f) centrale	*(dooh-blœ pAhzh sãhn-trAhl)*	center spread
double paie (f)	*(dOOh-blœ pEh)*	double time
doublure (f)	*(dooh-blOOhr)*	lining
doux (ce)	*(dOOh)*	soft
drap (m)	*(drAhp)*	sheet
draper	*(drah-pEh)*	drape (v)
drogue (f)	*(drOhg)*	drug
droit (m) ad valorem	*(drwAh ad valorem)*	duty ad valorem
droit antidumping	*(drwAh antidumping)*	anti-dumping duty
droit compensateur	*(drwAh kõhm-pãhn-sah-tŒhr)*	countervailing duty
droit (m) commercial	*(drwAh koh-mehr-syAhl)*	mercantile law
droit (m) d'auteur	*(drwAh doh-rŒhr)*	copyright
droit de l'accise	*(drwAh dœ lahk-sEEhz)*	excise license
droit de nantissement	*(drwAh dœ nãhn-teehs-mÃh)*	mechanic's lien
droit de passage	*(drwAh dœ pah-sAhz)*	right of way
droit de préemption	*(drwAh dœ preh-ehmp-syÕh)*	preemptive right

droit de recours	*(drwAh dœ ræh-kOOhr)*	right of recourse
droit de régie	*(drwAh dœ reh-zhEEh)*	excise duty, excise tax
droit de remise	*(drwAh dœ ræh-mEEhz)*	remission of duty
droit de succession	*(drwAh dœ soohk-seh-syÕh)*	inheritance tax
droit de vote	*(drwAh dœ vOht)*	voting right
droit spécifique	*(drwAh speh-seeh-fEEhk)*	specific duty
droits (mpl)	*(drwAh)*	rights, acquired rights, vested rights, duty
droits combinés	*(drwAh kõhm-beeh-nEh)*	combination duty
droits d'auteur (mpl)	*(drwAh doh-tŒhr)*	copyrights, royalties
droits d'exportation	*(drwAh dehks-pohr-tah-syÕh)*	export duty
droits d'importation	*(drwAh dæhm-pohr-tah-syÕh)*	import duty
droits de bassin	*(drwAh dœ bah-sÃEhn)*	wharfage charges
droits de dock	*(drwAh dœ dock)*	dock handling charges
droits de douane	*(drwAh dœ dooh-Ahn)*	customs duty
droits de douane à l'importation	*(drwAh dœ dooh-Ahn ah læhm-pohr-tah-syÕh)*	import tariff
droits (mpl) de l'homme	*(drwAh dœ lOhm)*	human rights
droits de mouillage	*(drwAh dœ mweeh-yAhzh)*	anchorage (dues)
droits de pilotage	*(drwAh dœ peeh-loh-tAhzh)*	pilotage
droits de succession	*(drwAh dœ soohk-seh-syÕh)*	estate tax
droits exclusifs	*(drwAh ehks-klooh-sEEhf)*	sole rights
droits portuaires	*(drwAh pohr-twEhr)*	harbor dues
dumping (m)		dumping
duopole (m)	*(dooh-oh-pOhl)*	duopoly
durée (f) d'un brevet	*(dooh-rEh dæhn bræh-vEh)*	life of a patent
durée d'une patente	*(dooh-rEh doohn pah-tÃhnt)*	life of a patent
durée de vie	*(dooh-rEh dœ vEEh)*	life cycle
durée de vie d'un produit	*(dooh-rEh dœ vEEh dæhn proh-dwEEh)*	product life
durée de vie moyenne	*(dooh-rEh dœ vEEh mwah-yEhn)*	average life
durée utile	*(dooh-rEh ooh-tEEhl)*	useful life
dureté (f)	*(dooh-ræh-tEh)*	toughness
dynamique (f) de groupe	*(deeh-nah-mEEhk dœ grOOhp)*	group dynamics
dynamique des produits	*(deeh-nah-mEEhk deh proh-dwEEh)*	product dynamics
dynamique du marché	*(deeh-nah-mEEhk dooh mahr-shEh)*	market dynamics

D

E

eaux (fpl) territoriales	*(Œh teh-reeh-toh-ryAhl)*	territorial waters
écart (m)	*(eh-kAhr)*	variance
écart de prix	*(eh-kAhr dœ prEEh)*	price differential
écart de tarif	*(eh-kAhr dœ tah-rEEhf)*	tariff differential
écart des cours	*(eh-kAhr deh kOOhr)*	spread
écart des cours brut	*(eh-kAhr deh kOOhr brOOh)*	gross spread
écart des salaires	*(eh-kAhr deh sah-lEhr)*	wage differential
écart net du cours	*(eh-kAhr nEht dooh kOOhr)*	net change
écart tarifaire	*(eh-kAhr tah-reeh-fEhr)*	tariff differential
écart type	*(eh-kAhr tEEhp)*	standard deviation
échange (m)	*(eh-shÃhnzh)*	trade-off
échange bancaire	*(eh-shÃhnzh bãhn-kEhr)*	bank exchange
échange de brevets	*(eh-shÃhnzh dœ brœh-vEh)*	cross licensing
échanger	*(eh-shãhn-zhEr)*	exchange
échantillon (m) aléatoire	*(eh-shãhn-teeh-yÕhn ah-leh-ah-twAhr)*	random sample
échantillonnage (m) divers	*(eh-shãhn-teeh-yoh-nAzh deeh-vEhr)*	mixed sampling
échantillonnage pour acceptation	*(eh-shãhn-teeh-yoh-nAzh poohr ahk-sehp-tah-syÕh)*	acceptance sampling
échantillonner	*(eh-shãhn-teeh-yoh-nEh)*	sample (v)
échantillons (mpl) provenant d'un même univers	*(eh-shãhn-teeh-yÕh proh-vœh-nÃhn dœhn mEhm ooh-neeh-vEhrs)*	matched samples
échappement (m)	*(eh-shahp-mÃh)*	exhaust
échéance (f)	*(eh-sheh-Ãhns)*	maturity
échéance originelle	*(eh-sheh-Ãhns oh-reeh-zheeh-nEhl)*	original maturity
échelle (f) des salaires	*(eh-shEhl deh sah-lEhr)*	wage scale
échelle mobile	*(eh-shEhl moh-bEEhl)*	sliding scale
échouer	*(eh-shooh-Eh)*	fail (v)
éclat (m)	*(eh-klAh)*	glow, sparkle
éclatant	*(eh-klah-tÃhn)*	glowing
écologie (f)	*(eh-koh-loh-zhEEh)*	ecology
écologique	*(eh-koh-loh-zhEEhk)*	ecological, environmentally friendly
écologiste (m/f)	*(eh-koh-loh-zhEEhst)*	environmentalist
économétrie (f)	*(eh-koh-noh-meh-trEEh)*	econometrics
économie (f)	*(eh-koh-noh-mEEh)*	economics
économie d'échelle	*(eh-koh-noh-mEEh deh-shEhl)*	economy of scale
économies (fpl) d'énergie	*(eh-koh-noh-mEEh deh-nehr-zhEEh)*	energy conservation

économie de main-d'œuvre	*(eh-koh-noh-mEEh dœ mÆhn dŒh-vrœ)*	labor-saving
économie dirigée	*(eh-koh-noh-mEEh deeh-reeh-zhEh)*	managed economy
économique	*(eh-koh-moh-mEEhk)*	economic
écran (m)	*(eh-krAhn)*	screen
écran (m) solaire	*(eh-krÃhn soh-lEhr)*	sun block
écriture (f) au grand livre	*(eh-kree-tOOhr oh grÃhn lEEh-vrœ)*	ledger entry
écriture au passif	*(eh-kreeh-tOOhr oh pah-sEEhf)*	debit entry
écriture de clôture	*(eh-kreeh-tOOhr dœ kloh-tOOhr)*	closing entry
ÉCU (m)	*(eh-kOOh)*	European Currency Unit
éditer	*(eh-deeh-tEh)*	edit (v)
éditeur (m)	*(eh-deeh-tŒhr)*	publisher
édition (f)	*(eh-deeh-syÕh)*	edition
effacer	*(eh-fah-sEh)*	delete (v)
effet (m)	*(eh-fEh)*	bill
effet à recevoir	*(eh-fEht ah rœh-seh-vwAhr)*	receivable note
effet à terme	*(eh-fEht ah tEhrm)*	time bill (of exchange)
effet avalisé	*(eh-fEht ah-vah-leeh-zEh)*	backed note
effet de commerce	*(eh-fEh dœ koh-mEhrs)*	draft
effet de levier	*(eh-fEh dœ lœh-vyEh)*	leverage
effet de serre (m)	*(eh-fEh dœ sEhr)*	greenhouse effect
effet (m) secondaire	*(eh-feh seh-kõhr-dEhr)*	side effect
efficacité (f)	*(eh-feeh-kah-seeh-tEh)*	efficiency
effondrement (m)	*(eh-fõn-drœ-mÃh)*	go down, slump
égaliser	*(eh-gah-leeh-zEh)*	level out
égalité (f) des salaires	*(eh-gah-leeh-tEh deh sah-lEhr)*	equal pay for equal work
égrappage (m)	*(eh-grah-pAhzh)*	stalking
élargir le fossé	*(eh-lahr-zhEEhr lœ foh-sEh)*	widen the gap (v)
élasticité (f)	*(eh-lahs-teeh-seeh-tEh)*	elasticity, resilience
élasticité des prix	*(eh-lahs-teeh-seeh-tEh deh prEEh)*	price elasticity
électricité (f)	*(eh-lehk-treeh-seeh-tEh)*	electricity
éléctrode (f)	*(eh-lehk-trOhd)*	electrode
électrolyse (f)	*(eh-lehk-troh-lEEhz)*	electrolysis
électron (m)	*(eh-lehk-trÕh)*	electron
électronique	*(eh-lehk-troh-nEEhk)*	electronic
électrophone (m)	*(eh-lehk-troh-fOhn)*	record player
électrostatique	*(eh-lehk-troh-stah-tEEhk)*	electrostatic
élégance (f)	*(eh-leh-gÃhns)*	elegance
élément (m)	*(eh-leh-mÃh)*	element

éléments (mpl) d'actif courus et non échus	*(eh-leh-mÃh dahk-tEEf kooh-rOOh eh nõn eh-shOOh)*	accrued assets
éléments d'actif productifs	*(eh-leh-mÃh dahk-tEEf proh-doohk-tEEhf)*	active assets
élimination (f) des déchets	*(eh-leeh-meeh-nah-syÕhn deh deh-shEht)*	waste disposal
emballage (m)	*(ãhm-bah-lAhzh)*	packaging
emballage (m) inviolable	*(ãhm-bah-lAhzh ãhn-vyoh-lAh-blœh)*	tamperproof package
emballé sous film rétractable	*(ãhm-bah-lEh sooh fEEhlm reh-trahk-tAh-blœ)*	shrink-wrapped
embargo (m)	*(ãhm-bahr-goh)*	embargo
embaucher	*(ãhm-boh-shEh)*	hire (v)
embrayage (m)	*(ãhm-brah-yAhzh)*	clutch
embrayage automatique	*(ãhm-brah-yAhzh oh-toh-mah-tEEhk)*	automatic gearshift
émettre	*(eh-mEh-trœ)*	issue (v), float (v) (issue stock)
émeute (f)	*(eh-mŒht)*	riot
émission (f)	*(eh-meeh-syÕhn)*	issue (stock), emission
émission d'obligations	*(eh-meeh-syÕh doh-bleeh-gah-syÕh)*	bond issue
émission de premier rang	*(eh-meeh-syÕh dœ prœh-myeh rÃhng)*	senior issue
émmission (f) en direct	*(eh-meeh-syÕhn ãhr deeh-rEhkt)*	live program
émission fiduciaire	*(eh-meeh-syÕh feeh-dooh-syEhr)*	fiduciary issue
émoluments (mpl)	*(eh-moh-looh-mÃh)*	salary
émulsion (f)	*(eh-moohl-syÕhn)*	emulsion
emploi (m)	*(ãhm-plwAh)*	job
emploi du temps	*(ãhm-plwAh dooh tÃh)*	timetable, work schedule
employé (m)	*(ãhm-plwah-yEh)*	employee
employé de bureau	*(ãhm-plwah-yEh dœ booh-rOh)*	white collar worker
emprunt (m)	*(ãhm-prŒhn)*	loan
emprunter	*(œhm-prœhn-tEh)*	borrow (v)
emprunts (mpl) nets	*(ãhm-prŒhn nEht)*	net borrowed reserves
en bonne santé	*(ãhn bohn sãhn-tEh)*	healthy
en compte	*(ãhn kÕhnt)*	on account
en consignation	*(ãhn kõhn-seeh-nyah-syÕh)*	on consignment
en dépôt	*(ãhn deh-pOh)*	on consignment
en exclusivité	*(ãhn ehksklooh-seeh-veeh-tEh)*	exclusive
en extérieur	*(ãhr ehk-steh-ryŒhr)*	on location
en franchise	*(ãhn frãh-shEEhz)*	duty free

en gras	(ãhn grAh)	boldface
en ligne	(ãhn lEEh-nyœh)	on-line
en réponse à	(ãhn reh-pÕhns ah)	in reply to
en retard	(ãhn rœh-tAhr)	overdue
en souffrance	(ãhn sooh-frÃhns)	past due
en transit	(ãhn trÃhn-zEEht)	in transit
encaissement (m)	(ãhn-kehs-mÃh)	cash entry
enceinte	(ãhn-sÆhnt)	pregnant
enchérir sur	(ãhn-sheh-rEEhr soohr)	improve upon (v)
encre (f)	(ãhn-krœ)	ink
endossataire (m)	(ãhn-doh-sah-tEhr)	endorsee
endossement (m)	(ãhn-dohs-mÃh)	endorsement
endossement de complaisance	(ãhn-dohs-mÃh dœ kõhn-pleh-zÃhns)	accommodation endorsement
endosser	(œhn-doh-sEh)	endorse (v)
énergie (f)	(eh-nehr-zhEEh)	energy, power
énergie (f) non polluante	(eh-nehr-zhEEh nõhn poh-lwÃhnt)	nonpolluting energy
énergie (f) solaire	(eh-nehr-zhEEh soh-lEhr)	solar energy
engagement (m)	(ãhn-gahzh-mÃh)	commitment, pledge, encumbrance (liens, liabilities, commitments)
enquêteur (m)	(ãhn-keh-tŒhr)	troubleshooter, investigator
enregistrement (m) initial	(ãhn-rœh-zheehs-trœ-mÃh eeh-neeh-syAhl)	original entry
enregistrer	(ãhn-rœh-zheehs-trEh)	record (v)
enregistreur (m)	(ãhn-rœh-zheehs-trŒhr)	tape recorder
ensemble des salaires (m)	(ãhn-sÃhm-blœ deh sah-lEhr)	payroll
entente (f)	(ãhn-tÃhnt)	understanding (agreement)
entièrement payé	(ãhn-tyehr-mÃh pah-yEh)	paid in full
entrée (f)	(ãhn-trEh)	input
entrée d'ordinateur	(ãhn-trEh dohr-deeh-nah-tŒhr)	computer input
entrée du grand livre	(ãhn-trEh dooh grãhn lEEh-vrœ)	ledger entry
entrée passive	(ãhn-trEh pah-sEEhv)	debit entry
entreposage (m)	(ãhn-trœ-poh-sAhzh)	storage
entreposage surveillé	(ãhn-trœ-poh-sAhzh soohr-veh-yEh)	field warehousing
entrepôt (m)	(ãhn-trœ-pOh)	warehouse
entrepôt autorisé	(ãhn-trœ-pOh oh-toh-reeh-zEh)	licensed warehouse
entrepôt régulier	(ãhn-trœ-pOh reh-gooh-lyEh)	regular warehouse
entreprendre	(ãhn-trœ-prãhn-drœ)	undertake (v)

E

entrepreneur (m)	*(ãhn-trœh-prœh-nŒhr)*	entrepreneur
entreprise (f)	*(ãhn-trœh-prEEhz)*	enterprise
entreprise commune	*(ãhn-trœh-prEEhz koh-mOOhn)*	joint venture
entreprise d'exportation	*(ãhn-trœh-prEEhz dehks-pohr-tah-syÕh)*	export house
entreprise de pointe	*(ãhn-trœh-prEEhz dœ pwÆhnt)*	high technology firm, leading firm
entreprise individuelle	*(ãhn-trœh-prEEhz æhn-deeh-veeh-dwEhl)*	sole proprietorship
entreprise non syndicalisée	*(ãhn-trœh-prEEhz nõh seehn-deeh-kah-leeh-zEh)*	open shop
entrer en vigueur	*(ãhn-trEh ãhn veeh-gŒhr)*	come into force (v)
entretien (m)	*(ãhn-trœh-tyEhn)*	maintenance
entretien préventif	*(ãhn-trœh-tyÆhn preh-vãhn-tEEhf)*	preventive maintenance
entrevue (f)	*(ãhn-trœh-vOOh)*	interview
environ	*(ãhn-veeh-rÕh)*	around
environnement (m)	*(ãhn-veeh-rohn-mÃhn)*	environment
envoi (m) contre remboursement	*(ãhn-vwAh kõhn-trœ rãhm-boohrs-mÃh)*	cash on delivery
enzyme (m)	*(ãhn-zEEhm)*	enzyme
épais	*(eh-pEh)*	thick
épargne (f)	*(eh-pAhr-nyœ)*	savings
épaulette (f)	*(eh-poh-lEht)*	shoulder pad
épiderme (m)	*(eh-peeh-dEhrm)*	skin
épreuve (f)	*(eh-prŒhv)*	galley, proof
éprouvette (f)	*(eh-prooh-vEht)*	test tube
épuiser	*(eh-pweeh-sEh)*	deplete (v)
équipe (f)	*(eh-kEEhp)*	shift (labor)
équipe de gestion	*(eh-kEEhp dœ zhœhs-tyÕh)*	management team
équipe des vendeurs	*(eh-kEEhp deh vÃhn-dŒhr)*	sales force
équipement (m)	*(eh-keehp-mÃh)*	equipment
équipement de traitement de texte	*(eh-keehp-mÃh dœ treht-mÃh dœ tEhk-stœ)*	word processor
ergonomie (f)	*(ehr-goh-noh-mEEh)*	ergonomics
érosion (f)	*(eh-roh-zyÕh)*	attrition
érosion (f) des sols	*(eh-roh-syÕhn deh sOhl)*	soil erosion
erreur (f)	*(eh-rŒhr)*	error
erreur de calcul	*(eh-rŒhr dœ kahl-kOOhl)*	miscalculation
erreur de traitement	*(eh-rŒhr dœ treht-mÃh)*	processing error
escalade (f) des armes nucléaires	*(ehs-kah-lAhd dez Ahrm nooh-kleh-Ehr)*	nuclear build up
escompte (m)	*(ehs-kÕhnt)*	discount
escompte d'usage	*(ehs-kÕhnt dooh-zAhzh)*	trade discount
escompte de caisse	*(ehs-kÕhnt dœ kEhs)*	cash discount
espèces (fpl)	*(ehs-pEhs)*	cash, liquidity
esquisse (f)	*(ehs-kEEhs)*	line drawing, rough draft

essai (m)	*(eh-sEh)*	assay, test
essence (f)	*(eh-sÃhns)*	gasoline
essor (m) économique	*(eh-sOhr eh-koh-moh-mEEhk)*	boom
estimation (f)	*(ehs-teeh-mah-syÕh)*	estimate, appraisal
estimation au jugé	*(ehs-teeh-mah-syÕh oh zhooh-zhEh)*	guesstimate
estimation de prix	*(ehs-teeh-mah-syÕh dœ prEEh)*	estimated price
estimation des immobilisations	*(ehs-teeh-mah-syÕh dehz eeh-moh-beeh-leeh-zah-syÕh)*	capital expenditure appraisal
estimation des ventes	*(ehs-teeh-mah-syÕh dehy vÃhnt)*	sales estimate
estimation linéaire	*(ehs-teeh-mah-syÕh leeh-neh-Ehr)*	lineal estimation
estimer	*(ehs-teeh-mEh)*	assess (v), estimate (v)
établir un prix	*(eh-tah-blEEhr œhn prEEh)*	price (v)
établissement (m) de la prime	*(eh-tah-bleehs-mÃh dœ lah prEEhm)*	premium pricing
établissement d'une liste	*(eh-tah-bleehs-mÃh doohn lEEhst)*	listing
étalagiste (m or f)	*(eh-tah-lah-zhEEhst)*	window dresser
étaler en faisant mousser	*(eh-tah-lEh ãhn feh-zÃhn mooh-sEh)*	lather (v)
étalon (m)	*(eh-tah-lÕh)*	yardstick
état (m)	*(eh-tAh)*	statement
état des pertes et profits	*(eh-tAh deh pEhrt eh proh-fEEh)*	profit-and-loss statement
état financier	*(eh-tAh feeh-nãhn-syEh)*	financial statement
État membre (m)	*(eh-tAh mÃhm-brœh)*	member state
état pro forma	*(eh-tAh proh-fOhr-mah)*	pro forma statement
état-major	*(eh-tAh mah-zhOhr)*	staff
éternuer	*(eh-tehr-nwEh)*	sneeze (v)
éthane (m)	*(eh-tAhn)*	ethane
éther (m)	*(eh-tEh)*	ether
étiquette (f)	*(eh-teeh-kEht)*	label
être à court	*(Eh-trœ ah kOOhr)*	be short of (v)
être compétitif	*(Eh-trœ kohm-peh-teeh-tEEhf)*	meet the price (v)
étude (f) de conception	*(eh-tOOhd dœ kõhn-sehp-syÕh)*	design engineering
étude de la rentabilité des investissements	*(eh-tOOhd dœ rãhn-tah-beeh-leeh-tEh dehz ãhn-vehs-teehs-mÃh)*	investment analysis
étude de la valeur	*(eh-tOOhd dœ lah vah-lŒhr)*	value engineering
étude de marché	*(eh-tOOhd dœ mahr-shEh)*	market research

E

étude de motivation	*(eh-tOOhd dœ moh-teeh-vah-syÕh)*	motivation study
étude de rentabilité	*(eh-tOOhd dœ rãhn-tah-beeh-leeh-tEh)*	profitability analysis
étude des besoins des consommateurs	*(eh-tOOhd deh bœh-zwÆhn deh kõhn-soh-mah-tŒhr)*	consumer research
étude des débouchés	*(eh-tOOhd deh deh-boohshEh)*	market survey
étude des méthodes	*(eh-tOOhd deh meh-tOhd)*	systems analysis
étude des ventes	*(eh-tOOhd deh vÃhnt)*	sales analysis
étude (f) d'opinion	*(eh-toohd doh-peeh-nÕyn)*	audience research
étude du produit	*(eh-tOOhd dooh proh-dwEEh)*	product analysis
étude du rapport coûts/profits	*(eh-tOOhd dooh rah-pOhr kOOht/proh-fEEh)*	cost-benefit analysis
étude du risque	*(eh-tOOhd dooh rEEhs-kœ)*	risk analysis
étui (m) à cigarettes	*(eh-twEEh ah seeh-gah-rEht)*	cigarette case
étui (m) à ciseaux	*(eh-twEEh ah seeh-zOh)*	scissor case
étui à lunettes	*(eh-twEEh ah looh-nEht)*	eyeglass case
étui à revolver	*(eh-twEEh ah rœh-vohl-vEh)*	holster
eurochèque (m)	*(eh-ooh-roh-shEhk)*	Eurocheque
eurocrate (m/f)	*(eh-ooh-roh-krAht)*	Eurocrat
eurodevise (f)	*(eh-ooh-roh-dœh-vEEhz)*	Eurocurrency
eurodollar (m)	*(eh-ooh-roh-doh-lAhr)*	Eurodollar
euromarché (m)	*(eh-ooh-roh-mahr-shEh)*	Euromarket
Euro-obligation (f)	*(eh-oh-roh-oh-bleeh-gah-syÕh)*	Eurobond
euthanasie (f)	*(eh-ooh-tah-nah-zEEh)*	euthanasia
évaluation (f)	*(eh-vah-lwah-syÕh)*	evaluation, appraisal, assessment, valuation, appreciation
évaluation (f) de la demande	*(eh-vah-lwah-syÕhn dœ lah dœh-mÃhnd)*	demand assessment
évaluation (f) de l'environnement	*(eh-vah-lwah-syÕhn dœ lãhn-veeh-rohn-mÃhn)*	environmental assessment
évaluation de l'impact d'une publicité	*(eh-vah-lwah-syÕh dœ lœahm-pAhkt doohn pooh-bleeh-seeh-tEh)*	copy testing
évaluation de la solvabilité	*(eh-vah-lwah-syÕh dœ sohl-vah-beeh-leeh-tEh)*	credit rating
évaluation de poste	*(eh-vah-lwah-syÕh dœ pOhst)*	job evaluation
évaluation des besoins	*(eh-vah-lwah-syÕh deh bœh-zwÆhn)*	needs analysis
évaluation des coûts	*(eh-vah-lwah-syÕh deh kOOht)*	cost analysis

E

évaluation des facteurs	*(eh-vah-lwah-syÕh deh fahk-tŒhr)*	factor rating
évaluation des investissements	*(eh-vah-lwah-syÕh dehz ãhn-vehs-teehs-mÃh)*	investment appraisal
évaluation du marché	*(eh-vah-lwah-syÕh dooh mahr-shEh)*	market appraisal, market rating
évaluation financière	*(eh-vah-lwah-syÕh feeh-nãhn-syEh)*	financial appraisal
évaporation (f)	*(eh-vah-poh-rah-syÕh)*	evaporation
examiner	*(ehk-zah-meeh-nEh)*	review (v)
ex-dividende (m)	*(ex-deeh-veeh-dÃhnd)*	ex dividend
ex-droits (mpl)	*(ex-drwAh)*	ex rights
excédent (m)	*(ehk-seh-dÃhn)*	overage
excédents (mpl)	*(ehk-seh-dÃhn)*	surplus goods
excès (mpl) de pouvoir	*(ehk-sEh dœ pooh-vwAhr)*	ultra vires acts
exclusivité d'opérations de change	*(ehks-klooh-seeh-veeh-tEh doh-peh-rah-syÕh dœ shÃhnzh)*	dealership
exécuteur (m) testamentaire	*(ehk-seh-kooh-tŒhr tehs-tah-mãhn-tEhr)*	executor
exemplaire (m)	*(ehk-zãhm-plEhr)*	copy (text)
exemplaire (m) de presse	*(ehk-zãhm-plEhr dœ prEhs)*	press book
exempt d'impôts	*(ehk-sÃhn dæhm-pOh)*	tax-free
exemption (f)	*(ehk-zãhm-syÕh)*	exemption
exemption personnelle	*(ehk-zãhm-syÕh per-soh-nEhl)*	personal exemption
exercice (m)	*(ehk-sœr-sEEhs)*	financial year, fiscal year
exercice comptable	*(ehk-sœr-sEEhs kõhn-tАh-blœ)*	accounting period
exercice financier	*(ehk-sœr-sEEhs feeh-nãhn-syEh)*	financial period, financial year
exercice fiscal	*(ehk-sœr-sEEhs feehs-kAhl)*	fiscal year
exiger	*(ehk-seeh-zhEh)*	demand (v)
exonération (f) fiscale	*(ehks-oh-neh-rah-syÕh feehs-kAhl)*	tax allowance
expansion (f) de l'entreprise	*(ehks-pãhn-syÕh dœ lãhn-træh-prEEhz)*	corporate growth
expéditeur (m)	*(ehks-peh-deeh-tŒhr)*	shipper
expédition (f)	*(ehks-peh-deeh-syÕh)*	consignment, shipment, dispatch
expédition directe	*(ehks-peh-deeh-syÕh deeh-rEhkt)*	drop shipment
expédition ferroviaire	*(ehks-peh-deeh-syÕh feh-roh-vyEhr)*	rail shipment
expédition, bordereau d'	*(ehks-peh-deeh-syÕh bohr-dœ-rOh)*	shipping memo
expéditions (fpl) illégales	*(ehks-peh-deeh-syÕh eeh-leh-gAhl)*	illegal shipments

E

expérience (f)	*(ehks-peh-ryÃhns)*	experiment
expérimental	*(ehks-peh-reeh-māhn-tAhl)*	experimental
expert (m) en gestion	*(ehks-pEhr āhn zhœhs-tyŌh)*	management consultant
expert-comptable	*(ehks-pEhr kōhn-tAh-blœ)*	certified public accountant, chartered accountant (Brit.)
exploitant (m)	*(ehks-plwah-tÃhnt)*	operator
exploiter les ressources forestière	*(ehks-plwah-tEh leh rœh-sOOhrs foh-rehs-tyEhr)*	tap the forest's wealth (v)
exportateur tiers	*(ehks-pohr-tah-tŒhr tyEhrs)*	third-party exporter
exportation (f) clef	*(ehks-pohr-tah-syŌh klEh)*	key exports
exportation de capitaux	*(ehks-pohr-tah-syŌh deh kah-peeh-tOh)*	capital exports
exporter	*(ehks-pohr-tEh)*	export (v)
expropriation (f)	*(ehks-proh-pryah-syŌh)*	expropriation
extrait (m) de titre de propriété	*(ehks-trEh dœ tEEh-trœ dœ proh-pryeh-tEh)*	abstract of title

---

F

fabricant (m)	*(fah-breeh-kÃh)*	manufacturer
fabrication (f) en série	*(fah-breeh-kah-syŌh āhn seh-rEEh)*	mass production
FACOB (traité facultatif obligatoire)	*(treh-tEh fah-koohl-tah-tEEhf oh-bleeh-gah-twAhr)*	open cover
facteur (m)	*(fahk-tŒhr)*	factor
facteur coût	*(fahk-tŒhr kOOht)*	cost factor
facteur profit	*(fahk-tŒhr proh-fEEh)*	profit factor
facteur rentabilité	*(fahk-tŒhr rāhn-tah-beeh-leeh-tEh)*	profit factor
factotum (m)	*(fahk-toh-tOOhm)*	man (gal) Friday
facturation (f) périodique	*(fahk-tooh-rah-syŌh peh-ryoh-dEEhk)*	cycle billing
facture (f)	*(fahk-tOOhr)*	invoice, bill
facture commerciale	*(fahk-tOOhr koh-mehr-syAhl)*	commercial invoice
facture pro forma	*(fahk-tOOhr proh-fOhr-mah)*	pro forma invoice
facultatif	*(fah-koohl-tah-tEEhf)*	optional
fade	*(fAhd)*	tasteless
faïence (f)	*(fah-eeh-Ãhns)*	chinaware, earthenware
faillite (f)	*(feh-yEEht)*	bankruptcy
faire cavalier seul	*(fEhr kah-vah-lyEh sŒhl)*	stay separate (v)
faire la grève	*(fEhr lah grEhv)*	strike (v)

faire la queue	*(fEhr la kOOh)*	stand in line (v)
faire obstacle	*(fEhr ohb-stAh-klœh)*	block (to)
faire passer une annonce	*(fehr pah-seh oohn ah-nÕhns)*	run an ad (v)
faire sauter le bouchon	*(fehr soh-tEh lœ booh-shÕhn)*	pop a cork (v)
faire un rabais	*(fEhr œhn rah-bEh)*	take off (v)
faire une offre	*(fEhr oohn Oh-frœ)*	put in a bid
fardage (m)	*(fahr-dAhzh)*	dunnage
fatigue (f) due au décalage horaire	*(fah-tEEhg dOOh oh deh-kah-lAzh oh-rEhr)*	jet lag
fautif	*(foh-tEEhf)*	negligent
faux frais (mpl)	*(fOh frEh)*	incidental expenses
faux frais divers	*(fOh frEh deeh-vEhr)*	contingencies
faux fret (m)	*(fOh frEht)*	dead freight
faveur (f) du public	*(fah-vŒhr dooh pooh-blEEhk)*	consumer acceptance
favorable à l'utilisateur	*(fah-voh-rAh-blœ ah looh-teeh-leeh-zah-tŒhr)*	user friendly
fenêtrage (m)	*(feh-neh-trAhzh)*	windowing
fer (m)	*(fEhr)*	iron
fer (m) à béton	*(fehr ah beh-tÕh)*	rebars
fer (m) à repasser	*(fehr ah rœh-pah-sEh)*	iron
ferment (m)	*(fehr-mÃh)*	ferment
fermentation (f) malolactique	*(fehr-mãhn-tah-syÕh mah-loh-lahk-tEEhk)*	biological diacidizing, malolactic fermentation
fermeture (f) éclair	*(fehr-mœh-tOOhr eh-klEhr)*	zipper
ferritique	*(feh-reeh-tEEhk)*	ferritic
ferro-alliages (mpl)	*(feh-roh-ah-lyAhzh)*	ferroalloys
ferrochrome (m) de charge	*(feh-roh-krOhm dœ shAhrzh)*	charge chrome
ferromanganèse (m)	*(feh-roh-mahn-gah-nEhz)*	ferromanganese
fête (f) légale	*(fEht leh-gAhl)*	legal holiday
feu (m) d'artillerie	*(fŒh dahr-teeh-yeh-rEEh)*	gun fire
feuille (f)	*(fŒh-yœ)*	sheet
feuille (f) de renseignements	*(fŒh-yœ dœ rãhn-seh-nyœ-mÃh)*	fact sheet
feuilleton (m)	*(fœh-yœh-tÕhn)*	serial film, series
fibre (f) optique	*(fEEh-brœ ohp-tEEhk)*	fiber optic
fibres (fpl) synthétiques	*(fEEh-brœ seehn-teh-tEEhk)*	manmade fibers
fichier (m)	*(feeh-shyEh)*	file
fidéicommis (m)	*(feeh-deh-eeh-koh-mEEh)*	trust
fiduciaire	*(feeh-dooh-syEhr)*	fiduciary
fiducie (f) active	*(feeh-dooh-sEEh ahk-tEEhv)*	active trust
fiducie révocable	*(feeh-dooh-sEEh reh-voh-kAh-blœ)*	revocable trust

fièvre (f)	*(fyEh-vrœh)*	fever
fil (m)	*(fEEhl)*	thread, yarn, wire
filament (m)	*(feeh-lah-mÃh)*	filament
filiale (f)	*(feeh-lyAhl)*	subsidiary, member firm
filtrage (m)	*(feehl-trAhzh)*	screening
filtre (m)	*(fEEhl-trœ)*	filter
filtre à air (m)	*(fEEhl-trœ ah Ehr)*	air filter
filtre (m) à huile	*(fEEhl-trœ ah wEEhl)*	oil filter
fin (f) d'année	*(fÆhn dah-nEh)*	year-end
fin d'exercice	*(fÆhn dehk-sœr-sEEhs)*	end of period
fin de série	*(fÆhn dœ seh-rEEh)*	broken lot
financement (m) à court terme	*(feeh-nãhns-mÃh ah koohr tEhrm)*	short-term financing
financement de départ	*(feeh-nãhns-mÃh dœ deh-pAhr)*	front-end financing
financement par le déficit	*(feeh-nãhns-mÃh pahr lœ deh-feeh-sEEht)*	deficit financing
financement spéculatif	*(feeh-nãhns-mÃh speh-kooh-lah-tEEhf)*	leveraged lease
financer	*(feeh-nãhn-sEh)*	finance (v)
finition (f)	*(feeh-neeh-syÕhn)*	finish
firme (f)	*(fEEhrm)*	firm
fixation (f) du prix	*(feehk-sah-syÕh dooh prEEh)*	price fixing
fixation du prix marginal	*(feehk-sah-syÕh dooh prEEh mahr-zheeh-nAhl)*	marginal pricing
fixé avec des lattes	*(feehk-sEh ah-vehk deh lAht)*	batten fitted
flacon (m) de parfum	*(flah-kÕhn doe pahr-fOOhm)*	perfume bottle
flanelle (f)	*(flah-nEhl)*	flannel
flotte (f) privée	*(flOht preeh-vEh)*	private fleet
flottement (m) dirigé	*(floht-mÃh deeh-reeh-zhEh)*	managed float
fluctuations (fpl) du personnel	*(floohk-twah-syÕh dooh pehr-soh-nEhl)*	labor turnover
flûte (f) à champagne	*(flOOht ah shahm-pÃh-nyœ)*	flute, champagne glass
fondé de pouvoir (m)	*(fõhn-dEh dœ pooh-vwAhr)*	attorney in fact, proxy
fonderie (f)	*(fõhn-dœh-rEEh)*	foundry
fond (m) de teint	*(fõhn dœ tÆhnt)*	base
fond (m) sonore	*(fÕhn soh-nOhr)*	background music
fonds (m)	*(fÕhn)*	fund
fonds (mpl) bloqués	*(fÕhn bloh-kEh)*	frozen assets
fonds (m) consultatif	*(fÕhn kõh-soohl-tah-tEEhf)*	advisory funds
fonds (m) tournant	*(fÕhn toohr-nÃh)*	revolving fund
fonds d'amortissement	*(fÕhn dah-mohr-eehs-mÃh)*	redemption fund, sinking fund

F

fonds d'assurance	*(fÕhn dah-sooh-rÃhns)*	insurance fund
fonds d'exploitation	*(fÕhn dehks-plwah-tah-syÕh)*	working funds
fonds (mpl) de cohésion	*(fÕhn dœ koh-eh-zyÕhn)*	cohesion funds
fonds de dépôt	*(fÕhn dœ deh-pOh)*	trust fund
fonds de prévoyance	*(fÕhn dœ preh-vwah-yÃhns)*	contingent fund
fonds de roulement	*(fÕhn dœ roohl-mÃh)*	working funds, working capital, revolving fund
fonds de roulement nets	*(fÕhn dœ roohl-mÃh nEht)*	net working capital
fonds hautement spéculatif	*(fÕhnz oht-mÃh speh-kooh-lah-tEEhf)*	go-go fund
fonds mutuel	*(fÕhn mooh-twEhl)*	trust fund
fonds publics (mpl)	*(fÕhn pooh-blEEhk)*	public funds
fonte (f)	*(fÕhnt)*	font, pig iron
fonte (f) coulée	*(fÕhnt kooh lEh)*	cast iron
force (f) de maintien de la paix	*(fohrs dœ mãehn-tyEhn dœ lah pEh)*	peace-keeping force
forêt (f) tropicale	*(foh-rEh troh-peeh-kAhl)*	rain forest
forfait (m)	*(fohr-fEh)*	package deal
format (m)	*(fohr-mAh)*	format
formater	*(fohr-mah-tEh)*	format (v)
formation (f) dans l'entreprise	*(fohr-mah-syÕh dãhn lãhn-trœh-prEEhz)*	on-the job training
formation de groupe	*(fohr-mah-syÕh dœ grOOhp)*	group training
formulaire (m)	*(fohr-mooh-lEhr)*	application form
formule (f)	*(fohr-mOOhl)*	formula
fouet (m)	*(fooh-Eh)*	whip
foulard (m)	*(fooh-lAhr)*	scarf
four (m)	*(fOOhr)*	furnace
four (m) à induction	*(fOOhr ah ãehn-doohk-synOh)*	induction furnace
four (m) électrique	*(fOOhr eh-lehk-trEEhk)*	electric arc furnace
four (m) sous vide	*(fOOhr sooh vEEhd)*	vacuum melting furnace
fourchette (f)	*(foohr-shEht)*	fork
fourchette (f) à trois dents	*(foohr-shEht ah trwah dAhn)*	three-pronged fork
fourchette (f) des prix	*(foohr-shEht deh prEEh)*	price range
fournisseur (m)	*(foohr-neeh-sŒhr)*	supplier, vendor
fournisseur à la commande	*(foohr-neeh-zŒhr ah lah koh-mÃhnd)*	job shop
fourniture (f) excédentaire	*(foohr-neeh-tOOhr ehk-seh-dãhn-tEhr)*	oversupply
fractionnement (m) des actions	*(frahk-syohn-mÃh dehz ahk-syÕh)*	stock split
fraîcheur (f)	*(freh-shŒhr)*	freshness

frais (mpl)	(frEh)	cost, charges, expenses
frais (mp) bancaires	(freh bãhn-kEhr)	bank charges
frais (mpl) communs	(frEh koh-mOOhn)	joint costs
frais contrôlés	(frEh kõhn-troh-lEh)	managed costs
frais d'administration	(frEh dad-meeh-neehs-trah-syÕh)	administrative expenses
frais d'arrimage	(frEh dah-reeh-mAhzh)	stowage charges
frais d'établissement	(frEh deh-tah-bleehs-mÃh)	start-up cost
frais d'expédition	(frEh dehks-peh-deeh-syÕh)	shipping expenses, shipping charges
frais d'exploitation	(frEh dehks-plwah-tah-syÕh)	operating expenses
frais d'installation	(frEh dǽhn-stah-lah-syÕh)	set-up costs
frais de banque	(frEh dœ bÃhnk)	bank charges
frais de couverture	(frEh dœ kooh-vehr-tOOhr)	cover charges
frais de débarquement	(frEh dœ deh-bahrk-mÃh)	landing charges
frais de déménagement	(frEh dœ dœ deh-meh-nahz-mÃh)	moving expenses
frais de distribution	(frEh dœ deehs-treeh-booh-syÕh)	distribution costs
frais de publicité	(frEh dœ pooh-bleeh-seeh-tEh)	advertising expenses
frais de quayage	(frEh dœ keh-yAhzh)	wharfage charges
frais de remplacement	(frEh dœ rãhm-plahs-mÃh)	replacement costs
frais de représentation	(frEh dœ rœh-preh-zãhn-tah-syÕh)	expense account
frais de reproduction	(frEh dœ rœ-proh-doohk-syÕh)	reproduction costs
frais de sauvetage	(frEh dœ soh-veh-tAhzh)	salvage charges
frais directs	(frEh deeh-rEhkt)	direct costs
frais évitables	(frEh eh-veeh-tAh-blœ)	avoidable costs
frais fixes	(frEh fEEhks)	standing costs, fixed costs
frais fonciers	(frEh fõhn-syEhr)	landed costs
frais généraux	(frEh zheh-neh-rOh)	overhead charges
frais généraux d'usine	(frEh zheh-neh-rOh dooh-zEEhn)	factory overhead
frais indirects	(frEh ǽhn-deeh-rEhkt)	indirect costs
frais mixtes	(frEh mEEhkst)	mixed costs
frais normaux	(frEh nohr-mOh)	standard costs
frais payés d'avance (bilan)	(frEh pah-yEh dah-vÃhns [beeh-lÃh])	prepaid expenses (balance sheet)
frais permanents	(frEh pehr-mah-nÃh)	standing charges
frais proportionnels	(frEh proh-pohr-syoh-nEhl)	direct expenses
frais reportés	(frEh rœh-pœhr-tEh)	switching charges
frais variables	(frEh vah-ryAh-blœ)	floating charge, variable costs

F

franc d'avaries particulières	(frÃhnk dah-vah-rEEh pahr-teeh-kooh-lyEhr)	free of particular average
franc-bord	(frãhnk-bOhr)	free board
franchise (f)	(frãh-shEEhz)	franchise
franchise, en	(frãh-shEEhz ãhn)	duty free
franco à bord	(frAhn-koh ah bOhr)	free on board
franco long du bord (F.L.B.)	(frAhn-koh lÕh dooh bOhr)	free alongside ship
franco quai	(frAhn-koh kEh)	free alongside ship
franco wagon	(frAhn-koh vah-gÕh)	free on rail
fraude (f)	(frOhd)	fraud
fraude fiscale	(frOhd feehs-kAhl)	tax evasion
frein (m)	(frÆhn)	brake, disincentive
fréquence (f)	(freh-kÃhns)	frequency
fret (m)	(frEht)	freight
fret à la cueillette	(frEht ah lah kœh-yEht)	berth terms
fret aérien	(frEht ah-eh-ryÆhn)	air freight
fret de retour	(frEht dœ rœh-tOOhr)	back haul
fret en tous genres	(frEht ãhn tooh zhÃhn-rœ)	freight of all kinds
fret inclus	(frEht æhn-klOOh)	freight included
fret transporté sur palettes	(frEht trãhnz-pohr-tEh soohr pah-lEht)	palletized freight
front (m)	(frÕhn)	forehead
fruité	(frweeh-tEh)	fruity
fuite (f)	(fwEEht)	leakage
fuseau (m) horaire	(fooh-zOh oh-rEhr)	time zone
fusée (f) de lancement	(fooh-zEh dœ lãhns-mÃhn)	booster rocket
fuselage (m)	(fooh-sœh-lAhzh)	fuselage
fusion (f)	(fooh-zyÕhn)	merger, amalgamation
fût de chêne (m)	(fOOh dœ shEhn)	oak barrel

G

gage (m)	(gAhzh)	pledge
gage de garantie confié à un tiers	(gAhzh dœ gah-rãhn-tEEh kõhn-fyEh ah œhn tyEhrs)	escrow
gages (mpl)	(gAhzh)	salary
gains (mpl)	(gÆhn)	earnings
gains au pourcentage	(gÆhn oh poohr-sãhn-tAhzh)	percentage earnings
gains horaires	(gÆhn oh-rEhr)	hourly earnings
gains non distribués	(gÆhn nõh deehs-treeh-bwEh)	retained earnings
galvanisation (f)	(gahl-vah-neeh-zah-syÕh)	galvanizing
gamme (f) de produits	(gAhm dœ proh-dwEEh)	product line
gamme des prix	(gAhm deh prEEh)	price range
gants (mpl)	(gÃhn)	gloves

garantie (f)	*(gah-rāhn-tEEh)*	guarantee, warranty, warrant, security, collateral
garantie de bonne exécution	*(gah-rāhn-tEEh dœ bOhn ehk-zeh-kooh-syŌh)*	performance bond
garanties (fpl) approuvées	*(gah-rāhn-tEEh ah-proohveh)*	approved securities
garanti four à micro-ondes	*(gah-rāhn-tEEh fOOhr ah meeh-kroh-Ōhnd)*	microwave safe
garanti lave-vaisselle	*(gah-rāhn-tEEh lahv-vehsEhl)*	dishwasher safe
gaz (m) asphyxiant	*(gahz ahs-feehk-syÃhn)*	nerve gas
gaz (m) entraînant l'effet de serre	*(gAhz æhn-treh-nÃhn lehfEh dœ sEhr)*	greenhouse gas
gaz (m) naturel	*(gAhz nah-tooh-rEhl)*	natural gas
gel (m)	*(zhEhl)*	gel
général	*(zheh-neh-rAhl)*	overhead
générateur (m)	*(zheh-neh-rah-tŒhr)*	generator
génie (m) civil	*(zheh-nEEh seeh-vEEhl)*	civil engineering
gérant (m) de fonds à court terme	*(zheh-rÃh dœ fŌhn ah koohr tEhrm)*	money manager
gérer	*(zheh-rEh)*	manage (v)
gestion (f)	*(zhœhs-tyŌh)*	administration, management
gestion commerciale	*(zhœhs-tyŌh koh-mehrsyAhl)*	market management
gestion d'entreprise	*(zhœhs-tyŌh dāhn-trœhprEEhz)*	business management
gestion de crédits	*(zhœhs-tyŌh dœ kreh-dEEh)*	credit management
gestion (m) de l'environnement	*(zhœhs-tyŌhn dœ lāhnveeh-rohn-mÃhn)*	environmental management
gestion de lignes	*(zhœhs-tyŌh dœ lEEh-nyœ)*	line management
gestion de portefeuille	*(zhœhs-tyŌh dœ pohrtfŒhyœ)*	portfolio management
gestion de produit	*(zhœhs-tyŌh dœ prohdwEEh)*	product management
gestion de trésorerie	*(zhœhs-tyŌh dœ treh-zohreh-rEEh)*	cash management
gestion (f) des déchets	*(zhœhs-tyŌhn deh dehshEht)*	waste management
gestion des stocks	*(zhœhs-tyŌh deh stocks)*	stock control, inventory control
gestion des systèmes	*(zhœhs-tyŌh dœ seehstEhm)*	systems management
gestion financière	*(zhœhs-tyŌh feeh-nāhnsyEh)*	financial management
gestion raisonnable	*(zhœhs-tyŌh reh-soh-nAhblœ)*	reasonable care
gestionnaire (m) de compte	*(zhehs-tyohn-nEhr dœ kŌhnt)*	account executive

G

gilet (m)	(zheeh-lEh)	vest
goulot (m)	(gooh-lOh)	neck (of bottle)
goût (m) de caoutchouc	(gOOh dœ kah-oh-shOOh)	rubbery
goût de moisi	(gOOh dœ mwah-zEEh)	moldy taste
goût de vinaigre	(gOOh dœ vãehn-Eh-grœh)	vinegar taste
goutte (f)	(gOOht)	drop
gouvernement (m)	(gooh-vehrn-mÃh)	government
grain (m)	(grÆhn)	grain
graissage (m)	(greh-sAhzh)	lubrication
gramme (m)	(grAhm)	gram
grand couturier (m)	(grãhn kooh-tooh-ryEh)	high fashion designer
grand livre (m)	(grãhn lEEh-vrœ)	ledger
grand magasin (m)	(grãhn mah-gah-zÆhn)	department store
graphique (m)	(graf-fEEhk)	graph
graphique circulaire "camembert"	(graf-fEEhk seehr-kooh-lEhr)	pie chart
graphique de flux	(graf-fEEhk dœ flOOhks)	flow chart
graphique des activités	(graf-fEEhk dehz ahk-teeh-veeh-tEh)	activity chart
graphique en tuyaux d'orgue	(graf-fEEhk ãhn tooh-yOh dOhr-gœ)	bar chart
grappe (f)	(grAhp)	grape bunch
gras	(grAh)	oily
gratification (f)	(grah-teeh-feeh-kah-syÕh)	gratuity, bonus
graver	(grah-vEh)	engrave (v)
greffe (f)	(grEhf)	transplant
grève	(grEhv)	strike
grève (f) générale	(grEhv zheh-neh-rAhl)	general strike
grille (f)	(grEEh-yœ)	grid
grille (f) des salaires	(grEEhyœ deh sah-lEhr)	wage differential
grille-pain (m)	(greeh-yœh-pÆhn)	toaster
gros plan (m)	(groh plÃhn)	close-up
grossesse (f)	(grohs-Ehs)	pregnancy
grossiste (m)	(groh-sEEhst)	wholesaler
grossiste-étalagiste	(groh-sEEhst eh-tah-lah-zhEEhst)	rack jobber
groupe de gestion	(grOOhp dœ zhœhs-tyÕh)	management group
groupe (m) de magasins à succursales multiples	(grOOhp dœ mah-gah-zÆhn ah sooh-koohr-sAhl moohl-tEEh-plœ)	chain store group
groupe de produits	(grOOhp dœ proh-dwEEh)	product group
groupe de travail	(grOOhp dœ trah-vAhyœ)	task force
groupeur (m)	(grooh-pŒhr)	forwarding agent
guelte (f)	(gEhlt)	commission
guérir	(geh-rEEhr)	cure (v)
guerre (f) conventionnelle	(gEhr kõhn-vãhn-syoh-nEhl)	conventional warfare
guerre des prix (f)	(gEhr deh prEEh)	price war
guerre (f) nucléaire	(gEhr nooh-kleh-Ehr)	nuclear war

G

guerre (f) tarifaire	*(gEhr tah-reeh-fEhr)*	tariff war
guichetier (m)	*(geehsh-tyEh)*	teller
guidage par laser	*(geeh-dAhzh pahr lah-zEhr)*	laser guidance

H

handicap (m)		handicap
hausse (f) des prix	*(Ohs deh prEEh)*	increased cost
haussier	*(oh-syEh)*	bull
haut de gamme	*(Oh dœ gAhm)*	top of the line, upmarket
haut-fourneau (m)	*(oht-foohr-nOh)*	blast furnace
haut-parleur (f)	*(Oht pahr-lŒhr)*	speaker
haute fidélité (f)	*(Oht feeh-deh-leeh-tEh)*	high fidelity
hauteur de nos demandes, à la	*(oh-tŒhr dœ noh dæh-mÃhnd)*	up to our expectations
hectare (m)	*(ehk-tAhr)*	hectare
hélicoptère (m)	*(eh-leeh-kohp-tEhr)*	helicopter
heure (f) de grande écoute	*(Œhr dœ grÃhnd eh-kOOht)*	prime time
heure (f) normale	*(Œhr nohr-mAhl)*	standard time
heure prévue d'arrivée	*(Œhr preh-vOOh dah-reeh-vEh)*	estimated time of arrival
heure prévue de départ	*(Œhr preh-vOOh dœ deh-pAhr)*	estimated time of departure
heures (fpl) de main-d'œuvre	*(Œhr dœ mÃhn dŒh-vrœ)*	man-hours
heures supplémentaires	*(Œhr sooh-pleh-mÃh-tEhr)*	overtime
hexachlorophène (m)	*(ehk-sah-kloh-roh-fEhn)*	hexachlorophene
holding (m)	*(holding)*	holding company
homme (m) de peine	*(Ohm dœ pEhn)*	journeyman
homéopathie (f)	*(oh-meh-oh-pah-tEEh)*	homeopathy
homogénéiser	*(oh-moh-zheh-neh-eeh-zEh)*	standardize (v)
homogénéité	*(oh-moh-zhœh-neh-eeh-tEh)*	homogeneity
honoraires (mpl) de participation	*(oh-noh-rEhr dœ pahr-teeh-seeh-pah-syÕh)*	participation fee
horaire (m)	*(oh-rEhr)*	timetable
horaire de travail	*(oh-rEhr dœ trah-vAhyœ)*	work hours
hormone (f)	*(ohr-mOhn)*	hormone
hors cote	*(ohr kOht)*	unlisted
hors-bourse	*(ohr-bOOhrs)*	off-board (stock market)
hospitalisation (f)	*(ohs-peeh-tah-leeh-zah-syÕhn)*	hospitalization
housse (f) de voyage	*(OOhs dœ vwah-yAhzh)*	garment bag
humecter	*(ooh-mehk-tŒhr)*	moisten (v)

humer	*(ooh-mEh)*	smell (v)
hydratant	*(eeh-drah-tÃhn)*	moisturizing
hydrater	*(eeh-drah-tEh)*	moisture (v)
hydrocarbure (m)	*(eeh-droh-kahr-bOOhr)*	hydrocarbon
hydrolyse (f)	*(eeh-droh-lEEhz)*	hydrolysis
hypothèque (f)	*(eeh-poh-tEhk)*	mortgage
hypothèque à taux variable	*(eeh-poh-tEhk ah tOh vah-ryAh-blœ)*	variable rate mortgage
hypothèque consentie au vendeur d'un immeuble par l'acheteur en immeuble garantie du montant du prêt non liquidé	*(eeh-poh-tEhk kõhn-sãhn-tEEh oh vÃhn-dŒhr dœhn eeh-mŒh-blœ pahr ahsh-tŒhr ãhn gah-rãhn-tEEh dooh mõhn-tÃh dooh prEht nõh leeh-keeh-dEh)*	purchase money mortgage
hypothèque de deuxième rang	*(eeh-poh-tEhk dœ dœh-zyEhm rÃhng)*	second mortgage
hypothèque sur les biens mobiles	*(eeh-poh-tEhk soohr leh byÆhn moh-bEEhl)*	chattel mortgage

I

illégal	*(eeh-leh-gAhl)*	illegal
illustration (f)	*(eeh-loohs-tra-syÕh)*	illustration
image (f) de marque d'une société	*(eeh-mAhzh dœ mAhr-kœ doohn soh-syeh-tEh)*	corporate image
imitation (f)	*(eeh-meeh-tah-syÕh)*	imitation
immobilisations (fpl)	*(eeh-moh-beeh-leeh-zah-syÕh)*	capital expenditure, fixed assets
impact (m) sur l'environnement	*(æm-pAhkt soohr læhn-veeh-rohn-mÃhn)*	environmental impact
impasse (f)	*(æhm-pAhs)*	deadlock
imperfection (f)	*(æhm-pehr-fehk-syÕhn)*	blemish
imperméable	*(æhm-pehr-meh-Ah-blœh)*	waterproof
implantation (f) d'une usine	*(æhm-plãhn-tah-syÕh doohn ooh-zEEhn)*	plant location
implication (f)	*(æhm-pleeh-kah-syÕh)*	implication
importateur inscrit	*(æhm-pohr-tah-tŒhr æhn-skrEEh)*	importer of record
importation (f)	*(æhm-pohr-tah-syÕh)*	import
imposable	*(æhm-poh-zAh-blœh)*	taxable
imposition (f)	*(æœhm-poh-zeeh-syÕh)*	taxation
imposition d'office	*(æhm-poh-zeeh-syÕh doh-fEEhs)*	assessment
imposition multiple	*(æhm-poh-zeeh-syÕh moohl-tEEh-plœ)*	multiple taxation
impôt (m)	*(æhm-pOh)*	tax
impôt différé	*(æhm-pOh deeh-feh-rEh)*	deferred tax
impôt foncier	*(æhm-pOh fõhn-syEhr)*	land tax

impôt indirect	*(æhm-pOh æhn-deeh-rEhkt)*	indirect tax
impôt régressif	*(æhm-pOh reh-greh-sEEhf)*	regressive tax
impôt sur le chiffre d'affaires	*(æhm-pOh soohr læ shEEh-fræ dah-fEhr)*	sales tax
impôt sur le revenu	*(æhm-pOh soohr læ ræhv-nOOh)*	income tax
impôt sur le revenu des personnes physiques	*(æhm-pOh soohr læ ræhv-nOOh deh pehr-sÕhn feeh-zEEhk)*	personal income tax
impôt sur les entreprises	*(æhm-pOh soohr lehz ãhn-træh-prEEhz)*	corporation tax
impôt sur les salaires	*(æhm-pOh soohr leh sah-lEhr)*	payroll tax
impôt sur les ventes au détail	*(æhm-pOh soohr leh vÃhnt oh deh-tAhyæ)*	retail sales tax
impôt variable à l'importation	*(æhm-pOh vah-ryAh-blæ ah lãhm-pohr-tah-syÕh)*	variable import levy
impôts (mpl) courus	*(æhm-pOh kooh-rOOh)*	accrued taxes
impôts locaux	*(æhm-pOh loh-kOh)*	local taxes
impression (f)	*(æhm-preh-syÕh)*	printing
impression (f) offset	*(æhm-præh-syÕh offset)*	offset printing
imprimante (f)	*(æhm-preeh-mÃhnt)*	printer
imprimante (f) à laser	*(æhm-preeh-mÃhnt ah lah-zEhr)*	laser printer
imprimé (m)	*(æhm-preeh-mEh)*	form, form letter, print
imprimés (mpl)	*(æhm-preeh-mEh)*	printed matter
impulser	*(æhm-poohl-sEh)*	boost (v)
impureté (f)	*(æhm-pooh-reeh-tEh)*	impurity
imputé	*(æhm-pooh-tEh)*	imputed
inadéquat	*(æhn-ah-deh-kAh)*	inadequate
incassable	*(æhn-kah-sAh-blæh)*	unbreakable
incidence (f) sur les bénéfices	*(æhn-seeh-dÃhns soohr leh beh-neh-fEEhs)*	profit impact
incidence sur le profit	*(æhn-seeh-dÃhns soohr læ proh-fEEh)*	impact profit
incinération (f)	*(æhn-sãehn-eh-rah-syÕhn)*	incineration
incorporer	*(æhn-kohr-poh-rEh)*	incorporate (v)
incurvé	*(æhn-koohr-vEh)*	curved
indemnité (f)	*(æhn-dehm-neeh-tEh)*	indemnity, compensation
indemnité de chômage	*(æhn-dehm-neeh-tEh dæ shoh-mAhzh)*	unemployment compensation
indemnité de dépréciation	*(æhn-dehm-neeh-tEh dæ deh-preh-syah-syÕh)*	depreciation allowance

I

indemnité de direction	*(æhn-dehm-neeh-tEh dœ deeh-rehk-syÕh)*	executive compensation
indemnité de lest	*(æhn-dehm-neeh-tEh dœ lEhst)*	ballast bonus
indemnité de licenciement	*(æhn-dehm-neeh-tEh dœ leeh-sāhn-seeh-mÃh)*	severance pay
indemnité pour frais professionnels	*(æhn-dehm-neeh-tEh poohr frEh proh-feh-syoh-nEhl)*	expense account
indépendant	*(æhn-deh-pāhn-dÃhnt)*	freelance, self-employed
indexation (f)	*(æhn-dehk-sah-syÕh)*	indexing, pegging
indicateur (m) d'alerte	*(æhn-deeh-kah-tŒr dah-lEhrt)*	warning indicator
indicateur (m) de marché	*(æhn-deeh-kah-tŒhr dœ mahr-shEh)*	leading indicator
indicateurs (mpl) économiques	*(æhn-deeh-kah-tŒhrz eh-koh-moh-mEEhk)*	economic indicators
indice (m)	*(æhn-dEEhs)*	index (indicator)
indice composite	*(æhn-dEEhs kohm-poh-zEEht)*	composite index
indice (m) d'écoute	*(æhn-dEEhs deh-kOOht)*	audience rating
indice de croissance	*(æhn-dEEhs dœ krwah-sÃhns)*	growth index
indice de prix	*(æhn-dEEhs dœ prEEh)*	price index
indice des actions	*(æhn-dEEhs dehz ahk-syÕh)*	stock index
indice des prix à la consommation	*(æhn-dEEhs deh prEEh ah lah kõhn-soh-mah-syÕh)*	consumer price index
indice du marché	*(æhn-dEEhs dooh mahr-shEh)*	market index
induction (f)	*(æhn-doohk-syÕh)*	induction
industrie (f)	*(æhn-doohs-trEEh)*	industry
industrie à prix libres	*(æhn-doohs-trEEh ah prEEh lEEh-brœ)*	free market industry
industrie de croissance	*(æhn-doohs-trEEh dœ krwah-sÃhns)*	growth industry
industrie lourde	*(æhn-doohs-trEEh lOOhrd)*	heavy industry
industrie mécanique	*(æhn-doohs-trEEh meh-kah-nEEhk)*	mechanical engineering
industrie naissante	*(æhn-doohs-trEEh neh-sÃhnt)*	infant industry
industriel (m)	*(æhn-doohs-tryEhl)*	manufacturer
inefficace	*(eehn-eh-feeh-kAhs)*	inefficient
inélasticité (f) de l'offre ou de la demande	*(æhn-eh-lahs-teeh-seeh-tEh dœ lOh-frœ ooh dœ lah dœh-mÃhnd)*	inelastic demand or supply
inexploité	*(æhn-ehks-plwah-tEh)*	undeveloped

I

infection (f) bactérienne	*(ǽhn-fehk-syÕhn bahk-teh-ryEhn)*	bacterial infection
inflation (f)	*(ǽhn-flah-syÕh)*	inflation
inflationniste	*(ǽhn-flah-syoh-nEEhst)*	inflationary
influencer	*(ǽhn-flooh-āhn-sEh)*	impact on (v)
informatique (f)	*(ǽhn-fohr-mah-tEEhk)*	computer science
informer	*(ǽhn-fohr-mEh)*	advise (v)
infrastructure (f)	*(eehn-frah-stroohk-tOOhr)*	infrastructure
ingénierie (f)	*(ǽhn-zheh-nyeh-rEEh)*	engineering
ingénierie industrielle	*(ǽhn-zheh-nyeh-rEEh ǽhn-doohs-tryEhl)*	industrial engineering
ingénieur (m)	*(ǽhn-zheh-nyŒhr)*	engineer
ingénieur mécanicien	*(ǽhn-zheh-nyŒhr meh-kah-neeh-syǼhn)*	mechanical engineer
injecteur (m)	*(ǽhn-zhehk-tŒhr)*	injector
injonction (f)	*(ǽhn-zhõhnk-syÕh)*	injunction
injuste	*(ǽhn-zhOOhst)*	unfair
innovation (f)	*(ǽh-noh-vah-syÕh)*	innovation
inodore	*(ǽhn-oh-dOhr)*	fragrance-free
inscription (f) comptable d'ajustement	*(ǽhn-skreehp-syÕh kõhn-tAh-blœ dah-zhOOhstœ-mÃh)*	adjusting entry
inscrire	*(ǽhn-skrEEhr)*	post (v) (bookkeeping)
insérer	*(ǽhn-seh-rEh)*	insert (v)
insertion (f)	*(ǽhn-sehr-syÕh)*	insert
insolvable	*(ǽhn-sohl-vAh-blœ)*	insolvent
inspecteur (m)	*(ǽhns-pehk-tŒhr)*	inspector
inspecteur de banque	*(ǽhns-pehk-tŒhr dœ bÃhnk)*	bank examiner
inspection (f)	*(ǽhn-spehk-syÕh)*	inspection
instabilité (f)	*(ǽhn-stah-beeh-leeh-tEh)*	instability
installer	*(ǽhn-stah-lEh)*	install (v)
institution (f) de crédit	*(ǽhn-steeh-tooh-syÕh dœ kreh-dEEh)*	credit bureau
instructions (fpl) d'expédition	*(ǽhn-stroohk-syÕh dehks-peh-deeh-syÕh)*	shipping instructions
instrument (m)	*(ǽhn-strooh-mÃhn)*	instrument
instruments (mpl)	*(ǽhn-strooh-mÃhn)*	tools
insuccès (m)	*(ǽhn-soohk-sEh)*	failure
insulateur (m)	*(ǽhn-sooh-lah-tŒhr)*	insulator
insuline (f)	*(ǽhn-sooh-lEEhn)*	insulin
intégration (f) verticale	*(ǽhn-teh-grah-syÕh vehr-teeh-kAhl)*	vertical integration
intérêt (m)	*(ǽhn-teh-rEh)*	interest
intérêt acquis	*(ǽhn-teh-rEh ah-kEEh)*	vested interest
intérêt composé	*(ǽhn-teh-rEh kohm-poh-zEh)*	compound interest

intérêt couru	*(æhn-teh-rEh kooh-rOOh)*	accrued interest
intérêt couru supplémentaire	*(æhn-teh-rEh kooh-rOOh sooh-pleh-mÃh-tEhr)*	plus accrued interest
intérêt incomplet	*(æhn-teh-rEh æhn-kohm-plEh)*	inchoate interest
intérim (m)	*(æhn-teh-rEEhm)*	interim
intermédiaire (m)	*(æhn-tehr-meh-dyEhr)*	middleman, inter-mediary, third-party exporter
intermédiaire (souvent ducroire)	*(æhn-tehr-meh-dyEhr sooh-vÃh dooh-krwAhr)*	factor
intermédiaire d'exportation	*(æhn-tehr-meh-dyEhr dehks-pohr-tah-syÕh)*	export middleman
interne	*(æhn-tEhrn)*	internal
intervenir	*(æhn-tehr-væh-nEEhr)*	intervene (v)
intervention (f) personnelle	*(æhn-tehr-vãhn-syÕh pehr-soh-nEhl)*	jawbone
intestat	*(æhn-tehs-tAh)*	intestate
introduire graduellement	*(æhn-troh-dwEEhr grah-dwehl-mÃh)*	phase in (v)
invalider	*(æhn-vah-leeh-dEh)*	invalidate (v)
invalidité (f)	*(æhn-vah-leeh-deeh-tEh)*	disability
inventaire (m)	*(æhn-vãhn-tEhr)*	inventory
inventaire comptable	*(æhn-vãhn-tEhr kõhn-tAh-blœ)*	book inventory
inventaire des marchandises	*(æhn-vãhn-tEhr dœ mahr-shãhn-dEEhz)*	physical inventory
inventaire périodique	*(æhn-vãhn-tEhr peh-ryoh-dEEhk)*	periodic inventory
inventaire perpétuel	*(æhn-vãhn-tEhr pœhr-peh-twEhl)*	perpetual inventory
inventaire physique	*(æhn-vãhn-tEhr feeh-zEEhk)*	physical inventory
inventaire tournant	*(æhn-vãhn-tEhr toohr-nÃhn)*	perpetual inventory
investigation (f)	*(æhn-vehs-teeh-gah-syÕh)*	action research
investir	*(æhn-vehs-tEEhr)*	invest (v)
investissement (m)	*(æhn-vehs-teehs-mÃh)*	investment
investissement brut	*(æhn-vehs-teehs-mÃh brOOh)*	gross investment
investissement budgétaire	*(æhn-vehs-teehs-mÃh booh-zheh-tEhr)*	budget investment
investissement direct	*(æhn-vehs-teehs-mÃh deeh-rEhkt)*	direct investment
investissement net	*(æhn-vehs-teehs-mÃh nEht)*	net investment
investissement privé	*(æhn-vehs-teehs-mÃh preeh-vEh)*	private placement

I

investissement réel	(ãehn-vehs-teehs-mÃh reh-Ehl)	real investment
investissements (mpl) en capital	(ãehn-vehs-teehs-mÃh ãhn kah-peeh-tAhl)	investments equity
investisseur (m) institutionnel	(ãehn-vehs-teeh-sŒhr ãehn-steeh-tooh-syÕh-nEhl)	institutional investor
invisibles (importations, exportations)	(ãehn-veeh-zEÃh-blœ), (ãehm-pohr-tah-syÕh, ehks-pohr-tah-syÕh)	invisibles
iode (f)	(yOhd)	iodine
irréalisable	(eeh-reh-ah-leeh-zAh-blœ)	unfeasible
irritation (f)	(eeh-reeh-tah-syÕhn)	irritation
isotope (m)	(eeh-zoh-tOhp)	isotope
italique	(eeh-tah-lEEhk)	italic
IVG (Interruption Volonatire de la Grossesse)	(ah-vay-zhee)	abortion

---

J

jaquette (f)	(zhah-kEht)	jacket
jetable	(zhœh-tAh-blœh)	disposable
joindre	(zhwãehn-drœ)	attach (v), enclose
jour (m) au lendemain, du	(zhOOhr oh lãhnd-mÃEhn)	overnight
jour de grève	(zhOOhr dœ grEhv)	strike day
jour de liquidation	(zhOOhr dœ leeh-keeh-dah-syÕh)	account day
jour férié	(zhOOhr feh-ryEh)	national holiday
jour ouvrable	(zhOOhr ooh-vrAh-blœ)	work day
journal (m)	(zhOOhr-nAhl)	journal
journal agricole	(zhOOhr-nAhl ah-greeh-kOhl)	agricultural paper
jours (mpl) de planche	(zhOOhr dœ plÃhnsh)	lay days
jugement (m)	(zhoohzh-mÃh)	adjudication
jupe (f)	(zhOOhp)	skirt
juridiction (f)	(zhooh-reeh-deehk-syÕh)	jurisdiction
jurisprudence (f)	(zhooh-reehs-prooh-dÃhns)	the law
jus (m) de raisin	(zhOOhs dœ reh-zÃEhn)	unfermented grape juice
justifier	(zhoohs-teeh-fyEh)	justify (v)

K

kilométrage (m)	(keeh-loh-meh-trAhzh)	mileage
kilowatt (m)		kilowatt
kyste (m)	(kEEhst)	cyst

I

L

l'imperméable (m)	*(ãehm-pehr-meh-Ah-blœ)*	raincoat
laborantin(e) (m)	*(lah-boh-rahn-tEEhn)*	laboratory technician
laboratoire (m)	*(lah-boh-rah-twAhr)*	laboratory
laboratoire (m) spatial	*(lah-boh-rah-twAhr spah-syAhl)*	spacelab
laine (f)	*(lEhn)*	wool
laisser faire		laissez-faire
lame (f)	*(lAhm)*	blade
laminé à chaud	*(lah-meeh-nEh ah shOhd)*	hot rolling
laminé à froid	*(lah-meeh-nEh ah frwAh)*	cold rolling
laminoir (m)	*(lah-meeh-nwAhr)*	rolling mill
laminoirs (mpl) de finition	*(lah-meeh-nwAhr deh feeh-neeh-syÕh)*	finishing mill
lancement (m) de nouveaux produits	*(lãhns-mÃh dœ nooh-vOh proh-dwEEh)*	new product development
lancer	*(lãhn-sEh)*	launch, boost (v)
langage (m) algorithmique	*(lãhn-gAhzh ahl-goh-reeht-mEEhk)*	algorithmic language
langage informatique	*(lãhn-gAhzh ãehn-fohr-mah-tEEhk)*	computer language
lanière (f)	*(lah-nyEhr)*	leather strap
lapin (m)	*(lah-pÆhn)*	rabbit
larcin (m)	*(lahr-sÆhn)*	pilferage
laser (m)	*(lah-zEhr)*	laser
le long de	*(lÕh dœ)*	alongside
lecteur (m) de disques	*(lehk-tŒhr dœ dEEhsk)*	disk drive
légalisation (f) (signature)	*(leh-gal-leeh-zah-syÕh), (seehg-nah-tOOhr)*	attestation
légende (f)	*(leh-zhÃhnd)*	caption
léger	*(leh-zhEh)*	light
législation du travail	*(leh-zheehs-lah-syÕh dooh trah-vAhyœ)*	labor law
legs (m)	*(lEhg)*	legacy, bequest
lésion (f)	*(leh-zyÕhn)*	lesion
lettre (f)	*(lEh-trœ)*	letter
lettre d'avis	*(lEh-trœ dah-vEEh)*	advice note
lettre d'introduction	*(lEh-trœ dãehn-troh-doohk-syÕh)*	letter of introduction
lettre de change sur l'étranger	*(lEh-trœ dœ shÃhnzh soohr leh-trãhn-zhEh)*	foreign bill of exchange
lettre de couverture	*(lEh-trœ dœ kooh-vehr-tOOhr)*	cover letter, binder
lettre de crédit	*(lEh-trœ dœ kreh-dEEh)*	letter of credit
lettre de crédit renouvelable	*(lEh-trœ dœ kreh-dEEh rœh-nooh-vœh-lAh-blœ)*	revolving letter of credit

lettre de garantie	*(lEh-trœ dœ gah-rãhn-tEEh)*	letter of guarantee
lettre de voiture	*(lEh-trœ dœ vwah-tOOhr)*	inland bill of lading, way bill
leucémie (f)	*(leh-ooh-seh-mEEh)*	leukemia
lever des taxes	*(lœh-vEh deh tAhks)*	levy taxes (v)
levier (m)	*(lœh-vyEh)*	gearing, lever
levier de commande	*(lœh-vyEh dœ koh-mÃhnd)*	control lever, joystick
levure (f)	*(lœh-vOOhr)*	yeast
liaison (f)	*(leeh-eh-zÕh)*	liaison
libérer (acquitter)	*(leeh-beh-rEh), (ah-keeh-tEh)*	pay up (v)
libre circulation (f)	*(lEEh-brœh seehr-kooh-lah-syÕhn)*	free movement
libre échange réciproque	*(lEEh-brœ eh-shÃhnzh reh-seeh-prOhk)*	fair trade
libre service (m)	*(lEEh-brœ sœr-vEEhs)*	self-service
libre-échange (m)	*(leeh-brœh-eh-shÃhnzh)*	free trade
licence (f) d'exportation	*(leeh-sÃhns dehks-pohr-tah-syÕh)*	export permit
licence d'importation	*(leeh-sÃhns d˜œhm-pohr-tah-syÕh)*	import licence
licenciement (m)	*(leeh-sãhn-seeh-mÃh)*	layoff
lieu d'exportation convenu	*(lyŒh dehks-pohr-tah-syÕh kõhn-vœh-nOOh)*	named point of exportation
lieu d'origine désigné	*(lyŒh doh-reeh-zhEEhn deh-zeeh-nyEh)*	named point of origin
lieu de destination convenu	*(lyŒh dœ dehs-teeh-nah-syÕh kõhn-vœh-nOOh)*	named point of destination
lieu de travail	*(lyŒh dœ trah-vAhyœ)*	workplace
ligne (f)	*(lEEh-nyœ)*	line
ligne (f) de direction	*(lEEh-nyœ dœ deeh-rehk-syÕh)*	executive line
ligne d'échantillons	*(lEEh-nyœ deh-shãhn-teeh-yÕh)*	sample line
ligne de crédit	*(lEEh-nyœ dœ kreh-dEEh)*	credit line
ligne de crédit à vue	*(lEEh-nyœ dœ kreh-dEEh ah vOOh)*	demand line of credit
ligne de production	*(lEEh-nyœ dœ proh-doohk-syÕh)*	production line
ligne de produits	*(lEEh-nyœ dœ proh-dwEEh)*	product line
ligne internationale de changement de date	*(lEEh-nyœ ãhn-tehr-nah-syoh-nAhl dœ shãhnzh-mÃh dœ dAht)*	International Date Line
limite (f)	*(leeh-mEEht)*	border
limite de négociation	*(leeh-mEEht dœ neh-goh-syah-syÕh)*	trading limit
linéaire	*(leeh-neh-Ehr)*	linear

L

lingot (m)	*(lǣhn-gOh)*	ingot
lingotière (f)	*(lǣhn-goh-tyEhr)*	ingot mold
liquidation (f)	*(leeh-keeh-dah-syÕh)*	liquidation
liquidation solde de tout compte	*(leeh-keeh-dah-syÕh sOhld dœ tooh kÕhnt)*	full settlement
liquider	*(leeh-keeh-dEh)*	liquidate (v)
liquidité (f)	*(leeh-keeh-deeh-tEh)*	liquidity
liquidités (fpl)	*(leeh-keeh-deeh-tEh)*	liquidate (v)
lisse	*(lEEhs)*	smooth
liste (f)	*(lEEhst)*	listing
liste d'adresses	*(lEEhst ah-drEhs)*	mailing list
liste d'exemptions	*(lEEhst dehk-zãhm-syÕh)*	free list (commodities without duty)
liste (f) de contrôle	*(lEEhst dœ kõhn-trOhl)*	checklist
liste imprimée	*(lEEhst ǣhm-preeh-mEh)*	printout
liste légale	*(lEEhst leh-gAhl)*	legal list
lit (m)	*(lEEh)*	bed
litige (m)	*(leeh-tĔĔhzh)*	litigation
litre (m)	*(lEEh-trœ)*	liter
livraison (f)	*(leeh-vreh-zÕh)*	delivery
livraison à terme	*(leeh-vreh-zÕh ah tEhrm)*	forward shipment
livraison immédiate	*(leeh-vreh-zÕh eeh-meh-dyAht)*	spot delivery
livraison incomplète	*(leeh-vreh-zÕh ǣhn-kohm-plEh)*	short delivery
livraison, de bonne	*(leeh-vreh-zÕh dœ bOhn)*	good delivery (securities)
livraisons (fpl) différées	*(leeh-vreh-zÕh deeh-feh-rEh)*	deferred deliveries
livre (m)	*(lEEh-vrœ)*	book
livre (m) de caisse	*(lEEh-vrœ dœ kEhs)*	cashbook
livret (m) de banque	*(lEEh-vrœ dœ bÃhnk)*	passbook
locataire (m/f) à bail	*(loh-kah-tEhr ah bAh-yœ)*	lessee
locaux (mpl)	*(loh-kOh)*	premises
logiciel (m)	*(loh-zheeh-syEhl)*	software
logistique (f)	*(loh-zhees-tEEhk)*	logistics
logo (m)	*(loh-gOh)*	logo
loi (f)	*(lwAh)*	law
loi (m) communautaire sur less armes à feu	*(lwAh koh-mooh-noh-tEhr soohr lehz Ahrm ah fŒh)*	common gun law
loi des rendements décroissants	*(lwAh deh rãhnd-mÃh deh-krwah-sÃh)*	law of diminishing returns
loi sur les brevets	*(lwAh leh brœh-vEh)*	patent law
lois (mpl) antitrust	*(lwAh anti-trust)*	antitrust laws
longueur (f)	*(lõhn-gŒhr)*	length
lot (m)	*(lOht)*	lot
lot irrégulier	*(lOht eeh-reh-gooh-lyEh)*	odd lot
lotion (f)	*(loh-syÕhn)*	lotion
lotion solaire	*(loh-syÕhn soh-lEhr)*	sun lotion

louche (f)	(lOOhsh)	soup ladle
louer	(looh-Eh)	lease (v), rent (v)
loutre (f)	(lOOh-trœ)	otter
loyer (m)	(loh-yEh)	rent
lutter	(looh-tEh)	fight (v)
lynx (m)	(lÆhnks)	lynx

M

machine (f) à coudre	(mah-shEEhn ah kOOh-drœ)	sewing machine
machine (f) à laver	(mah-shEEhn ah lah-vEh)	washing machine
machine de traitement de texte autonome	(mah-shEEhn dœ treht-mÃh dœ tEhk-stœ oh-toh-nOhm)	stand-alone text processor
machines (fpl)	(mah-shEEhn)	machinery
macroéconomie (f)	(mah-kroh-eh-koh-noh-mEEh)	macroeconomics
magasin (m)	(mah-gah-zÆhn)	store
magasin à succursales multiples	(mah-gah-zÆhn ah sooh-koohr-sAhl moohl-tEEh-plœ)	chain store
magasin de détail	(mah-gah-zÆhn dœ deh-tAhyœ)	retail outlet
magazine (m)	(mah-gah-zEEhn)	magazine
magnétophone (m)	(mah-nyeh-toh-fÕhn)	videocassette player
magnétoscope (m)	(mah-nyeh-toh-skOhp)	VCR
magnum (m)	(mahg-nOOhm)	magnum (2 bottles in one)
maigre	(mEh-grœh)	skinny
main-d'œuvre (f)	(mÆhn dŒh-vrœ)	manpower, workforce, labor
main-d'œuvre non qualifiée	(mÆhn dŒh-vrœ kah-leeh-feeh-Eh)	unskilled labor
maïs (m)	(mah-EEh)	maize, corn
maison (f) de commerce	(meh-zÕh dœ koh-mEhrs)	trade house, trade firm
maison (f) de production de vin	(meh-zÕhn dœ proh-doohk-syÕhn dœ vÆhn)	winery
maison mère	(meh-zÕh mEhr)	parent company, headquarters, head office
maître (m) de chais	(mEh-trœ dœ shEh)	winemaker
majoration (f)	(mah-zhoh-rah-syÕh)	increase
majuscule (f)	(mah-yoohs-kOOhl)	capital
mal (m) de tête	(mahl dœ tEht)	headache
malade	(mah-lAhd)	ill
maladie (f)	(mah-lah-dEEh)	disease

L

maladie (f) des caissons	*(mah-kah-dEEh deh keh-sÕh)*	bends
malentendu (m)	*(mah-lãhn-tãhn-dOOh)*	misunderstanding
malformation (f) congénitale	*(mahl-fohr-mah-syÕhn kõhn-zheh-neeh-tAhl)*	birth defect
malle (f)	*(mAhl)*	trunk
malléabilité (f)	*(mah-leh-ah-beeh-leeh-tEh)*	malleability
manches courtes (mpl)	*(mÃhnsh kOOhrt)*	short sleeves
manches (m) longues	*(mÃhnsh lÕhng)*	long sleeves
mandat (m)	*(mãhn-dAh)*	mandate
mandat bancaire	*(mãhn-dAh bãhn-kEhr)*	bank money order
mandat-poste	*(mãhn-dAh pOhst)*	money order
mandataire (m)	*(mÃhn-dah-tEhr)*	trustee, agent
manifeste (m)	*(mãh-neeh-fEhst)*	manifest
mannequin (m)	*(mah-nœh-kÆhn)*	model
manquer à ses engagements	*(mãhn-kEh ah sehz ãhn-gahzh-mÃh)*	default (v)
manteau (m)	*(mãhn-tOh)*	coat
manuscrit	*(mah-nooh-skrEEh)*	script
manutentionnaire (m)	*(mah-nooh-tãhn-syoh-nEhr)*	warehouseman, handler
maquette (f)	*(mah-kEht)*	dummy, mechanical, mock-up
maquillage (m)	*(mah-keeh-yAhzh)*	makeup
maquiller (se)	*(mah-keeh-yEh)*	make oneself up (v)
marasme (m)	*(mah-rAhz-mœ)*	slump
marchand (m)	*(mahr-shÃhn)*	merchant, dealer
marchand de titres	*(mahr-shÃhn-dœ tEEh-trœ)*	jobber
marchandise (f)	*(mahr-shãhn-dEEhz)*	merchandise
marchandises (fpl)	*(mahr-shãhn-dEEhz)*	goods
marchandises accompagnées	*(mahr-shãhn-dEEhz ah-kõhm-pah-nyEh)*	accompanied goods
marchandises de détail	*(mahr-shãhn-dEEhz dœ deh-tAh-yœ)*	retail merchandise
marchandises de luxe	*(mahr-shãhn-dEEhz dœ lOOhks)*	luxury goods
marchandises de qualité	*(mahr-shãhn-dEEhz dœ kah-leeh-tEh)*	quality goods
marchandises durables	*(mahr-shãhn-dEEhz dooh-rAh-blœ)*	durable goods
marchandises fongibles	*(mahr-shãhn-dEEhz fõhn-zhEEh-blœ)*	fungible goods
marchandises non accompagnées	*(mahr-shãhn-dEEhz nõhn ah-kõhm-pah-nyEh)*	unaccompanied goods
marchandises prohibées	*(mahr-shãhn-dEEhz proh-eeh-bEh)*	prohibited goods
marchandises rendues au port d'importation	*(mahr-shãhn-dEEhz rãhn-dOOh oh pOhr dæhm-pohr-tah-syÕh)*	ex dock

marchandises sèches (tissus [mpl], étoffes [fpl])	*(mahr-shãhn-dEEhz sEhsh), (teeh-sOOh), (eh-tOhf)*	dry goods
marchandises sous douane	*(mahr-shãhn-dEEhz sooh dooh-Ahn)*	bonded goods
marchandises telles quelles	*(mahr-shãhn-dEEhz tehl kEhl)*	as-is goods
marchandises vendues à terme	*(mahr-shãhn-dEEhz vãhn-dOOh ah tEhrm)*	futures
marché (m)	*(mahr-shEh)*	market, market place, bargain (stock exchange)
marché à deux niveaux	*(mahr-shEh ah dŒh neeh-vŒ)*	two-tiered market
marché à la baisse	*(mahr-shEh ah lah bEhs)*	bear market
marché à terme	*(mahr-shEh ah tEhrm)*	forward market
marché acheteur	*(mahr-shEh ahsh-tŒhr)*	buyer's market
marché au comptant	*(mahr-shEh oh kõhn-tÃhn)*	spot market
marché commun	*(mahr-shEh koh-mOOhn)*	common market
marche (f) dans l'espace	*(mAhrsh dãhn lehs-pAhs)*	spacewalk
marché de gros	*(mahr-shEh dœ grOh)*	wholesale market
marché de l'emploi	*(mahr-shEh dœ lãhm-plwAh)*	labor market
marché des actions	*(mahr-shEh dehz ahk-syÕh)*	stock market
marché des capitaux	*(mahr-shEh deh kah-peeh-tOh)*	capital market
marché (m) des obligations	*(mahr-shEh dehz oh-bleeh-gay-syÕhn)*	bond market
marché difficile	*(mahr-shEh deeh-feeh-sEEhl)*	tight market
marché du disponible	*(mahr-shEh deehs-poh-nEEh-blœ)*	spot market
marché haussier	*(mahr-shEh oh-syEh)*	bull market
marché instable	*(mahr-shEh æhn-stAh-blœ)*	volatile market
marché intérieur	*(mahr-shEh æhn-teh-reyŒhr)*	home market
marché inversé	*(mahr-shEh æhn-vehr-sEh)*	inverted market
marché libre	*(mahr-shEh lEEh-brœ)*	open market
marché marginal	*(mahr-shEh mahr-zheeh-nAhl)*	fringe market
marché (m) monétaire	*(mahr-shEh moh-neh-tEhr)*	money market
marché monopsone	*(mahr-shEh moh-nohp-sOhn)*	monopsony
marché noir	*(mahr-shEh nwAhr)*	black market
marché parallèle	*(mahr-shEh pah-rah-lEhl)*	gray market
marché primaire	*(mahr-shEh preeh-mEhr)*	primary market
marché réduit	*(mahr-shEh reh-dwEEh)*	thin market
marché secondaire	*(mahr-shEh sœh-kõhn-dEhr)*	secondary market

M

marché (m) unique	*(mahr-shEh ooh-nEEhk)*	single market
marché, au cours du	*(mahr-shEh, oh kOOhr dœ)*	at the market
marché-cible (m)	*(mahr-shEh-sEEh-blœ)*	target market
marge (f) à terme	*(mAhrzh ah tEhrm)*	forward margin
marge bénéficiaire	*(mAhrzh beh-neh-feeh-syEhr)*	profit margin
marge brute	*(mAhrzh brOOht)*	gross margin
marge brute actualisée	*(mAhrzh brOOht ahk-twah-leeh-zEh)*	discounted cash flow
marge brute d'autofinancement (M.B.A)	*(mAhrzh brOOht doh-toh-feeh-nãhns-mÃh)*	cash flow
marge brute négative	*(mAhrzh brOOht neh-gah-tEEhv)*	negative cash flow
marge brute nette	*(mAhrzh brOOht nEht)*	net cash flow
marge brute positive	*(mAhrzh brOOht poh-zeeh-tEEhv)*	positive cash flow
marge brute, relevé de la	*(mAhrzh brOOht, rœh-lœh-vEh dœ lah)*	cash flow statement
marge d'entretien	*(mAhrzh dãhn-trœh-ty̆Ehn)*	maintenance margin
marge de fluctuation entre monnaies	*(mAhrzh dœ floohk-twah-syÕh Ãhn-trœ moh-nEh)*	currency band
marge de prêt	*(mAhrzh dœ prEht)*	lending margin
marge de sécurité	*(mAhrzh dœ seh-kooh-reeh-tEh)*	margin of safety
marge nette	*(mAhrzh nEht)*	net margin
marge variable	*(mAhrzh vah-ryAh-blœ)*	variable margin
marges (fpl) requises	*(mAhrzh reh-kEEhz)*	margin requirements
marmotte (f)	*(mahr-mOht)*	marmot
maroquin (m)	*(mah-roh-kEEhn)*	Morroco leather
maroquinerie (f)	*(mah-roh-keeh-nœh-rEEh)*	leather goods
marque (f)	*(mAhr-kœ)*	brand
marque de distributeur	*(mAhr-kœ dœ deehs-treeh-booh-tŒhr)*	private label (or brand)
marque de fabrique	*(mAhr-kœ dœ fah-brEEhk)*	trademark
marque déposée	*(mAhr-kœ deh-poh-zEh)*	registered trademark
marque, acceptation de la	*(mAhr-kœ, ahk-sehp-tah-syÕh dœ lah)*	brand acceptance
marque, fidélité à la	*(mAhr-kœ, feeh-deh-leeh-tEh ah lah)*	brand loyalty
marque, identification de la	*(mAhr-kœ, eeh-dãhn-teeh-feeh-kah-syÕh dœ lah)*	brand recognition
marque, image de	*(mAhr-kœ, eeh-mAhzh dœ)*	brand image
mascara (m)	*(mahs-kah-rAh)*	mascara
masque (m)	*(mAhsk)*	mask

masse (f) monétaire	(mAhs moh-neh-tEhr)	money supply
mat		mat
matériaux (mpl)	(mah-teh-ryOh)	materials
matériel (m)	(mah-teh-ryEhl)	hardware
matériel (m) de traitement informatique	(mah-teh-ryEhl dœ treht-mÃhǽhn-fohr-mah-tEEhk)	hardware
matériel roulant	(mah-teh-ryEhl rooh-lÃh)	rolling stock
matières premiéres (fpl)	(mah-tyEhr prœh-myEhr)	raw materials
matrice (f)	(mah-trEEhs)	matrix
mécanicien (m)	(meh-kah-neeh-syÃ̃Ehn)	mechanic
mécanisme (m)	(meh-kah-nEEhz-mœ)	machinery
médecin (m)	(mehd-sǼhn)	physician
médecine (f) préventive	(mehd-sEEhn preh-vãhn-tEEhv)	preventive medicine
média (m)	(meh-dyAh)	mass media
médiane (f)	(meh-dyAhn)	median
médias publicitaire	(meh-dyAh pooh-bleeh-seeh-tEhr)	advertising media
médiateur (m)	(meh-dyah-tŒhr)	troubleshooter
médiation (f)	(meh-dyah-syÕh)	mediation
médicament (m)	(meh-deeh-kah-mÃh)	medication, medicine
mélanger	(meh-lãhn-zhEh)	blend (v)
mélangeur (m)	(meh-lãhn-zhŒhr)	mixer
membre (m) à vie	(mÃhm-brœ ah vEEh)	life member
membre d'un syndicat de garantie	(mÃhm-brœ dœhn seehn-deeh-kAh dœ gah-rãhn-tEEh)	underwriter
mémoire (f) à accès direct	(meh-mwAhr ah ahk-sEh deeh-rEhkt)	direct access storage
mémoire d'ordinateur	(meh-mwAhr dohr-deeh-nah-tŒhr)	computer memory, computer storage
mémoire magnétique	(meh-mwAhr mah-nyeh-tEEhk)	magnetic memory
mémoire (f) principale	(meh-mwAhr prǽhn-seeh-pAhl)	main memory
mémoire par série	(meh-mwAhr pahr seh-rEEh)	serial storage
mémoire vive	(meh-mwAhr vEEhv)	random access memory
mémorandum (m)	(meh-moh-rãhn-dOOhm)	memorandum
menacer	(meh-nah-sEh)	threaten (v)
meneur (m)	(mœh-nŒhr)	leader
mensonger	(mãhn-sõhn-zhEh)	misleading
mercantile	(mehr-kãhn-tEEhl)	mercantile
mère (f) porteuse	(mEhr pohr-tŒhz)	surrogate mother
mesurer	(mœh-zooh-rEh)	measure (v)
mesures (fpl) de relance de l'économie	(mœh-zOOhr dœ rœh-lÃhns dœ leh-koh-noh-mEEh)	pump priming

M

métaux (mpl)	*(meh-tOh)*	metals
méthane (m)	*(meh-tAhn)*	methane
méthode (f)	*(meh-tOhd)*	method
méthode (f) champenoise	*(meh-tOhd shāhm-peh-nwAhz)*	champagne method
méthode comptable	*(meh-tOhd kõhn-tAh-blœ)*	accounting method
méthode de forfait avec rectifications périodiques	*(meh-tOhd dœ fohr-fEh ah-vEhk rehk-teeh-feeh-kah-syŌh peh-ryoh-dEEhk)*	pay as you go
méthode de Monte Carlo	*(meh-tOhd dœ Monte Carlo)*	Monte Carlo technique
méthode des matrices	*(meh-tOhd deh mah-trEEhs)*	matrix management
méthode du report variable	*(meh-tOhd dooh rœh-pŒhr vah-ryAh-blœ)*	accrual method
métier (m)	*(meh-ttyEh)*	occupation
métrage (m)	*(meh-trAzh)*	footage
mettre à disposition	*(mEh-trœ ah deehs-poh-zeeh-syŌh)*	make available
mettre à jour	*(mEh-trœh ah zhoohr)*	update (v)
mettre au point	*(mEh-trœ oh pwÆh)*	to set, to focus
mettre en commun	*(mEh-trœ ãhn koh-mOOhn)*	pool (v)
mettre en commun ses ressources	*(mEh-trœh ãhn koh-mOOhn seh rœh-sOOhrs)*	pool one's resources (v)
mettre en œuvre	*(mEh-trœh ãhn Œh-vrœh)*	implement (to)
mettre en orbite	*(mEh-troe ãhn ohr-bEEht)*	put into orbit (v)
mettre en vigueur	*(mEh-trœh ãhn veeh-gŒhr)*	enforce (v)
mettre son veto	*(mEh-trœh sõhn vEh-toh)*	veto (v)
meulage (m)	*(mœh-lAhzh)*	grinding
micro-onde (m)	*(meeeh-kroh-Ohnd)*	microwave
micro-ordinateur (m)	*(meeh-kroh-ohr-deeh-nah-tŒhr)*	microcomputer
micro-plaquette (f)	*(meeh-kroh-plah-kEht)*	microchip
micro-processeur (m)	*(meeh-kroh-proh-seh-sŒhr)*	microprocessor
microfiche (f)	*(meeh-kroh-fEEsh)*	microfiche
millésime (m)	*(meeh-leh-zEEhm)*	vintage year
mince	*(mÆhns)*	thin
minerai (m)	*(meeh-neh-rEh)*	ore
minerai (m) de fer	*(meeh-neh-rEh dœ fEhr)*	iron ore
minerai (m) de manganèse	*(meeh-neh-rEh dœ mãhn-gah-nEhz)*	manganese ore
mini-ordinateur (m)	*(meeh-neeh-ohr-deeh-nah-tŒhr)*	minicomputer
minuscule (f)	*(meeh-neeh-skOOhl)*	lower case
mis en bouteille au château	*(mEEhz ãhn booh-tEh-yœ oh shah-tOh)*	estate bottled
mise (f) au point d'un produit	*(mEEhz oh pwÆh dœhn proh-dwEEh)*	product development
mise de fonds	*(mEEhz dœ fÕhn)*	outlay

mise en commun	*(mEEhz āhn koh-mOOhn)*	pool (of funds)
mise en commun d'intérêts	*(mEEhz āhn koh-mOOhn dǣhn-teh-rEh)*	pooling of interest
mise en forme	*(mEEhz āhn fOhrm)*	make-ready
mise (f) en mémoire	*(mEEhz āhn meh-nwAhr)*	storage
mise (f) en œuvre	*(mEEhz āhn Œh-vrœh)*	implementation
mise en page (f)	*(mEEhz-āhn pAhzh)*	page makeup
missile (m) air-air	*(meeh-sEEhl ehr-Ehr)*	air-to-air missile
missile (m) air-sol	*(meeh-sEEl ehr-sOhl)*	air-to-surface missile
mitrailleuse (f)	*(meeh-treh-yŒhz)*	machine gun
mixage (m)	*(meehk-sAhzh)*	audio mixing
mixeur (m)	*(meehk-sŒhr)*	blender
mobilité (f) de l'emploi	*(moh-beeh-leeh-tEh dœ lāhm-plwAh)*	mobility of labor
mode (f)	*(mOhd)*	fashion, mode
modèle (m)	*(moh-dEhl)*	layout, model, pattern
modem (m)	*(moh-dEhm)*	modem
modification (f)	*(moh-deeh-feeh-kah-syÕh)*	alteration
modulation (f) de fréquence	*(moh-dooh-lah-syÕh dœ freh-kÃhns)*	frequency modulation (FM)
modulation d'amplication	*(moh-dooh-lah-syÕh dahm-pleeh-kah-syÕh)*	amplitude modulation (AM)
moelleux	*(moeh-yŒh)*	soft, fluffy
moins-value (f)	*(mwǣh-vah-lOOh)*	drawdown
moins-value en capital	*(mwǣh-vah-lOOh āhn kah-peeh-tAhl)*	capital loss
moire (f)	*(mwAhr)*	moire
molaire	*(moh-lEhr)*	molar
mole (f)	*(mOhl)*	mole
molécule (f)	*(moh-leh-kOOhl)*	molecule
molybdène (m)	*(moh-leehb-dEhn)*	molybdenum
monde (m) des affaires	*(mÕhnd dehz ah-fEhr)*	marketplace
monnaie (f)	*(moh-nEh)*	mint
monnaie légale	*(moh-nEh leh-gAhl)*	legal tender
monogramme (m)	*(moh-noh-grAhm)*	monogram
monopole (m)	*(moh-noh-pOhl)*	monopoly
monopole légal	*(moh-noh-pOhl leh-gAhl)*	legal monopoly
montage (m)	*(mÕhn-tAhzh)*	stripping
montant (m)	*(mÕhn-tÃh)*	amount
montant dû	*(mÕhn-tÃh dooh)*	amount due
montant forfaitaire	*(mÕhn-tÃh fohr-feh-tEhr)*	lump sum
moral (m)	*(moh-rAhl)*	morale
morale (f)	*(moh-rAhl)*	morality
moratoire (m)	*(moh-rah-twAhr)*	moratorium
morphine (f)	*(mohr-fEEhn)*	morphine
mot (m)	*(mOh)*	byte
moteur (m)	*(moh-tŒhr)*	engine, motor

M

moteur à 4 cylindres	*(moh-tŒhr ah kÆh-trœ seeh-l Ẽhn-drœ)*	four-cylinder engine
moteur à 6 cylindres	*(moh-tŒhr ah sEEhs seeh-l Ẽhn-drœ)*	six-cylinder engine
moteur V.8	*(moh-tŒhr veeh wEEht)*	V8 engine
motion (f)	*(moh-syÕh)*	motion
mouchoir (m)	*(mooh-shwAhr)*	handkerchief
moule (m)	*(mOOhl)*	mold
moulin (m) à poivre	*(mooh-l Ẽhn ah pwAh-vrœ)*	pepper mill
moulu	*(mooh-lOOh)*	ground
mousse (f)	*(mOOhs)*	mousse
mousseline (f)	*(moohs-lEEhn)*	muslin
moût (m)	*(mOOht)*	dregs
moutardier (m)	*(mooh-tahr-dyEh)*	mustard pot
moyen (m) d'échange	*(mwah-yEhn deh-shÃhnzh)*	medium of exchange
moyen de fortune	*(mwah-yEhn dœ fohr-tOOhn)*	makeshift
moyen terme (m)	*(mwah-yEhn tEhrm)*	medium term
moyenne (f)	*(mwah-yEhn)*	average, mean
moyenne arithmétique	*(mwah-yEhn areeht-meh-tEEhk)*	arithmetic mean
moyenne mobile	*(mwah-yEhn moh-bEEhl)*	moving average
moyenne pondérée	*(mwah-yEhn põhn-deh-rEh)*	weighted average
moyenne, établissement d'une	*(mwah-yEhn, eh-tah-bleehs-mÃh doohn)*	averaging
moyens (mpl)	*(mwah-yEhn)*	facilities
multidevises (fpl)	*(moohl-teeh-dœh-vEEhz)*	multicurrency
multiples (mpl)	*(moohl-teeh-plœ)*	multiples
multiplet (m)	*(moohl-teeh-plEh)*	byte
multiplicateur (m)	*(moohl-teeh-pleeh-kah-tŒhr)*	multiplier
munition (f)	*(mooh-neeh-syÕhn)*	ammunition
mûr	*(mOOhr)*	ripe
muté	*(mooh-tEh)*	transferred
mutuelle (f) d'épargne	*(mooh-twEhl deh-pAhr-nyœ)*	mutual savings bank

N

nantissement (m)	*(nãhn-teehs-mÃh)*	collateral
nappe (f)	*(nAhp)*	tablecloth
nappes (fpl) phréatiques	*(nAhp freh-ah-tEEhk)*	groundwater reserves
narcotique (m)	*(nahr-koh-tEEhk)*	narcotic
nationalisme (m)	*(nah-syõhn-ah-lEEhz-mœ)*	nationalism
navette (f)	*(nah-vEht)*	shuttle
navire (m) de guerre	*(nah-vEEhr dœ gEhr)*	warship

N

navire (m) porte-allège	(nah-vEEhr pohrt-ah-lEhzh)	lash
négatif (m)	(neh-gah-tEEhf)	negative
négligent	(neh-gleeh-zhÃh)	negligent
négoce (m)	(neh-gOhs)	merchandising
négociable	(neh-goh-syAh-blœ)	negotiable
négociant (m)	(neh-goh-syÃh)	trader
négociant (m) en vins	(neh-goh-syÃh ãhn vǼhn)	vintner
négociateur (m)	(neh-goh-syah-tŒhr)	negotiator
négociation (f)	(neh-goh-syah-syÕh)	negotiation
négociation paritaire de convention collective	(neh-goh-syah-syÕh pah-reeh-tEhr dœ kÕhn-vÃhn-syÕh koh-lehk-tEEhv)	collective bargaining
négociations (fpl) tarifaires générales	(neh-goh-syah-syÕh tah-reeh-fEhr zheh-neh-rAhl)	across-the-board tariff negotiations
négocier	(neh-goh-syEh)	negotiate (v)
net	(nEht)	net
nettoyage (m)	(neh-twah-yAhzh)	clean-up
nettoyer	(nœh-twah-yEh)	clean (v)
neutralisation (f)	(nœh-trah-leeh-zah-syÕh)	neutralization
neutre	(nœh-trœ)	neutral
neutron (m)	(nœh-trÕh)	neutron
nitrate (m)	(neeh-trAht)	nitrate
nitrite (m)	(neeh-trEEht)	nitrite
niveau (m) de qualité acceptable	(neeh-vŒ dœ kah-leeh-tEh ahk-sehp-tAhblœ)	acceptable quality level
niveau (m) de toxicité	(neeh-vOh dœ tohk-seeh-tEh)	toxicity level
niveau d'investissement	(neeh-vŒ dæhn-vehs-teehs-mÃh)	investment grade
niveau de vie	(neeh-vŒ dœ vEEh)	standard of living
niveau des salaires	(neeh-vŒ deh sah-lEhr)	wage level
nocivité (f)	(noh-seeh-veeh-tEh)	noxiousness
nœud (m) papillon	(nŒh pah-peeh-yÕh)	bow tie
nœud (m)	(nŒh)	knot (nautical)
noir et blanc (m)	(nwAhr eh blÃhn)	black and white
nombre (m) d'exemptions par individu	(nÕhm-brœ dehk-zãhm-syÕh pahr ãhn-deeh-veeh-dOOh)	personal deduction
nomination (f)	(noh-meeh-nah-syÕh)	appointment
non connecté	(nÕh koh-nehk-tEh)	offline
non coté	(nÕh koh-tEh)	unlisted
non membre (m)	(nÕh mÃhm-brœ)	nonmember
non mentionné par ailleurs	(nÕh mãhn-syoh-nEh pahr ah-yŒhr)	not otherwise indexed by name
non polluant	(nÕhn poh-lwÃhn)	pollution-free
non raffiné	(nÕh rah-feeh-nEh)	crude
non-comptabilisé	(nÕhn-kÕhm-tah-beeh-leeh-zEh)	off-the-books
non-résident (m)	(nÕhn-reh-zeeh-dÃh)	nonresident

non toxique	(nõhn tohk-sEEhk)	nontoxic
normalisation (f)	(nohr-mah-leeh-zah-syÕh)	standardization
norme (f)	(nOhrm)	norm, standard
notaire (m)	(noh-tEhr)	notary
notation (f) binaire	(noh-tah-syÕh beeh-nEhr)	binary notation
note (f)	(nOht)	bill
note de colisage	(nOht dœ koh-leeh-zAhzh)	packing list
note de crédit	(nOht dœ kreh-dEEh)	credit note
note de débit	(nOht dœ deh-bEEh)	debit note
nouvelle émission (f)	(nooh-vEhl eh-meeh-syÕh)	new issue
novation (f)	(noh-vah-syÕh)	novation
nuageux	(nwah-zhŒh)	cloudy
nuisible	(nweeh-zEEh-blœh)	harmful
nul	(nOOhl)	void
nul et non avenu	(nOOhl eh nõhn ah-vœh-nOOh)	null and void
numérique	(nooh-meh-rEEhk)	differential
numéro (m) de commande	(nooh-meh-rOh dœ koh-mÃhnd)	order number
numéro de compte	(nooh-meh-rOh dœ kÕhnt)	account number
numéro de référence	(nooh-meh-rOh dœ reh-feh-rÃhns)	reference number

O

objectif (m)	(ohb-zhehk-tEEhf)	goal
obligation (f)	(oh-bleeh-gah-syÕh)	obligation, bond
obligation à faible rendement	(oh-bleeh-gah-syÕh ah fEh-blœ rãhnd-mÃh)	low-yield bond
obligation à intérêt conditionnel	(oh-bleeh-gah-synOh ah æhn-teh-rEh kõhn-deeh-syoh-nEhl)	revenue bond
obligation à rendement fixe	(oh-bleeh-gah-syÕh ah rãhnd-mÃh fEEhks)	flat bond
obligation à terme	(oh-bleeh-gah-syÕh ah tEhrm)	term bond
obligation amortissable	(oh-bleeh-gah-syÕh ah-mohr-teeh-sAh-blœ)	redeemable bond
obligation conjointe	(oh-bleeh-gah-syÕh kõhn-zhwÆhnt)	joint liability
obligation d'état	(oh-bleeh-gah-syÕh deh-tAh)	government bond
obligation hypothécaire	(oh-bleeh-gah-syÕh eeh-poh-teh-kEhr)	mortgage bond, mortgage debenture
obligation municipale	(oh-bleeh-gah-syÕh mooh-neeh-seeh-pAhl)	municipal bond

obligations (fpl) à intérêt conditionnel	*(oh-bleeh-gah-syÕh ah ãehn-teh-rEh kõhn-deeh-syoh-nEhl)*	income bonds
obligations convertibles	*(oh-bleeh-gah-syÕh kõhn-vehr-tEEh-blœ)*	convertible debentures
obligations échéant en série	*(oh-bleeh-gah-syÕh eh-sheh-Âhnt ãhn seh-rEEh)*	serial bonds
obligations non garanties	*(oh-bleeh-gah-syÕh nõh gah-rãhn-tEEh)*	debentures
observer	*(ohb-sehr-vEh)*	monitor (v)
obus (m)	*(oh-bOOhs)*	shell
octet (m)	*(ohk-tEht)*	byte
odeur (f) de fumée	*(oh-dŒhr dœ fooh-mEh)*	smoky smell
offre (f)	*(Oh-frœ)*	tender
offre et demande	*(Oh-frœ eh dœh-mÃhnd)*	supply and demand
offre globale	*(Oh-frœ gloh-bAhl)*	aggregate demand
offre publique	*(Oh-frœ pooh-blEEhk)*	public offering
offre (f) publique d'achat (OPA)	*(Oh-frœh pooh-blEEhk dah-shAh)*	takeover bid
offre secondaire	*(Oh-frœ sœh-kõhn-dEhr)*	secondary offering
offre supplémentaire	*(Oh-frœ sooh-pleh-mÃh-tEhr)*	premium offering
offrir	*(Oh-frEEhr)*	offer (v)
ogive (f)	*(oh-zhEEhv)*	warhead
ohm (m)		ohm
oligopole (m)	*(oh-leeh-goh-pOhl)*	oligopoly
oligopsonie (f)	*(oh-leeh-gohp-soh-nEEh)*	oligopsony
ombre (f) à paupières	*(Ohm-brœh ah poh-pyEhr)*	eye shadow
omettre	*(oh-mEh-trœ)*	omit (v)
onctueux	*(õhnk-tŒh)*	creamy, well-rounded
onde (f)	*(Ohnd)*	wave
onde courte	*(Ohnd kOOhrt)*	short wave
onguent (m)	*(õhn-gÃh)*	ointment
opaque	*(oh-pAhk)*	matt
opérateur (m) en bourse	*(oh-peh-rah-tŒhr ãhn bOOhrs)*	trader
opération (f)	*(oh-peh-rah-syÕhn)*	transaction
opération (f) annexe	*(oh-peh-rah-syÕh ah-nEhks)*	ancillary operation
opération au comptant	*(oh-peh-rah-syÕh oh kõhn-tÃhn)*	spot delivery
opération combinée: une vente, deux achats	*(oh-peh-rah-syÕh kõhm-beeh-nEh: ohn vÃhnt, dœhz ah-shAh)*	strapping
opération mixte (option d'achat plus option à la vente)	*(oh-peh-rah-syÕh mEEhkst), (ohp-syÕh dah-shAh ploohs ohp-syÕh ah lah vÃhnt)*	straddle

opération simultanée à terme	*(oh-peh-rah-syŌh seeh-moohl-tah-nEh ah tEhrm)*	forward
opérations (fpl) sur le marché libre	*(oh-peh-rah-syŌh lœ mahr-shEh lEEh-brœ)*	open market operations
opium (m)		opium
opossum (m)		opossum
option (f)	*(ohp-syŌh)*	option
option à terme	*(ohp-syŌh ah tEhrm)*	future option
option d'achat	*(ohp-syŌh dah-shAh)*	buyer's option
option de souscription	*(ohp-syŌh dœ sooh-skreehp-syŌh)*	stock option
option de vente	*(ohp-syŌh dœ vÃhnt)*	put option
option en bourse	*(ohp-syŌh ãhn bOOhrs)*	stock option
option indice	*(ohp-syŌh ǽhn-dEEhs)*	index option
optique	*(ohp-tEEhk)*	optic
ordinateur (m)	*(ohr-deeh-nah-tŒhr)*	computer
ordinateur analogique	*(ohr-deeh-nah-tŒhr ah-nah-loh-zhEEhk)*	analog computer
ordinateur hybride	*(ohr-deeh-nah-tŒhr eeh-brEEhd)*	hybrid computer
ordinateur numérique	*(ohr-deeh-nah-tŒhr nooh-meh-rEEhk)*	digital computer
ordonnance (f)	*(ohr-doh-nÃhns)*	prescription
ordre (m) à appréciation	*(Ohr-drœ ah ah-preh-syah-syŌh)*	discretionary order
ordre à terme	*(Ohr-drœ ah tEhrm)*	time order
ordre avec limites	*(Ohr-drœ ah-vEhk leeh-mEEht)*	limited order (stock market)
ordre d'achat	*(Ohr-drœ dah-shAh)*	purchase order
ordre de fabrication	*(Ohr-drœ dœ fah-breeh-kah-syŌh)*	work order, production order
ordre du jour	*(Ohr-drœ dooh zhOOhr)*	order of the day, agenda
ordre journalier	*(Ohr-drœ zhoohr-nah-lyEh)*	day order
ordre permanent	*(Ohr-drœ pehr-mah-nÃh)*	standing order
ordre révocable	*(Ohr-drœ reh-voh-kAh-blœ)*	open order
organigramme (m)	*(ohr-gah-neeh-grAhm)*	organization chart
organisateur (m) conseil	*(ohr-gah-neeh-zah-tŒhr kõhn-sEh-yœ)*	management consultant
organisation (f)	*(ohr-gah-neeh-zah-syŌh)*	organization
organisation des systèmes	*(ohr-gah-neeh-zah-syŌh deh seehs-tEhm)*	systems engineering
organisation industrielle	*(ohr-gah-neeh-zah-syŌh ǽhn-doohs-tryEhl)*	industrial engineering
organisation mixte (état-major et responsables sur le terrain)	*(ohr-gah-neeh-zah-syŌh mEEhks-tœ), (eh-tAh mah-zhOhr rehs-põhn-sAh-blœ soohr lœ tœ-rǼhn)*	staff and line

O

organisation scientifique du travail	*(ohr-gah-neeh-zah-syÕh syÃhn-teeh-fEEhk dooh trah-vAhyœ)*	time and motion
orientation (f) professionnelle	*(oh-ryãhn-tah-syÕh proh-feh-syoh-nEhl)*	employee counseling
oscillateur (m)	*(oh-seeh-lah-tŒhr)*	oscillator
OTAN (f)	*(oh-tAhn)*	NATO
ourlet (m)	*(oohr-lEh)*	hem
outils (mpl)	*(ooh-tEEhl)*	tools
outils de travail	*(ooh-tEEhl dœ trah-vAhyœ)*	working tools
ouverture (f), à l'	*(ooh-vehr-tOOhr)*	at the opening
ouvre-boîtes (m)	*(Œh-vrœh bwAht)*	can opener
ouvrier (m) mécanicien	*(ooh-vryEh meh-kah-neeh-sy Éhn)*	automotive worker

P

P.D.G. (m) (Président-Directeur Général)	*(preh-zeeh-dÃh deeh-rehk-tŒhr zheh-neh-rAhl)*	Chairman of the Board
P.N.B. (m) (Produit National Brut)	*(proh-dwEEh nah-syoh-nAhl brOOh)*	G.N.P. (Gross National Product)
pagination (f)	*(pah-zheeh-nah-syÕh)*	pagination, paging
paiement (m)	*(peh-mÃh)*	payment
paiement à la livraison	*(peh-mÃh ah lah eeh-vreh-zÕh)*	cash on delivery (C.O.D.)
paiement avant livraison	*(peh-mÃh ah-vÃh eeh-vreh-zÕh)*	cash before delivery
paiement bloqué	*(peh-mÃh bloh-kEh)*	stop-payment
paiement comptant des marchandises emportés	*(peh-mÃh kõhn-tÃhn mahr-shãhn-dEEhz œhm-pohr-tEh)*	cash and carry
paiement d'avance	*(peh-mÃh dah-vÃhns)*	cash in advance
paiement en bloc	*(peh-mÃh ãhn blOhk)*	balloon note
paiement en espèces	*(peh-mÃh ãhn ehs-pEhs)*	cash payment
paiement en souffrance	*(peh-mÃh ãhn sooh-frÃhns)*	suspended payment
paiement partiel	*(peh-mÃh pahr-syEhl)*	partial payment
paiement refusé	*(peh-mÃh rœh-fooh-zEh)*	payment refused
paiement supplémentaire	*(peh-mÃh sooh-pleh-mÃh-tEhr)*	additional payment
paiements (mpl) anticipés	*(peh-mÃh ãhn-teeh-seeh-pEh)*	advance payments
pair (m)	*(pEhr)*	par
palette (f)	*(pah-lEht)*	pallet
panneau (m)	*(pah-nOh)*	panel
panneau (m) d'affichage	*(pah-nOh dah-feeh-shAhzh)*	billboard
pansement (m)	*(pãhns-mÃh)*	dressing
pantalon (m)	*(pãhn-ah-lÕh)*	pants
paperasserie (f)	*(pah-peh-rah-seh-rEEh)*	red tape

papier (m)	*(pah-pyEh)*	journal newsprint, paper
papier (m) glacé	*(pah-pyEh glah-sEh)*	coated paper
papier à deux noms	*(pah-pyEh ah dŒh nÕh)*	two-name paper
papier direct	*(pah-pyEh deeh-rEhkt)*	direct paper
papier gommé	*(pah-pyEh goh-mEh)*	paper tape
paquet-poste (m)	*(pah-kEh-pOhst)*	parcel post
par action (m)	*(pahr ahk-syÕh)*	per share
par casier (m)	*(pahr kah-zyEh)*	written bid (stock exchange)

par express aérien	*(pahr ek-sprEhs ah-eh-ryẼhn)*	air express
par habitant	*(pahr ah-beeh-tÃh)*	per capita
par jour	*(pahr zhOOhr)*	per day
paradis (m) fiscal	*(pah-rah-dEEh feehs-kAhl)*	tax shelter, tax haven
pare-brise (m)	*(pahr-brEEhz)*	windshield
pare-choc (m)	*(pahr-shOhk)*	bumper
parité (f)	*(pah-reeh-tEh)*	parity
parité à crémaillère	*(pah-reeh-tEh ah kreh-mah-yEhr)*	crawling peg
parité de complaisance	*(pah-reeh-tEh dœ kõhn-pleh-zÃhns)*	accommodation parity
parité des taux d'intérêt	*(pah-reeh-tEh deh tOh d~œhn-teh-rEh)*	interest parity
parité fixe, mais ajustable	*(pah-reeh-tEh fEEhks meh ah-zhOOhs-tAh-blœ)*	adjustable peg
parité mobile	*(pah-reeh-tEh moh-bEEhl)*	sliding parity, moving parity
Parlement (m) européen	*(pahr-lœh-mÃhn eh-oh-roh-peh-Ehn)*	European Parliament
parrainer	*(pah-reh-nEh)*	sponsor (v)
part (f)	*(pAhr)*	allotment, share
part du marché (f)	*(pAhr dooh mahr-shEh)*	market share
participation (f) aux bénéfices	*(pahr-teeh-seeh-pah-syÕh oh beh-neh-fEEhs)*	profit sharing
participation majoritaire	*(pahr-teeh-seeh-pah-syÕh mah-zhoh-reeh-tEhr)*	majority interest, controlling interest
participation minoritaire	*(pahr-teeh-seeh-pah-syÕh meeh-noh-reeh-tEhr)*	minority interest
partie (f) remise	*(pahr-tEEh rœh-mEEhz)*	rain check
parts (fpl)	*(pAhr)*	parts
parts nominales	*(pAhr noh-meeh-nAhl)*	authorized shares
parvenir à un consensus	*(pahr-vœh-nEEhr ah œhn kõhn-sãhn-sOOh)*	reach a consensus (v)
passer commande	*(pah-sEh koh-mÃhnd)*	place an order (v)
passible de	*(pah-sEEh-blœ)*	liable to
passif (m)	*(pah-sEEhf)*	liability
passif éventuel	*(pah-sEEhf eh-vãhn-twEhl)*	contingent liability

passif pris en charge	*(pah-sEEhf preehz ãhn shАhrzh)*	assumed liability
pasteurisé	*(pahs-tœhr-eeh-zEh)*	pasteurized
pastille (f) pour la toux	*(pahs-tEEh-yœ poohr la tOOhs)*	cough drop
patine (f)	*(pah-tEEhn)*	luster
patron (m)	*(pah-trÕh)*	pattern
pause-café	*(pOhz-kah-fEh)*	coffee break
payable à la commande	*(pah-yAh-blœ ah lah koh-mÃhnd)*	payable to order
payable à la livraison	*(pah-yAh-blœ ah lah eeh-vreh-zÕh)*	collect on delivery
payable au porteur	*(pah-yAh-blœ oh pohr-tŒhr)*	payable to bearer
payable sur demande	*(pah-yAh-blœ soohr dœh-mÃhnd)*	payable on demand
payer	*(pah-yEh)*	pay (v)
payer d'avance	*(pah-yEh dah-vÃhns)*	prepay (v)
payer sous la table	*(pah-yEh sooh lah tAh-blœ)*	pay off (v)
payeur (m)	*(pah-yŒhr)*	payer
pays (m) à risque	*(pah-EEh ah rEEhs-kœ)*	country of risk
pays d'origine	*(pah-EEh doh-reeh-zhEEhn)*	country of origin
pays (mpl) en développement	*(pah-EEh ãhn deh-veh-lohp-mÃh)*	developing country
peau (f)	*(pOh)*	skin
peau (f) d'autruche	*(pOh doh-trOOhsh)*	ostrich (skin)
peau de chevreau	*(pOh dœ sheh-vrOh)*	kidskin
peau de lézard	*(pOh dœ leh-zAhr)*	lizard (skin)
peau de phoque	*(pOh dœ fOhk)*	sealskin
peau de porc	*(pOh dœ pOhr)*	pigskin
peau de serpent	*(pOh dœ sœhr-pÃh)*	snakeskin
peau de veau	*(pOh dœ vAhsh)*	calfskin
peau grasse	*(pOh grAhs)*	oily skin
peau normale	*(pOh nohr-mAhl)*	normal skin
peau sèche	*(pOh sEhsh)*	dry skin
peau sensible	*(pOh sãhn-sEEh-blœh)*	sensitive skin
pédale (f) d'embrayage	*(peh-dAhl dãhm-brah-yAhzh)*	clutch pedal
pédale de frein	*(peh-dAhl dœ frÆhn)*	brake pedal
peint(e) (f) à main	*(pÆhnt ah mÆhn)*	hand-painted
peinture (f)	*(pãhn-tOOhr)*	paint
pelle (f) à tarte	*(pEhl ah tAhrt)*	pastry server
pénétration (f) du marché	*(peh-neh-trah-syÕh dooh mahr-shEh)*	market penetration
pénicilline (f)	*(peh-neeh-seeh-lEEhn)*	penicillin
pénurie (f)	*(peh-nooh-rEEh)*	shortage
percée (f)	*(pehr-sEh)*	breakthrough
percepteur (m)	*(pehr-sehp-tŒhr)*	tax collector

perforatrice (f) à clavier	*(pehr-foh-rah-trEEhs ah klah-vyEh)*	keypunch
période (f) de détention	*(peh-ryOhd dœ deh-tãhn-syÕh)*	holding period
période d'intérêt	*(peh-ryOhd dãhn-teh-rEh)*	interest period
période de fermeture pour travaux	*(peh-ryOhd dœ fehr-mœh-tOOhr poohr trah-vOh)*	downtime
période de pointe	*(peh-ryOhd dœ pwÃEhnt)*	prime time
périphériques (mpl)	*(peh-reeh-feh-rEEhk)*	peripherals
permettre	*(pehr-mEh-trœ)*	allow (v)
permis (m)	*(pehr-mEEh)*	permit, license
permis de travail	*(pehr-mEEh dœ trah-vAhyœ)*	working papers
personne (f) en charge de comptes déterminés (responsable du budget)	*(pehr-sÕhn ãhn shArhzh dœ kÕhnt deh-tehr-meeh-nEh [rœhs-põhn-sΛh blœ dooh booh zhEh])*	account executive
personne morale	*(pehr-sÕhn moh-rAhl)*	legal entity
personnel (m)	*(pehr-soh-nEhl)*	staff
perspective (f)	*(pehrs-pehk-tEEhv)*	outlook
perte (f)	*(pEhrt)*	loss
perte brute	*(pEhrt brOOht)*	gross loss
perte d'avarie commune	*(pEhrt dah-vah-rEEh koh-mOOhn)*	general average loss
perte d'avarie particulière	*(pEhrt dah-vah-rEEh pahr-teeh-kooh-lyEhr)*	particular average loss
perte de conversion	*(pEhrt dœ kõhn-vehr-syÕh)*	exchange discount
perte nette	*(pEhrt nEht)*	net loss
perte sur le change	*(pEhrt soohr-lœ shÃhnzh)*	exchange loss
perte totale réelle	*(pEhrt toh-tAhl reh-Ehl)*	actual total loss
pesticide (m)	*(pehs-teeh-sEEhd)*	pesticide
pétillant (m)	*(peh-teeh-yÃhn)*	sparkling wine
petite annonce (f)	*(peh-tEEht ah-nÕhns)*	classified ad
petite entreprise (f)	*(pœh-tEEht ãhn-trœh-prEEhz)*	small business
petits profits (mpl)	*(pœh-tEEh proh-fEEh)*	perks
pétrochimique	*(peh-troh-keeh-mEEhk)*	petrochemical
pétrodollars (mpl)	*(peh-troh-doh-lAhr)*	petrodollars
pétrole (m)	*(peh-trOhl)*	petroleum
pharmaceutique	*(fahr-mah-seh-ooh-tEEhk)*	pharmaceutical
pharmacie (f)	*(fahr-mah-sEEh)*	drugstore
pharmacien(ne) (m)	*(fahr-mah-syÆEhn)*	pharmacist
phase (f) descendante	*(fAhz deh-sãhn-dÃhnt)*	downswing
phénol (m)	*(feh-nOhl)*	phenol
phosphate (m)	*(fohs-fAht)*	phosphate
photographe (m)	*(foh-toh-grAhf)*	photographer
pichet (m)	*(peeh-shEh)*	pitcher

pièce (f) justificative	*(pyEhs zhoohs-teeh-kah-tEEhv)*	voucher
pièce justificative de perte	*(pyEhs zhoohs-teeh-kah-tEEhv dœ pEhrt)*	proof of loss
pièces (fpl)	*(pyEhs)*	parts, documents, papers
pièces de rechange	*(pyEhs dœ rœh-shĀhnzh)*	replacement parts
pierre (f) à chaux	*(pyEhr ah shOh)*	limestone
pigment (m)	*(peehg-mĀh)*	pigment
pignon (m)	*(peeh-nyÕh)*	pinion
pilote (m) automatique	*(peeh-lOht oh-toh-mah-tEEhk)*	auto-pilot
pilule (f)	*(peeh-lOOhl)*	pill
pince (f)	*(pÆhns)*	dart
pince (f) à sucre	*(pÆhns ah sOOh-krœh)*	sugar tongs
piquet (m)	*(peeh-kEh)*	picket line
piqûre (f)	*(peeh-kOOhr)*	injection
piste (f)	*(pEEhst)*	runway
piston (m)	*(peehs-tÕh)*	piston
placement (m) à revenu fixe	*(plahs-mĀh ah rœhv-nOOh fEEhks)*	fixed investment
placement (m) à revenu variable	*(plahs-mĀhn ah rœh-vœh-nOOl vah-ryAh-blœh)*	variable yield investment
plafond (m)	*(plah-fÕhn)*	ceiling
plan commercial	*(plĀhn koh-mehr-syAhl)*	marketing plan
plan (m) d'action	*(plĀhn dahk-syÕh)*	action plan
planche (f) de contact	*(plĀhnsh dœ kõhn-tAhkt)*	contact sheet
plancher (m) (à la Bourse)	*(plĀhn-shEh ah lah bOOhrs)*	floor (of exchange)
planification (f)	*(plah-neeh-feeh-kah-syÕh)*	project planning
planification à long terme	*(plah-neeh-feeh-kah-syÕh ah lÕh tEhrm)*	long-range planning
planification budgétaire	*(plah-neeh-feeh-kah-syÕh booh-zheh-tEhr)*	financial planning
planification d'entreprise	*(plah-neeh-feeh-kah-syÕh dãhn-trœh-prEEhz)*	corporate planning
planification de la production	*(plah-neeh-feeh-kah-syÕh dœ lah proh-doohk-syÕh)*	production control
planification industrielle	*(plah-neeh-feeh-kah-syÕh ãhn-doohs-tryEhl)*	industrial planning
plantes (fpl)	*(plĀhnt)*	plants
plaque (f)	*(plAhk)*	plate
plaquette (f)	*(plah-kEht)*	chip
plat (m) creux	*(plAh krŒh)*	deep dish
plat (m) rond	*(plAh rÕhn)*	round platter
plateau (m)	*(plah-tŒh)*	tray
plateau (m) à fromage	*(plah-tOh ah froh-mAhzh)*	cheese-tray
pléthore (f)	*(pleh-tOhr)*	glut
pli	*(pleeh)*	pleat

pli (m) cacheté contenant une offre	*(pleeh kash-tEh kõhn-tœh-nÃhnt oohn Oh-frœ)*	sealed bid
plier à la législation européenne (se)	*(pleeh-Eh ah lah leh-zheehs-lah-syÕhn eh-oh-roh-peh-Ehn)*	comply with EC legislation (v)
plissé(e)	*(pleeh-sEh)*	pleated
pluie (f) acide	*(plwEEh ah-sEEhd)*	acid rain
plus offrant (m)	*(ploohz oh-frÃhn)*	highest bidder
plus-value (f)	*(plooh-vah-lOOh)*	appreciation, unearned increment, capital gain
plus-value des titres	*(plooh-vah-lOOh deh tEEh-trœ)*	stock profit
plus-value en capital	*(plooh-vah-lOOh ãhn kah-peeh-tAhl)*	capital gain
pneu (m)	*(nŒh)*	tire
pneu radial	*(nŒh rah dyΛhl)*	radial tire
poids (m)	*(pwAh)*	weight
poids brut	*(pwAh brOOh)*	gross weight
poignet (m) mousquetaire	*(pwah-nyEh moohs-keh-tEhr)*	French cuff
poil (m) de chameau	*(pwAhl dœ shAh-mOh)*	camel's hair
point (m)	*(pwÆhn)*	point, stitch
point d'équilibre	*(pwÆh deh-keeh-lEEh-brœ)*	break-even point
point de procédure	*(pwÆh dœ proh-seh-dOOhr)*	point of order
point de référence	*(pwÆh dœ reh-feh-rÃhns)*	basis point (1/100%)
point de sensibilité	*(pwÆh dœ sãh-seeh-beeh-leeh-tEh)*	break-even analysis
point (m) de vente	*(pwÆhn dœ vÃhnt)*	point-of-sale, retail outlet
pointage (m) des prix	*(pwæhn-tAhzh deh prEEh)*	price tick
points (mpl) de livraison	*(pwÆh dœ eeh-vreh-zÕh)*	delivery points
poivrière (f)	*(pwah-vryEhr)*	pepper shaker
police (f) d'assurance	*(poh-lEEhs dah-sooh-rÃhns)*	insurance policy
police d'assurance-vie	*(poh-lEEhs dah-sooh-rÃhns vEEh)*	life insurance policy
police (f) des caractères	*(poh-lEEhs deh kah-raht-tEhr)*	character font
police flottante	*(poh-lEEhs floh-tÃhnt)*	floater
police flotte	*(poh-lEEhs flOht)*	fleet policy
politique (f) agricole commune (PAC)	*(poh-leeh-tEEhk ah-greeh-kOhl koh-mOOhn)*	common agricultural policy (CAP)
politique (f) communautaire sur la drogue (f)	*(poh-leeh-tEEhk koh-mooh-nOh-tEhr soohr lah drOhg)*	common drug policy

P

politique (f) de distribution	(poh-leeh-tEEhk dœ deehs-treeh-booh-syÕh)	distribution policy
politique d'investissement	(poh-leeh-tEEhk dæhn-vehs-teehs-mÃh)	investment policy
politique de l'entreprise	(poh-leeh-tEEhk dœ lãhn-trœh-prEEhz)	business policy
politique de la porte ouverte	(poh-leeh-tEEhk dœ lah pOhrt ooh-vEhrt)	open door policy
politique de la société	(poh-leeh-tEEhk dœ lah soh-syeh-tEh)	company policy
politique monétaire	(poh-leeh-tEEhk moh-neh-tEhr)	monetary policy
polluant	(poh-lwÃhn)	pollutant
polluer	(poh-lwEh)	pollute (v)
pollution (f)	(poh-looh-syÕhn)	pollution
pollution (f) de l'air	(poh-looh-syÕhn dœ lEhr)	air pollution
pollution (f) des eaux	(poh-looh-syÕhn dehz Œh)	water pollution
pollution (f) par le bruit	(poh-looh-syÕhn pahr lah brwEEh)	noise pollution
polyester (m)	(poh-leeh-ehs-tEhr)	polyester
polymère (m)	(poh-leeh-mEhr)	polymer
pommade (f)	(poh-mAhd)	salve
pompe (f) à eau	(pOhmp ah Oh)	water pump
pompe à huile	(pOhmp ah wEEhl)	oil pump
ponction (f) fiscale	(põhnk-syÕh feehs-kAhl)	fiscal drag
pont (m) arrière	(pÕhnt ah-ryEhr)	rear axle
pontage (m)	(põhn-tAhzh)	bypass
popeline (f)	(pohp-lEEhn)	poplin
population (f) active	(poh-pooh-lah-syÕh ahk-tEEhv)	labor force
porcelaine (f)	(pohr-sœh-lEhn)	china, bone china
porcelaine (f) blanche	(pohr-sœh-lEhn blÃhnsh)	white porcelain
port (m) de débarquement convenu	(pOhrt dœ deh-bahrk-mÃh kõhn-vœh-nOOh)	named inland point in country of importation
port d'expédition convenu	(pOhr dehks-peh-deeh-syÕh kõhn-vœh-nOOh)	named port of shipment
port d'importation convenu	(pOhr dæhm-pohr-tah-syÕh kõhn-vœh-nOOh)	named port of importation
port dû	(pohrt dOOh)	freight collect
port franc	(pohrt frÃhnk)	free port
port payé d'avance	(pohrt pah-yEh dah-vÃhns)	freight prepaid
portatif	(pohr-tah-tEEhf)	laptop
porte-à-faux (m)	(pOhrt ah fOh)	overhang
porte-à-porte (m)	(pOhrt ah pOhrt)	door-to-door (sales)
porte-cartes (m)	(pohrt-kAhrt)	card case
porte-clés (m)	(pohrt-klEh)	key case
porte-couteau (m)	(pohrt-kooh-tOh)	knife rest

porte-monnaie (m)	*(pohrt-moh-nEh)*	purse
porte-passeport (m)	*(pohrt-pahs-pOhr)*	passport case
portefeuille (m)	*(pohrt-fŒh-yœ)*	pocketbook, portfolio
portefeuille de titres	*(pohrt-fŒhyœ dœ tEEh-trœ)*	stock portfolio
porter en compte	*(pohr-tEh ãhn kÕhnt)*	post (bookkeeping)
porteur (m)	*(pohrt-tŒhr)*	bearer
positif	*(poh-zeeh-tEEhf)*	positive
position (f)	*(poh-zeeh-syÕh)*	allotment
position à la baisse	*(poh-zeeh-syÕh ah lah bEhs)*	short position
position nette	*(poh-zeeh-syÕh nEht)*	net position (of a trade)
position sur le marché	*(poh-zeeh-syÕh soohr lœ mahr-shEh)*	market position
position-limite	*(poh-zeeh-syÕh leeh-mEEht)*	position limit
postdaté	*(pohst-dah-tEh)*	postdated
postdater	*(pohst-dah-tEh)*	postdate (v)
poste (m)	*(pOhst)*	post (bookkeeping), fixture (on balance sheet)
poste (m) de commandement	*(pOhst dœ koh-mãhnd-mÃhn)*	command station
poste de travail	*(pOhst dœ trah-vAhyœ)*	workstation
poste de travail autonome	*(pOhst dœ trah-vAhyœ oh-toh-nOhm)*	stand-alone workstation
pot-de-vin (m)	*(poh-dœ-vÃEhn)*	kickback
potentiel (m) de croissance	*(poh-tãhn-syEhl dœ krwah-sÃhns)*	growth potential
potentiel du marché	*(poh-tãhn-syEhl dooh mahr-shEh)*	market potential
potentiel inutilisé	*(poh-tãhn-syEhl æhn-ooh-teeh-leeh-zEh)*	idle capacity
pot (m) de crème	*(poh dœ krEhm)*	cream jar
poterie (f)	*(poh-tœh-rEEh)*	pottery
poterie en grès	*(poh-tœh-rEEh ãhn grEh)*	stoneware
pouce (m)	*(pOOhs)*	inch
poudre (f)	*(pOOh-drœh)*	powder
poudre de riz	*(pOOh-drœh dœ rEEhs)*	face powder
pour solde de tout compte	*(poohr sOhld dœ tooh kÕhnt)*	full settlement
pourboire (m)	*(poohr-bwAhr)*	tip
pourcentage (m) de sucre	*(poohr-sãhn-tAhzh)*	sugar content
pourparlers (mpl)	*(poohr-pahr-lEh)*	talks
pourtour des yeux (m)	*(poohr-tOOhr dehz yŒh)*	eye contour
pouvoir (m)	*(pooh-vwAhr)*	capacity, power
pouvoir d'achat	*(pooh-vwAhr dah-shAh)*	purchasing power

pouvoir d'émettre des obligations	*(pooh-vwAhr deh-mEh-træ dehz oh-bleeh-gah-syÕh)*	bond power
pouvoir de négociation	*(pooh-vwAhr dæ neh-goh-syah-syÕh)*	bargaining power
pouvoir pour le transfert et la vente d'actions	*(pooh-vwAhr poohr læ trãhnz-fEhr eh lah vÃhnt dahk-syÕh)*	stock-power
pratique	*(prah-tEEhk)*	practical
pratique (f) de l'escompte	*(prah-tEEhk dæ lehs-kÕhnt)*	discounting
préavis (m)	*(preh-ah-vEEh)*	advance notice
précipitations (fpl)	*(preh-seeh-peeh-tah-syÕhn)*	rainfall
préfabrication (f)	*(preh-fah-breeh-kah-syÕh)*	prefabrication
préface (f)	*(preh-fAhs)*	preface
préférence (f) pour la liquidité	*(preh-feh-rÃhns poohr lah leeh-keeh-deeh-tEh)*	liquidity preference
prélèvement (m)	*(preh-lehv-mÃh)*	appropriation
prélèvement des frais d'achat sur les premiers versements	*(preh-lehv-mÃh deh frEh dah-shAh soohr leh præh-myEh vehrs-mÃh)*	front-end loading
premier entré—premier sorti	*(præh-myEh ãhn-trEh), (præh-myEh sohr-tEEh)*	first in-first out
prendre en location	*(prÃhn-dræ ãhn loh-kah-syÕh)*	rent (v)
prendre note	*(prÃhn-dræ nOht)*	take down (v)
prescription (f) légale	*(preh-skreehp-syÕh leh-gAhl)*	statute of limitations
présentation (f) d'une vitrine	*(preh-zãhn-tah-syÕh doohn veeh-trEEhn)*	window dressing
préservatif (m)	*(preh-sehr-vah-tEEhf)*	condom
préservation (f)	*(preh-sehr-vah-syÕhn)*	preservation
président du conseil d'administration	*(preh-zeeh-dÃh dooh kõhn-sEh-yæ dad-meeh-neehs-trah-syÕh)*	chairman of the board
presse (f)	*(prEhs)*	press
pression (f)	*(præh-syÕh)*	pressure
pression (f) fiscale	*(præh-syÕh feehs-kAhl)*	tax burden
pressoir (m)	*(præh-swAhr)*	winepress
prêt (m)	*(prEht)*	loan
prêt à amortissement différé	*(prEht ah ah-mohr-eehs-mÃh deeh-feh-rEh)*	balloon
prêt à terme fixe	*(prEht ah tEhrm fEEhks)*	term loan
prêt au jour le jour	*(prEht oh zhOOhr læ zhOOhr)*	day loan
prêt (m) bancaire	*(prEht bãhn-kEhr)*	bank loan
prêt conditionnel	*(prEht kõhn-deeh-syoh-nEhl)*	tied loan
prêt en participation	*(prEht ãhn pahr-teeh-seeh-pah-syÕh)*	participation loan

prêt fiduciaire	*(prEht feeh-dooh-syEhr)*	fiduciary loan
prêt (m) hypothécaire	*(prEht eeh-poh-teh-kEhr)*	mortgage loan
prêt (m) non garanti	*(prEht nõhn gah-rãhn-tEEh)*	unsecured loan
prêt remboursable sur demande	*(prEht rãhm-boorh-sAh-blœ soohr dœh-mÃhnd)*	call loan
prêt-à-porter (m)	*(prEht ah pohr-tEh)*	ready-to-wear
prêter	*(preh-tEh)*	lend (v)
prêts (mpl) à faible intérêt	*(prEht ah fEh-blœ æhn-teh-rEh)*	low interest loans
prévenir le vieillissement	*(preh-vœh-nEEhr lœ vyeh-yeehz-mÃhn)*	prevent (v) aging
prévision (f)	*(preh-veeh-zyÕh)*	forecast
prévision budgétaire	*(preh-veeh-zyÕh booh-zheh-tEhr)*	budget forecast
prévision de marché	*(preh-veeh-zyÕh dœ mahr-shEh)*	market forecast
prévision de vente	*(preh-veeh-zyÕh dœ vÃhnt)*	sales forecast, sales estimate
prévision des bénéfices	*(preh-veeh-zyÕh deh beh-neh-fEEhs)*	profit projection
prévoir	*(preh-vwAhr)*	forecast (v)
prime (f)	*(prEEhm)*	bonus, premium
prime à la hausse	*(prEEhm ah lah Ohs)*	call option
prime d'assurance	*(prEEhm dah-sooh-rÃhns)*	insurance premium
prime de remboursement	*(prEEhm dœ rãhm-boohrs-mÃh)*	redemption premium
prime de remboursement anticipé	*(prEEhm dœ rãhm-boohrs-mÃh ãhn-teeh-seeh-pEh)*	acceleration premium
prime de sauvetage	*(prEEhm dœ soh-veh-tAhzh)*	salvage charges
prime pour l'acheteur	*(prEEhm poohr lahsh-tŒhr)*	buyer's premium
principale donnée (f) financiére	*(præhn-seeh-pAhl doh-nEh feeh-nãhn-syEhr)*	financial highlight
priorité (f)	*(preeh-oh-reeh-tEh)*	priority
prise (f) d'hypothèque mobilière	*(prEEhz deeh-poh-tEhk moh-beeh-lyEhr)*	hypothecation
prise de bénéfice	*(prEEhz dœ beh-neh-fEEhs)*	profit taking
prise (f) de vue	*(prEEhz dœ vOOh)*	take
privilège (m)	*(preeh-veeh-lEhzh)*	lien
privilège du constructeur	*(preeh-veeh-lEhzh dooh kõhn-stroohk-tŒhr)*	mechanic's lien
privilège du fournisseur	*(preeh-veeh-lEhzh dooh foohr-neeh-sŒhr)*	vendor's lien
prix (m)	*(prEEh)*	price
prix à l'unité	*(prEEh ah looh-neeh-tEh)*	unit price
prix à la livraison	*(prEEh ah lah leeh-vreh-zÕh)*	delivery price
prix brut	*(prEEh brOOh)*	gross price

prix CAF ajusté	*(prEEh ah-zhOOhs-tEh)*	adjusted CIF price
prix cible	*(prEEh sEEh-blœ)*	target price
prix compétitif	*(prEEh kohm-peh-teeh-tEEhf)*	competitive price
prix concurrentiel	*(prEEh kõhn-kooh-rãhn-syEhl)*	competitive price
prix contrôlé	*(prEEh kõhn-troh-lEh)*	pegged price
prix courant	*(prEEh kooh-rãhn)*	list price
prix d'achat	*(prEEh dah-shAh)*	purchase price
prix d'émission	*(prEEh deh-meeh-syÕh)*	issue price
prix de base	*(prEEh dœ bAhz)*	base price
prix de détail	*(prEEh dœ deh-tAhyœ)*	retail price
prix de gros	*(prEEh dœ grOh)*	wholesale price
prix de l'abonnement	*(prEEh dœ lah-bohn-mÃh)*	subscription price
prix de parité	*(prEEh dœ pah-reeh-tEh)*	parity price
prix de rachat	*(prEEh dœ rah-shAh)*	call price
prix de revient	*(prEEh dœ rœ-vyÃhn)*	prime cost
prix de revient complet	*(prEEh dœ rœ-vyÃhn kohm-plEh)*	absorption costing
prix de revient marginal	*(prEEh dœ rœ-vyÃhn mahr-zheeh-nAhl)*	incremental cost
prix de revient unitaire	*(prEEh dœ rœ-vyÃhn ooh-neeh-tEhr)*	unit cost
prix de souscription	*(prEEh dœ sooh-skreehp-syÕh)*	subscription price
prix demandé	*(prEEh dœh-mãhn-dEh)*	asking price
prix du marché	*(prEEh dooh mahr-shEh)*	market price
prix fort	*(prEEh fOhr)*	top price
prix limite	*(prEEh leeh-mEEht)*	price limit
prix nominal	*(prEEh noh-meeh-nAhl)*	nominal price
prix offert	*(prEEh oh-fEhr)*	offered price
prix réel	*(prEEh reh-Ehl)*	real price
prix rendu	*(prEEh rãhn-dOOh)*	delivered price
prix unitaire moyen	*(prEEh ooh-neeh-tEhr mwah-yEhn)*	average unit cost
problème (m)	*(proh-blÉhm)*	problem
problème d'analyse	*(proh-blÉhm dãh-nah-lEEhz)*	analysis problem
procédé (m)	*(proh-seh-dEh)*	process
procédé (m) électrolytique	*(proh-seh-dEh eh-leh-troh-leeh-tEEhk)*	electrolytic process
procédé (m) type	*(proh-seh-dEh tEEhp)*	standard practice
procédure (f) d'arbitrage	*(proh-seh-dOOhr dahr-beeh-trAhzh)*	grievance procedure
procès (m)	*(proh-sEh)*	lawsuit
procès intenté en cas de fraude	*(proh-sEh æhn-tãhn-tEh ãhn kAh dœ frOhd)*	penalty-fraud action
processeur (m)	*(proh-seh-sŒhr)*	processor
processus (m) d'ajustement	*(proh-seh-sOOh dah-zhOOhstœ-mÃh)*	adjustment process

processus de production	*(proh-seh-sOOh dœ proh-doohk-syÕh)*	production process
procuration (f)	*(proh-kooh-rah-syÕh)*	power of attorney, proxy
production (f)	*(proh-doohk-syÕh)*	production process, production
production en lots	*(proh-doohk-syÕh ãhn lOht)*	batch production
production globale	*(proh-doohk-syÕh gloh-bAhl)*	aggregate supply
production modulaire	*(proh-doohk-syÕh moh-dooh-lEhr)*	modular production
productivité (f)	*(proh-doohk-teeh-veeh-tEh)*	productivity
productivité marginale	*(proh-doohk-teeh-veeh-tEh mahr-zheeh-nAhl)*	marginal productivity
produit (m)	*(proh-dwEEh)*	product, merchandise
produit (m) classique	*(proh-dwEEh klah-sEEhk)*	conventional product
produit chimique	*(proh-dwEEh keeh-mEEhk)*	chemical
produit de base	*(proh-dwEEh dœ bAhz)*	commodity
produit de la vente	*(proh-dwEEh dœ lah vÃhnt)*	proceeds
produit des ventes	*(proh-dwEEh deh vÃhnt)*	return on sales
produit fini	*(proh-dwEEh feeh-nEEh)*	end product
produit intérieur brut	*(proh-dwEEh ãehn-teh-reyŒhr brOOh)*	gross domestic product
produit (m) long	*(proh-dwEEh lÕh)*	long product
produit national brut	*(proh-dwEEh nah-syoh-nAhl brOOh)*	gross national product
produits (mpl) agricoles	*(proh-dwEEh ah-greeh-kOhl)*	agricultural products
produits du pays	*(proh-dwEEh dooh pah-EEh)*	native produce
produits figurant au tarif douanier	*(proh-dwEEh feeh-gooh-rÃhnt oh tah-rEEhf dooh-ah-nyEh)*	tariff commodities
produits (mpl) finis	*(proh-dwEEh feeh-nEEh)*	finished products
produits industriels	*(proh-dwEEh ãehn-doohs-tryEhl)*	industrial goods
produits laitiers	*(proh-dwEEh leh-tyEhr)*	dairy products
produits (mpl) plats	*(proh-dwEEh plAht)*	flats products
produits (mpl) réfractaires	*(proh-dwEEh reh-frahk-tEhr)*	refractories
produits (mpl) spéciaux	*(proh-dwEEh speh-syOh)*	specialty goods
profession (f)	*(proh-feh-syÕh)*	profession
profil (m) de la clientèle	*(proh-feehl dœ lah kleeh-ãhr-tEhl)*	customer profile
profil (m) des acquisitions	*(proh-fEEhl dehz ah-keeh-zehh-syÕh)*	acquisition profile

profit (m) fictif	(proh-fEEh feehk-tEEhf)	paper profit
programmation (f) linéaire	(proh-grah-mah-syÕh leeh-neh-Ehr)	linear programming
programmation multiple	(proh-grah-mah-syÕh moohl-tEEh-plœ)	multiprogramming
programme (m)	(proh-grAhm)	program, schedule
programme d'action	(proh-grAhm dahk-syÕh)	action plan
programme d'investissement	(proh-grAhm dǣhn-vehs-teehs-mÃh)	investment program
programme d'ordinateur	(proh-grAhm dohr-deeh-nah-tŒhr)	computer program
programme de commercialisation	(proh-grAhm dœ koh-mehr-syah-leeh-zah-syÕh)	marketing plan
programme de complaisance	(proh-grAhm dœ kõhn-pleh-zÃhns)	accommodation platform
programme de production	(proh-grAhm dœ proh-doohk-syÕh)	production schedule
programmer	(proh-grah-mEh)	program (v)
projet (m)	(proh-zhEh)	plan, project, blueprint
projet commercial	(proh-zhEh koh-mehr-syAhl)	business plan, marketing plan
projeter	(proh-zheh-tEh)	project (v)
promotion (f)	(proh-moh-syÕh)	promotion
prononcer un jugement	(proh-nõhn-sEh œhn zhoohzh-mÃh)	adjudge (v)
proposition (f) de vente	(proh-poh-zeeh-syÕh dœ vÃhnt)	offer for sale
propriétaire (m)	(proh-pryeh-tEhr)	owner, proprietor
propriétaire absent	(proh-pryeh-tEhr ahb-sÃhn)	absentee ownership
propriétaire foncier	(proh-pryeh-tEhr fõhn-syEhr)	landowner
propriété (f)	(proh-pryeh-tEh)	property, ownership
propriété culturelle	(proh-pryeh-tEh koohl-tooh-rEhl)	cultural property
propriété exclusive	(proh-pryeh-tEh ehks-klooh-sEEhv)	proprietary
propriété foncière	(proh-pryeh-tEh fÕhn-syEhr)	estate
propriété immobilière	(proh-pryeh-tEh eeh-moh-beeh-lyEhr)	real estate
propriété publique	(proh-pryeh-tEh pooh-blEEhk)	public property
propulsion (f)	(proh-poohl-syÕh)	propulsion
prospectus (m)	(prohs-pehk-tOOh)	prospectus
protection (f) contre le risque de rembourse-ment anticipé	(kõhn-trœ lœ rEEhs-kœ dœ rãhm-boohrs-mÃh ãhn-teeh-seeh-pEh)	call protection
protectionnisme (m)	(proh-tehk-syoh-nEEhz-mœ)	protectionism

protéger	*(proh-teh-zhEh)*	protect (v)
protestation (f)	*(proh-tehs-tah-syÕh)*	protest (banking, law)
protêt (m)	*(proh-tEht)*	protest (banking, law)
proton (m)	*(proh-tÕh)*	proton
prototype (m)	*(proh-toh-tEEhp)*	prototype
provision (f) pour impôts	*(proh-veeh-zyÕhn poohr æhm-pOh)*	accrued taxes
public-cible (m)	*(pooh-blEEhk-sEEh-blœ)*	target audience
publicité (f)	*(pooh-bleeh-seeh-tEh)*	publicity, advertising
publicité collective	*(pooh-bleeh-seeh-tEh koh-lehk-tEEhv)*	cooperative advertising
publicité conjointe	*(pooh-bleeh-seeh-tEh kõhn-jwÆhnt)*	cooperative advertising
publicité (f) directe par correspondance	*(pooh-bleeh-see-tEh pahr koh-rehs-põhn-dÃhns)*	direct mail advertising
publicité de prestige	*(pooh-bleeh-seeh-tEh dœ prehs-tEEhzh)*	institutional advertising
puissance (f)	*(pweeh-sÃhns)*	power
puce (f)	*(pOOhs)*	chip
puissance (f)	*(pweeh-sÃhns)*	power
puissance (f) de combat	*(pweeh-sÃhns dœ kõhm-bAh)*	combat power
puits (m) asséché	*(pweeh ah-seh-shEh)*	dried up well
pull-over (m)		sweater
purgatif (m)	*(poohr-gah-tEEhf)*	purgative
purification (f)	*(pooh-reeh-feeh-kah-syÕh)*	purification
putois (m)	*(pooh-twAh)*	fitch

Q

quadrichromie (f)	*(kah-dreeh-kroh-mEEh)*	four colors
qualité (f), avoir qualité de	*(kah-leeh-tEh), (ah-vwAhr kah-leeh-tEh dœ)*	to have authority
qualité commerciale	*(kah-leeh-tEh koh-mehr-syAhl)*	commercial grade
qualité supérieure	*(kah-leeh-tEh sooh-peh-ryŒhr)*	top quality
quantité (f)	*(kÃhn-teeh-tEh)*	quantity
quantité économique d'approvisionnement	*(kÃhn-teeh-tEh eh-koh-moh-mEEhk dah-proh-veeh-zyohn-mÃh)*	economic order quantity
quasi-monnaie (f)	*(kah-zEEh moh-nÉh)*	near money
quitte et libre	*(kEEht eh lEEh-brœ)*	free and clear
quorum (m)	*(koh-rOOhm)*	quorum
quotidien (m)	*(koh-teeh-dyEhn)*	daily
quotité (f)	*(koh-teeh-tEh)*	round lot

R

rabais (m)	*(rah-bEh)*	price cutting
raccorder	*(rah-kohr-dEh)*	connect (v)
rachat (m)	*(rah-shAh)*	takeover (stock takeover)
racheter	*(rahsh-tEh)*	buy back (v), buy out (v)
radar (m)	*(rah-dAhr)*	radar
radio (f)	*(rah-dyOh)*	radio
radioactivité (f)	*(rah-dyoh-ahk-teeh-veeh-tEh)*	radioactivity
radiodiffuser	*(rah-dyoh-deeh-fooh-zEh)*	broadcast (v)
radiographie (f)	*(rah-dyoh-grah-fEEh)*	x-ray
raffermir	*(rah-fehr-mEEhr)*	firm (v)
raffiner	*(rah-feeh-nEh)*	refine (v)
raffinerie (f)	*(rah-feeh-nœh-rEEh)*	refinery
ragondin (m)	*(rah-gõhn-dÃEhn)*	nutria
raisin (m)	*(reh-zÃEhn)*	grape
rajeunir	*(rah-zhœh-nEEhr)*	rejuvenate (v)
ramassage (m) et livraison (f)	*(rah-mah-sAhzh eh lah leeh-vreh-zÕh)*	pick up and delivery
rame (f)	*(rAhm)*	ream
rapide	*(rah-pEEhd)*	prompt
rappel (m)	*(rah-pEhl)*	callback
rappel d'impôts	*(rah-pEhl dãhm-pOh)*	back taxes
rapport (m)	*(rah-pOhr)*	report
rapport (rendement)	*(rah-pOhr [rãhnd-mÃh])*	yield
rapport annuel	*(rah-pOhr ah-nwEhl)*	annual report
rapport financier	*(rah-pOhr feeh-nãhn-syEh)*	financial statement
rapport parité/revenu	*(rah-pOhr pah-reeh-tEh/ rœhv-nOOh)*	parity income ratio
rapport, par rapport à	*(rah-pOhr, pahr rah-pOhr ah)*	with regard to
ratio (m) comptable	*(rAh-syoh kõhn-tAh-blœ)*	accounting ratio
ratio de liquidité immédiate	*(rAh-syoh dœ leeh-keeh-deeh-tEh eeh-meh-dyAht)*	acid-test ratio
ratio sinistres-primes	*(rAh-syoh seeh-nEEhs-trœ prEEhm)*	loss-loss ratio
rationaliser	*(rah-syoh-nah-leeh-zEh)*	streamline (v)
rationnement (m)	*(rah-syohn-mÃh)*	rationing
ratios (mpl) de bilan	*(rah-syOh dœ beeh-lÃh)*	balance ratios
raton laveur (m)	*(rah-tÕh lah-vŒhr)*	raccoon
rayon (m)	*(rah-yÕh)*	beam
rayon (m) d'un grand magasin affermé en concession	*(rah-yÕh dœhn grãhn mah-gah-zÃEhn ãhn kõhn-seh-syÕh)*	leased department
rayonne (f)	*(rah-yOhn)*	rayon
réactif (m)	*(reh-ahk-tEEhf)*	reactant

réaction (f)	*(reh-ahk-syÕhn)*	feedback, response
réaction (f) allergique	*(reh-ahk-syÕhn ah-lehr-zhEEhk)*	allergic reaction
réagir réciproquement	*(reh-ah-zhEEhr reh-seeh-prohk-mÃh)*	interact (v)
réaliser l'unité	*(reh-ah-leeh-zEh)*	attain unity (v)
réassureur (m)	*(reh-ah-sooh-rEh)*	reinsurer
recapitalisation (f)	*(ræh-kah-peeh-tah-leeh-zah-syÕh)*	recapitalization
récepteur (m)	*(reh-sæhp-tŒhr)*	receiver
récession (f)	*(reh-seh-syÕh)*	downturn, recession
recette (f) fiduciaire	*(ræh-sEht feeh-dooh-syEhr)*	trust receipt
recette fiscale	*(ræh-sEht feehs-kAhl)*	internal revenue tax
recettes (fpl)	*(ræh-sEht)*	revenue
receveur (m) des douanes	*(ræh-seh-vŒhr deh dooh-Λhn)*	collector of customs
réchauffement (m) de la planète	*(reh-shohf-mÃhn dæ lah plah-nEht)*	global warming
recherche (f)	*(ræ-shEhrsh)*	research (n)
recherche de cadres	*(ræ-shEhrsh dæ kAh-dræ)*	executive search
recherche et développement	*(ræ-shEhrsh eh deh-veh-lohp-mÃh)*	research and development
recherche publicitaire	*(ræ-shEhrsh pooh-bleeh-seeh-tEhr)*	advertising research
réclamation (f)	*(reh-klah-mah-syÕh)*	claim
réclamation indirecte	*(reh klah mah-syÕh æhn-deeh-rEhkı)*	indirect claim
réclame (f)	*(reh-klAhm)*	advertising
récolte (f)	*(reh-kOhlt)*	yield, harvest
reconnaître (admettre)	*(ræ-koh-nEh-træ), (ahd-mEh-træ)*	acknowledge (v)
recours (m)	*(ræh-kOOhr)*	recourse, remedy (law)
recouvrement (m)	*(ræh-kooh-vræ-mÃh)*	recovery
rectifier	*(rehk-teeh-feeh-Eh)*	amend (v)
reçu (m)	*(ræh-sOOh)*	receipt, voucher
recuit	*(reh-kwEEh)*	annealing
recul (m)	*(ræh-kOOhl)*	recession, setback
récupérer	*(reh-kooh-peh-rEh)*	salvage (v), retrieve (v)
recyclable	*(ræh-seeh-klAh-blæh)*	recyclable
recycler	*(ræh-seel-klEh)*	recycle (v)
rédacteur (m)	*(reh-dahk-tŒhr)*	editor
rédacteur (-trice) publicitaire	*(reh-dahk-tŒhr pooh-bleeh-seeh-tEhr)*	copywriter
redevance (f)	*(ræh-dæh-vÃhns)*	royalty, license fee
redressement (m)	*(ræh-drehs-mÃh)*	upturn
réduction (f)	*(reh-doohk-syÕh)*	deduction, cutback

réduction (f) comptable	*(reh-doohk-syÕh kõhn-tAh-blœ)*	writedown
réduire	*(reh-dwEEhr)*	reduce (v)
réévaluation (f)	*(reh-eh-vah-lwah-syÕh)*	revaluation
réexportation (f)	*(reh-ehks-pohr-tah-syÕh)*	re-export
référence (f) de crédit	*(reh-feh-rÃhns dœ kreh-dEEh)*	credit reference
référence, année de	*(reh-feh-rÃhns, ah-nEh dœ)*	base year
refinancement (m)	*(rœh-feeh-nãhns-mÃh)*	refinancing
refondre les réglementations	*(rœh-fÕhn-drœh leh reh-glœh-mãhn-tah-syÕhn)*	overhaul (v) regulations
réforme (f) agraire	*(reh-fÕhrm ah-grEhr)*	land reform
refus (m) d'acceptation	*(rœh-fOOh dœ lahk-sehp-tah-syÕh)*	dishonor (as a check)
refuser l'acceptation	*(rœh-fooh-zEh lahk-sehp-tah-syÕh)*	refuse acceptance (v)
refuser le paiement	*(rœh-fooh-zEh lœ peh-mÃh)*	refuse payment (v)
région (f)	*(reh-zhÕh)*	country
règle (f) du remboursement	*(rEh-glœ dooh rãhm-boohrs-mÃh)*	call rule
règle sage	*(rEh-glœ sAhzh)*	prudent-man rule
réglement (m)	*(reh-glœh-mÃh)*	settlement
règlement intégral	*(reh-glœh-mÃh æhn-teh-grAhl)*	payment in full
réglementation (f)	*(reh-glœh-mãhn-tah-syÕh)*	regulation
réglementation à l'exportation	*(reh-glœh-mãhn-tah-syÕh ah lehks-pohr-tah-syÕh)*	export regulations
réglementation d'urbanisation	*(reh-glœh-mãhn-tah-syÕh doohr-bah-neeh-zah-syÕh)*	zoning law
réglementations (fpl) à l'importation	*(reh-glœh-mãhn-tah-syÕh ah læhm-pohr-tah-syÕh)*	import regulations
réglementations phytosanitaire	*(reh-glœh-mãhn-tah-syÕh feeh-toh-sah-neeh-tEhr)*	phytosanitary regulations
régler	*(reh-glEh)*	pay off(v), settle a bill
reinvestissement (m)	*(reh-æhn-vehs-teehs-mÃh)*	plow back (earnings)
relance (f) (par l'augmentation de la masse monétaire)	*(rœh-lÃhns pahr lohg-mãhn-tah-syÕh dœ lah mAhs moh-neh-tEhr)*	reflation
relancer	*(rœh-lãhn-sEh)*	follow up (v)
relations (fpl) avec les investisseurs	*(rœh-lah-syÕh ah-vEhk lehz æhn-vehs-teeh-sŒhr)*	investor relations
relations industrielles	*(rœh-lah-syÕh æhn-doohs-tryEhl)*	industrial relations
relations professionnelles	*(rœh-lah-syÕh proh-feh-syoh-nEhl)*	labor relations, employee relations

R

relations publiques	*(rœh-lah-syÕh pooh-blEEhk)*	public relations
relaxant (m) musculaire	*(reh-lahk-sÃhn moohs-kooh-lEhr)*	muscle relaxant
relecture (f)	*(rœh-lehk-tOOhr)*	proofreading
relevé (m) bancaire	*(rœh-lœh-vEh bãhn-kEhr)*	bank statement
relevé d'exploitation	*(rœh-lœh-vEh dehks-plwah-tah-syÕh)*	operating statement
relevé de compte	*(rœh-lœh-vEh dœ kÕhnt)*	statement of account
relevé pro forma	*(rœh-lœh-vEh proh fOhr-mah)*	pro forma statement
relevé provisoire	*(rœh-lœh-vEh proh-veeh-zwAhr)*	interest statement
reliquat (m)	*(reh-leeh-kAh)*	remainder, balance
reliure (f)	*(rœh-lyOOhr)*	perfect binding
remboursement (m)	*(rãhm-boohrs-mÃh)*	refund
remboursement anticipé	*(rãhm-boohrs-mÃh ãhn-teeh-seeh-pEh)*	advance refunding
remboursement des dépenses	*(rãhm-boohrs-mÃh deh deh-pãhns)*	recovery of expenses
remboursement lors de l'exportation des droits de douane payés à l'importation	*(rãhm-boohrs-mÃh lohr dœ lehks-pohr-tah-syÕh deh drwAh dœ dooh-Ahn pah-yEh ah lœhm-pohr-tah-syÕh)*	drawback
remboursement obligatoire	*(rãhm-boohrs-mÃh oh-bleeh-gah-twAhr)*	mandatory redemption
rembourser	*(rãhm-boohr-sEh)*	reimburse (v), repay (v)
rembourser un prêt	*(rãhm-boohr-sEh œhn prEht)*	pay back a loan (v)
remèdes (mpl)	*(rœh-mEhd)*	remedies
remerciement (m)	*(rœh-mœhr-seeh-mÃh)*	acknowledgment
remise (f)	*(rœh-mEEhz)*	rebate
remise à l'unité	*(rœh-mEEhz ah looh-neeh-tEh)*	unit load discount
remise de droits	*(rœh-mEEhz dœ drwAh)*	duty remission
remise pour quantité importante	*(rœh-mEEhz poohr kãhn-teeh-tEh œhm-pohr-tÃhnt)*	volume discount, quantity discount
remplacer	*(rãhm-plah-sEh)*	supersede (v)
remplir les obligations	*(rahm-plEEhr lehz oh-bleeh-gah-syÕhn)*	fulfill the obligations (v)
rémunération (f)	*(reh-mooh-neh-rah-syÕh)*	remuneration, compensation
rémunération du capital	*(reh-mooh-neh-rah-syÕh dooh kah-peeh-tAhl)*	return on capital
renard (m)	*(rœh-nAhr)*	fox

rendement (m)	*(rāhnd-mÃh)*	output, throughput, earnings yield, yield
rendement à l'échéance	*(rāhnd-mÃh ah leh-sheh-Ãhns)*	yield to maturity
rendement brut	*(rāhnd-mÃh brOOh)*	gross yield
rendement courant	*(rāhnd-mÃh kooh-rÃhn)*	current yield
rendement d'un dividende	*(rāhnd-mÃh doohn deeh-veeh-dÃhnd)*	dividend yield
rendement d'un investissement	*(rāhnd-mÃh dœhn ǣhn-vehs-teehs-mÃh)*	return on investment
rendement des fonds propres	*(rāhnd-mÃh deh fÕhn prOh-prœ)*	earning on assets
rendement des investissements	*(rāhnd-mÃh dehz ǣhn-vehs-teehs-mÃh)*	return on investment
rendement du capital	*(rāhnd-mÃh dooh kah-peeh-tAhl)*	return on capital
rendement du capital propre	*(rāhnd-mÃh dooh kah-peeh-tAhl prOh-prœ)*	return on equity
rendement du revenu	*(rāhnd-mÃh dooh rœhv-nOOh)*	income yield
rendement forfaitaire	*(rāhnd-mÃh fohr-feh-tEhr)*	flat yield
rendement marginal	*(rāhnd-mÃh mahr-zheeh-nAhl)*	marginal revenue
rendement moyen	*(rāhnd-mÃh mwah-yEhn)*	fair return
rendement nominal	*(rāhnd-mÃh noh-meeh-nAhl)*	nominal yield
rendement réel	*(rāhnd-mÃh reh-Ehl)*	effective yield
rendement, à faible	*(rāhnd-mÃh, ah fEh-blœ)*	low-income
rendez-vous (m)	*(rāhn-deh-vOOh)*	appointment
renégocier	*(rœh-neh-goh-syEh)*	renegotiate (v)
renouveler	*(rœh-noohv-lEh)*	renew (v)
rénovation (f) des zones urbaines	*(reh-noh-vah-syÕh deh zÕhn oohr-bEhn)*	urban renewal
rentabilité (f)	*(rāhn-tah-beeh-leeh-tEh)*	profitability, earnings performance
rentabilité d'un produit	*(rāhn-tah-beeh-leeh-tEh dœhn proh-dwEEh)*	product profitability
rentabilité des capitaux	*(rāhn-tah-beeh-leeh-tEh deh kah-peeh-tOh)*	return on equity
rentabilité du capital investi	*(rāhn-tah-beeh-leeh-tEh dooh kah-peeh-tAhl ǣhn-vœhs-tEEh)*	return on assets managed
rentabilité, analyse de	*(rāhn-tah-beeh-leeh-tEh āh-nah-lEEhz dœ)*	break-even analysis
rentable	*(rāhn-tAh-blœ)*	cost effective, profitable
rente (f)	*(rāhnt)*	rent, interest income

rentes (fpl)	*(rãhnt)*	unearned revenue
rentier (m) (rentière)	*(rãh-tyEh), (rãh-tyEhr)*	annuitant
réorganisation (f)	*(reh-ohr-gah-neeh-zah-syÕh)*	reorganization
réparer	*(reh-pah-rEh)*	repair (v)
répartition (f)	*(reh-pahr-teeh-syÕh)*	allotment
répartition des coûts	*(reh-pahr-teeh-syÕh deh kOOht)*	allocation of costs
répartition des responsabilités	*(reh-pahr-teeh-syÕh deh ræs-pohn-sah-beeh-leeh-tEh)*	allocation of responsibilities
répartition des ressources	*(reh-pahr-teeh-syÕh deh ræh-sOOhrs)*	resource allocation
repasser commande	*(ræh-pah-sEh koh-mÃhnd)*	reorder (v)
repères (mpl)	*(ræh-pEhr)*	register marks
répertorier	*(reh-pehr-toh-ryEh)*	index (v)
répondant (m)	*(reh-põhn-dÃhn)*	sponsor (of fund, partnership)
répondre	*(reh-pÕhn-dræ)*	reply (v)
report (m)	*(ræh-pŒhr)*	carryover
report à nouveau	*(ræh-pŒhr ah nooh-vOh)*	carryforward
report sur exercice précédent	*(ræh-pŒhr soohr ehk-sær-sEEhs preh-seh-dÃh)*	carryback
reportage (m) des médias	*(ræh-pohr-tAhzh deh meh-dyAh)*	media coverage
reprendre possession	*(ræh-prÃhn-dræ poh-seh-syÕh)*	repossess (v)
représentant (m)	*(ræh-preh-zãhn-tÃh)*	representative
représentant agréé	*(ræh-preh-zãhn-tAh ah-grEh)*	registered representative
représentant exclusif	*(ræh-preh-zãhn-tÃh ehks-klooh-sEEhf)*	exclusive representative
représentation (f) mathématique	*(ræh-preh-zãhn-tah-syÕh mah-teh-mah-tEEhk)*	mathematical model
reprise (f) (économique)	*(ræh-prEEhz eh-koh-moh-mEEhk)*	boom, upturn, rally
réputation (f)	*(reh-pooh-tah-syÕh)*	goodwill
réseau (m)	*(reh-zOh)*	network
réseau (m) de distribution	*(reh-zOh dæ deehs-treeh-booh-syÕh)*	distribution network, channel of distribution
réseau (m) étendre à l'ensemble du	*(reh-zOh eh-tÃhn-dræ ah lãhn-sÃhm-blæ dooh)*	network (n)
réserve (f)	*(reh-sEhrv)*	store, reserve
réserves de base	*(reh-zEhrv dæ bAhz)*	primary reserves
réserves de sécurité	*(reh-zEhrv dæ seh-kooh-reeh-tEh)*	minimum reserves
réserves (fpl) d'or	*(reh-zEhrv dOhr)*	gold reserves
résidu (m)	*(reh-zeeh-dOOh)*	residue
réservoir (m)	*(reh-zehr-vwAhr)*	gasoline tank

R

résilier	*(reh-zeeh-lEh)*	terminate (v)
résistance (f)	*(reh-seehs-tÃhns)*	resistance
résolution (f)	*(reh-zoh-looh-syÕh)*	resolution (legal documents)
résolution des problèmes	*(reh-zoh-looh-syÕh deh proh-blEhm)*	problem solving
résonance (f)	*(reh-zoh-nÃhns)*	resonance
résonance (f) magnétique nucléaire (RMN)	*(reh-soh-nÃhns may-nyeh-tEEhk nooh-kleh-Ehr)*	MRI
respecter une disposition	*(rœhs-pehk-tEh ooh deehs-poh-zeeh-syÕhn)*	abide by the provision (v)
respirer	*(rœhs-peeh-rEh)*	breathe (v)
responsabilité (f)	*(rœs-pohn-sah-beeh-leeh-tEh)*	accountability, liability
responsabilité de l'acheteur	*(rœs-pohn-sah-beeh-leeh-tEh dœ lahsh-tŒhr)*	buyer's responsibility
responsabilité individuelle	*(rœs-pohn-sah-beeh-leeh-tEh ãhn-deeh-veeh-dwEhl)*	personal liability
responsabilité (f) limitée	*(rehs-pohn-sah-beeh-leeh-tEh leeh-meeh-tEh)*	limited liability
ressort (m)	*(rœh-sOhr)*	spring
ressortissant (m) de la CE	*(rœh-sohr-teeh-sÃhn dœ lah sEh)*	EC national
ressources (fpl) humaines	*(rœh-sOOhrs ooh-mEhn)*	human resources
ressources (fpl) naturelles	*(rœh-sOOhrs nah-tooh-rEhl)*	natural resources
ressources renouvelables	*(rœh-sOOhrs rœh-nooh-vAh-blœh)*	renewable resources
ressources soutenables	*(rœh-sOOhrs sooh-tœh-nAh-blœh)*	sustainable resources
restriction (f)	*(rœhs-treehk-syÕh)*	cutback
restrictions (fpl) à l'exportation	*(rœhs-treehk-syÕh ah ehks-pohr-tah-syÕh)*	restrictions on export
restructurer	*(rœh-stroohk-tooh-rEh)*	restructure (v)
résultats (mpl) attendus	*(reh-soohl-tAh ah-tãhn-dOOh)*	expected results
résumer	*(reh-zooh-mEh)*	summarize
retard (m)	*(rœh-tAhr)*	delay
retarder	*(rœh-tahr-dEh)*	delay (v)
retenue (f) à la source (impôts)	*(rœh-tœh-nOOh ah lah sOOhrs [ãhm-pOh])*	withholding tax
retenue à la source, système de	*(rœh-tœh-nOOh ah lah sOOhrs, seehs-tEhm dœ)*	pay as you go
retirer	*(rœh-teeh-rEh)*	drop out (v), withdraw (v)
retombée (f)	*(rœh-tõhm-bEh)*	spin-off
retrait (le)	*(rœh-trEht)*	withdrawal
retraite (f)	*(rœ-trEht)*	retirement
rétribution (f)	*(reh-treeh-booh-syÕh)*	reward, salary

rétroactif	*(reh-troh-ahk-tEEf)*	retroactive
rétrogradation (f)	*(reh-troh-grah-dah-syÕh)*	demotion
réunion (f)	*(reh-ooh-nyÕh)*	meeting
réunion (f) au sommet	*(reh-ooh-nyÕhn oh soh-mEhr)*	summit meeting
réunion du conseil	*(reh-ooh-nyÕh dooh kõhn-sEh-yœ)*	board meeting
réunion pléniaire	*(reh-ooh-nyÕh pleh-nyEhr)*	plenary meeting
réutilisable	*(reh-ooh-teeh-leeh-zAh-blœh)*	reusable
revendeur (m) de logiciel	*(rœh-vÃhn-dŒhr)*	software broker
revente (f)	*(rœ-vÃhnt)*	resale, back selling
revenu (de l'impôt, etc.)	*(rœhv-nOOh [dœ lœhm-pOh])*	revenue, earnings
revenu (m) (personnes)	*(rœhv-nOOh [pehr-sÕhn])*	income
revenu brut	*(rœhv-nOOh brOOh)*	gross income
revenu couru	*(rœhv-nOOh kooh-rOOh)*	accrued income
revenu d'exploitation	*(rœhv-nOOh dehks-plwah-tah-syÕh)*	operating income
revenu différé	*(rœhv-nOOh deeh-feh-rEh)*	differed income
revenu disponible	*(rœhv-nOOh deehs-poh-nEEh-blœ)*	disposable income
revenu libre d'impôt	*(rœhv-nOOh lEEh-brœ dœhm-pOh)*	tax-free income
revenu net	*(rœhv-nOOh nEht)*	net income
revenu réel	*(rœhv-nOOh reh-Ehl)*	real income, actual income
revenu salarial ajusté	*(rœhv-nOOh sah-lah-ryAl ah-zhOOhs-tEh)*	adjusted earned income
revitalizer	*(rœh-veeh-tah-leeh-zEh)*	invigorate (v)
richesse (f)	*(reeh-shEhs)*	wealth
ride (f)	*(rEEhd)*	wrinkle
ridule (f)	*(reeh-dOOhl)*	fine line
rincer	*(rœhn-sEh)*	rinse (v)
risque (m)	*(rEEhs-kœ)*	risk
risque consolidé	*(rEEhs-kœ kõh-soh-leeh-dEh)*	aggregate risk
risque de change	*(rEEhs-kœ dœ shÃhnzh)*	exchange risk
risque du métier	*(rEEhs-kœ dooh meh-tyEh)*	occupational hazard
risque du transporteur	*(rEEhs-kœ dooh trãhnz-pohr-tŒhr)*	carrier's risk
risque (m) pour la santé	*(rEEhsk poohr lah sãhn-tEh)*	health hazard
risque pur	*(rEEhs-kœ pOOhr)*	pure risk
robe (f)	*(rOhb)*	dress
robot (m)	*(roh-bOh)*	robot
robuste		robust
roman (m)	*(roh-mÃh)*	novel
rond (m) de serviette	*(rÕhnd dœ sœhr-vyEht)*	napkin ring

ronger la couche arable	*(rõhn-zhEh lah koohsh ah-rAh-blœh)*	erode top soil (v)
rosé (m)	*(roh-zEh)*	rosé wine
rotation (f) de l'actif	*(roh-tah-syÕh dœ ahk-tEEf)*	turnover asset
rotation des capitaux	*(roh-tah-syÕh deh kah-peeh-tOh)*	asset turnover
rotation des stocks	*(roh-tah-syÕh deh stocks)*	inventory turnover, stock turnover, movement of goods
rotative offset (f)	*(roh-tah-tEEhv offset)*	web offset
roue (f)	*(rOOh)*	wheel
roue de secours	*(rOOh dœ sœeh-kOOhr)*	spare tire
rouge (f) à lèvres	*(rOOhzh ah lEh-vrœh)*	lipstick
rougeur (f)	*(rOOh-zhŒhr)*	rash
routine (f)	*(rooh-tEEhn)*	routine

S

S.M.I.C. (m)	*(smeehk)*	Index-Linked Guaranteed Minimum Wage
sac (m) à main	*(sAhk ah mÆhn)*	handbag
sac de voyage	*(sAhk dœ vwah-yAhzh)*	tote bag
saccharine (f)	*(sah-kah-rEEhn)*	saccharin
saigner	*(seh-nyEh)*	bleed (v)
sain	*(sÆhn)*	healthy
saisie (f) des données	*(seh-zEEh deh doh-nEh)*	data acquisition
saisie-arrêt	*(seh-zEEh-ah-rEht)*	garnishment
saisir	*(seh-zEEhr)*	impound (v)
saisonnier	*(seh-soh-nyEh)*	seasonal
saladier (m)	*(sah-lay-dyEh)*	salad bowl
salaire (m)	*(sah-lEhr)*	wage
salaire minimum	*(sah-lEhr meeh-neeh-mOOhm)*	minimum wage
salaire net	*(sah-lEhr nEht)*	take-home pay
salaire réel	*(sah-lEhr reh-Ehl)*	real wages
salarié (m)	*(sah-lah-ryEh)*	wage earner
salière (f)	*(sah-lyEhr)*	salt shaker
salle (f) de conférence	*(sAhl dœ kõhn-feh-rÃhns)*	conference room
salle de conseil	*(sAhl dœ kõhn-sEh-yœ)*	board room
sang (m)	*(sÃhn)*	blood
sans alcool	*(sãhnz ahl-kOOhl)*	alcohol-free
sans défaut	*(sãhn deh-fOh)*	flawless
sans imperfection	*(sãhnz æhm-pehr-fehk-syÕhn)*	flawless
sans plomb	*(sãhn plÕhm)*	leadfree
sans problème	*(sãh proh-blEhm)*	no problem
sans risque	*(sãhn rEEhsk)*	risk-free

sans valeur	*(sãh vah-lŒhr)*	worthless
sans valeur nominale	*(sãh vah-lŒhr noh-meeh-nAhl)*	no par value
saponification (f)	*(sah-poh-neeh-feeh-kah-syÕh)*	saponification
sas (m)	*(sAhs)*	airlock
satellite (m)	*(sah-teh-lEEkt)*	satellite
satisfaction (f) des consommateurs	*(sah-teehs-fahk-syÕh deh kõhn-soh-mah-tŒhr)*	consumer satisfaction
saturation (f) du marché	*(sah-tooh-rah-syÕh dooh mahr-shEh)*	market saturation
saucière (f)	*(soh-syEhr)*	gravy boat
sauvegarde (f)	*(sohv-gAhrd)*	safeguard
savoir-faire (m)	*(sah-vwAhr fEhr)*	know-how
savoureux	*(sah-vooh-rŒh)*	luscious
scanneur (m)	*(skah-nŒhr)*	scanner
scaphandre (m)	*(skah-fAhn-drœh)*	spacesuit
scintigraphie (f) osseuse	*(sæhn-teeh-grah-fEEh)*	bone scan
seau (m) à glace	*(sOh ah glAhs)*	ice bucket
sec	*(sEhk)*	dry
sécheresse (f)	*(seh-shoeh-rEhs)*	drought
secrétaire (m/f)	*(seh-kreh-tEhr)*	secretary
secrétaire de direction	*(seh-kreh-tEhr dœ deeh-rehk-syÕh)*	executive secretary
secteur (m) de vente	*(sehk-tŒhr dœ vÃhnt)*	sales territory
secteur public	*(sehk-tŒhr pooh-blEEhk)*	public sector
sécurité (f)	*(seh-kooh-reeh-tEh)*	security
sécurité de l'emploi	*(seh-kooh-reeh-tEh dãhm-plwAh)*	job security
sédatif	*(seh-dah-tEEhf)*	sedative
segment (m)	*(sehg-mÃh)*	ring
sel (m)	*(sEhl)*	salt
selle (f) de cheval	*(sEhl dœ shœh-vAhl)*	saddle
sellier (m)	*(seh-lyEh)*	saddler
sels (mpl)	*(sEhl)*	salts
semi-conducteur (m)	*(sœh-meeh-kõhn-doohk-tŒhr)*	semiconductor
semis (mpl)	*(sœh-mEEh)*	semis
séparation (f)	*(seh-pah-rah-syÕh)*	separation
séparation (f) couleur	*(seh-pah-rah-syÕh kooh-lŒhr)*	color separation
seringue (f)	*(sœh-rÆhng)*	syringe
serre-papier (m)	*(sehr-pah-pyEh)*	paper holder
sérum (m)	*(seh-rOOhm)*	serum
service (m)	*(sehr-vEEhs)*	department, dinnerware set
service après-vente	*(sœr-vEEhs ah-prEh-vÃhnt)*	after-sales service
service clients	*(sœr-vEEhs kleeh-Ãhn)*	customer service
service de comptabilité	*(sœr-vEEhs dœ kõhn-tah-beeh-leeh-tEh)*	accounting department

S

service de conseil	*(sær-vEEhs dæ kõhn-sEh-yœ)*	advisory service
service (m) de création	*(sæhr-vEEhs dæ kreh-ah-syÕhn)*	art department
service de documentation	*(sær-vEEhs dæ doh-kooh-mÃh-tah-syÕh)*	advisory service
service de ferroutage	*(sær-vEEhs dæ feh-rooh-tAhzh)*	piggyback service
service de livraison approuvé	*(sær-vEEhs dæ eeh-vreh-zÕh ah-prooh-vEh)*	approved delivery facility
service des ventes	*(sær-vEEhs deh vÃhnt)*	sales management
service du courrier	*(sær-vEEhs dooh kooh-ryEh)*	courier service
service du logement	*(sær-vEEhs dooh lohzh-mÃh)*	housing authority
service du personnel	*(sær-vEEhs dooh pehr-soh-nEhl)*	personnel department
service mer-route	*(sær-vEEhs mehr-rOOht)*	fishy-back service
service public	*(sær-vEEhs pooh-blEEhk)*	public utility
services (mpl) d'intendance	*(sær-vEEhs dæhn-tãhn-dÃhns)*	supply services
services financiers	*(sær-vEEhs feeh-nãhn-syEh)*	financial services
serviette (f)	*(sæhr-vyEht)*	napkin
session (f) pleinière	*(seh-syÕhn pleh-nyEhr)*	plenary session
seuil (m) de rentabilité	*(sŒhyœ dæ rãhn-tah-beeh-leeh-tEh)*	break-even point
sida (m)	*(sEEh-dah)*	AIDS
siège (m)	*(syEhzh)*	seat
siège (m) éjectable	*(syEhzh eh-zhehk-tAh-blœh)*	ejection seat
siège opérationnel	*(syEhzh oh-peh-rah-syoh-nEhl)*	operations headquarters
siège social	*(syEhzh soh-syAhl)*	headquarters, head office
sigle (m)	*(sEEh-glœ)*	acronym
signature (f)	*(seehg-nah-tOOhr)*	signature
signature autorisée	*(seehg-nah-tOOhr oh-toh-reeh-zEh)*	authorized signature
silicone (f)	*(seeh-leeh-kÕh)*	silicon
simuler	*(seeh-mooh-lEh)*	simulate (v)
sinus (m)	*(seeh-nOOhs)*	sinus
sirop pour (m) la toux	*(seeh-rOhp poohr la tOOh)*	cough syrup
situation (f) de non-endettement	*(seeh-twah-syÕh dæ nõhn-ãhn-deht-mÃh)*	debtlessness
slogan (m)	*(sloh-gÃhn)*	slogan
smoking (m)		tuxedo
sociétaire (m/f)	*(soh-syeh-tEhr)*	member of firm
société (f)	*(soh-syeh-tEh)*	corporation, company

société à capitaux étrangers	*(soh-syeh-tEh ah kah-peeh-tOh eh-trãhn-zhEh)*	foreign corporation
société affiliée	*(soh-syeh-tEh ah-feeh-lyEh)*	associate company
société anonyme par actions	*(soh-syeh-tEh ah-noh-nEEhm pahr ahk-syÕh)*	public company, joint stock company
société commerciale en nom collectif	*(soh-syeh-tEh koh-mehr-syAhl ãhn nOhm koh-lehk-tEEhv)*	general partnership
société d'investissement	*(soh-syeh-tEh dæ̃hn-vehs-teehs-mÃhn)*	investment company
société d'investissement à capital variable (SICAV)	*(soh-syeh-tEh dæan-vehs-teehs-mÃhn ah kah-peeh-tAhl vah-ryAh-blœ)*	mutual fund
société de cautionnement	*(soh-syeh-tEh dœ koh-syohn-mÃh)*	surety company, guaranty company
société de commerce	*(soh-syeh-tEh dœ koh-mEhrs)*	trading company
société de financement	*(soh-syeh-tEh dœ feeh-nãhns-mÃh)*	finance company
société de gestion active	*(soh-syeh-tEh dœ zhœhs-tyÕh ahk-tEEhv)*	living trust
société de portefeuille	*(soh-syeh-tEh dœ pohrt-fŒhyœ)*	holding company
société en commandite	*(soh-syeh-tEh ãhn koh-mahn-dEEht)*	limited partnership
société étrangère	*(soh-syeh-tEh eh-trãhn-zhEhr)*	foreign corporation, alien corporation
société multinationale	*(soh-syeh-tEh moohl-teeh-nah-syoh-nAhl)*	multinational corporation
société nationale	*(soh-syeh-tEh nah-syoh-nAhl)*	domestic corporation
société quasi-publique	*(soh-syeh-tEh kah-zeeh-pooh-blEEhk)*	quasi-public company
soie (f)	*(swAh)*	silk
soins (mpl) prénataux	*(swÆhn preh-nah-tOh)*	prenatal care
soirie (f)	*(swah-rEEh)*	silk factory
soiries (mpl)	*(swah-rEEh)*	silk goods
soldat (m)	*(sohl-dAh)*	soldier
solde (m) créditeur	*(sOhld kreh-deeh-tŒr)*	credit balance
solde à l'entrée	*(sOhld ah lãhn-trEh)*	opening balance
solde d'application d'une opération d'échange	*(sOhld dah-pleeh-kah-syÕh doohn oh-peh-rah-syÕh deh-shÃhnzh)*	applied proceeds swap
solde d'un compte	*(sOhld dæhn kÕhnt)*	account balance
solde de caisse	*(sOhld dœ kEhs)*	cash balance
solde de roulement	*(sOhld dœ roohl-mÃh)*	working balance
solde en banque	*(sOhld ãhn bÃhnk)*	bank balance

S

soldes (mpl)	*(sOhld)*	job lot
solubilité (f)	*(soh-looh-beeh-leeh-tEh)*	solubility
souillé	*(swee-yEh)*	spoiled
soluté (m)	*(soh-looh-tEh)*	solute
solution (f)	*(soh-looh-syÕh)*	solution
solvabilité (f)	*(sohl-vah-beeh-leeh-tEh)*	solvency, financial standing
solvant (m)	*(sohl-vÃh)*	solvent
somme (f)	*(sOhm)*	amount
somme due	*(sOhm dooh)*	amount due
sommelier (m)	*(soh-mœh-lyEh)*	wine steward
somnifère (m)	*(sohm-nee-fEhr)*	sleeping pill
somnolence (f)	*(sohm-noh-lÃhns)*	drowsiness
son (m)	*(sÕh)*	sound
sondage (m)	*(sõhn-dAhzh)*	public opinion poll
sortie (f) d'ordinateur	*(sohr-tEEh dohr-deeh-nah-tŒhr)*	computer output
soucoupe (f)	*(sooh-kOOhp)*	saucer
soumission (f)	*(sooh-meeh-syÕh)*	tender, sealed bid
soupage (f)	*(sooh-pAhzh)*	valve
soupière (f)	*(sooh-pyEhr)*	soup tureen
souple	*(sOOh-plœh)*	supple
source (f) digne de confiance	*(sOOhrs dEEh-nyœ dœ kõhn-feeh-Ãhns)*	reliable source
sourcil (m)	*(soohr-sEEhl)*	eyebrow
souris (f)	*(sooh-rEEh)*	mouse
sous directeur	*(sooh-deeh-rehk-tŒhr)*	assistant manager
sous les réserves d'usage	*(sooh leh reh-zEhrv dooh-zAhz)*	as, if and when
sous réserve de disponibilité	*(sooh reh-zEhrv dœ deehs-poh-neeh-beeh-leeh-tEh)*	subject to availability
sous-capitalisé	*(sooh-kah-peeh-tah-leeh-zEh)*	undercapitalized
sous-estimer	*(soohs-ehs-teeh-mEh)*	underestimate (v)
sous-évaluer	*(soohs-eh-vah-looh-Eh)*	undervalue (v)
sous-louer	*(sooh-looh-Eh)*	sublet (v)
sous-main (m)	*(sooh-mÆhn)*	blotter
sous-payé	*(sooh-pah-yEh)*	underpaid
sous-produit (m)	*(sooh-proh-dwEEh)*	by-product
sous-traitant (m)	*(sooh-treh-tÃh)*	subcontractor
souscripteur (m) d'assurance	*(sooh-skreehp-tŒhr dah-sooh-rÃhns)*	insurance underwriter
soussigné	*(sooh-seeh-nyEh)*	undersigned
soustraitance, donner en	*(sooh-treh-tÃhns, doh-nEh ãhn)*	farm out (v)
soutenir une entreprise	*(sooh-tœh-nEEhr ooh ãhn-trœh-prEEhz)*	back a venture (v)
soutien (m)	*(sooh-tyÆh)*	backing, support
soutien des prix	*(sooh-tyÆh deh prEEh)*	price support

S

soutien (m) financier	*(sooh-tyÊhn feeh-nãhn-syEh)*	financial backing
soutirer	*(sooh-teeh-rEh)*	draw off
souveraineté (f)	*(sooh-vrǽhn-tEh)*	sovereignty
soyeux (mpl)	*(swah-yŒh)*	silk manufacturers (Lyon), silky
spécialiste en certaines valeurs	*(speh-syah-lEEhst ãhn sæhr-tEhn vah-lŒhr)*	specialist (stock exchange)
spécialité (f) (d'une affaire)	*(speh-syah-leeh-tEh doohn ah-fEhr)*	line of business
spécimen (m)	*(speh-seeh-mEhn)*	complimentary copy
spectre (m)	*(spEhk-træ)*	spectrum
spéculateur (m)	*(speh-kooh-lah-tŒhr)*	speculator
spirale (f) des prix et des salaires	*(speeh-rAhl deh prEEh eh deh sah-lEhr)*	wage-price spiral
spot (m) publicitaire	*(spoht pooh-bleeh-seeh-tEhı)*	commercial
stagflation (f)	*(stahg-flah-syÕh)*	stagflation
stagiaire (m/f)	*(stah-zhEhr)*	trainee
station (f) d'observation	*(stah-syÕhn dohb-sehr-vah-syÕhn)*	tracking station
station (f) spatiale	*(stah-syÕhn spah-syAhl)*	space station
statistique (f)	*(stah-teehs-tEEhk)*	statistics
statut (m)	*(stah-tOOh)*	statute
statuts (d'une société)	*(stah-tOOh doohn soh-syeh-tEh)*	by-laws
stellage (m)	*(steh-lAhzh)*	put and call
stéréophonique	*(steh-reh-oh-foh-nEEhk)*	stereophonic
stimulant (m)	*(steeh-mooh-lÃh)*	incentive, stimulant
stimulant financier	*(steeh-mooh-lÃh feeh-nãhn-syEh)*	financial incentive
stipuler que	*(steeh-pooh-lEh kœh)*	provide that (v)
stock (m)		stock
stock de roulement	*(stock dœ roohl-mÃh)*	turnover stock
stock des produits finis	*(stock deh proh-dwEEh feeh-nEEh)*	finished goods inventory
stocks (mpl)	*(stocks)*	inventory
stocks et fournitures en magasin et fabrications en cours	*(stocks eh foohr-neeh-tOOhr ãhn mah-gah-zÃhn eh fah-breeh-kah-syÕh ãhn kOOhr)*	stock-in-trade
stratégie (f) de l'entreprise	*(strah-teh-zhEEh dœ lãhn-træh-prEEhz)*	business strategy
stratégie de l'investissement	*(strah-teh-zhEEh dãhn-vehs-teehs-mÃh)*	investment strategy
stratégie (f) publicitaire	*(strah-teh-zhEEh pooh-bleeh-seeh-tEhr)*	advertising strategy
structure (f) de l'entreprise	*(stroohk-tOOhr dãhn-træh-prEEhz)*	corporate structure

S

structure des salaires	*(stroohk-tOOhr deh sah-lEhr)*	wage structure
structure du capital	*(stroohk-tOOhr dooh kah-peeh-tAhl)*	capital structure
stupefiant (m)	*(stooh-peh-feeh-Ãh)*	drug
style (m)	*(stEEhl)*	style
styliste (f)	*(steeh-lEEhst)*	stylist
subalterne (en descendant la voie hiérarchique)	*(soohb-ahl-tEhrn ãhn deh-sãhn-dÃhn lah vwAh yeh-rahr-kEEhk)*	down the line
subtile	*(soohb-tEEhl)*	subtle
subvention (f)	*(soohb-vãhn-syÕhn)*	subsidy
subventionner	*(soohb-vãhn-syoh-nEh)*	subsidize (v)
succulent		luscious
succursale (f)	*(sooh-koohr-sAhl)*	branch office
sucrier (m)	*(sooh-kryEh)*	sugar bowl
suède (m)	*(swEhd)*	suede
suivant avis	*(sweeh-vÃh ah-vEEh)*	as per advice
sulfamide (m)	*(soohl-fah-mEEhd)*	sulphamide
sulfhydrate (m)	*(soohlf-eeh-drAht)*	hydrosulfate
sulfiter	*(soohl-feeh-tEh)*	sulfite (n)
super alliages (mpl)	*(sooh-pehr ah-lyAhzh)*	super alloys
super-dividende (m)	*(super-deeh-veeh-dÃhnd)*	extra dividend
superficie (f) maximale de terrains dont la production ouvre droit à subvention	*(sooh-pehr-feeh-sEEh mahk-seeh-mAhl dœ tœ-rÆhn dÕhn lah proh-doohk-syÕh OOh-vrœ drwAh ah soohb-vãhn-syÕh)*	acreage allotment
supprimer	*(sooh-preeh-mEh)*	delete, cancel
supprimer les contrôles douaniers	*(sooh-preeh-mEh leh kõhn-trOhl dooh-ah-nyEh)*	remove frontier controls (v)
supprimer peu à peu	*(sooh-preeh-mEh pœh ah pœh)*	phase out (v)
sur demande	*(soohr dœh-mÃhnd)*	at call, on demand
sur le tas	*(soohr lœ tAh)*	on-the-job training
sur-souscrit	*(soohr sooh-skrEEh)*	oversubscribed
surcapitalisé	*(soohr-kah-peeh-tah-leeh-zEh)*	overcapitalized
surcharge (f)	*(soohr-shAhrzh)*	surcharge, overcharge
surenchérir	*(sooh-rãhn-sheh-rEEhr)*	outbid (v)
surestarie (f)	*(sooh-rehs-tah-rEEh)*	demurrage, layday
surévalué	*(sooh-reh-vah-lwEh)*	overvalued
surpayé	*(soohr-pah-yEh)*	overpaid
surplomb (m)	*(soohr-plOhm)*	overhang
surplus de stock (m)	*(soohr-plOOh dœ stock)*	overstock
surplus (m) en capital	*(soohr-plOOh ãhn kah-peeh-tAhl)*	capital surplus
surplus versé	*(soohr-plOOh vehr-sEh)*	paid-in surplus

surtaxe (f)	*(soohr-tAhks)*	surtax
surveiller	*(soohr-veh-yEh)*	monitor (v)
survendu	*(soohr-vãhn-dOOh)*	overbought
susmentionné	*(soohs-mãhn-syoh-nEh)*	abovementioned
suspendu (le règlement, la règlementation)	*(soohs-pãhn-dOOh), (reh glœh-mÃh), (reh-glœh-mãhn-tah-syÕh)*	deregulated
suspension (f)	*(soohs-pãhn-syÕh)*	suspension
symptome (m)	*(sãehmp-tOhm)*	symptom
syndicat (m)	*(seehn-deeh-kAh)*	syndicate
syndicat de crédit	*(seehn-deeh-kAh dœ kreh-dEEh)*	credit union
syndicat industriel	*(seehn-deeh-kAh ãehn-doohs-tryEhl)*	industrial union
syndicat ouvrier	*(seehn-deeh-kAh ooh-vryEh)*	trade union, labor union
synthèse (f)	*(seehn-tEhz)*	synthesis
synthétique	*(sãehn-teeh-tEEhk)*	synthetic
système (m) de direction intégré	*(seehs-tEhm dœ deeh-rehk-syÕh ãehn-teh-grEh)*	integrated management system
système (m) de guidage	*(seehs-tEhm dœ geeh-dAhzh)*	guidance system
système des contingents	*(seehs-tEhm dœ kõhn-teehn-zhÃhn)*	quota system
système (m) immunitaire	*(seehs-tEhm eeh-mooh-neeh-tEhr)*	immune system
système (m) monétaire européen	*(seehs-tEhm moh-neh-tEhr eh-ooh-roh-peh-Ehn)*	European Monetary System

T

table des matières	*(tAh-blœ deh mah-tyEhr)*	table of contents
tableau (m) de bord	*(tah-blOh dœ bOhr)*	management chart, instrument panel
tableau de gestion	*(tah-blOh dœ zhœhs-tyÕh)*	management chart
tableau électronique	*(tah-blOh eh-lehk-troh-nEEhk)*	electronic whiteboard
tableau financier	*(tah-blOh feeh-nãhn-syEh)*	spreadsheet
tablette (f)	*(tah-blEht)*	tablet
taché	*(tah-shEh)*	blotchy
taffetas (m)	*(tah-feh-tAh)*	taffeta
taie (m) d'oreiller	*(tEh doh-reh-yEh)*	pillowcase
taille (f)	*(tAh-yœ)*	size
tailler	*(tah-yEh)*	cut (v)
tailleur (m)	*(tah-yŒhr)*	tailor
tanner	*(tah-nEh)*	tan (v)
tannerie (f)	*(tah-nœh-rEEh)*	tannery
tanneur (m)	*(tah-nŒhr)*	tanner
tannin (tanin) (m)	*(tah-nEEhn)*	tannin (tanin)

tantième (m)	*(tãhn-tyEhm)*	percentage of profit
tapis (m)	*(tah-pEEh)*	rug
tarif (m)	*(tah-rEEhf)*	tariff
tarif (m) de faible écoute	*(tah-rEEhf dœ fEl-blœh eh-kOOht)*	off-peak rate
tarif préférentiel	*(tah-rEEhf preh-feh-rãhn-syEhl)*	preferred tariff
tarif variable	*(tah-rEEhf vah-ryAh-blœ)*	flexible tariff
tarifs publicitaires (mpl)	*(tah-rEEhf pooh-bleeh-seeh-tEhr)*	advertising rates
tasse (f)	*(tAhs)*	cup
tasse (f) à thé	*(tahs ah tEh)*	teacup
taux (m)	*(tOh)*	rate
taux ajusté	*(tOh ah-zhOOhs-tEh)*	adjusted rate
taux central	*(tOh sãhn-trAhl)*	central rate
taux consenti	*(tOh kõhn-sãhn-tEEh)*	offered rate
taux d'acceptation	*(tOh Dahk-sehp-tah-syÕh)*	accession rate
taux d'approvisionnement	*(tOh dah-proh-veeh-zyohn-mÃh)*	feed ratio
taux (m) d'escompte	*(tOh deh-kÕhnt)*	discount rate
taux d'escompte bancaire préférentiel	*(tOh dehs-kÕhnt bãhn-kEhr preh-feh-rãhn-syEhl)*	prime rate
taux (m) d'intérêt	*(tOh dœhn-teh-rEh)*	interest rate
taux de base	*(tOh dœ bAhz)*	base rate
taux de base bancaire	*(tOh dœ bAhz bãhn-kEhr)*	bank rate
taux (m) de change	*(tOh dœ shÃhnzh)*	exchange rate
taux de change fixe	*(tOh dœ shÃhnzh fEEhks)*	fixed rate of exchange
taux de change flottant	*(tOh dœ shÃhnzh floh-tÃhn)*	floating exchange rate
taux de change multiple	*(tOh dœ shÃhnzh moohl-tEEh-plœ)*	multiple exchange rate
taux de croissance	*(tOh dœ krwah-sÃhns)*	growth rate
taux de l'argent au jour le jour	*(tOh dœ lahr-zhÃhn oh zhOOhr lœ zhOOhr)*	call rate
taux de majoration	*(tOh dœ mah-zhoh-rah-syÕh)*	rate of increase
taux de marge	*(tOh dœ mAhrzh)*	markup
taux de réescompte	*(tOh dœ reh-ehs-kÕhnt)*	rediscount rate
taux de rendement	*(tOh dœ rãhnd-mÃh)*	rate of return
taux de rendement du capital	*(tOh dœ rãhnd-mÃh dooh kah-peeh-tAhl)*	capital-output ratio
taux de rentabilité	*(tOh dœ rãhn-tah-beeh-leeh-tEh)*	rate of return
taux de rentabilité net	*(tOh dœ rãh-tah-beeh-lee-tEh)*	after-tax real rate of return
taux du jour	*(tOh dooh zhOOhr)*	current ratio
taux en vigueur	*(tOh ãhn veeh-nyŒhr)*	going rate
taux interne de rentabilité	*(tOh œhn-tEhrn dœ rãhn-tah-beeh-leeh-tEh)*	internal rate of return

T

taux mobile	(tOh moh-bEEhl)	floating rate
taux (m) préférentiel de l'escompte	(tOh preh-feh-rāhn-syEhl dœ lehs-kÕhnt)	prime rate
taux uniforme	(tOh ooh-neeh-fOhrm)	flat rate
taux variable	(tOh vah-ryAh-blœ)	variable rate
taxation (f)	(tahks-ah-syÕh)	taxation
taxe (f)	(tAhks)	tax, duty
taxe à l'achat	(tAhks ah lah-shAh)	sales tax
taxe à l'exportation	(tAhks ah lehks-pohr-tah-syÕh)	export tax
taxe à l'importation	(tAhks ah lǣhm-pohr-tah-syÕh)	import tax
taxe à la consommation	(tAhks ah lah kõhn-soh-mah-syÕh)	excise tax, use tax
taxe à la valeur ajoutée	(tAhks ah lahvah-lŒhr ah-zhooh-tEh)	value-added tax
taxe d'exportation	(tÃhks dehks-pohr-tah-syÕh)	export duty
taxe de luxe	(tAhks dœ lOOhks)	luxury tax
taxe sur le chiffre d'affaires	(tAhks soohr lœ shEEh-frœ dah-fEhr)	sales tax
technique (f) électrique	(tehk-nEEhk eh-lehk-trEEhk)	electrical engineering
technique pyramidale	(tehk-nEEhk peeh-rah-meeh-dAhl)	pyramiding
techniques (fpl) non-polluantes	(tehk-nEEhk nõhn poh-lwÃhnt)	clean technology
teindre	(tɛ̃hn-drœ)	dye (v)
teint (m)	(tɛ̃hnt)	complexion, tint
télécommande (f)	(teh-leh-koh-mÃhnd)	remote control
télécommunications (fpl)	(teh-leh-koh-mooh-neeh-kah-syÕh)	telecommunications
télétraitement (m)	(teh-leh-treht-mÃh)	teleprocessing
télévision (f)	(teh-leh-veeh-zyÕhn)	television
télévision (f) à câble	(teh-leh-veeh-zyÕh ah kAh-blœ)	cable television
télévision (f) par satellite	(teh-leh-veeh-zyÕhn pahr sah-teh-lEEht)	satellite TV
témoin	(teh-mwǢhn)	witness
température (f)	(tāhm-peh-rah-tOOhr)	temperature
temps (m) chômé	(tÃh shoh-mEh)	work stoppage
temps de présence	(tÃh dœ preh-zÃhns)	attended time
temps libre	(tÃh lEEh-brœ)	free time
temps mort	(tÃh mOhr)	downtime
temps normal	(tÃh nohr-mAhl)	standard time
temps partagé	(tÃh pahr-tah-zhEh)	time sharing
temps réel	(tÃh reh-Ehl)	real time
tendance (f)	(tahn-dÃhns)	trend
tendance (f) à la hausse	(tāhn-dÃhns ah lah Ohs)	upward trend
tendance future	(tāhn-dÃhns fooh-tOOhr)	wave of the future

T

tendances (fpl) du marché	*(tāhn-dÃhns dooh mahr-shEh)*	market trends, market forces
teneur (f)	*(tœh-nŒhr)*	content
teneur (f) en alcool	*(tœh-nŒhr āhn ahl-kOOhl)*	alcoholic content
teneur (f) en plomb	*(tœh-nŒhr āhn plÕhm)*	lead content
tenir au courant	*(tœ-nEEhr oh kooh-rÃhn)*	keep posted (v)
tenir compte de	*(tœ-nEEhr kÕhnt dœ)*	to take into account
tension (f) artérielle	*(tāhn-syÕhn ahr-teh-ryEhl)*	blood pressure
tension (f) des dirigeants	*(tāhn-syÕh deh deeh-reeh-zhÃh)*	management stress
termaillage (m)	*(tehr-mah-yAhzh)*	leads and lags
termes (mpl) de l'échange	*(tEhrm dœ leh-shÃhnzh)*	terms of trade
termes linéaires	*(tEhrm leeh-neh-Ehr)*	linear terms
terminal (m)	*(tehr-meeh-nAhl)*	terminal
terminal d'ordinateur	*(tehr-meeh-nAhl dohr-deeh-nah-tŒhr)*	computer terminal
terminer, se	*(tehr-meeh-nEh)*	terminate (v)
terre (f)	*(tEhr)*	land, earth
terreux	*(teh-rŒh)*	earthy
terrine (f)	*(teh-rEEhn)*	tureen
territoire (m)	*(teh-reeh-twAhr)*	territory
test en vue d'acceptation	*(test āhn vOOh dahk-sehp-tah-syÕh)*	acceptance test
testé par les dermatologues	*(tehs-tEh pahr leh dehr-mah-toh-lOhg)*	dermatologically tested
test psychologique	*(test seeh-koh-loh-zhEEhk)*	personality test
testament (m)	*(tehs-tah-mÃh)*	will
théière (f)	*(teh-yEhr)*	teapot
théorie (f) de portefeuille	*(teh-oh-rEEh dœ pohrt-fŒhyœ)*	theory portfolio
théorie keynésienne	*(teh-oh-rEEh keh-neh-zyEhn)*	Keynesian economics
thésaurisér	*(teh-zoh-reeh-zEh)*	hoard (v)
tiers porteur (m)	*(tyEhrs pohr-tŒhr)*	holder in due course
tirage (f)	*(teeh-rAhzh)*	print run, circulation
tirage à découvert	*(teeh-rAzh ah deh-kooh-vEhrt)*	kiting
tiré (m) d'un chèque	*(teeh-rEh dœhn shEhk)*	drawee
tiré d'une traite	*(teeh-rEh doohn trEht)*	drawer
tire-bouchon (m)	*(teehr booh-shÕhn)*	corkscrew
tirer	*(teeh-rEh)*	fire (v)
tirer une cuve	*(teeh-reh oohn kOOhv)*	draw off (v)
tireur (m)	*(teeh-rŒhr)*	maker (check, draft, etc.)
tireur d'un chèque	*(teeh-rŒhr dœhn shEhk)*	drawer
tireur d'une traite	*(teeh-rŒhr doohn trEht)*	drawer
tisserand (m)	*(teeh-sœh-rÃh)*	weaver
tissu (m)	*(teeh-sOOh)*	fabric

tissus (mpl)	*(teeh-sOOh)*	soft goods
titane (m)	*(teeh-tAhn)*	titanium
titrage (m)	*(teeh-trAzh)*	titration
titre (d'une solution) (m)	*(tEEh-trœ)*	concentration
titre (m)	*(tEEh-trœ)*	title
titre de bourse	*(tEEh-trœ dœ bOOhrs)*	stock certificate
titre de priorité non cumulatif	*(tEEh-trœ dœ preeh-oh-reeh-tEh nõh kooh-mooh-lah-tEEhf)*	noncumulative preferred stock
titre de second ordre	*(tEEh-trœ dœ seh-kÕhnd Ohr-drœ)*	junior security
titre nominatif	*(tEEh-trœ noh-meeh-nah-tEEhf)*	registered security
titre privilégié de premier ordre	*(tEEh-trœ preeh-veeh-leh-zhyEh dœ prœh-myEh Ohr-drœ)*	first preferred stock
titre sans frais de commission	*(tEEh-trœ sãh frEh dœ koh-meeh-syÕh)*	no-load fund
titres (mpl)	*(tEEh-trœ)*	securities, stock
titres en circulation	*(tEEh-trœ ãhn seehr-kooh-lah-syÕh)*	outstanding stock
titres négociables	*(tEEh-trœ neh-goh-syAh-)blœ)*	negotiable securities
titres privilégiés de participation	*(tEEh-trœ preeh-veeh-leh-zhyEh dœ pahr-teeh-seeh-pah-syÕh)*	participating pre-ferred stock
titres réalisables	*(tEEh-trœ reh-ah-leeh-zAh-blœ)*	marketable securities
titres sans droit de vote	*(tEEh-trœ sãh drwAh dœ vOht)*	nonvoting stock
titulaire (m) d'un passeport de la CE	*(teeh-tooh-lEhr doohn pahs-pOhr dœ lah sEh)*	EC passport holder
toile (f) cirée	*(twAhl seeh-rEh)*	oilcloth
toile de lin	*(twAhl dœ lEEhn)*	linen
toile écrue	*(twAhl eh-krOoh)*	unbleached linen
tôle (f)	*(tOhl)*	sheets
tôle (f) à chaudières	*(tOhl ah shoh-dyEhr)*	boilerplate
tolérance (f)	*(toh-leh-rÃhns)*	allowance
tonalité (f)	*(toh-nah-leeh-tEh)*	tone
tonicité (f)	*(toh-neeh-seeh-tEh)*	skin tone
tonnage (m)	*(toh-nAhzh)*	tonnage
tonne métrique	*(tOhn meh-trEEhk)*	long ton
tonnelier (m)	*(toh-neh-lyEh)*	cooper
tonneau (m)	*(toh-nOh)*	barrel
torchon (m)	*(tohr-shÕh)n*	dish towel
torpiller	*(tohr-peeh-yEh)*	torpedo (v)
touche (f)	*(tOOhsh)*	key
touche de commande	*(tOOhsh dœ koh-mÃhnd)*	control key
touche de fonction	*(tOOhsh dœ fõhnk-syÕhn)*	function key
tour (f) de contrôle	*(toohr dœ kõhn-trOhl)*	control tower

T

tournage (m)	*(toohr-nAhzh)*	shoot
tourner	*(toohr-nEh)*	shoot (film) (v)
tous frais compris	*(tooh frEh kõh-prEEh)*	all-in cost
tousser	*(tooh-sEh)*	cough (v)
toxicologie (f)	*(tohk-seeh-koh-loh-zhEEh)*	toxicology
toximanie (f)	*(tohk-seeh-mah-nEEh)*	drug addiction
toxine (f)	*(tohk-sEEhn)*	toxin
traction (f) avant	*(trahk-syÕh ah-vÃh)*	front-wheel drive
traducteur (m)	*(trah-doohk-tŒhr)*	translator
traite (f)	*(trEht)*	draft, bill of exchange
traité (m)	*(treh-tEh)*	treaty
traite à vue	*(trEht ah vOOh)*	sight draft
traite bancaire	*(trEht bãhn-kEhr)*	bank draft
traite de complaisance	*(trEht dœ kõhn-pleh-zÃhns)*	accommodation bill
traite documents contre acceptation	*(trEht doh-kooh-mÃh kõhn-trœ ahk-sehp-tah-syÕh)*	acceptance bill
traite intérieure	*(trEht ãehn-teh-reyŒhr)*	domestic bill
Traité (m) de Maastricht	*(treh-tEh dœ mehs-trEEhkt)*	Maastricht Treaty
traitement (m)	*(treht-mÃh)*	salary
traitement (m) de données	*(treht-mÃhn dœ don-nEh)*	data processing
traitemente (m) de longue durée	*(treht-mÃhn dœ lõhng dooh-rEh)*	long-term treatment
traitement de texte	*(treht-mÃhn dœ tEhkst)*	word processing
traitement (m) des eaux	*(treht-mÃh dehz Œh)*	water treatment
traiter	*(treh-tEh)*	process (v)
trame (f) de transmission	*(trAhm dœ trãhnz-meeh-syÕhn)*	transmission frame
tranche (f)	*(trÃhnsh)*	portion, installment, slice, range
tranche de revenus	*(trÃhnsh dœ rœhv-nOOh)*	income bracket
tranche (f) horaire	*(trÃhnsh oh-rEhr)*	time segment
transaction (f)	*(trãhn-zahk-syÕh)*	transaction, deal
transfert (m)	*(trãhnz-fEhr)*	transfer
transfert (m) des pouvoirs	*(trãhnz-fEhr deh pooh-vWAhr)*	transfer of powers
transfert télégraphique	*(trãhnz-fEhr teh-leh-graf-fEEhk)*	wire transfer, cable transfer
transformateur (m)	*(trãhnz-fohr-mah-tŒhr)*	transformer
transitaire (m)	*(trãhn-zeeh-tEhr)*	forwarding agent
transmetteur (m)	*(trãhnz-meht-tŒhr)*	transmitter
transmettre	*(trãhnz-mEh-trœ)*	assign (v)
transport (m) aérien	*(trãhns-pOhr ah-eh-ryÃhn)*	air shipments
transport ferroviaire	*(trãhns-pOhr feh-roh-vyEhr)*	railway transportation
transporteur (m)	*(trãhnz-pohr-tŒhr)*	conveyor, carrier

transporteur couvert par une caution	*(trãhnz-pohr-tŒhr kooh-vEhrt pahr oohn koh-syÕh)*	bonded carrier
transporteur public	*(trãhnz-pohr-tah-tŒhr pooh-blEEhk)*	common carrier
transporteur sous contrat	*(trãhnz-pohr-tŒhr kõhn-trAh)*	contract carrier
travail (m)	*(trah-vAhyœ)*	labor
travail à la pièce	*(trah-vAhyœ ah lah pyEhs)*	piecework
travail au noir	*(trah-vAhyœ oh nwAhr)*	moonlighting
travail indirect	*(trah-vAhyœ æhn-deeh-rEhkt)*	indirect labor
travail sous contrat	*(trah-vAhyœ sooh kõhn-trAh)*	work by contract
travailler	*(trah-vah-yEh)*	work (v)
travailleur (m)	*(trah-vah-yŒhr)*	laborer
travailleur à grande mobilité	*(trah-vah-yŒhr ah grÃhn moh-beeh-leeh-tEh)*	job hopper
travailleurs (mpl) manuels	*(trah-vah-yŒhr mah-nwEhl)*	manual workers, blue-collar workers
travaux (mpl) en cours	*(trah-vOh ãhn kOOhr)*	work in progress
travaux publics	*(trah-vOh pooh-blEEhk)*	public works
tremper	*(trãhm-pEh)*	quench (v)
trésorier (m)	*(treh-zoh-ryEh)*	treasurer
trésorier-payeur (m)	*(treh-zoh-ryEh pah-yŒhr)*	paymaster
trésorerie (f) positive	*(treh-soh-rœh-rEEh poh-zeeh-tEEhf)*	positive cash flow
trier	*(treeh-Eh)*	sort (v)
troc (m)	*(trOhk)*	barter
troisième guichet (m)	*(trwah-zyEhm geeh-shEht)*	third window
troquer	*(troh-kEh)*	barter (v)
trou (m) dans la couche d'ozone	*(trOOh dãhn lah kOOhsh doh-zOhn)*	hole in ozone layer
trou (m) noir	*(trooh nwAhr)*	black hole
trouble	*(trOOh-blœh)*	cloudy
trousse (f) à couture	*(trOOhs ah kooh-tOOhr)*	sewing kit
trousse à manucure	*(trOOhs ah mah-nah-kOOhr)*	manicuring kit
trousse à maquillage	*(trOOhs dœ mah-keeh-yAhzh)*	makeup case
trousse de toilette	*(trOOhs dœ twah-lEht)*	toilet kit
trucages (mpl) sonores	*(trooh-kAhzh soh-nOhr)*	sound effects
trust (m)		trust
tubes (mpl) et tuyauteries (fpl)	*(tOOhb eh tooh-yah-tœh-rEEh)*	pipes and tubes
tumeur (f) au cerveau	*(tooh-mŒhr oh sehr-vOh)*	brain tumor
tungstène (m)	*(toohng-stEhn)*	tungsten
tunnel sous la Manche (m)	*(tooh-nEhl sooh lah mÃhnsh)*	Channel tunnel

turbine (f)	(toohr-bEEhn)	turbine
tuyau (m)	(tooh-yOh)	tip (inside information)
typographie (f)	(teeh-poh-grah-fEEh)	letterpress

U

union (f) douanière	(ooh-nyÕh dooh-ah-nyEhr)	customs union
unité binaire (f)	(ooh-neeh-tEh beeh-nEhr)	bit
unité (f) centrale de traitement	(ooh-neeh-tEh sãhn-trAhl dœ treht-mÃh)	mainframe computer
unité de traitement centrale	(ooh-neeh-tEh dœ treht-mÃh sãhn-trAhl)	central processing unit
unité (f) monétaire	(ooh-neeh-tEh moh-neh-tEhr)	currency unit
urbanisation (f) effrénée	(oohr-bah-neeh-zah-syÕh eh-freh-nEh)	urban sprawl
urgence (f)	(oohr-zhÃhns)	emergency
usages (mpl) locaux	(ooh-zAhz loh-kOh)	local customs
usinage (m)	(ooh-zeeh-nAhzh)	machining
usine (f)	(ooh-zEEhn)	factory, plant
usine (f) de traitement	(ooh-zEEhn dœ treht-mÃhn)	recycling plant
usure (f) (d'une machine, etc.)	(ooh-zOOhr doohn mah-shEEhn)	wear and tear
usure (érosion)	(ooh-zOOhr [eh-roh-zyÕh])	attrition
usure (prêt avec intérêt)	(ooh-zOOhr [prEht ah-vEhk æhn-teh-rEh])	usury

V

V.P.C. (f) (vente par correspondance)	(vÃhnt pahr koh-rehs-põhn-dÃhns)	sale through mail order
vaccin (m)	(vahk-sÆhn)	vaccine
vachette	(vah-shEht)	cowhide
vaisseau (m) spatial	(veh-sOh spah-syAhl)	spacecraft
vaisselle (f)	(veh-sEhl)	dishes
valable	(vah-lAh-blœ)	valid
valeur (f)	(vah-lŒhr)	asset, value
valeur à neuf	(vah-lŒhr ah nŒhf)	replacement cost
valeur à revenu fixe	(vah-lŒhr ah ræhv-nOOh fEEhks)	fixed income security
valeur actuelle nette	(vah-lŒhr ahk-twElh nEht)	net present value
valeur au pair	(vah-lŒhr oh pEhr)	par value
valeur comptable	(vah-lŒhr kõhn-tAh-blœ)	book value
valeur comptable par action	(vah-lŒhr kõhn-tAh-blœ pahr ahk-syÕh)	book value per share

valeur d'échange	*(vah-lŒhr deh-shÃhnzh)*	exchange value
valeur de liquidation	*(vah-lŒhr dœ leeh-keeh-dah-syŌh)*	liquidation value, salvage value
valeur de premier ordre	*(vah-lŒhr dœ prœeh-myEh Ohr-drœ)*	gilt (Brit. govt. security)
valeur de rachat	*(vah-lŒhr dœ rah-shAh)*	cash surrender value
valeur douanière	*(vah-lŒhr dooh-ah-nyEhr)*	value for duty
valeur du chargement	*(vah-lŒhr dooh shahrzh-mÃh)*	carrying value
valeur en capital	*(vah-lŒhr ãhn kah-peeh-tAhl)*	asset value
valeur estimée	*(vah-lŒhr ehs-teeh-mEh)*	assessed valuation
valeur intrinsèque	*(vah-lŒhr ǽhn-trǽhn-sEhk)*	intrinsic value
valeur marchande	*(vah-lŒhr mahr-shÃhnd)*	market value
valeur marchande moyenne	*(vah-lŒhr mwah-yEhn)*	fair market value
valeur nette	*(vah-lŒhr nEht)*	net worth
valeur nette des placements en actions	*(vah-lŒhr nEht deh plahs-mÃh ãhn ahk-syŌh)*	net equity assets
valeur nominale	*(vah-lŒhr noh-meeh-nAhl)*	face value
valeur réelle au comptant	*(vah-lŒhr reh-Ehl oh kõhn-tÃhn)*	actual cash value
valeur résiduelle	*(vah-lŒhr reh-zeeh-dwEhl)*	salvage value
valeur saine	*(vah-lŒhr sEhn)*	going concern value
valeur (f) sûre	*(vah-lŒhr sOOhr)*	blue chip
valeurs (fpl)	*(vah-lŒhr)*	securities, stock
valeurs d'avenir	*(vah-lŒhr dah-vœh-nEEhr)*	growth stock
valeurs d'emprunt	*(vah-lŒhr dǽhm-prŒhnt)*	loan stock (govt. bonds)
valeurs de père de famille	*(vah-lŒhr dœ pEhr dœ fah-mEEh-yœ)*	safe investment
valeurs de premier ordre	*(vah-lŒhr dœ prœh-myEh Ohr-drœ)*	blue chip stock
valeurs de priorité cumulatives	*(vah-lŒhr dœ preeh-oh-reeh-tEh kooh-mooh-lah-tEEhv)*	cumulative preferred stock
valeurs de référence	*(vah-lŒhr dœ reh-feh-rÃhns)*	market-maker securities
valeurs étrangères	*(vah-lŒhr eh-trãhn-zhEhr)*	foreign securities
valeurs incorporelles	*(vah-lŒhr ǽhn-kohr-poh-rEhl)*	intangible assets
valeurs inscrites	*(vah-lŒhr ǽhn-skrEEht)*	listed securities
valeurs intangibles	*(vah-lŒhr ǽhn-tãhn-zhEEh-blœ)*	intangible assets
valeurs matérielles	*(vah-lŒhr mah-teh-ryEhl)*	tangible assets
valeurs mobilières	*(vah-lŒhr moh-beeh-lyEhr)*	stocks and bonds
valeurs non exigibles	*(vah-lŒhr nõhn ehk-seeh-zhEEh-blœ)*	noncurrent assets

valeurs privilégiées	*(vah-lŒhr preeh-veeh-leh-zhyEh)*	preferred stock
valeurs réalisables à court terme	*(vah-lŒhr reh-ah-leeh-zAh-blœ ah koohr tEhrm)*	accounts receivable
valeurs sûres	*(vah-lŒhr sOOhr)*	safe investment, blue chip
validation (f)	*(vah-leeh-dah-syŌh)*	probate
valider	*(vah-leeh-dEh)*	validate (v)
valise (f)	*(vah-lEEhz)*	suitcase
value nominale nette (valeur réelle nette)	*(vah-lOOh noh-meeh-nAhl nEht [vah-lŒhr reh-Ehl nEht])*	net asset value
vanadium (m)	*(vah-nah-dyOOhm)*	vanadium
vaporisateur (m)	*(vah-poh-reeh-zah-tŒhr)*	spray
vecteur (m)	*(vehk-tŒhr)*	vector
véhicule-plateau (m)	*(veh-eeh-kOOhl plah-tOh)*	flatcar
velouté	*(vœh-looh-tEh)*	velvety
vendanges (fpl)	*(vāhn-dAhzh)*	grape harvest
vendeur (m)	*(vĀhn-dŒhr)*	vendor
vendre	*(vĀhn-drœ)*	sell (v)
vendre directement	*(vĀhn-drœ deeh-rehkt-mĀh)*	sell direct (v)
vendre moins cher	*(vĀhn-drœ mwǼh shEhr)*	undercut (v)
vente (f) à découvert	*(vĀhnt ah deh-kooh-vEhr)*	short sale
vente à tempérament	*(vĀhnt ah tehm-peh-rah-mĀh)*	installment credit
vente au détail	*(vĀhnt oh deh-tAh-yœ)*	retail
vente aux enchères	*(vĀhnt oh āhn-shEhr)*	public auction
vente de choc	*(vĀhnt dœ shOhk)*	hard sell
vente directe	*(vĀhnt deeh-rEhkt)*	direct selling
vente (f) jumelée	*(vĀhnt zhooh-meh-lEh)*	composite package
vente négociée	*(vĀhnt neh-goh-syEh)*	negotiated sale
vente par correspondance	*(vĀhnt pahr koh-rehs-pōhn-dĀhns)*	direct mail
vente par des méthodes agressives	*(vĀhnt pahr deh meh-tOhd ah-greh-sEEhv)*	hard sell
vente par des méthodes de suggestion	*(vĀhnt deh meh-tOhd dœ sooh-zhœhs-tyŌh)*	soft sell
vente publique	*(vĀhnt pooh-blEEhk)*	public sale
vente pyramidale	*(vĀhnt peeh-rah-meeh-dAhl)*	pyramid selling
ventes (fpl)	*(vĀhnt)*	sales
ventes complémentaires	*(vĀhnt kōhn-pleh-mĀh-tEhr)*	add-on sales
ventes d'écoulement	*(vĀhnt deh-koohl-mĀh)*	turnover sales
ventes potentielles	*(vĀhnt poh-tāhn-syEhl)*	potential sales
ventes promotionnelles	*(vĀhnt proh-moh-syoh-nEhl)*	sales promotion
ver (m) à soie	*(vEhr ah swAh)*	silkworm
vérification (f)	*(veh-reeh-feeh-kah-syŌh)*	check

vérification annuelle	*(veh-reeh-feeh-kah-syÕh ah-nwEhl)*	annual audit
vérification des stocks	*(veh-reeh-feeh-kah-syÕh deh stocks)*	stock control
vérifier	*(veh-reeh-feeh-Eh)*	audit (v), check (v)
verre (m)	*(vEhr)*	glass
verre (m) à vin	*(vehr ah vÆhn)*	wine glass
verre soufflé	*(vEhr sooh-flEh)*	hand-blown glass
versement (m)	*(vehrs-mÃhn)*	installment
veste (f)	*(vEhst)*	blazer
vêtements (mpl)	*(vEht-mÃh)*	apparel
vêtements (mpl) de sport	*(veht-mÃh dœ spOhr)*	sportswear
vice-président (m)	*(veehs-preh-zeeh-dÃh)*	vice-president, deputy chairman
vide (m)	*(vEEhd)*	vacuum, void
vider	*(veeh-dEh)*	dump (v)
vie (f) économique	*(vEEh eh-koh-moh-mEEhk)*	economic life
vieillissement (m)	*(vyeh-yeehs-mÃh)*	obsolescence, aging
vieillissement calculé	*(vyeh-yeehs-mÃh kahl-kooh-lEh)*	planned obsolescence
vigneron (m), viticulteur (m)	*(veeh-nyeh-rÕh), (veeh-teeh-koohl-tŒhr)*	winegrower
vignoble (m)	*(veeh-nyOh-blœ)*	vineyard
VIH (m)	*(vay-ash-eeh)*	HIV
vilebrequin (m)	*(veehl-brœh-kEEhn)*	crankshaft
vin (m)	*(vÆhn)*	wine
vin (m) de cru	*(vÆhn dooh kr(Y(h)*	local wine
vin du terroir	*(vÆhn dooh teh-rwAhr)*	local wine
vin (m) mousseux	*(vÆhn mooh-sOh)*	sparkling wine
vin (m) sec	*(vÆhn sEhk)*	dry wine
virement (m) par câble	*(veehr-mÃh pahr kAh-blœ)*	cable transfer
virus (m)	*(veeh-rOOhs)*	virus
vison (m)	*(veeh-zÕh)*	mink
vitamine (f)	*(veeh-tah-mEEhn)*	vitamin
vitesse (f) de circulation	*(veeh-tEhs dœ seehr-kooh-lah-syÕh)*	velocity of money
viticulteur (m)	*(veeh-teeh-koohl-tŒhr)*	winemaker
viticulture (f)	*(veeh-teeh-koohl-tOOhr)*	viticulture
voie (f) hiérarchique	*(vwAh yeh-rahr-kEEhk)*	chain of command, official channels
voile (m)	*(vwah-lEht)*	veil
voiture (f)	*(vwah-tOOhr)*	car
volant (m)	*(voh-lÃhn)*	steering wheel
voler	*(voh-lEh)*	fly (v), steal
volonté (f)	*(voh-lõhn-tEh)*	will
voltage (m)	*(vohl-tAhzh)*	voltage
volume (m)	*(voh-lOOhm)*	volume
volume des ventes	*(voh-lOOhm deh vÃhnt)*	sales volume

volume réel du marché	*(voh-lOOhm reh-Ehl dooh mahr-shEh)*	actual market volume
vote (m) majoritaire	*(vOht mah-zhoh-reeh-tEhr)*	majority voting

W

watt (m)		watt

Z

zibeline (f)	*(zeeh-beh-lEEhn)*	sable
zinc (m)	*(zÆhnk)*	zinc
zone (f)	*(zOhn)*	zone
zone (f) d'exclusion aérienne	*(zohn dehk-sklooh-zyÕhn ah-eh-reeh-Ehn)*	no fly zone
zone franche	*(zOhn frÃhnsh)*	free zone
zones (fpl) d'entrepôt	*(zOhn dãhn-trœ-pOh)*	bond areas

V

KEY WORDS FOR KEY INDUSTRIES

The dictionary that forms the centerpiece of *French for the Business Traveler* is a compendium of more than 3,000 words that you are likely to use or encounter as you do business abroad. It will greatly facilitate fact-finding about the business possibilities that interest you, and will help guide you through negotiations as well as reading documents. To supplement the dictionary, we have added a special feature—groupings of key terms about sixteen industries. As you explore any of these industries, you'll want to have *French for the Business Traveler* at your fingertips to help make sure you don't misunderstand or overlook an aspect that could have a material effect on the outcome of your business decision. The industries covered in the vocabulary lists are the following:

- air/space/defense
- banking/finance/trading
- chemicals
- communications/advertising
- computers/electronic equipment
- cosmetics/beauty care
- environment
- European Community
- fashion
- home furnishings and tableware
- iron and steel
- leather goods
- motor vehicles
- pharmaceuticals/medical
- printing and publishing
- winemaking

AIR/SPACE/DEFENSE

English to French

aircraft	l'avion, l'appareil	*(ah-vyŌhn, ah-pah-rEhy)*
airlock	le sas	*(sAh)*
air-to-air missile	le missile air-air	*(meeh-sEEhl ehr-Ehr)*
air-to-surface missile	le missile air-sol	*(meeh-sEEhl ehr-sOhl)*
ally	l'allié	*(ah-yEh)*
ammunition	la munition	*(mooh-neeh-sŌhn)*
astronaut	l'astronaute	*(ahs-troh-nOht)*
auto-pilot	le pilote automatique	*(peeh-lOhl oh-toh-mah-tEEhk)*
automatic weapons	les armes automatiques	*(Ahrm oh-toh-mah-tEEhk)*
black hole	le trou noir	*(trooh nwAhr)*
blockade	le blocus	*(bloh-kOOh)*
bomb (v)	bombarder	*(bohm-bahr-dEh)*
bomber	le bombardier	*(bohm-bahr-dyEh)*
boost (v)	impulser, lancer	*(æhm-poohl-sEh), (lãhn-sEh)*
booster rocket	la fusée de lancement	*(fooh-zEh dœ lãhns-mÃhn)*
bullet	la balle	*(bAhl)*
cartridge	la cartouche	*(kahr-tOOsh)*
check (v)	vérifier, contrôler	*(veh-reeh-fyEh), (kõhn-troh-lEh)*
checklist	la liste de contrôle	*(lEEhst dœ kõhn-trOhl)*
cluster bomb	la bombe à fragmentation	*(bOhmb ah frahg-mãhn-tah-syŌhn)*
combat power	la puissance de combat	*(pweeh-sÃhns dœ kohm-bAh)*
command station	le poste de commandement	*(pOhst dœ koh-mãhnd-mÃhn)*
control tower	la tour de contrôle	*(toohr dœ kõhn-trOhl)*
convential warfare	la guerre conventionnelle	*(gEhr kõhn-vãhn-syoh-nEhl)*
countdown	le compte à rebours	*(kohmt ah ræh-bOOhr)*
defective	défectueux	*(deh-fehk-tŒh)*
delay (v)	retarder	*(ræh-tahr-dEh)*
demilitarize (v)	démilitariser	*(deh-meeh-leeh-tah-leeh-zEh)*
detonator	le détonateur	*(deh-toh-nah-tŒhr)*
device	le dispositif	*(deehs-poh-zeeh-tEEhf)*
disarmament	le désarmement	*(dehz-ahrmœh-mÃhn)*
ejection seat	le siège éjectable	*(syEhzh eh-zhehk-tAh-blœh)*
fall off (v)	se détacher	*(sœh deh-tah-shEh)*
fight (v)	lutter	*(looh-tEh)*
fire (v)	tirer	*(teeh-rEh)*

flight deck	la cabine de pilotage	*(kah-bEEhn dœ peeh-loh-tAhzh)*
fly (v)	voler	*(voh-lEh)*
fuselage	le fuselage	*(fooh-sœh-lAhzh)*
guidance system	le système de guidage	*(seehs-tEhm dœ geeh-dAhzh)*
gun fire	le feu d'artillerie	*(fœh dahr-teeh-yeh-rEEh)*
helicopter	l'hélicoptère	*(eh-leeh-kohp-tEhr)*
helmet	le casque	*(kAhsk)*
instrument panel	le tableau de bord	*(tah-blOh dœ bOhr)*
landing	l'atterrissage	*(ah-teh-reeh-sAhzh)*
laser guidance	guidage par laser	*(geeh-dAhzh pahr lah-zEhr)*
launch (v)	lancer	*(lãhn-sEh)*
long-range	à longue portée	*(ah lõhng pohr-tEh)*
machine gun	la mitrailleuse	*(meeh-trah-yŒhz)*
maintenance	l'entretien	*(ãhn-trœh-tyEhn)*
military	l'armée	*(ahr-mEh)*
monitor (v)	surveiller, observer	*(soohr-veh-yEh), (ohb-sehr-vEh)*
nerve gas	le gaz asphyxiant	*(gAhz ahs-feehks-yÃhn)*
no fly zone	la zone d'exclusion aérienne	*(zohn dehks-klooh-zyÕhn ah-eh-ryEhn)*
nuclear build-up	l'escalade des armes nucléaires	*(ehs-kah-lAhd dehz Ahrm nooh-kleh-Ehr)*
nuclear war	la guerre nucléaire	*(gEhr nooh-kleh-Ehr)*
peace-keeping force	la force de maintien de la paix	*(fohrs dœ mœhn-tyEhn dœ lah pEh)*
put into orbit (v)	mettre en orbite	*(mEht-rœh ãhn ohr-bEEht)*
remote control	la télécommande	*(teh-leh-koh-mÃhnd)*
retrieve (v)	récupérer	*(reh-kooh-peh-rEh)*
riot	l'émeute	*(eh-mŒht)*
runway	la piste	*(pEEhst)*
satellite	le satellite	*(sah-teh-lEEht)*
shell	l'obus	*(oh-bOOhs)*
short-range	à courte portée	*(ah koohrt pohr-tEh)*
shuttle	la navette	*(nah-vEht)*
soldier	le soldat	*(sohl-dAh)*
space station	la station spatiale	*(stah-syÕhn spah-syAhl)*
spacecraft	le vaisseau spatial	*(veh-sOh spah-syAhl)*
spacelab	le laboratoire spatial	*(lah-boh-rah-twAhr spah-syAhl)*
spacesuit	le scaphandre	*(skah-fAhn-drœh)*
spacewalk	la marche dans l'espace	*(mAhrsh dãhn leh-spAhs)*
take off (v)	décoller	*(deh-koh-lEh)*
tank	le char	*(ShAhr)*
torpedo (v)	torpiller	*(tohr-peeh-yEh)*
tracking station	la station d'observation	*(stah-syÕhn dœ ohb-sehr-vah-syÕhn)*
trigger (v)	déclencher	*(deh-klãhn-shEh)*

warhead	l'ogive	(oh-zhEEhv)
warship	le navire de guerre	(nah-vEEhr dœ gEhr)
weapon	l'arme	(Ahrm)
weightlessness	l'apesanteur	(ah-peh-sãh-tŒhr)

French to English

à courte portée	(ah koohrt pohr-tEh)	short-range
à longue portée	(ah lõhng pohr-tEh)	long-range
allié (m)	(ah-lyEh)	ally
apesanteur (f)	(ah-peh-zãhn-tŒhr)	weightlessness
appareil (m)	(ah-pah-rEhy)	aircraft
arme (f)	(Ahrm)	weapon
armée (f)	(ahr-mEh)	military
armes (fpl) automatiques	(Ahrm oh-toh-mah-tEEhk)	automatic weapons
astronaute (m)	(ahs-troh-nOht)	astronaut
atterrissage (m)	(ah-teh-reeh-sAhzh)	landing
avion (m)	(ah-vyÕhn)	aircraft
balle (f)	(bAhl)	bullet
blocus (m)	(bloh-kOOh)	blockade
bombarder	(bohm-bahr-dEh)	bomb (v)
bombardier (m)	(bohm-bahr-dyEh)	bomber
bombe (f) à fragmentation	(bOhmb ah frahg-mãhn-tah-syÕhn)	cluster bomb
cabine (f) de pilotage	(kah-bEEhn dœ neeh-loh-tAhzh)	flight deck
cartouche (f)	(kahr-tOOhsh)	cartridge
casque (m)	(kAhsk)	helmet
char (m)	(shAhr)	tank
compte (m) à rebours	(kOhmt ah rœh-bOOhr)	countdown
contrôler	(kõhn-troh-lEh)	check (v)
déclencher	(deh-klãhn-shEh)	trigger (v)
décoller	(del-koh-lEh)	take off (v)
défectueux	(deh-fehk-tŒh)	defective
démilitariser	(deh-meeh-leeh-tah-reel-zEh)	demilitarize (v)
désarmement (m)	(dehz-ahr-mœh-mÃhn)	disarmament
détacher (se)	(deh-tah-shEh, sœh)	fall off (v)
détonateur (m)	(deh-toh-nah-tŒhr)	detonator
dispositif (m)	(deehs-poh-zeeh-tEEhf)	device
émeute (f)	(eh-mŒht)	riot
entretien (m)	(ãhn-trœh-tyEhn)	maintenance
escalade (f) des armes nucléaires	(ehs-kah-lAhd dez Ahrm nooh-kleh-Ehr)	nuclear build up
feu (m) d'artillerie	(fŒh dahr-teeh-yeh-rEEh)	gun fire
force (f) de maintien de la paix	(fohrs dœ mãehn-tyEhn dœ lah pEh)	peace-keeping force
fuselage (m)	(fooh-sœh-lAhzh)	fuselage
fusée (f) de lancement	(fooh-zEh dœ lãhns-mÃhn)	booster rocket

gaz (m) asphyxiant	*(gahz ahs-feehk-syÃhn)*	nerve gas
guerre (f) conventionnelle	*(gEhr kõhn-vãhn-syoh-nEhl)*	conventional warfare
guerre (f) nucléaire	*(gEhr nooh-kleh-Ehr)*	nuclear war
guidage par laser	*(geeh-dAhzh pahr lah-zEhr)*	laser guidance
hélicoptère (m)	*(eh-leeh-kohp-tEhr)*	helicopter
impulser	*(æhm-poohl-sEh)*	boost (v)
laboratoire (m) spatial	*(lah-boh-rah-twAhr spah-syAhl)*	spacelab
lancer	*(lãhn-sEh)*	launch, boost (v)
liste (f) de contrôle	*(lEEhst dœ kõhn-trOhl)*	checklist
lutter	*(looh-tEh)*	fight (v)
marche (f) dans l'espace	*(mAhrsh dãhn lehs-pAhs)*	spacewalk
mettre en orbite	*(mEh-troe ãhn ohr-bEEht)*	put into orbit (v)
missile (m) air-air	*(meeh-sEEhl ehr-Ehr)*	air-to-air missile
missile (m) air-sol	*(meeh-sEEl ehr sOhl)*	air-to-surface missile
mitrailleuse (f)	*(meeh-treh-yŒhz)*	machine gun
munition (f)	*(mooh-neeh-syÕhn)*	ammunition
navette (f)	*(nah-vEht)*	shuttle
navire (m) de guerre	*(nah-vEEhr dœ gEhr)*	warship
observer	*(ohb-sehr-vEh)*	monitor (v)
obus (m)	*(oh-bOOhs)*	shell
ogive (f)	*(oh-zhEEhv)*	warhead
pilote (m) automatique	*(peeh-lOht oh-toh-mah-tÈÈhk)*	auto-pilot
piste (f)	*(pEEhst)*	runway
poste (m) de commandement	*(pOhst dœ koh-mãhnd-mÃhn)*	command station
puissance (f) de combat	*(pweeh-sÃhns dœ kõhm-bAh)*	combat power
récupérer	*(reh-kooh-peh-reh)*	retrieve (v)
retarder	*(rœh-tahr-dEh)*	delay (v)
sas (m)	*(sAhs)*	airlock
satellite (m)	*(sah-teh-lEEkt)*	satellite
scaphandre (m)	*(skah-fAhn-drœh)*	spacesuit
siège (m) éjectable	*(syEhzh eh-zhehk-tAh-blœh)*	ejection seat
soldat (m)	*(sohl-dAh)*	soldier
station (f) d'observation	*(stah-syÕhn dohb-sehr-vah-syÕhn)*	tracking station
station (f) spatiale	*(stah-syÕhn spah-syAhl)*	space station
surveiller	*(soohr-veh-yEh)*	monitor (v)
système (m) de guidage	*(seehs-tEhm dœ geeh-dAhzh)*	guidance system
tableau (m) de bord	*(tah-blOh dœ bOhr)*	instrument panel

télécommande (f)	*(teh-leh-koh-mÃhnd)*	remote control
tirer	*(teeh-rEh)*	fire (v)
torpiller	*(tohr-peeh-yEh)*	torpedo (v)
tour (f) de contrôle	*(toohr dœ kõhn-trOhl)*	control tower
trou (m) noir	*(trooh nwAhr)*	black hole
vaisseau (m) spatial	*(veh-sOh spah-syAhl)*	spacecraft
vérifier	*(veh-reeh-feeh-Eh)*	check (v)
voler	*(voh-lEh)*	fly (v)
zone (f) d'exclusion aérienne	*(zohn dehk-sklooh-zyÕhn ah-eh-reeh-Ehn)*	no fly zone

BANKING/FINANCE/TRADING

English to French

allowance (tax)	l'abattement	*(ah-baht-mÃhn)*
amortization	l'amortissement	*(ah-mohr-teehs-mÃhn)*
annuity	l'annuité	*(ah-nweeh-tEh)*
asset	l'actif	*(ahk-tEEhf)*
back a venture (v)	soutenir une entreprise	*(sooh-tœh-nEEhr oohn āhn-trœh-prEEhz)*
bank charges	les frais bancaires, les frais de banque	*(frEh bāhn-kEhr), (frEh-dœ bAhnk)*
bank check	le chèque bancaire	*(shEhk bāhn-kEhr)*
bank loan	le prêt bancaire	*(prEht bāhn-kEhr)*
bankruptcy	la faillite	*(feh-yEEht)*
blue chip	la valeur sûre	*(vah-lŒhr sOOhr)*
bond market	le marché des obligations	*(mahr-shEh dehz oh-bleeh-gah-syÕhn)*
borrow (v)	emprunter	*(æhm-prǣhn-tEh)*
buy out (v)	racheter	*(rah-shtEhr)*
capital	le capital	*(kah-peeh-tAhl)*
capital gain	la plus-value	*(ploohs-vah-lOOh)*
cash reserves	les liquidités	*(leeh-keeh-deeh-tEh)*
checking account	le compte chèque	*(kõhnt shEhk)*
clear off a debt	s'acquitter d'une dette	*(sah-keeh-tEh doohn dEht)*
collateral	la garantie	*(gah-rãhn-tEEh)*
credit	le crédit	*(kreh-dEEh)*
deferred	différé	*(deeh-feh-rEh)*
deficit	le déficit	*(deh-feeh-sEEht)*
deposit	le dépôt	*(deh-pOh)*
devaluation	la dévaluation	*(deh-vah-lwah-syÕhn)*
discount rate	le taux d'escompte	*(toh deh-kOhmt)*
endorse (v)	endosser	*(æhn-doh-sEh)*
exchange rate	le taux de change	*(toh dœ shÃhnzh)*
financial backing	le soutien financier	*(sooh-tyEhn feeh-nãhn-syEh)*
financial standing	la solvabilité	*(sohl-vah-beeh-leeh-tEh)*
fiscal year	l'année fiscale	*(ah-nEh feehs-kAhl)*
free trade	le libre-échange	*(leeh-brœh-eh-shÃhnzh)*
frozen credit	le crédit bloqué	*(kreh-deeh bloh-kEh)*
gross profit	le bénéfice brut	*(beh-neh-fEEhs brOOh)*
holding company	le holding	*(holding)*
installment	le versement	*(vehr-sœh-mÃhn)*
interest-free loan	le crédit gratuit	*(kreh-dEEh grah-twEEh)*
interest rate	le taux d'intérêt	*(toh-dæhn-teh-rEh)*
investment bank	la banque de placement	*(bÃhnk dœ plahs mÃhn)*
lend (v)	prêter	*(preh-teh)*
limited liability	la responsabilité limitée	*(rehs-pohn-sah-bleeh-leeh-teh leeh-meeh-teh)*

liquidate (v)	liquider	*(leeh-keeh-dEh)*
merger	la fusion	*(fooh-zyÕhn)*
money market	le marché monétaire	*(mahr-shEh mah-neh-tEhr)*
mortgage loan	le prêt hypothécaire	*(prEht eeh-poh-teh-kEhr)*
net asset	l'actif net	*(ahk-tEEhf nEht)*
overdraft	le découvert	*(deh-kooh-vEhr)*
pay back a loan (v)	rembourser un prêt	*(ræhn-boohr-sEh)*
pension fund	la caisse de retraite	*(kehs dœ ræh-trEht)*
portfolio	le portefeuille	*(pohrt-fŒh-yœh)*
positive cash flow	la trésorerie positive	*(treh-soh-ræh-rEEh)*
prime rate	le taux préférentiel de l'escompte	*(toh preh-feh-rãhn-syEhll dœ leh-kÕhnt)*
profitability	la rentabilité	*(rãhn-tah-beeh-leeh-tEh)*
profitable	rentable	*(rãhn-tAh-blœh)*
quotation	la cotation	*(koh-tah-syÕhn)*
reserve	la réserve	*(reh-sEhrv)*
revenue	le revenu, les recettes	*(ræhv-nOOh), (ræh-sEht)*
risk-free	sans risque	*(sãhn rEEhsk)*
savings account	le compte épargne	*(kÕhnt eh-pAhr-nyœh)*
self-financing	l'autofinancement	*(oh-toh-freeh-nahns-mÃhn)*
silent partner	le commanditaire	*(koh-mahn-deeh-tEhr)*
stock	l'action	*(ahk-syÕhn)*
Stock Exchange	la Bourse	*(bOOhrs)*
stockbroker	l'agent de bourse	*(ah-jÃhn dœ bOOhrs)*
subsidize (v)	subventionner	*(soohb-vãhn-syoh-nEh)*
takeover bid	l'offre publique d'achat (OPA)	*(Oh-fræh pooh-blEEhk dah-shAh)*
taxable	imposable	*(æhn-poh-zAh-blœh)*
tax-free	exempt d'impôts	*(ek-zÃhn dæhn-pOh)*
trade barrier	la barrière douanière	*(bah-ryEhr dooh-ah-nyEhr)*
trader	le cambiste	*(kãhn-bEEhst)*
transaction	l'opération	*(oh-peh-rah-syÕhn)*
treasury bill	le bon du trésor	*(bÕhn dooh treh-zOhr)*
trend	la tendance	*(tãhn-dÃhns)*
undercapitalized	sous-capitalisé	*(sooh-kah-peeh-tah-leeh-zEh)*
unsecured loan	le prêt non garanti	*(prEht nÕhn gah-rãhn-tEEh)*
upward trend	la tendance à la hausse	*(tãhn-dÃhns ah lah Ohs)*
variable yield investment	le placement à revenu variable	*(plahs-mÃhn ah ræh-væh-nOOh vah-ryAh-blœh)*
venture capital	le capital-risque	*(kah-peeh-tAhl rEEhsk)*
warning indicator	l'indicateur d'alerte	*(æhn-deeh-kah-tŒhr dah-lEhrt)*
withdraw (v)	retirer	*(ræh-teeh-rEh)*
withdrawal	le retrait	*(ræh-trEh)*

French to English

abattement (m)	*(ah-baht-mÃhn)*	allowance (tax)
acquitter (s') d'une dette	*(ah-keeh-tEh doohn dEht)*	clear off a debt (v)
actif (m)	*(ahk-tEEhf)*	asset
actif net (m)	*(ahk-tEEhf nEht)*	net assets
action (f)	*(ahk-syÕhn)*	stock
agent (m) de bourse	*(ah-zhÃhn dœ bOOhrs)*	stockbroker
amortissement (m)	*(ah-mohr-tees-mÃhn)*	amortization
année fiscale (f)	*(ah-nEh feehs-kAhl)*	fiscal year
annuité (f)	*(ah-nweeh-tEh)*	annuity
autofinancement (m)	*(ah-toh-feeh-nãhns-mÃhn)*	self-financing
banque (f) de placement	*(bãhnk dœ plahs-mÃhn)*	investment bank
barrière (f) douanière	*(bah-reEhr dooh-ah-nyEhr)*	trade barrier
bénéfice (m) brut	*(beh-neh-fEEhs)*	gross profit
bon (m) du trésor	*(bÕhn dooh treh-zOhr)*	treasury bill
Bourse (f)	*(bOOhrs)*	Stock Exchange
caisse (f) de retraite	*(kEhs dœ rœh-trEh)*	pension fund
cambiste (m)	*(kahm-bEEhst)*	trader, broker
capital (m)	*(kah-peeh-tAhl)*	capital
capital-risque (m)	*(kah-peeh-tahl rEEhsk)*	venture capital
chèque (m) bancaire	*(shEhk bãhn-kEhr)*	bank check
commanditaire (m)	*(koh-mãhn-deeh-tEhr)*	silent partner
compte (m) chèque	*(kÕhnt shEhk)*	checking account
compte (m) épargne	*(kÕhnt eh-pAhr-nyœh)*	savings account
cotation (f)	*(koh-tah-syÕhn)*	quotation
crédit (m)	*(krœh dEEh)*	credit
crédit (m) bloqué	*(kreh-deeh bloh-kEh)*	frozen credit
crédit (m) gratuit	*(kreh-deeh grah-twEEh)*	interest-free loan
découvert (m)	*(deh-kooh-vEhr)*	overdraft
déficit (m)	*(deh-feeh-sEEht)*	deficit
dépôt (m)	*(dep-pOh)*	deposit
dévaluation	*(deh-vah-lwah-syÕhn)*	devalution
différé	*(deeh-feh-rEh)*	deferred
emprunter	*(ãhm-prãehn-tEh)*	borrow (v)
endosser	*(ãhn-doh-sEh)*	endorse (v)
exempt d'impôts	*(ehk-sÃhn dãhm-pOh)*	tax-free
faillite (f)	*(feh-yEEht)*	bankruptcy
frais (mp) bancaires	*(freh bãhn-kEhr)*	bank charges
fusion (f)	*(fooh-zyÕhn)*	merger
garantie (f)	*(gah-rãhn-tEEh)*	collateral
holding (m)	*(holding)*	holding company
imposable	*(ãhm-poh-zAh-blœh)*	taxable
indicateur (m) d'alerte	*(ãhn-deeh-kah-tŒr dah-lEhrt)*	warning indicator
libre-échange (m)	*(leeh-brœh-eh-shÃhnzh)*	free trade
liquider	*(leeh-keeh-dEh)*	liquidate (v)
liquidités (fpl)	*(leeh-keeh-deeh-tEh)*	liquidate (v)

marché (m) des obligations	*(mahr-shEh dehz oh-bleeh-gay-syÕhn)*	bond market
marché (m) monétaire	*(mahr-shEh moh-neh-tEhr)*	money market
offre (f) publique d'achat (OPA)	*(Oh-frœh pooh-blEEhk dah-shAh)*	takeover bid
opération (f)	*(oh-peh-rah-syÕhn)*	transaction
placement (m) à revenu variable	*(plahs-mÃn ah rœh-vœh-nOOl vah-ryAh-blœh)*	variable yield investment
plus-value (f)	*(plooh-vah-lOOh)*	capital gain
portefeuille (m)	*(pohrt-fŒh-yœh)*	portfolio
prêt (m) bancaire	*(prEht bãhn-kEhr)*	bank loan
prêt (m) hypothécaire	*(prEht eeh-poh-teh-kEhr)*	mortgage loan
prêt (m) non garanti	*(prEht nõhn gah-rãhn-tEEh)*	unsecured loan
prêter	*(preh-tEh)*	lend (v)
racheter	*(rahsh-tEh)*	buy out (v)
recettes (fpl)	*(rœh-sEht)*	revenue
rembourser un prêt	*(rãhm-boohr-sEh œhn prEht)*	pay back a loan (v)
rentabilité (f)	*(rãhn-tah-beeh-leeh-tEh)*	profitability
rentable	*(rãhn-tAh-blœh)*	profitable
réserve	*(reh-sEhrv)*	reserve
responsabilité (f) limitée	*(rehs-pohn-sah-beeh-leeh-tEh)*	limited liability
retirer	*(rœh-teeh-rEh)*	withdraw (v)
retrait (le)	*(rœh-trEht)*	withdrawal
sans risque	*(sãhn rEEhsk)*	risk-free
solvabilité	*(sohl-rah-beeh-leeh-tEh)*	financial standing
sous-capitalisé	*(sooh-kah-peeh-tah-leeh-zEh)*	undercapitalized
soutenir une entreprise	*(sooh-tœh-nEEhr ooh ãhn-trœh-prEEhz)*	back a venture (v)
soutien (m) financier	*(sooh-tyÊhn feeh-nãhn-syEh)*	financial backing
subventionner	*(soohb-vãhn-syoh-nEh)*	subsidize (v)
taux (m) de change	*(tOh dœ shÃhnzh)*	exchange rate
taux (m) d'escompte	*(tOh deh-kÕhnt)*	discount rate
taux (m) d'intérêt	*(tOh dãehn-teh-rEh)*	interest rate
taux (m) préférentiel de l'escompte	*(tOh preh-feh-rãhn-syEhl dœ lehs-kÕhnt)*	prime rate
tendance (f)	*(tãhn-dÃhns)*	trend
tendance (f) à la hausse	*(tãhn-dÃhns ah lah Ohs)*	upward trend
trésorerie (f) positive	*(treh-soh-rœh-rEEh poh-zeeh-tEhf)*	positive cash flow
valeur (f) sûre	*(vah-lŒhr sOOhr)*	blue chip
versement (m)	*(vehrs-mÃhn)*	installment

CHEMICALS

English to French

acetic acid	l'acide acétique	*(ah-sEEhd ah-seh-tEEhk)*
acetone	l'acétone	*(ah-seh-tOhn)*
acid	l'acide	*(ah-sEEhd)*
amine	l'amine	*(ah-mEEhn)*
ammonia	l'ammoniac	*(ah-moh-nyAhk)*
analysis	l'analyse	*(ãh-nah-lEEhz)*
analytic chemistry	la chimie analytique	*(sheeh-mEEh ãh-nah-leeh-tEEhk)*
atom	l'atome	*(ah-tOhm)*
atomic	atomique	*(ah-toh-mEEhk)*
benzene	le benzène	*(bãhn-zEhn)*
biochemistry	la biochimie	*(beeh-oh-sheeh-mEEh)*
biologist	le biologiste	*(beeh-oh-loh-zhEEhst)*
biology	la biologie	*(beeh-oh-loh-zhEEh)*
buret	la burette	*(booh-rEht)*
carbon	le carbone	*(kahr-bOhn)*
catalyst	le catalyseur	*(kah-tah-leeh-zŒhr)*
chemical	chimique	*(sheeh-mEEhk)*
chemistry	la chimie	*(sheeh-mEEh)*
chloride	le chlorure	*(kloh-rOOhr)*
chloroform	le chloroforme	*(kloh-roh-fOhrm)*
component	le composant	*(kõhm-poh-zÃh)*
composition	la composition	*(kõhm-poh-zeeh-syÕh)*
compound	le composé	*(kõhm-poh-zEh)*
concentration	le titre (d'une solution)	*(tEEh-træ doohn soh-looh-syÕh)*
cracking	le cracking	
crystallization	la cristallisation	*(kreehs-tah-leeh-zah-syÕh)*
degree	le degré	*(dœh-grEh)*
density	la densité	*(dãhn-seeh-tEh)*
distillation	la distillation	*(deehs-teeh-lah-syÕh)*
dosage	le dosage	*(doh-zAhzh)*
electrolysis	l'électrolyse	*(eh-lehk-troh-lEEhz)*
electron	l'électron	*(eh-lehk-trÕh)*
element	l'élément	*(eh-leh-mÃh)*
engineer	l'ingénieur	*(ãehn-zheh-nyŒhr)*
enzyme	l'enzyme	*(ãehn-zhEEhm)*
ethane	l'éthane	*(eh-tAhn)*
ether	l'éther	*(eh-tEh)*
evaporation	l'évaporation	*(eh-vah-poh-rah-syÕh)*
experiment	l'expérience	*(ehks-peh-ryÃhns)*
experimental	expérimental	*(ehks-peh-reeh-mãhn-tAhl)*
formula	la formule	*(fohr-mOOhl)*
gram	le gramme	*(grAhm)*
homogeneity	l'homogénéité	*(oh-moh-zheh-neh-eeh-tEh)*

hydrocarbon	l'hydrocarbure	*(eeh-droh-kahr-bOOhr)*
hydrochloric acid	l'acide chloridrique	*(ah-sEEhd kloh-rEEhk)*
hydrolysis	l'hydrolyse	*(eeh-droh-lEEhz)*
hydrosulfate	le sulfhydrate	*(soohlf-eeh-drAht)*
impurity	l'impureté	*(æhm-pooh-reh-tEh)*
inorganic chemistry	la chimie minérale	*(sheeh-mEEh meeh-neh-rAhl)*
isotope	l'isotope	*(eeh-zoh-tOhp)*
laboratory	le laboratoire	*(lah-boh-rah-twAhr)*
methane	le méthane	*(meh-tAhn)*
molar	molaire	*(moh-lEhr)*
mole	la mole	*(mOhl)*
molecule	la molécule	*(moh-leh-kOOhl)*
natural gas	le gaz naturel	*(gAhz nah-tooh-rEhl)*
neutral	neutre	*(nŒh-træ)*
neutralization	la neutralisation	*(næh-trah-leeh-zah-syÕh)*
neutron	le neutron	*(næh-trÕh)*
nitric acid	l'acide nitrique	*(ah-sEEhd neeh-trEEhk)*
organic chemistry	la chimie organique	*(sheeh-mEEh ohr-gah-nEEhk)*
petroleum	le pétrole	*(peh-trOhl)*
phosphate	le phosphate	*(fohs-fAht)*
polymer	le polymère	*(poh-leeh-mEhr)*
product	le produit	*(proh-dwEEh)*
proton	le proton	*(proh-tÕh)*
purification	la purification	*(pooh-reeh-feeh-kah-synOh)*
reactant	le réactif	*(reh-ahk-tEEhf)*
reduction	la réduction	*(reh-doohk-syÕh)*
refine (v)	raffiner	*(rah-feeh-nEh)*
refinery	la raffinerie	*(rah-feeh-neh-rEEh)*
research	la recherche	*(ræh-shEhrsh)*
salt	le sel	*(sEhl)*
saponification	la saponification	*(sah-poh-neeh-feeh-kah-synOh)*
solubility	la solubilité	*(soh-looh-beeh-leeh-tEh)*
solute	le soluté	*(soh-looh-tE)*
solution	la solution	*(soh-looh-synOh)*
solvent	le solvant	*(sohl-vÃh)*
spectrum	le spectre	*(spEhk-træ)*
sulfuric acid	l'acide sulfurique	*(ah-sEEhd soohl-fooh-rEEhk)*
test tube	l'éprouvette	*(eh-prooh-vEht)*
titration	le titrage	*(teeh-trAzh)*
yield	le rendement	*(rãhnd-mÃh)*

French to English

acétone (m)	*(ah-seh-tOhn)*	acetone
acide (m)	*(ah-sEEhd)*	acid

acide acétique	*(ah-sEEhd ah-seh-tEEhk)*	acetic acid
acide chloridrique	*(ah-sEEhd kloh-rEEhk)*	hydrochloric acid
acide nitrique	*(ah-sEEhd neeh-trEEhk)*	nitric acid
acide sulfurique	*(ah-sEEhd soohl-fooh-rEEhk)*	sulfuric acid
amine (f)	*(ah-mEEhn)*	amine
ammoniac (m)	*(ah-moh-nyAhk)*	ammonia
analyse (f)	*(ãh-nah-lEEhz)*	analysis
atome (m)	*(ah-tOhm)*	atom
atomique	*(ah-toh-mEEhk)*	atomic
benzène (m)	*(bãhn-zEhn)*	benzene
biochimie (f)	*(beeh-oh-sheeh-mEEh)*	biochemistry
biologie (f)	*(beeh-oh-loh-zhEEh)*	biology
biologiste (m)	*(beeh-oh-loh-zhEEhst)*	biologist
burette (f)	*(booh-rEht)*	buret
carbone (m)	*(kahr-bOhn)*	carbon
catalyseur (m)	*(kah-tah-leeh-zŒhr)*	catalyst
chimie (f)	*(sheeh-mEEh)*	chemistry
chimie analytique	*(sheeh-mEEh ãh-nah-leeh-tEEhk)*	analytic chemistry
chimie minérale	*(sheeh-mEEh meeh-neh-rAhl)*	inorganic chemistry
chimie organique	*(sheeh-mEEh ohr-gah-nEEhk)*	organic chemistry
chimique	*(sheeh-mEEhk)*	chemical
chloroforme (m)	*(kloh-roh-fOhrm)*	chloroform
chlorure (m)	*(kloh-rOOhr)*	chloride
composant (m)	*(kõhm-poh-zÃh)*	component
composé (m)	*(kõhm-poh-zEh)*	compound
composition (f)	*(kõhm-poh-zeeh-syÕh)*	composition
cracking (m)		cracking
cristallisation (f)	*(kreehs-tah-leeh-zah-syÕh)*	crystallization
degré (m)	*(dœh-grEh)*	degree
densité (f)	*(dãhn-seeh-tEh)*	density
distillation (f)	*(deehs-teeh-lah-syÕh)*	distillation
dosage (m)	*(doh-zAhzh)*	dosage
électrolyse (f)	*(eh-lehk-troh-lEEhz)*	electrolysis
électron (m)	*(eh-lehk-trÕh)*	electron
élément (m)	*(eh-leh-mÃh)*	element
enzyme (m)	*(ãhn-zEEhm)*	enzyme
éprouvette (f)	*(eh-prooh-vEht)*	test tube
éthane (m)	*(eh-tAhn)*	ethane
éther (m)	*(eh-tEh)*	ether
évaporation (f)	*(eh-vah-poh-rah-syÕh)*	evaporation
expérience (f)	*(ehks-peh-ryÃhns)*	experiment
expérimental	*(ehks-peh-reeh-mãhn-tAhl)*	experimental
formule (f)	*(fohr-mOOhl)*	formula
gaz (m) naturel	*(gAhz nah-tooh-rEhl)*	natural gas
gramme (m)	*(grAhm)*	gram
homogénéité	*(oh-moh-zhœh-neh-eeh-tEh)*	homogeneity

hydrocarbure (m)	*(eeh-droh-kahr-bOOhr)*	hydrocarbon
hydrolyse (f)	*(eeh-droh-lEEhz)*	hydrolysis
impureté (f)	*(ǎhm-pooh-reeh-tEh)*	impurity
ingénieur (m)	*(ǎhn-zheh-nyŒhr)*	engineer
isotope (m)	*(eeh-zoh-tOhp)*	isotope
laboratoire (m)	*(lah-boh-rah-twAhr)*	laboratory
méthane (m)	*(meh-tAhn)*	methane
molaire	*(moh-lEhr)*	molar
mole (f)	*(mOhl)*	mole
molécule (f)	*(moh-leh-kOOhl)*	molecule
neutralisation (f)	*(nœh-trah-leeh-zah-syÕh)*	neutralization
neutre	*(nœh-trœ)*	neutral
neutron (m)	*(nœh-trÕh)*	neutron
pétrole (m)	*(peh-trOhl)*	petroleum
phosphate (m)	*(fohs-fAht)*	phosphate
polymère (m)	*(poh-leeh-mEhr)*	polymer
produit (m)	*(proh-dwEEh)*	product
proton (m)	*(proh-tÕh)*	proton
purification (f)	*(pooh-reeh-feeh-kah-syÕh)*	purification
raffiner	*(rah-feeh-nEh)*	refine (v)
raffinerie (f)	*(rah-feeh-nœh-rEEh)*	refinery
réactif (m)	*(reh-ahk-tEEhf)*	reactant
recherche (f)	*(rœh-shEhrsh)*	research
réduction (f)	*(reh-doohk-syÕh)*	reduction
rendement (m)	*(rãhnd-mÃh)*	yield
saponification (f)	*(sah-poh-neeh-feeh-kah-syÕh)*	saponification
sel (m)	*(sEhl)*	salt
solubilité (f)	*(soh-looh-beeh-leeh-tEh)*	solubility
soluté (m)	*(soh-looh-tEh)*	solute
solution (f)	*(soh-looh-syÕh)*	solution
solvant (m)	*(sohl-vÃh)*	solvent
spectre (m)	*(spEhk-trœ)*	spectrum
sulfhydrate (m)	*(soohlf-eeh-drAht)*	hydrosulfate
titrage (m)	*(teeh-trAzh)*	titration
titre (d'une solution) (m)	*(tEEh-trœ)*	concentration

COMMUNICATIONS/ADVERTISING

English to French

account executive	le chef de publicité	*(shef dœ pooh-bleeh-seeh-tEh)*
ad	la pub	*(poohb)*
advertising agency	l'agence de publicité	*(ah-zhÃhs dœ pooh-bleeh-seeh-tEh)*
advertising budget	le budget publicitaire	*(boo-zhEh pooh-bleeh-seeh-tEhr)*
advertising rates	les tarifs publicitaires	*(tah-rEEhf)*
advertising strategy	la stratégie publicitaire	*(strah-teh-zhEEh pooh-bleeh-seeh-tEhr)*
air date	la date de diffusion	*(daht dœ deer-fooh-ZyÕhn)*
art department	le service de création	*(sœr-vEEhs dœ kreh-sh-syÕhn)*
art director	le directeur artistique	*(deeh-rehk-tŒhr ahr-teehs-tEEhk)*
audience rating	l'indice d'écoute	*(ãhn-dEEhs deh-kOOht)*
audience research	l'étude d'opinion	*(eh-tOOhd doh-peeh-nyÕhn)*
audio mixing	le mixage	*(meehks-Ahzh)*
background	l'arrière-plan	*(ah-ryEhr plÃhn)*
background music	le fond sonore	*(fÕhn soh-nOhr)*
billboard	le panneau d'affichage	*(pah-noh dah-feeh-shAzh)*
broadcast (v)	diffuser	*(deeh-fooh-zEh)*
caption	la légende	*(leh-zhÃhnd)*
center spread	la double page centrale	*(dooh-blœ pah-zh sãhn-trAhl)*
classified ad	la petite annonce	*(pœh-tEEht- ãh-nÕhns)*
close-up	le gros plan	*(groh plÃhn)*
color transparency	la diapositive couleur	*(deeh-ah-poh-zeeh-tEEhv kooh-lŒhr)*
commercial	le spot publicitaire	*(sphot pooh-bleeh-seeh-tEhr)*
composite package	la vente jumelée	*(vÃhnt zhooh-mœh-lEh)*
computer-assisted	assisté par ordinateur	*(ah-seeh-tEh pahr ohr-deeh-nah-tŒhr)*
contact sheet	la planche de contact	*(plÃhnsh dœ kõhn-tAhkt)*
conventional product	le produit classique	*(proh-dwEEh klah-sEEhk)*
copywriter	le rédacteur (-trice) publicitaire	*(reh-dahk-tŒhr pooh-bleeh-seeh-tEhr)*
cover	la couverture	*(kooh-vehr-tOOhr)*
customer profile	le profil de la clientèle	*(proh-fEEhl dœ lah kleeh-ãhn-tEhl)*
deadline	la date limite	*(daht leeh-mEEht)*
demand assessment	l'évaluation de la demande	*(eh-vah-lwah-syÕhn dœ lah dœh-mÃhd)*

direct mail	la publicité directe par	*(pooh-bleeh-seeh-tEh*
advertising	correspondance	*deeh-rEhkt pahr koh-*
		rehs-põhn-dÃhns)
documentary	le documentaire	*(doh-kooh-mãhn-tEhr)*
dubbing	le doublage	*(dooh-blAzh)*
dummy	la maquette	*(mah-kEht)*
durable goods	les biens durables (m.p.)	*(byEhn dooh-rAh-blœh)*
exclusive	en exclusivité	*(ãhn ehks-klooh-seeh-*
		veeh-tEh)
eye-catching	accrocheur	*(ah-kroh-shŒhr)*
feedback	la réaction	*(reh-ahk-syÕhn)*
insert (to)	insérer	*(ãehn-seh-rEh)*
live program	l'émission en direct	*(eh-meeh-syÕhn ãhn deeh-*
		rEhkt)
logo	le logo	*(loh-gOh)*
magazine	le magazine	*(mah-gah-zEEhn)*
media coverage	le reportage des médias,	*(rœh-pohr-tAhzh deh meh-*
	la couverture	*dyÃh), (kooh-vehr-*
		tOOhr)
off-peak rate	le tarif de faible écoute	*(tah-rEEhf dœ fEh-blœ eh-*
		kOOht)
on location	en extérieur	*(ãhn ehks-teh-ryŒhr)*
photographer	le photographe	*(foh-toh-grAhf)*
point-of-sale	le point de vente	*(pwÆhn dœ vÃhnt)*
poster	l'affiche	*(ah-fEEhsh)*
press campaign	la campagne de presse	*(kahm-pÃhnyœ dœ prEhs)*
press clipping	la coupure de presse	*(kooh-pOOhr dœ prEhs)*
press release	le communiqué de presse	*(koh-mooh-neeh-kEh dœ*
		prEhs)
prime time	l'heure de grande écoute	*(Œhr dœ grÃhnd eh-*
		kOOht)
proof	l'épreuve	*(eh-prŒhv)*
prospective	le consommateur potentiel	*(kõhn-soh-mah-tŒhr poh-*
consumer		*tãhn-syEhl)*
random sample	l'échantillon aléatoire	*(eh-shãhn-teeh-yÕhn ah-*
		leh-ah-twAhr)
record (v)	enregistrer	*(ãhn-rœh-zheehs-trEh)*
response	la réaction	*(reh-ahk-syÕhn)*
rights	les droits	*(drwAh)*
royalties	les droits d'auteur	*(drwAh doh-tŒhr)*
run an ad (v)	faire passer une annonce	*(fehr pah-sEh oohn ah-*
		nÕhns)
satellite TV	la télévision par satellite	*(teh-leh-veeh-zyÕhn pahr*
		sah-teh-lEEht)
screen	l'écran	*(eh-krÃhn)*
serial film	le feuilleton	*(fœhy-tÕhn)*
shoot	le tournage	*(toohr-nAhzh)*
shoot (film) (v)	tourner	*(toohr-nEh)*
short film	le court-métrage	*(koohr-meh-trAzh)*
slogan	le slogan	*(sloh-gÃhn)*

sneak preview	l'avant-première	*(ah-vÃhn-prœh-myEhr)*
sound effects	les trucages sonores	*(trooh-kAhzh soh-nOhr)*
sound track	la bande son	*(bÃhnd sÕhn)*
space buying	l'achat d'espace	*(ah-shAh dehs-pAhs)*
speech bubble	la bulle	*(bOOhl)*
sponsor (v)	commanditer, parrainer	*(koh-mãhn-deeh-tEhr), (pah-reh-nEh)*
subscriber	l'abonné (e)	*(ah-boh-nEh)*
take	la prise de vue	*(prEEhz dœ vOOh)*
target audience	le public-cible	*(pooh-blEEhk sEEh-blœh)*
target market	le marché-cible	*(mahr-shEh sEEh-blœh)*
television	la télévision	*(teh-leh-veeh-zyÕhn)*
time segment	la tranche horaire	*(trÃhnsh oh-rEhr)*
top of the line	haut de gamme	*(Oht dœ gAhm)*
transit advertising	l'affichage transport	*(ah-feeh-shAhzh trãhns-pOhr)*

French to English

abonné (e)(m)	*(ah-boh-nEh)*	subscriber
accrocheur	*(ah-kroh-shŒhr)*	eye-catching
achat (m) d'espace	*(ah-shAh dehs-pAhs)*	space buying
affichage (m) transport	*(ah-feeh-shAhzh trãhns-pOhr)*	transit advertising
affiche (f)	*(ah-feehsh)*	poster
agence (f) de publicité	*(ah-zhÃhns dœ pooh-bleeh-seeh-tEh)*	advertising agency
annonce (f)	*(ah-nÕhns)*	ad
arrière-plan (m)	*(ah-ryEhr plÃhn)*	background
assisté par ordinateur	*(ah-seehs-tEh pahr ohr-deeh-nah-tŒhr)*	computer assisted
avant-première (f)	*(ah-vÃhn-prœh-myEhr)*	sneak preview
bande (f) son (m)	*(bÃhnd-sÕhn)*	sound track
biens durables (mpl)	*(byÆhn dooh-rAh-blœh)*	durable goods
budget (m) publicitaire	*(booh-zhEh pooh-bleeh-seeh-tEhr)*	advertising budget
bulle (f)	*(bOOhl)*	speech bubble
campagne (f) de presse	*(kahm-pÃh-nyœh dœ prEhs)*	press campaign
chef (m) de publicité	*(shEhf dœ pooh-bleeh-seeh-tEh)*	account executive
communiqué (m) de presse	*(koh-mooh-neeh-kEh dœ prEhs)*	press release
consommateur (m) potentiel	*(kõhn-soh-mah-tŒhr poh-tãhn-syEhl)*	prospective consumer
coupure (f) de presse	*(kooh-pOOhr dœ prEhs)*	press clipping
court-métrage (m)	*(koohr-meh-trAhzh)*	short film
couverture (f)	*(kooh-vehr-tOOhr)*	cover
date (f) de diffusion	*(daht dœ deeh-fooh-zyÕhn)*	air date
date (f) limite	*(daht leeh-mEEht)*	deadline

diapositive (f) couleur	*(deeh-ah-poh-zeeh-tEEhv kooh-lŒhr)*	color transparency
diffuser	*(deeh-fooh-zEh)*	broadcast (v)
directeur (m) artistique	*(deeh-rehk-tŒhr ahr-teehs-tEEhk)*	art director
documentaire (m)	*(doh-kooh-mãhn-tEhr)*	documentary
doublage (m)	*(dooh-blAhzh)*	dubbing
double page (f) centrale	*(dooh-blœ pAhzh sãhn-trAhl)*	center spread
droits (mpl)	*(drwAh)*	rights
droits d'auteur (mpl)	*(drwAh doh-tŒhr)*	royalties
échantillon (m) aléatoire	*(eh-shãhn-teeh-yÕhn ah-leh-ah-twAhr)*	random sample
écran (m)	*(eh-krAhn)*	screen
émission (f) en direct	*(eh-meeh-syÕhn ãhr deeh-rEhkt)*	live program
en exclusivité	*(ãhn ehksklooh-seeh-veeh-tEh)*	exclusive
en extérieur	*(ãhn ehk-steh-ryŒhr)*	on location
enregistrer	*(ãhn-rœh-zheehs-trEh)*	record (v)
épreuve (f)	*(eh-prŒhv)*	proof
étude (f) d'opinion	*(eh-toohd doh-peeh-nÕyn)*	audience research
évaluation (f) de la demande	*(eh-vah-lwah-syÕhn dœ lah dœh-mÃhnd)*	demand assessment
faire passer une annonce	*(fehr pah-seh oohn ah-nÕhns)*	run an ad (v)
feuilleton (m)	*(fœh-yœh-tÕhn)*	serial film, series
fond (m) sonore	*(fÕhn soh-nOhr)*	background music
gros plan (m)	*(groh plÃhn)*	close-up
haut de gamme	*(Oh dœ gAhm)*	top of the line
heure (f) de grande écoute	*(Œhr dœ grÃhnd eh-kOOht)*	prime time
indice (m) d'écoute	*(ãhn-dEEhs deh-kOOht)*	audience rating
insérer	*(ãhn-seh-rEh)*	insert (v)
légende (f)	*(leh-zhÃhnd)*	caption
logo (m)	*(loh-gOh)*	logo
magazine (m)	*(mah-gah-zEEhn)*	magazine
maquette (f)	*(mah-kEht)*	dummy
marché-cible (m)	*(mahr-shEh-sEEh-blœ)*	target market
mixage (m)	*(meehk-sAhzh)*	audio mixing
panneau (m) d'affichage	*(pah-nOh dah-feeh-shAhzh)*	billboard
parrainer	*(pah-reh-nEh)*	sponsor (v)
petite annonce	*(peh-tEEht ah-nÕhns)*	classified ad
photographe (m)	*(foh-toh-grAhf)*	photographer
planche (f) de contact	*(plãhnsh dœ kõhn-tAhkt)*	contact sheet
point (m) de vente	*(pwÆhn dœ vÃhnt)*	point-of-sale
prise (f) de vue	*(prEEhz dœ vOOh)*	take

produit (m) classique	*(proh-dwEEh klah-sEEhk)*	conventional product
profil (m) de la clientèle	*(proh-feehl dœ lah kleeh-ãhr-tEhl)*	customer profile
public-cible (m)	*(pooh-blEEhk-sEEh-blœ)*	target audience
publicité (f) directe par correspondance	*(pooh-bleeh-see-tEh pahr koh-rehs-põhn-dÃhns)*	direct mail advertising
réaction (f)	*(reh-ahk-syÕhn)*	feedback, response
rédacteur (-trice) publicitaire	*(reh-dahk-tŒhr pooh-bleeh-seeh-tEhr)*	copywriter
reportage (m) des médias	*(rœh-pohr-tAhzh deh meh-dyAh)*	media coverage
service (m) de création	*(sœhr-vEEhs dœ kreh-ah-syÕhn)*	art department
slogan (m)	*(sloh-gÃhn)*	slogan
spot (m) publicitaire	*(spoht pooh-bleeh-seeh-tEhr)*	commercial
stratégie (f) publicitaire	*(strah-teh-zhEEh pooh-bleeh-seeh-tEhr)*	advertising strategy
tarif (m) de faible écoute	*(tah-rEEhf dœ fEl-blœh eh-kOOht)*	off-peak rate
tarifs publicitaires (mpl)	*(tah-rEEhf pooh-bleeh-seeh-tEhr)*	advertising rates
télévision (f)	*(teh-leh-veeh-zyÕhn)*	television
télévision (f) par satellite	*(teh-leh-veeh-zyÕhn pahr sah-teh-lEEht)*	satellite TV
tournage (m)	*(toohr-nAhzh)*	shoot
tourner	*(toohr-nEh)*	shoot (film) (v)
tranche (f) horaire	*(trÃhnsh oh-rEhr)*	time segment
trucages (mpl) sonores	*(trooh-kAhzh soh-nOhr)*	sound effects
vente (f) jumelée	*(vÃhnt zhooh-meh-lEh)*	composite package

COMPUTERS AND ELECTRONIC EQUIPMENT

English to French

alternating current	le courant alternatif	*(kooh-rÃhnt ahl-tehr-nah-tEEhf)*
amplifier	l'amplificateur	*(ahm-pleeh-feeh-kah-tŒhr)*
amplitude modulation (AM)	la modulation d'amplication	*(moh-dooh-lah-syÕh dahm-pleeh-kah-syÕh)*
antenna	l'antenne	*(ãhn-tEhn)*
backup	la copie de sauvegarde	*(koh-pEEh dœ sohv-gAhrd)*
beam	le rayon	*(rah-yÕh)*
binary code	le code binaire	*(kOhd beeh-nEhr)*
bit	l'unité binaire	*(ooh-neeh-teh beeh-nEhr)*
broadcast (v)	radiodiffuser	*(rah-dyoh-deeh-fooh-zEh)*
byte	l'octet	*(ohk-tEht)*
cable television	la télévision à câble	*(teh-leh-veeh-zyÕh ah kAh-blœ)*
capacity	la capacité de mémoire	*(kah-pah-seh-tEh dœ meh-mwAhr)*
cartridge	le chargeur, la cartouche	*(shahr-zhŒhr), (kahr-tOOhsh)*
cassette	la cassette	*(kah-sEht)*
cathode	la cathode	*(kah-tOhd)*
channel	le canal	*(kah-nAhl)*
character font	la police des caractères	*(poh-lEEhs deh kah-rahk-tEhr)*
chip	la puce	*(pOOhs)*
circuit	le circuit	*(seehr-kwEEh)*
coaxial cable	le câble coaxial	*(kAh-blœ koh-ahk-syAhl)*
command	la commande	*(koh-mÃhnd)*
compatible	compatible	*(kõhn-pah-tEEh-blœh)*
computer	l'ordinateur	*(ohr-deeh-nah-tŒhr)*
computer science	l'informatique	*(œhn-fohr-mah-tEEhk)*
conductor	le conducteur	*(kõhn-doohk-tŒhr)*
connect (v)	raccorder	*(rah-kohr-dEh)*
control key	la touche de commande	*(tOOhsh dœ koh-mÃhnd)*
current	le courant	*(kooh-rÃhn)*
cursor	le curseur	*(koohr-sŒhr)*
data processing	le traitement de données	*(treht-mÃhn dœ doh-nEh)*
databank	la banque de données	*(bÃhnk dœ doh-nEh)*
database	la base de données	*(bAhz dœ doh-nEh)*
delete (v)	effacer	*(eh-fah-sEh)*
detector	le détecteur	*(deh-tehk-tŒhr)*
digital	le digital	*(deeh-zheeh-tAhl)*
diode	la diode	*(deeh-Ohd)*
disk drive	le lecteur de disques	*(lehk-tŒhr dœ dEEhsk)*
dump (v)	vider	*(veeh-dEh)*

electricity	l'électricité	*(eh-lehk-treeh-seeh-tEh)*
electrode	l'éléctrode	*(eh-lehk-trOhd)*
electron	l'électron	*(eh-lehk-trÕh)*
electronic	l'électronique	*(eh-lehk-troh-nEEhk)*
electrostatic	l'électrostatique	*(eh-lehk-troh-stah-tEEhk)*
erase (v)	effacer	*(eh-fah-sEh)*
fiber optic	la fibre optique	*(fEEh-brœ ohp-tEEhk)*
filament	le filament	*(feeh-lah-mÃh)*
file	le fichier	*(feeh-shyEh)*
filter	le filtre	*(fEEhl-trœ)*
floppy disk	la disquette	*(deehs-kEht)*
format (v)	formater	*(fohr-mah-tŒhr)*
frequency	la fréquence	*(freh-kÃhns)*
frequency modulation (FM)	la modulation de fréquence	*(moh-dooh-lah-syÕh dœ freh-kÃhns)*
function key	la touche de fonction	*(tOOhsh dœ fõhnk-syÕhn)*
generator	le générateur	*(zheh-neh-rah-tŒhr)*
hard disk	le disque dur	*(deehsk dOOhr)*
hardware	le matériel, le hardware	*(mah-teh-ryEhl)*
high fidelity	la haute fidélité	*(Oht feeh-deh-leeh-tEh)*
induction	l'induction	*(æhn-doohk-syÕh)*
insert (v)	insérer	*(æhn-seh-rEh)*
install (v)	installer	*(æhns-tah-lEh)*
insulator	l'insulateur	*(æhn-sooh-lah-tŒhr)*
integrated circuit	le circuit intégré	*(seehr-kwEEht æhn-teh-grEh)*
key	la touche	*(tOOhsh)*
keyboard	le clavier	*(klah-vyEh)*
kilowatt	le kilowatt	
laptop	le portatif	*(pohr-tah-tEEhf)*
laser	le laser	*(lah-zEh)*
laser printer	l'imprimante à laser	*(æhn-preeh-mÃhnt ah lah-zEh)*
main memory	la mémoire principale	*(meh-myAhr præhn-seeh-pAhl)*
microwave	le micro-onde	*(meeh-kroh-Ohnd)*
mixer	le mélangeur	*(meh-lãhn-zhŒhr)*
modem	le modem	*(moh-dEhm)*
motor	le moteur	*(moh-tŒhr)*
mouse	la souris	*(sooh-rEEh)*
network	le réseau	*(reh-zOh)*
off-line	autonome	*(oh-toh-nOhm)*
ohm	l'ohm	
on-line	en ligne	*(ãhn lEEhn-yœh)*
optic	l'optique	*(ohp-tEEhk)*
oscillator	l'oscillateur	*(oh-seeh-lah-tŒhr)*
paging	la pagination	*(pah-jeeh-nah-syÕhn)*
panel	le panneau	*(pah-nOh)*

parallel circuit	le circuit parallèle	*(seehr-kwEEh pah-rah-lEhl)*
power	la puissance, l'énergie	*(pweeh-sÃhns), (eh-nœhr-zhEEh)*
printed circuit	le circuit imprimé	*(seehr-kwEEht æhm-preeh-mEh)*
printer	l'imprimante	*(æhn-preeh-mÃhnt)*
processor	le processeur	*(proh-seh-sŒhr)*
program	le programme	*(proh-grAhm)*
program (v)	programmer	*(proh-grah-mEh)*
radar	le radar	*(rah-dAhr)*
radio	la radio	*(rah-dyOh)*
random access	l'accès aléatoire	*(ahk-sEh ah-leh-ah-twAhr)*
receiver	le récepteur	*(reh-sœhp-tŒhr)*
record	le disque	*(dEEhsk)*
record (v)	enregistrer	*(ãhn-rœh-zheehs-trEh)*
record player	l'électrophone	*(eh-lehk-troh-fÕhn)*
resistance	la résistance	*(reh-seehs-tÃhns)*
resonance	la résonance	*(reh-zoh-nÃhns)*
scanning	le balayage	*(bah-lah-yAhzh)*
screen	l'écran	*(eh-krAhn)*
semiconductor	le semi-conducteur	*(sœh-meeh-kõhn-doohk-tŒhr)*
short wave	l'onde courte	*(Ohnd- kOOhrt)*
silicon	la silicone	*(seeh-leeh-kÕh)*
software	le logiciel, le software	*(loh-zheeh-syEhl)*
sort (v)	trier	*(treeh-Eh)*
sound	le son	*(sÕh)*
speaker	le haut-parleur	*(Oht pahr-lŒhr)*
spellcheck	le contrôle orthographique	*(kõhn-trOhl ohr-toh-grah-fEEhk)*
stereophonic	stéréophonique	*(steh-reh-oh-foh-nEEhk)*
storage	la mise en mémoire	*(meehz ãhn meh-mwAhr)*
switch	le commutateur, l'interrupteur	*(koh-mooh-tah-tŒhr), (æhn-teh-roohp-tŒhr)*
tape recorder	l'enregistreur	*(ãhn-rœh-zheehs-trŒhr)*
transformer	le transformateur	*(trãhnz-fohr-mah-tŒhr)*
transmission frame	la trame de transmission	*(trAhm dœ trãhnz-meeh-syÕhn)*
transmitter	le transmetteur	*(trãhnz-meht-tŒhr)*
tone	la tonalité	*(toh-nah-leeh-tEh)*
turbine	la turbine	*(toohr-bEEhn)*
update (v)	mettre à jour	*(mEh-trœh ah zhOOhr)*
upgrade (v)	augmenter la puissance	*(ohg-mãhn-tEh lah pweeh-sÃhns)*
vacuum	le vide	*(vEEhd)*
VCR	le magnétoscope	*(mah-nyeh-toh-skOhp)*
vector	le vecteur	*(vehk-tŒhr)*
videocassette player	le magnétophone	*(mah-nyeh-toh-fÕhn)*

virus	le virus	*(veeh-rOOhs)*
voltage	le voltage	*(vohl-tAhzh)*
walkman	le baladeur	*(bah-lah-dŒhr)*
watt	le watt	
wave	l'onde	*(Ohnd)*
windowing	le fenêtrage	*(fœh-neh-trAhzh)*
wire	le fil	*(fEEhl)*
word processing	le traitement de texte	*(treht-mÃhn dœ tEhkst)*

French to English

accès (m) aléatoire	*(ahk-sEhs ah-leh-ah-twAhr)*	random access
amplificateur (m)	*(ahm-pleeh-feeh-kah-tŒhr)*	amplifier
antenne (f)	*(ãhn-tEhn)*	antenna
augmenter la puissance	*(ohg-mãhn-tEh lah pweeh-sÃhns)*	upgrade (v)
autonome	*(oh-tah-nOhm)*	off-line
baladeur (m)	*(bah-lah-dŒhr)*	walkman
balayage (m)	*(bah-lah-yAhzh)*	scanning
banque (f) de données	*(bÃhnk dœ doh-nEh)*	databank
base (f) de données	*(bahz dœ doh-nEh)*	database
câble (m) coaxial	*(kAh-blœ)*	coaxial cable
canal (m)	*(kah-nAhl)*	channel
capacité (f) de mémoire	*(kah-pah-seeh-tEh dœ meh-mwAhr)*	capacity
cartouche (f)	*(kahr-tOOhsh)*	cartridge
cassette (f)	*(kah-sEht)*	cassette
cathode (f)	*(kah-tOhd)*	cathode
chargeur (m)	*(shahr-zhŒhr)*	cartridge
circuit (m)	*(seehr-kwEEh)*	circuit
circuit imprimé	*(seehr-kwEEht ãhm-preeh-mEh)*	printed circuit
circuit intégré	*(seehr-kwEEht ãhn-teh-grEh)*	integrated circuit
circuit parallèle	*(seehr-kwEEh pah-rah-lEhl)*	parallel circuit
clavier (m)	*(klah-vyEh)*	keyboard
code (m) binaire	*(kOhd beeh-nEhr)*	binary code
commande (f)	*(koh-mÃhnd)*	command
commutateur (m)	*(koh-mooh-tah-tŒhr)*	switch
compatible	*(kõhn-pah-tEEh-blœh)*	compatible
conducteur (m)	*(kõhn-doohk-tŒhr)*	conductor
contrôle (m) orthographique	*(kõhn-trOhl ohr-toh-grah-fEEhk)*	spellcheck
copie (f) de sauvegarde	*(koh-pEEh dœ sohv-gAhrd)*	backup
courant (m)	*(kooh-rÃh)*	current
courant alternatif	*(kooh-rÃhnt ahl-tehr-nah-tEEhf)*	alternating current
curseur (m)	*(koohr-sŒhr)*	cursor
détecteur (m)	*(deh-tehk-tŒhr)*	detector
digital (m)	*(deeh-zheeh-tAhl)*	digital

diode (f)	*(deeh-Ohd)*	diode
disque (m)	*(deehs-kœ)*	record
disque (m) dur	*(deehsk dOOhr)*	hard disk
disquette (f)	*(deehs-kEht)*	floppy disk
écran (m)	*(eh-krAhn)*	screen
effacer	*(eh-fah-sEh)*	delete (v)
électricité (f)	*(eh-lehk-treeh-seeh-tEh)*	electricity
éléctrode (f)	*(eh-lehk-trOhd)*	electrode
électron (m)	*(eh-lehk-trÕh)*	electron
électronique	*(eh-lehk-troh-nEEhk)*	electronic
électrophone (m)	*(eh-lehk-troh-fOhn)*	record player
électrostatique	*(eh-lehk-troh-stah-tEEhk)*	electrostatic
en ligne	*(ãhn LEEh-nyœh)*	on-line
énergie (f)	*(eh-nehr-zhEEh)*	energy, power
enregistrer	*(ãhn-rœh-zheehs-trEh)*	record (v)
enregistreur (m)	*(ãhn-rœh-zheehs-trŒhr)*	tape recorder
fenêtrage (m)	*(feh-neh-trAhzh)*	windowing
fibre (f) optique	*(fEEh-brœ ohp-tEEhk)*	fiber optic
fichier (m)	*(feeh-shyEh)*	file
fil (m)	*(fEEhl)*	wire
filament (m)	*(feeh-lah-mÃh)*	filament
filtre (m)	*(fEEhl-trœ)*	filter
formater	*(fohr-mah-tEh)*	format (v)
fréquence (f)	*(freh-kÃhns)*	frequency
générateur (m)	*(zheh-neh-rah-tŒhr)*	generator
haut-parleur (f)	*(Oht pahr-lŒhr)*	speaker
haute fidélité (f)	*(Oht feeh-deh-leeh-tEh)*	high fidelity
imprimante (f)	*(æhm-preeh-mÃhnt)*	printer
imprimante (f) à laser	*(æhm-preeh-mÃhnt ah lah-zEhr)*	laser printer
induction (f)	*(æhn-doohk-syÕh)*	induction
informatique (f)	*(æhn-fohr-mah-tEEhk)*	computer science
insérer	*(æhn-seh-rEh)*	insert (v)
installer	*(æhn-stah-lEh)*	install (v)
insulateur (m)	*(æhn-sooh-lah-tŒhr)*	insulator
interrupteur (m)	*(æhn-teh-roohp-tŒhr)*	switch
kilowatt (m)		kilowatt
laser (m)	*(lah-zEhr)*	laser
lecteur (m) de disques	*(lehk-tŒhr dœ dEEhsk)*	disk drive
logiciel (m)	*(loh-zheeh-syEhl)*	software
magnétophone (m)	*(mah-nyeh-toh-fÕhn)*	videocassette player
magnétoscope (m)	*(mah-nyeh-toh-skOhp)*	VCR
matériel (m)	*(mah-teh-ryEhl)*	hardware
mélangeur (m)	*(meh-lãhn-zhŒhr)*	mixer
mémoire (f) principale	*(meh-mwAhr prãhn-seeh-pAhl)*	main memory
mettre à jour	*(mEh-trœh ah zhoohr)*	update (v)
micro-onde (m)	*(meeh-kroh-Ohnd)*	microwave

mise (f) en mémoire	*(mEEhz ãhn meh-mwAhr)*	storage
modem (m)	*(moh-dEhm)*	modem
modulation d'amplication	*(moh-dooh-lah-syÕh dahm-pleeh-kah-syÕh)*	amplitude modulation (AM)
modulation (f) de fréquence	*(moh-dooh-lah-syÕh dœ freh-kÃhns)*	frequency modulation (FM)
moteur (m)	*(moh-tŒhr)*	motor
octet (m)	*(ohk-tEht)*	byte
ohm (m)		ohm
onde (f)	*(Ohnd)*	wave
onde courte	*(Ohnd kOOhrt)*	short wave
optique	*(ohp-tEEhk)*	optic
ordinateur (m)	*(ohr-deeh-nah-tŒhr)*	computer
oscillateur (m)	*(oh-seeh-lah-tŒhr)*	oscillator
pagination (f)	*(pah-zheeh-nah-syÕhn)*	paging
panneau (m)	*(pah-nOh)*	panel
police (f) des caractères	*(poh-lEEhs deh kah-raht-tEhr)*	character font
portatif	*(pohr-tah-tEEhf)*	laptop
processeur (m)	*(proh-seh-sŒhr)*	processor
programme (m)	*(proh-grAhm)*	program
programmer	*(proh-grah-mEh)*	program (v)
puce (f)	*(pOOhs)*	chip
puissance (f)	*(pweeh-sÃhns)*	power
raccorder	*(rah-kohr-dEh)*	connect (v)
radar (m)	*(rah-dAhr)*	radar
radio (f)	*(rah-dyOh)*	radio
radiodiffuser	*(rah-dyoh-deeh-fooh-zEh)*	broadcast (v)
rayon (m)	*(rah-yÕh)*	beam
récepteur (m)	*(reh-sœhp-tŒhr)*	receiver
réseau (m)	*(reh-zOh)*	network
résistance (f)	*(reh-seehs-tÃhns)*	resistance
résonance (f)	*(reh-zoh-nÃhns)*	resonance
semi-conducteur (m)	*(sœh-meeh-kõhn-doohk-tŒhr)*	semiconductor
silicone (f)	*(seeh-leeh-kÕh)*	silicon
son (m)	*(sÕh)*	sound
souris (f)	*(sooh-rEEh)*	mouse
stéréophonique	*(steh-reh-oh-foh-nEEhk)*	stereophonic
télévision (f) à câble	*(teh-leh-veeh-zyÕh ah kAh-blœ)*	cable television
tonalité (f)	*(toh-nah-leeh-tEh)*	tone
touche (f)	*(tOOhsh)*	key
touche de commande	*(tOOhsh dœ koh-mÃhnd)*	control key
touche de fonction	*(tOOhsh dœ fõhnk-syÕhn)*	function key
traitement (m) de données	*(treht-mÃhn dœ doh-nEh)*	data processing
traitement de texte	*(treht-mÃhn dœ tEhkst)*	word processing
trame (f) de transmission	*(trAhm dœ trãhnz-meeh-syÕhn)*	transmission frame
transformateur (m)	*(trãhnz-fohr-mah-tŒhr)*	transformer

transmetteur (m)	*(trāhnz-meht-tŒhr)*	transmitter
trier	*(treeh-Eh)*	sort (v)
turbine (f)	*(toohr-bEEhn)*	turbine
unité binaire (f)	*(ooh-neeh-tEh beeh-nEhr)*	bit
vecteur (m)	*(vehk-tŒhr)*	vector
vide (m)	*(vEEhd)*	vacuum
vider	*(veeh-dEh)*	dump (v)
virus (m)	*(veeh-rOOhs)*	virus
voltage (m)	*(vohl-tAhzh)*	voltage
watt (m)		watt

COSMETICS/BEAUTY CARE

English to French

alcohol-free	sans alcool	*(sãhnz ahl-kOhl)*
aloe vera	l'aloès	*(ah-loh-Eh)*
amino acid	l'acide aminé	*(ah-seehd ah-mEEhn)*
apply (v)	appliquer	*(ah-pleeh-kEh)*
balm	le baume	*(bOhm)*
base	le fond de teint	*(fÕhn dœ tẼhnt)*
blemish	l'imperfection, le défaut	*(ãhm-pehr-fehk-syÕhn),* *(deh-fOh)*
blotchy	couvert de taches, taché	*(kooh-vEhr dœ tAhsh),* *(tah-shEh)*
clean (v)	nettoyer	*(nœh-twah-yEh)*
cleanser	le démaquillant	*(deh-mah-keeh-yÃhn)*
collagen	le collagène	*(koh-lah-jEhn)*
complexion	le teint	*(tẼhnt)*
cream jar	le pot de crème	*(poh dœ krEhm)*
creamy	onctueux	*(õhnk-tŒh)*
day cream	la crème de jour	*(krEhm dœ zhOOhr)*
dermatologically tested	testé par les dermatologues	*(tehs-tEh pahr leh dœhr-mah-toh-logh)*
dry	sec	*(sEhk)*
dry skin	la peau sèche	*(poh sEhsh)*
dryness	le dessèchement	*(doeh-sehsh-mÃhn)*
emulsion	l'émulsion	*(eh-mohl-syÕhn)*
extract	l'extrait	*(ehks-trEht)*
eye contour	le pourtour des yeux	*(poohr-tOOhr dehz yŒh)*
eye cream	la crème pour les yeux	*(krEhm poohr lehz yŒh)*
eye shadow	l'ombre à paupières	*(Ohm-brœh ah poh-pyEhr)*
eyebrow	le sourcil	*(soohr-sEEhl)*
eyelash	le cil	*(sEEhl)*
face cream	la crème pour le visage	*(krEhm poohr lœ veeh-zAhzh)*
face powder	la poudre de riz	*(pOOh-drœh dœ rEEhs)*
fine line	la ridule	*(reeh-dOOhl)*
firm (v)	raffermir	*(rah-fœhr-mEEhr)*
flaw	le défaut	*(deh-fOh)*
flawless	sans imperfection	*(sãhns œhm-pœhr-fehk-syÕhn)*
forehead	le front	*(frÕhn)*
fragrance-free	inodore	*(ãhn-oh-dOhr)*
freshness	la fraîcheur	*(freh-shŒhr)*
gel	le gel	*(zlEhl)*
glow	l'éclat	*(eh-klAh)*
glowing	éclatant	*(eh-klah-tÃhn)*
hand cream	la crème pour les mains	*(krEhm poohr leh mẼhn)*
harmful	nuisible	*(nweeh-zEEh-blœh)*
invigorate (v)	revitaliser	*(rœh-veeh-tah-leeh-zEh)*

irritant agent	l'agent irritant	*(ah-zhĀhn eeh-reeh-tĀhn)*
irritation	l'irritation	*(eeh-reeh-tah-syŌhn)*
lather (v)	étaler en faisant mousser	*(eh-tah-lEh āhn feh-zĀhn*
		mooh-sEh)
layer	la couche	*(kOOhsh)*
lipstick	le rouge à lèvres	*(rOOhzh ah lEh-vrœh)*
lotion	la lotion	*(loh-syŌhn)*
make oneself up	maquiller (se)	*(mah-keeh-leh)*
makeup	le maquillage	*(mah-keeh-lAhzh)*
mascara	le mascara	*(mahs-kah-rah)*
mask	le masque	*(mAhsk)*
moisten (v)	humecter	*(ooh-mehk-tEh)*
moisturize (v)	hydrater	*(eeh-drah-tEh)*
moisturizing	hydratant	*(eeh-drah-tĀhn)*
mousse	la mousse	*(mOOhs)*
night cream	la crème de nuit	*(krEhm dœ nwEEh)*
normal skin	la peau normale	*(pOh nohr-mAhl)*
oily	gras	*(grAh)*
oily skin	la peau grasse	*(pOh grAhs)*
perfume bottle	le flacon de parfum	*(flah-kŌhn dœ pahr-*
		fOOhm)
powder	la poudre	*(pOOh-drœ)*
prevent (v) aging	prévenir le vieillissement	*(preh-vœh-nEEhr lœ vyeh-*
		yeehs-mĀhn)
protect (v)	protéger	*(proh-teh-zhEh)*
rash	la rougeur	*(rooh-zhŒr)*
reduce (v)	réduire	*(reh-dwEEhr)*
rejuvenate (v)	rajeunir	*(rah-zhooh-nEEhr)*
repair (v)	réparer	*(rœh-pah-rEh)*
resilience	l'élasticité	*(eh-lahs-teeh-seeh-tEh)*
rinse (v)	rincer	*(rœhn-sEh)*
sensitive skin	la peau sensible	*(pOh sāhn-sEEh-blœh)*
silky	soyeux	*(swah-yŒh)*
skin	l'épiderme, la peau	*(eh-peeh-dEhr-mœh), (pOh)*
skin tone	la tonicité	*(toh-neeh-seeh-tEh)*
smooth	lisse	*(lEEhs)*
soft	doux (ce)	*(dOOh)*
spray	le vaporisateur, l'atomiseur	*(vah-poh-reeh-zah-tŒhr),*
		(ah-toh-meeh-zŒhr)
sun block	l'écran solaire	*(eh-krĀhn soh-lEhr)*
sun lotion	la lotion solaire	*(loh-syŌhn soh-lEhr)*
waterbased	à base d'eau	*(ah bAhz dOh)*
waterproof	imperméable	*(æhm-pœhr-meh-Ah-blœh)*
wrinkle	la ride	*(rEEhd)*

French to English

à base d'eau	*(ah bAhz dŒh)*	waterbased
acide (m) aminé	*(ah-sEEhd ah-meeh-nEh)*	amino acid
agent (m) irritant	*(ah-zhĀhn eeh-reeh-tAhn)*	irritant agent

aloès (m)	*(ah-loh-Ehs)*	aloe vera
appliquer	*(ah-pleeh-kEh)*	apply (v)
atomiseur (m)	*(ah-toh-meeh-zŒhr)*	spray
baume (m)	*(bOhm)*	balm
cil (m)	*(sEEhl)*	eyelash
collagène (m)	*(koh-lah-zhEhn)*	collagen
couche (f)	*(kOOhsh)*	layer
couvert de taches	*(kooh-vEhr dœ tAhsh)*	blotchy
crème (f) de jour	*(krEhm dœ zhOOhr)*	day cream
crème de nuit	*(krEhm dœ nweeh)*	night cream
crème pour le visage	*(krEhm poohr lœh veeh-zAhzh)*	face cream
crème pour les yeux	*(krEhm poohr lehz yŒh)*	eye cream
défaut (m)	*(deh-fOh)*	flaw, blemish
démaquillant (m)	*(deh-mah-keeh-yÃhn)*	cleanser
dessèchement (m)	*(deh-sehsh-mÃhn)*	dryness
doux (ce)	*(dOOh)*	soft
éclat (m)	*(eh-klÃh)*	glow
éclatant	*(eh-klah-tÃhn)*	glowing
écran (m) solaire	*(eh-krÃhn soh-lEhr)*	sun block
élasticité (f)	*(eh-lahs-teeh-seeh-tEh)*	resilience
émulsion (f)	*(eh-moohl-syÕhn)*	emulsion
épiderme (m)	*(eh-peeh-dEhrm)*	skin
étaler en faisant mousser	*(eh-tah-lEh ãhn feh-zÃhn mooh-sEh)*	lather (v)
flacon (m) de parfum	*(flah-kÕhn doe pahr-fOOhm)*	perfume bottle
fond (m) de teint	*(fõhn dœ tÆhnt)*	base
fraîcheur (f)	*(freh-shŒhr)*	freshness
front (m)	*(frÕhn)*	forehead
gel (m)	*(zhEhl)*	gel
gras	*(grAh)*	oily
humecter	*(ooh-mehk-tŒhr)*	moisten (v)
hydratant	*(eeh-drah-tÃhn)*	moisturizing
hydrater	*(eeh-drah-tEh)*	moisture (v)
imperfection (f)	*(æhm-pehr-fehk-syÕhn)*	blemish
imperméable	*(æhm-pehr-meh-Ah-blœh)*	waterproof
inodore	*(æhn-oh-dOhr)*	fragrance-free
irritation (f)	*(eeh-reeh-tah-syÕhn)*	irritation
lisse	*(lEEhs)*	smooth
lotion (f)	*(loh-syÕhn)*	lotion
lotion solaire	*(loh-syÕhn soh-lEhr)*	sun lotion
maquillage (m)	*(mah-keeh-yAhzh)*	makeup
maquiller (se)	*(mah-keeh-yEh)*	make oneself up (v)
mascara (m)	*(mahs-kah-rAh)*	mascara
masque (m)	*(mAhsk)*	mask
mousse (f)	*(mOOhs)*	mousse
nettoyer	*(nœh-twah-yEh)*	clean (v)
nuisible	*(nweeh-zEEh-blœh)*	harmful
ombre (f) à paupières	*(Ohm-brœh ah poh-pyEhr)*	eye shadow

onctueux	(õhnk-tŒh)	creamy
peau (f)	(pOh)	skin
peau grasse	(pOh grAhs)	oily skin
peau normale	(pOh nohr-mAhl)	normal skin
peau sèche	(pOh sEhsh)	dry skin
peau sensible	(pOh sãhn-sEEh-blœh)	sensitive skin
pot (m) de crème	(poh dœ krEhm)	cream jar
poudre (f)	(pOOh-drœh)	powder
poudre de riz	(pOOh-drœh dœ rEEhs)	face powder
pourtour des yeux (m)	(poohr-tOOhr dehz yŒh)	eye contour
prévenir le vieillissement	(preh-vœh-nEEhr lœ vyeh-yeehz-mÃhn)	prevent (v) aging
protéger	(proh-teh-zhEh)	protect (v)
raffermir	(rah-fehr-mEEhr)	firm (v)
rajeunir	(rah-zhœh-nEEhr)	rejuvenate (v)
réduire	(reh-dwEEhr)	reduce (v)
réparer	(reh-pah-rEh)	repair (v)
revitalizer	(rœh-veeh-tah-leeh-zEh)	invigorate (v)
ride (f)	(rEEhd)	wrinkle
ridule (f)	(reeh-dOOhl)	fine line
rincer	(rœhn-sEh)	rinse (v)
rouge (f) à lèvres	(rOOhzh ah lEh-vrœh)	lipstick
rougeur (f)	(rOOh-zhŒhr)	rash
sans alcool	(sãhnz ahl-kOOhl)	alcohol-free
sans imperfection	(sãhnz œhm-pehr-fehk-syÕhn)	flawless
sec	(sEhk)	dry
sourcil (m)	(soohr-sEEhl)	eyebrow
soyeux	(swah-yŒh)	silky
taché	(tah-shEh)	blotchy
teint (m)	(tÆhnt)	complexion
testé par les dermatologues	(tehs-tEh pahr leh dehr-mah-toh-lOhg)	dermatologically tested
tonicité (f)	(toh-neeh-seeh-tEh)	skin tone
vaporisateur (m)	(vah-poh-reeh-zah-tŒhr)	spray

ENVIRONMENT

English to French

acid rain	la pluie acide	*(plwEEh ah-sEEhd)*
additive	l'additif	*(ah-deeh-tEEhf)*
aerosol spray	l'aérosol	*(ah-eh-roh-sOhl)*
air pollution	la pollution de l'air	*(poh-looh-syÕhn dœ lEhr)*
atmosphere	l'atmosphère	*(aht-mohs-fEhr)*
biodegradable	biodégradable	*(beeh-oh-grah-dAh-blœh)*
biosphere	la biosphère	*(beeh-oh-sfEhr)*
clean technology	les techniques non-pollutantes	*(tehk-nEEhk nõhn poh-looh-tÃhnt)*
clean-up	le nettoyage	*(neh-twah-yAzh)*
conservation	la défense de l'environnement	*(deh-fÃhns dœ lõhn-veeh-rõhn-mÃhn)*
contaminate (v)	contaminer	*(kõhn-tah-meeh-nEh)*
decontamination	la décontamination	*(deh-kõhn-tah-meeh-nah-syÕhn)*
deforestation	la déforestation	*(deh-foh-rehs-tah-syÕhn)*
deplete (v)	épuiser	*(eh-pweeh-zEh)*
desertification	la désertification	*(deh-sehr-teeh-feeh-kah-syÕhn)*
device	le dispositif	*(deehs-poh-zeeh-tEEhf)*
dried up well	le puits asséché	*(pwEEhz ah-seh-shEh)*
drought	la sécheresse	*(seh-sheh-rEhs)*
dump	la décharge	*(deh-shAhrzh)*
dump (v)	déverser	*(deh-vehr-sEh)*
dumping	le déversement	*(deh-vehrs-mÃhn)*
ecological	écologique	*(eh-koh-loh-zhEEhk)*
ecology	l'écologie	*(eh-koh-loh-zhEEh)*
emission	l'émission	*(eh-meeh-syÕhn)*
energy conservation	les économies d'énergie	*(eh-koh-noh-mEEh deh-nehr-zhEEh)*
environment	l'environnement	*(æhn-veeh-rohn-mÃhn)*
environmental advantage	l'atout écologique	*(ah-tOOht eh-koh-loh-zhEEhk)*
environmental assessment	l'évaluation de l'environnement	*(eh-vah-lwah-syÕn dœ læhn-veeh-rohn-mÃhn)*
environmental damage	les atteintes à l'environnement	*(ah-tæhnt ah læhn-veeh-rohn-mÃhn)*
environmental impact	l'impact sur l'environnement	*(æhm-pAhkt soohr læhn-veeh-rohn-mÃhn)*
environmental management	la gestion de l'environnement	*(zhehs-tyÕhn dœ læhn-veeh-rohn-mÃhn)*
environmentalist	l'écologiste	*(eh-koh-loh-zhEEhst)*
environmentally friendly	écologique	*(eh-koh-loh-zhEEhk)*
erode top soil (v)	ronger la couche arable	*(rõhn-zhEh lah kOOhsh ah-rAh-blœh)*

fossil fuel	le combustible fossile	*(kohm-boohs-tEEh-blœh foh-sEEhl)*
global warming	le réchauffement de la planète	*(reh-shohf-mÃhn dœ lah plah-nEht)*
greenhouse effect	l'effet de serre	*(eh-fEh dœ sEhr)*
greenhouse gas	le gaz entraînant l'effet de serre	*(gAhz æhn-treh-nÃhn leh-fEh sEhr)*
groundwater reserves	les nappes phréatiques	*(nAhp freh-ah-tEEhk)*
harmful	nuisible	*(nweeh-zEEh-blœh)*
health hazard	le risque pour la santé	*(rEEhsk poohr lah sãhn-tEh)*
hole in ozone layer	le trou dans la couche d'ozone	*(trooh dãhn lah kOOhsh doh-zOhn)*
incineration	l'incinération	*(æhn-seeh-neh-rah-syÕhn)*
landfill site	la décharge	*(deh-shAhrzh)*
lead content	la teneur en plomb	*(teh-nŒhr ãhn plÕhm)*
leakage	la fuite	*(fwEEht)*
natural resources	les ressources naturelles	*(rœh-sOOhrs nah-tooh-rEhl)*
noise pollution	la pollution par le bruit	*(poh-looh-syÕhn pahr lœ brwEEh)*
nonpolluting energy	l'énergie non polluante	*(eh-nehr-zhEEh nohn poh-looh-Ãhnt)*
nontoxic	non toxique	*(nõhn tohk-sEEhk)*
noxiousness	la nocivité	*(noh-seeh-veeh-tEh)*
nuclear waste	les déchets nucléaires	*(deh-shEh rooh-kleh-Ehr)*
packaging	l'emballage	*(æhm-bah-lAhzh)*
pesticide	le pesticide	*(pehs-teeh-sEEhd)*
pollutant	polluant	*(poh-lwÃhn)*
pollute (v)	polluer	*(poh-lwEh)*
pollution	la pollution	*(poh-looh-syÕhn)*
polution-free	non polluant	*(nõhn poh-lwÃhn)*
preservation	la préservation	*(preh-sœhr-vah-syÕhn)*
protect (v)	protéger	*(proh-teh-zhEh)*
radioactivity	la radioactivité	*(rah-dyoh-ahk-teeh-veeh-tEh)*
rain forest	la forêt tropicale	*(foh-rEh troh-peeh-kAhl)*
rainfall	les précipitations	*(preh-seeh-peeh-tah-syÕhn)*
recyclable	recyclable	*(rœh-seeh-klAh-blœh)*
recycle	recycler	*(rœh-seeh-klEh)*
recycling center	le centre de recyclage	*(sÃhn-trœ dœ rœh-seeh-klAhzh)*
recycling plant	l'usine de traitement	*(ooh-zEEhn dœ treht-mÃhn)*
renewable resources	les ressources renouvelables	*(rœh-soohrs rœh-nooh-vAh-blœh)*
reusable	réutilisable	*(reh-ooh-teeh-zAh-blœh)*
soil erosion	l'érosion des sols	*(eh-roh-zyõhn deh sOhl)*

solar energy	l'énergie solaire	*(eh-nehr-zhEEh soh-lEhr)*
sustainable resources	les ressources soutenables	*(ræh-soohrs seeh-teh-nAh-blœh)*
tap the forest's wealth	exploiter les ressources forestières	*(ehks-plwah-tEh leh ræh-soohrs foh-rehs-tyEhr)*
threaten	menacer	*(meh-nah-sEh)*
toxicity level	le niveau de toxicité	*(neeh-vOh dœ tohk-seeh-tEh)*
waste disposal	l'élimination des déchets	*(eh-leeh-meeh-nah-syÕhn deh deh-shEt)*
waste disposal unit	le broyeur des déchets	*(brwah-yŒhr deh deh-shEt)*
waste management	la gestion des déchets	*(zhehs-tyÕhn deh deh-shEt)*
water pollution	la pollution des eaux	*(poh-looh-syÕhn dez Œh)*
water treatment	le traitement des eaux	*(treat-mÃh dez Œh)*

French to English

additif (m)	*(ah-deeh-tEEhf)*	additive
aérosol (m)	*(ah-eh-roh-sOhl)*	aerosol spray
atmosphère (f)	*(aht-moh-sfEhr)*	atmosphere
atout (m) écologique	*(ah-tOOh eh-koh-loh-zhEEhk)*	environmental advantage
atteintes (fpl) à l'environnement	*(ah-tÆhnt ah lãhn-veeh-rohn-mÃhn)*	environmental damage
biodégradable	*(beeh-oh-grah-dAh-blœh)*	biodegradable
biosphère (f)	*(beeh-oh-sfEhr)*	biosphere
broyeur (m) des déchets	*(brwah-yŒhr deh deh-shEht)*	waste disposal unit
centre (m) de recyclage	*(sÃhn-trœh dœ ræh-seeh-klAhzh)*	recycling center
combustible (m) fossile	*(kõhm-boohs-tEEh-blœh foh-sEEhl)*	fossil fuel
contaminer	*(kõhn-tah-meeh-nEh)*	contaminate (v)
décharge (f)	*(deh-shAhrzh)*	dump
déchets (mpl) nucléaires	*(deh-shEht nooh-kleh-Ehr)*	nuclear waste
décontamination (f)	*(deh-kõhn-tah-meeh-nah-syÕhn)*	decontamination
défense (f) de l'environnement	*(deh-fÃhns dœ lãhn-veeh-rohn-mÃhn)*	conservation
déforestation (f)	*(deh-foh-rehs-tah-syÕhn)*	deforestation
désertification	*(deh-sehr-teeh-feeh-kah-syÕhn)*	desertification
déversement (m)	*(deh-vehrs-mÃhn)*	dumping
déverser	*(deh-vehr-sEh)*	dump (v)
dispositif (m)	*(deehs-poh-zeeh-tEEhf)*	device
écologie (f)	*(eh-koh-loh-zhEEh)*	ecology

écologique	*(eh-koh-loh-zhEEhk)*	ecological, environmentally friendly
écologiste (m/f)	*(eh-koh-loh-zhEEhst)*	environmentalist
économies (fpl) d'énergie	*(eh-koh-noh-mEEh deh-nehr-zhEEh)*	energy conservation
effet de serre (m)	*(eh-fEh dœ sEhr)*	greenhouse effect
élimination (f) des déchets	*(eh-leeh-meeh-nah-syÕhn deh deh-shEht)*	waste disposal
emballage (m)	*(ãhm-bah-lAhzh)*	packaging
émission (f)	*(eh-meeh-syÕhn)*	emission
environnement (m)	*(ãhn-veeh-rohn-mÃhn)*	environment
énergie (f) non polluante	*(eh-nehr-zhEEh nõhn poh-lwÃhnt)*	nonpolluting energy
énergie (f) solaire	*(eh-nehr-zhEEh soh-lEhr)*	solar energy
épuiser	*(eh-pweeh-sEh)*	deplete (v)
érosion (f) des sols	*(eh-roh-syÕhn deh sOhl)*	soil erosion
évaluation (f) de l'environnement	*(eh-vah-lwah-syÕhn dœ lãhn-veeh-rohn-mÃhn)*	environmental assessment
exploiter les ressources forestières	*(ehks-plwah-tEh leh rœh-sOOhrs foh-rehs-tyEhr)*	tap the forest's wealth (v)
forêt (f) tropicale	*(foh-rEh troh-peeh-kAhl)*	rain forest
fuite (f)	*(fwEEht)*	leakage
gaz (m) entraînant l'effet de serre	*(gAhz æhn-treh-nÃhn leh-fEh dœ sEhr)*	greenhouse gas
gestion (m) de l'environnement	*(zhœhs-tyÕhn dœ lãhn-veeh-rohn-mÃhn)*	environmental management
gestion (f) des déchets	*(zhœhs-tyÕhn deh deh-shEht)*	waste management
impact (m) sur l'environnement	*(æm-pAhkt soohr læhn-veeh-rohn-mÃhn)*	environmental impact
incinération (f)	*(æhn-sãehn-eh-rah-syÕhn)*	incineration
menacer	*(meh-nah-sEh)*	threaten (v)
nappes (fpl) phréatiques	*(nAhp freh-ah-tEEhk)*	groundwater reserves
nettoyage (m)	*(neh-twah-yAhzh)*	clean-up
niveau (m) de toxicité	*(neeh-vOh dœ tohk-seeh-tEh)*	toxicity level
nocivité (f)	*(noh-seeh-veeh-tEh)*	noxiousness
non polluant	*(nõhn poh-lwÃhn)*	pollution-free
non toxique	*(nõhn tohk-sEEhk)*	nontoxic
nuisible	*(nweeh-zEEh-blœh)*	harmful
pesticide (m)	*(pehs-teeh-sEEhd)*	pesticide
pluie (f) acide	*(plwEEh ah-sEEhd)*	acid rain
polluant	*(poh-lwÃhn)*	pollutant
polluer	*(poh-lwEh)*	pollute (v)
pollution (f)	*(poh-looh-syÕhn)*	pollution
pollution (f) de l'air	*(poh-looh-syÕhn dœ lEhr)*	air pollution
pollution (f) des eaux	*(poh-looh-syÕhn dehz Œh)*	water pollution

pollution (f) par le bruit	*(poh-looh-syÕhn pahr lah brwEEh)*	noise pollution
précipitations (fpl)	*(preh-seeh-peeh-tah-syÕhn)*	rainfall
préservation (f)	*(preh-sehr-vah-syÕhn)*	preservation
protéger	*(proh-teh-zhEh)*	protect (v)
puits (m) asséché	*(pweeh ah-seh-shEh)*	dried up well
radioactivité (f)	*(rah-dyoh-ahk-teeh-veeh-tEh)*	radioactivity
réchauffement (m) de la planète	*(reh-shohf-mÃhn dœ lah plah-nEht)*	global warming
recyclable	*(rœh-seeh-klAh-blœh)*	recyclable
recycler	*(rœh-seel-klEh)*	recycle (v)
ressources (fpl) naturelles	*(rœh-sOOhrs nah-tooh-rEhl)*	natural resources
ressources renouvelables	*(rœh-sOOhrs rœh-nooh-vAh-blœh)*	renewable resources
ressources soutenables	*(rœh-sOOhrs sooh-tœh-nAh-blœh)*	sustainable resources
réutilisable	*(reh-ooh-teeh-leeh-zAh-blœh)*	reusable
risque (m) pour la santé	*(rEEhsk poohr lah sãhn-tEh)*	health hazard
ronger la couche arable	*(rõhn-zhEh lah koohsh ah-rAh-blœh)*	erode top soil (v)
sécheresse (f)	*(seh-shoeh-rEhs)*	drought
techniques (fpl) non-polluantes	*(tehk-nEEhk nõhn poh-lwÃhnt)*	clean technology
teneur (f) en plomb	*(tœh-nŒhr ãhn plÕhm)*	lead content
traitement (m) des eaux	*(treht-mÃh dehz Œh)*	water treatment
trou (m) dans la couche d'ozone	*(trOOh dãhn lah kOOhsh doh-zOhn)*	hole in ozone layer
usine (f) de traitement	*(ooh-zEEhn dœ treht-mÃhn)*	recycling plant

EUROPEAN COMMUNITY

English to French

abide by a provision (v)	respecter une disposition	*(ræhs-pehk-tEh oohn deehs-poh-zeeh-syÕhn)*
apply (v)	déposer une demande d'adhésion	*(deh-poh-zEh oohn dœh-mÃhnd dah-deh-zyÕhn)*
aspirant member	le candidat à l'adhésion	*(kÃhn-deeh-dah ah lah-deh-zyÕhn)*
attain unity (v)	réaliser l'unité	*(reh-ah-leeh-zEh looh-neeh-tEh)*
block (to)	faire obstacle	*(fehr ohb-stAh-klœh)*
breakthrough	la percée	*(pehr-sEh)*
Channel tunnel	le tunnel sous la Manche	*(tooh-nEhl sooh lah mÃhnsh)*
clause	la clause	*(klOhz)*
cohesion funds	le fonds de cohésion	*(fÕhn dœ koh-eh-zyÕhn)*
come into force (v)	entrer en vigueur	*(ãhn-trEh ãhn veeh-gŒhr)*
common agricultural policy (CAP)	la politique agricole commune (PAC)	*(poh-leeh-tEEhk ah-greeh-kOhl koh-mOOhn)*
common drug policy	la politique communautaire sur la drogue	*(poh-leeh-tEEhk koh-mooh-noh-tEhr soohr lah drOhg)*
common gun law	la loi communautaire sur les armes à feu	*(lwah koh-mooh-noh-tEhr soohr lehz Ahrm ah fŒh)*
competition	la concurrence	*(kõhn-kooh-rÃhns)*
comply with EC legislation (v)	se plier à la législation européenne	*(sœ pleeh-Eh ah lah leh-zheehs-lay-syÕhn eh-roh-peh-Ehn)*
Council of Europe	le Conseil de l'Europe	*(kõhn-sEh dœ leh-ooh-rOhp)*
currency unit	l'unité monétaire	*(ooh-neeh-tEh moh-neh-tEhr)*
deadline	la date limite	*(dAht leeh-mEEht)*
deregulation	la déréglementation	*(deh-reh-glœh-mahn-tah-syÕhn)*
devalue (v)	dévaluer	*(deh-vah-lwEh)*
EC national	le ressortissant de la CE	*(ræh-sohr-teeh-sÃhn dœ lah seh-Eh)*
EC passport holder	le titulaire d'un passeport de la CE	*(teeh-tooh-lEhr dœhn pahs-pOhr dœ lah seh-Eh)*
empowered to	abilité à	*(ah-beeh-leh-tEh ah)*
enforce (v)	appliquer, mettre en vigueur	*(ah-pleeh-kEh, mEh-træh ãhn veeh-gŒhr)*
Eurocheque	l'eurochèque	*(eh-ooh-roh-shEhk)*
Eurocrat	l'eurocrate	*(eh-ooh-roh-krAht)*

Eurocurrency	l'eurodevise	*(eh-ooh-roh-dœh-vEEhz)*
Eurodollar	l'eurodollar	*(eh-ooh-roh-doh-lAhr)*
Euromarket	l'euromarché	*(eh-ooh-roh-mahr-shEh)*
European citizenship	la citoyenneté européenne	*(seeh-twah-yehn-tEh eh-ooh-roh-peh-Ehn)*
European Community (EC)	la Communauté européenne (CE)	*(koh-mooh-noh-tEh eh-ooh-roh-peh-Ehn)*
European Currency Unit	l'ÉCU	*(eh-kOOh)*
European Monetary System	le système monétaire européen	*(seehs-tEhm moh-neh-tEhr eh-ooh-roh-peh-Ehn)*
European Parliament	le Parlement européen	*(pahr-lœh-mÃhn eh-ooh-roh-peh-Ehn)*
foreign affairs	les affaires étrangères	*(ah-fEhr eh-trãhn-zhEhr)*
free movement	la libre circulation	*(lEEh-brœh seehr-kooh-lah-syÕhn)*
fulfill the obligations (v)	remplir les obligations	*(rãhm-plEEhr lehz oh-bleeh-gah-syÕhn)*
grant (v)	accorder	*(ah-kohr-dEh)*
growth	la croissance	*(krwah-sÃhns)*
human rights	les droits de l'homme	*(drwAh dœ lOhm)*
implement (to)	metter en œuvre	*(mEh-trœh ãhn Œh-vrœh)*
implementation	la mise en œuvre	*(mEEhz ãhn Œh-vrœh)*
increase tension (v)	accroître la tension	*(ah-krwAh-trœh lah tãhn-syÕhn)*
Maastricht Treaty	le Traité de Maastricht	*(treh-tEh dœh mehs-trEEht)*
majority voting	le vote majoritaire	*(vOht mah-zhoh-reeh-tEhr)*
member state	l'État membre	*(eh-tAh mãhm-brœh)*
MEP	le député européen	*(deh-pooh-tEh eh-ooh-roh-peh-Ehn)*
NAFTA	l'ALÉNA	*(ah-leh-nAh)*
NATO	l'OTAN	*(oh-tAhn)*
negotiator	le négociateur	*(neh-goh-syah-tŒhr)*
on the agenda	à l'ordre du jour	*(ah lOhr-drœh dooh zhOOhr)*
overhaul regulations (v)	refondre les réglementations	*(rœh-fÕhn-drœh leh reh-glœh mãhn-tah-syÕhn)*
patent registering	le dépôt des brevets	*(deh-pOh deh brœh-vEht)*
play host (v)	accueillir	*(ah-kweh-yEEhr)*
plenary session	la session pléinière	*(seh-syÕhn pleh-nyEhr)*
political framework	le cadre politique	*(kAh-drœh poh-leeh-tEEhk)*
pool one's resources (v)	mettre en commun ses ressources	*(meh-trœh ãhn koh-mOOhn seh-rœh-soohrs)*
provide that (v)	stipuler que	*(steeh-pooh-lEh kœh)*

reach a	parvenir à un consensus	*(pahr-vœh-nEEhr ah œ̃hr*
consensus (v)		*kõhn-sãhn-sooh)*
relaxation of	l'assouplissement des	*(ah-sooh-pleehs-mÃhn deh*
restraints	restrictions	*rœhs-treehk-syÕhn)*
remove frontier	supprimer les contrôles	*(sooh-preeh-mEh leh kõhn-*
controls (v)	douaniers	*trOhl dooh-ah-nyEh)*
review (v)	examiner	*(ehk-zah-meeh-nEh)*
seat	le siège	*(syEhzh)*
single market	le marché unique	*(mahr-shEh ooh-neeh-kEh)*
sovereignty	la souveraineté	*(sooh-vrœ̃hn-oeh-tEh)*
standard	la norme	*(nOhrm)*
standardize (v)	homogénéiser	*(oh-moh-zheh-neh-eeh-zEh)*
stay separate (v)	faire cavalier seul	*(fehr kah-vah-lyEh sŒhl)*
subsidize (v)	subventionner	*(sooh-vãhn-syoh-nEh)*
subsidy	la subvention	*(soohb-vãhn-syÕhn)*
summit meeting	la réunion au sommet	*(reh-ooh-nyÕhn oh soh-mEh)*
talks	les pourparlers	*(poohr-pahr-lEh)*
tax break	l'avantage fiscal	*(ah-vãhn-tAhzh feehs-kAhl)*
trade barrier	la barrière douanière	*(bah-ryEhr dooh-ah-nyEhr)*
transfer of powers	le transfert des pouvoirs	*(trãhns-fEhr deh pooh-vwAhr)*
veto (v)	mettre son veto	*(mEh-trœh sÕhn veh-tOh)*
widen the gap (v)	élargir le fossé	*(eh-lahr-zhEEhr lœh foh-sEh)*

French to English

abilité à	*(ah-beeh-leeh-tEh ah)*	empowered to
accorder	*(ah-kohr-dEh)*	grant (v)
accroître la tension	*(ah-krwAh-trœh lah*	increase tension (v)
	tãhn-syÕhn)	
accueillir	*(ah-kweh-yEEhr)*	play host (v)
affaires (fpl) étrangères	*(ah-fEhr eh-trãhn-zhEh)*	foreign affairs
ALÉNA (m)	*(al-leh-nAh)*	NAFTA
à l'ordre du jour	*(ah lOhr-drœh dooh*	on the agenda
	zhOOhr)	
appliquer	*(ah-pleeh-kEh)*	enforce (v)
assouplissement (m) des	*(ah-sooh-pleehs-mÃhn deh*	relaxation of
restrictions	*rœhs-treehk-syÕyn)*	restraints
avantage (m) fiscal	*(ah-vãhn-tAhzh fees-kAhl)*	tax break
barrière (f) douanière	*(bah-ryEhr dooh-ah-nyEhr)*	trade barrier
cadre (m) politique	*(kAh-drœ poh-leeh-tEEhk)*	political framework
candidat (m) à l'adhésion	*(kãhn-deeh-dAh ah lah-*	aspirant member
	deh-zyÕhn)	
citoyenneté (f)	*(seeh-twah-yehn-tEh eh-*	European
européenne	*ooh-roh-peh-Ehn)*	citizenship

clause (f)	(klOhz)	clause
Communauté (f) Européenne (CE)	(koh-mooh-noh-tEh eh-ooh-roh-peh-Ehn)	European Community (EC)
concurrence (f)	(kõhn-kooh-rÃhns)	competition
Conseil (m) de l'Europe	(kõhn-sEh-yœh dœ leh-ooh-rOhp)	Council of Europe
croissance (f)	(krwa-sAhns)	growth
date (f) limite	(daht leeh-mEEht)	deadline
déposer une demande d'adhésion	(deh-poh-zEh oohn dœ-mÃhnd dah-deh-zyÕhn)	apply (v)
dépôt (m) des brevets	(deh-pOh deh breh-vEht)	patent registering
député (m) européen	(deh-pooh-tEh eh-ooh-roh-peh-Ehn)	MEP
déréglementation (f)	(deh-rehg-lœh-mãhn-tah-syÕhn)	deregulation
dévaluer	(deh-vah-lwEh)	devalue (v)
droits (mpl) de l'homme	(drwAh dœ lOhm)	human rights
ÉCU (m)	(eh-kOOh)	European Currency Unit
élargir le fossé	(eh-lahr-zhEEhr lœ foh-sEh)	widen the gap (v)
entrer en vigueur	(ãhn-trEh ãhn veeh-gŒhr)	come into force (v)
eurochèque (m)	(eh-ooh-roh-shEhk)	Eurocheque
eurocrate (m/f)	(eh-ooh-roh-krAht)	Eurocrat
eurodevise (f)	(eh-ooh-roh-dœh-vEEhz)	Eurocurrency
eurodollar (m)	(eh-ooh-roh-doh-lAhr)	Eurodollar
euromarché (m)	(eh-ooh-roh-mahr-shEh)	Euromarket
État membre (m)	(eh-tAh mÃhm-brœh)	member state
examiner	(ehk-zah-meeh-nEh)	review (v)
faire cavalier seul	(fEhr kah-vah-lyEh sŒhl)	stay separate (v)
faire obstacle	(fEhr ohb-stAh-klœh)	block (to)
fonds (mpl) de cohésion	(fÕhn dœ koh-eh-zyÕhn)	cohesion funds
homogénéiser	(oh-moh-zheh-neh-eeh-zEh)	standardize (v)
libre circulation (f)	(lEEh-brœh seehr-kooh-lah-syÕhn)	free movement
loi (m) communautaire sur les armes à feu	(lwAh koh-mooh-noh-tEhr soohr lehz Ahrm ah fŒh)	common gun law
marché (m) unique	(mahr-shEh ooh-nEEhk)	single market
mettre en communn ses ressources	(mEh-trœh ãhn koh-OOhn seh rœh-sOOhrs)	pool one's resources (v)
mettre en œuvre	(mEh-trœh ãhn Œh-vrœh)	implement (to)
mettre en vigueur	(mEh-trœh ãhn veeh-gŒhr)	enforce (v)
metter son veto	(mEh-trœh sõhn vEh-toh)	veto (v)
mise (f) en œuvre	(mEEhz ãhn Œh-vrœh)	implementation
négociateur (m)	(neh-goh-syah-tŒhr)	negotiator
norme (f)	(nOhrm)	standard
OTAN (f)	(oh-tAhn)	NATO

Parlement (m) européen	*(pahr-lœh-mÃhn eh-oh-roh-peh-Ehn)*	European Parliament
parvenir à un consensus	*(pahr-vœh-nEEhr ah œhn kõhn-sãhn-sOOh)*	reach a consensus (v)
percée (f)	*(pehr-sEh)*	breakthrough
plier à la législation européenne (se)	*(pleeh-Eh ah lah leh-zheehs-lah-syÕhn eh-oh-roh-peh-Ehn)*	comply with EC legislation (v)
politique (f) agricole commune (PAC)	*(poh-leeh-tEEhk ah-greeh-kOhl koh-mOOhn)*	common agricultural policy (CAP)
politique (f) communautaire sur la drogue	*(poh-leeh-tEEhk koh-mooh-nOh-tEhr soohr lah drOhg)*	common drug policy
pourparlers (mpl)	*(poohr-pahr-lEh)*	talks
réaliser l'unité	*(reh-ah-leeh-zEh)*	attain unity (v)
refondre les réglementations	*(rœh-fOhn-drœh leh reh-glœh-mãhn-tah-syÕhn)*	overhaul regulations (v)
remplir les obligations	*(rahm-plEEhr lehz oh-bleeh-gah-syÕhn)*	fulfill the obligations (v)
respecter une disposition	*(rœhs-pehk-tEh ooh deehs-poh-zeeh-syÕhn)*	abide by the provision (v)
ressortissant (m) de la CE	*(rœh-sohr-teeh-sÃhn dœ lah sEh)*	EC national
réunion (f) au sommet	*(reh-ooh-nyÕhn oh soh-mEhr)*	summit meeting
session (f) pléinière	*(seh-syÕhn pleh-nyEhr)*	plenary session
siège (m)	*(syEhzh)*	seat
souveraineté (f)	*(sooh-vrǣhn-tEh)*	sovereignty
stipuler que	*(steeh-pooh-lEh kœh)*	provide that (v)
subvention (f)	*(soohb-vãhn-syÕhn)*	subsidy
subventionner	*(soohb-vãhn-syoh-nEh)*	subsidize (v)
supprimer les contrôles douaniers	*(sooh-preeh-mEh leh kõhn-trOhl dooh-ah-nyEh)*	remove frontier controls (v)
système (m) monétaire européen	*(seehs-tEhm moh-neh-tEhr eh-ooh-roh-peh-Ehn)*	European Monetary System
titulaire (m) d'un passeport de la CE	*(teeh-tooh-lEhr doohn pahs-pOhr dœ lah sEh)*	EC passport holder
Traité (m) de Maastricht	*(treh-tEh dœ mehs-trEEhkt)*	Maastricht Treaty
transfert (m) des pouvoirs	*(trãhnz-fEhr deh pooh-vWAhr)*	transfer of powers
tunnel sous la Manche (m)	*(tooh-nEhl sooh lah mÃhnsh)*	Channel tunnel
unité (f) monétaire	*(ooh-neeh-tEh moh-neh-tEhr)*	currency unit
vote (m) majoritaire	*(vOht mah-zhoh-reeh-tEhr)*	majority voting

FASHION

English to French

angora	l'angora	*(ãhn-goh-rAh)*
bathing suit	le maillot de bain	*(mah-yoh duh ban)*
blazer	blazer	
belt	la ceinture	*(sæhn-tOOhr)*
blouse	le chemisier	*(shœh-meeh-zyEh)*
bow tie	le nœud papillon	*(nŒh pah-peeh-yŌh)*
button	le bouton	*(booh-tŌh)*
buttonhole	la boutonnière	*(booh-toh-nyEhr)*
camel's hair	le poil de chameau	*(pwAhl dœ shAh-mOh)*
cashmere	le cachemire	*(kahsh-eh-mEEhr)*
coat	le manteau	*(mãhn-tOh)*
collar	le col	*(kOhl)*
color	la couleur	*(kooh-lŒhr)*
collection	la collection	*(koh-lehk-syŌh)*
cuff link	le bouton de manchette	*(booh-tŌhn dœ mãhn-shEht)*
cut (v)	tailler	*(tah-yEh)*
design (v)	dessiner	*(dœh-seeh-nEh)*
designer	le couturier	*(kooh-tooh-ryEh)*
drape (v)	draper	*(drah-pEh)*
dress	la robe	*(rOhb)*
elegance	l'élégance	*(eh-leh-gÃhns)*
fabric	le tissu	*(teeh-sOOh)*
fashion	la mode	*(mOhd)*
fashionable	à la mode	*(ah lah mOhd)*
flannel	la flanelle	*(flah-nEhl)*
footage	le métrage	*(meh-trAhzh)*
hem	l'ourlet	*(oohr-lEht)*
high fashion designer	le grand couturier	*(grãhn kooh-tooh-ryEh)*
hood	la capuche	*(kah-pOOhsh)*
jacket	la veste	*(vehst)*
jewel	le bijou	*(beeh-zhOOh)*
length	la longueur	*(lõhn-gŒhr)*
lining	la doublure	*(dooh-blOOhr)*
long sleeves	les manches longues	*(mÃhnsh lÕhng)*
model	le mannequin	*(mah-nœh-kÆhn)*
moire	la moire	*(mwAhr)*
muslin	la mousseline	*(moohs-lEEhn)*
out of style	démodé	*(deh-moh-dEh)*
pants	le pantalon	*(pãhn-tah-lÕh)*
panty hose	les collants	*(koh-lAhn)*
pattern	le patron	*(pah-trÕh)*
pleat	le pli	*(plEEh)*
pleated	plissé(e)	*(pleeh-sEh)*
polyester	le polyester	*(poh-leeh-ehs-tEhr)*

poplin	la popeline	*(pohp-lEEhn)*
print	l'imprimé	*(æhm-preeh-mEh)*
raincoat	l'imperméable	*(æhm-pehr-meh-Ah-blœ)*
rayon	la rayonne	*(rah-yOhn)*
ready-to-wear	le prêt-à-porter	*(prEht-ah-pohr-tEh)*
sample	l'échantillon (m)	*(lay-shahn-tee-yohn)*
scarf	le foulard	*(fooh-lAhr)*
sewing machine	la machine à coudre	*(mah-shEEhn ah kOOh-drœ)*
shirt	la chemise	*(shœh-mEEhz)*
shoe	la chaussure	*(shoh-sOOhr)*
short sleeves	les manches courtes	*(mÃhnsh kOOhrt)*
shoulder pad	l'épaulette	*(eh-poh-lEht)*
silk	la soie	*(swAh)*
size	la taille	*(tAh-yœ)*
skirt	la jupe	*(zhOOhp)*
socks	les chaussettes	*(shoh-sEht)*
solid color	la couleur unie	*(kooh-lŒhr ew-nEE)*
sportswear	les vêtements sport	*(veht-mÃh spOhr)*
stitch	le point	*(pwÆhn)*
striped	à rayures	*(ah rah-yewr)*
style	le style	*(stEEhl)*
stylist	le styliste	*(steeh-lEEhst)*
suede	le daim	*(dEhm)*
suit	le complet	*(kõhm-plEh)*
sweater	le pull-over	
synthetic	synthétique	*(sæhn-teeh-tEEhk)*
tie	la cravate	*(krah-vAht)*
tuxedo	le smoking	
underwear	les sous-vêtements	*(soo veht-mahn)*
veil	le voile	*(vwah-lEht)*
vest	le gilet	*(zheeh-lEh)*
window dresser	l'étalagiste	*(eh-tah-lah-zhEEhst)*
wool	la laine	*(lEhn)*
zipper	la fermeture éclair	*(fehr-mœh-tOOhr eh-klEhr)*

French to English

à la mode	*(ah lah mOhd)*	fashionable
à rayures	*(ah rah-yewr)*	striped
angora	*(ãhn-goh-rAh)*	angora
bijou (m)	*(beeh-zhOOh)*	jewel
blazer		blazer
bouton (m)	*(booh-tÕh)*	button
bouton (m) de manchette	*(booh-tÕhn dœ mãhn-shEht)*	cuff link
boutonnière (f)	*(booh-toh-nyEhr)*	buttonhole
cachemire (m)	*(kahsh-eh-mEEhr)*	cashmere
capuche (f)	*(kah-pOOhsh)*	hood

ceinture (f)	*(sæhn-tOOhr)*	belt
chaussettes (m)	*(shoh-sEht)*	socks
chaussure (f)	*(shoh-sOOhr)*	shoe
chemise (f)	*(shœh-mEEhz)*	shirt
chemisier (m)	*(shœh-meeh-zyEh)*	blouse
col (m)	*(kOhl)*	collar
collants (mpl)	*(koh-lAhn)*	panty hose
collection (f)	*(koh-lehk-syÕh)*	collection
complet (m)	*(kõhm-plEh)*	suit
couleur (f)	*(kooh-lŒhr)*	color
couleur unie (f)	*(kooh-lŒhr ew-nEE)*	solid color
couturier (m)	*(kooh-tooh-ryEh)*	designer
cravate (f)	*(krah-vAht)*	tie
daim (m)	*(dEhm)*	suede
démodé	*(deh-moh-dEh)*	out of style
dessiner	*(dœh-seeh-nEh)*	design (v)
doublure (f)	*(dooh-blOOhr)*	lining
draper	*(drah-pEh)*	drape (v)
échantillon (m)	*(ay-shahn-tee-yohn)*	sample
élégance (f)	*(eh-leh-gÃhns)*	elegance
épaulette (f)	*(eh-poh-lEht)*	shoulder pad
étalagiste (m/f)	*(eh-tah-lah-zhEEhst)*	window dresser
fermeture (f) éclair	*(fehr-mœh-tOOhr eh-klEhr)*	zipper
flanelle (f)	*(flah-nEhl)*	flannel
foulard (m)	*(fooh-lAhr)*	scarf
gilet (m)	*(zheeh-lEh)*	vest
grand couturier (m)	*(grãhn kooh-tooh-ryEh)*	high fashion designer
imprimé	*(æhm-preeh-mEh)*	print
jupe (f)	*(zhOOhp)*	skirt
l'imperméable (m)	*(æhm-pehr-meh-Ah-blœ)*	raincoat
laine (f)	*(lEhn)*	wool
longueur (f)	*(lõhn-gŒhr)*	length
maillot de bain	*(mah-yoh duh ban)*	bathing suit
manches courtes (mpl)	*(mÃhnsh kOOhrt)*	short sleeves
manches (m) longues	*(mÃhnsh lÕhng)*	long sleeves
mannequin (m)	*(mah-nœh-kÆhn)*	model
manteau (m)	*(mãhn-tOh)*	coat
métrage (m)	*(meh-trAzh)*	footage
mode (f)	*(mOhd)*	fashion
moire (f)	*(mwAhr)*	moire
mousseline (f)	*(moohs-lEEhn)*	muslin
noeud (m) papillon	*(nŒh pah-peeh-yÕh)*	bow tie
ourlet (m)	*(oohr-lEh)*	hem
pantalon (m)	*(pãhn-ah-lÕh)*	pants
patron (m)	*(pah-trÕh)*	pattern
pli (m)	*(plEeh)*	pleat
plissé(e)	*(pleeh-sEh)*	pleated
poil (m) de chameau	*(pwAhl dœ shAh-mOh)*	camel's hair
point (m)	*(pwÆhn)*	stitch

polyester (m)	*(poh-leeh-ehs-tEhr)*	polyester
popeline (f)	*(pohp-lEEhn)*	poplin
prêt-à-porter (m)	*(prEht-ah-pohr-tEh)*	ready-to-wear
pull-over (m)		sweater
rayonne (f)	*(rah-yOhn)*	rayon
robe (f)	*(rOhb)*	dress
smoking (m)		tuxedo
soie (f)	*(swAh)*	silk
sous-vêtements	*(soo veht-mahn)*	underwear
style (m)	*(stEEhl)*	style
styliste (f)	*(steeh-lEEhst)*	stylist
synthétique	*(sǽhn-teeh-tEEhk)*	synthetic
taille (f)	*(tAh-yœ)*	size
tailler	*(tah-yEh)*	cut (v)
tissu (m)	*(teeh-sOOh)*	fabric
vêtements (mpl) de sport	*(veht-mÃh dœ spOhr)*	sportswear
veste (f)	*(vEhst)*	blazer
voile (m)	*(vwah-lEh)*	veil

HOME FURNISHINGS AND TABLEWARE

ashtray	le cendrier	*(sāhn-dryEh)*
bed	le lit	*(lEEh)*
blade	la lame	*(lAhm)*
blender	le mixeur	*(meek-sŒhr)*
bone china	la porcelaine	*(pohr-seh-lEhn)*
bowl	le bol	*(bOhl)*
breadbasket	la corbeille à pain	*(kohr-bEh-yœ ah pÆhn)*
butter dish	le beurrier	*(bœh-ryEh)*
can opener	l'ouvre-boîtes	*(Œhv-rœh bwAht)*
candlestick	le chandelier	*(shāhn-dœh-lyEh)*
carving knife	le couteau à découper	*(kooh-tOh ah dœh-kooh-pEh)*
chafing dish	le chauffe-plat	*(shOht plAh)*
champagne glass	la flûte à champagne	*(flOOht ah sham-pÃh-nyœ)*
cheese-tray	le plateau à fromage	*(plah-tOh ah froh-mAhzh)*
china	la porcelaine	*(pohr-seh-lEhn)*
chinaware	la faïence	*(fah-eeh-Ãhns)*
coaster	les dessous de verre	*(dœ-sOOh dœ vEhr)*
coffeepot	la cafetière	*(kah-feh-tyEhr)*
corkscrew	le tire-bouchon	*(teehr booh-shÕhn)*
couch	le canapé	*(kah-nah-pEh)*
crystal	le cristal	*(kreehs-tAhl)*
crystal glass manufacturing	la cristallerie	*(kreehs-tah-lœh-rEEh)*
cup	la tasse	*(tAhs)*
curved	incurvé	*(æhn-koohr-vEh)*
cutlery	la coutellerie	*(kooh-teh-lœh-rEEh)*
decanter	la carafe	*(kah-rAhf)*
deep dish	le plat creux	*(plah krŒh)*
dessert plate	l'assiette à dessert	*(ah-syEht ah dœh-sEhr)*
dinner plate	l'assiette plate	*(ah-syEht plAht)*
dinnerware set	le service	*(sœhr-vEEhs)*
dish towel	le torchon	*(tohr-shÕhn)*
dishes	la vaisselle	*(veh-sEhl)*
dishwasher safe	garanti lave-vaisselle	*(gah-rāhn-tEEh lahv-veh-sEhl)*
earthenware	la faïence	*(fah-eeh-Ãhns)*
espresso cup	la demi-tasse	*(dœh-mEEh tAhs)*
finish	la finition	*(feeh-neeh-syÕhn)*
flatware	les couverts	*(kooh-vEhr)*
flawless	sans défaut	*(sāhn deh-fOh)*
flute	la flûte à champagne	*(flOOht ah sham-pÃh-nyœ)*
fork	la fourchette	*(foohr-shEht)*
gilded	doré	*(doh-rEh)*
glass	le verre	*(vEhr)*
gravy boat	la saucière	*(soh-syEhr)*
hand-blown glass	le verre soufflé	*(vEhr sooh-flEh)*

hand-glued handles	les anses collées à la main	*(Ahns koh-lEh ah lah mÃEhn)*
hand-painted	peint(e) à la main	*(pãehnt ah lah mÃEhn)*
ice bucket	le seau à glace	*(sOh ah glAhs)*
iron	le fer à repasser	*(fEhr ah rœh-pah-sEh)*
kettle	la bouilloire	*(booh-lwAhr)*
knife	le couteau	*(kooh-tOh)*
knife handle	le manche de couteau	*(mÃhnsh dooh kooh-tOh)*
knife rest	le porte-couteau	*(pOhrt-kooh-tOh)*
lace	la dentelle	*(dãhn-tEhl)*
leadfree	sans plomb	*(sãhn plÕhn)*
lid	le couvercle	*(kooh-vEhr-klœh)*
linen	la toile de lin	*(twAhl dœ lEEhn)*
luster	la patine	*(pah-tEEhn)*
microwave safe	garanti four à micro-ondes	*(gah-rãhn-tEEh foohr ah meeh-kroh-Õhnd)*
mold	le moule	*(mOOhl)*
monogram	le monogramme	*(moh-roh-grAhm)*
mustard pot	le moutardier	*(mooh-tahr-dyEh)*
napkin	la serviette	*(sœhr-vyEht)*
napkin ring	le rond de serviette	*(rõhnd dœ sœhr-vyEht)*
oilcloth	la toile cirée	*(twAhl seeh-rEh)*
pastry server	la pelle à tarte	*(pEhl ah tAhr-tœ)*
pepper mill	le moulin à poivre	*(mooh-lÃEhn ah pwAh-vrœ)*
pepper shaker	la poivrière	*(pwah-vryEhr)*
pillowcase	la taie d'oreiller	*(tEh doh-reh-yEh)*
pitcher	le pichet	*(peeh-shEh)*
place setting	le couvert	*(kooh-vEhr)*
plate	l'assiette	*(ah-syEht)*
pottery	la poterie	*(poh-teh-rEEh)*
round platter	le plat rond	*(plAh rÕhn)*
rug	le tapis	*(tah-pEEh)*
salad bowl	le saladier	*(sah-lah-dyEh)*
salad plate	l'assiette à salade	*(ah-syEht ah sah-lAhd)*
salt shaker	la salière	*(sah-lyEhr)*
saucer	la soucoupe	*(sooh-kOOhp)*
shade	l'abat-jour	*(ah-bah-zhOOhr)*
sheet	le drap	*(drAh)*
silverware	l'argenterie	*(ahr-zhãhn-tœh-rEEh)*
soup dish	l'assiette creuse	*(ah-syEht krŒhz)*
soup ladle	la louche	*(lOOhsh)*
soup tureen	la soupière	*(sooh-pyEhr)*
sparkle	l'éclat	*(eh-klAh)*
spoon	la cuiller, cuillère	*(kooh-yEhr)*
spout	le bec verseur	*(bEhk vehr-sŒhr)*
stoneware	la poterie en grès	*(poh-teh-rEEh ãhn grEh)*
sugar bowl	le sucrier	*(sooh-kryEh)*
sugar tongs	la pince à sucre	*(pÃEhns ah sOOh-krœh)*
tablecloth	la nappe	*(nAhp)*

tablespoon	la cuiller à soupe	*(kooh-yEhr ah sOOhp)*
teacup	la tasse à thé	*(tAhs ah tEh)*
teapot	la théière	*(teh-yEhr)*
teaspoon	la cuiller à cafe	*(kooh-yEhr ah kah-fEh)*
three-pronged fork	la fourchette à trois dents	*(foohr-shEht ah trwah dÃhn)*
toaster	le grille-pain	*(grEEh-yœh-pÃ̃Ehn)*
tray	le plateau	*(plah-tŒh)*
tureen	la terrine	*(teh-rEEhn)*
unbleached linen	la toile écrue	*(twAhl eh-krOOh)*
unbreakable	incassable	*(æhn-kah-sAh-blœh)*
vacuum cleaner	l'aspirateur	*(ahs-peeh-rah-tŒhr)*
washing machine	la machine à laver	*(mah-shEEhn ah lah-vEh)*
white porcelain	la porcelaine blanche	*(pohr-sœh-lEhn blÃhnsh)*
wine glass	le verre à vin	*(vEhr ah vÃ̃Ehn)*

French to English

abat-jour (m)	*(ah-bah zhOOhr)*	shade
anses (fpl) collées à la main	*(Ãhns koh-lEh ah lah mÃ̃Ehn)*	hand-glued handles
argenterie (f)	*(ahr-zhãhn-teh-rEEh)*	silverware
aspirateur (m)	*(ahs-peeh-rah-tŒhr)*	vacuum cleaner
assiette (f)	*(ah-syEht)*	plate
assiette à dessert	*(ah-syEht ah dœh-sEhr)*	dessert plate
assiette à salade	*(ah-syEht ah sah-lAhd)*	salad plate
assiette creuse	*(ah-syEht krŒhz)*	soup dish
assiette plate	*(ah-syEht plAht)*	dinner plate
bec (m) verseur	*(bEhk vehr-sŒhr)*	spout
beurrier (m)	*(bœh-ryEh)*	butter dish
bol (m)	*(bOhl)*	bowl
bouilloire (f)	*(booh-lwAhr)*	kettle
cafetière (f)	*(kah-feh-tyEhr)*	coffeepot
canapé (m)	*(kah-nah-pEh)*	couch
carafe (f)	*(kah-rAhf)*	decanter
cendrier (m)	*(sãhn-dryEh)*	ashtray
chandelier (m)	*(shãhn-dœh-lyEh)*	candlestick
chauffe-plat (m)	*(shohf-plAh)*	chafing dish
corbeille (f) à pain	*(kohr-bEh-yœ ah pÃ̃Ehn)*	breadbasket
couteau (m)	*(kooh-tOh)*	knife
couteau à découper	*(kooh-tOh ah deh-kooh-pEh)*	carving knife
coutellerie (f)	*(kooh-teh-yœh-rEEh)*	cutlery
couvercle (m)	*(kooh-vEhr-klœh)*	lid
couvert (m)	*(kooh-vEhrt)*	place setting
cristal (m)	*(kreehs-tAhl)*	crystal
cristallerie (f)	*(kreehs-tah-lœh-rEEh)*	crystal glass manufacturing
cuiller, cuillère (f)	*(kooh-yEhr)*	spoon
cuiller (f) à café	*(kooh-yEhr ah kah-fEh)*	teaspoon

cuiller à soupé	*(kooh-yEhr ah sOOhp)*	tablespoon
demi-tasse (f)	*(deh-mEEh tAhs)*	espresso cup
dentelle (f)	*(dāhn-tEhl)*	lace
dessous (m) de verre	*(dœh-sOOh dœ vEhr)*	coaster
doré	*(doh-rEh)*	gilded
drap (m)	*(drAhp)*	sheet
éclat (m)	*(eh-klAh)*	sparkle
faïence (f)	*(fah-eeh-Ãhns)*	chinaware, earthenware
fer (m) à repasser	*(fehr ah rœh-pah-sEh)*	iron
finition (f)	*(feeh-neeh-syÕhn)*	finish
flûte (f) à champagne	*(flOOht ah shahm-pÃh-nyœ)*	flute, champagne glass
fourchette (f)	*(foohr-shEht)*	fork
fourchette (f) à trois dents	*(foohr-shEht ah trwah dAhn)*	three-pronged fork
garanti four à micro-ondes	*(gah-rāhn-tEEh fOOhr ah meeh-kroh-Õhnd)*	microwave safe
garanti lave-vaisselle	*(gah-rāhn-tEEh lahv-veh-sEhl)*	dishwasher safe
grille-pain (m)	*(greeh-yœh-pÃ̈hn)*	toaster
incassable	*(ã̈hn-kah-sAh-blœh)*	unbreakable
incurvé	*(ã̈hn-koohr-vEh)*	curved
lame (f)	*(lAhm)*	blade
lit (m)	*(lEEh)*	bed
louche (f)	*(lOOhsh)*	soup ladle
machine (f) à laver	*(mah-shEEhn ah lah-vEh)*	washing machine
mixeur (m)	*(meehk-sŒhr)*	blender
monogramme (m)	*(moh-noh-grAhm)*	monogram
moule (m)	*(mOOhl)*	mold
moulin (m) à poivre	*(mooh-lÃ̈hn ah pwAh-vrœ)*	pepper mill
moutardier (m)	*(mooh-tahr-dyEh)*	mustard pot
nappe (f)	*(nAhp)*	tablecloth
ouvre-boîtes (m)	*(Œh-vrœh bwAht)*	can opener
patine (f)	*(pah-tEEhn)*	luster
peint(e) (f) à la main	*(pÃ̈hnt ah lah mÃ̈hn)*	hand-painted
pelle (f) à tarte	*(pEhl ah tAhrt)*	pastry server
pichet (m)	*(peeh-shEh)*	pitcher
pince (f) à sucre	*(pÃ̈hns ah sOOh-krœh)*	sugar tongs
plat (m) creux	*(plAh krŒh)*	deep dish
plat (m) rond	*(plAh rÕhn)*	round platter
plateau (m)	*(plah-tŒh)*	tray
plateau (m) à fromage	*(plah-tOh ah froh-mAhzh)*	cheese-tray
poivrière (f)	*(pwah-vryEhr)*	pepper shaker
porcelaine (f)	*(pohr-sœh-lEhn)*	china, bone china
porcelaine (f) blanche	*(pohr-sœh-lEhn blÃhnsh)*	white porcelain
porte-couteau (m)	*(pohrt-kooh-tOh)*	knife rest
poterie (f)	*(poh-tœh-rEEh)*	pottery
poterie en grès	*(poh-tœh-rEEh ãhn grEh)*	stoneware
rond (m) de serviette	*(rÕhnd dœ sœhr-vyEht)*	napkin ring

saladier (m)	*(sah-lay-dyEh)*	salad bowl
salière (f)	*(sah-lyEhr)*	salt shaker
sans défaut	*(sãhn deh-fOh)*	flawless
sans plomb	*(sãhn plŌhm)*	leadfree
saucière (f)	*(soh-syEhr)*	gravy boat
seau (m) à glace	*(sOh ah glAhs)*	ice bucket
service (m)	*(sehr-vEEhs)*	dinnerware set
serviette (f)	*(sœhr-vyEht)*	napkin
soucoupe (f)	*(sooh-kOOhp)*	saucer
soupière (f)	*(sooh-pyEhr)*	soup tureen
sucrier (m)	*(sooh-kryEh)*	sugar bowl
taie (m) d'oreiller	*(tEh doh-reh-yEh)*	pillowcase
tapis (m)	*(tah-pEEh)*	rug
tasse (f)	*(tAhs)*	cup
tasse (f) à thé	*(tahs ah tEh)*	teacup
terrine (f)	*(teh-rEEhn)*	tureen
théière (f)	*(teh-yEhr)*	teapot
tire-bouchon (m)	*(teehr booh-shŎhn)*	corkscrew
toile (f) cirée	*(twAhl seeh-rEh)*	oilcloth
toile de lin	*(twAhl dœ lEEhn)*	linen
toile écrue	*(twAhl eh-krOoh)*	unbleached linen
torchon (m)	*(tohr-shŎhn)*	dish towel
vaisselle (f)	*(veh-sEhl)*	dishes
verre (m)	*(vEhr)*	glass
verre (m) à vin	*(vehr ah vÃEhn)*	wine glass
verre soufflé	*(vEhr sooh-flEh)*	hand-blown glass

IRON AND STEEL

English to French

alloy steel	l'acier allié	*(ah-syEh ah-lyEh)*
annealing	recuit	*(reh-kwEEh)*
bars	les barres	*(bAhr)*
billets	les billettes	*(beeh-yEht)*
blast furnace	le haut-fourneau	*(oht-foohr-nOh)*
carbon steel	l'acier au carbone	*(ahs-yEh oh kahr-bOhn)*
cast iron	la fonte coulée	*(fÕhnt kooh-lEh)*
charge chrome	le ferrochrome de charge	*(feh-roh-krOhm dœ shAhrzh)*
chromium	le chrome	*(krOhm)*
coal	le charbon	*(shahr-bÕh)*
coil	la bobine	*(boh-bEEhn)*
cold rolling	le laminé à froid	*(lah-meeh-nEh ah frwAh)*
continuous caster	la coulée continue	*(kooh-lEh kõhn-teeh-nOOh)*
conveyor	le transporteur	*(trãhnz-pohr-tah-tŒhr)*
conveyor belt	la chaîne de montage	*(shEhn dœ mõhn-tAhzh)*
copper	le cuivre	*(kwEEh-vrœ)*
crucible	le creuset	*(krœh-zEht)*
cupola	le cubilot	*(kooh-beeh-lOh)*
electric arc furnace	le four électrique	*(fOOhr eh-lehk-trEEhk)*
electrodes	les électrodes	*(eh-lehk-trOhd)*
electrolytic process	le procédé électrolytique	*(proh-seh-dEh eh-leh-troh-leeh-tEEhk)*
ferritic	ferritique	*(feh-reeh-tEEhk)*
ferroalloys	les ferro-alliages	*(feh-roh-ah-lyAhzh)*
ferromanganese	le ferromanganese	*(feh-roh-mahn-gah-nEhz)*
finished products	les produits finis	*(proh-dwEEh feeh-nEEh)*
finishing mill	les laminoirs de finition	*(lah-meeh-nwAhr deh-feeh-neeh-syÕh)*
flats products	les produits plats	*(proh-dwEEh plAh)*
foundry	la fonderie	*(fõhn-dœh-rEEh)*
furnace	le four	*(fOOhr)*
galvanizing	la galvanisation	*(gahl-vah-neeh-zah-syÕh)*
grinding	le meulage	*(mœh-lAhzh)*
hardness	le diamètre	*(deeh-ah-meh-trEEh)*
heat	la charge	*(shAhrzh)*
hot rolling	le laminé à chaud	*(lah-meeh-nEh ah shOhd)*
induction furnace	le four à induction	*(fOOhr ah æhn-doohk-synOh)*
ingot mold	la lingotière	*(lǽhn-goh-tyEhr)*
ingot	le lingot	*(lǽhn-gOh)*
iron ore	le minerai de fer	*(meeh-neh-rEh dœ fEhr)*
limestone	la pierre à chaux	*(pyEhr ah shOh)*
long product	le produit long	*(proh-dwEEh lÕh)*

malleability	la malléabilité	*(mah-leh-ah-beeh-leeh-tEh)*
manganese ore	le minerai de manganèse	*(meeh-neh-rEh dœ māhn-gah-nEhz)*
molybdenum	le molybdène	*(moh-leehb-dEhn)*
nitrogen	l'azote	*(ah-zOht)*
ore	le minerai	*(meeh-neh-rEh)*
pickling	le décapage	*(deh-kah-pAhzh)*
pig iron	la fonte	*(fÕhnt)*
pipes and tubes	les tubes et tuyauteries	*(tOOhb eh tooh-yah-tœh-rEEh)*
plate	la plaque	*(plAhk)*
powder	la poudre	*(pOOh-drœ)*
pressure	la pression	*(prœh-syÕh)*
process	le procédé	*(proh-seh-dEh)*
quench (v)	tremper	*(trāhm-pEh)*
rebars	le fer à béton	*(fehr ah beh-tÕh)*
refractories	les produits réfractaires	*(proh-dwEEh reh-frahk-tEhr)*
rod	la baguette	*(bah-gEht)*
rolling mill	le laminoir	*(lah-meeh-nwAhr)*
scale	la balance	*(bsah-lÃhns)*
scrap	les déchets ou la ferraille	*(deh-shEht ooh feh-rAh-yœ)*
semis	les semis	*(sœh-mEEh)*
sheets	la tôle	*(tOhl)*
slabs	les brames	*(brAhm)*
specialty steels	les aciers spéciaux	*(ahs-yEh speh-syOh)*
stainless steel	l'acier inoxydable	*(ahs-yEh æhn-ohk-seeh-dAh-blœ)*
steel mill	l'acierie	*(ahs-yeh-rEEh)*
structural shapes	l'acier de construction	*(ahs-yEh dœ kÕhn-stroohk-syÕh)*
super alloys	les super alliages	*(sooh-pehr ah-lyAhzh)*
titanium	le titane	*(teeh-tAhn)*
toughness	la dureté	*(dooh-rœh-tEh)*
tungsten	le tungstène	*(toohng-stEhn)*
vacuum melting furnace	le four sous vide	*(fOOhr sooh vEEhd)*
vanadium	le vanadium	*(vah-nah-dyOOhm)*
wire	le fil	*(fEEhl)*

French to English

acier (m) allié	*(ah-syEh ah-lyEh)*	alloy steel
acier (m) au carbone	*(ahs-yEh oh kahr-bOhn)*	carbon steel
acier (m) de construction	*(ahs-yEh dœ kÕhn-stroohk-syÕh)*	structural shapes
acier (m) inoxydable	*(ahs-yEh æhn-ohk-seeh-dAh-blœ)*	stainless steel

acierie (f)	(ahs-yeh-rEEh)	steel mill
aciers (mpl) spéciaux	(ahs-yEh speh-syOh)	specialty steels
azote	(ah-zOht)	nitrogen
baguette (f)	(bah-gEht)	rod
balance (f)	(bah-lÃhns)	scale
barres (fpl)	(bAhr)	bars
billettes (fpl)	(beeh-yEht)	billets
bobine (f)	(boh-bEEhn)	coil
brames (fpl)	(brAhm)	slabs
chaîne (f) de montage	(shEhn dœ mõhn-tAhzh)	conveyor belt
charbon (m)	(shahr-bÕh)	coal
charge (f)	(shAhrzh)	heat
chrome (m)	(krOhm)	chromium
coulée (f) continue	(kooh-lEh kõhn-teeh-nOOh)	continous caster
creuset (m)	(krœh-zEht)	crucible
cubilot (m)	(kooh-beeh-lOh)	cupola
cuivre (m)	(kwEEhv-rœ)	copper
décapage (m)	(deh-kah-pAhzh)	pickling
déchets (m) ou ferraille (f)	(deh-shEht ooh feh-rAh-yœ)	scrap
diamètre (m)	(deeh-ah-mEh-trœ)	hardness
dureté (f)	(dooh-rœh-tEh)	toughness
électrodes (fpl)	(eh-lehk-trOhd)	electrodes
fer (m) à béton	(fehr ah beh-tÕh)	rebars
ferritique	(feh-reeh-tEEhk)	ferritic
ferro-alliages (mpl)	(feh-roh-ah-lyAhzh)	ferroalloys
ferrochrome (m) de charge	(feh-roh-krOhm dœ shAhrzh)	charge chrome
ferromanganèse (m)	(feh-roh-mahn-gah-nEhz)	ferromanganese
fil (m)	(fEEhl)	wire
fonderie (f)	(fõhn-dœh-rEEh)	foundry
fonte (f)	(fÕhnt)	pig iron
fonte (f) coulée	(fÕhnt kooh-lEh)	cast iron
four (m)	(fOOhr)	furnace
four (m) à induction	(fOOhr ah æ̃hn-doohk-synOh)	induction furnace
four (m) électrique	(fOOhr eh-lehk-trEEhk)	electric arc furnace
four (m) sous vide	(fOOhr sooh vEEhd)	vacuum melting furnace
galvanisation (f)	(gahl-vah-neeh-zah-syÕh)	galvanizing
haut-fourneau (m)	(oht-foohr-nOh)	blast furnace
laminé à chaud	(lah-meeh-nEh ah shOhd)	hot rolling
laminé à froid	(lah-meeh-nEh ah frwAh)	cold rolling
laminoir (m)	(lah-meeh-nwAhr)	rolling mill
laminoirs (mpl) definition	(lah-meeh-nwAhr deh-feeh-neeh-syÕh)	finishing mill
lingot (m)	(læ̃hn-gOh)	ingot
lingotière (f)	(læ̃hn-goh-tyEhr)	ingot mold
malléabilité	(mah-leh-ah-beeh-leeh-tEh)	malleability
meulage (m)	(mœh-lAhzh)	grinding
minerai (m)	(meeh-neh-rEh)	ore

minerai (m) de fer	(meeh-neh-rEh dœ fEhr)	iron ore
minerai (m) de manganèse	(meeh-neh-rEh dœ māhn-gah-nEhz)	manganese ore
molybdène (m)	(moh-leehb-dEhn)	molybdenum
pierre (f) à chaux	(pyEhr ah shOh)	limestone
plaque (f)	(plAhk)	plate
poudre (f)	(pOOh-drœ)	powder
pression (f)	(prœh-syŌh)	pressure
procédé (m)	(proh-seh-dEh)	process
procédé (m) électrolytique	(proh-seh-dEh eh-leh-troh-leeh-tEEhk)	electrolytic process
produit (m) long	(proh-dwEEh lŌh)	long product
produits (mpl) finis	(proh-dwEEh feeh-nEEh)	finished products
produits (mpl) plats	(proh-dwEEh plAht)	flats products
produits (mpl) réfractaires	(proh-dwEEh reh-frahk-tEhr)	refractories
recuit	(reh-kwEEh)	annealing
semis (mpl)	(sœh-mEEh)	semis
super alliages (mpl)	(sooh-pehr ah-lyAhzh)	super alloys
titane (m)	(teeh-tAhn)	titanium
tôle (f)	(tOhl)	sheets
transporteur (m)	(trāhnz-pohr-tah-tŒhr)	conveyor
tremper	(trāhm-pEh)	quench (v)
tubes (mpl) et tuyauteries (fpl)	(tOOhb eh tooh-yah-tœh-rEEh)	pipes and tubes
tungstène (m)	(toohng-stEhn)	tungsten
vanadium (m)	(vah-nah-dyOOhm)	vanadium

LEATHER GOODS

English to French

ankle boots	les bottines	*(boh-tEEhn)*
astrakan	l'astrakan	*(ahs-trah-kãhn)*
attache case	l'attaché-case, la serviette	*(ah-tah-shEh kAhs), (sœhr-vyEht)*
beaver	le castor	*(kahs-tOhr)*
belt	la ceinture	*(sæhntOOhr)*
billfold	le porte-billets	*(pohrt-beeh-yEh)*
blotter	le sous-main	*(sooh-mÆhn)*
boot shop	la botterie	*(boh-teh-rEEh)*
bootmaker	le bottier	*(boh-tyEh)*
boots	les bottes	*(bOht)*
briefcase	la serviette	*(sœhr-vyEht)*
calfskin	la vachette	*(vah-shEht)*
card case	le porte-cartes	*(pohrt-kAhrt)*
cigarette case	l'étui à cigarettes	*(eh-twEEh ah seeh-gah-rEht)*
cowhide	la vachette	*(vah-shEht)*
crocodile	le crocodile	*(kroh-koh-dEEhl)*
dye (v)	teindre	*(tÆhn-drœ)*
eyeglass case	l'étui à lunettes	*(eh-twEEh ah looh-nEht)*
fox	le renard	*(rœh-nAhr)*
garment bag	la housse de voyage	*(OOhs dœ vwah-yAhzh)*
gloves	les gants	*(gÃhn)*
handbag	le sac à main	*(sAhl ah mÆhn)*
holster	l'étui à revolver	*(eh-twEEh ah rœh-vohl-vEh)*
key case	le porte-clés	*(pOhrt klEh)*
kidskin	le chevreau	*(shœh-vrOh)*
lambskin	l'agneau	*(ah-nyOh)*
leather	le cuir	*(kwEEhr)*
leather goods	la maroquinerie	*(mah-roh-keeh-neh-rEEh)*
leather jacket	le blouson de cuir	*(blooh-zÕh dœ kwEEhr)*
leather strap	la lanière	*(lah-nyEhr)*
lizard (skin)	le lézard	*(leh-zAhr)*
lynx	le lynx	*(lÆhnks)*
makeup case	la trousse à maquillage	*(trOOhs ah mah-keeh-yAhzh)*
manicuring kit	la trousse à manucure	*(trOOhs ah mah-nooh-kOOhr)*
marmot	la marmotte	*(mahr-mOht)*
mink	le vison	*(veeh-zÕh)*
nutria	le ragondin	*(rah-gõhn dÆhn)*
paper holder	le serre-papier	*(sEhr pah-pyEh)*
passport case	le porte-passeport	*(pohrt-pahs-pOhrt)*
pigskin	le porc	*(pOhr)*

portfolio	le porte-documents	*(pohrt-doh-kooh-mÃh)*
purse	le porte-monnaie	*(pohrt-moh-nEh)*
rabbit	le lapin	*(lah-pÆhn)*
raccoon	le raton laveur	*(rah-tÕh lah-vŒhr)*
sable	la zibeline	*(zeeh-beh-lEEhn)*
saddle	la selle de cheval	*(sEhl dœ shœh-vAhl)*
saddler	le sellier	*(seh-lyEh)*
scissor case	l'étui à ciseaux	*(eh-twEEh ah seeh-zOh)*
scratch resistant	non vulnérable aux éraflures	*(nõhn voohl-neh-rAh-blœh oh eh-rah-flOOhr)*
shoe	la chaussure	*(shoh-sOOhr)*
slippers	les chaussons	*(shoh-sÕh)*
snakeskin	le serpent	*(sœhr-pÃh)*
suede	le suède	*(swEhd)*
suede jacket	le blouson de daim	*(blooh-zÕh dœ dEhm)*
suitcase	la valise	*(vah-lEEhz)*
tan (v)	tanner	*(tah-nEh)*
tanner	le tanneur	*(tah-nŒhr)*
tannery	la tannerie	*(tah-neh-rEEh)*
tannin (tanin)	le tannin (le tanin)	*(tah-nÆhn)*
toilet kit	la trousse de toilette	*(trOOhs dœ twah-lEht)*
tote bag	le sac de voyage	*(sahk dœ vwah-yAhzh)*
trunk	la malle	*(mAhl)*
wallet	le porte-feuille	*(pohrt-fŒh-yœ)*
watch band	le bracelet de montre	*(brah-sœh-lEht dœ mÕhn-trœ)*

French to English

agneau (m)	*(ah-nyOh)*	lamb
astrakan (m)	*(ahs-trah-kAhn)*	astrakan
attaché-case (m)	*(ah-tah-shEh kAhs)*	attache case
blouson (m) de cuir	*(blooh-zÕh dœ kwEEhr)*	leather jacket
blouson de daim	*(blooh-zÕh dœ dEhm)*	suede jacket
botterie (f)	*(boh-teh-rEEh)*	boot shop
bottes (fpl)	*(bOht)*	boots
bottier (m)	*(boh-tyEh)*	bootmaker
bottines	*(bOh-tEEhn)*	ankle boots
bracelet (m) de montre	*(brahs-lEh dœ mÕhn-trœ)*	watch band
castor (m)	*(kahs-tOhr)*	beaver
ceinture (f)	*(sæhn-tOOhr)*	belt
chaussons (mpl)	*(shoh-sÕh)*	slippers
chaussure (f)	*(shoh-sOOhr)*	shoe
chevreau (m)	*(sheh-vrOh)*	kidskin, cowhide
crocodile (m)	*(kroh-koh-dEEhl)*	crocodile
cuir (m)	*(kwEEhr)*	leather
daim (m)	*(dan)*	suede
étui (m) à cigarettes	*(eh-twEEh ah seeh-gah-rEht)*	cigarette case
étui (m) à ciseaux	*(eh-twEEh ah seeh-zOh)*	scissor case

étui à lunettes	*(eh-twEEh ah looh-nEht)*	eyeglass case
étui à revolver	*(eh-twEEh ah rœh-vohl-veh)*	holster
gants (mpl)	*(gÃhn)*	gloves
housse (f) de voyage	*(OOhs dœ vwah-yAhzh)*	garment bag
lanière (f)	*(lah-nyEhr)*	leather strap
lapin (m)	*(lah-pÆhn)*	rabbit
lézard (m)	*(leh-zAhr)*	lizard (skin)
malle (f)	*(mAhl)*	trunk
marmotte (f)	*(mahr-mOht)*	marmot
maroquinerie (f)	*(mah-roh-keeh-nœh-rEEh)*	leather goods
non vulnérable aux éraflures	*(nõhn voohl-neh-rAh-blœh oh eh-rah-flOOhr)*	scratch resistant
peau (f) d'autruche	*(pOh doh-trOOhsh)*	ostrich (skin)
peau de phoque	*(pOh dœ fOhk)*	sealskin
porc (m)	*(pOhr)*	pigskin
porte-cartes (m)	*(pohrt-kAhrt)*	card caæ
porte-clés (m)	*(pohrt-klEh)*	key case
porte-documents (m)	*(pohrt-doh-kooh-mÃh)*	portfolio
porte-feuille (m)	*(pohrt-fŒh-yœ)*	pocketbook
porte-monnaie (m)	*(pohrt-moh-nEh)*	purse
porte-passeport (m)	*(pohrt-pahs-pOhr)*	passport case
raton laveur (m)	*(rah-tÔh lah-vŒhr)*	raccoon
renard (m)	*(rœh-nAhr)*	fox
sac (m) à main	*(sAhk ah mÆhn)*	handbag
sac de voyage	*(sAhk dœ vwah-yAhzh)*	tote bag
selle (f) de cheval	*(sEhl dœ shœh-vAhl)*	saddle
sellier (m)	*(seh-lyEh)*	saddler
serpent (m)	*(sœhr-pÃh)*	snakeskin
serre-papier (m)	*(sehr-pah-pyEh)*	paper holder
serviette (f)	*(sœhr-vyEht)*	briefcase, attache case
sous-main (m)	*(sooh-mÆhn)*	blotter
tanner	*(tah-nEh)*	tan (v)
tannerie (f)	*(tah-nœh-rEEh)*	tannery
tanneur (m)	*(tah-nŒhr)*	tanner
tannin (tanin) (m)	*(tah-nEEhn)*	tannin (tanin)
teindre	*(tÆhn-drœ)*	dye (v)
trousse à manucure	*(trOOhs ah mah-nah-kOOhr)*	manicuring kit
trousse à maquillage	*(trOOhs dœ mah-keeh-yAhzh)*	makeup case
trousse de toilette	*(trOOhs dœ twah-lEht)*	toilet kit
vachette (f)	*(vah-shEht)*	calfskin
valise (f)	*(vah-lEEhz)*	suitcase
vison (m)	*(veeh-zÕh)*	mink
zibeline (f)	*(zeeh-beh-lEEhn)*	sable

MOTOR VEHICLES

English to French

air filter	le filtre à air	*(fEEhl-trœ ah Ehr)*
alternator	l'alternateur	*(ahl-tehr-nah-tŒhr)*
assembly line	à la chaine	*(ah lah shEhn)*
automatic gearshift	l'embrayage automatique	*(ãhm-brah-yAhzh oh-toh-mah-tEEhk)*
automobile	l' automobile	*(oh-toh-moh-bEEhl)*
automotive worker	l'ouvrier mécanicien	*(ooh-vryEh meh-kah-neeh-syÆhn)*
battery	la batterie	*(bah-teh-rEEh)*
belt	la courroie	*(kooh-rwAh)*
body	la carrosserie	*(kah-roh-seh-rEEh)*
brake	le frein	*(frÆhn)*
brake pedal	la pédale de frein	*(peh-dAhl dœ frÆhn)*
bumper	le pare choc	*(pahr-shOhk)*
camshaft	l'arbre à came	*(Ahr-brœ ah kAhm)*
car	la voiture	*(vwah-tOOhr)*
carburetor	le carburateur	*(kahr-booh-rah-tŒhr)*
chassis	le châssis	*(shah-sEEh)*
clutch	l'embrayage	*(ãhm-brah-yAhzh)*
clutch pedal	la pédale d'embrayage	*(peh-dAhl dãhm-brah-yAhzh)*
connecting rod	la bielle	*(byEh-yœ)*
convertible	la décapotable	*(deh-kah-poh-tAh-blœ)*
crankshaft	le vilebrequin	*(vEEhl-brœh-kEEhn)*
cylinder	le cylindre	*(seeh-lãhn-drœ)*
defroster	le dégivreur	*(deh-geeh-vrŒhr)*
designer	le dessinateur	*(deh-seeh-nah-tŒhr)*
diesel	le diésel	*(deeh-zEhl)*
disc	le disque	*(dEEhsk)*
distributor	le distributeur	*(deehs-treeh-booh-tŒhr)*
driver	le conducteur	*(kõhn-doohk-tŒhr)*
engine	le moteur	*(moh-tŒhr)*
engineer	l'ingénieur	*(æhn-zheh-nyŒhr)*
exhaust	l'échappement	*(eh-shAhp-mÃh)*
fender	l'aile	*(Ehl)*
four-cylinder engine	le moteur à 4 cylindres	*(moh-tŒhr ah kÆh-trœ seeh-lÆhn-drœ)*
front-wheel drive	la traction avant	*(trahk-syÕh ah-vÃh)*
gas consumption	la consommation	*(kõhn-soh-mah-syÕh)*
gas pedal	l'accélérateur	*(ahk-seh-leh-rah-tŒhr)*
gasoline	l'essence	*(eh-sÃhns)*
gasoline tank	le réservoir	*(reh-zehr-vwAhr)*
gearshift	le changement de vitesse	*(shãhnzh-mÃh dœ veeh-tEhs)*
generator	le générateur	*(zheh-neh-rah-tŒhr)*
grille	la calandre	*(kah-lÃhn-drœ)*

horsepower	les chevaux, la cylindrée	*(shœ-vOh), (seeh-lǣhn-drEhr)*
ignition	le contact	*(kõhn-tAhkt)*
injector	l'injecteur	*(ǣhn-zhehk-tŒhr)*
inspection	l'inspection	*(ǣhn-spehk-syÕh)*
lubrication	le graissage	*(greh-sAhzh)*
mechanic	le mécanicien	*(meh-kah-neeh-syǢhn)*
mechanical engineer	l'ingénieur mécanicien	*(ǣhn-zheh-nyŒhr meh-kah-neeh-syǢhn)*
mileage	le kilométrage	*(keeh-loh-meh-trAhzh)*
model	le modèle	*(moh-dEhl)*
odometer	le compte-tours	*(kÕnt-tOOhr)*
oil filter	le filtre à huile	*(fEEhl-trœ ah wEEhl)*
oil pump	la pompe à huile	*(pOhmp ah wEEhl)*
paint	la peinture	*(pǣhn-tOOhr)*
pinion	le pignon	*(peeh-nyÕh)*
piston	le piston	*(peehs-tÕh)*
power steering	la direction assistée	*(deeh-rehk-syÕh ah-seehs-tEh)*
propulsion	la propulsion	*(proh-poohl-syÕh)*
prototype	le prototype	*(proh-toh-tEEhp)*
radial tire	le pneu radial	*(nŒh rah-dyAhl)*
rear axle	l'essieu arrière	*(eh-syuh ah-ryEhr)*
ring	le segment	*(seg-mnAhn)*
robot	le robot	*(roh-bOh)*
seat	le siège	*(syEhzh)*
sedan	la berline	*(behr-lEEhn)*
shock absorber	l'amortisseur	*(ah-mohr-teeh-sŒhr)*
six-cylinder engine	le moteur à six cylindres	*(moh-tŒhr ah sEEhs seeh-lǢhn-drœ)*
spare tire	la roue de secours	*(rOOh dœ sœh-kOOhr)*
spark plug	la bougie	*(booh-zhEEh)*
speedometer	le compteur de vitesse	*(kõhmp-tŒhr dœ veeh-tEhs)*
spring	le ressort	*(rœh-sOhr)*
starter	le démarreur	*(deh-mah-rŒhr)*
steering	la direction	*(deeh-rehk-syÕh)*
steering wheel	le volant	*(voh-lÃh)*
suspension	la suspension	*(soohs-pãhn-syÕh)*
tire	le pneu	*(nŒh)*
torque	le couple	*(kOOh-plœ)*
V8 engine	le moteur V.8	*(moh-tŒhr veh wEEht)*
valve	la soupape	*(sooh-pAhp)*
water pump	la pompe à eau	*(pOhmp-ah Oh)*
wheel	la roue	*(rOOh*
windshield	le pare-brise	*(pahr brEEhz)*

French to English

à la chaine (f)	*(ah lah shEhn)*	assembly line
accélérateur (m)	*(ahk-seh-leh-rah-tŒhr)*	gas pedal
aile (f)	*(Ehl)*	fender
alternateur (m)	*(ahl-tehr-nah-tŒhr)*	alternator
amortisseur (m)	*(ah-mohr-teeh-sŒhr)*	shock absorber
arbre (m) à came	*(Ahr-brœ ah kAhm)*	camshaft
automobile (f)	*(oh-toh-moh-bEEhl)*	automobile
batterie (f)	*(bah-teh-rEEh)*	battery
berline (f)	*(behr-lEEhn)*	sedan
bielle (f)	*(byEh-yœ)*	connecting rod
bougie (f)	*(booh-zhEEh)*	spark plug
calandre (f)	*(kah-lÃhn-drœ)*	grille
carburateur (m)	*(kahr-booh-rah-tŒhr)*	carburetor
carrosserie (f)	*(kah-roh-seh-rEEh)*	body
changement (m) de vitesse	*(shãhnzh-mÃh dœ veeh-tEhs)*	gearshift
châssis (m)	*(shah-sEEh)*	chassis
chevaux (mpl)	*(shœh-vOh)*	horsepower
compte-tours (m)	*(kÕnt-tOOhr)*	odometer
compteur (m) de vitesse	*(kõhmp-tŒhr dœ veeh-tEhs)*	speedometer
conducteur (m)	*(kõhn-doohk-tŒhr)*	driver
consommation (f)	*(kõhn-soh-mah-syÕh)*	gas consumption
contact (m)	*(kÕhn-tAhkt)*	ignition
couple (m)	*(kOOh-plœ)*	torque
courroie (f)	*(kooh-rwAh)*	belt
cylindre (m)	*(seeh-lÆhn-drœ)*	cylinder
cylindree (f)	*(seeh-lǽhn-drEh)*	horsepower
décapotable (f)	*(deh-kah-poh-tAh-blœ)*	convertible
dégivreur (m)	*(deh-geeh-vrŒhr)*	defroster
démarreur (m)	*(deh-mah-rŒhr)*	starter
diésel (m)	*(dEEh-zehhl)*	diesel
direction (f)	*(deeh-rehk-syÕh)*	steering
direction (f) assistée	*(deeh-rehk-syÕh ah-seehs-tEh)*	power steering
disque (m)	*(dEEhsk)*	disc
distributeur (m)	*(deehs-treeh-booh-tŒhr)*	distributor
échappement (m)	*(eh-shahp-mÃh)*	exhaust
embrayage (m)	*(ãhm-brah-yAhzh)*	clutch
embrayage automatique	*(ãhm-brah-yAhzh oh-toh-mah-tEEhk)*	automatic gearshift
essence (f)	*(eh-sÃhns)*	gasoline
essieu (m) arrière	*(eh-syuh ah-ryEhr)*	rear axle
filtre à air (m)	*(fEEhl-trœ ah Ehr)*	air filter
filtre (m) à huile	*(fEEhl-trœ ah wEEhl)*	oil filter
frein (m)	*(frǼhn)*	brake
générateur (m)	*(zheh-neh-rah-tŒhr)*	generator
graissage (m)	*(greh-sAhzh)*	lubrication
ingénieur (m)	*(ǽhn-zheh-nyŒhr)*	engineer

ingénieur mécanicien	*(æhn-zheh-nyŒhr meh-kah-neeh-syÆhn)*	mechanical engineer
injecteur (m)	*(æhn-zhehk-tŒhr)*	injector
inspection (f)	*(æhn-spehk-syÕh)*	inspection
kilométrage (m)	*(keeh-loh-meh-trAhzh)*	mileage
mécanicien (m)	*(meh-kah-neeh-syÆhn)*	mechanic
modèle (m)	*(moh-dEhl)*	model
moteur (m)	*(moh-tŒhr)*	engine
moteur à 4 cylindres	*(moh-tŒhr ah kÆh-trœ seeh-lÆhn-drœ)*	four-cylinder engine
moteur à 6 cylindres	*(moh-tŒhr ah sEEhs seeh-lÆhn-drœ)*	six-cylinder engine
moteur V.8	*(moh-tŒhr veeh wEEht)*	V8 engine
ouvrier (m) mécanicien	*(ooh-vryEh meh-kah-neeh-syÆhn)*	automotive worker
pare-brise (m)	*(pahr-brEEhz)*	windshield
pare-choc (m)	*(pahr-shOhk)*	bumper
pédale (f) d'embrayage	*(peh-dAhl dãhm-brah-yAhzh)*	clutch pedal
pédale de frein	*(peh-dAhl dœ frÆhn)*	brake pedal
peinture (f)	*(pæhn-tOOhr)*	paint
pignon (m)	*(peeh-nyÕh)*	pinion
piston (m)	*(peehs-tÕh)*	piston
pneu (m)	*(nŒh)*	tire
pneu radial	*(nŒh rah-dyAhl)*	radial tire
pompe (f) à eau	*(pOhmp ah Oh)*	water pump
pompe à huile	*(pOhmp ah wEEhl)*	oil pump
propulsion (f)	*(proh-poohl-syÕh)*	propulsion
prototype (m)	*(proh-toh-tEEhp)*	prototype
réservoir (m)	*(reh-zehr-vwAhr)*	gasoline tank
ressort (m)	*(rœh-sOhr)*	spring
robot (m)	*(roh-bOh)*	robot
roue (f)	*(rOOh)*	wheel
roue de secours	*(rOOh dœ sœeh-kOOhr)*	spare tire
segment (m)	*(sehg-mÃh)*	ring
siège (m)	*(syEhzh)*	seat
soupage (f)	*(sooh-pAhzh)*	valve
suspension (f)	*(soohs-pãhn-syÕh)*	suspension
traction (f) avant	*(trahk-syÕh ah-vÃh)*	front-wheel drive
vilebrequin (m)	*(veehl-brœh-kEEhn)*	crankshaft
voiture (f)	*(vwah-tOOhr)*	car
volant (m)	*(voh-lÃhn)*	steering wheel

PHARMACEUTICALS/MEDICAL

English to French

abortion	l'avortement, (m) l'IVG	*(ah-vohrt-mÃhn), (eeh-veh-jeh)*
AIDS	le SIDA	*(see-dAh)*
allergic reaction	la réaction allergique	*(reh-ahk-syÕhn ah-lehr-zhEEhk)*
anesthesia	l'anesthésie	*(ah-nehs-teh-zEEh)*
anesthetic	l'anesthétique	*(ãh-nehs-teh-tEEhk)*
analgesic	l'analgésique	*(ãh-nahl-zheh-zEEhk)*
antacid	l'antiacide	*(ahn-teeh-ah-sEEhd)*
antibiotic	l'antibiotique	*(ahn-teeh-beeh-oh-tEEhk)*
anticholinergic	l'anticholinergique	*(ahn-teeh-koh-leeh-nehr-zhEEhk)*
anticoagulant	l'anticoagulant	*(ahn-teeh-koh-ah-gooh-lÃh)*
antidepressant	l'antidépresseur	*(ahn-teeh-deh-preh-sOOhr)*
anti-inflammatory	l'anti-inflammatoire	*(ahn-teeh-ãehn-flah-mah-twAhr)*
antiseptic	l'antiseptique	*(ahn-teeh-sehp-tEEhk)*
aspirin	l'aspirine	*(ahs-peeh-rEEhn)*
bacterial infection	l'infection bactérienne	*(ãehn-fehk-syÕhn bahk-teh-ryEhn)*
barbiturate	le barbiturique	*(bahr-beeh-tooh-rEEhk)*
biopsy	la biopsie	*(beeh-ohp-sEEh)*
birth control	le contrôle des naissances	*(kõhn-trOhl deh neh-sÃhns)*
birth defect	la malformation congénitale	*(mahl-fohr-mah-syÕhn kõhn-zheh-neeh-tAhl)*
bleed (v)	saigner	*(seh-nyEh)*
blood	le sang	*(sÃhn)*
blood pressure	la tension artérielle	*(tãhn-syÕhn ahr-teh-ryEhl)*
blood test	l'analyse de sang	*(ah-nah-lEEhz deh sAhn)*
bone scan	la scintigraphie osseuse	*(sãehn-teeh-grah-fEEh ohs-Œhz)*
botanic	la botanique	*(boh-tah-nEEhk)*
brain tumor	la tumeur au cerveau	*(tooh-mŒhr oh sehr-vOh)*
breast cancer	le cancer du sein	*(kãhn-sEhr dooh sEhn)*
burn, burning	la brûlure	*(brooh-lOOhr)*
bypass	le pontage	*(põhn-tahzh)*
calcium	le calcium	*(kahl-syOOhm)*
capsule	la capsule	*(kahp-sOOhl)*
catch (v)	attraper	*(ah-trah-pEh)*
cell	la cellule	*(seh-lOOhl)*
cervical cancer	le cancer du col	*(kãhn-sEhr dooh kOhl)*

cirrhosis of the liver	la cirrhose du foie	*(seehr-Ohz dooh fwAh)*
compounds	les composés	*(kõhm-poh-zEh)*
condom	le préservatif	*(preh-zehr-vah-tEEhf)*
contagious	contagieux	*(kõhn-tah-zhŒh)*
contaminate (v)	contaminer	*(kõhn-tah-meeh-nEh)*
contraceptive	le contraceptif	*(kõhn-trah sehp-tEEhf)*
contraindication	la contre-indication	*(kõhn-trœh-œhn-deeh-kah-syÕhn)*
cortisone	la cortisone	*(kohs-teeh-zOhn)*
cough (v)	tousser	*(tooh-sEh)*
cough drop	la pastille pour la toux	*(pahs-tEEh-yœ poohr lah tOOh)*
cough syrup	le sirop pour la toux	*(seeh-rOhp poohr lah tOOh)*
cure (v)	guérir	*(geh-rEEhr)*
cyst	le kyste	*(kEEhst)*
delivery	l'accouchement	*(ah-koohsh-mÃhn)*
density	la densité	*(dãhn-seeh-tEh)*
diabetes	le diabète	*(deeh-ah-bEht)*
digitalis	la digitaline	*(deeh-zheeh-tah-lEEhn)*
disability	l'invalidité	*(ãehn-vah-leeh-deeh-tEh)*
disease	la maladie	*(mah-lah-dEEh)*
disposable	jetable	*(zhœh-tAh-blœh)*
diuretic	la diurétique	*(deeh-ooh-reh-tEEhk)*
donor	le donneur	*(doh-nŒhr)*
dose	la dose	*(dOhz)*
dressing	le pansement	*(pãhns-mÃh)*
drop	la goutte, la pastille	*(gOOht), (pahs-tEEh-yœ)*
drowsiness	la somnolence	*(sohm-noh-lÃns)*
drug	la drogue, le stupéfiant	*(drOhg), (stooh-peh-feeh-Ãh)*
drug addiction	la toximanie	*(tohk-seeh-mah-nEEh)*
drugstore	la pharmacie	*(fahr-mah-sEEh)*
emergency	l'urgence	*(oohr-zhÃhns)*
euthanasia	l'euthanasie	*(eh-ooh-tah-nah-zEEh)*
eyedrop	le collyre	*(koh-lEEhr)*
fever	la fièvre	*(fyEh-vrœh)*
headache	le mal à la tête	*(mahl ah lah tEht)*
healthy	sain, en bonne santé	*(sÆhn, ãhn bohn sãhn-tEh)*
heart attack	la crise cardiaque	*(krEEhz kahr-deeh-Ahk)*
hexachlorophene	l'hexachlorophène	*(ehk-sah-kloh-roh-fEhn)*
HIV	VIH	*(vay-ash-eeh)*
homeopathy	l'homéopathie	*(oh-meh-oh-pah-tEEh)*
hormone	l'hormone	*(ohr-mOhn)*
hospitalization	l'hospitalisation	*(ohs-peeh-tah-leh-zah-syÕhn)*
ill	malade	*(mah-lAhd)*

immune system	le système immunitaire	*(seehs-tEhm eeh-moh-neeh-tEhr)*
injection	la piqûre	*(peeh-kOOhr)*
insulin	l'insuline	*(ãhn-sooh-lÆhn)*
intravenous feeding	l'alimentation intraveineuse	*(ah-leeh-mãhn-tah-syÕhn æhn-trah-veh-nŒhz)*
iodine	l'iode	*(yOhd)*
iron	le fer	*(fEhr)*
itching	la démangeaison	*(deh-mãhn-zheh-sÕhn)*
laboratory technician	le laborantin(e)	*(lah-boh-rahn-tEEhn)*
lesion	la lésion	*(leh-zyÕhn)*
leukemia	la leucémie	*(leh-ooh-seh-mEEh)*
long-term treatment	le traitement de longue durée	*(treht-mÃhn dœ lÕhng dooh-rEh)*
lung cancer	le cancer du poumon	*(kãhn-sEhr dooh pooh-mÕhn)*
medicine	le médicament, la médicine	*(meh-deeh-kah-mÃh), (mayd-sseen)*
medication	le médicament	*(meh-deeh-kah-mÃh)*
morphine	la morphine	*(mohr-fEEhn)*
MRI	la résonance magnétique nucléaire (RMN)	*(reh-soh-nÃhns mah-nyeh-tEEhk nooh-kleh-Ehr)*
muscle relaxant	le relaxant musculaire	*(reh-lahk-sÃhn moohs-kooh-lEhr)*
narcotic	le narcotique	*(nahr-koh-tEEhk)*
nitrate	le nitrate	*(neeh-trAht)*
nitrite	le nitrite	*(neeh-trEEht)*
ointment	la pommade	*(poh-mAhd)*
opium	l'opium	
pellet	le grain	*(grÆhn)*
penicillin	la pénicilline	*(peh-neeh-seeh-lEEhn)*
pharmaceutical	pharmaceutique	*(fahr-mah-seh-ooh-tEEhk)*
pharmacist	le pharmacien(ne)	*(fahr-mah-syÆhn)*
phenol	le phénol	*(feh-nOhl)*
physician	le médecin, le physicien	*(mehd-sÆhn), (feeh-zeeh-syÆhn)*
pill	la pilule	*(peeh-lOOhl)*
plants	les plantes	*(plÃhnt)*
pregnancy	la grossesse	*(grohs-Ehs)*
prenatal care	les soins prénataux	*(swÆhn preh-nah-tOh)*
prescription	l'ordonnance	*(ohr-doh-nÃhns)*
preventive medicine	la médecine préventive	*(meh-deeh-sEEhn preh-vãhn-tEEhv)*
purgative	le purgatif	*(poohr-gah-tEEhf)*
remedies	les remèdes	*(rœh-mEhd)*
saccharin	la saccharine	*(sah-kah-rEEhn)*
salve	la pommade	*(poh-mAhd)*
screening	le dépistage	*(deh-peehs-tAhzh)*

sedative	le sédatif	*(seh-dah-tEEhf)*
serum	le sérum	*(seh-rOOhm)*
side effect	l'effet secondaire (m)	*(eh-fEh seh-kohn-dEhr)*
sinus	le sinus	*(seeh-nOOhs)*
sleeping pill	le somnifère	*(sohm-nee-fehr)*
sneeze (v)	éternuer	*(eh-tœhr-nwEh)*
starch	l'amidon	*(ah-meeh-dÕh)*
stimulant	le stimulant	*(steeh-mooh-lÃh)*
sulphamide	le sulfamide	*(soohl-fah-mEEhd)*
surgery	la chirurgie	*(sheeh-roohr-zhEEh)*
surrogate mother	la mére porteuse	*(mEhr pohr-tŒhz)*
symptom	le symptome	*(sœhn-tOhm)*
synthesis	la synthèse	*(seehn-tEhz)*
syringe	la seringue	*(sœh-rǼhng)*
tablet	le comprimé	*(kohn-pree-may)*
tamperproof package	l'emballage inviolable	*(ǽhm-bah-lAhzh ǽhn-vyoh-lAh-blœh)*
toxicology	la toxicologie	*(tohk-seeh-koh-loh-zhEEh)*
toxin	la toxine	*(tohk-sEEhn)*
tranquilizer	le calmant	*(kahl-mÃh)*
transplant	la greffe	*(grEhf)*
vaccine	le vaccin	*(vahk-sEEhn)*
vitamin	la vitamine	*(veeh-tah-mEEhn)*
x-ray	la radiographie	*(rah-dyoh-grah-fEEh)*
zinc	le zinc	*(zǼhnk)*

French to English

accouchement (m)	*(ah-koohsh-mÃhn)*	delivery
alimentation (f) intraveineuse	*(ah-leeh-mãhn-tah-syÕhn ǽhn-trah-veh-nŒhz)*	intravenous feeding
amidon (m)	*(ah-meeh-dÕh)*	starch
analgésique (m)	*(ãh-nahl-zheh-zEEhk)*	analgesic
analyse (f) de sang	*(ah-nah-lEEhz dœ sÃhn)*	blood test
anesthésie (f)	*(ah-nehs-teh-zEEh)*	anesthesia
anesthétique (m)	*(ãh-nehs-teh-tEEhk)*	anaesthetic
antibiotique (m)	*(ahn-teeh-beeh-oh-tEEhk)*	antibiotic
anticholinergique	*(ahn-teeh-koh-leeh-nehr-zhEEhk)*	anticholinergic
anticoagulant (m)	*(ahn-teeh-koh-ah-gooh-lÃh)*	anticoagulant
antidépresseur (m)	*(ahn-teeh-deh-preh-sOOhr)*	antidepressant
antiseptique (m)	*(ahn-teeh-sehp-tEEhk)*	antiseptic
anti-inflammatoire	*(ahn-teeh-ǽhn-flah-mah-twAhr)*	anti-inflammatory
arthrite (f)	*(ahr-trEEht)*	arthritis
aspirine (f)	*(ahs-peeh-rEEhn)*	aspirin
attraper	*(ah-trah-pEh)*	catch (v)
avortement (m)	*(ah-vohrt-mÃhn)*	abortion
barbiturique (m)	*(bahr-beeh-tooh-rEEhk)*	barbiturate

biopsie (f)	(beeh-ohp-sEEh)	biopsy
botanique (f)	(boh-tah-nEEhk)	botanic
brûlure (f)	(brooh-lOOhr)	burn, burning
calcium (m)	(kahl-syOOhm)	calcium
calmant (m)	(kahl-mÃh)	tranquilizer
cancer du poumon	(kãhn-sEh dooh pooh-mÕhn)	lung cancer
cancer du sein	(kãhn-sEh dooh sÆhn)	breast cancer
cancer (m) du col	(kãhn-sEh dooh kOhl)	cervical cancer
capsule (f)	(kahp-sOOhl)	capsule
cellule (f)	(seh-lOOhl)	cell
chirurgie (f)	(sheeh-roohr-zhEEh)	surgery
cirrhose (f) du foie	(seehr-Ohz dooh fwAh)	cirrhosis of the liver
collyre (m)	(koh-lEEhr)	eyedrop
composés (mpl)	(kõhm-poh-zEh)	compounds
comprimé	(kohn-pree-may)	tablet
contagieux	(kõhn-tah-zhŒEh)	contagious
contaminer	(kõhr-tah-meeh-nEh)	contaminate (v)
contraceptif (m)	(kõhn-trah-sehp-tEEhf)	contraceptive
contre-indication (f)	(kõhn-trœh-œhn-deeh-kah-syÕhn)	contraindication
contrôle (m) des naissances	(kõhn-trOhl deh neh-sÃhns)	birth control
cortisone (f)	(kohr-teeh-zOhn)	cortisone
crise (f) cardiaque	(krEEhz kahr-deeh-Ahk)	heart attack
démangeaison (f)	(deh-mãhn-zheh-sÕhn)	itching
densité (f)	(dãhn-seeh-tEh)	density
dépistage (m)	(deh-peehs-tAhzh)	screening
diabète (m)	(deeh-ah-bEht)	diabetes
digitaline (f)	(deeh-zheeh-tah-lEEhn)	digitalis
diurétique (f)	(deeh-ooh-reh-tEEhk)	diuretic
donneur (m)	(doh-nŒhr)	donor
dose (f)	(dOhz)	dose
drogue (f)	(drOhg)	drug
effet (m) secondaire	(eh-feh seh-kõhr-dEhr)	side effect
emballage (m) inviolable	(æhm-bah-lAhzh æhn-vyoh-lAh-blœh)	tamperproof package
en bonne santé	(ãhn bohn sãhn-tEh)	healthy
enceinte	(ãhn-sÆhnt)	pregnant
éternuer	(eh-tehr-nwEh)	sneeze (v)
euthanasie (f)	(eh-ooh-tah-nah-zEEh)	euthanasia
fer (m)	(fEhr)	iron
fièvre (f)	(fyEh-vrœh)	fever
goutte (f)	(gOOht)	drop
greffe (f)	(grEhf)	transplant
grossesse (f)	(grohs-Ehs)	pregnancy
guérir	(geh-rEEhr)	cure (v)
hexachlorophène (m)	(ehk-sah-kloh-roh-fEhn)	hexachlorophene
homéopathie (f)	(oh-meh-oh-pah-tEEh)	homeopathy

hormone (f)	*(ohr-mOhn)*	hormone
hospitalisation (f)	*(ohs-peeh-tah-leeh-zah-syÕhn)*	hospitalization
infection (f) bactérienne	*(æhn-fehk-syÕhn bahk-teh-ryEhn)*	bacterial infection
insuline (f)	*(æhn-sooh-lEEhn)*	insulin
invalidité (f)	*(æhn-vah-leeh-deeh-tEh)*	disability
iode (f)	*(yOhd)*	iodine
IVG	*(eeh-veh-jeh)*	abortion
laborantin(e) (m)	*(lah-boh-rahn-tEEhn)*	laboratory technician
jetable	*(zhœh-tAh-blœh)*	disposable
kyste (m)	*(kEEhst)*	cyst
lésion (f)	*(leh-zyÕhn)*	lesion
leucémie (f)	*(leh-ooh-seh-mEEh)*	leukemia
mal (m) de tête	*(mahl dœ tEht)*	headache
malade	*(mah-lAhd)*	ill
malformation (f) congénitale	*(mahl-fohr-mah-syÕhn kõhn-zheh-neeh-tAhl)*	birth defect
maladie (f)	*(mah-lah-dEEh)*	disease
médecin (m)	*(mehd-sÆhn)*	physician
médecine (f) préventive	*(mehd-sEEhn preh-vãhn-tEEhv)*	preventive medicine
médicament (m)	*(meh-deeh-kah-mÃh)*	medication, medicine
mère (f) porteuse	*(mEhr pohr-tŒhz)*	surrogate mother
morphine (f)	*(mohr-fEEhn)*	morphine
narcotique (m)	*(nahr-koh-tEEhk)*	narcotic
nitrate (m)	*(neeh-trAht)*	nitrate
nitrite (m)	*(neeh-trEEht)*	nitrite
opium (m)		opium
ordonnance (f)	*(ohr-doh-nÃhns)*	prescription
pansement (m)	*(pãhns-mÃh)*	dressing
pastille (f)	*(pahs-tEEh-yœ)*	drop
pastille (f) pour la toux	*(pahs-tEEh-yœ poohr la tOOhs)*	cough drop
pénicilline (f)	*(peh-neeh-seeh-lEEhn)*	penicillin
pharmaceutique	*(fahr-mah-seh-ooh-tEEhk)*	pharmaceutical
pharmacie (f)	*(fahr-mah-sEEh)*	drugstore
pharmacien(ne) (m)	*(fahr-mah-syÆhn)*	pharmacist
phénol (m)	*(feh-nOhl)*	phenol
physicien (m)	*(feeh-zeeh-syÆhn)*	physician
pilule (f)	*(peeh-lOOhl)*	pill
piqûre (f)	*(peeh-kOOhr)*	injection
plantes (fpl)	*(plÃhnt)*	plants
pommade (f)	*(poh-mAhd)*	salve, ointment
pontage (m)	*(põhn-tAhzh)*	bypass
préservatif (m)	*(preh-sehr-vah-tEEhf)*	condom
purgatif (m)	*(poohr-gah-tEEhf)*	purgative

radiographie (f)	(rah-dyoh-grah-fEEh)	x-ray
réaction (f) allergique	(reh-ahk-syÕhn ah-lehr-zhEEhk)	allergic reaction
relaxant (m) musculaire	(reh-lahk-sÃhn moohs-kooh-lEhr)	muscle relaxant
remèdes (mpl)	(rœh-mEhd)	remedies
résonance (f) magnétique nucléaire (RMN)	(reh-soh-nÃhns may-nyeh-tEEhk nooh-kleh-Ehr)	MRI
saccharine (f)	(sah-kah-rEEhn)	saccharin
saigner	(seh-nyEh)	bleed (v)
sain	(sÆhn)	healthy
sang (m)	(sÃhn)	blood
scintigraphie (f) osseuse	(sæhn-teeh-grah-fEEh)	bone scan
sédatif	(seh-dah-tEEhf)	sedative
sérum (m)	(seh-rOOhm)	serum
sels (mpl)	(sEhl)	salts
seringue (f)	(sœh-rÆhng)	syringe
SIDA (m)	(sEEh-dah)	AIDS
sinus (m)	(seeh-nOOhs)	sinus
sirop pour (m) la toux	(seeh-rOhp poohr la tOOh)	cough syrup
soins (mpl) prénataux	(swÆhn preh-nah-tOh)	prenatal care
somnifère	(sohm-nee-fehr)	sleeping pill
somnolence (f)	(sohm-noh-lÃhns)	drowsiness
stimulant (m)	(steeh-mooh-lÃh)	stimulant
stupéfiant (m)	(stooh-peh-feeh-Ãh)	drug
sulfamide (m)	(soohl-fah-mEEhd)	sulphamide
symptome (m)	(sæhmp-tOhm)	symptom
synthèse (f)	(seehn-tEhz)	synthesis
système (m) immunitaire	(seehs-tEhm eeh-mooh-neeh-tEhr)	immune system
teneur (f)	(tœh-nŒhr)	content
tension (f) artérielle	(tãhn-syÕhn ahr-teh-ryEhl)	blood pressure
tousser	(tooh-sEh)	cough (v)
toxicologie (f)	(tohk-seeh-koh-loh-zhEEh)	toxicology
toximanie (f)	(tohk-seeh-mah-nEEh)	drug addiction
toxine (f)	(tohk-sEEhn)	toxin
traitement (m) de longue durée	(treht-mÃhn dœ lõhng dooh-rEh)	long-term treatment
tumeur (f) au cerveau	(tooh-mŒhr oh sehr-vOh)	brain tumor
urgence (f)	(oohr-zhÃhns)	emergency
vaccin (m)	(vahk-sÆhn)	vaccine
VIH (m)	(vay-ash-eeh)	HIV
vitamine (f)	(veeh-tah-mEEhn)	vitamin
zinc (m)	(zÆhnk)	zinc

PRINTING AND PUBLISHING

English to French

acknowledgment	le remerciement	*(rœh-mehr-seeh-mÃh)*
adhesive binding	le reliure sans couture	*(reh-lwEEhr sãhn kooh-tOOhr)*
binding	la reliure	*(reh-lwEEhr)*
black and white	le noir et blanc	*(nwAhr eh blÃhn)*
blowup	l'agrandissement	*(ah-grãhn-deehs-mÃh)*
boldface	en gras	*(ãhn grAh)*
book	le livre	*(lEEh-vrœ)*
bookbinder	le relieur	*(reh-lyŒhr)*
capital	la majuscule	*(mah-yoohs-kOOhl)*
chapter	le chapitre	*(shah-pEEh-trœ)*
circulation	le tirage	*(teeh-rAhzh)*
coated paper	le papier glacé	*(pah-pyEh glah-sEh)*
color separation	la séparation couleur	*(seh-pah-rah-syÕh kooh-lŒhr)*
copy	l'exemplaire	*(ehk-zãhm-plEhr)*
copy (v)	copier	*(koh-pyEhr)*
copyright	le droit d'auteur	*(drwAh doh-tŒhr)*
cover	la couverture	*(kooh-vehr-tOOhr)*
crop	la coupe	*(kOOhp)*
daily	le quotidien	*(koh-teeh-dyEhn)*
desktop publishing	le publication assisteé par ordinateur	*(pooh-bleeh-kah-syÕhn ah-seehs-tEh pahr ohr-deeh-nah-tŒhr)*
distribution	la distribution	*(deehs-treeh-booh-syÕh)*
drop out (v)	retirer	*(rœh-teeh-rEh)*
dummy	la maquette	*(mah-kEht)*
edit (v)	éditer	*(eh-deeh-tEh)*
edition	l'édition	*(eh-deeh-syÕh)*
editor	le rédacteur	*(reh-dahk-tŒhr)*
embossed	gaufré	*(gOh-frœh)*
engrave (v)	graver	*(grah-vEh)*
font	la fonte	*(fÕhnt)*
form	l'imprimé	*(ãehm-preeh-mEh)*
format	le format	*(fohr-mAh)*
four colors	la quadrichromie	*(kah-dreeh-kroh-mEEh)*
galley	l'épreuve	*(eh-prŒhv)*
glossy	brillant, glacé	*(breeh-yÃh), (glah-sEh)*
grain	le grain	*(grEhn)*
grid	la grille	*(grEEh-yœ)*
hardcover	cartonné	*(kahr-toh-rˈEh)*
headline	à la une	*(ah lah OŨhn)*
illustration	l'illustration	*(eeh-loohs-trah-syÕh)*
inch	le pouce	*(pOOhs)*
ink	l'encre	*(Ãhn-krœ)*

insert	l'insertion	*(ǣhn-sehr-synOh)*
italic	l'italique	*(eeh-tah-lEEhk)*
jacket	la jaquette	*(zhah-kEht)*
justify (v)	justifier	*(zhoohs-teeh-fyEh)*
layout	le modèle	*(moh-dEhl)*
letter	le caractère	*(kah-rahk-tEhr)*
letterpress	la typographie	*(teeh-poh-grah-fEEh)*
line	la ligne	*(lEEh-nyœ)*
line drawing	l'esquisse	*(ehs-kEEhs)*
lower case	la minuscule	*(meeh-neehs-kOOhl)*
matrix	la matrice	*(mah-trEEhs)*
matt	mat	*(maht)*
mechanical	la maquette	*(mah-kEht)*
misprint	la coquille	*(koh-kEEh-yœh)*
negative	le négatif	*(neh-gah-tEEhf)*
newsprint	le papier journal	*(pah-pyEh zhoohr-nAhl)*
novel	le roman	*(roh-mÃhn)*
out of print	épuisé	*(eh-pweeh-sEh)*
packing	l'emballage	*(ãhm-bah-yAhzh)*
page makeup	la mise en page	*(mEEhz ãhn pAhzh)*
pagination	la pagination	*(pah-zheeh-nah-syÕh)*
pamphlet	la brochure	*(broh-shOOhr)*
paper	le papier	*(pah-pyEh)*
paperback	broché	*(broh-shEh)*
perfect binding	la reliure	*(rœh-lyOOhr)*
pica	le cicéro	*(seeh-seh-rOh)*
pigment	le pigment	*(peehg-mÃh)*
plate	le cliché, la plaque	*(kleeh-shEh), (plAhk)*
point	le corps	*(kOhr)*
positive	positif	*(poh-zeeh-tEEhf)*
preface	la préface	*(preh-fAhs)*
press book	l'exemplaire de presse	*(ehk-zãhm-plEhr dœ prEhs)*
print run	la tirage	*(teeh-rAhzh)*
printing	l'impression	*(ǣhm-preh-syÕh)*
proofreader	le correcteur	*(koh-rehk-tŒhr)*
proofreading	la relecture	*(rœh-lehk-tOOhr)*
publisher	l'éditeur	*(eh-deeh-tŒhr)*
ream	la rame	*(rAhm)*
register marks	les repères	*(rœh-pEhr)*
roman	le romain	*(roh-mÃy)*
scanner	le scanneur	*(skah-nŒhr)*
scoring	la coordination	*(koh-ohr-deeh-nah-syÕh)*
screen	l'écran	*(eh-krÃhn)*
sewn	broché	*(broh-shEh)*
sheet	la feuille	*(fŒh-yœ)*
size	la dimension	*(deeh-mãhn-syÕh)*
soft cover	la couverture souple	*(kooh-vehr-tOOhr sOOh-plœ)*
spine	le dos	*(dOhs)*

stripping	le montage	*(mõhn-tAhzh)*
table of contents	la table des matières	*(tAh-blœ deh mah-tyEhr)*
title	le titre	*(tEEh-trœ)*
vellum paper	le papier velin	*(pah-pyEhl vœh-lÆ̃hn)*
web offset	la rotative offset	*(roh-tah-tEEhv offset)*

French to English

à la une	*(ah lah OOhn)*	headline
agrandissement (m)	*(ah-grãhn-deehz-mÃh)*	blowup
brillant	*(breeh-yÃh)*	glossy
broché	*(broh-shEh)*	paperback, sewn
brochure (f)	*(broh-shOOhr)*	pamphlet
caractère (m)	*(kah-rahk-tEhr)*	letter
cartonné	*(kahr-toh-nEh)*	hardcover
chapitre (m)	*(shah-pEEh-trœ)*	chapter
cicéro (m)	*(seeh-seh-rOh)*	pica
cliché (m)	*(kleeh-shEh)*	plate
coordination (f)	*(koh-ohr-deeh-nah-syÕh)*	scoring
copier	*(koh-pyEh)*	copy (v)
coquille (f)	*(koh-kEEh-yœh)*	misprint
corps (m)	*(kOhr)*	point
correcteur (m)	*(koh-rehk-tŒhr)*	proofreader
coupe (f)	*(kOOhp)*	crop
couverture (f)	*(kooh-vehr-tOOhr)*	cover
couverture (f) souple	*(kooh-vehr-tOOhr sOOh-plœ)*	soft cover
dimension (f)	*(deeh-mãhn-syÕh)*	size
distribution (f)	*(deehs-treeh-booh-syÕh)*	distribution
dos (m)	*(dOhs)*	spine
droit (m) d'auteur	*(drwAh doh-rŒhr)*	copyright
écran (m)	*(eh-krÃhn)*	screen
éditer	*(eh-deeh-tEh)*	edit (v)
éditeur (m)	*(eh-deeh-tŒhr)*	publisher
édition (f)	*(eh-deeh-syÕh)*	edition
emballage (m)	*(ãhm-bah-lAhzh)*	packing
en gras	*(ãhn grAh)*	boldface
encre (f)	*(ãhn-krœ)*	ink
épreuve (f)	*(eh-prŒhv)*	gally
épuisé	*(eh-pweeh-sEh)*	out of print
esquisse (f)	*(ehs-kEEhs)*	line drawing
exemplaire (m)	*(ehk-zãhm-plEhr)*	copy
exemplaire (m) de presse	*(ehk-zãhm-plEhr dœ prEhs)*	press book
feuille (f)	*(fŒh-yœ)*	sheet
fonte (f)	*(fÕhnt)*	font
format (m)	*(fohr-mAh)*	format
gaufré	*(gOh-frœh)*	embossed
grain (m)	*(grEhn)*	grain
graver	*(grah-vEh)*	engrave (v)
grille (f)	*(grEEh-yœ)*	grid

illustration (f)	*(eeh-loohs-tra-syÕh)*	illustration
impression (f)	*(æhm-preh-syÕh)*	printing
imprimé (m)	*(æhm-preeh-mEh)*	form
insertion (f)	*(æhn-sehr-syÕh)*	insert
italique	*(eeh-tah-lEEhk)*	italic
jaquette (f)	*(zhah-kEht)*	jacket
justifier	*(zhoohs-teeh-fyEh)*	justify (v)
ligne (f)	*(lEEh-nyœ)*	line
livre (m)	*(lEEh-vrœ)*	book
majuscule (f)	*(mah-yoohs-kOOhl)*	capital
maquette (f)	*(mah-kEht)*	dummy, mechanical
mat	*(maht)*	matt
matrice (f)	*(mah-trEEhs)*	matrix
minuscule (f)	*(meeh-neeh-skOOhl)*	lower case
mise en page (f)	*(mEEhz- ãhn pAhzh)*	page makeup
modèle (m)	*(moh-dEhl)*	layout
montage (m)	*(mõhn-tAhzh)*	stripping
négatif (m)	*(neh-gah-tEEhf)*	negative
noir et blanc (m)	*(nwAhr eh blÃhn)*	black and white
pagination (f)	*(pah-zheeh-nah-syÕh)*	pagination
papier (m)	*(pah-pyEh)*	paper, journal newsprint
papier (m) glacé	*(pah-pyEh glah-sEh)*	coated paper
papier velin (m)	*(pah-pyEhl væh-lẪhn)*	vellum paper
pigment (m)	*(peehg-mÃh)*	pigment
plaque	*(plAhk)*	plate
positif	*(poh-zeeh-tEEhf)*	positive
pouce (m)	*(pOOhs)*	inch
préface (f)	*(preh-fAhs)*	preface
publication assistée par ordinateur (f)	*(pooh-bleeh-kah-syÕhn ah-seehs-tEh pahr ohr-deeh-nah-tŒhr)*	desktop publishing
quadrichromie (f)	*(kah-dreeh-kroh-mEEh)*	four colors
quotidien (m)	*(koh-teeh-dyEhn)*	daily
rame (f)	*(rAhm)*	ream
rédacteur (m)	*(reh-dahk-tŒhr)*	editor
relecture (f)	*(ræh-lehk-tOOhr)*	proofreading
relieur (m)	*(reh-lyŒhr)*	bookbinder
reliure (f)	*(ræh-lyOOhr)*	binding, perfect binding
reliure sans couture (f)	*(reh-lwEEhr sãhn kooh-tOOhr)*	adhesive binding
remerciement (m)	*(ræh-mœhr-seeh-mÃh)*	acknowledgment
repères (mpl)	*(ræh-pEhr)*	register marks
retirer	*(ræh-teeh-rEh)*	drop out (v)
romain (m)	*(roh-mÃh)*	roman
roman (m)	*(roh-mÃhn)*	novel
rotative offset (f)	*(roh-tah-tEEhv offset)*	web offset
scanneur (m)	*(skah-nŒhr)*	scanner

séparation (f) couleur	*(seh-pah-rah-syÕh kooh-lŒhr)*	color separation
table des matières (f)	*(tAh-blœ deh mah-tyEhr)*	table of contents
tirage (f)	*(teeh-rAhzh)*	print run, circulation
titre (m)	*(tEEh-trœ)*	title
typographie (f)	*(teeh-poh-grah-fEEh)*	letterpress

WINEMAKING

English to French

acid content	le degré d'acidité	*(deh-grEh dah-seeh-deeh-tEh)*
aftertaste	l'arrière-goût	*(ah-ryEhr gOOht)*
aging	le vieillissement	*(vyeh-yeehs-mÃh)*
alcohol	l'alcool	*(ahl-kOhl)*
alcoholic content	la teneur en alcool	*(tœ-nŒr ãhn ahl-kOOl)*
A.O.C.	Appellation d'Origine Contrôlée	*(ah-peh-lah-syÕh doh-reeh-zheen kõhn-troh-lEh)*
aroma	l'arôme	*(ah-rOhm)*
barrel	le tonneau	*(toh-nOh)*
batch	la cuvée	*(kooh-vEh)*
bitter	amer	*(ah-mEhr)*
blend (v)	mélanger	*(meh-lãhn-zhEh)*
biological diacidizing	la fermentation malolactique	*(fehr-mãhn-tah-syÕh mah-loh-lahk-tEEhk)*
body	le corps	*(kOhr)*
bottle	la bouteille	*(booh-tEh-yœ)*
bouquet	le bouquet	*(booh-kEh)*
breathe (v)	respirer	*(rœhs-peeh-rEh)*
case	la caisse	*(kEhs)*
cask (225 litres)	la barrique	*(bah-rEEhk)*
centiliter	le centilitre	*(sãhn-teeh-lEEh-trœ)*
chalky	crayeux	*(kreh-yŒh)*
champagne	le champagne	*(shahm-pAh-nyœ)*
champagne method	la méthode champenoise	*(meh-tOhd shãhm-peh-nwAhz)*
character	le caractère	*(kah-rahk-tEhr)*
climate	le climat	*(kleeh-mAh)*
cloudy	nuageux, trouble	*(nwah-zhŒh), (trOOh-blœh)*
cooper	le tonnelier	*(toh-neh-lyEh)*
cork	le bouchon	*(booh-shÕh)*
corkscrew	le tire-bouchon	*(teehr-booh-shÕh)*
country	la région	*(reh-zhÕh)*
distil (v)	distiller	*(deehs-teeh-lEh)*
draw off	soutirer, tirer une cuve	*(sooh-teeh-rEh), (teeh-rEh ooh kOOhv)*
dregs	le moût	*(mOOht)*
drink (v)	boire	*(bwAhr)*
dry	sec	*(sEhk)*
dry wine	le vin sec	*(vÆhn sEhk)*
earthy	terreux	*(teh-rOe)*
estate (or chateau)	le château	*(shah-tOh)*
estate bottled	mis en bouteille au château	*(mEEhz ãhn booh-tEh-yœ oh shah-tOh)*

ferment	le ferment	*(fehr-mÃh)*
fruity	fruité	*(frweeh-tEh)*
full-bodied	corsé	*(kohr-sEh)*
grape	le raisin	*(reh-zÆhn)*
grape bunch	la grappe	*(grAhp)*
grape harvest	les vendanges	*(vãhn-dAhzh)*
guaranteed classified vintage	l'appellation contrôlée	*(ah-peh-lah-syÕh kõhn-troh-lEh)*
heady	capiteux	*(kah-peeh-tOh)*
hectare	l'hectare	*(ehk-tAhr)*
label	l'étiquette	*(eh-teeh-kEht)*
light	léger	*(leh-zhEh)*
liter	le litre	*(lEEh-trœ)*
local wine	le vin du cru, du terroir	*(vÃEhn dooh krOOh, dooh teh-rwAhr)*
luscious	savoureux, succulent	*(sah-vooh-rŒh)*
magnum (2 bottles in one)	le magnum	*(mahg-nOOhm)*
malolactic fermentation	la fermentation malolactique	*(fehr-mãhn-tah-syÕh mah-loh-lahk-tEEhk)*
moldy taste	le goût de moisi	*(gOOh dœ mwah-zEEh)*
neck (of bottle)	le goulot	*(gooh-lOh)*
oak barrel	le fût de chêne	*(fOOh dœ shEhn)*
pasteurized	pasteurisé	*(pahs-tœh-reeh-zEh)*
pop a cork (v)	faire sauter le bouchon	*(fehr soh-tEh loe booh-shÕhn)*
production	la production	*(proh-doohk-synOh)*
residue	le résidu	*(reh-zeeh-dOOh)*
ripe	mûr	*(mOOhr)*
robust	charpenté, robuste	*(shahr-pãhn-tEh)*
room temperature	chambré	*(shãhm-brEh)*
rosé wine	le rosé	*(roh-zEh)*
rubbery	le goût de caoutchouc	*(gOOh dœ kah-oh-shOOh)*
smell (v)	humer	*(ooh-mEh)*
smoky smell	l'odeur de fumée	*(oh-dŒhr dœ fooh-mEh)*
sour	l'acre	*(Ah-krœ)*
sparkling wine	le vin mousseux	*(vÆhn mooh-sOh)*
spoiled	altéré	*(ahl-teh-rEh)*
stalking	l'égrappage	*(eh-grah-pAhzh)*
subtle	subtile	*(soohb-tEEhl)*
sulfite (v)	sulfiter	*(soohl-feeh-tEh)*
sugar content	le pourcentage de sucre	*(poohr-sãhn-tAhzh dœ sOOh-krœ)*
supple	souple	*(sOOh-plœh)*
sweet and sour	aigre-doux	*(Eh-greoh dOOh)*
tannin	le tannin (tanin)	*(tah-nÆhn)*
tart	acide, âpre	*(ah-sEEhd), (Ah-prœh)*
taste (v)	déguster	*(deh-goohs-tEh)*
tasteless	fade	*(fAhd)*

tasting	la dégustation	*(deh-goohs-tah-syÕh)*
temperature	la température	*(tãhm-peh-rah-tOOhr)*
thick	épais	*(eh-pEh)*
thin	mince, maigre	*(mÆhns), (mEh-groeh)*
tint	la teinte, la couleur	*(tÆhnt), (kooh-lŒhr)*
type of vine	le cépage	*(seh-pAhzh)*
uncork (v)	déboucher	*(deh-booh-shEh)*
unfermented grape juice	le jus de raisin	*(zhOOhs dœ reh-zÆhn)*
vat	la cuve	*(kOOhv)*
velvety	velouté	*(vœh-looh-tEh)*
vine	le cep	*(sEhp)*
vinegar taste	le goût de vinaigre	*(gOOh dœ vœhn-Eh-greoh)*
vineyard	le vignoble	*(veeh-nyOh-blœ)*
vintage	le cru	*(krOOh)*
vintage year	le millésime	*(meeh-lEh-zEEhm)*
vintner	le négociant en vins	*(neh-goh-syÃh ãhn vÆhn)*
vintry	le chais	*(shEh)*
viticulture	la viticulture	*(veeh-teeh-koohl-tOOhr)*
well-rounded	moelleux, onctueux	*(mœh-yŒh), (õhnk-tŒh)*
wine	le vin	*(vÆhn)*
wine cellar	la cave à vin	*(kahv ah vÆhn)*
wine cooperative	la coopérative vinicole	*(koh-oh-peh-rah-tEEhv veeh-neeh-kOhl)*
wine steward	le sommelier	*(soh-meh-lyEh)*
winegrower	le vigneron, le viticulteur	*(veeh-nyeh-rÕh), (veeh-teeh-koohl-tŒhr)*
winemaker	le maître de chais, le viticulteur, le vigneron	*(mEh-trœ dœ shEh), (vee-teeh-koohl-tŒhrt), (veeh-nyeh-rÕh)*
winepress	le pressoir	*(preh-swAhr)*
winery	la maison de production de vin	*(meh-zÕhn dœ proh-doohk-syÕhn dœ vÆhn)*
yeast	la levure	*(lœh-vOOhr)*
yield	la récolte, le rendement	*(reh-kOhlt), (rãhnd-mÃhn)*

French to English

acide	*(ah-sEEhd)*	tart
acre	*(Ah-krœ)*	sour
aigre-doux	*(Eh-grœh dOOh)*	sweet and sour
alcool (m)	*(ahl-kOhl)*	alcohol
altéré	*(ahl-teh-rEh)*	spoiled
amer	*(ah-mEhr)*	bitter
appellation (f) contrôlée	*(ah-peh-lah-syÕh kõhn-troh-lEh)*	guaranteed classified vintage
Appellation d'Origine Contrôlée	*(ah-peh-lay-syÕhn doh-reeh-zhEEhn kõhn troh-lEh)*	A.O.C.

âpre	*(Ah-præh)*	tart
arôme (m)	*(ah-rOhm)*	aroma
arrière-goût (m)	*(ah-ryEhr gOOht)*	aftertaste
barrique (f)	*(bah-rEEhk)*	cask (225 litres)
boire	*(bwAhr)*	drink (v)
bouchon (m)	*(booh-shÕh)*	cork
bouquet (m)	*(booh-kEh)*	bouquet
bouteille (f)	*(booh-tEh-yæ)*	bottle
caisse (f)	*(kEhs)*	case
capiteux	*(kah-peeh-tOh)*	heady
caractère (m)	*(kah-rahk-tEhr)*	character
cave (f) à vin	*(kahv ah vÆhn)*	wine cellar
cépage (m)	*(seh-pAhzh)*	type of vine
centilitre (m)	*(sãhn-teeh-lEEh-træ)*	centiliter
cep (m)	*(sEhp)*	vine
château (m)	*(shah-tOh)*	estate (or chateau)
chais (m)	*(shEh)*	vintry
chambré	*(shãhm-brEh)*	room temperature
champagne (m)	*(sham-pAh-nyæ)*	champagne
charpenté	*(shahr-pãhn-tEh)*	robust
climat (m)	*(kleeh-mAh)*	climate
collage (m)	*(koh-lAhzh)*	clearing
coopérative (f) vinicole	*(ko-oh-peh-rah-tEEhv veeh-neeh-kOhl)*	wine cooperative
corps (m)	*(kOhr)*	body
corsé	*(kohr-sEh)*	full-bodied
couleur (f)	*(kooh-lŒhr)*	tint
cru (m)	*(krOOh)*	vintage
crayeux	*(kreh-yŒh)*	chalky
cuve (f)	*(kOOhv)*	vat
cuvée (f)	*(kooh-vEh)*	batch
déboucher	*(deh-booh-shEh)*	uncork (v)
degré (m) d'acidité	*(deh-grEh dah-seeh-deeh-tEh)*	acid content
dégustation (f)	*(deh-goohs-tah-synOh)*	tasting
déguster	*(deh-goohs-tEh)*	taste (v)
distiller	*(deehs-teeh-lEh)*	distil (v)
égrappage (m)	*(eh-grah-pAhzh)*	stalking
épais	*(eh-pEh)*	thick
étiquette (f)	*(eh-teeh-kEht)*	label
fade	*(fAhd)*	tasteless
faire sauter le bouchon	*(fehr soh-tEh læ booh-shÕhn)*	pop a cork (v)
ferment (m)	*(fehr-mÃh)*	ferment
fermentation (f) malolactique	*(fehr-mãhn-tah-syÕh mah-loh-lahk-tEEhk)*	biological diacidizing, malolactic fermentation
fruité	*(frweeh-tÊh)*	fruity

fût de chêne (m)	*(fOOh dœ shEhn)*	oak barrel
goulot (m)	*(gooh-lOh)*	neck (of bottle)
goût (m) de caoutchouc	*(gOOh dœ kah-oh-shOOh)*	rubbery
goût de moisi	*(gOOh dœ mwah-zEEh)*	moldy taste
goût de vinaigre	*(gOOh dœ vãhn-Eh-grœh)*	vinegar taste
grappe (f)	*(grAhp)*	grape bunch
hectare (m)	*(ehk-tAhr)*	hectare
humer	*(ooh-mEh)*	smell (v)
jus (m) de raisin	*(zhOOhs dœ reh-zÆhn)*	unfermented grape juice
léger	*(leh-zhEh)*	light
levure (f)	*(lœh-vOOhr)*	yeast
litre (m)	*(lEEh-trœ)*	liter
magnum (m)	*(mahg-nOOhm)*	magnum (2 bottles in one)
maigre	*(mEh-grœh)*	thin
maison (f) de production de vin	*(meh-zÕhn dœ proh-doohk-syÕhn dœ vÆhn)*	winery
maître (m) de chais	*(mEh-trœ dœ shEh)*	winemaker
mélanger	*(meh-lãhn-zhEh)*	blend (v)
méthode (f) champenoise	*(meh-tOhd shãhm-peh-nwAhz)*	champagne method
millésime (m)	*(meeh-leh-zEEhm)*	vintage year
mince	*(mÆhns)*	thin
mis en bouteille au château	*(mEEhz ãhn booh-tEh-yœ oh shah-tOh)*	estate bottled
moelleux	*(moeh-yŒh)*	well-rounded
moût (m)	*(mOOht)*	dregs
mûr	*(mOOhr)*	ripe
négociant (m) en vins	*(neh-goh-syÃh ãhn vÆhn)*	vintner
nuageux	*(nwah-zhŒh)*	cloudy
odeur (f) de fumée	*(oh-dŒhr dœ fooh-mEh)*	smoky smell
onctueux	*(Õhnk-tŒh)*	well-rounded
pasteurisé	*(pahs-tœhr-eeh-zEh)*	pasteurized
peau (f)	*(pOh)*	skin
pétillant (m)	*(peh-teeh-yÃhn)*	sparkling wine
pourcentage (m) de sucre	*(poohr-sãhn-tAhzh)*	sugar content
pressoir (m)	*(prœh-swAhr)*	winepress
production (f)	*(proh-doohk-syÕh)*	production
raisin (m)	*(reh-zÆhn)*	grape
récolte (f)	*(reh-kOhlt)*	yield
région (f)	*(reh-zhÕh)*	country
rendement (m)	*(rãhnd-mÃhn)*	yield
respirer	*(rœhs-peeh-rEh)*	breathe (v)
résidu (m)	*(reh-zeeh-dOOh)*	residue
robust		robust
rosé (m)	*(roh-zEh)*	rosé wine
savoureux	*(sah-vooh-rŒh)*	luscious
sec	*(sEhk)*	dry
sommelier (m)	*(soh-mœh-lyEh)*	wine steward

souple	(sOOh-plœh)	supple
soutirer	(sooh-teeh-rEh)	draw off
subtile	(soohb-tEEhl)	subtle
sulfiter	(soohl-feeh-tEh)	sulfite (n)
tannin (tanin) (m)	(tah-nÆhn)	tannin
teint (m)	(tÆhnt)	tint
température (f)	(tãhm-peh-rah-tOOhr)	temperature
teneur (f) en alcool	(tœh-nŒhr ãhn ahl-kOOhl)	alcoholic content
terreux	(teh-rŒh)	earthy
tire-bouchon (m)	(teehr-booh-shÕh)	corkscrew
tirer une cuve	(teeh-reh oohn kOOhv)	draw off (v)
tonneau (m)	(toh-nOh)	barrel
tonnelier (m)	(toh-neh-lyEh)	cooper
trouble	(trOOh-blœh)	cloudy
velouté	(vœh-looh-tEh)	velvety
vendanges (fpl)	(vãhn-dAhzh)	grape harvest
vieillissement (m)	(vyeh-yeehs-mÃh)	aging
vigneron (m)	(veeh-nyeh-rÕh)	winegrower
vignoble (m)	(veeh-nyOh-blœ)	vineyard
vin (m)	(vÃhn)	wine
vin (m) du cru	(vÃhn dooh-krOOh)	local wine
vin du terroir	(vÃhn dooh teh-rwAhr)	local wine
vin (m) mousseux	(vÃhn mooh-sOh)	sparkling wine
vin (m) sec	(vÃhn sEhk)	dry wine
viticulteur (m)	(veeh-teeh-koohl-tŒhr)	winemaker
viticulture (f)	(veeh-teeh-koohl-tOOhr)	viticulture

V. GENERAL INFORMATION

ABBREVIATIONS

a.a.   always afloat
a.a.r.   against all risks
a/c   account
A/C   account current
acct.   account
a.c.v.   actual cash value
a.d.   after date
a.f.b.   air freight bill
agcy.   agency
agt.   agent
a.m.t.   air mail transfer
a/o   account of
A.P.   accounts payable
A/P   authority to pay
approx.   approximately
A.R.   accounts receivable
a/r   all risks
A/S, A.S.   account sales
a/s   at sight
at. wt.   atomic weight
av.   average
avdp.   avoirdupois
a/w   actual weight
a.w.b.   air waybill

bal.   balance
bar.   barrel
bbl.   barrel
b/d   brought down
B/E, b/e   bill of exchange
b/f   brought forward
B.H.   bill of health
bk.   bank
bkge.   brokerage
B/L   bill of lading
b/o   brought over
B.P.   bills payable
b.p.   by procuration
B.R.   bills receivable
B/S   balance sheet
b.t.   berth terms
bu.   bushel
B/V   book value

ca.   circa; centaire
C.A.   chartered accountant
c.a.   current account
C.A.D.   cash against documents
C.B.   cash book
C.B.D.   cash before delivery
c.c.   carbon copy
c/d   carried down
c.d.   cum dividend
c/f   carried forward
cf.   compare
c & f   cost and freight
C/H   clearing house
C.H.   custom house
ch. fwd.   charges forward
ch. pd.   charges paid
ch. ppd.   charges prepaid
chq.   check, cheque
c.i.f.   cost, insurance, freight
c.i.f. & c.   cost, insurance, freight, and commission
c.i.f. & e.   cost, insurance, freight, and exchange
c.i.f. & i.   cost, insurance, freight, and interest
c.l.   car load
C/m   call of more
C/N   credit note
c/o   care of
co.   company
C.O.D.   cash on delivery
comm.   commission
corp.   corporation
C.O.S.   cash on shipment
C.P.   carriage paid
C/P   charter party
c.p.d.   charters pay duties
cpn.   corporation
cr.   credit; creditor
C/T   cable transfer
c.t.l.   constructive total loss
c.t.l.o.   constructive total loss only
cum.   cumulative

cum div.   cum dividend
cum. pref.   cumulative preference
c/w   commercial weight
C.W.O.   cash with order
cwt.   hundredweight

D/A   documents against acceptance;
    deposit account
DAP   documents against payment
db.   debenture
DCF   discounted cash flow
d/d   days after date; delivered
deb.   debenture
def.   deferred
dept.   department
d.f.   dead freight
dft.   draft
dft/a.   draft attached
dft/c.   clean draft
disc.   discount
div.   dividend
DL   dayletter
DLT   daily letter telegram
D/N   debit note
D/O   delivery order
do.   ditto
doz.   dozen
D/P   documents against payment
dr.   debtor
Dr.   doctor
d/s, d.s.   days after sight
d.w.   deadweight
D/W   dock warrant
dwt.   pennyweight
dz.   dozen

ECU   European Currency Unit
E.E.T.   East European Time
e.g.   for example
encl.   enclosure
end.   endorsement
E. & O.E.   errors and omissions
    excepted
e.o.m.   end of month
e.o.h.p.   except otherwise herein
    provided
esp.   especially
Esq.   Esquire
est.   established
ex   out

ex cp.   ex coupon
ex div.   ex dividend
ex int.   ex interest
ex h.   ex new (shares)
ex stre.   ex store
ex whf.   ex wharf

f.a.a.   free of all average
f.a.c.   fast as can
f.a.k.   freight all kinds
f.a.q.   fair average quality; free
    alongside quay
f.a.s.   free alongside ship
f/c   for cash
f c. & s.   free of capture and seizure
f.c.s.r. & c.c.   free of capture,
    seizure, riots, and civil
    commotion
F.D.   free delivery to dock
f.d.   free discharge
ff.   following; folios
f.g.a.   free of general average
f.i.b.   free in bunker
f.i.o.   free in and out
f.i.t.   free in truck
f.o.b.   free on board
f.o.c.   free of charge
f.o.d.   free of damage
fol.   following; folio
f.o.q.   free on quay
f.o.r.   free on rail
f.o.s.   free on steamer
f.o.t.   free on truck(s)
f.o.w.   free on wagons; free on
    wharf
F.P.   floating policy
f.p.   fully paid
f.p.a.   free of particular average
frt.   freight
frt. pd.   freight paid
frt. ppd.   freight prepaid
frt. fwd.   freight forward
ft.   foot
fwd.   forward
f.x.   foreign exchange

g.a.   general average
g.b.o.   goods in bad order
g.m.b.   good merchantable brand
g.m.q.   good merchantable quality

G.M.T. Greenwich Mean Time
GNP gross national product
g.o.b. good ordinary brand
gr. gross
GRT gross register ton
gr. wt. gross weight
GT gross tonnage

h.c. home consumption
hgt. height
hhd. hogshead
H.O. head office
H.P. hire purchase
HP horsepower
ht. height

IDP integrated data processing
i.e. that is
I/F insufficient funds
i.h.p. indicated horsepower
imp. import
Inc. incorporated
incl. inclusive
ins. insurance
int. interest
inv. invoice
I.O.U. I owe you

J/A, j.a. joint account
Jr. junior

KV kilovolt
KW kilowatt
KWh kilowatt hour

L/C, l.c. letter of credit
LCD telegram in the language of
  the country of destination
LCO telegram in the language of
  the country of origin
ldg. landing; loading
l.t. long ton
Ltd. limited
l. tn. long ton

m. month
m/a my account
max. maximum
M.D. memorandum of deposit
M/D, m.d. months after date

memo. memorandum
Messrs. plural of Mr.
mfr. manufacturer
min. minimum
MLR minimum lending rate
M.O. money order
m.o. my order
mortg. mortgage
M/P, m.p. months after payment
M/R mate's receipt
M/S, m.s. months' sight
M.T. mail transfer
M/U making-up price

n. name; nominal
n/a no account
N/A no advice
n.c.v. no commercial value
n.d. no date
n.e.s. not elsewhere specified
N/F no funds
NL night letter
N/N no noting
N/O no orders
no. number
n.o.e. not otherwise enumerated
n.o.s. not otherwise stated
nos. numbers
NPV no par value
nr. number
n.r.t. net register ton
N/S not sufficient funds
NSF not sufficient funds
n. wt. net weight

o/a on account
OCP overseas common point
O/D, o/d on demand; overdraft
o.e. omissions excepted
o/h overhead
ono. or nearest offer
O/o order of
O.P. open policy
o.p. out of print; overproof
O/R, o.r. owner's risk
ord. order; ordinary
O.S., o/s out of stock
OT overtime

p. page; per; premium

P.A., p.a.   particular average; per annum

P/A   power of attorney; private account

PAL   phase alternation line

pat. pend.   patent pending

PAYE   pay as you earn

p/c   petty cash

p.c.   percent; price current

pcl.   parcel

pd.   paid

pf.   preferred

pfd.   preferred

pkg.   package

P/L   profit and loss

p.l.   partial loss

P/N   promissory note

P.O.   post office; postal order

P.O.B.   post office box

P.O.O.   post office order

p.o.r.   pay on return

pp.   pages

p & p   postage and packing

p. pro   per procuration

ppd.   prepaid

ppt.   prompt

pref.   preference

prox.   proximo

P.S.   postscript

pt.   payment

P.T.O., p.t.o.   please turn over

ptly. pd.   partly paid

p.v.   par value

qlty.   quality

qty.   quantity

r. & c.c.   riot and civil commotions

R/D   refer to drawer

R.D.C.   running down clause

re   in regard to

rec.   received; receipt

recd.   received

red.   redeemable

ref.   reference

reg.   registered

retd.   returned

rev.   revenue

R.O.D.   refused on delivery

R.P.   reply paid

r.p.s.   revolutions per second

RSVP   please reply

R.S.W.C.   right side up with care

Ry   railway

s.a.e.   stamped addressed envelope

S.A.V.   stock at valuation

S/D   sea damaged

S/D, s.d.   sight draft

s.d.   without date

SDR   special drawing rights

sgd.   signed

s. & h. ex   Sundays and holidays excepted

shipt.   shipment

sig.   signature

S/LC, s. & l.c.   sue and labor clause

S/N   shipping note

s.o.   seller's option

s.o.p.   standard operating procedure

spt.   spot

Sr.   senior

S.S., s.s.   steamship

s.t.   short ton

ster.   sterling

St. Ex.   stock exchange

stg.   sterling

s.v.   sub voce

T.A.   telegraphic address

T.B.   trial balance

tel.   telephone

temp.   temporary secretary

T.L., t.l.   total loss

T.L.O.   total loss only

TM   multiple telegram

T.O.   turn over

tr.   transfer

TR   telegram to be called for

TR, T/R   trust receipt

TT, T.T.   telegraphic transfer (cable)

TX   Telex

UGT   urgent

u.s.c.   under separate cover

U/ws   underwriters

v.   volt

val.   value

v.a.t.   value-added tax
v.g.   very good
VHF   very high frequency
v.h.r.   very highly recommended

w.   watt
WA   with average
W.B.   way bill
w.c.   without charge
W.E.T.   West European Time
wg.   weight guaranteed
whse.   warehouse
w.o.g.   with other goods
W.P.   weather permitting; without
   prejudice

w.p.a.   with particular average
W.R.   war risk
W/R, wr.   warehouse receipt
W.W.D.   weather working day
wt.   weight

x.c.   ex coupon
x.d.   ex dividend
x.i.   ex interest
x.n.   ex new shares

y.   year
yd.   yard
yr.   year
yrly.   yearly

WEIGHTS AND MEASURES

U.S. UNIT	METRIC EQUIVALENT
mile	1.609 kilometers
yard	0.914 meters
foot	30.480 centimeters
inch	2.540 centimeters
square mile	2.590 square kilometers
acre	0.405 hectares
square yard	0.836 square meters
square foot	0.093 square meters
square inch	6.451 square centimeters
cubic yard	0.765 cubic meters
cubic foot	0.028 cubic meters
cubic inch	16.387 cubic centimeters
short ton	0.907 metric tons
long ton	1.016 metric tons
short hundredweight	45.359 kilograms
long hundredweight	50.802 kilograms
pound	0.453 kilograms
ounce	28.349 grams
gallon	3.785 liters
quart	0.946 liters
pint	0.473 liters
fluid ounce	29.573 milliliters
bushel	35.238 liters
peck	8.809 liters
quart	1.101 liters
pint	0.550 liters

TEMPERATURE AND CLIMATE

Temperature Conversion Chart

DEGREES CELSIUS	DEGREES FAHRENHEIT
–5	23
0	32
5	41
10	50
15	59
20	68
25	77
30	86
35	95
40	104

Average Temperatures for Major Cities

	JAN	APR	JULY	OCT
Paris	37°F (3°C)	60°F (15°C)	77°F (25°C)	60°F (15°C)
Bordeaux	45°F (7°C)	61°F (16°C)	77°F (25°C)	63°F (17°C)
Marseille	46°F (8°C)	63°F (17°C)	80°F (27°C)	66°F (18°C)
Geneva	38°F (4°C)	58°F (15°C)	68°F (20°C)	58°F (15°C)
Brussels	38°F (4°C)	55°F (13°C)	72°F (21°C)	58°F (15°C)

COMMUNICATIONS CODES

Telephone

The entire French telephone system is automatic and connected to the international dialing system. Public pay phones are located at post offices, cafés, airports, and on the streets. They accept mainly phone cards and, unlike the old system that needed a token, international and long distance calls may be placed from them.

The modern phones need a special card that can be purchased at any post office or tobacco store (including the airports) for about $10 (U.S.). It can be used for local, long distance, or international calls until the 50-franc credit is used up. The computer will automatically deduct the cost of the call from your card and tell you your remaining balance.

In France telephone numbers consist of eight digits.

For calls to another part of France, dial 16 + area code + telephone number. To dial direct to the U.S., you must dial 19 + 1 + area code + telephone number. To call a number in Geneva (Switzerland) from France, dial 19 + 41 + 22 + number. To call Lausanne from France, dial 19 + 41 +

21 + number. To call a number in Brussels (Belgium) from France, dial 19 + 32 + 02 + number. In Switzerland and in Belgium, the telephone system is similar to France's.

Public pay phones in both of these countries can be found at post offices, in cafés, and on the streets. They accept coins and cards. The Swiss telephone numbers have six digits. Belgian telephone numbers have seven digits.

telephone booth	cabine téléphonique
public phone	téléphone public
telephone directory	annuaire téléphonique
local call	appel local; appel en ville
long-distance call	appel interurbain; appel à l'extérieur
person-to-person call	appel avec préavis
collect call	appel téléphonique en P.C.V.

Area Codes within France

Bordeaux	56	Marseille	91
Clermont-Ferrand	73	Nantes	40
Dijon	80	Nice	93
Grenoble	76	Paris	1
Lille	20	Strasbourg	88
Lyon	78	Toulouse	61

Area Codes for Other French-Speaking Cities

Antwerp	31	Liege	41
Bruges	50	Geneva	22
Brussels	2	Lausanne	21
Ghent	91	Montreal	514

International Country Codes

Algeria	213	Hungary	36
Argentina	54	Iceland	354
Australia	61	India	91
Austria	43	Ireland	353
Belgium	32	Israel	972
Brazil	55	Italy	39
Canada	1	Japan	81
Chile	56	Kuwait	965
Colombia	57	Luxembourg	352
Denmark	45	Malta	356
Finland	358	Mexico	52
France	33	Morocco	212
Germany	37	Netherlands	31
Gibraltar	350	New Zealand	64
Greece	30	Norway	47
Hong Kong	852	Philippines	63

Poland	48	Sweden	46
Portugal	351	Switzerland	41
Russia	7	Taiwan	886
Saudi Arabia	966	Thailand	255
Singapore	33	Tunisia	216
South Africa	37	Turkey	90
South Korea	49	United Kingdom	44
Spain	34	USA	1
Sri Lanka	94	Venezuela	58

POSTAL SERVICES

In France

The French postal service (P&T) handles mail, telephone service, and telegrams. Most offices are open Monday through Friday from 8 A.M. to 7 P.M. and until noon on Saturday. The main post office in Paris (52, rue du Louvre, 75001) is open 24 hours. Key branches in Paris are:

71, Avenue des Champs-Elysées 75008   Accepts telegrams and cables until 11:30 P.M. except Sundays and holidays (10 A.M. to noon and from 2 P.M. to 8 P.M.).

Orly Airport (South)   Open 24 hours.

Orly Airport (West)   Open 6:30 A.M. to 11 P.M.

Charles de-Gaulle Airport   Open 6:30 A.M. to 11 P.M. except Sundays and holidays (8:30 A.M. to 6:30 P.M.).

Stamps may be bought at a post office, at a tobacconist's, or at your hotel. If you collect stamps, you can buy all the French stamps by correspondence from Service Philatélique des P&T, 61-63, rue de Douai, 75346 Paris Cedex 09. You can also buy them at Musée de la Poste, Maison de la Poste et la Philatelie, 34 boulevard de Vaugirard, 75015.

In Belgium

Post offices are separate from telegram and telephone services. Hours for post offices are approximately 8 A.M. to 7 P.M., Monday through Friday and until noon on Saturday. There is a 24-hour post office at 48A, avenue Fonsny (Gare du Midi). The main post office in Brussels is at 1, place de la Monnaie.

In Switzerland

The postal service is highly efficient and delivery of regular mail ordinarily takes one day. Post offices are open from 7:30 A.M. to noon and 1:30 P.M. to 6:30 P.M., Monday through Friday; 9:30 A.M. to 11 A.M. on Saturday. Facilities offer postal, telephone, and telegram service. In Geneva, the office at rue de Lausanne is open from 6:30 A.M. to 11 P.M., every day.

TIME ZONES

Note that in Europe official time is based on the 24-hour clock as follows:

1:00 P.M. = 13h00 treize heures
1:30 P.M. = 13h30 treize heures trente

Use the table on the following page to know the time difference between where you are and other major cities. Note, however, that during April through September, you will also have to take Daylight Savings Time into account. Since there are four time zones for the United States, eleven zones for the former U.S.S.R., and three for Australia, we've listed major cities for these countries.

MAJOR HOLIDAYS

January 1	New Year's Day	Le Jour de l'An
March–April	Good Friday	Le Vendredi saint
	Easter	Pâques
	(Monday)	le lundi de Pâques
40 days after Easter	Ascension	L'Ascension
7 Mondays after Easter	Whitmonday	Lundi de la Pentecôte
May 1	Labor Day	La Fête du Travail
July 14	Bastille Day	La Fête Nationale
August 15	Assumption Day	L'Assomption
November 1	All Saints' Day	La Toussaint
November 11	Armistice Day	L'Armistice
December 25	Christmas	Noël

CURRENCY INFORMATION

Major Currencies of the World

Andorra	French Franc
Austria	Schilling
Belgium	Belgian Franc
Denmark	Danish Krone
Finland	Finnmark
France	Franc
Germany	Mark (DM)
Greece	Drachma
Hungary	Forint
Iceland	Krone
Ireland	Punt
Israel	Shekel
Italy	Lira
Liechtenstein	Swiss Franc
Luxembourg	Luxembourg Franc
Malta	Maltese Lira
Monaco	French Franc
Netherlands	Guilder

−8 HOURS	−6 HOURS	−5 HOURS	GREEN-WICH MEAN TIME	+1 HOURS	+2 HOURS	+3 HOURS	+ ADDITIONAL HOURS
Los Angeles San Francisco	Chicago Dallas Houston	Boston New York Washington, D.C.	Great Britain Iceland Ireland Portugal	Austria Belgium Denmark France Germany Hungary Italy Luxembourg Malta Monaco Netherlands Norway Poland Spain Sweden Switzerland	Finland Greece Romania South Africa	Turkey Moscow	Sydney (10 hours) New Zealand (10 hours)

Norway	Norwegian Krone
Portugal	Escudo
Russia	Ruble
Spain	Peseta
Sweden	Swedish Krone
Switzerland	Swiss Franc
Turkey	Lira
United Kingdom	Pound Sterling

Major Commercial Banks

In France

Banque Nationale de Paris
16, boulevard des Italiens
75009 Paris

Caisse Nationale de Crédit Agricole
91/93, boulevard Pasteur
75015 Paris

Crédit Lyonnais
19, boulevard des Italiens
75002 Paris

Société Générale
29, boulevard Haussmann
75009 Paris

In Belgium

Banque Bruxelles Lambert
24 avenue Marnix
B-1050 Brussels

Kredietbank
19 Grote Markt
B-1000 Brussels

Société Générale de Banque
(Generale Bank)
3 Montaigne du Parc
B-1000 Brussels

In Switzerland

Union Bank of Switzerland (UBS)
Bahnhofstrasse 45
Postfach
CH-8021 Zurich

Swiss Bank Corporation
Postfach
CH-4002 Basle

Crédit Suisse
Paradeplatz 8
Postfach
CH-8021 Zurich

MAJOR BUSINESS PERIODICALS

The *International Herald Tribune* is the leading English-language newspaper sold in Europe. It is available at most hotels and newsstands. The *Journal of Commerce* is also widely available.

Newspapers

In France

Les Echos
Le Figaro
Libération
Le Matin de Paris
Le Monde
Le Quotidien (de Paris)

In Belgium

Le Soir
La Libre Belgique
L'Echo de la Bourse
Le Lloyd Anversois
La Lanterne
La Dernière Heure
La Wallonie

In Switzerland

(All major business newspapers in
Switzerland are in German.)
Neue Zuercher Zeitung
Schweiz. Handelszeitung
Finanz und Wirtschaft
La Tribune de Genève
La Gazette de Lausanne

Magazines

In France

Le Nouvel Observateur
Le Nouvel Economiste
L'Expansion
L'Express
Le Point
L'Usine Nouvelle
L'Auto-Journal
L'Evénement du Jeudi

In Belgium

Trends Tendance
Libelle/Rosita
Femmes d'aujourd'hui
Pourquoi-Pas?
BMB
Cine Revue
The Bulletin (in English)
Prospects (in English)

ANNUAL TRADE FAIRS

This is a partial list of annual events. Changes may occur from year to year, as
well as during the year, and it is advisable to consult local tourist offices and
the Government Tourist Offices abroad for up-to-date information.

Paris

January	International Furniture Exhibition
	Furniture Manufacturer's Exhibition
	Show for KD Furniture and Take-Home Goods for Home
	International Lighting Exhibition
	Commercial and Professional Arts and Gifts Exhibition
	Jewelry, Gold and Silver, Clocks Exhibition
	International Paris Boat Show
	Games and Toys Exhibition
	Confectionary, Chocolate and Biscuit Trade Exhibition
	Stationery Exhibition
	Household Appliances Exhibition
February	Men's and Boy's Wear Trade Show
	Children's Fashion Exhibition
	Knitwear Exhibition
	Ladies Ready-to-Wear Exhibition
	Franchise Show
	Retail Trades Equipment Show

March	Mechanical Components and Systems for Machine Construction Show*
	Agricultural Show
	Agricultural Machinery Show
	Leisure Power Cultivation Show
	International Sound Festival
	Woodworking Machinery Exhibition
	Fur Industries Exhibition
May	International Handling Equipment Exhibition
	Wallcoverings, Furnishing, Textiles and Linens Show
	Carpet and Floor Coverings Exhibition
June	Dairy Equipment Exhibition
September	Commercial and Professional Arts and Gifts Exhibit
	Jewelry, Gold and Silver, Clocks Exhibition
	Children's Fashion Exhibition
	Men's and Boy's Wear Trade Show
	Sports Goods and Leisure Equipment Exhibition
	International Leather Week
	Hardware, Tools, Gardening and Domestic Hardware Exhibition
	Data Processing and Communications Show
	Ladies Ready-to-Wear Clothing Exhibition
October	Laundry, Dry Cleaning Machinery Exhibit
	Hotel and Catering Equipment Exhibition
	Food Products Exhibition*
	Optical Equipment Exhibition
November	Food Manufacturing Processing Exhibition*
	Machinery and Technics for Meat Industry Exhibition*
	Packaging Exhibition*
	Environment Exhibition*
December	Laboratory Exhibition*
	Chemical Engineering and Equipment Exhibition*

Paris Convention Center
2, place de la Porte-Maillot
75017 Paris
Tel: (1) 46-40-22-22
Telex: 660235 F.

Parc des Expositions de la Porte de
Versailles
Porte de Versailles
75015 Paris

Parc des Expositions de Villepinte
93420 Villepinte

Palais des Congrès
2, place de la Porte-Maillot
75017 Paris

CNIT-La Défense
Puteaux
92092 Paris

---

* Held every two years
Note: For additional information, contact PromoSalons, International Trade Exhibitions in France, Inc., 8 West 40th Street, Suite 1505, New York, New York 10018 (212) 869-1720; Telex 427 563 FRSHOWS. In Paris, the address is 17, rueDaru, 75008; telephone (1) 267-26-53; telex MLR 648 256 F.

Brussels

February	Material and Equipment for Florists Trade Show
	Crystalware, Chinaware, Ceramics, Jewelry, Toys, Gifts, and Home Decoration Trade Show
March	Exhibition of Touring, Aviation, Caravans, Motorhomes
	Sports Show
	Brussels Trade Fair—All Consumer Goods: Foodstuffs, Home Decoration, Fashion, Home Comfort
	Garden and Swimming Pool Exhibition
April	Medical and Hospital Equipment Trade Show
May	International Industrial Equipment Exhibition
	International Packaging Show
	International Exhibition of Public Services Equipment
	International Sub-contracting Trade Show
	Handling, Hoisting, and Storage Trade Show
	Forum of New Technologies
	Hydraulic and Pneumatic Components Trade Show
	Industrial Electricity Trade Show
	Automation Show
July	International Congress on Thrombosis and Haemostasis
September	International Congress of International Fiscal Association
	Crystalware, Chinaware, Ceramics, Jewelry, Toys, Gifts, and Home Decoration Trade Show
	Material and Equipment for Florists Trade Show
	International Hardware and Household Goods Fair
	World Road Congress and Exhibition
	International Symposium on Industrial Robots and Technical Exhibition
October	European Professional Fair for Hotels, Restaurants, Pubs, Communities, and Ice Cream Trade
November	European Exhibition for Heating, Drying, Ventilation, Air Conditioning and Refrigeration
	Symposium on Air Conditioning and Refrigeration
	International Brussels Travel Fair
	Water Technics Exhibition
	Applications of Synthetic Materials and Composites Exhibition
	International Woodworking Show
	Horses and Horseriding Equipment Trade Show
	Do-it-Yourself Exhibition
	Worldfair for Inventions
December	Investment and Saving Exhibition

Parc des Expositions
Place de Belgique
B-1020 Brussels
Tel: 02-478-48-60
Telex: 23643 b

Geneva

January	International Commercial Vehicles Show
February	National Cycle and Motorcycle Exhibition
March	International Motor Show
April	Exhibition of Inventions and New Techniques
May	Car Model Exchange
	Vehicle Industry Suppliers Exhibition
June	European Nuclear Conference and Trade Fair
	Banking Services Exhibition
September	Data and Text Processing Applications Fair
November	Ideal Home Exhibition
	Geneva Antiques Fair
December	Pest Control Exhibition

Palexpo Exhibition and Conference Center

For more information, contact Foundation for the Promotion and Organization of Trade Exhibitions, Case postale 112, CH-1218 Grand-Saconnex, Geneva; telephone: 022/98 11 11; telex; 422784 EXPO CH.

TRAVEL TIMES

To France

Most international flights to Paris arrive at Roissy-Charles-de-Gaulle Airport, though charter flights usually head to Orly Airport. Charles-de-Gaulle Airport is 26 km from Paris; Orly is 16 km. Connections are made easily to Paris from either airport.

Air Terminals

Maillot terminal 2, place de la Porte-Maillot, 75017 Paris Tel. (1) 42 99 20 18 and (1) 42 99 21 49
Invalides terminal 2, rue Esnault-Pelterie, 75007 Paris Tel. (1) 42 23 97 10 and (1) 43 23 87 79

Air France Buses

From all airports to Maillot, Hôtel Méridien, Les Invalides, Montparnasse (check with Air France, your travel agent, or at the airport upon your arrival).

Railways

Orly Rail (Railway services connecting boulevard Victor, Javel, Champ-de-Mars, Alma, Invalides, Orsay, Saint-Michel and Austerlitz with Orly-South and West Airports). Departures every 15 minutes from 5:30 A.M. to 8:45 P.M. and every 30 minutes from 8:45 P.M. to 10:45 P.M.
Roissy-Rail (Railway services connecting Cité Universitaire, Denfert-Rochereau, Port Royal, Luxembourg, Châtelet, Gare du Nord with Charles-de-Gaulle Airport). Departures every 15 minutes from 5:30 A.M. to 11:30 P.M.

Buses (RATP)

350 Gare de l'Est/Gare du Nord to Le Bourget Airport and Charles-de-Gaulle Airport (6 tickets).
351 Nation to Charles-de-Gaulle Airport (6 tickets).
215 Denfert-Rochereau to Orly-South and Orly-West Airports (3 tickets).
183 A Porte de Choisy to Orly-South Airport (4 tickets).

To Belgium

Flights to Belgium arrive at Brussels' Zaventem Airport, 12 km from the center of the city. The easiest way to reach the city is to take the train to Gare Centrale, which runs every 20 minutes.

To Switzerland (Geneva)

Flights to Geneva arrive at Cointrin Airport, located about 4 km from the center of the city. Taxis are quick but you can also take the airport bus to the Air Terminal at Gare Cornavin. The airport bus runs every 20 minutes.

Approximate Flying Times to Key French-Speaking Cities

New York–Paris	7 hours
New York–Geneva	7 $\frac{1}{2}$ hours
New York–Brussels	6 $\frac{1}{2}$ hours
Montreal–Paris	8 $\frac{1}{2}$ hours
Montreal–Geneva	9 hours
Montreal–Brussels	9 hours
Los Angeles–Paris	12 hours
London–Paris	2 hours
Sydney–Paris	13 $\frac{1}{2}$ hours

Average Flying Times Between Major French-Speaking Cities

Paris–Geneva	1 hour
Paris–Bordeaux	1 hour
Paris–Lyon	1 hour
Paris–Marseille	1 hour, 20 minutes
Geneva–Brussels	1 hour
Paris–Brussels	50 minutes

Air Inter
Air Inter is the French domestic airline. Air Inter flies in and out of both Orly and Charles-de-Gaulle Airport, as well as to Nice, Marseille, Toulouse, Bordeaux, Lyon, Strasbourg, Mulhouse/Basle, Montpellier, and Nantes. Reservations: (1) 45 39 25 25.

Air Littoral
Flights serving the south of France, Italy, and Spain. Telephone: 67 64 72 72.

Brit Air
Specializing in flights to Brittany and Normandy. Telephone: 98 62 10 22.

Euralair International
Executive jet flights and charter flights. Telephone: (1) 48 38 92 73.

Stellair
Passenger and freight charter flights. Telephone: 40 04 04 62.

Belgium has no large domestic airline. In Switzerland, the major domestic airlines are listed below:

Balair AG
Flugplatz Basle-Muelhausen
CH-4002 Basle

CTA
Case Postale 110
CH-1215 Geneva

Crossair
Postfach 630
CH-8058 Zurich

Rail Travel

France is covered by a dense network of railroad lines connecting large cities.

FOR INFORMATION AND RESERVATIONS APPLY TO S.N.C.F.	
INFORMATION	RESERVATION
Paris-Austerlitz Tel. (1) 45.84.16.16	(1) 45.84.15.20
Paris-Est Tel. (1) 42.08.49.90	(1) 42.40.11.22
Paris-Gare de Lyon Tel. (1) 43.45.92.22	(1) 42.45.93.33
Paris-Montparnasse Tel. (1) 45.38.52.29	(1) 45.38.52.39
Paris-Nord Tel. (1) 42.80.03.03	(1) 48.78.87.54
Paris-St-Lazare Tel. (1) 45.38.52 29	(1) 43.87.91.70

NEW! Special phone number for SNCF rail information in English.
From Paris and its region, call: (1) 43.80.50.50.
From other regions of France call: (1) 43.80.50.50
From foreign countries call: (33-l) 43.80.50.50

Thanks to the T.G.V. (Train à grande vitesse, or highspeed train), Lyon is only two hours from Paris, four hours from Marseille, and three and a half hours from Geneva.

There are more than twenty-five departures daily for Lyon, nine for Marseille, and five for Geneva, every day of the week. Reservations can be made and tickets can be bought in the United States at any office of the French Railroads or at a travel agency, one week prior to departure. For more information, please call the French Railroads at (914) 682-2999, (800) 438-7245, (800) 868-7245.

In Belgium, trains link up with major cities in Europe, and train travel is quick and efficient. There are three main stations: Gare du Midi, Gare Centrale, Gare du Nord.

In Switzerland, all trains to Geneva arrive at Gare Cornavin, which is conveniently located in the center of the city. There are also link-ups with other major Swiss cities, as well as other European cities.

TRAVEL TIPS

On the Plane

1. Be aware that the engine noise is less noticeable in the front part of the plane. Try to sleep. Some frequent travelers bring along earplugs, eye-shades, and slippers.
2. Wear comfortable, loose-fitting clothing.
3. Walk up and down the aisles, when permitted, at least five minutes every hour to maintain body circulation.
4. Limit alcohol intake—altitude heightens the intoxicating effect.

Jet Lag

Disruption of the body's natural cycles can put a lingering damper on your travels, so take the following precautions:

1. *Avoid loss of sleep* by taking a flight that will get you to your destination early in the evening, if at all possible. Get a good night's sleep at home the night before your departure.
2. *Rearrange your daily routine* and sleeping schedule to harmonize with a normal body clock at your destination.
3. *Avoid stress and last-minute rush.* You're going to need all your strength.

Shopping

Most shops open at 9 A.M. and close between 6:30 and 7:00 P.M. in France. In Belgium stores are open until 6:00 P.M.; in Switzerland until 6:30 P.M. Except for department stores and most of the boutiques in Paris, most shops close for an hour or two around noon. Most shops are closed on Sundays. In France, shops generally close at 5:00 P.M. on Saturday.

We suggest that, while in Paris, you do your shopping (especially perfume) in one of the big department stores instead of the duty-free shops at the airport. They are much less expensive, even when we are talking duty-free. For example, *Les Galeries Lafayette* has an extensive choice of perfumes and gifts of all kinds. You can pay with a major credit card and they will immediately credit your account in the amount of the V.A.T. (approximately 15% of the paid amount), which you are not supposed to pay if you are not a resident of France. This is true for all stores in France. (You will, of course, be billed in American dollars according to the current rate of exchange.) You can also be reimbursed at the airport customs office before leaving France, on presentation of your passport and the bill given to you by the store. Have the items in question with you in case the customs officer asks for them.

Clothing Sizes

In Europe, clothing sizes vary from country to country. Basically, for men, a suit size is "10" more than the American size; thus, an American 40 is a European or Continental 50. For women, the conversion is the American size plus "28"; thus, an American size 10 is a Continental 38.

Tipping

Tipping, of course, varies with the individual and the situation. The following amounts are typical: In hotels in France, Belgium, and Switzerland, 10–15% is included in the bill; porter (per bag): 45 francs in Belgium, 5 francs in France, and 1 franc in Switzerland; for the maid (per week): 150 francs in Belgium, 10 francs in France, and in Switzerland the tip is included in the price of the room. In restaurants, 10–15% is usually included in the check. Lavatory and coat check attendants expect a few francs. Taxi drivers and hairdressers receive 5%; ushers and guides expect lesser amounts.

Taxis

Taxi drivers in Paris are generally helpful and willing to get you to your destination in record time. You can catch a taxi at a taxi stand, identified by signs that say Tête de Station and/or Taxi, on a first-come, first-served basis. If both roof lights are lit, it's available; if just one is lit, it's taken. You can call for taxis—42 05 77 77 or 42 03 99 99 are two of many numbers to call—but getting a taxi at a taxi stand is usually faster.

MAJOR HOTELS

Paris

Ambassador (9th)
16, boulevard Haussmann
Tel: 42 46 92 63
Fax: 40 22 08 74
Major credit cards accepted
Restaurant

Bristol (8th)
112, rue du Faubourg St-Honoré
Tel: 42 66 91 45
Fax: 42 66 68 68
(Indoor pool)
Major credit cards accepted
Restaurant: Le Bristol (two stars)

Château Frontenac (8th)
54, rue Pierre Charron
Tel: 47 23 55 85
Fax: 47 23 03 32
Major credit cards accepted
Restaurant

Claridge Bellman (8th)
37, rue Francois ler
Tel: 47 23 90 03
Fax: 47 23 08 84
Major credit cards accepted
Restaurant

Commodore (9th)
12, boulevard Haussmann
Tel: 42 46 72 82
Fax: 47 70 23 81
Major credit cards accepted
Restaurant

Crillon (Hôtel de) (8th)
10, place de la Concorde
Tel: 42 65 24 24
Fax: 44 71 15 02
Major credit cards accepted
Restaurant: Les Ambassadeurs (two
stars)

George V (8th)
31, avenue George-V
Tel: 47 23 54 00
Fax: 47 20 40 00
Major credit cards accepted
Restaurant: Les Princes

Hilton (15th)
18 avenue de Suffren
Tel: 42 73 92 00
Fax: 47 83 62 66
Major credit cards accepted
(Indoor pool)
Restaurants: Le Western and Le Toit
de Paris

Holiday-lnn (11th)
10, place de la République
Tel: 43 55 44 34
Fax: 47 00 32 34
Major credit cards accepted
Restaurant: Belle Epoque; Coffee-
shop: Le Jardin d'Hiver

Inter-Continental (1st)
3, rue la Castiglione
Tel: 42 60 37 80
Fax: 44 77 15 60
Major credit cards accepted

Lancaster (8th)
7, rue de Berri
Tel: 43 59 90 43
Fax: 42 89 22 71
Major credit cards accepted
Restaurant

L'Hotel Guy-Louis Duboucheron
13, rue des Beaux-Arts
Tel: 43 25 27 22
Major credit cards accepted
Restaurant

Lutétia (6th)
45, boulevard Raspail
Tel: 45 44 38 10
Fax: 49 54 46 00
Major credit cards accepted
Restaurant: Le Paris (one star)

Lotti (1st)
7, rue de la Castiglione
Tel: 42 60 37 34
Fax: 40 15 93 56
Major credit cards accepted
Restaurant

Louvre-Concorde (1st)
Place André Malraux
Tel: 42 61 56 01
Fax: 44 58 38 01
Major credit cards accepted
Restaurant

Meurice (1st)
228, rue de Rivoli
Tel: 42 60 38 60
Fax: 44 58 10 15
Major credit cards accepted

Meridien Montparnasse Park (14th)
19, rue Cdt Mouchette
Tel: 43 20 15 51
Fax: 44 36 49 00
Major credit cards accepted
Restaurant: La Ruche

Nikko (15th)
61, quai de Grenelle
Tel: 45 75 62 62
Fax: 45 75 42 35
Major credit cards accepted
(Indoor pool)
Restaurant: Les Célèbrités (one star)

Pont Royal Best Western (7th)
7, rue de Montalembert
Tel: 45 44 38 27
Fax: 45 44 92 07
Major credit cards accepted
Restaurant

Prince de Galles-Sheraton (8th)
33, avenue George-V
Tel: 47 23 55 11
Fax: 47 20 96 92
Major credit cards accepted
Restaurant

Ritz (1st)
15, place Vendôme
Tel: 42 60 38 30
Fax: 42 60 23 71
Major credit cards accepted
Restaurant: L'Espadon (two stars)

Scribe (9th)
1, rue Scribe
Tel: 47 42 03 40
Fax: 42 65 39 97
Major credit cards accepted
Restaurant: Le Jardin des Muses

Sofitel Paris (15th)
8, rue L. Armand
Tel: 45 54 95 00
Fax: 45 57 04 22
Major credit cards accepted
(Indoor pool)
Restaurant: Le Relais (one star)

La Trémoille (8th)
14, rue de la Trémoille
Tel: 47 23 34 20
Fax: 40 70 01 08
Major credit cards accepted

Victoria Palace (6th)
6, rue Blaise-Desgoffe
Tel: 45 44 38 16
Fax: 45 49 23 75
Major credit cards accepted
Restaurant

Warwick (8th)
5, rue de Berri
Tel: 45 63 14 11
Fax: 45 63 75 81
Major credit cards accepted
Restaurant: La Couronne (one star)

Westminster (2nd)
13 rue de la Paix
Tel: 42 61 57 46
Fax: 42 60 30 66
Major credit cards accepted
Restaurant: Le Celadon (one star)

Bordeaux

Frantel
5, rue R-Lateulade
Tel: 56 90 92 37
Telex 540565
Major credit cards accepted
Restaurant: Le Mériadeck

Grand Hôtel et Café de Bordeaux
2, place Comédie
Tel: 56 90 33 44
Telex 541658
Major credit cards accepted

Novotel-Mérignac (near Airport)
Tel: 56 34 10 25
Telex 540320
Major credit cards accepted
(Outdoor pool)
Restaurant

La Réserve (near Airport)
Av. Bourgailh
Tel: 56 07 13 28
Telex 560585
American Express, Visa accepted
Restaurant

Sofitel Aquitania (near Parc des
    Expositions)
Tel: 56 50 83 80
Telex 570557
Major credit cards accepted
(Outdoor Pool)
Restaurants: Le Flore, Le Pub

Lyon

Grand Hôtel des Beaux-Arts
75, rue Président E-Herriot, 69002
Tel: 78 38 09 50
Telex 330442
Major credit cards accepted

Grand Hôtel Concorde
11, rue Grolée, 69002
Tel: 78 42 56 21
Telex 330244
Major credit cards accepted
Restaurant: Le Florelle

Grand Hôtel de la Paix
41, rue Président
    Edouard Herriot
Tel: 78 37 17 17
Major credit cards accepted

Royal
20, place Bellecour, 69002
Tel: 78 37 57 31
Telex 310785
Major credit cards accepted
Restaurant

Sofitel
20, quai Gailleton, 69002
Tel: 78 42 72 50
Telex 330225
Major credit cards accepted
Restaurants: Les Trois Dômes, Sofi
    Shop

Marseille

Concorde-Palm Beach (on the
    Corniche)
2, promenade Plage, 13008
Tel: 91 76 20 00
Telex 401894
Major credit cards accepted
(Outdoor pool)
Restaurants: La Réserve, Les Voiliers

Concorde-Prado
11, avenue Mazargues, 13008
Tel: 91 76 51 11
Telex 420209
American Express, Visa accepted
Restaurant

Frantel
Rue Neuve St-Martin, 13001
Tel: 91 91 91 29
Telex 401886
Major credit cards accepted
Restaurants: L'Oursinade,
    L'Oliveraie

Le Petit Nice (on the Corniche)
Anse de Maldormé, 13007
Tel: 91 52 14 39
Telex 401565
American Express, Visa accepted
(Outdoor pool)
Restaurant

Résidence Bompard
2, rue Flots-Bleus, 13007
Tel: 91 52 10 93
Telex 400430
American Express accepted

Sofitel Vieux Port
36, boulevard Ch.-Livon, 13007
Tel: 91 52 90 19
Telex 401270
Major credit cards accepted
(Outdoor pool)
Restaurant

Nice

Abe la Hôtel
223, promenade des Anglais
Tel: 93 37 17 17
Fax: 93 71 21 71

Brussels

Amigo
rue Amigo 1, 1000
Tel: 511 5910
Telex 21618
Major credit cards accepted
Restaurant

Hyatt Regency Brussels
rue Royale 250, 1210
Tel: 219 4640
Telex 61871
Major credit cards accepted
Restaurant

Astoria
rue Royale 103, 1000
Tel: 217 6290
Telex 20540
Major credit cards accepted
Restaurant: Palais Royal

Jolly Hotel Atlanta
boulevard A. Max 7, 1000
Tel: 217 0120
Telex 21475
Major credit cards accepted

Brussels-Sheraton
place Rogier 3, 1210
Tel: 219 3400
Telex 26887
Major credit cards accepted
Restaurant

President World Trade Center
boulevard Emile Jacqmain 180, 1210
Tel: 217 2020
Telex 61417
Major credit cards accepted
Restaurant

Hilton-International Brussels
boulevard Waterloo 38, 1000
Tel: 513 8877
Telex 22744
Major credit cards accepted
Restaurant: Plein Ciel (27th Fl.)

Royal Windsor Hotel
rue Duquesnoy 5, 1000
Tel: 511 4215
Telex 62905
Major credit cards accepted
Restaurant

Geneva

Beau Rivage
13, quai Mont Blanc, 1201
Tel: 31 02 21
Telex 23362
Major credit cards accepted
Restaurant: Le Chat Botté (one star)

Les Bergues
33, quai Bergues, 1201
Tel: 31 50 50
Telex 23383
Major credit cards accepted
Restaurants: Le Pavillon and
l'Amphitryon

Grand Pré
35, rue Grand-Pré, 1202
Tel: 33 91 50
Telex 23284
Major credit cards accepted

Intercontinental
7, Petit Saconnex, 1211
Tel: 34 60 91
Telex 23130
Major credit cards accepted
(Indoor pool)
Restaurant: Les Continents

Noga Hilton
19, quai Mont-Blanc, 1201
Tel: 31 98 11
Telex 289704
Major credit cards accepted
(Indoor pool)
Restaurant: Le Cygne (one star)

Paix
11, quai Mont Blanc, 1201
Tel: 32 61 50
Telex 22552
Major credit cards accepted
Restaurant

Président
47, quai Wilson, 1200
Tel: 31 10 00
Telex 22780
Major credit cards accepted
Restaurant: La Palmeraie

Ramada Renaissance
19, rue Zurich, 1201
Tel: 31 02 41
Telex 289109
Major credit cards accepted
Restaurants: La Toquade and la
Cortille

Rhône
quai Turrettini, 1201
Tel: 31 98 31
Telex 22213
Major credit cards accepted
Restaurant: La Rôtisserie le Neptune
(one star)

Richemond
Brunswick Garden, 1201
Tel: 31 14 00
Telex 22598
Major credit cards accepted
Restaurant: Le Gentilhomme (one star)

Métropole
34, quai Général Guisan, 1204
Tel: 21 13 44
Telex 421550
Major credit cards accepted
Restaurant: L'Arlequin (one star)

If you are traveling to cities other than the ones mentioned here, you may wish to call SOFITEL/NOVOTEL or HOTELS MÉRIDIEN in Paris, at the following numbers, which are the main reservation offices: 60 77 27 27 (Sofitel/Novotel) and 42 56 01 01 (Méridien). Sofitel/Novotel and Méridien have hotels in many towns in France and in many European cities.

MAJOR RESTAURANTS

Paris

Bristol—two stars
112, rue du Faubourg St-Honoré
(8th)
Tel: 42 66 91 45
Major credit cards accepted

Chez Pauline—two stars
5, rue Villedo (1st)
Tel: 42 96 20 70
Major credit cards accepted

Chiberta—two stars
3, rue Arsène-Houssaye (8th)
Tel: 45 63 77 90
Major credit cards accepted

Le Divellec—two stars
107, rue de l'Université (7th)
Tel: 45 51 91 96
Major credit cards accepted

Faugeron—two stars
52, rue de Longchamp (16th)
Tel: 47 04 24 53

Lasserre—two stars
17, avenue Franklin Roosevelt (8th)
Tel: 43 59 53 43

Laurent—one star
41, Avenue Gabriel (8th)
Tel: 42 25 00 39
Major credit cards accepted

La Marée—two stars
1, rue Daru (8th)
Tel: 47 63 52 42
Major credit cards accepted

Michel Rostang—two stars
20, rue Rennequin
Tel: 47 63 40 77
Visa accepted

Le Pré Catelan—two stars
Route de Suresnes
Bois de Boulogne (16th)
Tel: 45 24 55 58
Major credit cards accepted

Relais Louis XIII—two stars
1, rue Pont de Loti (6th)
Tel: 43 26 75 96
Major credit cards accepted

Tour d'Argent—three stars
15, quai Tournelle (5th)
Tel: 43 54 23 21

Bordeaux

La Chamade—one star
20 rue Piliers de Tutelle
Tel: 56 48 13 74
American Express accepted

Dubern—one star
42, allées Tourny
Tel: 56 48 03 44
Major credit cards accepted

Le Rouzic—two stars
34 Cours du Chapeau rouge
Tel: 56 44 39 11
Major credit cards accepted

Le St-James—two stars
Place C. Hosteins (at Bouliac)
Tel: 56 20 52 19
Major credit cards accepted

Lyon

Léon de Lyon—two stars
1 rue Pleney
Tel: 78 28 11 33

Orsi—two stars
3 place Kléber
Tel: 78 89 57 68
American Express, Visa accepted

Paul Bocuse—three stars
Pont de Collonges N
Tel: 78 22 01 40
Major credit cards accepted

Tour Rose—two stars
16 rue Boeuf
Tel: 78 37 25 90
Major credit cards accepted

Marseille

Calypso
3 rue Catalans
Tel: 91 52 64 22
Visa accepted

Jambon de Parme—one star
67 rue la Palud
Tel: 91 54 37 98
Major credit cards accepted

Max Caizergues—one star
11 rue G-Ricard
Tel: 91 33 58 07
Major credit cards accepted

Michel—one star
6 rue Catalans
Tel: 91 52 64 22
Visa accepted

Brussels

Bruneau—two stars
avenue Broustin, 73, 1080
Tel: 427 6978
Major credit cards accepted

Carlton—two stars
boulevard Waterloo, 28, 1000
Tel: 513 7831
Major credit cards accepted

Comme Chez Soi—three stars
place Rouppe 23, 1000
Tel: 512 2921
Major credit cards accepted

Cravache d'Or—three stars
place A. Leemans, 10, 1050
Tel: 538 3746
Major credit cards accepted

L'Ecaillier du Palais Royal—two
    stars
rue Bodenbroek, 18, 1000
Tel: 512 8751
Major credit cards accepted

Eddie Van Maele—two stars
Chaussée Romaine, 964, 1810
Tel: 478 5445

La Maison du Cygne—two stars
Grand Place, 9, 1000
Tel: 511 8244
Major credit cards accepted

Villa Lorraine—two stars
avenue Vivier-d'oie, 75, 1180
Tel: 374 3163
Major credit cards accepted

Geneva

L'Arlequin—one star
34, quai Général Guisan 1204
Tel: 21 13 44
Major credit cards accepted

Le Bearn
4, quai de la Poste, 1204
Major credit cards accepted

Le Chat Botté—one star
13, quai Mont-Blanc, 1201
Tel: 31 65 32
Major credit cards accepted

Le Cygne—two stars
19, quai Mont-Blanc, 1201
Tel: 31 98 11
Major credit cards accepted

Le Gentilhomme—one star
Brunswick Garden, 1201
Tel: 31 14 00
Major credit cards accepted

Parc des Eaux Vives—one star
82, quai Gustave-Ador, 1207
Tel: 35 41 40
Major credit cards accepted

La Perle du Lac—one star
128, route de Lausanne, 1202
Tel: 31 79 35
Major credit cards accepted

Le Pont Route
(Hostellerie de la Vendée)
28, chemin Vendée
Tel: 92 04 11
Major credit cards accepted

Le Vieux Moulin—two stars
89, route de Drize
Tel: 42 29 56
Major credit cards accepted

Ratings extracted from the *Red Michelin Guide*, 1992.

USEFUL ADDRESSES

In France (Paris)

Paris Chamber of Commerce and
  Industry
27, avenue de Friedland
75008

Centre National du Commerce
  Extérieur
10, avenue d'Iena
75016

French-American Chamber of
  Commerce
7, rue Jean Goujon
75008

American Chamber of Commerce in
  France
21, avenue George V
75008

Customs Information Service
182, rue St.-Honore
75001

Ministry of Industry and Foreign
  Trade
101, rue de Grenelle
75007

Export and Import Licenses Bureau
42, rue de Clichy
75436

French Industrial Development
  Agency
DATAR
1, avenue Charles Floquet
75007

ANIT (Public Information Service)
8, avenue de l'Opéra
75001

International Chamber of Commerce
38, cours Albert-ler
75008

International Monetary Fund
66, avenue d'Iéna
75016

French Chamber of Commerce of
Canada
11, avenue Franklin-Roosevelt
75008

British Chamber of Commerce
6, rue Halévy
75009

In Belgium (Brussels)

Belgian Foreign Trade Office
Boulevard Emile Jacqumain 162
B-1000

Ministry of Economic Affairs
Square de Meeus 23
B-1000

Belgium National Tourist Office
61, rue du Marché aux Herbes
1000

In Switzerland (Zurich)

Swiss-American Chamber of
Commerce
Talacker 49
8001

Swiss National Tourist Office
Bellariastrasse 38
8027

Swiss Federation of Commerce and
Industry
Borenstrasse 25
8022

In the United States

S.O.F.T.E. General Representative
610 Fifth Avenue
New York, New York 10020

French American Chamber of
Commerce
1350 Avenue of the Americas
New York, New York 10019

F.I.D.A.
610 Fifth Avenue
New York, New York 10020

French Embassy/Commercial
Counselor
40 West 57th Street
New York, New York 10019

Belgian American Chamber of
Commerce
350 Fifth Avenue, Suite 703
New York, New York 10118

Consulate General of Switzerland
444 Madison Avenue
New York, New York 10022

In Canada and Great Britain

S.O.F.T.E. General Representative
1981 McGill College, Suite 490
Montreal, Quebec H3A 2W9

S.O.F.T.E. General Representative
Department 178 Piccadilly
London W 1 V OA 1

French Embassy
Commercial Section
12 Stanhope Gate
London W 1

French Chamber of Commerce
54, Conduit Street
London W 1

MAPS

The maps of Europe, France, Switzerland, and Belgium on the following pages will be useful in doing business in French-speaking areas.

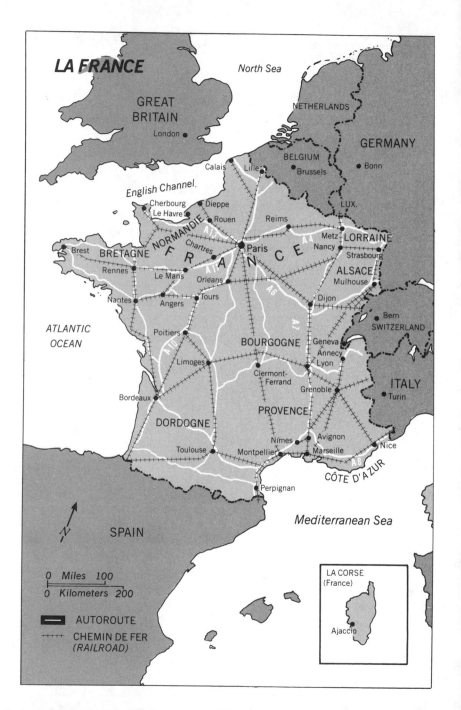

LA FRANCE

North Sea

GREAT
BRITAIN

London

NETHERLANDS

GERMANY

Calais   Lille   BELGIUM   Bonn
                   Brussels

English Channel.

Cherbourg   Dieppe   LUX.
Le Havre   Rouen   Reims   Metz   LORRAINE
NORMANDIE   Chartres   Nancy
Brest   BRETAGNE   F R A N C E   Paris   Strasbourg
Rennes   Le Mans   Orleans   ALSACE   Mulhouse
Nantes   Angers   Tours   Dijon
                                        Bern
ATLANTIC   Poitiers   SWITZERLAND
OCEAN
            Limoges   BOURGOGNE   Geneva
                                    Annecy
                       Clermont-   Lyon
            Bordeaux   Ferrand   Grenoble   ITALY
                                                Turin
DORDOGNE   PROVENCE
            Toulouse   Nîmes   Avignon
                       Montpellier   Marseille   Nice
                                      CÔTE D'AZUR
            Perpignan

Mediterranean Sea

SPAIN

N

0   Miles   100
0   Kilometers   200

███ AUTOROUTE
+++ CHEMIN DE FER
     (RAILROAD)

LA CORSE
(France)

Ajaccio

386

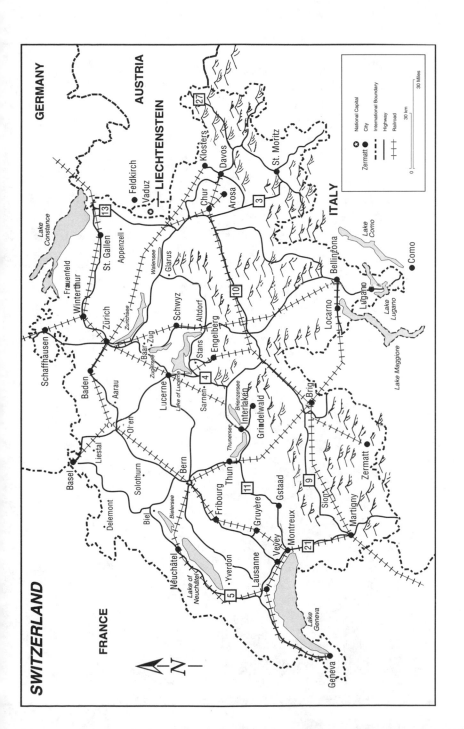

SWITZERLAND

GERMANY

AUSTRIA

LIECHTENSTEIN

ITALY

FRANCE

N

Lake Constance

Frauenfeld
Winterthur
Schaffhausen
Zürich
Baden
Aarau
Olten
Liestal
Basel
Delemont
Solothurn
Biel
Bielersee
Neuchâtel
Lake of Neuchâtel
Yverdon
Fribourg
Bern
Thun
Thunersee
Gruyère
Lausanne
Vevey
Montreux
Lake Geneva
Geneva
Gstaad
Sion
Martigny
Zermatt
Brig
Interlaken
Grindelwald
Brienzersee
Sarnen
Lucerne
Lake of Lucerne
Stans
Engelberg
Altdorf
Schwyz
Baar
Zug
Zugersee
Glarus
Walensee
Appenzell
St. Gallen
Zürichsee

Feldkirch
Vaduz
Klosters
Davos
Chur
Arosa
St. Moritz

Bellinzona
Locarno
Lugano
Lake Lugano
Lake Maggiore
Lake Como
Como

13
27
3
10
4
11
5
21
9

National Capital
City
International Boundary
Highway
Railroad
Zermatt

0   30 km
0   30 Miles

Europe

Europe

⊛ National capital

• City or village

--- International boundary

| 0 | 100 | 200 | 300 | 400 |
Scale in Miles

| 0 | 100 | 200 | 300 | 400 |
Scale in Kilometers

Polycanic Projection

©Copyright 1994 by
Barron's Educational Series, Inc.

PARIS
Points of Interest

N

Cimetière Montmartre

Place de Clichy

BATIGNOLLES

Moulin Rouge

AV. CHARLES DE GAULLE

AV. DES TERNES

Pl. des Ternes

BD. DE COURCELLES

Bois de Boulogne

GRANDE ARMEE

R. DU FAUBOURG ST. HONORE

Gare St. Lazare

BD. HAUSSMANN

Pl. Charles de Gaulle

Arc de Triomphe

AV. FOCH

AV. DES CHAMPS ELYSEES

Pl. de l'Opéra

Opér

LES G

BD. SUCHET

VICTOR HUGO

AV. KLEBER

Ste. Madeleine

AV. DE L'OPER

Palais de la Découverte

Grand Palais

Musée Jeu de Paume

Musée de l'Art Moderne

Petit Palais

Pl. de la Concorde

Jardin des Ju

Comédie Française

Pl. du Trocadéro

QUAI D'ORSAY

Palais de Chaillot

AV. DE NEW YORK

QUAI BRANLY

Munsée D'Orsay

Assemblée Nationale

Musée du Louvre

AV. KLEBER

Tour Eiffel

Champ de Mars

Hôtel des Invalides

BD. RASPAIL

Seine

SUFFREN

BD. DES INVALIDES

RUE DE SEVRES

RENNES

BD. DE GRENELLE

EMILE ZOLA

Palais d Luxemb

R. DE LA CONVENTION

RUE LECOURBE

VAUGIRARD

R. DE

BD. RASPAIL

Jarc Luxen

BD. DU MONTPARNAS

BD. VICTOR

R. DE

R. D'ALESIA

Cimetière Montparnasse

AV. DU MAINE

Sacré Coeur

Pl. Pigalle

BD. DE MAGENTA

Gare du Nord

RUE DE FLANDRE

AVE. JEAN JAURES

Parc des Buttes Chaumont

RUE LAFAYETTE

Gare de l'Est

RUE DE BELLEVILLE

Folies Bergère

DS. BOULEVARDS

R. REUMUR

Pl. de la République

AV. DE LA REPUBLIQUE

BD. DE SEBASTOPOL

Palais Royal

BD. VOLTAIRE

RUE DE RIVOLI

Centre Pompidou

BD. BEAUMARCHAIS

Cimetière du Père-Lachaise

Hôtel de Ville

Ile de la Cité

Institut de France

Notre Dame

BD. BASTILLE

Pl. de la Bastille

Opera Bastille

Théâtre l'Odéon

BD. ST-GERMAIN

Sorbonne

Panthéon

QUAI D'AUSTERLITZ

BD. ST. MICHEL

GAY-LUSSAC

Jardin des Plantes

AVE. DAUMESNIL

Gare de Lyon

Gare d'Austerlitz

QUAI DE LA GARE

PORT-ROYAL

ST. MARCEL

BD. DE L'HOPITAL

BD. ARAGO

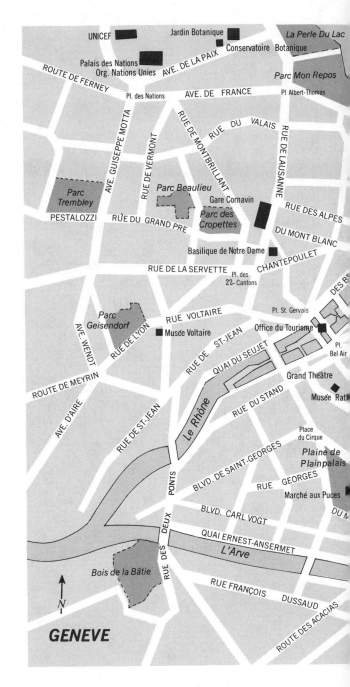

UNICEF

Jardin Botanique

La Perle Du Lac

Conservatoire Botanique

Palais des Nations
Org. Nations Unies — AVE. DE LA PAIX

ROUTE DE FERNEY

Parc Mon Repos

Pl. des Nations

AVE. DE FRANCE

Pl Albert-Thomas

AVE. GUISEPPE MOTTA

RUE DE VERMONT

RUE DE MONTBRILLANT

RUE DU VALAIS

RUE DE LAUSANNE

Parc Beaulieu

Gare Cornavin

Parc
Trembley

Parc des
Cropettes

PESTALOZZI   RUE DU GRAND PRE

RUE DES ALPES

DU MONT BLANC

Basilique de Notre Dame

CHANTEPOULET

RUE DE LA SERVETTE   Pl. des
22- Cantons

DES B

Parc
Geisendorf

RUE VOLTAIRE

Pl. St. Gervais

AVE. WENDT

RUE DE LYON

■ Musée Voltaire

Office du Tourisme

RUE DE ST-JEAN

QUAI DU SEUJET

Pl.
Bel Air

ROUTE DE MEYRIN

Grand Théâtre

AVE. D'AIRE

Le Rhône

RUE DU STAND

Musée Rath

RUE DE ST-JEAN

Place
du Cirque

Plaine de
Plainpalais

PONTS

BLVD. DE SAINT-GEORGES

RUE GEORGES

Marché aux Puces

DU M

DEUX

BLVD. CARL VOGT

QUAI ERNEST-ANSERMET

RUE DES

L'Arve

Bois de la Bâtie

RUE FRANÇOIS

DUSSAUD

N

ROUTE DES ACACIAS

GENEVE

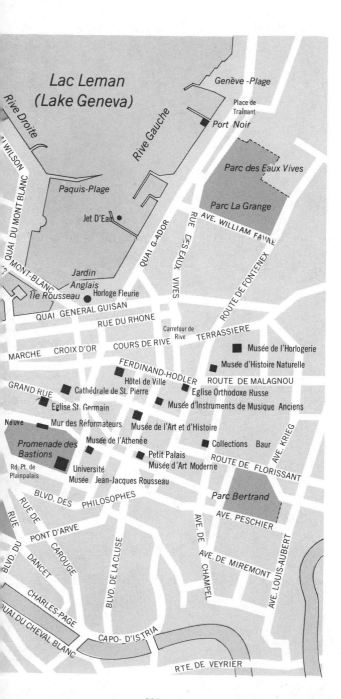

Lac Leman
(Lake Geneva)

Rive Droite

Rive Gauche

Genève -Plage

Place de
Traînant

Port Noir

Parc des Eaux Vives

Parc La Grange

QUAI DU MONT BLANC

RUE WILSON

Paquis-Plage

Jet D'Eau

QUAI G-ADOR

RUE DES EAUX VIVES

AVE. WILLIAM FAVRE

ROUTE DE FONTENEX

MONT-BLANC

Jardin
Anglais

Île Rousseau

Horloge Fleurie

QUAI GENERAL GUISAN

RUE DU RHONE

Carrefour de
Rive

TERRASSIERE

MARCHE

CROIX D'OR

COURS DE RIVE

Musée de l'Horlogerie

FERDINAND-HODLER

Musée d'Histoire Naturelle

ROUTE DE MALAGNOU

GRAND RUE

Hôtel de Ville

Cathédrale de St. Pierre

Eglise Orthodoxe Russe

Eglise St. Germain

Musée d'Instruments de Musique Anciens

Neuve

Mur des Réformateurs

Musée de l'Art et d'Histoire

Promenade des
Bastions

Musée de l'Athenée

Collections Baur

AVE. KRIEG

Rd. Pt. de
Plainpalais

Université

Petit Palais

Musée d'Art Moderne

ROUTE DE FLORISSANT

Musée Jean-Jacques Rousseau

BLVD. DES PHILOSOPHES

Parc Bertrand

RUE DE

AVE. PESCHIER

RUE DU BLVD.

PONT D'ARVE

CAROUGE

DANCET

BLVD. DE LA CLUSE

AVE. DE CHAMPEL

AVE. DE MIREMONT

AVE. LOUIS-AUBERT

CHARLES-PAGE

QUAI DU CHEVAL BLANC

CAPO- D'ISTRIA

RTE. DE VEYRIER

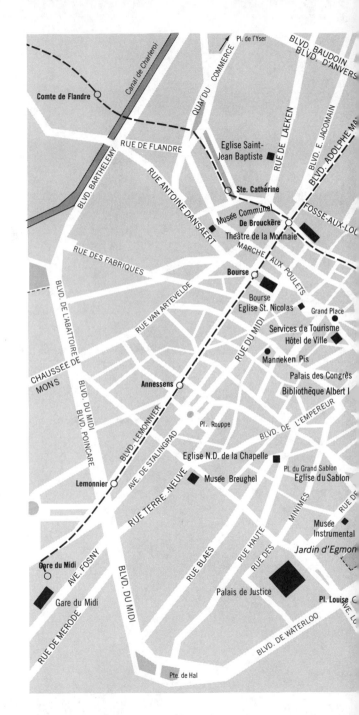

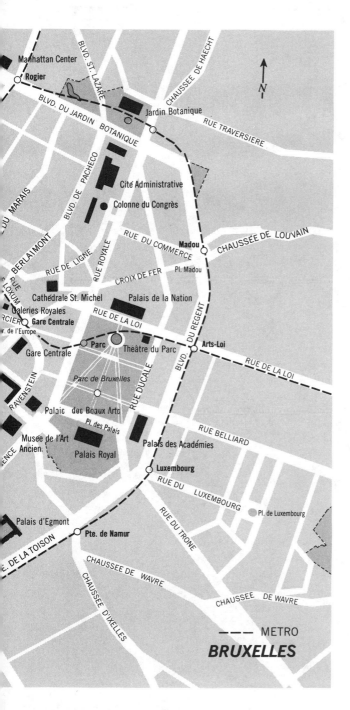

Manhattan Center

Rogier

BLVD. ST. LAZARE

BLVD. DU JARDIN BOTANIQUE

CHAUSSÉE DE HAECHT

N

Jardin Botanique

RUE TRAVERSIERE

BLVD. DE PACHECO

Cité Administrative

Colonne du Congrès

DU MARAIS

BERLAIMONT

RUE DE LIGNE

RUE ROYALE

RUE DU COMMERCE

Madou

CHAUSSÉE DE LOUVAIN

RUE LOXUM

CROIX DE FER

Pl. Madou

Cathédrale St. Michel

Palais de la Nation

Galeries Royales

RUE DE LA LOI

RCIER

Gare Centrale

r. de l'Europe

Parc

Théâtre du Parc

BLVD. DU REGENT

Arts-Loi

RUE DE LA LOI

Gare Centrale

RAVENSTEIN

Parc de Bruxelles

RUE DUCALE

Palais des Beaux Arts

Pl. des Palais

RUE BELLIARD

Musée de l'Art Ancien

Palais Royal

Palais des Académies

ENCE

Luxembourg

RUE DU LUXEMBOURG

Pl. de Luxembourg

Palais d'Egmont

RUE DU TRONE

E. DE LA TOISON

Pte. de Namur

CHAUSSÉE DE WAVRE

CHAUSSÉE D'IXELLES

CHAUSSÉE DE WAVRE

——— METRO

BRUXELLES

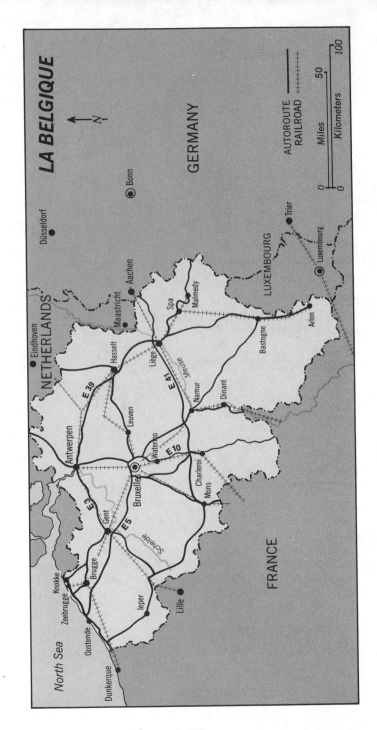